The First Oration Of Cicero Against Cataline: Being The Latin Text ... With A Literal Interlinear Translation, And With An Elegant Translation In The Margin, And Footnotes In Which Every Word Is Completely Parsed ...

Marcus Tullius Cicero, Archibald A. Maclardy

Cicero, Marcus Tullius
II

Completely Parsed Classics

THE FIRST ORATION

OF

CICERO AGAINST CATILINE

Being the Latin Text in the Original Order ;
with a Literal Interlinear Translation ; and with an Elegant
Translation in the Margin ;

AND

FOOTNOTES IN WHICH EVERY WORD IS COMPLETELY PARSED, THE CON-
STRUCTIONS AND CONTEXT EXPLAINED, WITH REFERENCES TO
THE REVISED GRAMMARS OF ALLEN & GREENOUGH,
BENNETT, GILDERSLEEVE, AND HARKNESS

BY

ARCHIBALD A. MACLARDY, B.A.

FORMERLY CLASSICAL SCHOLAR OF WADHAM COLLEGE, OXFORD

HINDS & NOBLE, Publishers

31-33-35 WEST 15TH STREET, NEW YORK CITY

Schoolbooks of all publishers at one store

PREFACE.

WITH this book *any one* can learn not only *about* the Latin language, but can learn *the language itself*.

The editor has designed it as an aid to three classes of learners, and it is his confident belief that *they* will find it in practice to be of really invaluable service — first, *teachers*, both those rusty in Latin, who nevertheless find themselves called upon to teach Cicero without much time for preparation, and also those who are "up" in Cicero, but still may benefit greatly, at the first, by having at their elbow a model for teaching and drilling which, like this, sets forth to the most minute detail each step in the parsing and the translation of every word in the text; then *clergymen* whose opportunities may not have permitted the acquisition of Latin, but who yet desire to possess themselves rapidly of so much of this language as a minister really needs for etymological and philological and literary purposes, as well as for the simple satisfaction of emerging from a state of ignorance regarding a language so familiar to the educated; then *students*, both those who are not so situated as to have an instructor, but are still ambitious enough to study Latin without a teacher, and also students who, though members of a class, yet need the help of a complete model for translation and analysis, to be used, of course, under wise guidance. Again, it is not wholly unlikely that the perfectly competent teacher of Latin will find this book useful, not because of any need for assistance, but because of the advantage of comparing one's own ways and opinions with the methods and views of another competent teacher, even if, or rather, particularly if that other's ideas are not always in accord with one's own.

The following suggestions are made to aid any *learner* who may wish to use this book as a BEGINNER'S LATIN BOOK: Take any one of the Latin grammars referred to farther on in this preface; learn from it to distinguish and to decline the five Latin declensions of nouns; the first and second, and the third declension of adjectives; study the comparison of adjectives and adverbs, and become familiar with the different kinds of pronouns; learn also how to distinguish the four conjugations of the verbs, and how to inflect the verbs; read attentively Latin Syntax, especially the coarse print portion of it. With this equipment, turn to any nude text of the First Catilinarian Oration — the TUTORIAL, for instance, or any other. Read a line or sentence or paragraph, noting carefully the cases and numbers of the nouns, pronouns, and adjectives, and the persons and numbers of the verbs. If without knowledge of the *meaning* of the words, turn to the interlined translation in this volume, using it *now* as a vocabulary; and then turning from this back to the nude text, *translate* the line, sentence, or paragraph — always in the Latin order of the words. Compare your version with the interlinear translation. After this transpose your line, sentence, or paragraph into the English order of the words, making as good English as possible, and then, not till then, compare your perfected whole with the English *translation in the margin.* Finally, look up the grammatical references as given in the footnotes, and examine the synonyms carefully, and thus develop a critical scholarship. Not only will rapid progress be made in the facility to translate Latin, but a certain degree of culture will be attained as the outcome of the process.

The text of this FIRST ORATION AGAINST CATILINE follows with only occasional variations the text of Professor Wilkins's English edition, which is based upon the original German commentary of Karl Halm. The editor has compared the texts of the best-known

American editions of this speech, and in the footnotes has directed the students' attention to all important and essential differences of lection, though these are happily very few.

The text is accompanied by a rigidly literal interlinear translation according to the Latin order of the words, and a passably literal translation in the order of English idiom in the margin. The difficulties in the way of giving a literal and at the same time a pleasing version of Cicero's speeches are very great, not less so than the temptation to reconstruct here and there a sentence, and render it by a flowing paraphrase; but in the marginal translation absolute accuracy has been aimed at, and wherever elegance and accuracy have appeared hard to combine, the former has been sacrificed to the latter, lest the student should be misled by a too free version.

The footnotes are both explanatory and critical. Every word of the text is parsed; and when the construction seems to require it, reference is made to the Latin grammars of Allen & Greenough's Revised Edition, Bennett, Gildersleeve revised by Lodge, and Harkness's Revised Standard Edition. Historical and constitutional allusions are treated at sufficient length for a correct understanding of the subject matter of the text. Moreover, brief biographical details are included in the notes, so that the student may gain a clear idea of the character and importance of the persons mentioned in the speech.

Latin synonyms have been noticed wherever they occur, and hints as to critical word study are given on every page. Grammatical references, and occasionally derivations and synonyms, are repeated, especially in the first part of the book, in order that principles, grammatical and philological, may be kept continually before the reader's eye.

The rhetorical character of the speech has been kept in mind, and the student is directed to observe the development of the great orator's scathing denunciation of the guilty conspirator.

In order properly to understand the occasion of this speech, and the various allusions which occur in the text to such matters as Catiline's earlier career, governmental institutions, the nature and powers of the different magistrates, and the like, the student needs more connected information than can be conveyed in footnotes mainly devoted to parsing and syntax, and therefore the editor has added an Introduction, which will, it is hoped, give a sufficiently clear outline of the actual environment of the speech.

This volume will be followed shortly by a companion volume in the same series, viz., THE SECOND ORATION OF CICERO AGAINST CATILINE, which will in every way resemble this first oration with regard to parsing and translation; the only modification of method being that the student's progress will not be hampered by full and unnecessary repetition in the footnotes of ordinary simple grammatical rules and references which have been already treated at length and repeated in the first oration, and with which the most backward student who has used this book might reasonably be expected to be conversant.

Finally, the editor wishes to express his grateful acknowledgment of the invaluable assistance and the unfailing courtesy of the publishers, Messrs. Hinds and Noble, who have spared no pains to help him in making of this book what it has been claimed to be at the beginning of the preface.

ARCHIBALD A. MACLARDY.

INTRODUCTION.

THE CONSPIRACY OF CATILINE.

LUCIUS SERGIUS CATILINA, descended from an old and once important patrician family, was born about the year 108 B.C. He was distinguished for his physical strength and powers of endurance, as well as for his mental abilities; and so great was the influence of his magnetic personality that, in spite of his notorious indulgence in every kind of vicious pleasure and extravagance, he retained till late in his career the friendship of some of Rome's noblest and most respected citizens.

His first appearance in public life was at the time of the Sullan proscriptions, when his cruelty and rapacity brought him into unenviable prominence. Among other scandalous crimes he is said to have caused the name of his brother, whom he had previously murdered, to be placed on the list of the condemned, so that he might escape prosecution for the murder. He was suspected of wife-murder, and it was alleged that he killed his own son in order that no encumbrance might hinder his marriage with the beautiful but profligate Aurelia Orestilla. In 73 B.C. he was accused of incest with a vestal virgin, but, owing to the intercession of a noble of good repute, Q. Lutatius Catulus, he escaped conviction.

Catiline served as *quaestor* and afterward as *legatus*, and in 69 B.C. was elected *praetor* for the following year.

In the year 67 B.C. he governed the province of Africa as *propraetor*, returning to Rome in 66 B.C., to sue for election to the consulship for 65 B.C. His candidature was rendered illegal by the fact that preliminary measures were taken for prosecuting him on the well-supported charge of provincial extortion and misgovernment.

The So-called First Conspiracy. — The successful candidates in the consular elections for 65 B.C. were P. Antronius Paetus and P. Cornelius Sulla, but both were convicted of bribery, and their rivals, L. Aurelius Cotta and L. Manlius Torquatus, were elected in their stead. Upon this Antronius and Catiline conspired together, and made arrangements to have the consuls and several other notable senators assassinated, and to take by violence the consular position and authority. The date fixed for the massacre was Jan. 1, 65 B.C., but the disclosure of certain details necessitated a postponement.

In these schemes the conspirators were assisted by a young patrician firebrand, named Cn. Calpurnius Piso, whose part was to be the raising of an army and the seizure of the province of Spain. The second attempt of the conspirators, arranged for Feb. 5th, failed, as Catiline gave the signal before a sufficient number of his followers had gathered together.

The above is the common account of this plot; but in the light of its description by Suetonius, it is very probable that Catiline's part in it was overstated by his political enemies. Suetonius represents, not Antronius and Catiline, but Caesar and Crassus, as the chief figures in the conspiracy, and there is good reason to suppose that this was the case.

In 65 B.C. the trial, which had been pending, came on; and though Catiline bribed his accuser, Clodius, and the judges, and won acquittal, yet the proceedings had been protracted into the autumn, and consequently the consular elections for the year 64 B.C. were over.

Disappointed in 66 and in 65, Catiline made every possible effort to secure election as consul in 64 B.C. When the elections came on, there were in all seven candidates, the most important being Catiline, C. Antonius Hybrida, and the great orator, M. Tullius Cicero. The two former, being heavily in debt, worked together to keep Cicero out, and had at least the tacit support of Caesar and Crassus. Cicero was largely handicapped by the fact that he was a *novus homo* and unpopular with the nobility. But the political intrigues entered upon by Catiline and Antonius, and the extent of their promises and bribes to the electors, were so outrageous that the Senate became indignant, and Cicero seized the opportunity to deliver, a few days before the election, a scathing denunciation of the character, practices, and designs of his formidable rivals. In this speech, the *oratio in toga candida*, Cicero alarmed the aristocrats by his hardly veiled hints that Catiline and Antonius were only puppets, and that the constitution itself was in danger. Whereupon the Senate overcame its repugnancy and voted for Cicero, who was returned as consul, with Antonius as his colleague. Thus once more was Catiline defeated, though he carried only a few votes less than Antonius.

It should here be stated that Sallust assigns to June, 64 B.C., a speech delivered by Catiline in the presence of his most devoted adherents, in which he advocated a conspiracy, promised *novae tabulae*, — *i.e.* a general cancelling of all debts, — and urged an armed rising against the constitutional authorities. But we cannot believe that Catiline was plotting revolution so early, while he yet had strong democratic influence behind him and good hopes of winning power by constitutional methods. It is far more credible that he was driven into revolutionary schemes for retrieving his fortunes by the desperation occasioned by his electoral defeat and his increased pecuniary embarrassments.

After the elections Catiline was again prosecuted, on this occasion for taking part in Sulla's proscriptions. Caesar was president at the trial, and Catiline was acquitted. But from this time on we hear of nothing pointing to political association between Catiline and the rising democratic leaders, Caesar and Crassus.

The Great Conspiracy. — Catiline now resolved upon revolution, and found many who were ready, for various reasons, to take up arms against the state. Among his followers were dissipated patrician youths, who hoped to profit by bloodshed and anarchy in the same way as Sulla's supporters had done; men of high position but ruined fortunes, numerous not only in Rome but also in the country towns; Sulla's veterans, who had been granted lands in the north of Italy, but had exhausted their wealth in riotous extravagance; farmers and others, who had been dispossessed of their property to make room for Sulla's old soldiers; and, lastly, the dregs of the Roman populace, men who delighted in rapine and murder.

Catiline organized a wide conspiracy, and at one of several secret meetings delivered the speech, mentioned above, which Sallust assigns incorrectly to the year 64 B.C. At the same time Catiline canvassed for the consular elections of 63 B.C. On the day preceding the elections Cicero spoke strongly in the Senate, and described the extent of the dangers besetting the constitution. Thereupon the alarmed senators decided to postpone the elections, and discuss the question of public safety. Cicero related what he knew of the conspiracy, and challenged Catiline, who was present, to refute his accusations. The latter insolently replied that there were two bodies in the state, the one weak and with a feeble head (the Senate and Cicero), the other strong but without a head (the people); he declared that he himself would become the head, and champion the people against oppression.

When the election day arrived, Cicero came on the scene with an armed body-guard, and so Catiline, although attended by a crowd of ruffians, did not dare to make a riot. Lucius Licinius Murena and Decimus Junius Silanus were declared consuls elect for 62 B.C.

After this the conspirators worked actively to raise money and collect forces and munitions of war; and Gaius Manlius, who had served as centurion under Sulla, took up a position at Faesulae in Etruria, with instructions to declare war on the state on Oct. 27th. It was further arranged that Cicero and other Roman nobles should be massacred on the 28th of October. Cicero, learning of these arrangements from his spies, called a meeting of the Senate on Oct. 21st, and the senators discussed the state's peril on that and the following day, finally issuing the *senatus consultum ultimum*, whereby the consuls were empowered to take any and every step to preserve the state from harm. Not long afterward news came that Manlius had set up the standard of revolt, and that slave risings were taking place in certain districts. Driven into immediate action, the consuls despatched generals to the threatened parts of Italy, and caused Catiline, who was still in Rome, to be prosecuted on the charge of riot (*de vi*). Catiline, with his usual audacity, assuming innocence, offered to place himself in the custody of some prominent noble, but intended, nevertheless, to leave Rome for Faesulae as soon as all his plans were ready.

Meeting at Laeca's House. — On the night of Nov. 6th Catiline held a secret assembly of conspirators at the house of Marcus Porcius Laeca, and made the final preparations for revolt, expressing his impatient desire to join the camp of Manlius. He laid great stress on the necessity of doing away with Cicero, whereupon two men, the senator Lucius Vargunteius and the knight Gaius Cornelius, agreed to murder him that same night. According to Cicero's account, the attempt was made, but failed, owing to the fact that Cicero had information of all the conspirators' actions from a woman named Fulvia, the mistress of one of Catiline's associates.

The First Catilinarian Oration was delivered on Nov. 8th before the Senate, which Cicero summoned to meet in the temple of

Jupiter Stator. Catiline's boldness is well shown by the fact that he attended the meeting. The gist of Cicero's speech was that Catiline should retire into voluntary exile. Catiline ventured to defend himself against his accuser, protesting his innocence, and supplicating the Senate not to give credence to the charges of an upstart alien. But the senators loudly upbraided Catiline as a traitor, whereupon he rushed from the meeting, and after concluding his intrigues with some of his supporters left Rome the same night, ostensibly to go into exile at Massilia, but in reality to join the rebel forces under Manlius.

The Second Catilinarian Oration was delivered next day, Nov. 9th, before a mass-meeting of the people. The orator explained his course of action the preceding day, and strove, by dwelling on the resolute measures taken by the state to quell the revolt, to frighten all would-be conspirators from throwing in their lot with Catiline.

It was announced shortly after that Catiline, attended by the *fasces*, had joined Manlius. Forthwith the Senate declared Catiline and Manlius enemies of their country, at the same time offering pardon to all who would at once leave the rebel ranks.

The consul Antonius, whom Cicero had long since won from his adherence to Catiline by the promise of the government of the rich province of Macedonia, was given the chief command of the army, and sent into the field. Meanwhile Cicero remained at Rome to cope with the growing machinations of the conspirators in the city, who were led by P. Cornelius Lentulus and C. Cornelius Cethegus. Sallust informs us that their plot was to denounce Cicero as the cause of the war through the mouth of one of the tribunes, to murder Cicero and many other influential citizens, to set the city on fire in several parts, and to cause a general massacre and tumult.

The danger of the state cannot be overestimated, but a happy accident averted the crisis and ruined the hopes of the conspirators.

This fortunate result was due to the following circumstances. Some envoys of the Allobroges, a tribe of Transalpine Gaul, had come to Rome to petition the Senate for relief from certain oppressions to which their tribe was subjected; and the conspirators, aware of their mission, hoped to secure their armed assistance in the revolt. Lentulus and Cethegus gave them letters bearing their seals and signatures, promising rewards for their aid, and also a letter directed to Catiline. The envoys had at first hesitated, but eventually consulted their Roman patron, who advised them to disclose everything to Cicero. Thus the envoys played a double part, and when they left Rome to return home offered no resistance to the force sent by Cicero to arrest them at the Mulvian Bridge. With them was arrested one of the conspirators, named Titus Volturcius. They were all led before Cicero and the Senate, and were joined by Lentulus, Cethegus, Statilius, Gabinius, and other leading conspirators, whom Cicero had summoned to meet him. Denial of guilt was useless, as Volturcius, the envoys, and their own letters and signatures unmistakably proclaimed them traitors. Lentulus was obliged to resign his praetorship, and the offenders were placed under private arrest.

The Third Catilinarian Oration was delivered on Dec. 3d, after the meeting described above, and informed the people of all that had taken place. The mob had been hitherto uncertain, but now extolled the consul, and loudly praised his energy. Strong measures were taken to prevent the rescue of the prisoners, and the Senate was convoked in the temple of Concordia on Dec. 5th. In the debate the consul elect, D. Silanus, advocated the punishment of death. Caesar caused the senators to waver by proposing instead the confiscation of the prisoners' property, and imprisonment for life. Then Cicero, whose fate lay in the balance just as much as that of the conspirators, arose, and delivered **the Fourth Catilinarian Oration**. With much preamble he gave his vote for death; but it remained for the young Cato to decide the meeting by a most eloquent speech, which rang the knell of doom over the prisoners. The same night the latter were led to the Tullianum and strangled.

The last scene of the tragedy took place at Pistaria in Etruria, where Catiline fought a desperate battle with M. Petreius, the lieutenant of Antonius. No less than three thousand of the rebels were killed, and among them their intrepid leader, Catiline.

NOTE. — Some writers, notably Professor E. S. Beesly, in his disquisition on "Catiline, Clodius, and Tiberius," give Catiline a very different character from that which Cicero gives him. They claim, not without reason, that nearly all the worst charges against him rest upon Cicero's unsupported evidence, especially upon statements in the *oratio in toga candida*. Professor Beesly very ingeniously represents Catiline as a true democratic leader, forced by a selfish aristocracy into armed protest in the same way as C. Gracchus, Saturninus, and Marius. But the general features of the conspiracy as described by Cicero, find an unprejudiced witness in Sallust, who was a democrat, and so opposed to Cicero in political sympathies.

The Date of the First Oration against Catiline.

There is some uncertainty as to whether the speech was made on Nov. 7th or Nov. 8th. The latter date now finds the most support, and has been adopted in the NOTES in this volume. From a passage in Cicero's speech *pro Sulla*, we learn that the meeting at Laeca's house took place on the night between Nov. 6th and 7th, and that the attempt on Cicero's life was arranged for the early morning of Nov. 7th. Now in Chap. I, ll. 13 and 14, a distinction is made between *proxima nox* and *superior nox; proxima nox* = the night preceding the delivery of the speech, and *superior nox* = the second night before the speech. If the speech was, as we suppose, delivered on Nov. 8th, then *proxima nox* = night between Nov. 7th and 8th, and *superior nox* = the night between Nov. 6th and 7th, *i.e.* the night of the secret meeting. We know that Cicero heard of this meeting almost as soon as it broke up, and informed several others of the schemes formed at it. Moreover, Cicero's spies would scarcely fail to keep a keen watch on Catiline's movements on the following night. Therefore *proxima nox* and *superior nox* conveyed very definite ideas to the orator's audience. But if the speech was delivered on Nov. 7th, immediately after the attempted murder, *proxima nox* = the night of the secret assembly, and *superior nox* = the night between Nov. 5th and 6th, concerning which we have no information at all. It may be objected that Cicero would not delay his denunciation of the conspiracy even for a day, after his narrow escape from assassination; but a reasonable reply to this objection is found in the conjecture that the consul fully expected Catiline to leave Rome on the night between Nov. 7th and 8th, and, seeing that the refrain of the first oration is "leave Rome," he would have been satisfied if Catiline had gone away.

Catiline was given the chance to depart unmolested, but as he refused it and his presence in Rome was a constant menace to Cicero, the latter was forced to call the Senate on Nov. 8th and disclose the character of the plot.

Some editors assign the speech to Nov. 7th on the authority of Asconius, who states that it was delivered on the eighteenth day after the passing of the *decretum ultimum*. They accept the supposition that the decree was passed on Oct. 21st. But Dio Cassius distinctly says that the discussion in the Senate occupied two days, Oct. 21st and 22d, the decree being resolved upon the second day.

The settlement of the date of the attempted murder of Cicero helps us to some extent in determining the date of the speech. In this book the attempt is assigned to the early morning of Nov. 7th, for reasons which will be found in the notes to various statements in the text. But there are several scholars who maintain that the attempt was made on the morning of Nov. 8th; they account for the delay by supposing that the secret meeting at Laeca's house lasted too long for Cornelius and Vargunteius to venture on their plan at once. If this opinion is correct, the speech could not have been delivered earlier than Nov. 8th.

ROMAN GOVERNMENT.

After the expulsion of the kings, the regulation of the state was intrusted to the Senate, the people, and the magistrates. These three bodies were not to wield independent power, for the theory was that in so far as they worked harmoniously together the government would be sound and good. While Rome was extending its power in Italy, the Senate gradually came to be recognized as the supreme source of government, and its authority continued until it proved itself incapable of managing an oversea empire. The Gracchi were among the first to question the validity of its assumed power, and others, imbued with democratic principles, soon followed. The bitterness of the struggle is well exemplified by the civil war and misery which marked the career of Saturninus, Marius, and Cinna. Sulla was strong enough to re-establish the Senate in its old position, but it was clear that after his death a change must take place, and that the rule of a single man was only a question of time. During Cicero's life the Senate was tottering to its fall, and the people asserting its power by arming individuals with extraordinary authority, which foreshadowed the absolute, if disguised, sway of the emperor.

A. **The Senate.** — Under the republic the Senate theoretically continued to be what it had been under the kings, viz. an advising body of elders. It was consulted by the magistrates, and being the only body in which debate was possible, it soon usurped the functions of preparing bills for the *comitia* to vote upon, and discussing and managing foreign policy. Moreover, the collegiate character of the magistracies and the fact that, whereas the magistrates were only annual, the Senate was permanent, inevitably resulted in the assumption of the supreme power by the latter. The senators were originally chosen by the censor, but after the *lex Ovinia* was passed all curule magistrates became *ex officio* members of the Senate. The Senate could not meet unless at a magistrate's summons. It could not propose and pass laws, but only frame them for the people to accept or reject; yet a *senatus consultum*, or decree of the Senate, virtually had the force of law, if assented to by the tribunes. The Senate usually met in the *curia*, but frequently for special reasons met in a temple or other consecrated spot.

B. **The Comitia,** *i.e.* the assemblies of the people.

(1) COMITIA CENTURIATA. — This was an assembly, originally for military purposes and therefore held in the Campus Martius, of the people by property classes. It elected the consuls, praetors, and censors, and voted on *rogationes* put before it by a magistrate with the Senate's approval. When a Roman citizen's life was at stake, the condemned might appeal to the *comitia centuriata*, whose verdict was final.

(2) COMITIA TRIBUTA. — This assembly was an outgrowth from the *concilia plebis*, which were called by a *tribunus plebis*. The people voted by tribes. After 449 B.C. the assembly was recognized as constitutional, and it elected tribunes, quaestors, aediles, and lesser magistrates. It was empowered to make laws known as *plebiscita*, but it is doubtful when these laws became binding on all the citizens; originally they were only binding on the *plebs*. In 287 B.C. at the latest the *plebiscita* were universally valid.

(3) COMITIA CURIATA. — It originally consisted of thirty curies, each *curia* having one vote. Its originally important powers vanished soon after the expulsion of the kings, and in Cicero's time the assembly only existed to attend to certain religious formalities, and to confer *imperium* on the consuls and the praetors.

C. **The Magistrates.** — The regular magistrates held office for one year, except the censors, whose authority lasted for five years.

The elections for all except the tribunes, quaestors, and aediles usually fell in July. No one man could hold two different magistracies in the same year. The *lex Villia Annalis* of 180 B.C. fixed the age of office-holders and the order of offices, but as this law was often overridden, Sulla established that thirty was to be the earliest age for quaestor, forty for praetor, and forty-three for consul. Every magistrate held *potestas, i.e.* authority to perform the functions of his office, but only the consuls, praetors, and dictators could enjoy the right of *imperium, i.e.* the right to command an army.

The magistrates may be divided into two classes, regular and extraordinary. The regular magistrates consisted of the consuls, the praetors, the aediles, the quaestors, the censors, the tribunes of the *plebs*. The extraordinary magistrates included dictators and masters of the horse (*magistri equitum*). The student will find their duties and powers described in any Roman history.

ABBREVIATIONS.

abl.	= ablative.	*impers.*	= impersonal.
abs. or *absol.*	= absolute.	*ind.*	= indicative.
acc.	= accusative.	*indecl.*	= indeclinable.
act.	= active.	*indef.*	= indefinite.
adj.	= adjective.	*infin.* or *inf.*	= infinitive.
adv.	= adverb.	*interrog.*	= interrogative.
appos.	= apposition.	*intrans.*	= intransitive.
A. & G.	= Allen & Green-	*l.*	= line.
	ough's Latin	*ll.*	= lines.
	Grammar, Re-	*m.*	= masculine.
	vised Ed.	*n.* or *neut.*	= neuter.
B.	= Bennett's Latin	*neg.*	= negative.
	Grammar.	*nom.*	= nominative.
Chap.	= chapter.	*num.*	= numeral.
cf. (*cōnfer*)	= compare.	*obj.*	= object.
comp.	= compound.	*p.*	= page.
conj.	= conjunction.	*pp.*	= pages.
cop.	= copulative.	*part.*	= participle.
dat.	= dative.	*pass.*	= passive.
decl.	= declension.	*perf.*	= perfect.
dem.	= demonstrative.	*pers.*	= personal.
dep.	= deponent.	*pluperf.*	= pluperfect.
disc.	= discourse.	*plur.*	= plural.
distrib.	= distributive.	*poss.*	= possessive.
=	= *equals, equivalent*	*pred.*	= predicate.
	to, or *denotes.*	*prep.*	= preposition.
e.g. (*exemplī*		*pres.*	= present.
grātiā)	= for example.	*pron.*	= pronoun.
etc. (*et caetera*)	= and so forth.	*rel.*	= relative.
f. or *fem.*	= feminine.	*sc.* (*scīlicet*)	= that is to say;
ff.	= following.		sometimes =
fr.	= from.		supply.
fut.	= future.	*sing.*	= singular.
G.	= Gildersleeve's	*subj.*	= subject.
	Latin Gram.,	*subjunct.*	= subjunctive
	Revised Ed.	*subst.*	= substantive.
gen.	= genitive.	*superl.*	= superlative.
gov.	= governs; some-	*trans.*	= transitive.
	times = gov-	*viz.* (*vidēlicet*)	= namely.
	erned.	*1, 2, 3, 4*	
H.	= Harkness's Latin	with verbs	= 1st, 2d, 3d, 4th,
	Grammar, Rev.		conjugation.
	Stand. Ed.	*1st, 2d, 3d, 4th,*	
i.e. (*id est*)	= that is.	*5th*	= 1st, 2d, 3d, 4th,
imperf.	= imperfect.		5th, declension.

1 I. Quō   ūsque   tandem   abūtēre,
      How far (lit. *whither up to*) *at length*   *will you abuse,*

2 Catilīna, patientiā nostrā?   quam diū etiam
   Catiline,   *patience   our?*   *how   long   still*

I. How far pray,
Catiline, will you
abuse our patience?
How much longer is

LINE 1. **Quō**, interrog. adv.; limiting *abūtēre*. In origin *quō* is the abl. sing. n. of the interrog. pron. *quis*, or of the rel. pron. *quī*, used adverbially; cf. *quā*.——**ūsque**, adv. of extent in time or place; here modifies *quō*, and is sometimes written with it in a single word, *quoūsque*, = *how long, up to what point?* Similarly other combinate expressions occur, e.g. *quam diū* (*quamdiū*), *rēs pūblica* (*rēspūblica*), etc. *Ūsque* = *right on, as far as*, and may modify (1) adverbs, e.g. *usque eō*, of place, *quō usque* of time; (2) preps., e.g. *usque ad urbem* = *even* (*right on*) *to the city. Usque* sometimes governs the acc. as a prep., = *as far as, up to.*——**tandem** (*tam* = *so far*, + demonstr. suffix -*dem*), adv., usually of time, = *at length*, often standing in close conjunction with another adv., e.g. *iam tandem, aliquandō tandem.* Here *tandem* strengthens *quō ūsque*, and emphasizes the whole question, for rhetorical effect. It corresponds very nearly to the Greek particle δή, e.g. τίς δή = *who exactly?* For this usage cf. Sallust, *Cat.* XX, 9: *quae* (= *and this*) *quō ūsque tandem patiēminī? Tandem* is sometimes found with imperatives; cf. Chap. IV, l. 1, *Recognōsce tandem.* A. & G. 210, *f*; B. and G. omit any reference; H. 351, 4.——**abūtēre**, 2d pers. sing. fut. ind. of the deponent verb *abūtor* (*ab* + *ūtor*), *abūtī, abūsus sum*, 3; agrees with the subj. *tū* implied by the personal ending. A. & G. 135; B. 112; G. 113, 220; H. 231. Observe that *abūtēre* is future, as the parallel tenses following, *ēlūdet* and *iactābit*, show; distinguish from the pres. *abūtĕre.* Cicero uses the 2d pers. sing. ending -*re* far more often than the ordinary -*ris* in the fut. ind. pass., prefers -*re* also in the pres. subjunct. pass., but in the pres. ind. pass. -*ris* is almost invariably used.

LINE 2. **Catilīna**, voc. sing. of *Catilīna, -ae*, m. 1st; the case of the person addressed. The meeting of the Senate took place on November 8th in the temple of Jupiter Stator, which was guarded by Roman knights. Catiline attended the meeting, his object being, according to Sallust, either to disguise his treason (*dissimulandī causā*) or to clear himself (*suī expurgandī causā*).——**patientiā**, abl. sing. of *patientia, -ae*, f. 1st (from *patiēns*, pres. part. of *patior*, 3, deponent); direct obj. of *abūtēre.* A few verbs require their objects in the abl. case, viz. *fungor, fruor, ūtor, abūtor, vescor, potior, dīgnor, supersedeō* (also the adjectives *dīgnus, indīgnus*, and the noun *opus*). A. & G. 249; B. 218, 1; G. 407; H. 421, I.——**nostrā**, abl. sing. f. of the poss. adj. *noster, nostra, nostrum* (*nōs*, the 1st personal pron. plur.); agrees with *patientiā.*——**quam** (originally acc. f. of rel. pron. *quī*), interrog. adv., modifying *diū;* the compound interrog. adv. *quam diū* limits the predicate *ēlūdet. Quam diū* is sometimes written as one word, *quamdiū.* Other uses of *quam* are: (1) in exclamations, = *how*, e.g. *quam mīrābile!* (2) correl. of *tam*, e.g. *tam . . . quam*, = *so . . . as;* (3) in extension of (2) with superl. adjectives and adverbs, e.g. *quam celerrimē* = (*tam*) *celerrimē quam* (*potuit*); (4) after comparative adjectives and adverbs, and a few words like *aliter, secus*, etc., e.g. *haec arbor altior est quam illa;* (5) with adjectives and adverbs, introducing indirect questions; (6) conjoined with or following *ante* or *prius* (*antequam* or *ante . . . quam*), as temporal conjunct. taking ind. mood.—— **diū** (originally locative of *diēs;* cf. *noctū*, from *nox*), temporal adv., in composition with *quam* modifying *ēlūdet. Diū* admits of comparison, compar. degree *diūtius*, superl. *diūtissimē.*——**etiam** (*et* + *iam*), adv., intensifying *quam diū.* The original force of *etiam* is temporal, especially in connection with other temporal adverbs, e.g. *etiam nunc. Etiam* is also common as an intensive sociative conjunction, = *also, and even*, being usually post-positive (cf. *igitur* and *tamen*) and rather more emphatic than *quoque.* A. & G. 151, *a*; B. 347, 1; G. 478, 479; H. 554, I, 4.

that madness of yours to make a mock of us? Up to what bound	furor	iste	tuus	nōs	ēlūdet?	quem	ad	finem 3
	frenzy	*that*	*your*	*us*	*will mock?*	*what*	*to*	*limit*

LINE 3. **furor**, nom. sing. of *furor, -ōris,* m. 3d (from *furō = I rage*); subj. of *ēlūdet. Furor* is a strong term (*insanīre = to be out of one's mind; furere = to be raving mad*), and represents Cicero's estimate of the state of mind of Catiline, boldly and deliberately choosing the role of murderer and traitor.——**iste**, nom. sing. m. of *iste, ista, istud,* demonstr. adj. and pron. of the 2d pers.; agrees with and modifies *furor.* The gen. sing. of *iste* is *istīus,* dat. *istī,* in classical Latin, though Plautus has a gen. *istī,* and a dat. fem. *istae. Iste* appears to be derived from *is* + suffix *te* (akin to the Greek δε in ὅδε). As an adj., *iste = that* or *this of yours,* and may have either a good or a bad sense, according to the context; thus in Chap. VII, l. 20, *istō factō, istō = such* (i.e. *so vile*), whereas in Chap. I, l. 38, *ista . . . virtūs = such* (i.e. *so distinguished*) *virtue.* As a pron., *iste = he, that person* (to whom the attention of the person addressed is directed); it is more often used in a bad sense than a good one, chiefly from the adoption of the word in the courts to denote the defendant (*iste = that fellow,* contemptuously). A. & G. 102, *c*; B. 87, and 246, 4; G. 306, and NOTE; H. 450, 1, and NOTE.——**tuus**, nom. sing. m. of *tuus, -a, -um,* the poss. adj. of the 2d pers. pron. *tū*; agrees with *furor.* The addition of *tuus* helps to define *iste* (as referring to the 2d pers.), and also indicates that *iste* above has more than its mere demonstrative significance and expresses strong disgust.——**nōs**, acc. plur. of *nōs* (gen. *nostrum* or *nostrī,* dat. and abl. *nōbīs*), the 1st personal pron. plur.; direct obj. of *ēlūdet; nōs* here embraces the Senate and all Roman citizens. The feeling of Cicero's audience towards Catiline was shown by their desertion of the part of the Senate where he sat. Several editions omit *nōs,* on the ground that a subsequent writer who quotes this passage does not give it. But this scarcely justifies us in ignoring Ms. evidence for the word, and it would also make the construction less simple; see *ēlūdet* below.——**ēlūdet**, 3d pers. sing. fut. ind. act. of *ēlūdō, -ere, ēlūsī, ēlūsum,* 3 (*ē =away + lūdō*); agrees with its subj. *furor. Ēlūdō = I mock, I dodge,* and is more often trans. than intrans. If *nōs* above be omitted, it would still be possible to regard *ēlūdet* as trans., understanding from *patientiā* in the preceding sentence *patientiam nostram* as its object. Some editors, however, regard it as absolute, and compare Livy, II, 45, *hostis ēlūdēbat,* for a similar usage.——**quem**, acc. sing. m. of the interrog. pron. and adj. *quis, quae, quid* (gen. *cūius,* dat. *cui,* and declined like the rel. pron. *quī*); agrees with *finem,* and introduces a question. The difference between the interrog. adj. *quis,* and the interrog. adj. *quī* (declined like the rel. pron.) may be exemplified thus: *quis homō = what man?, quī homō = what kind of man?* The neut. adjectival form of *quis* is *quod, quid* being pronominal only. As *quis* and *quī,* as adjectives, are only distinguishable in the nom. m. sing., many prefer to regard *quis* as wholly pronominal; thus in *quis homō, homō* is an appositive, = *who* (being, or as) *a man?*——**ad**, prep. and acc.; governs *finem. Ad* expresses motion with the acc., but sometimes also rest, e.g. *ad flūmen,* = *by,* or *near the river,* and also has many idiomatic relations. Distinguish between: (1) *ergā = to, towards,* of direction rather than limit of motion; (2) *ad = to, up to* the boundary of a place, e.g. *ad urbem = to the city,* i.e. the exterior of it; (3) *in = to, into,* denoting penetration within the boundary. A. & G. 153; B. 182, 3; G. 416, 1; H. 433, I, AD.——**finem**, acc. sing. of *finis, -is,* m. 3d (probably = *the separating thing,* akin to *findō,* = *I cleave*); governed by the prep. *ad;* the phrase *quem ad finem* is synonymous with *quō ūsque* and *quam diū.* Note three points respecting *finis;* (1) its abl. sing. is *fine,* rarely *finī,* (2) its gender is mas. in classical Latin, fem. in ante-classical and post-classical writers and poets, (3) in the sing. it = *limit, boundary, end* (less commonly *summit* of a series, *design*), in the plur. it = *borders,* hence *territory, country.*

4 sēsē effrēnāta iactăbit　　audācia?　　Nihilne　tē | will your unbridled
itself　unbridled　will show off　your boldness?　Not at all　you | effrontery display it-
self?　Have you not

LINE 4. **sēsē**, acc. sing. of the reflexive pron. of the 3d pers. ; direct obj. of *iac-tăbit.* When reference is made in the oblique cases to the subject of the sentence (the subject being a noun or a pron. of the 3d pers.), the reflexive pron. is regularly employed. *Sēsē* is a strengthened form (by reduplication) of the simple *sĕ,* no nom. or voc., acc. *sĕ* or *sēsē,* gen. *suī,* dat. *sibĭ,* abl. *sĕ* or *sēsē,* = *himself, herself, itself,* or in plur. *themselves;* it is akin to the Sanskrit *sva* = *one's own self,* and the Greek reflexive pron. acc. ἔ, gen. οὗ, dat. οἷ. A. & G. 196; B. 85 and 244; G. 309; H. 448.——**effrēnāta,** nom. sing. f. of *effrēnātus, -a, -um,* adj. (originally perf. part. pass. of *effrēno,* 1 = *I unbri-dle,* from *ex* = *away* + *frēnum* = *a bridle, bit*); qualifies *audācia,* = *unbridled boldness.* The metaphor is, of course, taken from an unmanageable horse, one that cannot be *held* in check, for *frēnum* is etymologically akin to *tenēre. Effrēnātus* soon lost all parti-cipial force, and we find it as an adj. in the superl. degree in Seneca, e.g. *effrēnātissimī affectūs.*——**iactăbit,** 3d pers. sing. fut. ind. act. of *iacto, -āre, -āvī, -ātum,* 1 (frequenta-tive of *iacĭō*); agrees with its subj. *audācia.* Frequentative verbs express repeated action, and are formed by adding *-tō* or *-sō* to supine stems (e.g. *iacĭō,* supine *iact-um,* frequent. *iactō; dīcō,* supine *dict-um,* frequent. *dictō*), or by adding *-itō* or *-itor* to clipt stems (e.g. *clām-ō,* frequent. *clāmitō; dict-ō,* frequent. *dictitō,* i.e. a frequentative from a frequentative). But *agitō* (instead of *actō*) from *agō,* supine *act-um,* shows that fre-quentatives originally came from nouns of agency in *-ta,* cf. *nauta.* A. & G. 167, *b;* B. 155, 2; G. 191, 1; H. 336. *Iactō = I toss about, I utter, I show off,* etc.; *sĕ iactāre =* *to boast oneself.* A passage in Isaiah well illustrates this use, x, 15, "Shall the axe *boast* *itself* against him that heweth therewith? . . . as if the rod should *shake itself* against them that lift it up."——**audācia,** gen. *audāciae,* f. 1st (from *audeō* = *I dare,* through adj. *audāx*), nom. sing., subj. of *iactăbit. Audācia =* (1) *boldness, courage;* (2) in a bad sense, *insolence, effrontery;* (3) *a bold deed.* Cicero is fond of applying this quality to Catiline, and always in sense (2) above. However, a lurking admiration or at least appreciation of Catiline's assurance and daring shows itself in the speeches, and Sallust, XXXI, says that the first Oration was prompted either by fear due to Catiline's daring in attending the Senate or by indignation.——**nihil,** acc. sing. of *nihil* (contracted form *nīl*), indecl. n.; used adverbially, to modify more emphatically (than *nōn*) the predi-cate *mōvĕrunt. Nihil* is an apocopated form of *nihilum, -ī,* n. 2d, which is derived from *ne* = *not* + *hilum* (old form of *fīlum* = *a thread*), and = lit. *not a thread,* hence *not a trifle, not at all.* The adverbial use of the neut. acc. of pronouns and adjectives is common in Latin, and in many cases the acc. is really a kind of cognate acc. in which the relationship of the acc. and the verb has become so dim as to leave the former almost a real adverb. A. & G. 240, *a;* B. 176, 3; G. 442, NOTE 2; H. 378, 2.——**ne,** enclitic interrog. particle; introduces a question, and is appended to the emphatic word, as to *nihil* here. A simple question may be introduced: (1) by an interrog. pron. adj. or adv., e.g. *quis, quantus, cur;* (2) by *ne,* which simply asks for information; (3) by *nōnne* (*nōn* + *ne*), which expects an affirmative answer; (4) by *num,* which expects a nega-tive answer; (5) occasionally without any introductory particle or word at all. Distinguish *ne* enclitic from: (1) *nē* = ναί, νή, interjection, = *truly, indeed;* (2) *nĕ,* adv., = *not,* e.g. *nĕ . . . quidem = not . . . even;* (3) *nē,* final conj., = *in order that not, lest.* A. & G. 210, *a, b, c;* B. 162, 2, *a, b, c, d;* G. 453-456; H. 351, 1-3.——**tē,** acc. sing. of the 2d pers. pron. *tū* (Greek σύ; gen. *tuī,* dat. *tibĭ,* abl. *tē*); direct obj. of *mōvit,* understood from *mōvĕrunt,* below which is in agreement with the composite subj. *praesidium, vigi-liae, timor,* etc. *Tē* must be understood as obj. thus: *nihil urbis vigiliae* (*tē*) (*mōvē-runt*), *nihil timor populī* (*tē*) (*mōvit*), and so on.

been impressed at all by the night-guard on the Palatine hill,	nocturnum praesidium	Palātī,	nihil	urbis 5
nightly	*the guard*	*of the Palatine,*	*not at all*	*of the city*

LINE 5. **nocturnum**, nom. sing. n. of the adj. *nocturnus, -a, -um* (from *nox*, gen. *noctis*, f. 3d) ; qualifies *praesidium*. That greater precautions for securing the safety of the Palatine hill should be taken at night than in the daytime was a self-evident necessity.——**praesidium**, gen. *praesidii* or contracted *praesidī*, n. 2d (from adj. *praesēs*, for *praesids*, gen. *praesidis*, which is derived from *praesideō = prae, before,* + *sedeō, I sit*, hence *I guard*); subj. of *movit*, understood from *movērunt* below, or it may be regarded as one of the subjects of *movērunt*, which see. *Praesidium* has various meanings: (1) *help, defence*, properly, and figuratively if defining persons, (2) *garrison*, (3) *escort, guard*, (4) *picket, outpost*, (5) *a camp, an intrenchment*. The central position, the height, and the wall-defences of the Palatine hill made it a very important post, and one that Catiline would be most anxious to seize as a base. The Senate, alarmed by Cicero's depositions respecting Catiline, after passing the ultimatum (*videant cōnsulēs*, etc.) made minute provisions for the safety of the city, posting guards in important positions under the direction of the lower magistrates (Sallust, *Cat.* XXX, *ad fin.*).——**Palātī** (contracted from *Palātiī*), gen. sing. of *Palātium*, n. 2d; poss. gen. (= *the Palatine's garrison*) or perhaps objective gen. (= *guard over the Palatine*), limiting *praesidium*. For the objective gen. consult A. & G. 217; B. 200; G. 363, 2; H. 396, III. Observe that the contracted gen. in *-ī* is preferred before the gen. in *-iī* of 2d decl. nouns ending in *-ius* or *-ium*. Allen & Greenough state that the gen. in *-iī* is found frequently in Ovid, only twice in Vergil, and never in Cicero, but many most eminent scholars, e.g. Prof. Wilkins, do not accept this rule as universal, and keep the gen. in *-iī*. A. & G. 40, *b*, and footnote; B. 25, 1, 2; G. 33, REM. 1; H. 51, 5. The derivation of *Palātium* (also called *mōns Palātīnus*) is a very open question: (1) Corssen derives it from a root *pal = to guard*, in reference to its having been the fort of early Rome and continuing to be its strongest post; (2) others derive from *Palēs*, the tutelary goddess of shepherds, or from a root *pal* (akin to *Palēs*) = *pā*, Latin *pascere*, signifying *to pasture;* (3) others derive from some supposed people called *Palātīnī* who originally occupied the hill; (4) others from *bālāre* or *pālāre, = to bleat;* (5) others from *palāntēs* (*pālor = I wander*). Of the above, (1) is much the best, and (2) appears to come next in probability. This hill was the original Rome, was the largest of Rome's seven hills, and was built and fortified in the shape of a square, hence often called *Rōma quadrāta*. The magnificent mansions of Catiline, M. Cicerō, Q. Cicerō, Clōdius, etc., stood upon it; there Tullus Hostīlius had had his residence, and there Augustus lived and held his court (hence our word *palace, =* a monarch's residence) in the house that had belonged to the orator Hortensius ; here too stood fine public buildings, e.g. the *Palātīnae Balneae* (= Palatine Baths), and the temple of Jupiter Stator, wherein the Senate is assembled to hear Cicero denounce Catiline.——**nihil**, adverbial acc. of *nihil*, indecl. n. (see *nihil* above); modifying *movērunt*, the pred. of *vigiliae*. Observe the repetition of *nihil* with each member of the composite subject of *movērunt*. This repetition is called *anaphora*, and the repeated word stands first in each sentence. *Anaphora* is a favorite rhetorical device, adding much emphasis to what is said, and often conjunctions are omitted, as here (*asyndeton*), in order to make the repeated word yet more pointed. For *anaphora*, consult A. & G. 344, *f*; B. 350, 11, *b*; G. 636, NOTE 4; H. 636, III, 3. For *asyndeton*, consult A. & G. 208, *b*; B. 346; G. 473, REM.; H. 636, I, 1.——**urbis**, gen. sing. of *urbs*, f. 3d; poss. gen., or perhaps objective (the *Palātī* above), limiting *vigiliae*. *Urbs* = all the space included within the boundary of Servius Tullius, which remained unchanged for 800 years. The suburbs outside the wall also doubtless had *vigiliae*.

6 vigiliae,	nihil	timor	populī,	nihil	the city watches, the
the watches,	*not at all*	*the fear*	*of the people,*	*not at all*	people's fear, the
7 concursus		bonōrum	omnium,	nihil hīc	thronging together of
the assemblage		*of good (citizens)*	*all,*	*not at all this*	all who are loyal, this

LINE 6. **vigiliae**, nom. plur. of *vigilia, -ae*, f. 1st (formed, as also the verb *vigilō*, from the adj. *vigil*); subj. of *mōvērunt*. The plur. *vigiliae* is often used by Caesar in a concrete sense, = *sentinels, watchmen*, and has this meaning here. The other senses of *vigilia* are: (1) *a state of wakefulness* or *watchfulness*, (2) *vigilance, watching*, (3) *watching*, at religious festivals, (4) *a watch*, in military division of time, = a 4th part of a night. Refer to the note on *praesidium* above for Sallust's mention of city-watches. *Vigiliae* includes the subordinates of the aediles and minor officials whose duty it was to keep the peace in Rome, guard against fire, and the like; in imperial times there was a *praefectus urbis*, and under him a *praefectus vigilum.*——**nihil**, adverbial acc.; modifies *mōvit* understood from *mōvērunt*, l. 10, as pred. of *timor.*——**timor**, gen. *timōris*, m. 3d (from *timeō*), subj. of *mōvit* understood from *mōvērunt*, l. 10, or a member of the composite subj. of *mōvērunt*. Synonyms: *timor* = *fear*, due to timidity or cowardice and expresses the simple emotion; *metus* = *anxiety*, due to foresight of imminent evil (defined by Cicero as *opīniō impendentis malī, quod intolerābile esse videātur = expectation of imminent evil seemingly unbearable*); *pavor* = *mind-disturbing fear (metus locō movēns mentem,* Cicero); *formīdō* = *terror (metus permanēns,* Cic.); *verēcundia* = *awe, reverential fear* (sometimes = *modest shyness*); *horror* = *shuddering fear* (from *horrescō = I bristle, I tremble*); *trepidātiō* = *consternation, agitated fear* (from *trepidō = I hurry to and fro in alarm*). Sallust, *Cat.* XXXI, *ad init.* pictures the alarm in Rome, how dejection and terror supplanted the usual gayety, how men distrusted each other, how women lamented, prayed to the gods, and trembled as they asked for information. ——**populī**, gen. sing. of *populus*, m. 2d (from a root *par* or *pal*, Latin *ple = to fill;* cf. Greek πλῆθος and Latin *plēnus*); poss. gen., limiting *timor*. *Pŏpŭlus* (old form *poplus*) = *people; pōpŭlus, -ī*, f. 2d = *poplar tree*. *Populus* = (1) *a people*, generic; (2) *the Roman people*, usually + *Rōmānus;* (3) *the Roman people*, as distinguished from *senātus;* (4) *a multitude, a throng*. Synonyms: (1) *populus = the people*, i.e. all citizens, senators, knights, and populace (*plēbs*), regarded collectively as a political whole; (2) *plēbs = the commons*, as opposed to patricians, senators, and knights; (3) *vulgus = the rabble;* (4) *gēns = a race*, the generic term, e.g. *gēns Germāna;* (5) *nātiō = a people, a tribe*, i.e. of barbarians, properly a subdivision of a *gēns*, e.g. the *Suēvī*, a *nātiō* of the *gēns Germāna;* (6) *hominēs =* the English colloquial *people*, i.e. *persons.*——**nihil**, adverbial acc.; modifies the predicate, as above.

LINE 7. **concursus**, gen. *concursūs*, m. 4th (from *concurrō, con = together + currō = I run*); nom. sing., a subj. of *mōvērunt*, l. 10, or of *mōvit* understood. The allusion is in part to the crowded Senate, but particularly to the throng of citizens (many of them carrying weapons) which had gathered round about the temple of Jupiter Stator, cf. Chap. VIII, ll. 54–56, *illī equitēs Rōmānī . . . cēterīque fortissimī cīvēs, quī circumstant senātum, ff.* These *bonī* had gathered to protect the meeting and support the city's cause against the mob violence of the conspirators. Quintilian, IX, 3, 30, reads *cōnsēnsus = agreement, unanimity*, for *concursus*, but the latter is preferable. In epistles *ad Atticum*, IV, 1, 4, Cicero states that the law repealing his banishment, which was his reward for the execution of Lentulus and other comrades of Catiline, was carried *incrēdibilī concursū Ītaliae.*——**bonōrum**, gen. plur. of the plur. noun *bonī*, m. 2d (strictly the mas. plur. of the adj. *bonus, -a, -um*, used substantively); poss. gen., modifying *concursus*. The substantival use of adjectives is very common in Latin, e.g. *multī = many men, multa = many things*, and in some cases the former use is much more

strongly protected spot for the holding of the Senate's meet-	mūnītissimus *excellently fortified*	habendī *of holding* (lit. *to be held*)	senātūs *the Senate*	locus, 8 *place,*

general than the latter, e.g. *amīcus = a friend.* A. & G. 188, 189; B. 236–238; G. 204, NOTES 1–4; H. 441. *Bonī* in Cicero = *good* or *loyal citizens*, especially members of his own party, the *Optimātēs*, composed mainly of knights and senators; Cicero's name for the chief opposing party is *populārēs* (the proletariat, which preferred a single leader of the state, e.g. Pompey, or Caesar), though often he calls it *improbī*, especially when it diverged at all from political morality and offended against the constitution. Aristocracies are fond of labelling their politics with complimentary epithets; thus in Rome the so-called *nobilēs* became known in politics as *bonī virī*, or stronger still as *optimī*, *optimātēs;* so in Athens the oligarchical party assumes the title of καλοὶ κάγαθοί, or stronger ἄριστοι, βέλτιστοι, and strongest χρηστοί, describing the democrats as μοχθηροί, or πονηροί (= lit. *villains*). From much usage these terms gradually lost moral significance, and served merely as party titles. Similarly the English *Whig* and *Tory* (now supplanted by *Liberal* and *Conservative*), which came into use in 1680 A.D., mean respectively a Scotch farmer and an Irish plunderer. —— **omnium**, gen. plur. m. of the 3d decl. adj. *omnis, -e;* agrees with *bonōrum*. Of course *omnium* adds rhetorical effect, but is not literally true, for there were many more *bonī cīvēs* in the country districts of Italy than in the city of Rome. —— **nihil**, adverbial acc.; modifies the predicate like *nihil*, l. 4. —— **hīc**, nom. sing. m. of the demonstr. pron. *hīc, haec, hōc* (gen. *hūius*, dat. *huic*); agrees with *locus*, and as spoken was probably accompanied by a gesture. It will be remembered that *hīc* denotes something near the speaker in place, thought, or time, and is therefore called the demonstr. of the 1st person; *iste* denotes something near or belonging to the person addressed, and is the demonstr. of the 2d person; *ille* denotes something remote, and is the demonstr. of the 3d pers. A. & G. 101; B. 87; G. 104; H. 186.

LINE 8. **mūnītissimus**, nom. sing. m. of the adj. *mūnītissimus, a-, -um*, superl. degree of *mūnītus, -a, -um*, perf. part. pass. of *mūniō, -īre, -īvī, -ītum*, 4 (from a root *mu = to bind, enclose, protect*, cf. Greek ἄμυνα = *defence*, *moenia*, *mūrus*, etc.); agrees with and modifies *locus*. The reference is to the strong guard of *equitēs* which surrounded the temple, as well as generally to the natural and artificially increased strength of the Palatine hill, the central hill of Rome. —— **habendī**, gen. sing. m. of *habendus, -a, -um*, gerundive of *habeō, -ēre, -uī, -itum*, 2; agrees with *senātūs* in the gerundival attraction construction. The gerundive and the gerund are respectively the adjectival and the substantival forms of a participle ending in *-ndus;* the gerund is a verbal noun, supplementing the inf. act. (which can be subj. or obj. of a sentence), and has the following cases, acc. (only used after prepositions), gen., dat., and abl.; the gerundive is declined in full like a 1st and 2d decl. adjective. The gerundive construction is a development of the use of the gerund (as verbal) with a direct object, the object being attracted into the case of the gerund, and the gerund taking adjectival inflections and agreeing with the object in gender and number; e.g. (1) gerund, *causā pācem petendī*, = *for the sake of seeking peace*, (2) gerundive, *causā pācis petendae*. Observe that the gerundive construction is preferably used in all cases where the gerund with direct object may be used; (1) after a prep., e.g. *ad pācem petendam*, much better than *ad pācem petendum;* (2) gen., as above; (3) dat., *praeesse agrīs colendīs*, = *to supervise the tilling of the fields;* (4) abl., *bellō gerendō*, = *by waging war*, or with prep., *dē pāce petendā*, = *about seeking peace. Ūtor, fruor*, and other verbs taking the abl. are used in the gerundive construction exactly as if they were transitive verbs governing an acc. case. Other uses of the gerundive are: (*a*) as an attribute, e.g. *volvenda diēs*, = *the rolling day;* (*b*) personally, as a pass. part. in a periphrastic pass. tense, e.g. *pāx*

9   nihil   hōrum   ōra   vultūsque | ing, the faces and ex-
                                                            pressions of the sena-
not at all   *of these (senators)*   *the faces*   *and expressions* | tors here among us?

petenda est = peace is to be sought (i.e. *must be* or *ought to be sought*); (*c*) as a kind of complement, after certain verbs like *cūrō, dō,* etc., e.g. *templum aedificandum cūrāvit,* = *he had a temple built.* A. & G. 296–301; B. 337, 7, and 339; G. 115, 3, and 427–433; H. 543, 544.——**senātūs,** gen. sing. of *senātus,* m. 4th (from *senex,* gen. *senis,* = *old,* cf. Greek ἕνος = *old*); subjective gen., in the gerundive construction with *habendī,* limiting *locus.* The gen. of the gerund or gerundive is sometimes subjective, sometimes objective, e.g. (1) *vīvendī fīnis est optimus,* = *it is the best end of living* (subjective), (2) *neque cōnsiliī habendī neque arma capiendī spatiō datō,* = *time being given neither for forming plans nor for taking arms* (objective). [Examples quoted from A. & G.] *Senātus* here = *a meeting of the Senate;* usually it = *the senators* regarded collectively, i.e. *the Senate.*——**locus,** gen. sing. *locī,* m. 2d; nom. sing., a subj. of *mōvērunt,* l. 10, or of *mōvit* understood. *locus* has two plurals: (1) *locī,* m., which = *places,* mentioned singly; (2) *loca,* n., = *places* connected with one another, hence *region, district.* The common senses of *locus* are: (1) *a place, spot;* (2) *a position, post;* (3) *room, occasion;* (4) *a topic,* which is being discussed; (5) *rank.* The place of meeting on this occasion was the temple of *Jupiter Stator,* on the Palatine, chosen instead of the usual *Cūria Hostīlia* because it was safer. The *cūria Hostīlia* was called after *Tullus Hostīlius,* and stood in the northern part of the *Forum Rōmānum,* between the Palatine and Capitoline hills. It was burnt down in 52 B.C., but the son of the great Sulla rebuilt it and called it *cūria Cornēlia.* Caesar demolished it, and began a new *cūria,* finished by Augustus, and known as *cūria Iūlia.* There was another senate-house, viz. the *cūria Pompēia,* built by Pompey in the *campus Martius,* in which Caesar was murdered in 44 B.C. The magistrate who called the meeting appointed where it should take place; but it could only be held in a *templum,* i.e. a building sanctioned by auspices. Note, however, that any place might be made a *templum,* if there was an augur present to take auspices and pronounce the place *inaugurātum.*

    LINE 9. **nihil,** adverbial acc.; modifies the pred. *mōvērunt,* l. 10.——**hōrum,** gen. plur. m. of the demonstr. pron. of the 1st pers. *hīc, haec, hōc;* poss. gen., limiting *ōra vultūsque; hōrum* refers to the senators present at the meeting, to whose numbers and expressions Cicero would draw Catiline's notice by the rhetorical artifice of a pause, a wide glance around, or a gesture.——**ōra,** nom. plur. of the 3d decl. noun *ōs, ōris,* n. (from Sanskrit root = *to eat,* hence *the eating part,* i.e. *the mouth;* gen. plur. not in use); subj. of *mōvērunt.* Distinguish *ōs, ōris,* from *os, ossis,* n. 3d = *a bone.* Synonyms: (1) *ōs,* by metonomy = *features, countenance,* and practically the same as (2); (2) *faciēs = face,* i.e. the form of the features, whereby we distinguish one person from another; *faciēs* in poetry often = *form,* i.e. the whole bodily appearance; (3) *vultus = the countenance,* i.e. the face as a medium expressive of mental passions and emotions; thus Cicero speaks of *vultūs simulātōs = feigned looks.* Hence it is clear that *ōra vultūsque* = *the expressions of the faces,* an instance of *Hendiadys* (ἓν διὰ δυοῖν = *one thing by means of two).* Hendiadys is the expression of a single idea, which would ordinarily require a noun + an adj. or an attributive gen., by two substantives joined by a copulative conjunction; cf. the well-known Vergilian example, *paterīs lībāmus et aurō = we make libation with bowls and gold* (i.e. *with golden bowls* or *with bowls of gold).* A. & G. 385; B. 374, 4; G. 698; H. 636, III, 2. For the attitude of the Senate towards Catiline, cf. Chap. VII, ll. 5–8, describing the silence that marked his entry and the vacation of the benches next to Catiline's seat.——**vultūs,** nom. plur. of *vultus, -ūs,* m. 4th (etymology doubtful, but perhaps akin to *volō*); joined by *que* to *ōra,* and a member of the composite subj. of *mōvērunt.*——**que** (akin to Greek τέ), enclitic cop. conj., joining *ōra*

Are you not conscious that your designs are open to the light?	mōvērunt?	Patēre	tua	cōnsilia	nōn 10
	have they moved?	*To be exposed*	*your*	*plans*	*not*

and *vultūs*. The copulative conjunctions: *que* joins together two members which have a close internal connection; *et* simply connects words or sentences; *atque* (*ac* before words beginning with any consonant except *c, g, qu*) adds emphasis to the second of the members it connects, and frequently introduces a third and important member of a series. A. & G. 156, *a*; B. 341; G. 475–477; H. 554, I.

LINE 10. **mōvērunt**, 3d pers. plur. perf. ind. act. of *moveō, -ēre, mōvī, mōtum*, 2; agrees with the subj. *ōra vultūsque* and understood with *praesidium, vigiliae, timor, concursus*, and *locus*, though all these nouns may be regarded as the composite subject. *Moveō* here has the figurative sense, *I move, affect, influence, impress*. The verb elsewhere has several meanings, e.g. *I set in motion, dislodge, remove, repulse, produce, revolve* and *declare* (poetical), *disturb*, etc. —— **Patēre**, pres. inf. act. of *pateō, -ēre, -uī*, no supine, 2 (akin to Greek πετάννυμι); agrees with its subj.-acc. *cōnsilia* in the acc. and inf. construction after *sentīs*, a verb of perception. Observe that *tua cōnsilia patēre*, the whole phrase, is the real object of *sentīs*, and that this is a simpler form of indirect discourse (*ōrātiō oblīqua*), viz. that in which the acc. and inf. is used without dependent clauses, and serves (1) as subj. of principal verb, e.g. *hominēs mortālēs esse manifestum est*, (2) as obj., e.g. *cōnsilia patēre* above. The direct thought is *tua cōnsilia patent*, and after the introductory verb *sentīs* the subj. *cōnsilia* becomes a subj.-acc., and the verb *patent* becomes an infinitive. This construction is always used after a verb of *saying, knowing, thinking, feeling*, and the like, when the verb expresses a direct thought or statement in an indirect manner. The term *indirect discourse* refers in a narrower sense to speeches or narratives reported at length, as in Livy or Caesar. In every kind of indirect discourse, the verbs of dependent clauses have the subjunct. mood, following the general rule of tense sequence with certain modifications determined by the tense of the leading verb. A. & G. 272 and REM., and 336; B. 313–318, and 330, 331; G. 508, 527, 531; H. 534, *ff*. With regard to the tense of the inf., observe that when the action of the verb in the indirect discourse is prior to that of the introductory verb of *feeling* or *saying*, the perf. inf. is used; when it is subsequent, the fut. inf.; when the time of the action of both verbs is the same, the inf. is present. So here the action of *patēre* is contemporaneous with that of *sentīs*.—— **tua**, acc. plur. n. of the poss. adj. *tuus, -a, -um* (poss. of *tū*); agrees with *cōnsilia*. —— **cōnsilia**, acc. plur. of *cōnsilium, -ī*, n. 2d (from *cōnsulō*); subj.-acc. of *patēre* above in the acc. and inf. construction after *sentīs*. Here *cōnsilia = plans, designs;* other meanings of *cōnsilium* are (1) *advice*, (2) *resolution*, (3) *deliberation*, (4) *deliberative body*, i.e. *council*. Distinguish from *concilium, -ī*, n. 2d = *an assembly* (probably from *con = together + calō* or *kalō*, Greek καλέω, = *I call*). The *cōnsilia* are general and particular; the *general* being the creation of a revolution, during which Catiline hoped to secure the chief power, overthrow the constitution, cancel all debts, and exercise a despotic oppression after the example of Marius and Sulla; the *particular* being those plans formed at Laeca's house (*vidē* Chap. IV, ll. 26–36), viz. to murder Cicero and prominent Romans, fire the city, organize the rebel army, and seize important military stations in Italy.—— **nōn** (originally *noenum*, for *ne + oenum = ūnum = not one*), neg. adv., limiting *sentīs*. *Nōn* is the common negative adverb; *haud* (= *not*) is very common with adjectives and adverbs, but is rare with verbs, except *sciō* in the expression *haud sciō an = perhaps*. *Haud* is often found limiting verbs in early writers, and reappears in Livy and Tacitus; Caesar only uses it once, viz. in *haud sciō an;* Cicero uses it in *haud sciō an*, and also has *haud dubitō, haud ignōrō, haud dubium est*, and a few other like expressions. *Nōn* may limit not only verbs, but also words and phrases.

11 sentīs?	cōnstrictam	iam	hōrum	omnium	Do you not see that
do you feel?	*held firm*	*already*	*of these (men here)*	*all*	your conspiracy is already fast held and
12 scientiā	tenērī	coniūrātiōnem		tuam	bound in the knowl-
by the knowledge	*to be checked*	*conspiracy*		*your*	edge of all who are

LINE 11. **sentīs**, 2d pers. sing. pres. ind. act. of *sentiō, -īre, sensī, sensum*, 4; the subj. implied by the personal ending is *tū*, i.e. Catiline. Observe that this simple sentence has no interrogative particle; the omission of *ne, num*, etc., occurs when the question conveys the speaker's indignation, wonder, disgust, or censure. A. & G. 210, *b*; B. 162, 2, *d*; G. 453; H. 351, 3. *Nōn sentīs* expects the affirmative answer, for *nōnne* is a compound of *nōn* and the unexpressive enclitic *ne;* refer to *ne*, l. 4.——**cōn-strictam**, acc. sing. f. of *cōnstrictus, -a, -um*, perf. part. pass. of *cōnstringō, -ere, cōn-strinxī, cōnstrictum*, 3 (*con = together + stringō = I press close*, hence *I check, repress*); agrees with *coniūrātiōnem*, and must be taken predicatively with *tenērī; cōnstrictam . . . tenērī = cōnstrictam esse et cōnstringī*, i.e. the participle (whose action is prior to that of the verb *cōnstringī*) in the predicate serves to compress two co-ordinate predications into one single predication. In English the opposite idiom is preferred, so translate *is bound firmly and held*. A. & G. 292, REM.; B. 336, 3, and 337, 2; G. 437; H. 549, 5. Cicero makes frequent use of this metaphor, which appears to be derived from the capture and caging of wild beasts.——**iam** (probably = *eam*, f. sing. of *is*), temporal adv., modifying the predicate *cōnstrictam tenērī. Iam* has a very large number of different shades of meaning, of which the chief are: (1) *now, already*, as above; (2) *now, at this time;* (3) *forthwith, at once;* (4) *just now, a moment ago;* (5) preceded by a neg., e.g. *nōn iam = no longer;* (6) in transitions, *moreover, besides;* (7) in several combinations, e.g. *iam iam = at this very moment, iam nunc*, and *iam tum (prīdem, dūdum*, etc.), where it intensifies another adverb.——**hōrum**, gen. plur. m. of the demonstr. pron. *hīc, haec, hōc;* poss. gen., limiting *conscientiā;* as in l. 9 above, *hōrum* refers to the senators; some editors arrange *omnium hōrum* for *hōrum omnium*.——**omnium**, gen. plur. m. of the 3d decl. adj. *omnis, -e* (etymology doubtful, but perhaps akin to Greek ἀμφί = *around*); agrees with *hōrum*. Synonyms: (1) *omnis = all*, or *the whole*, when number is implied and opposed to *nūllus*, but is sometimes used for *tōtus*, e.g. *omne coelum, tōtamque terram*, Cic.; (2) *tōtus = the whole*, without subtraction. Quintilian distinguishes *tōtus* and *omnēs* thus, the former as meaning *the whole* collectively, the latter as meaning *all* in detail and particularity; (3) *cunctus* or *cunctī = all*, together and in one mass (*coacervātim = in a heap*, as Apuleius says), as opposed to *sēiunctī* or *dīversī*, whereas *omnēs* might refer to far scattered units; (4) *ūnī-versī = all* (lit. *turned into one*, from *ūnus* and *vertō*), in regard to same time or unanimity, and in opposition to *singulī*, cf. *ūniversum = the universe*, Cic.; (5) *integer* (= lit. *untouched*, from *in = not + tangō = I touch*) = *the whole*, entire and without division.

LINE 12. **scientiā**, abl. sing. of *scientia, -ae*, f. 1st (from *sciēns*, pres. part. act. of *sciō*, 4 = *I know, discern*); abl. of the means or instrument with *tenērī*. It will be remembered that the instrument is expressed by the simple abl. case. A. & G. 248, *c*; B. 218; G. 401; H. 420. *Sciō (scientia), secō = I cut*, and *saxum = a rock*, are all kindred words from a root *sak* or *ski = to split, cleave, distinguish;* cf. Greek κεάζω = *I split*. There is another reading *cōnscientia* (a compound with *cum = together*) which would imply that many of the senators shared the knowledge of the conspiracy, for Schütz defines *cōnscientia* as *commūnis inter complūrēs reī alicūius nōtitia*.——**tenērī**, pres. inf. pass. of *teneō, -ēre, -uī, tentum*, 2 (akin to *tendō* and Greek τείνω = *I stretch*); agrees with its subj.-acc. *coniūrātiōnem* in the acc. and inf. construction after *vidēs*, a *verbum sentiendī;* the construction is exactly similar to that of *patēre tua cōnsilia*, l. 10.

| present here? As regards what you did last night, what the | nōn
not | vidēs?
do you see? | Quid
What | proximā,
on the preceding (night), | quid 13
what |

Tenērī in this metaphor = *dēprehendī*, for as Ernesti explains, those are said *tenērī* (*to be caught*) who have been convicted of some charge and cannot clear themselves from the meshes of the prosecutor. This verb is a favorite with Cicero, who uses it in several different connections, for which consult a reliable dictionary.——**coniūrātiōnem**, acc. sing. of *coniūrātiō, -ōnis,* f. 3d (*con = together* + *iūrō = I swear; lit. I bind myself,* from a root *iu* or *yu = to bind,* cf. *iungō* and Greek ζεύγνυμι = *I join*); subj.-acc. of *tenērī* in the acc. and inf. construction dependent on *vidēs. Coniūrātiō* rarely has the good sense of *union, agreement;* in Cicero it = *a conspiracy,* or by metonymy *a band of conspirators.*——**tuam**, acc. sing. f. of the poss. adj. *tuus, -a, -um;* agrees with *coniūrātiōnem;* Cicero calls the plot *yours* (*tuam*) because Catiline was recognized as the prime leader and the moving spirit of disaffection, as had been apparent from his behavior since his first failure to secure the consulship, and especially after the election of Decimus Jūnius Sīlānus and L. Licinius Mūrēna as consuls for 62 B.C.

LINE 13. **nōn**, negative adv. (see l. 10 above for derivation and use); limits *vidēs,* and as in *nōn sentīs* the omission of *ne* (*nōnne*) shows that the question demands an affirmative reply, and is brimful of indignation and surprise.——**vidēs**, 2d pers. sing. pres. ind. act. of *videō, -ēre, vīdī, vīsum,* 2 (from a root *vid,* Greek Ιδ, or with the *digamma* ϝιδ = *to see;* cf. the Greek εἶδον = *I saw,* for ἔϝιδον); the implied subj. is *tū,* i.e. Catiline. Synonyms: (1) *videō = I see,* the general word; (2) *cernō = I see clearly,* so as to be able to discriminate; (3) *animadvertō = I notice, turn my attention to,* as opposed to overlooking anything; (4) *aspicere* (= *ad* + *speciō*) = *to look at,* whether with or without intent; (5) *spectāre = to look at steadily,* as at the movement of the stars; (6) *intuērī = to gaze at carefully.*——**Quid**, acc. sing. n. of the interrog. pron. *quis, quae, quid* (see *quem,* l. 3); direct obj. of *ēgeris,* understood from *ēgeris,* l. 14. What Catiline had done on the night before the speech was delivered was known to Cicero from information furnished by Fulvia, the mistress of Quintus Curius, one of the conspirators; Cicero by large promises also induced Curius himself to disclose details of the plot. The historian Ihne has, not without reason, described this evidence as very untrustworthy, but Cicero certainly saved his own life through information received from Fulvia. The order may be thus simplified: *quem nostrum īgnōrāre arbitrāris quid proximā (nocte ēgeris), quid superiōre nocte ēgeris,* etc.——**proximā**, abl. sing. f. of the superl. adj. *proximus, -a, -um;* modifies *nocte,* understood from *nocte,* l. 14. *Proximus* (*proxumus*) is a superl. formed from the adv. and prep. *prope, = near;* no positive; comparative *propior* (cf. *summus* from *super,* and *īmus* from *īnfer,* though these have rare positives, *superus* and *īnferus*). *Prope, proximus, prīmus, prīdem,* etc., are all descended from an Indo-European root *pra = before,* cf. Greek πρό = *before,* πρῶτος = *first. Proximus = nearest,* hence often substantively = *a neighbor;* in point of time *proximus* may = *nearest* in the future or in the past, but in contrast to *posterus,* e.g. *posterō diē = on the next day* (*following*), usually = *nearest,* i.e. in the past, e.g. here *proximā nocte = on the night before* (preceding this day). This speech was delivered in the Senate on Nov. 8th, B.C. 63 (for the evidence, see the Introduction); *proximā* therefore refers to the preceding night, viz. Nov. 7th. Thus *superiōre* would refer to the *next before last,* i.e. Nov. 6th, the night of the meeting at Laeca's house. If it be considered that the attempt on Cicero's life was made in the early morning of Nov. 7th, directly after the meeting at Laeca's house broke up, we must account for Cicero's inaction in not calling the Senate together earlier. The main arguments in favor of the view that Vargunteius and Cornēlius tried to obtain access to Cicero on the 7th are as follows: (1) the clear statement (*illā ipsā nocte*) in Chap. IV, which certainly gives the impression

14 **superiōre　　nocte　　ēgeris,　ubi　fueris,　quōs**| night before, where
　last but one　on the night　you did,　where you were,　whom| you were, what men

that the attempt was made on the 7th; (2) Sallust, XXVII *ad fin.* and XXVIII *ad init.* describes the meeting at Laeca's house, the promise to kill Cicero that same night, the hasty communication of the plot through Fulvia to Cicero, so as to set him on his guard, and concludes "and so, as they (the would-be murderers) were refused admission, they undertook the very desperate deed all in vain"; (3) Catiline was anxious to leave Rome and join Manlius immediately, and it was unlikely that Vargunteius and Cornēlius would wait at the meeting and allow it to grow so late as to have to defer the attempt till the next morning (the 8th); (4) Cicero very likely thought Catiline would set off on the night of the 7th of Nov., whether the consul were murdered or not, and as the 1st Oration aims only at driving Catiline from Rome, Cicero would have been satisfied with his departure. This would account for deferring the Senate's meeting till the 8th. (5) Cicero had every movement of Catiline watched, and so in referring to "last night" (*proximā nocte*) he is merely trying to terrify Catiline by the evidence of his carefulness. For the evidence in favor of the view that Cicero's life was threatened on the 8th (Mommsen's view), see the note on *hesternō* (*diē*), Chap. VI, of the 2d Oration.—— *quid*, acc. sing. n. of the interrog. pron. *quis, quae, quid;* direct obj. of *ēgeris*, l. 14; introduces an indirect question after *īgnōrāre*, exactly like *quid* above. Observe that the indirect clauses follow one another without any connecting conjunctions, whereby they are made more emphatic (*asyndeton*). A. & G. 208, *b*; B. 346; G. 473, REM.; H. 636, I, 1. The stock example of *asyndeton* is Caesar's letter to Rome, consisting of three words, — *vēni, vīdi, vīci.*

LINE 14. **superiōre**, abl. sing. of the comparative adj. *superior, -ius*, 3d decl.; modifies *nocte* below. *Superior* is the comparative of the rare positive *superus*, chiefly found in the poets (though Cic. speaks of *supera, īnfera*, both rare), derived from the adv. or prep. *super* (not from *suprā*, which = *superā*, adverbial f. of *superus*); in the plur. *superī* = *the gods above*, just as *īnferī* = *the gods below;* the superl. has two forms (1) *suprēmus* = *last*, (2) *summus* = *highest*. In origin *super* = Greek ὑπέρ, and so of place *superior* = *upper;* of time *earlier, older, previous* (special, *next before last*); of quality, *superior, higher, more distinguished*. As stated above, *superiōre nocte* = Nov. 6th, as we assume the Senate to have met on the 8th. If, however, we suppose the first speech to have been delivered on Nov. 7th (and there is a fair amount of support for this view; see the Introduction, and II, Chap. VI, *hesternō diē) proximā*, l. 13 would refer to Nov. 6th when Laeca's house was the conspirators' rendezvous, and *superiōre* here and *priōre* Chap. IV, l. 5, to Nov. 5th. But we have no definite information about what happened, on Nov. 5th.—— **nocte**, abl. sing. of *nox, noctis*, f. 3d (akin to Greek νύξ, and Ind.-Eur. root *nak*); abl. of *time when*. *Time when* is expressed by the abl. without a preposition, *time within which* by the abl. with or without the prep. *in.* A. & G. 256; B. 230; G. 393; H. 429. We have no information as to the time when the meeting at Laeca's house on Nov. 6th began or ended. Prof. Wilkins contents himself with saying it was held on the night of Nov. 6th-7th, i.e. probably continuing till the early morning hours of the 7th. Mommsen (see Introduction) argues that it lasted so long, that Vargunteius and Cornēlius were unable to attend Cicero's morning levée.—— **ēgeris**, 2d pers. sing. perf. subjunct. act. of *agō, -ere, ēgī, actum*, 3 (from a root *ag*, Greek ἄγ = *to drive, put in motion*, hence *do;* cf. Greek ἄγω = *I lead, drive*, etc.); the subj. implied by the personal ending is *tū* = Catiline. The root *ag* has many different meanings, which accounts for the multiplicity of the senses of *agō*, e.g. *I lead, do, guide, rob, chase, spend* (*time*), *treat* (*with* some one), etc.; Martial devotes a whole epigram to the illustration of some of these, concluding with the phrase *actum est dē* (*aliquō*) = *it is all over with* (*some one*). For Catiline's doings, refer to the introduction, on Catiline's conspi-

you summoned to-gether, what scheme you took in hand,	convocāveris, quid cōnsilī cēperis, quem 1 *you called together, what (of) design you undertook, whom*

racy. *Ēgeris* is subjunct. in the indirect question *quid ēgeris* dependent on the inf. *ignōrāre;* the simple question would be *quid ēgistī = what did you do?* NOTE. Indirect questions: (1) are introduced by an interrog. pronoun, adjective, or adverb; (2) give the substance of a question contained within the whole compound sentence, but not retaining the form of a direct question; (3) are connected with some verb or verbal expression, either as subj. or obj., e.g. as subj. *quis sīs mihi nōtum est*, as obj. *sciō quis sīs;* (4) the verb of the contained question is put in the subjunct. mood, and conforms to the rule of tense sequence. A. & G. 334; B. 300; G. 467; H. 528, 2, and 529, I. The rule of tense sequence is: that *primary* tenses of the ind. in the principal clause (fut., perf., and fut. perf.) are followed by *primary* in the subjunct. of the subordinate clause (pres., perf., and periphrastic fut., e.g. *actūrus sim*), and *historic* or *secondary* in the ind. (imperf., pluperf., and perf. indefinite or *aorist*) by *historic* in the subjunct. (imperf., pluperf., and periphrastic fut., e.g. *actūrus essem*). A. & G. 286; B. 267, 268; G. 509, *ff;* H. 491.——ubĭ, for *quo-bi*, akin to the rel. *quī*, and Greek ποῦ = *where*, from a root *ka*, in Latin *quo*, in Greek κο or πο), interrog. adv. of place; introduces the indirect question *ubĭ fueris*, dependent on *ignōrāre. Ubĭ* is in origin a rel. local adv., corresponding to the demonstr. *ibĭ = there.* Its uses: (1) rel., e.g. *ibĭ . . . ubĭ = there . . . where;* (2) temporal conj. = *when*, e.g. *haec ubĭ dicta* (*sunt*), Vergil; (3) rel. with regard to antecedent persons or things = *by, with, which* or *whom;* (4) interrog. of place or time = *when? where?* Cicero tells us (Chap. IV, ll. 4–6) where Catiline was on Nov. 6th, and here implies knowledge of his movements on the 7th also, though he does not describe them.——fueris, 2d pers. sing. perf. subjunct. of the verb *sum, esse, fuī;* the implied subj. is *tū.* The tense is perf., describing past events in subordinate sequence after a primary principal verb, *ignōrāre arbitrāris;* for references, consult note on *ēgeris* above.——quōs, acc. plur. m. of the interrog. pron. *quis, quae, quid;* direct obj. of *convocāveris*, and introduces an indirect question. Sallust (chapter 17) gives a list of the conspirators at Laeca's house, including 11 prominent men (given by name) of patrician rank, 4 of equestrian (named), and many men of influence from the colonies and *mūnicĭpia.*

LINE 15. convocāveris, 2d. pers. sing. perf. subjunct. act. of *convocō, -āre, -āvī, -ātum,* 1 (*con = together,* + *vocō = I call*, from a root *vak = to speak, call*); the implied subj. is *tū;* the construction is similar to that of *ēgeris* and *fueris* above. Those who assign this speech to Nov. 7th consider that this refers to Catiline's occupation *superiōre nocte,* Nov. 5th.——quid, acc. sing. n. of the interrog. pron. *quis, quae, quid;* direct obj. of *cēperis*, and introduces an indirect question.——cōnsilī, gen. sing. of *cōnsilium* (see *cōnsilia*, l. 10) n. 2d; partitive gen., after *quid.* The partitive gen. represents the whole to which a part is assigned, and so is a branch of the ordinary poss. gen. It may be used with nouns, e.g. *pars mīlitum;* pronouns, e.g. *iī nostrum = those of us;* adjectives, especially numerals, e.g. *multī* or *ūnus mīlitum;* comparatives and superlatives, e.g. *fortior* or *fortissimus mīlitum* (*fortior = braver*, of two); many neut. adjectives and pronouns, e.g. *nihil novī = nothing new;* and even adverbs, e.g. *ubĭ terrārum = where on earth.* A. & G. 216, 3; B. 201, 2; G. 369; H. 397, 3. For the contraction of the gen. from *-iī* to *-ī,* refer to the note and references under *Palātī,* l. 5.——cēperis, 2d pers. sing. perf. subjunct. act. of *capiō, -ere, -cēpī, captum,* 3 (from an Ind.-Eur. root *kap = to take hold of;* cf. Greek κώπη = *a handle*); the subj. understood is *tū;* the verb is in the subjunc. because the question *quid cēperis* is indirect, the construction being like that of *quid ēgeris,* l. 14.——quem, acc. sing. m. of the interrog. pron. *quis, quae, quid;* direct obj. of *arbitrāris,* and subj.-acc. of *ignōrāre,* which is a *verbum sentiendi.* Observe that

16	nostrum	īgnōrāre	arbitrāris?	Ō	tempora,	whom of us do you
	of us	*to be ignorant of*	*do you think?*	*Oh*	*the times,*	suppose to be igno-rant? What an age,
17	ō	mōrēs!	senātus	haec	intellegit,	what conduct are ours! The Senate
	oh	*the manners!*	*The senate*	*these things*	*understands,*	perceives these evils,

quem introduces a direct question, *quem īgnōrāre arbitrāris?* = *whom do you think not to know?* whereas *quid ēgeris*, etc., are indirect and dependent on *īgnōrāre*. The question here is rhetorical, and = an emphatic statement, *nēmō nostrum īgnōrat*. There could scarcely be any senator who was not aware of the conspiracy, at least after the consuls were empowered by the Senate to protect the state from harm (Oct. 21st, *circ.*).

LINE 16. **nostrum**, gen. plur. of the 1st pers. pron. *ego*, plur. *nōs* (cf. Greek ἐγώ); partitive gen., after *quem*, cf. *quid cōnsilī* above. Observe that *ego* and *tū* have two forms of the gen. plur., viz. *nostrī* and *nostrum*, and *vestrī* and *vestrum ;* as a general rule the form in *-um* is *partitive*, and the form in *-ī objective*. A. & G. 194, *b* ; B. 241, 2 ; G. 364, REM. ; H. 446, NOTE 3.——**īgnōrāre**, pres. inf. at. of *īgnōrō, -āre, -āvī, -ātum,* 1 (from *in = not* + root *gna* or *gno = to know,* cf. *īgnārus, noscō*, etc., and Greek γνῶσις); agrees with the subj.-acc. *quem* in the simple acc. and inf. construction dependent on *arbitrāris*, the tense being present because the action of *īgnōrāre* and of *arbitrāris* is contemporaneous ; refer to the note on *patēre*, l. 10. The negative use of the particle *in-* should be noted ; this particle is akin to the Sanskrit *a*, the Greek α(ἀνα-, ἀν-) privative, as in ἄπειρος = *inexperienced,* the English *un-, in-, im-,* as in *unnecessary, intolerable, impossible.*——**arbitrāris**, 2d pers. sing. pres. ind. of the deponent verb *arbitror, -ārī, -ātus sum,* 1 (from *arbiter = lit. one who goes to see,* hence *spectator,* or *one who goes to inquire into something,* hence *an arbiter, judge*); the implied subj. is *tū*. The active form *arbitrō, -āre,* no perf., *-ātum,* 1, is found in Plautus, etc. = (1) *to decide ;* (2) *to think ;* but is little used by Cicero. *Arbitror* and *arbiter* are derived from *ar = ad, to,* + root *bi* or *bit = to go ;* cf. Greek βάσις, ἔ-βη-ν ; the Latin root sometimes appears as *bu* and *ven,* cf. *am-bu-lō, ven-iō.* Synonyms : (1) *rērī* = *to think, to consider as a fact ;* (2) *opīnārī = to think, to form an opinion,* not implying real knowledge ; (3) *arbitrārī = to think, to decide,* from an examination of disputed matters, and differs from *rērī* and *opīnārī,* as it denotes the expression of an opinion, whereas they denote merely the entertainment ; (4) *exīstimāre = to think,* after logical consideration ; (5) *cēnsēre = to think, to resolve,* in an official sense, as of the Senate ; (6) *iūdicāre = to judge ;* (7) *putāre = lit. to clear up,* hence *to settle, to think,* sometimes *to suspect.*——**Ō**, interjection, used to express joy, sorrow, desire, wonder, indignation, and other emotions. Here *ō* is attached to the acc. *tempora* in an exclamation. *Ō* is often found : (1) with the voc., to emphasize the address and command attention ; (2) with the nom., to emphasize a characteristic ; (3) with *sī* (*ō sī = utinam*), followed by the subjunct. of desire (*optative*) ; (4) *ō* precedes the word it emphasizes, but in poetry sometimes stands after it, e.g. *spēs ō fīdissima Teucrūm,* Vergil.——**tempora**, acc. plur. of *tempus, temporis,* n. 3d (from an Ind.-Eur. root *tam,* Latin *tem = to cut,* cf. Greek τέμ-νω = *I cut ;* hence *tem-pus = lit. a section* of time); exclamatory acc. ; cf. *mē miserum = wretched me !* A. & G. 240, *d* ; B. 183 ; G. 343, 1 ; H. 381. This acc. may be used with or without an interjection, as *ō, prō,* etc. Cicero uses this same exclamation elsewhere, e.g. in his speech against Verrēs. *Tempora* here = *the times,* i.e. the condition of present circumstances ; the commonest sense is simply *time ;* sometimes *tempus = emergency.*

LINE 17. **ō**, exclamatory interjection, emphasizing *mōrēs.*——**mōrēs**, acc. plur. of ·
mōs, mōris, m. 3d ; exclamatory acc., like *tempora* above. In the sing. *mōs = custom, way, fashion ;* in the plur. *manners, morals,* and very often *character.*——**senātūs**, gen.

| the consul sees them, | cōnsul | videt: | hīc | tamen | vīvit. 18 |
| — yet this fellow | *the consul* | *sees (them):* | *this man* | *nevertheless* | *lives.* |

senātus, m. 4th (from *senex = old*); nom. sing., subj. of *intellegit; senātus* here has its common collective sense, *the Senate,* i.e. all the senators. —— **haec**, acc. plur. n. of the demonstr. pron. *hīc, haec, hōc;* direct obj. of *intellegit;* under *haec* are included the signs of the conspiracy mentioned in ll. 13-15. —— **intellegit**, 3d pers. sing. pres. ind. act. of *intellegō, -ere, intellexī, intellectum,* 3 (from *inter = between,* + *legō = I choose;* hence *I perceive, understand*); agrees with its subj. *senātus.* It is better to regard this verb as a compound of *legō = I choose,* although the commoner meanings are *I gather, I read,* and although *legō* is the usual verb = *I choose;* but in point of fact both *legō* and *lēgō* are from one root *lag* (Latin *leg,* Greek λεγ) = *to collect,* cf. Greek λέγω = (1) *I pick, count, collect,* (2) *I speak, tell. Intellegō, neglegō,* and *aequeparō* are often incorrectly written as *intelligō, negligō,* and *aequiparō;* cf. Prof. Mayor, quoting Ritschl, Prolegoma, page XCVII, " *Nec antīquitās . . . formās nōvit, sed in hīs e vōcālem probāvit sōlam,*" = " *antiquity was not acquainted with the forms* (in *i*), *but sanctioned only the vowel e in these verbs.*" Synonyms: (1) *intellegere = to perceive* by the senses or understanding; (2) *nōscere = to know* things or attributes as the objects of perception, e.g. *nōvī hominem = I know the man;* (3) *cōgnōscere = to know, to recognize, to ascertain;* (4) *percipere = lit. to seize,* hence *to hear, to comprehend;* (5) *sciō,* and its neg. *nesciō = to know* facts or truths, as the objects of conviction, e.g. *sciō quis sit.* The above verbs express mental selection or perception, as opposed to sensual perception, for which refer to *videt* in the following line.

LINE 18. **cōnsul**, gen. *cōnsulis,* m. 3d (from *cōnsulō = I consult,* because the consuls were executive officers, who summoned the Senate to consult it and carry out its orders); nom. sing., subj. of *videt.* Observe the *asyndeton,* whereby greater stress is laid upon the facts of the Senate's knowledge and the consuls' perception of the conspiracy. Either Cicero is referring to himself impersonally when he uses *cōnsul* in the sing. and is ignoring his colleague in office, or he is using the noun in an abstract sense in reference to the magistracy rather than the magistrate. Cicero's colleague in the consulship was Gāius Antōnius, the younger son of the orator Marcus Antōnius, and the brother of Marcus Antōnius Crēticus, the great triumvir's father. He was a man of dissolute life which made him acquainted with Catiline and also caused his expulsion from the Senate in 70 B.C. He was Cicero's colleague in the praetorship in 65 B.C., and stood with him for the consulship in 64 B.C. He was then implicated in Catiline's plot, but Cicero won him over to his own side by offering him the rich province of Macedonia for government as proconsul. Being appointed to lead the Roman army against Catiline, he preferred to send his legate Marcus Petreius against his former friend. He misgoverned Macedonia, where he was in command for two years, and in B.C. 59 was accused on this count and on the charge of complicity in Catiline's plot. In spite of Cicero's defence he was found guilty and went into exile to Cephallēnia, whence he was afterwards recalled, for he was in Rome in 44 B.C. —— **videt**, 3d pers. sing. pres. ind. act. of *videō, -ēre, vīdī, vīsum,* 2 (root *vid,* cf. Greek εἶδον = εϝιδον); agrees with its subj. *cōnsul.* For synonyms, refer to the note on *vidēs,* l. 13. —— **hīc**, nom. sing. m. of the demonstr. pron. *hīc, haec, hōc;* subj. of *vīvit; hīc* is deictic and very emphatic. —— **tamen**, adv. or adversative conj., introducing an idea opposed to what has preceded. Adversative particles: (1) *tamen,* = *yet, however,* etc. *Tamen* is usually prepositive, i.e. stands first in the sentence, but when a particular word is to be emphasized (as *hīc* above) *tamen* is postpositive; *tamen* may or may not be preceded by a concessive clause with *etsī* or *etiamsī,* to which *senātus intellegit, consul videt* is equivalent; (2) *sed = but,* strongest of the adversative particles, *sed* and *tamen* being the only ones that are really adversative; *sed* may be used in two ways, (*a*) in a strong sense, *but* contradictory; (*b*) in a weaker sense, introducing a

19	Vīvit?	Immō	vērō	etiam	in	senātum	lives!	Lives, did I
	He lives?	*Nay more*	*but*	*even*	*into*	*the senate*	say?	Nay, he even

new idea; it is often strengthened by the conjunction of *tamen, autem, enim*, or *vērō*; (3) *vērum* and *vērā* are somewhat weaker than *sed*, often = *indeed;* the former usually stands first in the sentence, the latter second; (4) *at* introduces some new and lively objection, and so does its stronger form *atquī* (most common in argumentative sentences); (5) *cēterum* = *besides, for the rest*, occurs once in Terence and once in Cicero, but is fairly common in Sallust and later writers; (6) *autem* is the weakest of all the adversatives, and is often scarcely anything more than connective. A. & G. 156, *b*; B. 343, I; G. 483–491; H. 554, III.——vīvit, 3d pers. sing. pres. ind. act. of *vīvō, -ere, vīxī, victum*, 3 (from a root *gi, gviv*, = *to live;* cf. Greek βίος from root βι); agrees with the subj. *hic*.

LINE 19. Vīvit, 3d pers. sing. pres. ind. act. of *vīvō* (as above); the subj. implied is a pron. referring to Catiline. Observe that ll. 16–24 are spoken aside or rather addressed to the senators. Also note that the question *vīvit* has no interrog. particle; this is because the question is rhetorical and expresses intense indignation; refer to the note on *sentīs*, l. 11, for references. Though Cicero here and in several other places hints or says that Catiline should have been executed long ago, yet it is clear from the speeches that he did not dare to employ extreme measures until he had documentary and irrefragable proof of the conspiracy. The real object of this speech was to drive Catiline from Rome into manifest rebellion. It is true that on or about Oct. 21st the Senate had empowered the consuls to take any measures to protect the state, but even when the conspiracy was fully proved the authority of this *senātūs cōnsultum ultimum* is open to strong dispute (see Introduction), and Cicero's execution of Lentulus and others caused his banishment.——Immō, adv., partly correcting and partly emphasizing what has been already said, and when so used often strengthened by *vērō*, cf. Greek μὲν οὖν. Observe the rhetorical figure (*correctiō*) of a question immediately followed by an emphatic statement. Other uses of *immō* are: (1) in replies, = *no indeed*, or *yes indeed;* (2) in the phrase *immō sī sciās (audiās)* = *yes* (or *no*) *if you only knew (heard)*, found in Plautus, and implying that the condition was not realized; (3) corrective, in the middle of sentences, e.g. Livy, *simulācra deūm, deōs immō ipsōs* = *the images of the gods, nay the gods themselves.*——vērō, adv., = *truly, however, but in fact*, here strengthening *immō*. Some of the older editors omit *vērō*, but the best editions retain it. In origin *vērō* is the adverbial abl. n. sing. of the adj. *vērus, -a, -um*, just as *vērum* is the adverbial acc. n. sing. of the same adjective; cf. *subitō*. A. & G. 148, *e*; B. 77, 2; G. 91, 2, *c*; H. 304, II.——etiam, adv., intensifying *venit in senātum*. For the uses of *etiam*, and grammatical references, see the note on *etiam*, l. 2.——in, prep. with the acc.; governs *senātum. In* = *to, into*, i.e. into the interior; *ad* = *to, towards*, i.e. to the borders.—— senātum, acc. sing. of *senātus, -ūs*, m. 4th; governed by the prep. *in; senātum* here = the meeting place of the Senate, just as *cūriam* might be used. Cicero pictures Catiline's audacities in an ascending manner; he says first that he ought to be dead, but not being dead he actually enters the Senate; but he does not enter the Senate to make a petition for mercy, but to consult on the general welfare as if he were an honest citizen; as a climax of effrontery, he is present to see and make a note of the men who best uphold the constitution, intending to have them murdered. By the legislation of Sulla the Senate was confined to acting and past magistrates, and though in 70 B.C. the censors' authority was revived and 64 senators were expelled, yet its constitution was little affected. Accordingly, as an ex-praetor, Catiline could attend the Senate as a member, being classified as a *vir praetōrius* (cf. *virī cōnsulārēs, quaestōriī*, etc.). As one who had held a curule office, he wore the *mulleus*, which was a purple shoe, and the *toga praetexta*. All ordinary senators wore the *calceus senātōrius*, which was a peculiar kind of half-boot, and the *tunica lāticlāvia* (with wide purple edges).

| enters the Senate, shares in the deliberations of the commonwealth, marks and picks out with his eyes each of us | venit, he comes, | fit he becomes | pūblicī public | cōnsilī of the deliberation | particeps, 20 a sharer, |
| | notat he observes | et and | dēsīgnat marks out | oculīs with his eyes | ad caedem 21 for murder |

LINE 20. **venit**, 3d pers. sing. pres. ind. act. of *veniō, -īre, vēnī, ventum*, 4 (from an Ind.-Eur. root *ga, va*, etc., Latin *bi, bu*, or *ven*, = *to go;* cf. Greek βαίνω = *I go*, from root *βα*); agrees with the implied pron.-subj. referring to Catiline. Observe that the present tense is here used of a past act in order to make it vivid and emphatic; this is called the *historic* present, and is very common in emotional speeches and graphic descriptions (as in Livy's battle-scenes). A. & G. 276, *d*; B. 259, 3; G. 229; H. 467, III. That the tense is present and not perfect (*vēnit*) is obvious from a comparison of the coördinate verbs *fit* below, and *notat* and *dēsīgnat* in the next line.——**fit**, 3d pers. sing. pres. ind. of *fiō, fierī, factus sum*, irreg. and intrans. (used (1) = *to become, happen*, (2) as pass. of *faciō = to be done*); the implied subj. is a pron. referring to Catiline. *Faciō* and *fiō* are derived from an Ind.-Eur. root *dha*, Latin *fa(c)*, = *to do, make*, or *place*. The tense is *historic* present, like *venit* above.——**pūblicī**, gen. sing. n. of the adj. *pūblicus, -a, -um* (from root *par* or *pal*, Latin *ple*, Greek πλα or πλε = *to fill*, being a contraction of *populicus*, = pertaining to the *populus, people;* cf. Greek πλέος = *full*, and πλῆθος = *throng*); agrees with and modifies *cōnsilī*. As its origin implies, *pūblicus* always refers to something affecting the state, e.g. *equus pūblicus*, the horse *provided by the state* for an *equus;* so *rēs pūblica* = lit. *the interest* or *weal of the state*, hence often = *the state*. As an attribute of an individual, *pūblicus* denotes one holding office in the state, as opposed to *prīvātus (homō)*, i.e. one who is not a magistrate; thus *pūblicē sepelīrī = to be buried with a state funeral*, as opposed to *prīvātim*. The same distinction is noteworthy in Greek between κοινός = *public*, and ἴδιος = *private*.——**cōnsilī** (contracted from *cōnsiliī*), gen. sing. of *cōnsilium*, n. 2d (see *cōnsilī*, l. 15); objective gen., limiting *particeps*. This gen. is found limiting adjectives expressing *fulness, sharing, power, memory, knowledge*, etc. A. & G. 218, *a*; B. 204, 1; G. 374; H. 399, I. In post-classical Latin *particeps* is frequently found with the dative case. *Cōnsilī* might = here (1) *counsel, deliberation*, or (2) *the deliberating body;* the second meaning is not uncommon, but there is no necessity for insisting on it here, as Upcott does. The rest of Upcott's note, however, is worth notice, wherein he says that any state-constituted body of men gathered together for deliberation was called *cōnsilium pūblicum*, as for example the board of *iūdicēs* who met to try a law-case.——**particeps**, gen. *participis*, 3d decl. adj. often used substantively as here (from *pars = a part*, + *capiō = I take*, hence *sharing*); nom. sing. m., complement in the predicate of the *copulative* verb *fit*. It should be remembered that the *copula sum*, and verbs signifying *to be named, to be made* (*elected*, etc.), *to become, to seem*, and the like, are used with a predicate noun or adj. so as to make a complete predication; the predicate noun or adj. is in the same case as its subject. Observe that *sum = I am* is *copulative;* but *sum = I exist* is the *substantive* verb, making a complete predicate. A. & G. 176; B. 233, 2; G. 205, 206; H. 360.

LINE 21. **notat**, 3d pers. sing. pres. ind. act. of *notō, -āre, -āvī, -ātum*, 1 (from *nota = a mark*, from root *gna (gno) = to know*, hence *that by which something is known*); the implied subj.-pron. refers to Catiline. *Notat = marks, singles out*, so as to know with a view to destroying in the future. Observe the absence of conjunctions between these coördinate sentences (*asyndeton*).——**et**, copulative conj., connecting *notat* and *dēsīgnat*. In etymology *et* and *atque* seem to be akin to one another, and also to the Greek ἔτι = *still*. For the cop. conjunctions, refer to the note on *que*, l. 9.——

22 **ūnum quemque nostrum. Nōs autem, fortēs** | individually for mas-
one   each   of us.   We   however,   brave | sacre. While we, men

dēsīgnat, 3d. pers. sing. pres. ind. act. of *dēsīgnō, -āre, -āvī, -ātum*, 1 (*dē + sīgnō*, from *sīgnum = a mark*); its subj. is a pron. understood. *Dēsīgnō* = lit. *I mark out*, e.g. Vergil, *urbem dēsīgnat arātrō;* hence *I mark, select*, e.g. officially *cōnsul dēsīgnātus = the consul elect.* —— **oculīs**, abl. plur. of *oculus, -ī*, m. 2d (from a root *ak*, Latin *oc*, Greek ὄπ, cf. Greek ὄμμα (= ὄπμα) = *sight*); abl. of the means or instrument, extending the pred. *notat et dēsīgnat. Oculus* has a diminutive form *ocellus*, used as a term of endearment. Cicero's ideas of Catiline's daring are exaggerated by his excitement and his fear of the man ; Sallust seems to explain Catiline's attendance more reasonably by imputing it to the desire of appearing ingenuously innocent or else of clearing himself of any charges that might be made against him. —— **ad**, prep. with the acc. ; governs *caedem*, and = *for*, expressing purpose. *Ad* has many applications which it is instructive to note : (1) motion, *to*, or direction, *towards;* (2) reference, *as regards;* (3) manner, *according to;* (4) place, *at* or *near;* (5) time, *at*, generally of future time; (6) with numbers, *about;* (7) *ad* occurs in many phrases, and after Cicero *ad* + the acc. becomes to some extent a substitute for the dat. case. For examples, consult A. & G. 153, under AD ; B. 182, 3 ; G. 416, 1 ; H. 433, I, AD. —— **caedem**, acc. sing. of *caedēs, -is,* f. 3d (from *caedō = I cut, I kill;* Sanskrit root *khid*, Greek σχιδ, cf. σχίζω and *scindō = I split*); governed by the prep. *ad.* The prose authors use *caedēs* of (1) *slaughter*, in battle, (2) *murder*, by an assassin ; the second meaning is the one that keeps recurring in these speeches.

    LINE 22. **ūnum**, acc. sing. m. of the cardinal numeral adj. *ūnus, -a, -um*, gen. *ūnīus*, dat. *ūnī* (old forms *oinus* and *oenos*, akin to Greek εἷς, gen. ἐν-ός = *one*, and οἴνη, *the ace* on dice); agrees with and modifies emphatically *quemque.* —— **quemque**, acc. sing. m. of the indef. pron. *quisque, quaeque, quidque* (when used adjectively the neut. is *quodque*); direct obj. of *notat* and *dēsīgnat; quemque ūnum* = not *all of us*, but *each of us singly*, i.e. individually, for Cicero does not mean to say that Catiline will destroy every senator, but such individuals among them as he has marked as enemies, cf. Sect. IV, ll. 11, 12, wherein Cicero says that some of Catiline's accomplices are present in the Senate. Special uses of *quisque* are : (1) with superlatives, e.g. *fortissimus quisque = all the bravest* men ; (2) with ordinal numerals, to express generality, e.g. *tertiō quōque verbō = at every third word;* (3) with *prīmus*, e.g. *prīmō quōque tempore*, Cic. = *on the very first occasion;* (4) rarely, *quisque = each* of two, instead of *uterque;* and in Plautus *quisque* appears as feminine. —— **nostrum**, gen. plur. of 1st pers. pron. *ego* (plur. *nōs*) ; — partitive gen., limiting *quemque.* For *nostrum* partitive, and *nostrī* objective, etc., refer to the note on *nostrum*, l. 16. —— **Nōs**, nom. plur. of *ego;* subj. of *vidēmur*, l. 23. When the subj. is a personal pron., it is not usually expressed, except for the purpose of emphasis or contrast ; *nōs* here is emphatic and scornful. —— **autem**, adversative conj. (see note on *tamen*, l. 18); introducing a contrast to the previous statement — Catiline is a bold murderer, *but we* are shrinking cowards. —— **fortēs**, nom. plur. m. of the adj. *fortis, -e*, 3d decl. (akin to *fīrmus*, and *frēnum*, from a root *dhar* (*dhra*) = *to support*); modifies *virī;* some editors arrange *virī fortēs. Fortēs* is ironical here, for Cicero really charges himself and the Senate with timidity for not having already brought Catiline to account for his crimes. Synonyms : (1) *fortis = brave*, chiefly with regard to strength and firmness of mind, though sometimes of mere physical strength ; as applied to statesmen (*virī fortēs* or *fortissimī*) *fortis* denotes a character that cannot be driven from duty by fear, but must express itself freely in the face of peril ; (2) *animōsus = spirited*, an attribute of the spiritual and emotional part of a man (*animus*); as distinguished from *fortis, animōsus = animī vehementiam habēns;* (3) *strenuus = strong, energetic*, and always refers to action, as an attribute of one characterized by deeds of prowess.

of courage, think we are fulfilling our obligation to the state if	virī,	satis	facere	reī pūblicae	vidēmur, 23
	men,	enough	to do	for the weal common	seem,

LINE 23. **virī**, nom. plur. of *vir, virī,* m. 2d (gen. plur. *virōrum* sometimes contracted to *virūm*); in apposition with the subj. *nōs.* An appositive is a noun not in the predicate describing another noun, and standing in the same case. A. & G. 184; B. 169; G. 320, *ff*; H. 359, NOTE 2. Synonyms: (1) *vir = a man,* as distinguished from a woman, hence frequently *husband;* a special sense is *hero,* as in Vergil, *Aen.* I, 1, *Arma virumque canō;* vir, as regards adjectival attribution, is used only with reference to good qualities, e.g. *vir fortis* or *cōnstāns;* (2) *homō = a man,* as distinguished from *deī* on one side and *bestiae* on the other; it is used with regard to virtues or vices, birth, intelligence, etc., e.g. *homō improbus, nōbilis, īndoctus,* etc.; in the plur., *hominēs = mankind,* including men and women. —— **satis** (or *sat*), adv. (from a root *sat,* akin to Greek ἅδ, cf. *satiō,* 1 = *I satisfy* and Greek ἁδ-έω); modifies *facere* and with it becomes one idea *to satisfy,* hence often written in one *satisfacere;* or *satis* may be taken as an indecl. noun, the direct obj. of *facere. Satis* appears to have three distinct uses: (1) as adjective; thus it has a comparative degree *satius = better;* (2) indecl. noun; (3) adverb. *Satis* occurs in many phrases: (1) *satis accipere vel dare = to take or to give sufficient bail;* (2) *satis facere = to satisfy,* often in a mercantile sense = *to pay a creditor;* another sense is *to give satisfaction, to apologize.* —— **facere**, pres. inf. act. of *faciō, -ere, fēcī, factum,* 3 (from the same root as *fit,* l. 20); *prolative* inf., with *vidēmur.* Certain verbs, e.g. *to seem, dare, be able, begin, hesitate, learn, know how,* etc., which suggest a further action of the same subject, require an inf. (without any subj.-acc.) to complete their meaning. This inf. is variously called *complementary, prolative, epexegetic,* and *explanatory,* though some grammarians reserve the names *prolative* and *epexegetic* for an extended poetical use of the inf. instead of the subjunct. with *ut.* A. & G. 271; B. 326; G. 423; H. 533. *Satisfacere reī pūblicae = lit. to do enough for the state,* i.e. *to fulfil our duty to the state.* —— **reī**, dat. sing. of *rēs, reī,* f. 5th; dat. of the indirect obj. with *satis* in *satis facere. Rēs* has many different meanings: (1) *event, thing, circumstance;* (2) *a real thing, fact,* as *rē vērā = in truth;* (3) in plur., *property, possessions;* (4) *benefit, advantage;* (5) *cause, ground, reason;* (6) *an affair, business;* (7) *a case* in law, *cause, suit;* (8) very many phrases, e.g. *rēs pūblica = good of the community, administration,* and often = *cīvitas, the state.* The context is the only guide for the rendering of *rēs.* In combinations, observe especially *rēs prosperae (adversae) = prosperity (adversity);* rēs *gestae = achievements, facts* of history; *rēs mīlitāres = the art of war; rēs novae = revolution; rēs familiāris = property; rērum potīrī = to become master of the government; rēs ratiōnēsque = business relations.* The above are only a small fraction of the Ciceronian idioms in which *rēs* bears a part. —— **pūblicae**, dat. sing. f. of the adj. *pūblicus, -a, -um* (see *pūblicī,* l. 20); modifies *reī;* when *pūblica* occurs in combination with *rēs,* many editors write in one *rēspūblica; cf. quamdiū, senātūscōnsultum.* —— **vidēmur**, 1st pers. plur. pres. ind. of *videōr* used as deponent (properly pass. of *video, -ēre, vīdī, vīsum,* 2; see *vidēs,* l. 13); agrees with its subj. *nōs,* l. 22. *Videor* is generally used = *I seem,* though sometimes *I am seen;* the impersonal *vidētur = it seems good.* Note that only the personal construction is allowable with the passives of verbs of feeling or saying such as *vidērī* and *dīcī;* thus *it seems (is said) that Cicero was consul* cannot be rendered *viaētur (dīcitur) Cicerōnem fuisse cōnsulem,* but *Cicerō vidētur (dīcitur) fuisse cōnsul.* With other verbs of *saying,* etc., the personal construction is preferred, except in the compound tenses, e.g. *trāditum est Homērum caecum fuisse = tradition relates that Homer was blind,* but *trāditur Homērus caecus fuisse.* For the two ways of explaining the ind. *vidēmur satis facere* of the principal clause followed by the subjunct. *vīēmus* of the subordinate, refer to the note on *vidēmus,* l. 24.

24 **sī** **istīus** **furōrem** **ac** **tēla** **vītēmus.** | we manage to escape
if *of that (fellow)* *the frenzy* *and* *the weapons* *we avoid.* | the ruffian's frenzied
　　　　　　　　　　　　　　　　　　　　　　　　　　　| assaults. Long ago,
25 **Ad** **mortem** **tē,** **Catilīna,** **dūcī** **iussū** | Catiline, you ought to
To *death* *you,* *Catiline,* *to be led* *by order* | have been conducted

LINE 24. **sī**, conditional or hypothetical conj. followed by ind. or subjunct. (akin to Greek *el = if*); introducing the subordinate clause *sī . . . vītēmus*, which is the *protasis* in the condition. Uses of *sī :* (1) = *if*, in the *protasis* of a conditional sentence ; sometimes strengthened *sī quidem = if indeed;* sometimes introducing an adverse condition, *quod sī = but if;* (2) the sense *if* sometimes in Caesar passes into the causal *since*, when the condition is realized, and in Vergil into *when ;* (3) *sī* rarely introduces indirect question, except in poetry ; (4) *sī +* the subjunct. sometimes = *to see if*, denoting purpose. A conditional sentence consists of two parts : (a) *protasis*, the dependent clause stating the condition with *if*, (b) the *apodosis*, the main clause, stating the conclusion. But in origin a conditional sentence was the mere statement of two independent ideas, for *sī = if* is a weak demonstrative akin to *sīc (thus)* and = *in some way.* Thus *sī audīre volētis, reperiētis (if you will listen, you will find) = you will listen in some way, you will find*, two distinct statements united into one modified statement. For a general survey of the kinds of conditions, with various tenses of the ind. or subjunct., consult A. & G. 304-309 ; B. 301-304 ; G. 589, 594, *ff* ; H. 507-512.——istīus, gen. sing. m. of *iste, ista, istud;* poss. gen., limiting *furōrem* and *tēla. Istīus* is here used with its acquired forensic implication of scorn = *of that villain;* see the note and references under *iste,* l. 3. —— **furōrem**, acc. sing. of *furor, -ōris*, m. 3d (from *furō = I rave*, sometimes of madness, sometimes of inspiration); direct obj. of *vītēmus.*—— **ac** (shortened form of *atque*), cop. conj., connecting *furōrem* and *tēla. Ac* is used instead of *atque* before words beginning with any consonant except *c, g,* and *qu.* For its use, and for the other cop. conjunctions, see the note on *que,* l. 9. —— **tēla,** acc. plur. of *tēlum, -i*, n. 2d ; joined by *ac* to *furōrem*, and direct obj. of *vītēmus. Tēlum =* (1) *a missile, spear, dart, arrow,* etc. ; (2) *a weapon, sword,* etc. The derivation from τῆλε = *afar* (hence *something sent from afar, a missile*) is exploded ; others refer to *tendō = to hurl*, in poetry, as if for *tend-lum ;* but the best etymology is from an Ind.-Eur. root *tak*, or *tuk = to prepare, to hit, to generate.* Thus *tēlum = tec-lum ;* cf. Greek τόξον = *a bow.* —— **vītēmus,** 1st pers. plur. pres. subjunct. act. of *vītō, -āre, -āvī, -ātum,* 1 (= *vic-i-tō*, from a root *vik = to yield;* cf. Greek εἰκ-ω = *I yield*, and *vicissitude*) ; the subj. *nōs* is implied by the personal ending. There are two ways of explaining the subjunct. mood of *vītēmus*, and the second appears preferable : (1) *vidēmur satis facere* is regarded as slightly stronger than the potential subjunct. *satis faciāmus.* Thus the whole sentence is a remote future condition, which may or may not come true = *we should fulfil our duties . . . if we should avoid his weapons.* A similar contingency is expressed by the ind. in II, Chap. XI, *sī . . . contendere velīmus . . . intellegere possumus* (= *intellēgāmus*). A. & G. 307, *b* ; B. 303 ; G. 596, 1 ; H. 509. According to this explanation the statement of the compound sentence is ironical throughout. (2) The subjunct. is used, not because the sentence is a hypothetical one, but because the condition is a reported one in virtual indirect discourse. *Vidēmur* then = *we seem (nōbīs, to ourselves)*, i.e. *we think we are fulfilling*, etc., *if we avoid*, etc. ; the direct condition is *satisfacimus, sī vītāmus*, and according to the rule that the indicative of dependent clauses becomes subjunct. in indirect discourse, *vītāmus* becomes *vītēmus* after the primary *vidēmur.* A. &. G. 336, 2 ; B. 314, 1 ; G. 650 ; H. 524.

LINE 25. **Ad**, prep. with the acc. ; governs *mortem ; ad mortem* combines the idea of motion after *dūcī, to death*, with one of purpose, *for* death ; observe the emphatic position of *ad mortem.*—— **mortem,** acc. sing. of *mors, mortis*, f. 3d (from a root *mar*

| to your death at the consul's command; upon your own head | cōnsulis *of the consul* | iam *already* | prīdem *long ago* | oportēbat, *it behooved,* | in *against* | tē *you* | 26 |

= *to waste away;* cf. Greek μάρανσις = *decay*); gov. by the prep. *ad.* Had Cicero really on his own authority as consul put Catiline to death, and not with the authority of the Senate, as it fell out later, he would indisputably have broken the laws of the state. The *Lēx Valēria* (509 B.C.) gave the defendant the right to appeal from a magistrate's decision to the people; and this law was reënacted and made more stringent by the *Lēx Porcia* (197 B.C.), and by the *Lēx Semprōnia* of Gāius Gracchus (122 B.C.). All these laws made it clear that no magistrate could scourge or put to death a citizen without the consent of the people, and the people generally preferred a condemned citizen to retire into exile and free them from the responsibility of dealing with him.——**tē**, acc. sing. of the 2d pers. pron. *tū;* direct obj. of *oportēbat,* l. 26. Observe here that while *tē* is object of *oportēbat,* it is subj.-acc. of *dūcī* below, and the whole acc. and inf. *tē dūcī* is the subj. of *oportēbat.*——**Catilīna**, voc. sing. of *Catilīna, -ae,* m. 1st; case of the person addressed. Cicero turns from the senators and addresses Catiline directly.——**dūcī**, pres. inf. pass. of *dūcō, -ere, dūxī, ductum,* 3 (from a root *du(k)*), in Latin *dūc* or *dŭc,* cf. *ēdŭcō* = *I train up*); agrees with its subj.-acc. *tē.* Observe that, if *oportet tē* + the inf. be rendered in English by *you ought,* the tense is expressed by the inf. as *ought* is auxiliary, e.g. *you ought to be led* (pres. or fut.) and *you ought to have been led* (past); but in Latin the tense is expressed by the verb itself, e.g. *oportēbit* (fut.), *oportēbat* and *oportuit* (past), *oportet* (pres.) *tē dūcī;* but for a common variation see the note on *oportēbat* below.——**iussū**, adverbial abl. of *iussus, -ūs,* m. 4th (only found in this abl.; so *iniussū;* from *iubeō,* 2 = *I order*); modifies *dūcī.* Though used adverbially, *iussū* may be accompanied by a poss. adj., e.g. *meō iussū,* and both *iussū* and *iniussū* by a limiting gen., as *cōnsulis* below. *Iubeō* (and its derivatives *iussum, -ī,* n. 2d and *iussū*) is from the root *yu* = *to bind,* and may perhaps be a compound of *iūs,* n. 3d (also from root *yu*), and *habeō.*

LINE 26. **cōnsulis**, gen. sing. of *cōnsul,* m. 3d; poss. gen., limiting *iussū; cōnsulis* seems to refer to Cicero himself, but may be used of the office. Cicero evidently means that he might have acted on the strength of the Senate's decree of Oct. 21st, which armed the consuls with extraordinary power to enable them to ward off danger from the state. The precedents for executing traitors which he proceeds to cite are very unhappy, for Tiberius Gracchus was murdered by an unruly mob, and Servīlius Ahāla had to retire into exile for obeying the dictator's order to kill Maelius.——**iam**, temporal adv., strengthening *prīdem* = *already long ago, this long time.*——**prīdem** (from a root *pra* = *before;* cf. Greek πρό, πρίν, etc., and Latin *prae, prīmus, princeps,* and many more), temporal adv. = *long ago,* modifying *oportēbat.* Cicero was probably thinking of Catiline's first conspiracy (see Introduction).——**oportēbat**, 3d pers. sing. imperf. ind. act. of the impersonal verb *oportet, oportēre, oportuit,* 2; the real subj. is the acc. and inf. *tē dūcī. Oportet* is used: (1) with the subjunct. without *ut* (later writers add *ut*) in a substantive clause of purpose; (2) with the inf., with or without a subj.-acc. For the difference between the Latin and English constructions of *I ought* and *oportet mē,* refer to the note on *dūcī,* l. 25. But past obligation is sometimes expressed by the perf. part. pass., instead of the pres. inf., with or without *esse,* and a past tense of *oportēre,* cf. Chap. II, 40, *quod iam prīdem factum esse oportuit,* and consult the note and references under *interfectum,* l. 20 of Chap. I. The imperf. tense with *iam diū,* etc., denotes an action begun in the past and continuing in it. A. & G. 277, *b*; B. 260, 4; G. 234; H. 469, II, 2.——**in**, prep. with the acc.; gov. *tē; in tē* is very emphatic by position. *In* + the acc. = *to, into,* of place; *for, into,* of time; *towards,* often *against,* of disposition; *in, after,* of manner.——**tē**, acc. sing. of *tu;* gov. by the prep. *in.*

27 cōnferrī	istam	pestem,	quam	tū	should have been
(it behooved) to be applied	that	ruin,	which	you	heaped the ruin which you are plot-
28 in	nōs	māchināris.	An	vērō	vir	ting for us. You will
against	us	are contriving.	Or	truly	the man	admit, I suppose, that

LINE 27. **conferrī**, pres. inf. pass. of *cōnferō, cōnferre, contulī, collātum*, irreg. (compound of *con + ferō* = lit. *I bring together, collect*); agrees with its subj.-acc. *pestem*, in construction after *oportēbat* understood from l. 23. *Cōnferre* = (1) *to collect*, (2) *to compare*, hence *to match against*, (3) *to employ, bring*, as here, (4) *to bestow, grant, assign*, (5) *to postpone;* (6) *sē cōnferre = to betake oneself, to go.* —— **istam**, acc. sing f. of the demonstr. pron. *iste, ista, istud;* agrees with *pestem* and modifies it emphatically; many editors omit *istam*, but if retained it adds much to the force of the passage, as Cicero is wishing that Catiline may be "hoist with his own petard." *Istam* = not *your* but *devised by you*, for *iste* refers to what appertains to the person addressed in any relation. —— **pestem**, acc. sing. of *pestis, -is,* f. 3d; obj. of *oportēbat* understood, and subj.-acc. of *cōnferrī.* Synonyms: (1) *perniciēs = destruction*, the general word; (2) *pestis* = (a) *plague*, (b) *ruin, destruction*, (c) *bane*, of one causing ruin; (3) *exitium* = *destruction*, lit. *a going to naught;* (4) *dāmnum* = simply *loss, hurt;* (5) *caeaēs* = *destruction, slaughter*, from *caedō = I kill;* (6) *clāaēs = ruin, defeat*, often of warfare; (7) *strāgēs* = lit. *overthrow*, especially of armies, hence *massacre, carnage;* (8) *interitus = annihilation, extermination.* —— **quam**, acc. sing. f. of the rel. pron. *quī, quae, quod;* direct obj. of *māchināris.* It should be remembered that the rel. pron. agrees in gender and number with its antecedent, but its case depends on its function in its own clause; the verb in the rel. clause agrees in number and person with the subj., e.g. *ego quī audiō, tū quī audīs.* A. & G. 198; B. 250, 1; G. 614; H. 445. —— **tū**, nom. sing. of the 2d pers. pron.; subj. of *māchināris*, and emphatic.

LINE 28. **in**, prep. with the acc. (see *in* above); gov. *nōs.* —— **nōs**, acc. plur. of the 1st pers. pron.; governed by *in;* *nōs* includes the senators and Roman citizens in general. —— **māchināris**, 2d pers. sing. pres. ind. of the deponent verb *māchinor, -ārī, -ātus sum*, 1 (from *māchina*, f. 1st, akin to Greek μηχανή); agrees with its subj. *tū.* Cicero uses this verb in a good sense = *to skilfully devise*, in reference to the works of nature, and in a bad sense, as here, = *to plot, scheme;* he also has nouns *māchinātiō*, and *māchinātor;* and Livy employs *māchināmentum = a military engine.* For deponents, refer to *abūtere*, l. 1. Observe the ending in *-ris*, which Cicero prefers for the pres. ind. passive. —— **An**, conj., introducing a question with *interfēcit*, l. 32. *An* is properly a conj. introducing a second or subsequent clause in direct disjunctive questions, and so = *or*, the first clause being introduced by *utrum, ne* enclitic, or by no special word, e.g. (1) *utrum hōc falsum est an vērum?* (2) *hōcne falsum est an vērum?* (3) *hōc falsum an vērum est?* Sometimes *-ne* is added to *an* pleonastically, e.g. *utrum hōc falsum anne vērum est?* When the second member is a mere negative, *nōn* is added to *an*, e.g. *utrum hōc falsum annōn (or not)?* Occasionally *an = or rather*, or *on the contrary*, emphasizing the second clause. In indirect disjunctive questions, *an* introduces a second clause in the same way as in direct, e.g. *quaerō utrum hōc vērum an falsum sit*, and in rare instances leads the first clause instead of *utrum, num*, and the other regular particles. But in the passage before us there is only one question, and that is scarcely more than an exclamation. When so used in direct question, *an* is regarded as introducing an elliptical double question, with the first clause suppressed or involved. We may supply the suppression thus : "*am I mistaken in my recollection* or did that most illustrious man, P. Scipio, really kill Tiberius Gracchus ?" As such direct questions with *an* are expressive of some emotion, e.g. surprise, indignation, or are remonstrative in character, *an* may be left untranslated and the question be rendered as an exclamation—

| the illustrious Publius Scipio, supreme pon- | amplissimus, *most honorable,* | P. Scīpiō, *Publius Scipio,* | pontifex *high-priest* | maximus, 29 *supreme,* |

surely Scīpiō killed Gracchus.   *An* is used in early Latin in direct questions, and there is some reason for supposing it was originally a simple particle of interrogation.   A. & G. 211, *b* ; B. 163, 4, *a* ; G. 457, 1 ; H. 353, NOTE 4.——vērō, adv., with slight adversative force (originally n. of adj. *vĕrus, -a, -um*).   See *vĕrō*, l. 19.——vir, gen. *virī*, m. 2d ; appositive of *Scīpiō*.   When in English we attribute a quality to the name of a person, the Latin idiom is to add *vir* or *homō* as an appositive and to attribute the quality to the appositive, e.g. *the brave Brūtus = Brūtus, vir fortis (fortissimus).*   *Vir* is only used with reference to a man's good qualities ; refer to the note on *virī*, l. 23.

LINE 29.   **amplissimus,** nom. sing. m. of the superl. degree of the adj. *amplus, -a, -um* (from *am = ambi = around + plus* from *pleō = I fill,* hence *full all round ; ambi* is a prep. only used in composition, cf. Greek ἀμφί) ; qualifies *vir.*   As distinguished from *māgnus* and *ingēns, amplus = wide, spacious ;* in the positive, and esp. in the superl., this adj. is much used as a term of honorable compliment, referring in particular to a man's high standing in respect of birth and office.   Scīpiō was *amplissimus* in nobility, as he belonged to the great Cornelian family ; in office, as he was *pontifex māximus* and probably the only Roman elected to this office without being present at the election, and he had been consul in 138 B.C. ; in character, if we follow Cicero, who in many passages praises him very highly.——**Pūblius** (abbreviated P.), gen. *Pūblī,* m. 2d ; nom. sing., the *praenōmen* or forename of *Scīpiō.*   The Romans had three names each, one for himself, one for his *gēns,* and one for his family : thus *Pūblius Cornēlius Scīpiō Nasīca Serāpiō : Pūblius* is the *praenōmen,* serving as a Christian name in English ; *Cornēlius* is the *nōmen,* showing Publius to belong to the *gēns Cornēlia,* founded by a certain Cornēlius ; *Scīpiō,* the family name or *cōgnōmen,* is, as often (cf. *Cicerō = chick-pea,* from *cicer*), a nickname = *a staff,* which name was supposed to have been given to the founder because he guided his blind father ; any extra title is an *agnōmen (ad + (g)nōmen = name in addition),* as *Nasīca (= with pointed nose)* and *Serāpiō ; agnōmina* were often given for military success, e.g. *Africānus,* given to another great Scīpiō. Women had no Christian names, only the *nōmen* of the house, e.g. *Cornēlia ;* sisters, if two in number, were distinguished as *Cornēlia māior* and *minor,* but if more, as (1) *Cornēlia,* (2) *Cornēlia secunda,* (3) *Cornēlia tertia,* and so on.   There were only some 18 *praenōmina* to choose from.   The most common are : *Aulus (A.), Gāius (C.), Marcus (M.), Lūcius (L.), Quintus (Q.), Mānius (M'.), Gnaeus (Cn.), Tītus (T.),* and *Pūblius (P.).*——**Scīpiō,** gen. *Scīpiōnis,* m. 3d ; nom. sing., subj. of *interfēcit,* l. 32.   Pūblius Cornēlius Scīpiō Nasīca Serāpiō was the son of Scīpiō Nasīca Corculum, and grandson of Scīpiō Nasīca who was considered the most virtuous man in Rome.   He was consul in 138 B.C., and later *pontifex māximus.*   His private character is said to have been eminently noble.   In politics he was leader of the senatorial party, and when Tiberius Gracchus sought reëlection in 133 B.C. as tribune Scīpiō defied the law and led the riot in which Gracchus met his death.   The populace demanded reparation for this crime, whereupon Scīpiō was sent on a mission to Asia and never returned to Rome, i.e. he went into voluntary exile.——**pontifex,** gen. *pontificis,* m. 3d (*pōns + faciō,* hence originally *bridge-builders,* one of whose duties would be "to appease the deities on whose domains the bridges or roads intruded," *Prof. Gow*) ; nom. sing., in apposition with *P. Scīpiō.*   The *pontificēs* were founded as a college by Numa, the king (as afterwards the emperor) being president (*pontifex māximus*).   Under the republic the *Pontifex Māximus* and the *Rēx Sacrōrum* divided the king's priestly functions, the *Rēx Sacrōrum* (with 15 other *flāminēs,* i.e. priests of particular deities) being appointed by the *Pontifex Māximus.*   The pontifical duties were to choose Vestal Virgins, keep the calendar, announce festivals, preside over religious marriages (by *cōn-*

80 **Ti.   Gracchum,   mediocriter   labefactantem** | tiff, although not a
~ *Tiberius   Gracchus,   to a slight extent   undermining* | magistrate, killed Ti-
berius Gracchus be-
cause of his not very
81 **statum   rei pūblicae,   prīvātus** | grave disturbance of
the constitution   of the commonwealth,   (as) a private (citizen) | the settled order of

---

farreātiō), and superintend all religious affairs not specially attended to by priestly clubs, e.g. the *Lupercī*, the *Saliī*. The number of *pŏntifĭcĕs* was 9 at first; Sulla added 6 more, and Caesar yet another. By the *lēx Ogulnia* (300 B.C.) a plebeian might be elected *supreme pontiff*, and soon after the people secured the right of electing to this dignity. The *pŏntĭfĕx mặximus* was elected for life, and was the superior of the *rēx sacrōrum.* —— **măximus**, nom. sing. m. of the adj. *măximus, -a, -um* (superl. of *magnus, -a, -um ;* comp. *māior*); qualifies *pŏntĭfĕx.* There is some doubt as to whether *Scīpio* was high-priest at the time of the riot. The office was certainly held for life, but there may have been methods of resignation.

LINE 30. **Tiberium** (= Ti. or Tib. abbreviated), acc. sing. of *Tiberius, -ĭ*, m. 2d ; *praenōmen* of the elder Gracchus, and here direct obj. of *interfĕcit.* —— **Gracchum**, acc. sing. m. of *Gracchus, -ĭ*, m. 2d (the name of a famous family of the *gēns Semprōnia*) ; direct obj. of *interfĕcit.* Tiberius Semprōnius Gracchus was the elder son of his father of the same name, and Cornēlia, the daughter of the Scīpiō who conquered Hannibal. He was an earnest social reformer, and as tribune of the people in 133 B.C. he proposed an agrarian law reënacting the old Licinian Rogations which forbade *lătĭfundia* or large estates. The opposition of the capitalist Senate drove him against his will to use unconstitutional methods and depose a fellow-tribune who vetoed his measures, and he carried his law. When against precedent he sought reëlection, he and 300 of his followers met a violent death in a party riot. Nasīca led the senatorial rioters, but P. Saturnius and L. Rūfus laid claim to the murder. Tiberius and his more famous brother Gāius are sometimes alluded to in the plural, *Gracchī =* the Gracchī; for Gāius, see the note on Chap. II, l. 5. —— **mediocriter** (from the adj. *mediocris, -e*, 3d), adv. of manner, limiting *labefactantem.* Cicero speaks of the Gracchī with varying degrees of severity, according to the object he has in mind; here he calls Tiberius a mild offender, arguing from the less to the greater, in order to prove Catiline worthy of death. Cicero's prejudice prevented him from seeing that, if the Senate had not forced Tiberius into illegality, Italy would have had self-supporting citizen-farmers, who with the abolition of large estates and the consequent diminution of slave labor would have infused new life into the constitution of the state. —— **labefactantem**, acc. sing. m. of *labefactāns, -antis*, pres. part. act. of *labefactō, -āre, -āvī, -ātum*, 1 (frequentative form of *labefaciō*, from *labō + faciō,* hence *I make to reel*) ; agrees with *Gracchum* in participial enlargement of the subject ; *mediocriter labefactantem* of Gracchus is purposely mild, being contrasted with *orbem terrae . . . vāstāre cupientem* of Catiline.

LINE 31. **statum**, acc. sing. of *status, -ūs*, m. 4th (from *stō = I stand*, hence *standing, condition*); direct obj. of *labefactantem = quī statum . . . labefactāvit ;* the metaphor is taken from causing something previously standing firm to spin from its support and totter, ready to fall, on the brink. —— **rei**, gen. sing. of *rēs*, f. 5th ; poss. gen., limiting *statum.* —— **pūblicae**, gen. sing. f. of the adj. *pūblicus, -a, -um ;* agrees with *reī*, forming one idea = *the commonwealth;* refer to *reī pūblicae*, l. 23. Quintilian (VIII, 4, 13) remarks on the elaborate contrast thus : " a comparison is made between Catiline and Gracchus ; the state's organization and the whole world ; a slight disturbance and massacre, fire, and devastation ; a private citizen and the consuls." —— **prīvatus**, nom. sing. m. of the adj. *prīvātus, -a, um* (originally perf. part. pass. of *prīvō*, hence *set apart* from the state, *private*), agrees with the subj. *Scīpiō*, but modifies the verb *interfĕcit* adverb-

| public affairs: and shall we, we the consuls, endure Catiline, whose cherished aim is to make the whole | interfēcit: *killed:* | Catilīnam, *Catiline,* | orbem *the circle* | terrae 32 *of the earth* |
| | caede *with slaughter* | atque *and* | incendiīs *with conflagrations* | vāstāre 33 *to lay waste* |

ially = *in a private (unofficial) capacity.* The adjs. most often used adverbially are: *prīmus, prior, volēns, tōtus, ūnus, sōlus,* and *ultimus,* but any adjective may be so used, e.g. *prīmus vēnī = I came first, laetī audiēre = they heard with gladness.* A. & G. 191; B. 239; G. 325, REM. 6; H. 443. For *prīvātus,* as opposed to *pūblicus,* see note on *pūblicī,* l. 20. *Scīpiō* is called *prīvātus* because, if he was not high-priest in 133 B.C., yet he held no other office; while, even if he was *pontifex māximus,* this office was not among the *magistrātūs.* For this latter reason the *pontifex māximus* might be a candidate for a magistracy; Jūlius Caesar held the high-priesthood at the same time that he was dictator. It is worth while noting that if *Scīpiō* was high-priest in 133 B.C. his act was sacrilegious in being a party to the death of Gracchus (who, as some say, fell by his hand), and the more so as a tribune's person was inviolable (*sacrōsānctus*); he further broke the laws by retiring for safety on a pretended mission to Asia, for the *pontifex māximus* was not allowed to leave Italy.

LINE 32. **interfēcit,** 3d pers. sing. perf. ind. act. of *interficiō, -ere, interfēcī, interfectum,* 3 (*inter* + *faciō* = lit. *to make* something be *between* the parts of anything, so as to sunder and destroy it); agrees with the subj. *Scīpiō,* l. 29. Observe the coördination of the clauses, "was Tiberius Gracchus killed? (*and*) shall we endure Catiline?" In English it is better to subordinate the first clause, e.g. *if (while)* Gracchus was killed, etc.—— **Catilīnam,** acc. sing. of *Catilīna, -ae,* m. 1st; direct obj. of *perferēmus,* l. 34. Old editions used to read *vērō* after *Catilīnam,* but, as it has occurred in l. 28, and as Quintilian does not quote it, it is better omitted.—— **orbem,** acc. sing. of *orbis, -is,* m. 3d (= (1) *circle,* (2) *region,* (3) *circuit,* (4) *wheel*); direct obj. of *vāstāre* in the participial clause *vāstāre cupientem; orbem terrae* is in strong contrast with *statum reī pūblicae* above. *Orbis terrae = the world;* the more usual expression is *orbis terrārum* (cf. *ubī terrārum = where in the world?*), but Cicero uses both without any discrimination of sense; cf. Chap. IV, l. 16 and l. 20. Synonyms: (1) *orbis terrae* or *terrārum* = *the world, the whole earth,* cf. *imperium orbis terrārum = universal empire;* (2) *mundus* = *the universe.*—— **terrae,** gen. sing. of *terra,* f. 1st (probably from a root *tars* = *to be dry,* cf. Greek τερσαίνω = *I make dry,* and *torreō* = *I burn*); poss. gen., limiting *orbem;* Schütz reads *terrārum* as quoted by Quintilian, but most prefer *terrae.* Synonyms: (1) *terra* = *the earth,* as opposed to sky and sea, *the dry land;* (2) *tellūs = the earth,* as the globe (poetical chiefly, but once in Cicero); *Tellūs* personified = the Greek goddess Γαῖα, also known as Cybelē, Cerēs, etc.; (3) *humus = the ground, the surface earth,* as the low (*humilis*) part of the visible world, cf. *humī iacēre = to lie on the ground;* (4) *solum* = *the firm ground,* cf. *solō aequāre = to level with the ground;* (5) *ager = cultivated ground.*

LINE 33. **caede,** abl. sing. of *caedēs -is,* f. 3d (from *caedō = I kill,* from a Sanskrit root *khid* = *to cut*); abl. of the means or instrument with *vāstāre.* There is often scarcely any difference between this abl. and the abl. of manner, though manner requires the abl. with *cum* unless it be modified by an adjective; many grammarians class *vī et armīs,* a similar phrase, as an abl. of manner. For the synonyms of *caedēs,* refer to the note on *pestem,* l. 27.—— **atque,** cop. conj., joining *caede* and *incendiīs. Atque,* a compound of *ad* = *at* + *que* = *and also, as well as, and specially,* and usually introduces something important. For the cop. conjunctions, refer to the note on *que,* l. 9.—— **incendiīs,** abl. plur. of *incendium, -ī,* n. 2d (from *incendō = I set on fire,* for *incandō,* from a root *kan* = *to burn,* cf. Greek καίω); abl. of the means or instrument, with *vāstāre,* joined by *atque* to *caede.* The allusion in *caede atque incendiīs* is to one part of Catiline's scheme,

34	cupientem,	nōs	cōnsulēs	perferēmus?	Nam
	desiring,	*we*	*the consuls*	*shall (we) endure?*	*For*
35	illa	nimis	antīqua	praetereō,	quod
	those (instances)	*too*	*ancient*	*I pass by,*	*that (= how)*

world desolate with fire and murder? I pass over the famous precedents, too far back in the past, how

---

viz. to set fire to Rome in several different places, and in the general confusion slaughter all who opposed revolution, secure plunder, and seize with armed men the strongest parts of Rome, e.g. the Palatine hill.—— **vāstāre**, pres. inf. act. of *vāstō, -āre, -āvī, -ātum*, I (= *I make vāstus*, i.e. desolate, *vāstus*, being probably akin to *vacuus = empty*); *complementary* inf. with *cupientem*, of which it is the object. See the note on *facere*, l. 23. Synonyms: (1) *vāstāre = to render desolate* or *waste* (by emptying), particularly in regard to the country, houses, fields, etc.; (2) *dēpopulārī (dē + populus) = to destroy the people, to depopulate*, but it often loses its strict application and denotes plunder and destruction of inhabitants and property like *vāstāre*.

LINE 34. **cupientem**, acc. sing. m. of *cupiēns, -entis*, pres. part. act of *cupiō, -ere, cupīvī* or *cupiī, cupītum*, 3 (akin to Sanskrit root *kup* = (1) *to be angry*, (2) *to desire strongly*); in agreement with and participial enlargement of *Catilīnam*, l. 32; *Catilīnam . . . vāstāre cupientem* = a rel. clause *quī vāstāre cupit*, and is in contrast with *Gracchum . . . labefactantem*, l. 30. Synonyms: (1) *cupiō = I desire passionately*, cf. English *cupidity;* with the dat. *cupiō = I wish (well)* for some one, hence *I favor;* (2) *volō = I wish*, but in a weaker sense, hence often *I am willing;* the distinction is well marked in the complimentary expression *cupiō omnia quae vīs = I strongly desire* (for you) *what you wish for* (Horace); (3) *expetō = I wish, crave*, especially of desiring to reach something, e.g., *dīvitiās*, as opposed to *fugiō;* (4) *optō* = lit. *I choose*, cf. *optiō = choice*, hence *I wish* as the result of rational choice; (5) *dēsīderō (dē + root sid = vid = to look*, hence *to look for* something absent), *I yearn for, I miss*.—— **nōs**, nom. plur. of the 1st pers. pron.; subj. of *perferēmus*, and emphatic because contrasted with *Scīpiō prīvātus*.—— **cōnsulēs**, nom. plur. of *cōnsul, cōnsulis*, m. 3d; in apposition with the subj. *nōs; cōnsulēs* is contrasted with *prīvātus*, l. 31. Cicerō, the *equēs* and *novus homō*, was much impressed by the dignity of the office of consul.—— **perferēmus**, 1st pers. plur. fut. ind. act. of *perferō, perferre, pertulī, perlātum*, irreg. (*per = through*, i.e. to the end + *ferō = I bear*); agrees with the subj. *nōs;* this question is coördinate with the first one (see *interfēcit* above) and implies an indignant negative answer.—— **Nam**, causal conj., explaining the unexpressed idea that the recent fate of Gracchus was sufficient precedent for severe measures against Catiline, and assigning their remoteness as a reason for not multiplying instances. The causal particles are *nam* (prae-positive), *enim* (post-positive), *namque* and *etinim* (both as a rule first in the sentence). *Nam* is used: (1) with its original asseverative force, assigning a reason; (2) as in the present passage, to pass over a subject; Cicero uses it so frequently; (3) in close connection with interrogative words, emphasizing them, e.g. *ubinam gentium sumus*, Chap. IV, l. 13. A. & G. 156, *d;* B. 345; G. 498, A; H. 310, 5, and 554, V.

LINE 35. **illa**, acc. plur. n. of the demonstr. pron. of the 3d pers., *ille, illa, illud;* direct obj. of *praetereō. Ille* is used: (1) of what is remote from the speaker and his audience = *that yonder;* (2) = *that famous*, or *that well known*, in which case it usually follows the noun it qualifies; (3) sometimes, as here, *ille* is used like the Greek ἐκεῖνος with reference to what follows. A. & G. 102, *b;* B. 246, 2; G. 307, esp. 3 and 4; H. 450, esp. 3. When the neut. of adjectives or demonstr. prons. is found in Latin, English idiom often requires the addition of a noun suitable to the context; so *illa = those (precedents)*, cf. *multa cōnātus est = he made many attempts*.—— **nimis**, (*ni-, ne- + root ma = measure*, hence *beyond measure*), adv. of degree, limiting *antīqua*.—— **antīqua**, acc. plur. n. of the adj. *antīquus, -a, -um* (akin to *ante*); agrees with *illa*. Observe that *illa*

Gaius Servīlius Ahala with his own hand	C. Servīlius Ahāla Sp. Maelium, *Gaius Servilius Ahala Spurius Maelius,*	novīs 86 *new*

antīqua is plural, but yet only one instance is given by Cicero, viz. the case of Ahāla ; it is implied that several other precedents of ancient date might be cited. But the plural may be due to another cause, for the Mss. read *quodque Servīlius*, and the *que* of *quodque* may connect the example of Servīlius with that of another person which was originally also introduced by *quod* and has somehow been lost from the text. Cicero states his desire to rely on modern precedents, but the insecurity of his ground causes him to ignore at least three important facts: (1) that Scīpiō had to leave Rome to avoid trial for the death of Tiberius Gracchus ; (2) that L. Opīmius was brought to trial (though not convicted) for causing the death of C. Gracchus ; (3) that C. Rabīrius was accused in this very year, 63 B.C., of implication in the murder of Sāturnīnus, which took place nearly 40 years before ; he was condemned by his judges, but appealed to the people, with Cicero as his advocate ; nevertheless the people would have condemned him if the trial had been allowed to run its course, but Rabīrius' friends saved him by obstruction.

—— **praetereō**, 1st pers. sing. pres. ind. act. of *praetereō, praeterīre, praeteriī, praeteritum*, irreg. (*praeter = beyond + eō = I go*) ; the subj. *ego* is implied by the personal ending. Observe that the intrans. verb *eō* by composition with *praeter* acquires a transitive force, and governs the acc. case. Similar to *praetereō* are all compounds of *per, circum, trāns,* and *subter ;* many compounds of other prepositions likewise govern a direct object, e.g. *adeō, antegredior.* A. & G. 228, *a* ; B. 175, 2, *a* ; G. 331 ; H. 372.

—— **quod** (acc. sing. n. of *quī*), conj., introducing a substantival clause *quod . . . occīdit* in partitive apposition with *illa.* Observe that *quod* is not strictly causal here (*because*), but must rather be rendered *the fact that.* Such substantival clauses may act as the subj. or obj. of the main verb, and *quod . . . occīdit*, being in apposition with *illa*, is a direct obj. of *praetereō.* The antecedent demonstr. of the *quod* clause may be either a pron. e.g. *illud, illa,* or an adv., e.g. *inde.* A. &. G. 333, and NOTE ; B. 299, 1, *a* ; G. 525, 2 ; H. 540, IV, NOTE. *Quod* causal = *because* takes the ind. or subjunct., according to whether the statement rests on the speaker's or another's authority. For partitive apposition, consult A. & G. 184, *a* ; B. 169, 5 ; G. 322, 323 ; H. 364.

LINE 36. **Gāius** (abbreviated = C.), gen. *Gāiī*, m. 2d ; nom. sing., the *praenōmen* of Ahāla. *Gāius* is often less correctly written *Cāius ;* cf. *Cn.* the abbreviation of *Gnaeus.* For Roman names, refer to the note on *Pūblius*, l. 29. The old reading here was *Q = Quintus*, but Ernesti restored the true reading *C.* —— **Servīlius**, gen. *Servīlī*, m. 2d ; nom. sing., the *nōmen* of Ahāla, signifying that he belonged to the *gēns Servīlia.* —— **Ahāla**, gen. *Ahālae*, m. 1st ; nom. sing., the *cognōmen* or family-name of Gāius above, subj. of *occīdit* below. *Gāius* appears to be his proper *praenōmen*, though in another oration of Cicero it appears as *Marcus.* According to the tradition *Ahāla* was the *magister equitum* or master-of-horse of the dictator L. Quintius Cincinnātus, when the latter was in 439 B.C. for the second time raised to that extraordinary office for the purpose of coping with the supposed regal designs of Maelius. When Maelius refused to appear before Cincinnātus to meet accusations, Ahāla went in search of him, and killed him as he was inciting his friends of the populace to protect him. Ahāla was prosecuted for this murder, and retired into voluntary exile ; but he was subsequently recalled and elected to the highest office in the state. —— **Spurium** (originally = *illegitimate ;* abbreviation = *Sp.*), acc. case sing. of *Spurius, -ī,* m. 2d, the *praenōmen* of Maelius. —— **Maelium**, acc. sing. of *Maelius, -ī,* m. 2d ; the *nōmen* of Spurius above, and the direct obj. of *occīdit* below. Spurius Maelius was a very wealthy plebeian knight, and in 440 B.C. when the price of food in Rome was so high as to occasion famine, Maelius employed his wealth in buying in Etrūria large quantities of corn, which he either sold to the Roman people at a nominal price or distributed free. He aspired to the consulship, but was not

87 rēbus   studentem,   manū   suā | slew Spurius Maelius
   things (= *revolution*) *being eager for,*   *with hand*   *his own* | who was promoting a
                                                              | revolution. Yet there
88 occīdit.   Fuit,   fuit   ista   quondam   in | was once, at one time
   slew.   *There was,* *there was* *that* (= *such*)   *once*   *in* | in our state's history,

elected, and being suspected of designs to make himself supreme in Rome, he was denounced before the Senate, which created Cincinnātus dictator to deal with the dangerous situation. He was killed as described in the note above. Some used to consider Maelius an injured benefactor, but according to Livy he was a revolutionist. He is interesting as anticipating C. Gracchus, who employed free corn largesses to win a following in Rome, and made empire necessary, even if he did not aspire to it himself. —— **novīs**, dat. plur. f. of the adj. *novus, -a, -um* (akin to the Greek *véos* = *new*); agrees with *rēbus. Novae rēs* = lit. *new things,* i.e. politically *revolution;* cf. the similar Greek verb *νεωτερίζειν* = *to make a revolution,* which is derived from *νεώτερος,* the comparative degree of the adj. *véos.*

LINE 37. **rēbus**, dat. plur. of *rēs, reī,* f. 5th; obj. of *studentem.* The object of intransitive verbs is put in the dative case, e.g. *persuadeō, pareō, īgnōscō,* and many others. Most of these verbs are intrans. in Latin, though trans. in English; they cannot therefore be used personally in the passive. For special lists of such verbs, consult A. & G. 227; B. 187, II, and *a;* G. 346; H. 385, I, II. For the extensive use of *rēs,* refer to l. 23, *reī.* —— **studentem**, acc. sing. m. of *studēns, -entis,* pres. part. act. of *studeō, -ēre, -uī,* no supine, 2 (probably akin to Greek *σπουδή* = *zeal,* and *σπουδάζειν* = *to be zealous*); agrees with *Maelium,* which it enlarges; *studentem* = a rel. clause *quī studēbat.* —— **manū**, abl. sing. of *manus, -ūs,* f. 4th (from a root *ma* = *to measure,* hence *the measuring* thing, *the shaper, the hand*); abl. of the means or instrument, extending the pred. *occīdit.* Note that *mānus* (rare) = *good;* also that *mănus* is one of the few exceptions to the general rule that nouns of the 4th declension are masculine. —— **suā**, abl. sing. f. of the reflexive poss. adj. of the 3d pers., *suus, -a, -um* (akin to *sē,* and the Greek *ἑ, ἑός,* and *ἴδιος*); agrees with *manū.*

LINE 38. **occīdit**, 3d pers. sing. perf. ind. act. of *occīdō, -ere, occīdī, occīsum,* 3 (*ob + caedō*); agrees with the subj. *C. Servīlius Ahāla.* Distinguish *occīdō* = *I cut down, I kill,* from *occīdō, -ere, occĭdī, occāsum,* 3 intrans. (*ob + cădō*) = *I fall down.* Synonymous verbs of *killing:* (1) *interficiō,* the generic verb; (2) *caedō* and *occīdō* = *I cut down,* esp. of hand to hand conflict, as in battle; (3) *necō,* = *I slay,* usually in a terrible way, e.g. *verberibus* = *by scourging;* (4) *trucīdāre* = *to butcher,* e.g. *captīvōs;* (5) *iugulāre* (from *iugulum* = *the throat*) = *to cut the throat, to kill* in bandit fashion; (6) *interimere* and *ē mediō tollere* = *to make away with;* (7) *perimere* = *to destroy, annihilate;* (8) *percutere* = *to strike dead,* e.g. *fulmine* = *by lightning,* or *secūrī* = *by the axe* of the executioner. —— **Fuit**, 3d. pers. sing. perf. ind. of the copula *sum, esse, fuī,* no supine, irreg.; agrees with its subj. *virtūs;* the perf. here has special significance, denoting that the state of things mentioned as existing in the past no longer exists now, cf. the Vergilian *Trōia fuit.* —— **fuit** (see above), repeated by *anaphora,* in order to emphasize the contrast between political cowardice and immorality in the present and the blunt uprightness of Roman statesmen in the past. A. & G. 344 *f;* B. 350, II, *b;* G. 636, NOTE 4; H. 636, III, 3. —— **ista**, nom. sing. f. of the demonstr. pron. *iste, ista, istud;* agrees with *virtūs.* Observe that *ista* in this passage is not used in the usual Ciceronian way in contempt, but on the contrary is laudatory, = *such; illa,* the demonstr. pron. of the 3d pers., would be more natural here, and Cicero might have used it but for the fact that *illa* occurs just before in l. 35. Refer to *iste,* l. 4, for usage and references. —— **quondam** (*quom,* old form of *cum,* + suffix *dam*), temporal adv., modifying *fuit.* —— **in**, prep. with the acc. and abl.; gov. the abl. *rē pūblicā.*

such loyal spirit that men of character checked a dangerous citizen with severer punishment than (they meted out to) the bitterest foreign enemy. Directed					
hāc	rē pūblicā	virtūs,	ut	virī	fortēs 89
this	*commonwealth*	*virtue,*	*that*	*men*	*brave*
ācriōribus	suppliciīs	cīvem			perniciōsum 40
sharper	*with punishments*	*a citizen*			*harmful*
quam acerbissimum hostem coërcērent. Habēmus 41					
than *most bitter* *the enemy* *repressed.* *We have*					

LINE 39. **hāc**, abl. sing. f. of the demonstr. pron. *hĭc, haec, hōc;* agrees with *rē pūblicā.*——**rē**, abl. sing. of *rēs, reī,* f. 5th; governed by the prep. *in.*——**pūblicā**, abl. sing. f. of the adj. *pūblicus, -a, -um;* agrees with *rē.*——**virtūs**, gen. *virtūtis,* f. 3d (from *vir, a man,* hence *manliness*); nom. sing., subj. of *fuit. Virtūs* has two chief meanings, (1) *manliness,* hence *courage;* (2) *moral worth, virtue, merit;* personified *Virtūs* = the goddess of manly valor, who had a temple in Rome. Synonyms of the two senses of *virtūs* above should be noted. A. (1) *virtus = courage,* the generic term; (2) *fortitūdō = courageous endurance* of dangers and troubles; (3) *audācia = boldness,* and differs from the first two as it implies no moral principle or regard for the value of the object; it is sometimes used favorably, but Cicero calls it a vice, and says *imitātur audācia fortitūdinem:* B. (1) *virtūs = the true worth* of a manly man; (2) *praestantia = worth,* or *excellence,* in a comparative sense.——**ut** (originally *utī*), conj., here followed by the subjunct. *coërcērent* expressing consequence or result, = *so that.* Observe the five rules of the conj. *ut* or *utī:* (1) *consecutive,* or expressing result, = *so that,* being the rel. of an antecedent demonstr. adj. or adv., e.g. *tālis, tantus, tam, ita,* etc.; when the result clause is negative, *ut nōn* is used; the verb of the result clause is always in the subjunct. mood; (2) *final,* or expressing purpose, = *in order that;* the negative is not *ut nōn,* but *nē;* the verb of the purpose clause is always in the subjunct. mood; (3) *ut concessive,* or making some admission, = *although,* followed by the subjunct. mood; *ut* is here elliptical for *fac ut,* = *suppose that;* (4) *ut* = *that not* after verbs of fearing, and expresses apprehension that something will not happen, e.g., *timeō ut veniat = I fear that he will not come;* (5) temporal, = *when, as,* often + *prīmum,* = *as soon as,* followed by the ind. mood, and usually by the *historic pres.* or *perf.* tenses, less commonly the imperf. and pluperf. *Ut* or *utī* is also used adverbially: (*a*) of place, = *where,* (*b*) of manner, both interrog. and rel., = *how;* (*c*) relatively in comparisons, *as, as if,* often followed by *ita;* (*d*) exclamatory, = *how!;* (*e*) in wishes *ut* is used like *utinam,* the verb always being in the subjunct. mood. For *ut* in result clauses, consult A. & G. 319; B. 284; G. 552; H. 500.——**virī**, nom. plur. of *vir, virī,* m. 2d; subj. of *coërcērent.*——**fortēs**, nom. plur. of the adj. *fortis, -e,* 3d (akin to *firmus,* from a root *dhar = to support*); qualifies the subj. *virī.*

LINE 40. **ācriōribus**, abl. plur. n. of *ācrior, ācrius,* the compar. of the 3d decl. adj. *ācer, ācris, ācre,* superl. *ācerrimus, -a, -um* (from a root *ak = sharp, swift,* cf. Greek ἄκων = *a javelin,* and ὠκύς = *swift*); agrees with *suppliciīs.*——**suppliciīs**, abl. plur. of *supplicium, -ī,* n. 2d (from the adj. *supplex, sub + plicō,* denoting bending the knee to make entreaty or receive punishment); abl. of the means, extending the pred. *coërcērent.* ——**cīvem**, acc. sing. of *cīvis, -is,* m. 3d; direct obj. of *coërcērent;* Cicero contrasts a secret revolutionist at home with an open foreign enemy.——**perniciōsum**, acc. sing. m. of the adj. *perniciōsus, -a, -um* (from the noun *perniciēs,* a compound of *per* and the root *nak,* in Latin *nec* or *noc = to destroy,* cf. *necō, noceō*); agrees with *cīvem.*

LINE 41. **quam**, adv., in comparative sentence; connects *cīvem* and *hostem* after the compar. *ācriōribus;* for the use of *quam,* refer to the note on *quam,* l. 2.——**acerbissimum**, acc. sing. m. of the adj. *acerbissimus, -a, -um,* superl. of the adj. *acerbus, -a, -um* (from root *ak = sharp,* akin to *ācer*); agrees with *hostem.*——**hostem**, acc. sing.

42 senātūs	cōnsultum	in	tē,	Catilīna,	against you, Catiline,
of the senate	*a decree*	*against*	*you,*	*Catiline,*	we have a stern and forcible decree of the
43 vehemēns	et	grave;	nōn	deest	Senate; the state
forcible	*and*	*severe;*	*not*	*is wanting*	does not lack the
44 reī pūblicae		cōnsilium	neque	auctōritās	counsel and the sanc-
to the commonwealth	*the deliberation*		*nor*	*the authority*	tion of this order

of *hostis, -is,* m. 3d ; direct obj. of *coërcērent,* and joined by *quam* to *cīvem.* Synonyms : *hostis* = *a public enemy,* a state's opponent, in war ; *inimīcus* = a private or personal enemy.—— **coërcērent,** 3d pers. plur. imperf. subjunct. act. of *coërceō, -ēre, -uī, -itum,* 2 (*cum + arceō* = *I confine on all sides,* hence *I check, curb*) ; agrees with the subj. *virī* above, and is subjunct. because expressing result with *ut,* l. 39 above. The tense is imperf. in sequence with the historic perf. *fuit* of the main clause. A. & G. 286 ; B. 267, 268 ; G. 509 *ff* ; H. 491.—— **Habēmus,** 1st pers. plur. pres. ind. act. of the verb *habeō, -ēre, -uī, -itum,* 2 ; the subj. *nōs* is implied by the personal ending.

LINE 42. **senātūs,** gen. sing. of *senātus,* m. 4th (from *senex* = *old*) ; poss. gen., limiting the noun *cōnsultum,* and so closely connected with it as to be often written in one, *senātūscōnsultum.*—— **cōnsultum,** acc. sing. of the noun. *cōnsultum, -ī,* n. 2d (originally the neut. sing. of the perf. part. *cōnsultus, -a, -um,* of the verb *consulō,* hence something *resolved upon*) ; direct obj. of *habēmus.* The *senātūs cōnsultum* (or *aēcrētum*), often called the *aēcrētum ultimum,* was the formula *videant cōnsulēs nē quid dētrimentī rēs pūblica capiat.* This resolution of the Senate was an acknowledgment that the state was in danger, and by it the Senate directed the consuls to provide for the public safety ; whether dictatorial powers of life and death were thereby given to the consuls is a disputed question ; see the Introduction. The conjectured date of this decree is Oct. 21, 63 B.C., but the chronology is very unsettled. A *senātūs cōnsultum* or *decision of the Senate,* if formally carried, was an instruction to the magistrate who had summoned the meeting, and if it was accepted by the magistrate who asked for it and was not vetoed by any magistrate entitled to do so, it had the force of law ; if, however, it was vetoed, it became only a *senātūs auctōritās,* and had no force at all except as an expression of the opinion of the Senate.—— **in,** prep. with the acc. or abl. ; gov. the acc. *tē.*—— **tē,** acc. sing. of the 2d pers. pron. *tū ;* governed by the prep. *in.*—— **Catilīna,** voc. sing. of *Catilīna, -ae,* m. 1st ; the person addressed.

LINE 43. **vehemēns,** acc. sing. n. of the adj. *vehemēns, -entis,* 3d (probably a lengthened form of *vēmēns,* the inseparable negative particle *vē + mēns,* = lit. *not having mind,* hence *unreasonable, violent*) ; agrees with the obj. *cōnsultum.*—— **et,** cop. conj., joining *vehemēns* and *grave.*—— **grave,** acc. sing. n. of the adj. *gravis, -e,* 3d (= *gar-vis,* from a root *gar* or *bar,* cf. Greek βαρ-ύς = *heavy*) ; agrees with *cōnsultum,* and is joined by *et* to *vehemēns.*—— **nōn,** negative adv., limiting *cōnsilium deest.*—— **deest,** 3d pers. sing. pres. ind. of *dēsum, deesse, dēfuī,* no supine (compound of *dē* and *sum*), irreg. and intrans. ; agrees with the subj. *cōnsultum,* and is understood with *auctōritās.* Observe that *dēsum* is used with the dative of the indirect object.

LINE 44. **reī,** dat. sing. of *rēs, reī,* f. 5th ; dat. of the indirect obj. with the intrans. verb *deest.*—— **pūblicae,** dat. sing. f. of the adj. *pūblicus, -a, -um ;* agrees with *reī.*—— **cōnsilium,** gen. *cōnsilī,* n. 2d ; nom. sing., subj. of *deest.* Observe that *cōnsilium* here = *advice,* or *deliberation ;* elsewhere it = *a council,* or deliberative assembly, and especially *plan* as in line 15 ; *concilium* is always concrete = *council, assembly.* The notion conveyed by this passage is that the Senate has done its duty as far as it could, as it had given its deliberate advice (*cōnsilium*) and its sanction (*auctōritās*) in advance to any measures the consuls might take ; the deliberative body was therefore free of all blame,

(the Senate): I say	hūius ōrdinis: nōs, nōs, dīcō apertē, cōnsulēs 45
it openly, it is we,	*this of order: we, we, I say openly, the consuls*
we the consuls, who	dēsumus. 46
fail to help her.	*are wanting (= remiss).*
II. On one occa-	II. Dēcrēvit quondam senātus, ut L. 1
sion the Senate gave	*Decreed once the senate, that Lucius*
a decree that Lucius	

the executive officers (*cōnsulēs*) were alone remiss in their duties. Sallust calls the authority given the consuls by the *dēcrētum ultimum* "the highest ever vested in a magistrate by the Senate according to the Roman constitution, viz. to enroll an army, carry on war, control citizens and allies in every way, and exercise supreme military and judicial power." The question still remains whether the consuls, even thus empowered, could usurp the people's prerogative of deciding sentences affecting a citizen's life and death. —— **neque** (*ne + que*), neg. cop. conj., = *and . . . not;* *neque* here connects *nōn deest cōnsilium* with *auctōritās* (*deest*). *Neque* is often used correlatively, in the following ways : (1) *neque* (*nec*) . . . *neque* (*nec*), (2) *neque* . . . *nec*, (3) *nec* . . . *neque* (rare). In this passage *neque* merely illustrates copulation by means of a negative, cf. *et nōn.* A. & G. 156, *a* ; B. 341, 1, *d* ; G. 480 ; H. 310, 1. —— **auctōritās**, gen. *auctōritātis*, f. 3d (from the noun *auctor*) ; nom. sing., <u>subj.</u> of *deest* to be supplied from *deest* in the preceding line. *Auctōritās* here refers in general to the decree of the Senate, and does not have the special sense of a decree of the Senate rendered legally forceless by the interposition of a tribune's veto.

LINE 45. **hūius**, gen. sing. m. of the demonstr. pronominal adj. *hīc, haec, hōc* ; agrees with *ōrdinis.* —— **ōrdinis**, gen. sing. of *ōrdō*, m. 3d (= *senātūs*) ; poss. gen., limiting *cōnsilium* and *auctōritās.* The meanings of *ōrdō* are : (1) *row, line;* (2) *rank, order, grade;* (3) *series, array;* (4) *body,* or *class,* as in this passage. —— **nōs**, gen. *nostrī* or *nostrum;* nom. plur. of the 1st personal pron., subj. of *dēsumus.* Observe the three ways in which emphasis is thrown upon this word : (1) by its presence in the sentence, for the nom. case of the personal pronouns is usually omitted and the subj. implied by the verbal termination, except where strong emphasis or contrast is intended ; (2) by the omission of a conjunction connecting the sentence with the previous one (*asyndeton*). A. & G. 208, *b* ; B. 346 ; G. 473, REM. ; H. 636, I. 1 ; (3) by the repetition of *nōs.* —— **dīcō**, 1st pers. sing. pres. ind. act. of *dīcō, -ere, dīxī, dictum,* 3 (from a root *dak,* in Latin *dic = to show,* cf. Greek δείκνυμι *= I show*) ; the subj. *ego* (Cicero) is implied by the personal ending. *Dīcō apertē* is inserted here parenthetically. —— **apertē**, adv. from the adj. *apertus, -a, -um;* modifies *dīcō.* —— **cōnsulēs**, nom. plur. of *cōnsul, cōnsulis,* m. 3d ; in apposition with the subj. *nōs.* Cicero did not yet dare to apprehend and put to death Catiline ; Antōnius was not important, even as consul, and had a certain attachment for the conspirator.

LINE 46. **dēsumus**, 1st pers. plur. pres. ind. of *aĕsum, deesse, dēfuī,* no supine, irreg. (see *deest,* l. 43) ; agrees with the subj. *nōs.*

LINE 1. **Dēcrēvit**, 3d pers. sing. perf. ind. act. of *dēcernō, -ere, dēcrēvī, dēcrētum,* 3 (*dē + cernō*) ; agrees with the subj. *senātus.* In 121 B.C., when Gāius Gracchus had failed to be reëlected as tribune, and his opponents began to repeal some of his measures, Gracchus himself appeared in the *forum* to oppose them and a riot occurred ; whereupon the Senate met and passed the *aĕcrētum ultimum.* Cicero here leaves the *nimis antīqua* precedents for others more recent. —— **quondam** (*quom,* old form of *cum + -dam*), temporal adv., modifying *dēcrēvit.* —— **senātus**, gen. *senātūs,* m. 4th ; nom.

2 Opīmius	cōnsul	vidēret	nē	quid	rēs	Opimius, the consul,
Opimius	the consul	should see	that not	anything	the	should see that the
3 pūblica	dētrīmentī	caperet	nox	nūlla		state suffered no
commonwealth	of harm	(should experience)	night	no		harm. Before a single night passed some

sing., subj. of *dēcrēvit*. The Senate were acting in an intensely partisan spirit on this occasion, and the death of Gracchus was doubtless intended ; yet their course was justifiable, seeing that Gāius, like his brother Tiberius, had trampled on constitutional principles. —— ut, final conj., introducing a complementary or substantival final clause *ut . . . vidēret*, after the leading verb *dēcrēvit*, which belongs to the class of *verba studii et voluntātis* (verbs of *will* and *desire*); the verb is subjunct. in accordance with the regular rule of *ut* in final clauses ; see *ut*, l. 39 of Chap. I. The student should note that final sentences fall into three divisions: (1) pure, when *ut* or *nē* expresses the purpose ; (2) complementary, when the leading verb expresses the purpose, as *dēcrēvit;* (3) *ut* or *nē* after verbs of *fearing*. A. & G. 331 ; B. 295, esp. 4, and 296 ; G. 546 ; H. 498. —— Lūcius (abbreviated = L.), gen. *Lūcī*, m. 2d ; nom. sing., the *praenōmen* of Opīmius.

LINE 2. Opīmius, gen. *Opīmī*, m. 2d ; nom. sing., the *nōmen* of Lūcius, and the subj. of *vidēret* in the final clause with *ut*. He was consul in 121 B.C., and was a devoted and unscrupulous member of the aristocratic party. The Senate enlarged his powers as consul by passing the *dēcrētum ultimum*. This is the only instance of a single consul having his authority so increased, and the reason is that his colleague in the office, Q. Fabius Māximus, was absent from Rome, conducting a campaign in southern Gaul. Opimius led the senatorial mob in the riot in which C. Gracchus was killed. In 109 B.C. he was convicted on the charge of receiving bribes from Jugurtha, king of Numidia, and went into exile, finally dying in great poverty and misery. The year of his consulship was very fruitful in wine, and two centuries after some of the vintage of 121 B.C. was obtainable ; thus the name of Opīmius descends in the expression *vīnum Opīmiānum*. —— cōnsul, gen. *cōnsulis*, m. 3d ; nom. sing., in appos. with *Opīmius*. —— vidēret, 3d pers. sing. imperf. subjunct. act. of *video, -ēre, vīdī, vīsum*, 2 ; agrees with its subj. *Opīmius*, and is in the subjunct. because it is in the complementary final clause with *ut;* the tense sequence is historic, because *dēcrēvit* is historic. —— nē (a strengthening of *nĕ*, the primitive negative, e.g. *nĕque*), negative final conj. = *that . . . not, lest*, introducing the substantival final clause *nē . . . caperet* in dependence on *vidēret;* the construction is similar to that of *dēcrēvit . . . ut . . . cōnsul vidēret* above, the only difference being that this is negative ; *vidēret* as leading verb belongs to the class of verbs of *caution* or *effort*, which is a subdivision of the wide class of verbs of *will* and *desire*. *Nē* as an adv. occurs in phrases, e.g. *nĕ . . . quidem* = *not even, nēdum* = *much less*, etc. As a conj., *nē* has the following chief uses : (1) as the neg. of *ut* final, in pure and complementary purpose clauses, and in final object clauses after verbs of fearing — the mood of the verb is always subjunctive ; (2) with the perf. subjunct., less commonly in pres., in prohibitions, e.g. *nē hōc fēceris = do not do this;* (3) in wishes, e.g. *(utinam) nē fiat !* (4) in restrictions, generally with *dum* or *modo*, with the subjunct.; cf. *nē dīcam* in parentheses ; (5) in concessions = *granted that . . . not*, with the subjunct.; (6) with the imperative mood, pres. imperative in poetry, and the fut. imperative in legal and moral maxims. —— quid, acc. sing. n. of the indef. pron. *quis, quae*, and *qua, quid;* direct obj. of *caperet*. The indef. pron. is very rarely used in Latin except in clauses introduced by *si* or *nē;* it occurs, however, in compounds, e.g. *quisquam*. —— rēs, gen. *reī*, f. 5th ; nom. sing., subj. of *caperet*.

LINE 3. pūblica, nom. sing. f. of the adj. *pūblicus, -a, -um ;* agrees with *rēs*. —— dētrīmentī, gen. sing. of *dētrīmentum*, n. 2d (from the verb *dēterō = I rub away*, hence

suspicion of treasonable disaffection brought his death	intercessit;	interfectus	est	propter	quāsdam 4
	intervened;	*was killed*		*on account of*	*certain*

a rubbing away, impairment); <u>partitive gen.</u> with *quid,* cf. *nihil novī = nothing new.* This genitive is common with the neuter of adjectives and pronouns. A. & G. 216, 3; B. 201, 2; G. 369; H. 397, 3. —— **caperet,** 3d pers. sing. imperf. subjunct. act. of *capiō, -ere, cēpī, captum,* 3 (from a root *kap = to seize,* cf. Greek κώπη = *a handle,* i.e. something *to take hold of*); agrees with the subj. *rēs pūblica;* the mood is subjunct. because *nē . . . caperet* is a final object clause dependent on *vidēret.* Compare the wording of this decree with that passed in 121 B.C. which Cicero quotes in the eighth Philippic, *cēnsuērunt utī L. Opīmius cōnsul rem pūblicam dēfenderet.* —— **nox,** gen. *noctis,* f. 3d (from a root *nak = to injure,* night being regarded as "no man's friend," cf. Greek νύξ); nom. sing., subj. of *intercessit.* —— **nūlla,** nom. sing. f. of the adj. *ūllus, -a, -um (ne + ūllus)*; qualifies *nox.*

LINE 4. **intercessit,** 3d pers. sing. perf. ind. act. of *intercēdō, -ere, intercessī, intercessum,* 3, intrans. (*inter = between + cēdō = I come*); agrees with the subj. *nox.* Observe the coördination of this and the two following clauses, viz. *interfectus est . . . Gracchus* and *occīsus est . . . Fulvius;* subordination of clauses is usual in Latin, but in this instance Cicero gives his statements more rhetorical effect by employing crisp, unconnected sentences. —— **interfectus est,** 3d pers. sing. perf. ind. pass. of *interficiō, -ere, interfēcī, interfectum,* 3 (*inter + faciō,* i.e. to *make* something come *between* the parts of a thing, so as to break it up and destroy it); agrees with the subj. *Gracchus;* it will not be necessary to remark again that the perf., fut. perf., and pluperf. tenses passive are periphrastic, being compounded of the perf. part. passive and the pres., fut., and imperf. tenses (respectively) of the ind. of *sum.* There is no contrast between this sentence and the preceding one, though the cross order (*chiasmus*) might suggest it, viz. *nox . . . intercessit, interfectus est . . . Gracchus; interfectus est* is transferred from its usual place (at the end of the sentence) to the beginning for sake of emphasis, and as compensation for the omission of a conjunction (*asyndeton*). —— **propter,** prep. with the acc. (contracted for *propiter,* from *prope*); gov. *suspīciōnēs.* As an adv., *propter = near,* like *prope;* as a prep., it = *on account of, because of.* Rarely it has the meaning (1) *near,* prep.; (2) *by means of,* e.g. *propter quōs vīvit = through whom he lives.* As a prep., *propter* may occasionally stand after its object. —— **quāsdam,** acc. plur. f. of the indef. pron. *quīdam, quaedam, quiddam* (adjectival neut. *quoddam*); agrees with *suspīciōnēs.* Cicero, who really thought the proceedings of the Gracchi grave offences against the constitution (though he appreciated their ability and some of their aims for social improvement), here purposely speaks mildly of *certain* (i.e. some vague) *suspicions,* in order to add weight to his argument; he implies that if Gāius Gracchus, a mere seditious suspect, was killed in consequence of a senatorial decree, there is no excuse for sparing the life of an undoubted revolutionist such as Catiline. The indef. pronouns *quīdam* and *aliquis* often have a weakening or apologetic force; cf. Chap. VI, l. 47, *quādam dēclīnātiōne,* where he apologizes for the use of the noun, and Chap. VI, l. 38, *nōn mentem aliquam.* Indefinite pronouns: (1) *aliquis,* absolutely indefinite and undiscriminating = *any one, some one or other* (i.e. not known at all), in opposition to *nēmō;* (2) *nesciō quis* is similar to *aliquis,* but less vague; (3) *quīdam,* though indefinite, does discriminate, e.g. *quīdam Antōnius = a certain Antōnius,* i.e. a definite person named Antōnius, but otherwise unknown; in fact, *quīdam = some one, a certain one,* implying that something more is known but reserved unstated; (4) *quīvis* and *quīlibet = any one you like,* without distinction; (5) *quis* is purely indef., being used in clauses introduced by *nē* or *sī;* (6) *quisquam = any one at all,* and occurs usually in negative sentences, or sentences (chiefly interrogative) implying a negative; (7) *quisque = each;* for use, refer to note on *quemque,*

5 sēditiōnum	suspīciōnēs	C.	Gracchus,	upon Gaius Gracchus,
of treasonable practices	*suspicions*	*Gaius*	*Gracchus,*	the son, grandson,
6 clārissimō		patre,	avō,	and descendant of
(descended) most famous		*from a father,*	*grandfather,*	men of the highest

Chap. I, l. 22 ; (8) *quicumque,* and all compounds of *cumque* are universal in character = *whosoever,* etc.

LINE 5. **sēditiōnum,** gen. plur. of *sēditiō, -ōnis,* f. 3d (from *sē* or *sĕd,* denoting separation and *itiō* from *eō,* hence *a going apart;* others less probably derive from *sē* = *apart + dō = I put*); objective gen., limiting *suspīciōnēs. Sēditiō* generally has a political sense, = *internal schism, insurrection,* and the word was largely used by speakers of aristocratic sympathies to designate the aims of democrats.——**suspīciōnēs,** acc. plur. of *suspīciō, -ōnis,* f. 3d (from *sub + speciō,* probably implying *looking* at some one from *under* knit eyebrows, i.e. with mistrust); gov. by the prep. *propter.*——**Gāius** (abbreviated = C ; cf. *Cn.* for *Gnaeus*), gen. *Gāiī,* m. 2d ; nom. sing., *praenōmen* of Gracchus.——**Gracchus,** gen. *Gracchī,* m. 2d ; nom. sing., *cōgnōmen* of Gāius and subj. of *interfectus est.* Gāius Semprōnius Gracchus was the younger brother of Tiberius referred to in l. 30 of Chap. I. He held the office of tribune of the people in the years 123 and 122 B.C. His reforms went much further than his brother's, for he not only revived the agrarian legislation of Tiberius, but also struck a severe blow at the Senate by raising the rich merchants to a class (*Equitēs*) and giving them sole judicial power. He also organized colonies, and strove to extend the Roman franchise in Italy. Mommsen credits him with anticipating many of the chief principles embodied and fulfilled in the Empire. The Senate undermined his influence with the people by having a senatorial puppet, M. Livius Drusus, elected tribune, who outdid Gracchus in the unsound practice of corn-largesses, and promised more colonies. Gracchus and his party took up their position on the Aventine when the riot of 121 B.C. (see note on *dēcrēvit,* l. 1) took place ; a massacre ensued, and 3000 of the Gracchan supporters were killed, and many more imprisoned and strangled.

LINE 6. **clārissimō,** abl. sing. m. of the superl. *clārissimus, -a, -um,* of the adj. *clārus, -a, -um ;* agrees with *patre.*——**patre,** abl. sing. of *pater, patris,* m. 3d (from a root *pa = to nourish,* cf. Greek πατήρ); abl. of quality = (*a man*) *of most famous paternal descent, ancestry,* etc. A. & G. 251 ; B. 224 ; G. 400 ; H. 419, II. This ablative may be used only when a modifying adj. like *clārissimō* or limiting gen. accompanies it ; the abl. modifies the substantive, e.g. *Gracchus,* by describing it, and is often called the *descriptive* ablative. It is possible here to consider *clārissimō patre* (1) abl. of attendant circumstances, = *though his father was most renowned,* or (2) abl. of origin, supplying *descended from ;* Prof. Wilkins regards it as an abl. of origin, but quotes in support an abl. which is rather one of quality. The father of the brothers Tiberius and Gāius was Tiberius Semprōnius Gracchus, a man of high character and ability. He was twice chosen consul, and once censor. As tribune in 187 B.C. he acquitted himself nobly, and P. Cornēlius Scīpiō Āfricānus gave him his youngest daughter, Cornēlia, in marriage. They had 12 children, but none lived long except Tiberius and Gāius, and a daughter, Cornēlia, who married the younger Scīpiō Āfricānus. The elder Cornēlia was renowned for her learning and virtue, and carefully educated her two sons, and after her death was honored by the people with a statue, inscribed "Cornēlia, mother of the Gracchī."—— **avō,** abl. sing. of *avus, -ī,* m. 2d ; abl. of quality, modified by *clārissimō,* which, being an attribute of several nouns, agrees with the nearest and is understood (as here) with the rest. The maternal grandfather of Gāius was the famous Pūblius Cornēlius Scīpiō Āfricānus Māior, one of Rome's greatest names. He rendered Rome great service against Hannibal in Italy after Cannae ; later he drove the Carthaginians out of Spain.

renown; and Marcus Fulvius, an ex-consul, was killed, and his children with him. By a like decree of	māiōribus; / occīsus est cum līberīs M. 7

renown; and Marcus Fulvius, an ex-consul, was killed, and his children with him. By a like decree of | māiōribus; / occīsus est cum līberīs M. 7
(and) ancestors; was slain with his children Marcus
Fulvius cōnsulāris. Similī senātūs 8
Fulvius (a man) of consular rank. Similar of the senate

In 205 B.C. he became consul, though legally debarred by age and the *cursus honōrum*. He carried the war against Carthage into Africa, and won a decisive victory at Zama, B.C. 202. He was later elected censor, and the consul for the second time, and overrode a charge of misapplication of money by appealing to the people's gratitude for his services. He remained to his death the idol of the people.

LINE 7. **māiōribus**, abl. plur. of *māiōrēs, māiōrum,* m. 3d, the plural of the compar. degree *māior* (of the adj. *māgnus, -a, -um*), used substantively; abl. of quality, with *clārissimīs* understood as modifier, describing *Gāius Gracchus.* With *māiōrēs* the abl. of specification *nātū = by birth* is understood. *Nātū minor* (*māior*) and *nātū mini- mus* (*māximus*) are used as the compar. and superl. of *iuvenis* (*senex*); *senex* and *iuvenis* also have comparatives *senior* and *iunior.* The Gracchī had distinguished ancestors on their father's as well as their mother's side, e.g. Tiberius Semprōnius Gracchus, who fought in the second Punic War; the family of the *Scīpiōnēs* included many famous names, among them being great generals, consuls, a *magister equitum,* and a dictator. —— **occīsus est**, 3d pers. sing. perf. ind. pass. of *occīdō, -ere, occīdī, occīsum,* 3 (*ob + caedō*); agrees with the subj. *M. Fulvius;* observe the *asyndeton* and the emphatic position of the verb, as in the previous clause. —— **cum**, prep. with the abl.; gov. the abl. *līberīs. Cum* is used as an enclitic and affixed to the abl. of the personal, reflexive, and relative pronouns; when it is used with a noun modified by an adj., the best order is (1) adj., (2) prep., (3) noun, e.g. *māgnō cum exercitū.* —— **līberīs**, abl. plur. of *līberī,* gen. *liberōrum* or *liberūm,* m. 2d (the specialized substantial use of the adj. *līber, -a, -um, = free,* hence *free people,* and specially *children* of free parents); gov. by the prep. *cum.* Synonyms : (1) *puerī = children,* considered with reference to age, hence *disciplīna puerōrum = the training of children;* (2) *līberī = children* (*free- born*) considered with reference to their parents; the sing. of *līberī* would be *fīlius* or *fīlia; puerī* might be used to describe children of slave parents born into slavery as well as the children of free citizens, but *līberī* can only mean the latter. The children referred to are the two sons of Fulvius, of whom the elder was killed in the riot in which Gāius Gracchus perished, and the younger, who had been sent to Opīmius under a flag of truce to propose an adjustment of difficulties, was apprehended, and after the massacre ruthlessly put to death. —— **Marcus** (abbreviated = *M.*), gen. *Marcī,* m. 2d; nom. sing., *praenōmen* of *Fulvius.*

LINE 8. **Fulvius**, gen. *Fulvī,* m. 2d; nom. sing., the *nōmen* or clan name (*gēns Fulvia*) of *Marcus,* subj. of *occīsus est;* the full name was *Marcus Fulvius Flaccus, Flaccus* being the *cōgnōmen* or family name. Fulvius commanded a division in the fight with the senatorial forces, but the archers of Opīmius caused such slaughter that he and his men fled; he was found hiding, and killed together with his elder son. Fulvius was a special object of hatred to the Senate, as he was one of the commission of three appointed to carry out the agrarian law of Tiberius Gracchus. —— **cōnsulāris**, nom. sing. m. of the adj. *cōnsulāris, -e,* 3d (from the noun *cōnsul*); qualifies *Fulvius; cōnsulāris = of consular rank,* cf. *praetōrius = of praetorian rank;* there were special seats in the Sen- ate for the various grades. Fulvius was consul in the year 125 B.C. —— **Similī**, abl. sing. n. of the adj. *similis, -e,* 3d (from a root in Latin *sim = like,* in Greek ἁμ or ὁμ, cf. ὅμοιος = *like*); agrees with *cōnsultō;* the similarity consists in the fact that the decrees were both *dēcrēta* (*cōnsulta*) *ultima.* This decree, as quoted elsewhere by Cicero, instead of vaguely empowering the consuls to protect the state from danger, specifically instructed

9 cōnsultō	C.	Mariō	et	L.	Valeriō
by a decree	*Gaius*	*to Marius*	*and*	*Lucius*	*to Valerius*

10 cōnsulibus	est	permissa	rēs	pūblica :
the consuls	*was*	*entrusted*	*the weal*	*common :*

11 num	ūnum	diem	posteā	L.	Sāturnīnum
surely not one		*for day*	*afterwards*	*Lucius*	*Saturninus*

the Senate the consuls Gaius Marius and Lucius Valerius were entrusted with the care of the state; and did death, the state's avenger, there-

them to *employ all the tribunes and praetors they thought advisable* and also to uphold the authority and dignity of the Roman people ; all the tribunes were made use of except Saturninus, all the praetors except Glaucia, Saturninus and Glaucia being the authors of the city's peril. —— **senātūs**, gen. sing. of *senātus*, m. 4th ; poss. gen. limiting *cōnsultō*.

LINE 9. **cōnsultō**, abl. sing. of *cōnsultum, -ī*, n. 2d ; abl. of means with *permissa est*, or more likely abl. of manner = *similiter*. Manner may be expressed by an adverb, or by the abl. case with the prep. *cum ;* *cum* must be used if the abl. is not modified by an adjective, but it is often omitted when there is an adj., e.g. *magnā curā* or *magnā cum curā = with great care.* A. & G. 248 ; B. 220 ; G. 399 ; H. 419, III. —— **Gāiō** (abbreviated in all cases *C.*), dat. sing. of *Gāius, -ī*, m. 2d ; *praenōmen* in apposition with *Mariō.* —— **Mariō**, dat. sing. of *Marius, -ī*, m. 2d ; dat. of the indirect obj. with *permissa est ;* Marius is the *nōmen* of the plebeian *gēns* to which Gāius belonged. C. Marius was born 157 B.C., and became one of Rome's greatest generals. He served with distinction in Spain, and in 106 B.C. conquered Jugurtha's stubborn resistance to Rome. He saved Rome from destruction by vast barbarian hordes by defeating the *Teutonēs* near *Aquae Sextiae* (102 B.C.) and the *Cimbrī* near *Vercellae* (101 B.C.) Up to this time his career is notable for three things : (1) though a plebeian, he rose to high office, being elected consul five times to take command of the army against strong enemies of Rome ; (2) he married the sister of Jūlius Caesar ; (3) he reorganized and immensely improved the Roman army. For the sixth time in 100 B.C. he gained the consulship, by employing the demagogues Sāturnīnus and Glaucia. In 88 B.C. his aristocratic rival Sulla won the command against Mithridātēs, and Marius, who got the people to reverse this decision, was driven from Rome. In 87 B.C. Marius returned, and with the aid of Cinna, who led the democrats in his absence, instituted a general massacre of Sulla's party. Marius and Cinna declared themselves consuls for 86 B.C., and Marius died on the eighteenth day of his seventh consulship. —— **et**, cop. conj., joining *Mariō* and *Valeriō.* —— **Lūciō** (abbreviated = *L.*), dat. sing. of *Lūcius, -ī*, m. 2d ; *praenōmen* in apposition with *Valeriō.* **Valeriō**, dat. sing. of *Valerius, -ī*, m. 2d ; dat. of the indirect obj. with *permissa est ;* *Valeriō* is the *nōmen* of Lūcius, showing him to be a member of the *gēns Valeria.* Lūcius Valerius Flaccus (Flaccus being the *cōgnōmen* or family name) was consul with Marius in 100 B.C., and it was he who fulfilled the Senate's wishes as expressed in the decree by inciting the mob to kill Sāturnīnus and Glaucia, for Marius was politically allied with these two and owed his election as consul to their help. In 86 B.C. Valerius was chosen consul in the place of Marius, and was sent to Asia against Mithridātēs ; his own soldiers, prompted by Fimbria, murdered him.

LINE 10. **cōnsulibus**, dat. plur. of *cōnsul, -is*, m. 3d ; in appos. with *Mariō* and *Valeriō.* —— **est permissa**, 3d pers. sing. perf. ind. pass. of *permittō, -ere, permīsī, permissum*, 3 (*per + mittō*); agrees with its subj. *rēs pūblica ; permittere* here = *to entrust, to surrender*, a sense which it bears much more frequently than *to permit, to allow* (*sincere, patī*, or *cōncēdere*). —— **rēs**, gen. *reī*, f. 5th ; nom. sing., subj. of *est permissa ; rēs* and *pūblica* (*rēspūblica*) represent only one idea, viz. *the state.* —— **pūblica**, nom. sing. f. of the adj. *pūblicus, -a, -um ;* agrees with *rēs.*

LINE 11. **num**, interrogative adv., introducing a question to which a negative answer is expected. It has no English equivalent, and so the question it introduces may be

after allow a single	tribūnum	plēbis	et	C.	Servīlium 12
day's respite to the	*the tribune*	*of the people*	*and*	*Gaius*	*Servīlius*

treated as follows: *num* . . . *interfēcit* = (1) *he did not kill* . . . , *did he?* or (2) *surely he did not kill*, a statement implying a question and expecting the challenge of a reply if incorrect. A. & G. 210, *c*; B. 162, 2, *b*; G. 456; H. 351, 1 and 2. *Numne* is found in Cicero, but is rare; *numnam* (*num* + *nam*) occurs chiefly in early Latin. *Num* may be used to introduce simple indirect questions, losing its negative force altogether = *whether;* it is not used in indirect disjunctive questions. For the other interrogative particles, see note on *ne*, l. 4 of Chap. I. —— **ūnum**, acc. sing. n. of the numeral adj. *ūnus, -a, -um* (old forms *oinos* and *oenos;* akin to Greek οἴνη = *the ace* on dice, and εἷς, gen. ἑνός); agrees with *diem*. —— **diem**, acc. sing. of *diēs, diēī*, m. 5th (from a root *di, div*, or *dyu = to be bright, to shine*, cf. Greek δῖος = *divine* and *dīvus = a god;* Ζεύς, gen. Δι-ός, and *Iuppiter*, gen. *Iovis = Djovis; diū dūdum*, etc.); acc. of duration of time. This acc. may be used with or without *per*, accompanying the verb, and answering a question, *how long?*; without *per* the acc. is a survival of the original meaning of the case which is older than prepositions, expressing *motion to* or *motion over*. A. & G. 256; B. 181; G. 336; H. 379. Observe that *dies* is commonly masculine (fem. when it means a period of time) in the sing., and always in the plur. *Num unum diem*, etc., implies that Sāturnīnus and Glaucia were killed on the very day on which the decree was passed. —— **posteā**, temporal adv.; defines *ūnum diem* more closely, the whole phrase being an adverbial extension of the pred. *remorāta est*. *Posteā* is a compound of *post* and *eā;* Corrsen thinks that the final vowel was originally short, and that *ea* is the acc. plur. n. of the demonstr. pron. *is, ea, id;* some regard *eā* as an abl., whose connection with *post* dates from a time when *post*, etc., could be used with that case; others less probably make *ea = eam*, the acc. f. of *is;* cf. similar adverbs *anteā* and *praetereā*. —— **Lūcium** (abbreviated = *L.*), acc. sing. of *Lūcius, -ī*, m. 2d; *praenōmen* and appositive of *Sāturnīnum*. —— **Sāturnīnum**, acc. sing. of *Sāturnīnus, ī-*, m. 2d; direct obj. of *remorāta est;* for the reading *Sāturnīnī*, see the note under *remorāta est*. The full name was Lūcius Appuleius (i.e. of the *gēns Appuleia*) Sāturnīnus (the family *cōgnōmen*). This demagogue was a violent democrat, who used the worst of the devices of C. Gracchus to gain popularity and power, and did little of service to the country except to promote the foundation of colonies. He was quaestor in 104 B.C., and tribune of the *plēbs*, 102 B.C. He was a second time tribune in 100 B.C., having secured the murder of his opponent. In the elections held in this year he secured reëlection as tribune, but the aid which he extended to his friend and fellow-democrat Glaucia cost the life of both.

LINE 12. **tribūnum**, acc. sing. of *tribūnus, -ī*, m. 2d (from *tribus = a tribe*); appositive of *Sāturnīnum;* Sāturnīnus was doubly a tribune, as holding the office and being elected again for the next year. In 494 B.C., after the secession of the *plēbs* to the Mōns Sacer, the *tribūnī plēbis* were appointed, being inviolable in their persons and empowered to rescue prisoners held by the consuls; soon they acquired the additional right of the *intercessiō*, for which and other details see the Introduction. —— **plēbis**, gen. sing. of *plēbs, plēbis*, f. 3d (with another form *plēbēs, plēbeī*, f. 5th; this gen. in combination with *tribūnus, scītum*, etc., often appears as *plēbī*, the final *-ī* being = to *-ei* scanned as one syllable); poss. gen., limiting *tribūnus*. *Plēbs* has no plural; as a political term it = *the plebeian citizens*, regarded as a class, in opposition to the patricians, senators, and knights. The word has the same etymological origin as *populus;* for difference of meaning, etc., see the note on *populī*, l. 6 of Chap. I. —— **et**, cop. conj., connecting *Servīlium* with *Sāturnīnum*. —— **Gāium**, acc. sing. of *Gāius, -ī*, m. 2d; *praenōmen* of Servīlius. —— **Servīlium**, acc. sing. of *Servīlius, -ī*, m. 2d; the *nōmen* of Gāius, direct ob. of *remorāta est;* observe that all *nōmina* are adjective forms ending in- *ius* used substantively, e.g. masc. *Servīlius*, fem. *Servīlia*. It is noteworthy that Cicero

13 praetōrem	mors	ac	reī pūblicae	tribune of the people,
the praetor	*death*	*and*	*of the commonwealth*	Lucius Saturninus, or to Gaius Servilius, the
14 poena	remorāta est?	At	vērō nōs	praetor? But as for
the penalty	*did keep waiting?*	*But*	*indeed we*	us, we have for these

speaks of Glaucia by the name of his *gens* (*Servīlia*) and remarks that he held the important office of *praetor*, implying that the state's vengeance could overtake all, even the noblest-born and the highest officials. Gāius Servīlius Glaucia was *praetor* in 100 B.C., in which year he sought to be elected as consul for the one following. There was, however, an influential rival candidate, C. Memmius, whom the tribune Sāturnīnus, wishing to ensure his friend's election, caused his armed ruffians to murder openly in the streets. This act of violence alienated the people's sympathies, and by the Senate's decree Marius and Valerius, the consuls, were directed to guard the state from harm. Marius wished to spare his political adherents, but Valerius and many others were averse to this, and inflamed the mob's fury. Glaucia and Sāturnīnus fled to the Capitol, but soon, through failure of food and water, surrendered to Marius, who removed them to the *Cūria Hostīlia* for safety. But the mob tore off tiles from the roof, and pelted the two offenders to death.

LINE 13. **praetōrem**, acc. sing. of *praetor, -ōris*, m. 3d (from *prae + eō = one who goes before, a leader*); acc. in apposition with *C. Servīlium*. In 366 B.C., when the Licinian Rogations of 367 B.C. revived the consulship and enacted that one consul at least must be plebeian, the patricians tried to prevent the plebeians from acquiring too great power by transferring the judicial powers of the consuls to a new magistrate called *praetor;* but in 337 B.C. this office was also opened to the *plēbs*. In 241 B.C. a second praetor was appointed to try disputes in which a foreigner was a party; this new *praetor* was called *peregrīnus*, and the original one *urbānus*. For the functions, increase in number, etc., of the praetors, refer to the Introduction.——**mors**, gen. *mortis*, f. 3d (from a root *mar*, in Greek and Latin *mar* or *mor*, = *to waste away*, cf. *morior = I die, marceō = I wither*, μάρ-ανσις = *decay*, etc.); nom. sing., subj. of *remorāta est*.——**ac**, cop. conj., connecting *mors* and *poena;* see *ac*, l. 24 of Chap. I. *Ac* is here explanatory; see *poena* below.——**reī**, gen. sing. of *rēs*, f. 5th; subjective poss. gen., limiting *poena; reī pūblicae poena = penalty inflicted by the state*.——**pūblicae**, gen. sing. of the adj. *pūblicus, -a, -um;* modifies *reī*.

LINE 14. **poena**, gen. *poenae*, f. 1st (cf. Greek ποινή = *a penalty*, from a root *pu = to purify, to cleanse;* akin are *putō, pūrus, purgō, pūniō*); nom. sing., joined by *ac* to the subj. *mors*, more clearly defining *mors* as a state-inflicted punishment; in English *ac* is better left untranslated, *death, the penalty of the state*. *Mors ac poena* may be considered as a case of *hendiadys*, i.e. two connected nouns expressing a single idea which might be expressed by one noun accompanied by modifiers, e.g. *death of the avenging state's infliction*. A. & G. 385; B. 374, 4; G. 698; H. 636, III, 2. Observe that both *mors* and *poena* are here personified, as if avenging deities watching over the safety of the state.——**remorāta est**, 3d pers. sing. perf. ind. of the deponent verb *remoror, -ārī, -ātus sum*, 1 (*re = back, + moror = I delay*); agrees with the fem. subj. *mors*, and here governs a direct obj., viz. *Sāturnīnum*, l. 11, and *Servīlium*, l. 12. *Remoror* is often used: (1) intransitively, = *I stay, linger*, (2) transitively = *I hold back, detain, retard*. There is therefore nothing forced about the rendering *did death keep them waiting a single day?* i.e. *did death fail to overtake them* (or *give them respite*) *for a single day?* Though rather uncommon in this sense, *remoror* has parallel instances in other authors. —NOTE. Some editors, who doubt the Latinity of such an expression as *poena remorātur aliquem* and think that *remoror*, transitive, can only be used in the sense *I delay, retard, = retineō*, reconstruct the passage as follows: (1) *num ūnum diem posteā L. Sāturnīnī*

| last twenty days been | vīcēsimum | iam | diem | patimur | hebēscere 15 |
| passively allowing the | twentieth | already | for the day | are allowing | to grow blunt |

tribūnī plēbis et C. Servīlī praetōris mortem reī pūblicae poena remorāta est? changing the case of the proper names and appositives to poss. gen. limiting *mortem*, the nom. *mors* to acc. *mortem*, direct obj. of *remorāta est*, omitting *ac*, and keeping *poena reī pūblicae* as sole subject, = *did the state's vengeance delay, for a single day after, the death of Lūcius Sāturnīnus, tribune of the plēbs, or of Gāius Servīlius the praetor?* The change of *mors ac* to *mortem* is somewhat violent. (2) Ernesti recommends that the acc. case of the proper names and appositives be changed to gen., and that the verb *remorāta est* be considered intransitive, = *did the death (and), the penalty of the state, of Lūcius Sāturnīnus the tribune,* etc., *and of Servīlius,* etc., *tarry for a single day thereafter?* This makes very good sense, but the necessity for changing the common reading is not apparent. ——**At**, adversative conj. (see note on *tamen*, l. 18 of Chap. I); introducing a statement in emphatic contradiction of the idea that any one was remiss in duty except the consuls, and resuming the contention of ll. 45, 46 of Chap. I. ——**vērō** (originally abl. n. of *vērus*), asseverative adv. or adversative conj., intensifying the contradiction introduced by *at;* see note on *tamen*, l. 18 of Chap. I. Some editors omit *vērō* here. ——**nōs**, nom. plur. of the 1st pers. pron.; subj. of *patimur*, and very emphatic in contrast with the consuls Marius and Valerius.

LINE 15. **vīcēsimum**, acc. sing. m. of the ordinal numeral adj. *vīcēsimus, -a, -um* (contracted from *vigintēsimus*, from the cardinal numeral *vigintī*, indeclinable ; other forms *vigēsimus* and *vicensimus* sometimes occur ; akin is the Greek εἴκοσι, Boeotian ϝίκατι, = twenty); agrees with *diem ; vīcēsimum* is approximate only, for supposing the *cōnsultum* to have been passed on Oct. 22d, the second day of the Senate's meeting, and not on Oct. 21st (and Dion Cassius supports our argument), Nov. 8th was only the 18th day ; and if the decree was passed on Oct. 21st, as some hold, then Nov. 8th is only the 19th day after, reckoning inclusively. An orator always likes to use round numbers; so Cicero speaks of "40 years" in his speech against Pīsō, where he should have said "36 years."——**iam**, temporal adv., modifying *vīcēsimum*, as may be seen from its close proximity. ——**diem**, acc. sing. of *diēs, -ēī*, m. 5th ; acc. of duration of time ; see *diem*, l. 11 above. ——**patimur**, 1st pers. plur. pres. ind. of the deponent verb *patior, patī, passus sum*, 3 ; agrees with the subj. *nōs*. Synonyms : (1) *patī* = *to allow*, implying non-interference (*cum patientiā sinere*); (2) *sinere* = *to allow*, with indifference ; *sinere* is purely negative, in opposition to (3) *permittere* = *to give permission* (*potestātem dare*) ; (4) *concēdere* = *to allow*, in yielding compliance with a request. *Patī* often = *to suffer, endure;* note the following synonyms : (1) *patī* = *to suffer*, entirely passively, and differs from (2) *ferre* = *to bear*, inasmuch as the latter implies some energy ; cf. in English "he *suffered* misfortunes and *bore* them well ; " (3) *sustinēre* = *to endure, to bear up*, and implies greater energy and a heavier burden or evil than *ferre;* (4) *tolerāre* = *to support, endure*, with subjective regard to the state of mind of the person who is enduring. —— **hebēscere**, pres. inf. act. of *hebēscō, -ere*, no perf., no supine, 3, intrans. (from the verb *hebēre = to be dull*); object-inf. agreeing with the subj.-acc. *aciem*. Observe that the real object of *patimur* is the whole phrase *aciem . . . hebēscere;* the inf. is really a kind of complementary one, helped into existence by the leading verb, as commonly after verbs of *creation, will, power, effort*, etc. The termination in *-scō* expresses the beginning of an action, e.g. Vergil *mītēscent saecula = the ages will grow gentle;* verbs ending in *-scō* are called *inceptive* or *inchoative*. A. & G. 167, *a*; B. 155, 1; G. 133, V; H. 337. The student should note that, no matter what may be the conjugation of the original verb, the inceptive is always of the 3d conjugation, e.g. *obdormiō, -īre* and *obdormīscō, -ere;* but frequently inceptives are formed directly from adjectives or nouns, cf. *mītēscō* from the adj. *mītis*, and *lapidēscō* from the substantive *lapis*.

16 aciem	hōrum	auctōritātis.	Habēmus	weapon of this coun-
the edge	*of these (senators)*	*of the authority.*	*We have*	cil's sanction to lose its sharpness. For

17 enim	hūius	modī	senātūs	cōnsultum,	we, too, have a sena-
for	*this*	*of kind*	*of the senate*	*a decree,*	torial decree of this kind, thrust away, it

18 vērum	inclūsum	in	tabulīs,	tamquam	in	is true, among the
but in truth	*shut up*	*in*	*the records,*	*as if*	*in*	archives, like a sword

LINE 16. **aciem,** acc. sing. of *aciēs, acieī,* f. 5th (from root *ak = sharp,* akin to *ācer, acūtus,* etc.); may be correctly called the direct obj. of *patimur* (with *hebēscere* as complementary inf.), or subj.-acc. of the obj.-inf. *hebēscere* after *patimur. Aciēs* has several meanings, e.g. (1) *point, sharp edge;* (2) *brightness;* (3) *battle order* or *array;* (4) *a battle, an engagement;* (5) *sharp sight* (rare). The metaphor is taken from a sword, to which the authority of the Senate is likened. —— **hōrum,** gen. plur. m. of the demonstr. pron. *hīc, haec, hōc;* poss. gen., limiting *auctōritātis; hōrum* is deictic = *senātōrum quī hīc adsunt.* —— **auctōritātis,** gen. sing. of *auctōritās,* f. 3d (from *auctor*); poss. gen., limiting *aciem.* —— **Habēmus,** 1st pers. plur. pres. ind. act. of *habeō, -ēre, -uī, -itum,* 2; agrees with the subj. *nōs* implied; cf. *habēmus,* l. 41 of Chap. I.

LINE 17. **enim,** causal conj., introducing an explanation of the statement that the consuls are slow in doing their duty (end of Chap. I), a fact which Cicero has been illustrating in Chap. II. The causal particles are : (1) *enim,* post-positive, though in early Latin it often stood first; *enim* is often strengthened by another particle, e.g. *atenim, vērumenim, enimvērō;* (2) *nam,* praepositive, except sometimes in poetry; see *nam,* Chap. I, l. 34; (3) *namque,* standing first, and not very common in classical Latin, though Livy uses it considerably; (4) *etenim,* standing first, is very common in classical Latin, especially in Cicero, but rare in ante-classical and post-classical literature. A. & G. 156, *d*; B. 345; G. 498; H. 310, 5, and 554, V. —— **hūius,** gen. sing. m. of the demonstr. pron. *hīc, haec, hōc;* agrees with *modī; hūius* and *ēius,* when used with *modī,* are often combined, e.g. *ēiusmodī = such.* The reading *hūiusce (hūius + ce)* is adopted in some editions, *-ce* being a deictic particle appended to emphasize the demonstrative (cf. French *ce-ci = this here*). *Hīc, haec, hōc,* combines in full with *-ce* in early Latin, but in classical Latin the following are the forms most found, *hōsce, hāsce, hūiusce* (esp. + *modī*), and *hīsce. Ille* and *iste* also combine with *-ce,* and the neut. *istuc* is more common than *istud* in classical Latin. Note that *ce* is often shortened to *c,* as *istic, illic,* etc., and that the *c* of *hīc, haec, hōc* is an abbreviation of the same particle. —— **modī,** gen. sing. of *modus,* m. 2d (from a root *mad* or *med, = to measure,* cf. μέδιμνος *= a measure,* and English *mode, mood;* whence *modus =* (1) *measure,* (2) *moderation,* (3) *limit,* (4) *rhythm,* (5) *mode, manner;* descriptive gen., limiting *cōnsultum; hūius modī* is an adjectival phrase. —— **senātūs,** gen. sing. of *senātus,* m. 4th; poss. gen., limiting *cōnsultum.* —— **cōnsultum,** acc. sing. of *cōnsultum, -ī,* n. 2d; direct obj. of *habēmus.* The idea intended is that the decree empowering Cicero and his colleague is just as efficient as that empowering Marius and Valerius; the latter put to death Glaucia, and so should Catiline long ago have been put to death.

LINE 18. **vērum,** adversative conj. (see note on *tamen,* Chap. I, l. 18); introducing something slightly opposed to what has been said. Some read *vērumtamen,* but the best editions omit *tamen.* —— **inclūsum,** acc. sing. n. of *inclūsus, -a, -um,* perf. part. pass. of *inclūdō, -ere, inclūsī, inclūsum,* 3 (*in + claudō*); agrees with and enlarges the object *cōnsultum.* It is plain that Cicero's aim is to frighten Catiline, not to convince the senators; he warns Catiline that he holds the warrant for his arrest, and that its production from among the official documents is equivalent to drawing the weapon of execution from its resting-place. —— **in,** prep.; gov. the abl. *tabulīs.* —— **tabulīs,** abl. plur.

concealed within the scabbard; and by the authority of this de-	vāgīnā reconditum, quō ex senātūs 1
	a scabbard sheathed (lit. *hidden*), *which according to of the senate*

of *tabula, -ae*, f. 1st; obj. of the prep. *in*. The *tabulae* referred to are the minutes or records of the questions discussed, resolutions passed, and general business transacted in the Senate. These records (*acta senātūs*) were in Caesar's time written out by shorthand scribes and published (59 B.C.); previously they were stored in the treasury (*aerarium*) under the care of the quaestors. Other meanings of *tabula* are : (1) *a board*, or *plank* of plane surface, the original sense; hence, (2) *a tablet*, of wood, etc., smeared with wax and used for writing; hence, (3) according to the nature of the writing, *a will* (Ovid), *a list* of proscribed persons (Juvenal), *a map* (Cicero), *an auction* (Cicero); (4) *a voting-tablet*, on which voters at the *comitia* registered their *punctum;* (5) *a painted panel, a picture* (Cicero); (6) *a board*, used for games such as dice, draughts, etc. ; (7) *a votive tablet*, for dedication in a temple ; (8) in plur., *tabulae* often = XII *tabulae*, the famous *twelve tables* of laws, which were published in 450 B.C., and gave some sort of form to traditional law; these were the foundation of Roman law. —— **tamquam** (*tam + quam*, = lit. *so . . . as*, i.e. *as if*), adv. implying comparison; introducing the simile *in vāgīnā reconditum. Tamquam* and *quasi* as conjunctions are used in direct comparison with the ind. mood, and as the verb is likely to be the same in both the clauses it is usually left out. In regular conditional sentences of comparison, *tamquam, tamquam sī, velut, velut sī, ut sī, āc sī*, and *quam sī* are the particles used, and the verb in the comparative clause is subjunctive. Observe that in this passage *tamquam* is not a conj., but an adverb ; thus it qualifies *reconditum. Tamquam* is now and then used by Cicero as the attribute of a noun, and the same author uses *tum, saepe*, and *quasi* in similar fashion. —— **in**, prep.; gov. the abl. *vāgīnā.*

˚ LINE 19. **vāgīnā**, abl. sing. of *vāgīna, -ae*, f. 1st; obj. of the prep. *in;* the metaphor of the *sword* (cf. *aciem* above) of the Senate's authority is here further elaborated. The noun *gladium* is not found in the best MSS. and editions, but some insert it after *tamquam*, and Ernesti approves it because *inclūsum* has already been used of *cōnsultum;* thus the sentence would read (*the Senate's decree*) *shut up in the archives, like a sword hidden in the scabbard.* —— **reconditum**, acc. sing. n. of *reconditus, -a, -um*, perf. part. pass. of *recondō, -ere, recondidī, reconditum*, 3 (*re = back + condō, condō* being a compound of *cum* and *dō = I put, place*); agrees with and enlarges attributively *cōnsultum* (or, if *gladium* be inserted after *tamquam*, agrees with *gladium*). Observe the force of *re* or *red* in composition : (1) = *back*, e.g. *redūcō = I lead back, removeō = I move back;* (2) = *again*, e.g. *revīsō = I visit again, revisit, repetō = I seek again.* —— **quō**, abl. sing. n. of the rel. pron. *quī, quae, quod;* agrees with *cōnsultō; ex quō* would have been sufficient in itself, *quō* agreeing in gender and number with the antecedent *cōnsultum*, l. 17, but the antecedent is repeated in the rel. clause to make the meaning clear (as often in legal statements) and emphasize the argument. The repetition of the antecedent in the rel. clause is very common in the best Latin, and Caesar often indulges in it. A. & G. 200, *a* ; B. 251, 3 ; G. 615 ; H. no reference. —— **ex**, prep. with the abl. ; gov. *cōnsultō;* here used of reference = *according to. Ex* may be used before words beginning with a vowel or a consonant, *ē* only before words whose initial letter is a consonant. It is used also of (1) time = *from*, (2) origin = *from*, (3) place = *out of, from*, (4) manner, in phrases, e.g. *ex ordine*, (5) after verbs of receiving = *from*, (6) in many phrases, e.g. *ex parte.* A. & G. 152, *b* ; B. 142, 2 ; G. 417 ; H. 434. The prep. strictly stands next to the noun it governs, but *senātūs* intervenes here because it is so closely connected with *cōnsultō*, forming a single idea and often written as one word, e.g. *senātūscōnsultō.* —— **senātūs**, gen. sing. of *senātus*, m. 4th ; poss. gen., limiting *cōnsultō*, with which it expresses a single notion.

20 cōnsultō　　cōnfēstim　　interfectum　　tē
　 decree　　*immediately*　　*killed*　　*(that) you*

21 esse,　　　　　　Catilīna,　　　　convēnit.
　 should have been (lit. *to be*),　*Catilina,*　*it was fitting.*

22 Vīvis, et vīvis nōn ad dēpōnendam, sed
　 You live, and you live not for laying aside, but

cree, you, Catiline,
might have been very
properly put to death
on the instant. You
live yet, and live, not
to put your insolence

LINE 20.　cōnsultō, abl. sing. of *cōnsultum, -ī,* n. 2d ; governed by *ex.*——cōnfēstim (probably a compound of *cum* and adj. *festīnus = hastening;* others think *cōnfestim = cōnfer-tim,* from *cōnferō*), adv. of manner, modifying *interfectum esse.*——interfectum, acc. sing. m. of *interfectus, -a, -um,* perf. part. pass. of *interficiō, -ere, interfēcī, interfectum,* 3 (*inter + faciō*), forming with *esse* below the perf. inf. pass. ; the inf. *interfectum esse* agrees with the subj.-acc. *tē* after the leading verb *convēnit* below. As stated in the notes on *dūcī,* l. 25, and *oportēbat,* l. 26 of Chap. I, the tense is expressed by the inf. in English when an auxiliary verb, e.g. *might, ought,* is used ; but in Latin the tense is given in the leading verb, and the pres. inf. is used after it. In this passage the usual construction would have been *tē interfīcī . . . convēnit (oportuit).* A. & G. 288, *a* ; B. 270, 2 ; G. 535 ; H. 537, 1. Observe that the acc. and inf. constitute the real subject of the sentence. After verbs of *obligation* and *desire* the perf. inf. pass. or the perf. part. pass. without *esse* may be often found, as in this passage ; cf. *nōllem factum = I could wish it not done,* and esp. l. 40, *quod iam prīdem factum esse oportuit.* Allen and Greenough remark that the part. (with or without *esse*) is "rather in predicate agreement than used to form a strict perf. infinitive." A. & G. 288, *d* and NOTE ; B. 270, 2, *a* ; G. 280, 2, *a,* REM. 2 ; H. no reference. In the case of *oportet,* another construction is also used, viz. the consecutive subjunct., usually with *ut* omitted.——tē, acc. sing. of the 2d personal pron. *tū ;* obj. of *convēnit,* and subj.-acc. of *interfectum esse.*

LINE 21.　esse, pres. inf. of *sum,* perf. *fuī ;* constitutes with *interfectum* the perf. inf. pass. of *interficiō,* and agrees with the subj.-acc. *tē.*——Catilīna, voc. sing. of *Catilīna, -ae,* m. 1st ; case of person addressed.——convēnit, 3d pers. sing. pres. ind. act. of the impersonal verb *convenit, convenīre, convēnit,* 4 (a form of the personal verb *conveniō, -īre, convēnī, conventum,* 4, *cum + veniō*) ; the logical subj. of *convēnit* is the clause *tē interfectum esse ;* observe that *convēnit* is perf., referring to obligation in the past.

LINE 22.　Vīvis, 2d pers. sing. pres. ind. act. of *vīvō, -ere, vīxī, victum,* 3 ; agrees with the implied subj. *tū,* i.e. Catiline.——et, cop. conj. ; connecting the first unmodified *vīvis* with the second *vīvis* which is extended by *nōn . . . audāciam.* In ordinary prose the second *vīvis* would be omitted, and possibly *et* also ; or *et* would have been strengthened *et quidem = aye indeed;* the repetition of *vīvis* is rhetorical.——vīvis, 2d pers. sing. pres. ind. act. of *vīvō* (as above).——nōn, negative adv. (see *nōn,* l. 10 of Chap. I) ; negatives *ad dēpōnendam (audāciam).*——ad, prep. with the acc. ; gov. *dēpōnendam (audāciam)* in the gerundial construction, expressing purpose. Purpose may be expressed in the following ways in Latin : (1) *ad* with the acc. in the gerundial construction ; (2) *causā* with the gen. of the gerund, or the gen. in the gerundial construction, e.g. *causā pugnandī vel pācis petendae ;* (3) *ut* or *quī* final + the subjunct., e.g. *lēgātōs ut* or (*quī*) *pacem peterent mīsit ;* (4) occasionally the fut. part. act., e.g. *lēgātōs pacem petītūrōs mīsit ;* (5) the supine in *-um* after verbs implying *motion,* e.g. *lēgātī vēnērunt pācem petītum ;* (6) in Tacitus the gen. of the gerundial construction without *causā,* the gen. limiting and defining the whole clause, e.g. *vītandae suspīciōnis = in order to avoid suspicion.*——dēpōnendam, acc. sing. f. of *dēpōnendus, -a, -um,* gerundive of *dēpōnō, -ere, dēposuī, dēpositum,* 3 (*dē = from, aside + pōnō = I lay*) ; agrees with *audāciam* understood from *ad cōnfirmandam audāciam* below, in the construction

from you, but to increase its daring. I am anxious, Conscript Fathers, to be forbearing; I am anx-	ad cōnfīrmandam audāciam. Cupiō, patrēs 23		
	for	*strengthening*	*your audacity.*	*I desire,*	*fathers*

| | cōnscrīptī, | mē | esse | clēmentem, | cupiō | in 24 |
| | *enrolled,* | *myself* | *to be* | *forbearing,* | *I desire* | *in* |

of gerundival attraction. Refer to the note and grammatical references under *habendī*, Chap. I, l. 8. —— **sed**, adversative conj., connecting *dēpōnendam* and *cōnfīrmandam*, and introducing a contradiction of the former.

LINE 23. **ad**, prep. with the acc.; governs *audāciam* in the gerundial construction. —— **cōnfīrmandam**, acc. sing. f. of *cōnfīrmandus, -a, -um*, gerundive of *cōnfīrmō, -āre, -āvī, -ātum*, 1 (*cum + firmō*); agrees with *audāciam* in the gerundival-attraction construction. —— **audāciam**, acc. sing. of *audācia, -ae*, f. 1st; obj. of *ad*, expressing purpose in the gerundial construction. —— **Cupiō**, 1st pers. sing. pres. ind. act. of *cupiō, -ere, cupīvī (cupiī), cupītum*, 3; the subj. *ego* is implied in the personal ending; for synonyms, see note on *cupientem*, Chap. I, l. 34. Observe the rhetorical repetition of *cupiō* in the next line instead of the natural connection of the two object-clauses of *cupiō*, e.g. *cupiō mē esse clēmentem neque tamen . . . dissolūtum vidērī;* the two object clauses are antithetical, which fact would have been marked in Greek by μέν inserted in the first and δέ in the second. —— **patrēs**, voc. plur. of *pater, patris*, m. 3d; case of address. The *patrēs* or senators were chosen out of the *patriciī*, who were the descendants of the ancient *gentēs;* plebeians became eligible under the Republic. Not all *patrēs familiās* became *patrēs* or senators, but only such as were chosen by the king, consul, or censor, or succeeded to a seat in the Senate by virtue of having held a curule magistracy.

LINE 24. **cōnscrīptī**, voc. plur. m. of *cōnscrīptus, -a, -um*, perf. part. pass. of *cōnscrībō, -ere, cōnscrīpsī, cōnscrīptum*, 3 (*cum + scrībō*); agrees with *patrēs*. NOTE. (1) The old explanation is that *patrēs cōnscrīptī = patrēs et cōnscrīptī*, i.e. *senators* (patrician) *and enrolled* (plebeians), in allusion to the enrolment of 160 plebeians in 509 B.C. Mommsen holds that the *cōnscrīptī* did not become full senators, and had no share in giving *auctōritās*, sharing discussion, or doing anything at all except voting in silence, i.e. he identifies the *cōnscrīptī* with the *pedāriī*, though most scholars think that the term *pedāriī* applies to all senators who were not present or past curule officers, *cōnsulārēs, praetōriī*, etc. This explanation is very doubtful, for *et* is never found to connect *patrēs* and *cōnscrīptī*, and besides *adscrīptī* would be more suitable to *additional* members. (2) It is better to regard *patrēs cōnscrīptī* as = *enrolled fathers*, the epithet *cōnscrīptī* being the distinguishing mark between those *patrēs* (patricians) or *patrēsfamiliās* who were senators and those who were not. —— **mē**, acc. sing. of the 1st pers. pron. *ego;* obj. of *cupiō* and subj.-acc. of *esse;* instead of the usual *cupiō clēmēns esse*. —— NOTE. Verbs of *will* and *desire* (e.g. *cupiō*) admit of two constructions : (1) with *ut* or *nē* and the subjunct. (complementary final clauses); (2) with the object acc. and infinitive, as in this passage. With regard to (2), note (*A*) that, *when the subj. of the inf. and of the verb of wishing is the same*, the subj. of the inf. is not usually expressed, but is understood in the nom. case, and so predicate words referring to the subj. must be in the nom. case. (*B*) But when the subj. of the inf. and verb of *wishing* is the same, and when the action expressed by the inf. is outside the power of the subj., then the subj. is put in the acc. case ; this is common when the inf. is passive or = a passive (e.g. *esse* here nearly = *habērī* or *existimārī*), cf. *māluit* SĒ DĪLIGĪ *quam* METUĪ = *he preferred being loved to being feared.* (*C*) When the subj. of the inf. is not the same as the subj. of the verb of *wishing*, it is invariably expressed in the acc. case, e.g. *tē tuā fruī virtūte cupimus = we desire that you should enjoy your virtue*. A. & G. 331, *b*, NOTE; B. 331, IV, *a*; G. 532, REM. 2; H. 535, II. —— **esse**, pres. inf. of *sum;* agrees with the subj.-acc. *mē* after *cupiō;* esse

25	tantīs	reī	pūblicae	perīculīs	mē	nōn
	so great	*of the commonwealth*		*dangers*	*myself*	*not*

26	dissolūtum	vidērī,	sed	iam	mē	ipse
	negligent	*to appear,*	*but*	*now*	*myself*	*in person*

27	inertiae	nēquitiaeque	condemnō.	Castra
	for inactivity	*and inefficiency*	*I condemn.*	*A camp*

ious in this the state's hour of grievous peril not to seem neglectful, but I do now convict myself of remissness and slowness to act. A camp has

may almost be rendered *to be considered.*—— **clēmentem**, acc. sing. m. of the adj. *clēmēns, -entis*, 3d ; complement of *esse* in the pred., and agrees with the subj.-acc. *mē.* —— **cupiō**, 1st pers. sing. ind. act. (see *cupiō* above). The rhetorical repetition of *cupiō* at the beginning of this sentence is called *anaphora ;* see note on *nihil*, Chap. I, l. 5. —— **in**, prep. ; gov. the abl. *perīculīs.*

Line 25. **tantīs**, abl. plur. n. of the demonstr. adj. *tantus, -a, -um ;* agrees with *perīculīs.* —— **reī**, gen. sing. of *rēs*, f. 5th ; poss. gen., limiting *perīculīs.* —— **pūblicae**, gen. sing. of the adj. *pūblicus, -a, -um ;* agrees with *reī.* Observe the position of *reī pūblicae ;* a single word in the gen. case preferably stands immediately before the noun which it limits, when the latter is modified by an adjective, and the adj. then precedes the limiting genitive. —— **perīculīs**, abl. plur. of *perīculum, -ī*, n. 2d ; obj. of the prep. *in.* —— **mē**, acc. sing. of *ego ;* subj.-acc. of *vidērī* in the object clause dependent on *cupiō.* —— **nōn**, negative adv., modifying *vidērī dissolūtum.*

Line 26. **dissolūtum**, acc. sing. m. of the adj. *dissolūtus, -a, -um*, properly perf. part. pass. of *dissolvō, -ere, dissolvī, dissolūtum,* 3 (*dis = apart + solvō = I loose*, hence *loosed apart, loose, remiss, dissolute*); completes the pred. with *vidērī*, and agrees with the subj.-acc. *mē. Dissolūtus* is a synonym of *neglegēns*, but implies that the vice has become a permanent habit of mind ; it is opposed to *sevērus et iūstus* (Ernesti). *Dis-* or *dī-* is an inseparable prep. only met in compound words as a prefix, = *asunder, apart, between ;* sometimes negative = *not*, e.g. *difficilis ;* sometimes with intensive force developed from the notion of separation, = *utterly*, e.g. *disperdō = I waste* (destroy) *utterly. Dis-* is its form before *s, c, p, φ,* and *t ; dif-* before *f* (by assimilation), e.g. *differō ; dī* before *b, d, g, m, n, l, v, r,* and *s* followed by another consonant, e.g. *dīvellō, discrībō ; dir-* before vowels, e.g. *dirimō* (= *dis + emō*); *dis-* or *dī-* before *i* consonantal, e.g. *disiungō, dīiūdicō.* —— **vidērī**, pres. inf. of the deponent verb *videor, -ērī, vīsus sum,* 2 (the pass. form of *video, -ēre, vīdī, vīsum*, 2, and sometimes so used, = *I am seen*); agrees with the subj.-acc. *mē ; vidērī* requires the complement *dissolūtum* to make a predicate, being a copulative verb. The copulative verbs include those of *seeming (appearing)*, *becoming, making, calling, thinking, showing,* and *choosing.* —— **sed**, adversative conj., introducing an idea opposed to what has been stated. —— **iam**, temporal adv., modifies *condemnō.* —— **mē**, acc. sing. of *ego ;* direct obj., used reflexively, of *condemnō.* When the subj. acts upon itself and is a personal pron. of the 1st or 2d pers., the oblique forms of *tū* and *ego* are used ; the reflexive pron. of the 3d person is *sē*, gen. *suī* (poss. adj. reflexive *suus*). —— **ipse**, nom. sing. m. of the intensive pron. *ipse, ipsa, ipsum*, gen. *ipsīus* (*is, + pse = pte*, a suffix from the same root as *potis = able,* cf. *suōpte* (= *suō + pte*)); subj. of *condemnō*, or rather intensifies the subj. *ego* implied. *Ipse* is a determinative pron., and is used (1) as an intensive adj. agreeing with a noun or another pron., e.g. *Caesar ipse = Caesar himself, ego ipse = I myself,* or (2) independently, in which case the word intensified is suggested by the verb or the context, e.g. *ipse condemnō :* it may be variously translated, *-self, very, actually, in person,* etc., to suit the context. It is never used reflexively, though it may intensify a reflexive pron., e.g. *mē ipsum condemnō.* A. & G. 102, *e* ; B. 88 ; G. 103, 3 ; H. 186, and 452.

Line 27. **inertiae**, gen. sing. of *inertia*, f. 1st (from the adj. *iners = in, not + ars,* *skilled in production*, from a root *ar = to join ;* akin are *ars, sollers, arma,* ἀρετή, ἄρθρον,

been established in	sunt	in	Ītaliā	contrā	populum 28
Italy, in a mountain	*has been*(lit. *is*)*in*		*Italy*	*against*	*the people*
gorge of Etruria, to	Rōmānum	in	Etrūriae	faucibus	collocāta, 29
threaten the Roman	*Roman*	*in*	*of Etruria*	*the passes*	*established,*

etc.); objective gen. of the *charge* with *condemnō*. Judicial verbs, i.e. of *accusing, convicting, condemning,* and *acquitting,* govern the acc. of the person, and the gen. of the charge; verbs of *condemning* govern the gen. of the *penalty* also, esp. when it is stated indefinitely, e.g. *duplī = at double,* but the abl. when the *penalty* is definite, e.g. *damnārī decem mīlibus = to be fined ten thousand* (coins); cf. English *guilty of death.* Common variations from the gen. construction are: (1) abl. of charge or penalty; (2) *nōmine* or *crīmine* + the gen. of the charge; (3) *aē* + the abl., e.g. *aē vī accūsāre.* A. & G. 220; B. 208, 1, and 2, *a*; G. 378; H. 409, II. Synonyms: (1) *inertia = indolence,* originally from lack of skill; (2) *īgnāvia = idleness, cowardice,* from *īgnāvus* (= *in, not* + (*g*)*nāvus* = *active*); (3) *segnitia* (*segnis*) = *sluggishness;* (4) *dēsidia = sloth,* from *aēsideō = I sit idle;* (5) *pigritia* (from *piger,* cf. *piget = it displeases, disgusts*) = *apathy, listlessness.* —— **nēquitiae,** gen. sing. of *nēquitia,* f. 1st (from *nēquam,* indecl. adj. = *worthless*); gen. of the *charge,* joined by *que* to *inertiae.* The usual sense of *nēquitia* is *worthlessness, depravity;* here it = *inexcusable negligence;* in Chap. XI, ll. 38–40, it is contrasted with *sevēritās.* —— **que,** enclitic cop. conj.; joins *inertiae* and *nēquitiae.* —— **condemnō,** 1st pers. sing. pres. ind. act. of *condemnō, -āre, -āvī, -ātum,* I (*cum* + *damnō*); agrees with its subj. (*ego*) *ipse.* —— **Castra,** gen. *castrōrum,* n. 2d plur. (sing. *castrum, -ī = a fortress,* plur. = *a camp,* from root *ska = to cover*); nom. plur., subj. of *collocāta sunt;* the camp is that of the revolutionist Manlius; when modified by a numeral, the distributive is used, e.g. *bīna castra = two camps.*

LINE 28. **sunt,** 3d pers. plur. pres. ind. or *sum, esse, fuī;* agrees with the subj. *castra,* and probably forms with *collocāta* below the perf. tense ind. pass. of *collocō.* —— **in,** prep.; gov. the abl. *Italiā.* —— **Ītaliā,** gen. *Italiae,* f. 1st; abl. sing., obj. of the prep. *in; in Italiā* is emphatic and expresses indignation that Italy and Rome should be assailed from within. —— **contrā,** prep. (originally and often adv.) with the acc.; gov. *populum.* —— **populum,** acc. sing. of *populus, -ī,* m. 2d; obj. of *contrā; populus Rōmānus* is often abbreviated *P. R.,* esp. in *S. P. Q. R.* (= *senātus populusque Rōmānus*).

LINE 29. **Rōmānum,** acc. sing. m. of the adj. *Rōmānus, -a, -um* (from *Rōma*); qualifies *populum; contrā populum Rōmānum* expresses indignation like *in Italiā* above, and modifies *collocāta sunt.* —— **in,** prep.; gov. the abl. *faucibus.* —— **Etrūriae,** gen. sing. of *Etrūria,* f. 1st (sometimes *Etrūria*); poss. gen., limiting *faucibus.* Etrūria (Tuscia), called by the Greeks Tyrrhēnia, was a country of central Italy, west of the Tiber and south of the Po. The Etruscans' origin is doubtful; some think them a Lydian colony, others a Rhaetian race which settled from over the Alps. They had a confederacy of twelve cities, and were so powerful in early times that they dominated Rome, for the last three kings of Rome were Etruscan. Sulla's military colonies completely Romanized Etrūria. —— **faucibus,** abl. of *faucēs, -ium,* f. 3d plur. (abl. sing. *fauce* is rare); obj. of prep. *in; faucēs* is the regular word for a *mountain pass, defile,* or *gorge,* formed by two mountain spurs. The camp of Mānlius was near Faesulae (now Fiesole), on a ridge of the western Apennines, and commanded a road to Cisalpine Gaul; it was thus strategically well chosen, especially as it was in the centre of the districts inhabited by Sulla's old veterans. —— **collocāta,** nom. plur. n. of *collocātus, -a, -um,* perf. part. pass. of *collocō, -āre, -āvī, -ātum,* I (*cum* + *locō,* through *con = col* by assimilation); agrees with the subj. *castra,* either in participial enlargement, or rather as perf. ind. pass. 3d pers. plur. with *sunt* above. The extension of *collocāta* by the adverbial phrases *in Italia, contrā populum Rōmānum,* etc., is very effective.

30 **crēscit**	**in**	**diēs**	**singulōs**	**hostium**
grows	*to*	*days*	*separate* [= *daily*] *of the enemy*	

31 **numerus,**	**eōrum**	**autem**	**castrōrum**	**imperātōrem**
the number,	*that*	*but*	*of camp*	*the general*

32 **ducemque**	**hostium**	**intrā**	**moenia**	**atque**
and the leader	*of the enemy*	*within*	*our city-walls*	*and*

people. With each day the numbers of the enemy grow larger; and now you see the ruling officer of that camp, the leader of that enemy, within your walls and

LINE 30. **crēscit**, 3d pers. sing. pres. ind. act. of *crēscō, -ere, crēvī, crētum,* 3 (Latin root *cre* or *cer* + inceptive termination -*scō*; root *kar* = *to do, make,* cf. *Cĕrēs,* as goddess of *creation*); agrees with the subj. *numerus;* note the absence of a conjunction (*asyndeton*).——**in**, prep. ; gov. the acc. *diēs*.——**diēs**, acc. plur. of *diēs, dieī,* m. (also sometimes f. in sing.), 5th ; obj. of *in ; in diēs* is an idiomatic phrase, expressing daily increase, and differing from *cotīdiē,* inasmuch as the latter expresses mere daily repetition without any comparative force accompanying, e.g. *in diēs* (with or without *singulōs*) *litterās breviōrēs scrībō* = *from day to day I write shorter letters* (i.e. the letter is shorter each day), but *cotīdiē litterās scrībō* = *I write letters daily.* The comparative idea in this passage is contained in *crescit = māior fit.*——**singulōs**, acc. plur. of the distributive adj. *singulī, -ae, -a,* plur. (sing. very rare); agrees with *diēs. Singulī* properly = *one each, single,* hence *single, separate, individual,* without exact distribution.——**hostium**, gen. plur. of *hostis, -is,* m. 3d ; poss. gen., limiting *numerus; hostium* = the conspirators led by Mānlius.

LINE 31. **numerus**, gen. *numerī,* m. 2d (root *nam* = *to allot, number,* or *pasture ;* cf. *nummus* = *a coin,* νέμω = *I distribute*); nom. sing. subj. of *crescit.*——**eōrum**, gen. plur. n. of the determinative pron. *is, ea, id;* agrees with *castrōrum.*——**autem**, weak adversative conj. (see note on *tamen,* Chap. I, l. 18); introduces something in opposition. ——**castrōrum**, gen. of *castra,* plur. nom., n. 2d ; poss. gen., limiting *imperātōrem.*—— **imperātōrem**, acc. sing. of *imperātor, -ōris,* m. 3d (from verb *imperō*); direct obj. of *viaĕtis. Dux* and *imperātor* are often used without discrimination = *general,* but in so far as they are distinguishable *imperātor* = *general in chief,* and *dux* = *the leader (of a brigade),* being the highest of the inferior officers and holding an important command. *Imperātor* was originally given as a title of honor to a successful general by his soldiers, and could only be held by a *cōnsul, prōcōnsul,* on *praetor* or *prōpraetor* actually in the field. Caesar first assumed it as a permanent title, and Augustus did likewise in B.C. 40 as his heir. This title was formally assigned to Augustus by the Senate about 29 B.C., and henceforth was adopted by all his successors in the Principate. From *imperātor,* through the French *empereur,* comes the English *emperor.*

LINE 32. **ducem**, acc. sing. of *dux, ducis,* m. 3d (root *du* or *duk* = *to lead, draw,* cf. *dūcō*); direct obj. of *vidētis.*——**que**, enclitic cop. conj.; connects *imperātōrem* and *ducem,* the two objects of *viaĕtis.*——**hostium**, gen. plur. of *hostis, -is,* m. 3d ; poss. gen., limiting *ducem.*——**intrā** (originally adv., contracted from *interā* + *parte* supplied = *on the inside,* from obsolete adj. *interus,* whose compar. *interior* and superl. *intimus* survive), prep. with the acc. ; gov. *moenia. Intra* is etymologically akin to *in, inter, intestīnus,* ἐν, εἰς, ἐντός, etc.——**moenia**, acc. plur. of *moenia, -ium,* n. 3d (akin to *mūniō* and *mūrus*); obj. of the prep. *intrā.* Synonyms: (1) *moenia* = *the city-walls,* fortified against an enemy's attack ; (2) *mūrus* = *wall,* the generic word, used of a city-wall or any kind of wall except the inner walls of a house ; (3) *pariēs* = *the partition-wall* of a house.——**atque**, cop. conj. ; here, as often, introducing something of importance, viz. *adeō in senātū* and connecting it with *intrā moenia. Atque* adds emphasis to the second of the words it connects, and sometimes introduces a third and important member of a series.

even in the Senate plotting every day from within some disaster to the state. If I order you, Catiline, to be at once arrested and put to	**adeō in senātū vidētis intestīnam aliquam** 33 *further in the senate you see internal some* **cotīdiē perniciem reī pūblicae mōlientem.** 34 *daily destruction for the commonwealth contriving.* **Sī tē iam, Catilīna, comprehendī, sī interficī** 35 *If you now, Catiline, to be seized, if to be killed*

LINE 33. **adeō** (*ad + eō*), adv. = lit. *so far*, and + *atque* = *and still further*, emphasizing the idea introduced by *atque*. —— **in**, prep.; gov. the abl. *senātū*. —— **senātū**, abl. sing. of *senātus, -ūs*, m. 4th; obj. of the prep. *in; senātū = the senate*, in the sense of the meeting-place of the Senate, *senate-house*. —— **vidētis**, 2d pers. plur. pres. ind. act. of *videō, -ēre, vīdī, vīsum*, 2; the subj. *vōs* is implied in the personal ending, i.e. *you, the senators*. —— **intestīnam**, acc. sing. f. of the adj. *intestīnus, -a, -um* (see *intrā* above); agrees with *perniciem. Intestīnus* is local in signification, being used of that which is *intus = within*, in opposition to *externus*, which is also entirely local = *foreign*, belonging to those *outside;* cf. *intestīnum bellum = civil war* within a state. —— **aliquam**, acc. sing. f. of the indef. pronominal adj. *aliquī, aliqua, aliquod* (*alius + quī;* the pron. pure is *aliquis, aliqua, aliquid*, i.e. *alius + quis*); agrees with *perniciem*, the nature of which is rendered vague by *aliquam*. For the indef. pronouns consult the note on *quasdam*, l. 4.

LINE 34. **cotīdiē** (*quot + dies*), temporal adv., extending *mōlientem*. This word is often written *quotīdiē*, but there is no authority for the form; on the other hand, *cotīdiē*, though very common and adopted by Halm on Cicero, is not so old nor so well established as *cottīdiē*. See the note under *diēs*, l. 30. —— **perniciem**, acc. sing. of *perniciēs, perniciēī*, f. 5th (*per + nex*); direct obj. of *mōlientem;* see the synonyms in the note on *pestem*, Chap. I, l. 27. —— **reī**, dat. sing. of *rēs, reī*, f. 5th; dat. of interest (indirect obj.) after *mōlientem*. —— **pūblicae**, dat. sing. f. of the adj. *pūblicus, -a, -um;* agrees with *reī*, forming one idea = *for the state*. —— **mōlientem**, acc. sing. m. of *mōliēns, -entis*, pres. part. of the deponent verb *mōlior, -īrī, -ītus sum*, 4 (from noun *mōlēs = a mass, labor*); agrees with *ducem*, the direct obj. of *vidētis*, instead of the ordinary inf. which is used with the acc. after verbs *sentiendī*, e.g. *video*. The participle after verbs of perception is more vivid than the inf., and represents the actual state of the object; but the construction is not originally Latin, being found only once in early writers. It is a development from the common Greek construction of verbs of emotion and perception and participles. Cicero and Sallust made it popular in Latin, and other writers, esp. poets, were quick to follow. A. & G. 292, *e*; B. 336, **2**; G. 536; H. 535, I, 4.

LINE 35. **Sī**, conditional conj., introducing the *protasis*, the *apodosis* being *erit verendum mihi nē nōn*, etc. A. & G. 304; B. 301; G. 589; H. 506. The conditional sentence that follows is of the logical kind, which does not consider whether the condition or conclusion be true or not, possible or not, but merely states that under given conditions, there will be such and such a conclusion. A. & G. 306; B. 302; G. 595; H. 508, 4. —— **tē**, acc. sing. of *tū;* direct obj. of *iusserō*. —— **iam**, temporal adv., modifying *iusserō; sī iam iusserō = if I shall at once order*, i.e. departing *now* from the mode of action followed *till now*. —— **Catilīna**, voc. sing. of *Catilīna, -ae*, m. 1st; the case of address. —— **comprehendī**, pres. inf. pass. of *comprehendō, -ere, comprehendī, comprehensum*, 3 (*cum + prehendō, prehendō* being from a Latin root *hend* = root *ghad* = *to seize;* cf. *praeda* [= *prae-hend-a*], *booty*); agrees with subj.-acc. *tē* in the object clause *tē . . . comprehendī* dependent on *iusserō*. Convicted criminals were not imprisoned long after arrest, for the *Tulliānum* was not used as a place of long detention;

xussi te piripheastic

36	iussērō,	crēdō,	~~erit~~	~~verendum~~	mihi,	death, I shall have
	I shall order,	*I suppose,*	*it will have*	*to be feared*	*by me,*	to fear, I suppose,
37	nē	nōn	potius	hōc	omnēs	~~not so much~~ that all
	that	*not*	*rather this (to have been done)*		*all*	who are loyal will

the execution followed with little or no delay. —— **sī**, conditional conj., repeated for effect instead of a cop. conj. connecting *comprěhendī* and *interficī.* —— **interficī**, pres. inf. pass. of *interficiō, -ere, interfēcī, interfectum,* 3 (*inter* + *faciō*) ; agrees with the subj.-acc. *tē* (understood from *tē* in preceding *sī* clause), *tē interficī* being direct obj. of *iussērō.* Three *lēgēs Porciae* of B.C. 198, 195, and 194 abolished altogether the flogging and execution of Roman citizens, and only foreigners, soldiers on active service, and slaves were henceforth so punished ; voluntary exile, with confiscation, was allowed as a substitute for the death penalty. Less grave crimes were punished by *īnfāmia* (= loss of citizenship), or merely by a fine (*multa*).

LINE 36. **iussērō**, 1st pers. sing. fut. perf. ind. act. of *iubeō, -ēre, iussī, iussum,* 2 (perhaps = *ius* + *habeō*) ; the subj. *ego* is implied in the termination. In logical conditional sentences, the tense used in the *protasis* or the *apodosis* depends upon the sense ; Cicero often uses *fut.* in both clauses, and *fut. perf.* in both clauses. The fut. perf. (*iussērō*) and fut. (*erit verendum*) are easily explained : *if (supposing that) I shall just now have ordered you to be executed, I shall have to fear* (now and henceforth), etc. —— **crēdō**, 1st pers. sing. pres. ind. act. of *crēdō, -ere, crēdidī, crēditum,* 3 (Sanskrit *çrat* = *trust* + root *dha* = *to place,* as in *con-dō, ab-dō,* etc.) ; the subj. is *ego* understood ; *crēdō* is parenthetical, and, moreover, ironical, and being ironical it reverses the order of the criticisms which Cicero says he will have to fear. Thus " I shall have to fear, *I suppose,* that all loyal citizens will not say I have acted too late rather than that any one should say that I have acted too cruelly " = " I shall have to fear that all loyal citizens will say that I have acted too late rather than that any one may say I have acted too cruelly." —— **erit**, 3d pers. sing. fut. ind. act. of *sum ;* used impersonally, and forming the fut. tense in the pass. periphrastic conjugation, with *verendum,* = *it will have to be feared.* The tense rule is the regular one, e.g. *est (erat) verendum = it is (was) to be feared.* —— **verendum**, nom. sing. n. of *verendus, -a, -um,* gerundive of the deponent verb *vereor, -ērī, -itus sum,* 2 (root *var* = *to be wary,* cf. Greek root ὁρ, ϝορ in ὁράω = *I see,* φρουρός = προ-ορός = *a watcher*) ; used impersonally with *erit* in the periphrastic pass. conjugation. The verb in this conjugation may also be used personally, e.g. *hōc faciendum est.* A. & G. 113, *d* ; B. 337, 7, *b*, 1 ; G. 251 ; H. 234, and 466, NOTE. For the uses of the gerundive, refer to the note on *habendī,* Chap. I, l. 8. —— **mihi**, dat. sing. of *ego ;* dat. of the agent with *verendum erit.* The agent is regularly in the dat. case after the gerundive, except when the gerundive is that of a verb which governs a dative in the active (and of course used impersonally in the pass.), e.g. *mihi tibi persuādendum est* is not found, because it might = *I must persuade you,* or *you must persuade me ;* hence the agent must be expressed in the usual way, e.g. *ā mē tibi* (or *ā tē mihi*) *persuādendum est.* A. & G. 232 ; B. 189, 1 ; G. 354, 355 ; H. 388. The dat. of the agent is also frequent after compound passive tenses, or the perf. part. passive. A. & G. 232, *a* ; B. 189, 2 ; G. 354 ; H. 388.

LINE 37. **nē**, conj. *nē nōn* in combination introducing the final clause *nē nōn . . . dīcat* as object of the verb of *fearing, verendum erit.* The verb of the object-clause is always subjunct. ; of the tenses, the pres. subjunct. = pres. and fut. ind., the perf. subjunct. = perf. ind., and the pres. and perf. subjunct. become imperf. and pluperf. subjunct. respectively after a past tense of the verb of fearing. *Nē* is used of what it is feared may happen ; *nē nōn* or *ut* of what it is feared may not happen. *Ut* was more common than *nē nōn* till Cicero, but the latter becomes more frequent thenceforward.

| denounce my action for coming too late as that there may be some individual who will call it barbarously severe. But, | bonī
the good (may say) | sērius
too late | ā
by | mē
me | quam 88
than (that) |
| | quisquam
any one | crūdēlius
too cruelly | factum
(it) to have been | esse
done | dīcat. 89
may say. |

Nē nōn is always used : (1) when the verb of *fearing* has a negative, e.g. *nōn vereor nē mihi nōn respondeat* = *I do not fear he will not answer me ;* (2) when some particular word is negatived, e.g. *vereor nē (dum dēfendam meōs) nōn parcam tuīs,* = *I fear that (while defending my own) I may not spare yours.* *Ut* is rarely found except with *vereor* (though often with *metuō* in early Latin). The subjunct. was originally independent, expressing a wish ; e.g. *vereor, nē veniat* = *I fear ; may he not come !* and *vereor, ut veniat* = *I fear ; O may he come !* A. & G. 331, *f* ; B. 296, 2, and *a* ; G. 550 ; H. 498, III, and NOTE 2. —— nōn, neg. adv., with *nē* after the verb of *fearing, erit verendum ; nōn* qualifies the particular word *sērius*. —— potius (akin to *potis* = *able*), comparative adv. ; either strengthens the comparative *sērius*, or *potius quam* = *potius quam nē*. —— hōc, acc. sing. n. of the demonstr. pron. *hīc, haec, hōc* ; subj.-acc. of *factum esse* (understood from below) as object of the verb of *saying, dīcant* (agreeing with subj. *omnēs bonī* and understood from *dīcat* below); the construction is the simple acc. and infinitive after a verb of *thinking, feeling, perceiving,* or *saying.* *Hōc* refers to the fulfilment of the threat conveyed by *sī interficī iusserō,* l. 35. —— omnēs, nom. plur. m. of the adj. *omnis, -e,* 3d ; agrees with *bonī,* which is substantival.

LINE 38. bonī, nom. plur. m. of *bonus, -a, -um ;* used substantively, as a political term = *loyal citizens,* i.e. those of the aristocratic party (see note on *bonōrum,* Sect. I, l. 7) ; subj. of *dīcant* understood from *dīcat* in the comparative clause. So *bonus* = *a good man ; bona,* the neut. plur., = *goods, property.* —— sērius, comparative adv., = *too late ;* modifies *factum esse ;* very emphatic, contrasted with *crūdēlius. Sērius* is the comparative degree of the adv. *sērō* (originally, as all adverbs in -*ō,* e.g. *subitō,* the abl. sing. n. of the adj. *sērus, -a, -um*); superl. *sērissimē.* The comparative, apart from its ordinary denotation of a greater degree in a quality, has two uses : (1) expressing a *considerable* degree, e.g. *tristior* = *rather sad ;* (2) expressing an *excessive* degree, = *too,* e.g. *sērius,* as above. A. & G. 93, *a* ; B. 240, 1 ; G. 297, 2, and 298 ; H. 444, 1. —— ā, prep. with the abl. ; gov. the abl. *mē ;* written *ā* or *ab* before consonants, *ab* before vowels or *h.* —— mē, abl. sing. of *ego ;* abl. of the agent, gov. by the prep. *ā.* —— quam, adv., introducing the comparative clause *quisquam . . . dīcat.* After *quam,* in comparative clauses, *ut* is frequently idiomatically omitted or understood, the construction being then similar to that with *prius . . . quam,* etc. ; so here *nē* is understood from *nē nōn* above. See note on *quam,* Chap. I, l. 2.

LINE 39. quisquam, nom. sing m. of the indef. pron. and adj. *quisquam, quaequam, quidquam* or *quicquam ;* subj. of *dīcat* in the comparative clause ; *quisquam* = *any individual at all ;* in contrast with *omnēs bonī. Quisquam* is generally used in negative sentences, or rhetorical questions equivalent to a negative statement ; here *quisquam* is used in much the same way as in l. 46, where see note. —— crūdēlius, comparative adv.; modifies *factum esse* in the comparative clause, being contrasted with *sērius factum esse* in the first clause. *Crūdēlius* is the compar. degree of the adv. *crūdēliter* (from the adj. *crūdēlis,* 3d, cf. *crūdus,* probably from root *kru* = *to be cold,* hence *unfeeling,* and not, as some think, from Sanskrit root *krudh* = *to be wrathful*) ; the comparative is used as in *sērius,* superl. *crūdēlissimē.* A. & G. 92 ; B. 76, 2, and 77, 1 ; G. 93 ; H. 306. —— factum, acc. sing. n. of *factus, -a, -um,* perf. part. of *fīō,* used as pass. of *faciō ;* agrees with the subj.-acc. *hōc,* l. 37, and with the next word *esse (factum esse)* = the perf. inf. pass. of *faciō,* in the obj. clause dependent on *dīcat.* The sentence with ellipses supplied

						for myself, I am not
40 Vērum	ego	hōc,	quod	iam prīdem factum		yet inclined to do
But	*I*	*this*	*which*	*already*	*long ago*	*to have been*

what ought to have

41 esse	oportuit,	certā	dē	causā	nōndum	been done a long
done	*it was necessary,*	*definite*	*from*	*a reason*	*not yet*	time ago, for a defi-

42 addūcor	ut	faciam.		Tum	dēnique	nite reason. Then,
am induced	*that*	*I should do.*		*Then*	*at last*	and only then, will

would read: *nē nōn potius hōc omnēs bonī sērius ā mē factum esse dīcant quam nē quis-quam crūdēlius factum esse dīcat.* —— **esse**, pres. inf. of *sum ;* forms the perf. inf. of *fīō*, being combined with *factum ; factum esse* agrees with the subj.-acc. *hōc.* —— **dīcat**, 3d pers. sing. pres. subjunct. act. of *dīcō, -ere, dīxī, dictum,* 3 ; agrees by attraction with the subj. *quisquam* in the clause containing the comparison, rather than with the subj. in the earlier clause *omnēs bonī* (with which *dīcant* must be understood). Mr. Wilkins well compares Philippics, IV, Chap. 9, *quis illum igitur cōnsulem nisi latrōnēs putant,* the verb agreeing with the subj. in the *nisi* clause, and understood with the first subj. *quis. Dīcat* is subjunct., because it is the verb of the final object clause (with *nē nōn*) dependent on *erit verendum ;* the tense is pres., as it refers to the future.   A. & G. 286; B. 267, 268; G. 509, *ff;* H. 491.

LINE 40. **Vērum**, adversative conj. (see note on *tamen,* Chap. I, l. 18); introducing an oppositional statement. —— **ego**, nom. sing. of the 1st personal pron.; subj. of *addū-cor ;* inserted for emphasis. —— **hōc**, acc. sing. n. of *hīc, haec, hōc ;* direct obj. of *faciam ;* the reference is the same as in *hōc,* l. 37. —— **quod**, acc. sing. n. of the rel. pron. *quī, quae, quod;* agrees with the antecedent *hōc,* and is subj.-acc. of *factum esse* in depend-ence on *oportuit ;* for the usual construction, and especially for the perf. *factum esse,* see note on *interfectum,* II. 20. —— **iam**, temporal adv., strengthening *prīdem. Iam prīdem, iam diū,* etc., are often used + the historic pres. or imperf. to denote the con-tinuation of an action begun in the past. —— **prīdem** (*prī = before* + *-dem*), adv., modifying *factum esse.* —— **factum**, acc. sing. n. of *factus, -a, -um,* perf. part. of *fīō* (used as a pass. of *faciō*) ; agrees with subj.-acc. *quod,* and appears to form the perf. inf. with *esse.* But refer to the quotation from Allen and Greenough, and to other references under *interfectum,* II. 20.

LINE 41. **esse**, pres. inf. of *sum ;* forms the perf. inf. pass. of *faciō,* agreeing with *quod* in construction after *oportuit.* —— **oportuit**, 3d pers. sing. pres. ind. of the imper-sonal verb *oportet,* inf. *oportere,* 2 ; the virtual subj. is the clause *quod iam prīdem factum esse.* —— **certā**, abl. sing. f. of the adj. *certus, -a, -um* (old part. of *cernō*); agrees with *causā.* Cicero gives the reason in general terms in ll. 42-46 and in Chap. XII states that if he killed Catiline at once, the latter's friends would make him out an innocent man sacrificed to the consul's tyranny, and moreover Catiline's accomplices would still remain a constant menace to Rome. —— **dē**, prep. with the abl. ; gov. *causā.* —— **causā**, abl. sing. of *causa, -ae,* f. 1st ; obj. of the prep. *dē.* —— **nōndum** (*nōn* + *dum*), temporal adv. ; may modify either *addūcor* or *faciam.*

LINE 42. **addūcor**, 1st pers. sing. pres. ind. pass. of *addūcō, -ere, addūxī, adductum,* 3 (*ad* + *dūcō*); the implied subj. is *ego.* —— **ut**, conj., introducing the complementary consecutive clause *ut . . . faciam* in dependence on *addūcor ;* see *ut,* Chap. I, l. 39. —— **faciam**, 1st pers. sing. pres. subjunct. act. of *faciō, -ere, fēcī, factum,* 3 ; the implied subj. is *ego ; faciam* is a consecutive subjunct., complementary or substantival. A. & G. 319; B. 284; G. 552; H. 500. —— **Tum**, temporal adv., modifying *interficiēre* and being the demonstr. antecedent of *cum.* —— **dēnique**, adv., of time or order, modifying *interficiēre ; dēnique* is often made more exact by combination with *nunc* or *tum,* and similar definite adverbial expressions of time.

you be put to death	interficiĕre,	cum	iam	nēmō	tam	improbus,	43
when there can at	*you will be slain,*	*when*	*at length*	*no one*	*so*	*depraved,*	
last be found no one							
so depraved, so aban-	tam	perditus,	tam	tuī	similis	invenīrī	44
doned, so like your-	*so*	*abandoned,*	*so*	*to you*	*like*	*to be found*	
self, as to decline the	poterit,	quī	id	nōn	iūre	factum	45
admission that my	*will be able,*	*who*	*that (deed)*	*not*	*by right*	*to have been*	

LINE 43. **interficiĕre**, 2d pers. sing. fut. ind. pass of *interficiō, -ere, interfĕcī, inter-fectum,* 3; the subj. implied is *tū,* i.e. Catiline; the reading *interficiĕre* is that of the best MSS, though some read *interficiam tē.* —— **cum**, temporal conj., defining the point of time intended by *tum.* A. & G. 325, and NOTE; B. 288, 1, A; G. 580; H. 521, I. As a temporal conj., *cum* is used with the subjunct. of the imperf. and pluperf. tenses, and the ind. of others. It is also used to introduce: (1) causal clauses = *since, as,* and is followed by the subjunct. mood in every tense; (2) concessive clauses, the mood being always subjunctive. A. & G. 325, 326; B. 286, 2; 288; 309, 3; G. 580–587; H. 515, III; 517, 521. —— **iam**, temporal adv., modifying *invenīrī poterit.* —— **nēmō** (*ne + homō*), nom. sing. m. and f. 3d (acc. *nĕminem,* dat. *nĕminī* or *nūllī,* abl. *nūllō,* gen. *nūllīus*); subj. of *poterit.* *Nēmō* is an universal negative, and supplies the cases it wants from *nūllus, -a, -um,* as above; observe that *nōn nēmō* = *somebody,* and that *nēmō nōn* = *everybody.* —— **tam**, demonstr. adv., modifying *improbus;* its correlative is *quam.* —— **improbus**, nom. sing. m. of the adj. *improbus, -a, -um* (*in* = *not + probus* = *virtuous*); agrees with *nēmō,* and is predicative with *invenīrī poterit* = *erit.*

LINE 44. **tam**, adv., modifying *perditus.* —— **perditus**, nom. sing. m. of *perditus, -a, -um,* adj. (originally perf. part. pass. of *perdō, -ere, perdidī, perditum,* 3 = *I lose, destroy*); agrees with *nēmō,* and is predicative like *improbus.* —— **tam**, adv.; modifies *similis.* —— **tuī**, gen. sing. of *tū;* objective gen., with *similis.* *Similis* and *dissimilis* are generally used by Cicero with the gen. of living objects, with the dat. of things. Others say that the gen. expresses a resemblance of nature or constitution (internal), while the dat. expresses an external resemblance. No hard and fast rule can be laid down, but the gen. was most used in early Latin, and in the case of the personal pronouns the gen. is almost invariably found. A. & G. 234, *d,* 2; B. 204, 3; G. 359, REM. I; H. 391, II, 4. —— **similis**, nom. sing. m. of the adj. *similis, -e,* 3d; predicative, agrees with *nēmō.* *Similis* has the superl. *simillimus,* instead of following the rule and having the termination *-issimus;* so also *dissimilis, humilis, facilis, difficilis,* and *gracilis;* all others make the superl. in *-issimus,* e.g. *amābilis, amābilior, amābilissimus.* —— **in-venīrī**, pres. inf. pass. of *inveniō, -īre, invēnī, inventum,* 3 (*in + veniō*); objective complementary inf. after *poterit;* this inf. is required to complete the meaning of such verbs as *to be able, to know how, to dare, to learn,* etc. A. & G. 271; B. 326; G. 423; H. 533.

LINE 45. **poterit**, 3d pers. sing. fut. ind. act. of *possum, posse, potuī,* no supine, irreg. (adj. *potis* = *able* + *sum,* through *pot* + *sum,* the *t* of *pot* changing to *s* by assimilation); agrees with the subj. *nēmō* in the temporal clause with *cum.* For mood, see note on *cum.* —— **quī**, nom. sing. m. of the rel. pron. *quī, quae, quod;* agrees with the antecedent *nēmō,* and is subj. of *fateātur* in the rel. clause of result. —— **id**, acc. sing. n. of the determinative pron. *is, ea, id;* subj.-acc. of *factum esse* in the acc. and inf. object clause dependent on the notion of *thinking* or *saying* implied in *fateātur; id* = *hōc* in ll. 37 and 40, i.e. the execution of Catiline. —— **nōn**, negative adv.; modifies *fateātur.* When *quī* is *characteristic* and introduces a result clause, *nōn* is frequently combined = *quin;* but this *quin* must be distinguished from *quin* (= *quī,* abl. of rel. pron. + *ne*) used after verbs of *hindering* or *doubting.* —— **iūre**, adverbial abl. of *iūs, iūris,* n. 3d; modifies *factum esse.* *Iūre* (and sometimes *inūriā*) resembles *forte* in being practically an

46 esse	fateātur.	Quam	diū	quisquam	action was justly
done	*may confess.*	*As*	*long (as)*	*any one*	taken. As long as
47 erit	quī	tē	dēfendere	audeat,	there is one man who
there will be	*who*	*you*	*to defend*	*may dare,*	dares to defend you, you will live; but you
48 vīvēs,	sed	vīvēs	ita,	ut	vīvis,
you will live,	*but*	*you will live*	*so,*	*as you are living,*	living now, beset by

adverb; the usual rule is that the abl. can only express manner with *cum*, but may omit *cum* if there is an adj. qualifying the ablative. —— **factum**, acc. sing. n. of *factus, -a, -um*, perf. part. of *fīō*; agrees with *id*; *factum* + *esse* = the perf. inf. of *fīō*.

LINE 46. **esse**, pres. inf. of *sum*; *factum esse* agrees with the subj.-acc. *id*, in the simple acc. and inf. construction after *fateātur*. —— **fateātur**, 3d pers. sing. pres. subjunct. of the deponent verb *fateor, -ērī, fassus sum*, 2 (from root *bha* = *to make known, declare*; cf. *fārī* = *to speak, faciēs, fāma*, φημί = *I say*, etc.); agrees with the subj. *quī*; *fateātur* is a consecutive subjunct. with *quī* = *ut*, in the result clause *quī nōn fateātur*. *Quī* may be used = *ut* consecutive, when the main clause is interrogative or negative. A. & G. 319, 2, and *ff*; B. 284, 2; G. 552, 1; H. 500, 1.—— **Quam**, adv.; + *diū, quam diū* (*quamdiū*) is a temporal conj., and may be used: (1) interrogatively, as in Chap. I, l. 2; (2) as a conj. of contemporaneous action = *as long as*, denoting complete coëxtension of action; it is used so in this passage. The particles used in clauses of contemporaneous action are *dum, dōnec, quoad*, and *quamdiū*, taking the ind. mood of all tenses. *Quamdiū* was first used in this way by Cicero.—— **diū**, temporal adv. (akin to *diēs*); *diū* + *quam* = *quam diū*, the temporal conjunction.—— **quisquam**, nom. sing. m. of the indef. pron. *quisquam, quaequam, quicquam* (*quidquam*); subj. of *erit*. *Quisquam* is most often used in negative sentences or interrogative sentences which imply a negation; but it is here used in an affirmative sentence, and denotes the barest minimum *any one at all* (i.e. the nearest approach to the negative, implying that there are none or only a very few).

LINE 47. **erit**, 3d pers. sing. fut. ind. of *sum*; agrees with the subj. *quisquam*. Observe the tense and mood; the future, because Cicero is considering a state of things that may come to pass (*as long as there is any one* is an instance of English carelessness); the ind., because the action of *erit* is contemporaneous in extent with that of *vīves* (see *quam* above), i.e. Cicero implies that, so soon as people (if there are any who now believe Catiline innocent) cease to question the consul's justice in ordering Catiline's execution, Catiline's life will terminate. —— **quī**, nom. sing. m. of the rel. pron.; subj. of *audeat*; *quī* is here *characteristic*, i.e. denotes a tendency = *of a sort to*, and is therefore followed by the subjunct. mood *audeat*. The antecedent of *quī* may be (1) definite, e.g. *idōneus, dignus, tālis, sōlus, tam*, etc., or (2) as here, indefinite, e.g. *multī* (*quīdam, nōnnūllī*) *sunt quī*, etc., or (3) without a stated antecedent, e.g. *est quī, sunt quī*. A. & G. 320; B. 283; G. 631, 2; H. 503, I.—— **tē**, acc. sing. of *tū*; direct obj. of *dēfendere*. —— **dēfendere**, pres. inf. act. of *dēfendō, -ere, dēfendī, dēfensum*, 3 (*dē* + obsolete *fendō*); prolative inf., with *audeat*.—— **audeat**, 3d pers. sing. pres. subjunct. of the semi-deponent verb *audeō, -ēre, ausus sum*, 2 (akin to *audiō* and *avidus*); agrees with the subj. *quī*; the potential subjunct. with *quī* expresses tendency. Semi-deponents form the present-stem tenses regularly in the active; but, as they have no perf. act. stem, the perf. stem tenses are passive in form, as in deponents; the meaning is active. A. & G. 136; B. 114, 1; G. 167, 1; H. 268, 3, and 465, 2, NOTE 2.

LINE 48. **vīvēs**, 2d pers. sing. fut. ind. act. of *vīvō, -ere, vīxī, victum*, 3; the implied subj. is *tū*, i.e. Catiline.—— **sed**, adversative conj.; joins the sentence of *vīvēs* above with that of *vīvēs* below.—— **vīvēs** (parsed as above).—— **ita** (from pronominal root *i*), adv.

my watchmen, many	multīs	meīs	et	fīrmīs	praesidiīs	obsessus,	49
and faithful, that you	*many*	*my*	*and*	*secure*	*by guards*	*invested,*	
may find it impossi-	nē	commovēre	tē	contrā	rem	pūblicam	50
ble to take any move	*lest*	*to set in motion*	*yourself*	*against*	*the*	*commonwealth*	
against the state.	possīs.		Multōrum	tē	etiam	oculī	51
And further, the eyes	*you may be able.*		*Of many men*	*you*	*also*	*the eyes*	
and ears of many,	et	aurēs	nōn	sentientem,	sicut	adhūc	52
though you see it	*and*	*the ears*	*not*	*perceiving (it),*	*just as*	*up to now*	
not, will hold you in							

of manner or degree ; *ita ut vīvis* is an adverbial enlargement of the pred. *vīvēs* immediately preceding. *Ita* (so *sīc* and *item*) are demonstr., and often have a correlative *ut*
=*so . . . as.*—— **ut,** adv. of manner ; correlative of *ita ; ut vīvis* defines *ita,* and is itself
further explained by *multīs . . . possīs.*—— **vīvis,** 2d pers. sing. pres. ind. act. of *vīvō*
(see *vīvēs*) ; the personal ending implies that the subj. is *tū.*

LINE 49. **multīs,** abl. plur. n. of the adj. *multus, -a, -um ;* agrees with *praesidiīs.*
—— **meīs,** abl. plur. n. of the poss. pronominal adj. *meus, -a, -um ;* agrees with *praesidiīs ; meīs* is emphatic, and = *multīs et fīrmīs praesidiīs quae ego parāvī.*—— **et,** cop.
conj., connecting *multīs* and *fīrmīs ;* when *multus* is one of two adjectives qualifying the
same noun, it is regularly connected with the other by a cop. conjunction.—— **fīrmīs,**
abl. plur. n. of the adj. *fīrmus, -a, -um* (from root *dhar = to support*) ; agrees with *praesidiīs.*—— **praesidiīs,** abl. plur. of *praesidium, -ī,* n. 2d ; abl. of the means, with
obsessus.—— **obsessus,** nom. sing. m. of *obsessus, -a, -um,* perf. part. pass. of *obsideō, -ere,
obsēdī, obsessum,* 2 (*ob + sedeō = I sit in the way of,* esp. metaphorically of one investing
a town) ; agrees with and extends the subj. *tū* (implied in *vīvis*). There is another reading *oppressus = crushed,* being the perf. part. pass. of *opprimō, -ere, oppressī, oppressum,*
3 (*ob + premō*), but *obsessus* is generally preferred. The allusion is to the precautions
taken by Cicero in Rome, and in the colonies and municipalities.

LINE 50. **nē,** final conj. = *lest, in order that . . . not,* expressing purpose with the
subjunct. *possīs.* A. & G. 317 ; B. 282 ; G. 545 ; H. 497.—— **commovēre,** pres. inf. act.
of *commoveō, -ēre, commōvī, commōtum,* 2 (*cum + moveō*) ; prolative inf., completing the
predication of *possīs.*—— **tē,** acc. sing. of the 2d personal pron. *tū ;* direct obj. of *commovēre ; tē* is reflexive, as the subj. of *commovēre possīs* is *tū* (Catiline).—— **contrā,** prep.
with the acc. ; gov. *rem pūblicam.*—— **rem,** acc. sing. of *rēs, reī,* f. 5th ; obj. of the prep.
contrā.—— **pūblicam,** acc. sing. f. of the adj. *pūblicus, -a, -um ;* agrees with *rem.*

LINE 51. **possīs,** 2d pers. sing. pres. subjunct. of *possum, posse, potuī,* no supine,
irreg. (*potis + sum*) ; the implied subj. is *tū ;* the subjunct. is final.—— **multōrum,** gen.
plur. m. of the adj. *multus, -a, -um ; multōrum* is substantival = *of many men,* and is
a poss. gen. limiting *oculī* and *aurēs.* Observe the position of *multōrum* in the sentence
and in regard to the nouns it modifies ; it is very emphatic.—— **tē,** acc. sing. of *tū ;*
direct obj. of *speculābuntur ; tē* is made emphatic by being placed out of the object's
usual place between the subj. and the verb, and set in juxtaposition with *multōrum.*——
etiam, adv. or cop. conj. ; connects the sentence with the preceding one, and strengthens the new idea ; see note on *etiam,* Chap. I, l. 2.—— **oculī,** nom. plur. of *oculus, -ī,* m.
2d (root *ak = to see*) ; subj. of *speculābuntur.* Observe that *oculī* and *aurēs* are here
personified, one of the kinds of freedom with which Cicero embellishes Latin prose, but
which are avoided by the stricter Latin writers.

LINE 52. **et,** cop. conj., joining *oculī* and *aurēs.*—— **aurēs,** nom. plur. of *auris, -is,*
f. 3d (= *aus-is,* from Latin root *aus =* the Ind.-Eur. root *av = to hear + s ;* cf. Greek
οὖς = *ear*) ; joined by *et* to *oculī ;* a subj. of *speculābuntur.*—— **nōn,** negative adv. ; modifies *sentientem.*—— **sentientem,** acc. sing. m. of *sentiēns, -entis,* pres. part. act. of *sentiō,*

| 53 | fēcērunt, | speculābuntur | atque | custōdient. | watch and bond, as they have done hitherto. |
| | *they have done,* | *will watch* | *and* | *will guard.* | |

1	III.	Etenim quid est, Catilīna, quod iam	III. For indeed, Catiline, what is there now that you can look for further, seeing that neither can night hide your
		For indeed what is there, Catiline, *which* *now*	
2	amplius	exspectēs, sī neque nox	
	further	*you may await,* *if* *neither* *night*	

-īre, sensī, sensum, 4 ; agrees with and enlarges *tē,* the obj. of *speculābuntur.* —— **sīcut** (often *sīcutī ; sīc + ut* or *utī*), adv., introducing the clause *adhūc fēcērunt* as an adverbial (manner) modification of the main clause. —— **adhūc** (*ad + hūc*), adv. of time, modifying *fēcērunt.*

LINE 53. **fēcērunt,** 3d pers. plur. perf. ind. act. of *faciō, -ere, fēcī, factum,* 3 ; the implied subj. is a pron. referring to *oculī et aurēs.* It is noteworthy that the use of *fēcērunt* in this passage resembles that of the English auxiliary *did,* i.e. *as they have done up to the present.* —— **speculābuntur,** 3d pers. plur. fut. ind. of the deponent verb *speculor, -ārī, -ātus sum,* 1 (from *specula = a watch-tower ;* root *spak = to spy*) ; agrees with the subj. *oculī et aurēs.* —— **atque,** cop. conj., joining *speculābuntur* and *custōdient.* —— **custōdient,** 3d pers. plur. fut. ind. act. of *custōdiō, -īre, -īvī, -ītum,* 4 (from *custōs = a guardian*) ; joined by *atque* to *speculābuntur ;* agrees with subj. *oculī* and *aurēs.*

LINE 1. **Etenim,** causal conj. ; *et* intensive + *enim ;* see note on *enim,* Chap. II, l. 17. *Etenim quid est* and the following are explanatory of *vīvēs ita ut vīvis ff,* l. 48 of Chap. II. —— **quid,** nom. sing. n. of the interrog. pron. *quis, quae, quid ;* subj. of *est ;* the question is rhetorical, and = a negative statement *nihil est quod expectēs,* etc. —— **est,** 3d pers. sing. pres. ind. of *sum ;* agrees with the subj. *quid.* —— **Catilīna,** voc. sing. of *Catilīna, -ae,* m. 1st ; the case of address. —— **quod,** acc. sing. n. of the rel. pron. *quī, quae, quod ;* direct obj. of *expectēs ; quod* is characteristic (hence the consecutive subjunct. *expectēs*) with an indef. antecedent *quid,* with which it agrees in number and gender. A. & G. 320 ; B. 283 ; G. 631, 2 ; H. 503, I. —— **iam,** temporal adv. ; modifies the pred. *expectēs.*

LINE 2. **amplius,** comparative adv. ; modifies the pred. *expectēs.* The adv. *amplē = abundantly, magnificently ;* compar. *amplius = further, besides ;* superl. *amplissimē = most abundantly.* —— **expectēs,** 2d pers. sing. pres. subjunct. act. of *expectō, -āre, -āvī, -ātum,* 1 (*ex + spectō,* = lit. *I look out for*) ; the ending implies *tū* as subject ; *expectēs* is a subjunct. of result with *quod.* —— **sī,** conditional particle, introducing the condition *sī . . . potest.* The force of *sī* is here almost causal, for *if night cannot hide your meetings* practically = *as night cannot,* etc. —— **neque** (*ne + que*), cop. coördinating conj., used correlatively with *neque* below, *neque . . . neque = neither . . . nor* (corresponding to affirmative *et . . . et = both . . . and*). The following combinations are found : (1) *neque . . . neque,* (2) *nec* (abbreviation of *neque*) . . . *nec,* (3) *neque . . . nec,* (4) *nec . . . neque* (rare). Of mixed negative and positive combinations, note the following : (*a*) *neque . . . et,* common in Cicero and thenceforward ; (*b*) *et . . . neque,* common in Cicero, but not in later writers ; (*c*) *neque . . . que,* rare ; (*d*) *neque . . . atque* (*āc*), rare, starts with Tacitus. A. & G. 155, *a* ; B. 341, 3 ; G. 480, NOTE 3 ; H. 554, I, 5. —— **nox,** gen. *noctis,* f. 3d (cf. Greek νύξ) ; nom. sing., subj. of *obscūrāre* (*potest*). The allusion is to the meeting that was held at the house of Laeca, when Cicero's murder was planned, and when all the arrangements prior to open revolution were discussed and agreed upon.

impious meetings	tenebrīs	obscūrāre	coetūs	nefāriōs 3
with its cloak of dark-	*with its darkness*	*to hide*	*your meetings*	*nefarious*
ness nor yet a pri-	neque	prīvāta	domus	parietibus	continēre 4
vate dwelling shut in	*nor*	*private*	*a house*	*with its walls*	*to enclose*
within its walls your	vōcēs	coniūrātiōnis	tuae	potest?	sī 5
treason's utterance,	*the voices*	*of conspiracy*	*your*	*is able?*	*if*
—seeing that every-				

LINE 3. **tenebrīs**, abl. plur. of the plur. noun *tenebrae, -ārum*, f. 1st; abl. of the means, with *obscūrāre*.——**obscūrāre**, pres. inf. act. of *obscūrō, -āre, -āvī, -ātum*, 1 (through the adj. *obscūrus*, from root *sku = to cover;* cf. *scūtum = a shield*, and σκῦτος *= skin; ska*, a kindred root *= to cover*, hence σκία *= shadow*, and *casa = a cottage*); objective complementary inf., + *potest*. Cicero's knowledge of Laeca's meeting was derived from Fulvia (see Introduction).——**coetūs**, acc. plur. of *coetus, -ūs*, m. 4th (from *co = con + eō*); direct obj. of *obscūrāre*. Another reading is *coeptūs = undertakings;* but *coeptus, -ūs* m. 4th, is a comparatively rare word, and less applicable here, where the reference is obviously to the night-meeting (*nox*) in Laeca's house.—— **nefāriōs**, acc. plur. m. of the adj. *nefārius, -a, -um* (*ne = not + fārius* from *fas = not right* by divine law, hence *execrable; fas* is akin to *fārī, fānum*, etc.); agrees with *coetūs*.

LINE 4. **neque**, cop. conj., connecting the coördinate sentences *nox obscūrāre* (*potest*) and *domus continēre potest*.——**prīvāta**, nom. sing. f. of the adj. *prīvātus, -a, -um* (perf. part. pass. of *prīvō, -āre, -āvī, -ātum*, 1); agrees attributively with *domus*. ——**domus**, gen. *domūs*, f. 4th (root *dam = to build;* cf. Greek δόμος); nom. sing., subj. of *continēre potest*. *Domus* is declined completely in the 4th declension, though the abl. *domū* is scarce : the following 2d decl. cases are found (1) gen. sing. *domī* (rare), (2) dat. and abl. *domō*, (3) acc. plur. *domōs*, (4) gen. plur. *domōrum*, (5) old locative case, *domī = at home*, cf. *rūrī = in the country*. The acc. and abl. are often used without prepositions, *domum = home*, denoting the limit, *domō = from home*, denoting *place whence*, in each case with verbs of motion. Note that *domus* is an exception to the rule of masculine gender in the 4th declension.——**parietibus**, abl. plur. of *pariēs, parietis*, m. 3d; abl. of the means, with *continēre*. *Pariēs* usually *= a party-wall*, as opposed to *mūrus = wall* in general, and often *city-wall*, though *moenia* is the proper word for the latter.——**continēre**, pres. inf. act. of *contineō, -ēre, -uī, contentum*, 2 (*con + teneō*); complementary inf. with *potest*.

LINE 5. **vōcēs**, acc. plur. of *vōx, vōcis*, f. 3d (root *vak = to sound, speak, call;* cf. *vocō* and Greek ἔπος, *a word, =* ϝέπος); direct obj. of *continēre*. A few read *vōcem* here, considering that *coniūrātiōnis* should be personified, *= conspiracy's voice;* they contend that *vōcēs* would spoil the effect of the personification.——**coniūrātiōnis**, gen. sing. of *coniūrātiō*, f. 3d (*coniūrō*); poss. gen., limiting *vōcēs*. *Coniūrātiōnis* is to be considered : (1) personified, *= Conspiracy's utterances*, or better (2) as concrete *= a band of conspirators = coniūrātōrum; servitium = servī* is common, and *latrōcinium = latrō-nēs;* Prof. Wilkins adduces *advocātiō* used in concrete sense, and also *salūtātiō*, quoting from one of Cicero's letters, *ubi salūtātiō dēfluxit (= ubi salūtātōrēs dēfluxērunt) litterīs mē involvō, = when my morning-callers have disappeared, I envelop myself with correspondence*.——**tuae**, gen. sing. of the poss. adj. *tuus, -a, -um;* agrees with *coniūrātiōnis*.——**potest**, 3d pers. sing. pres. ind. act. of *possum, posse, potuī*, no supine, irreg. (*potis + sum*); agrees with the subj. *domus; potest* is understood with the subj. *nox* in the preceding sentence, as is the general rule when two coördinate sentences have the same verb.——**sī**, conditional conj., introducing *illūstrantur* in a semi-causal way, in dependence on the main clause *etenim . . . expectēs*, ll. 1 and 2; the construction is similar to that of *sī neque nox*, etc., l. 2.

6 illūstrantur,	sī	ērumpunt	omnia ?	Mūtā iam
are made clear,	*if*	*break out*	*all things?*	*Change now*
7 istam	mentem,	mihi	crēde :	oblīvīscere
that of yours	*purpose,*	*to me*	*trust :*	*become forgetful*
8 caedis	atque	incendiōrum.		Tenēris
of slaughter	*and*	*of burnings.*		*You are held*
9 undique ;	lūce	sunt	clāriōra	nōbis
on every side ; than daylight		*are*	*clearer*	*to us*

thing is made manifest and bursts out into sight? Take my advice, change your purposes at once: think no longer of massacre and incendiarism. You are hemmed in on every side; all your schemes are clearer

LINE 6. il̲l̲u̲s̲t̲r̲a̲n̲t̲u̲r̲, 3d pers. plur. pres. ind. pass. of *illūstrō, -āre, -āvī, -ātum*, I (*in*, intensive, + *lustrō* = *I light up ;* root *luk* = *to light, shine*, cf. *luc-eō, lūna* (= *luc-na*), *lūmen* (= *luc-men*), and Greek λύχ-νος = *a lamp*); agrees with the subj. *omnia* understood from the next clause which is practically coördinate. Observe that *illūstrantur* is opposed to *obscūrāre* above, and that *ērumpunt* similarly opposes *continēre.* —— sī, conditional conj., repeated by *anaphora ; illūstrantur* and *ērumpunt* are practically coördinate, but the repetition of *sī* is much more effective than copulation by *et.* A. & G. 344, *f* ; B. 350, 11, *b* ; G. 636, NOTE 4 ; H. 636, III, 3. —— ērumpunt, 3d pers. plur. pres. ind. act. of *ērumpō, -ere, ērūpī, ēruptum*, 3 (*ē = ex*, + *rumpō ;* root *rup*, Greek λυπ, = *to break, trouble*, cf. Greek λύπη = *pain*); agrees with the subj. *omnia.* —— omnia, nom. plur. n., used substantively, of the adj. *omnis, -e*, 3d ; subj. of *ērumpunt*, and understood as subj. of *illūstrantur ;* cf. *bonī* = *good men*, and *multa* = *many things*, and consult A. & G. 188, 189 ; B. 236–238 ; G. 204, NOTES 1–4 ; H. 441. —— Mūtā, 2d pers. sing. pres. imperative act. of *mūtō, -āre, -āvī, -ātum*, I (a frequentative form, = *movitō ;* root *mav* = *to push out of place*, cf. *moveō, mōmentum*, and Greek ἀ-μείβ-ω = *I change*); the implied subj. is *tū.* —— iam, temporal adv., modifying *mūtā ; iam* is emphatic, *change now*, i.e. even at the eleventh hour.

LINE 7. istam, acc. sing. f. of the demonstr. pron. *iste, ista, istud ;* agrees with *mentem ;* see note on *iste*, Chap. I, l. 3. —— mentem, acc. sing. of *mēns, mentis*, f. 3d (root *ma* or *man*, = (a) *to strive*, (b) *to be excited, to think, to be wrathful*, (c) *to remain*, i.e. like one thinking deeply, (d) *to remember*); direct obj. of *mūtā.* —— mihi, dat. sing. of *ego ;* indirect obj. of *crēde.* A. & G. 227 ; B. 187, II ; G. 346 ; H. 384, I, and 385, I, II. —— crēde, 2d pers. sing. pres. imperative act. of *crēdō, -ere, crēditī, crēditum*, 3 (Sanskrit *çrat* = *trust*, + root *dha* = *to place*); the implied subj. is *tū*, i.e. Catiline. *Mihi crēde* = *believe me*, i.e. that it is better for you to repent now (*iam*), *take my advice.* This phrase is very common in Cicero, but the same inverted (*crēde* mihi) occurs only four times in his writings. —— oblīvīscere, 2d pers. sing. pres. imperative of the deponent verb *oblīviscor, -ī, oblītus sum*, 3 (*ob* + *līveō* = *I am dark-hued*, hence of a mind darkened ; others derive from *ob* + Sanskrit root *li* = *to make to melt*); agrees with the implied subj. *tū.* Distinguish *oblīvīscere* (parsed above) from *oblīvīscēre* = 2d pers. sing. fut. ind., and part. *oblītus* from *oblītus* = *smeared* (*oblinō*).

LINE 8. caedis, gen. sing. of *caedēs*, f. 3d ; obj. of *oblīvīscere.* Verbs of *remembering* and *forgetting* take the gen. of the object when it is a person, the gen. or the acc. of the object when it is a thing. A. & G. 219 ; B. 206 ; G. 376 ; H. 406, II, and 407. —— atque, cop. conj., joining *caedis* and *incendiōrum ;* adds something important, viz. destruction of property, to destruction of life. —— incendiōrum, gen. plur. of *incendium, -ī*, n. 2d (from *incendō* = *I set on fire*); joined by *atque* to *caedis ;* obj. of *oblīvīscere.* —— Tenēris, 2d pers. sing. pres. ind. pass. of *teneō, -ēre, -uī, tentum*, 2 ; the implied subj. is *tū.*

LINE 9. undique (*unde* + *que*), adv. of place ; modifies *tenēris.* —— lūce, abl. sing. of *lūx, lūcis*, f. 3d ; abl. of comparison, with the compar. adj. *clāriōra.* Comparison may

than daylight to us,	tua	cōnsilia	omnia,	quae	iam	mēcum	10
and these you may	*your*	*plans*	*all,*	*which*	*now*	*with me*	
review with me now.	licet	recōgnōscas.		Meministine		mē	11
Do you remember	*it is permitted*	*you may review.*		*Do you remember*		*me*	

be expressed (1) by the compar. degree and *quam*, the noun compared being in the same case as that with which it is compared, or (2) *quam* may be omitted, and the abl. of the noun in the comparative clause used instead. A. & G. 247, and footnote; B. 217; G. 296; H. 417. The abl. of comparison is especially common after a negative. Synonyms: (1) *lūmen* (= *luc-men*, from root *luc* = *to shine*) is strictly a *light-giving body;* (2) *lūx* = *the light* which emanates from a *lūmen*, hence often *daylight.* —— **sunt**, 3d pers. plur. pres. ind. of *sum;* agrees with the subj. *cōnsilia.* —— **clāriōra**, nom. plur. n. of the adj. *clārior, -ius* (compar. of *clārus, -a, -um* = strictly *well audible*, hence *clear, brilliant,* from root *klu* = *to hear,* cf. Greek κλύω = *I hear,* and Latin *cluō* = *I hear myself called, glōria, laus* (= *claus*), in the pred. with *sunt;* agrees with the subj. *cōnsilia.* —— **nōbīs**, dat. plur. of the 1st personal pron. *ego* (plur. *nōs*); dat. of the indirect obj. with *clāriōra sunt.*

LINE 10. **tua**, nom. plur. n. of the poss. adj. *tuus, -a, -um;* agrees with *cōnsilia;* observe the contrast heightened by the juxtaposition of *nōbīs* and *tua.* —— **cōnsilia**, nom. plur. of *cōnsilium, -ī,* n. 2d; subj. of *clāriōra sunt.* —— **omnia**, nom. plur. n. of the adj. *omnis, -e,* 3d decl.; agrees with *cōnsilia.* —— **quae**, acc. plur. n. of the rel. pron. *quī, quae, quod;* direct obj. of *recōgnōscās;* agrees with the antecedent *cōnsilia.* —— **iam**, adv.; modifies *recōgnōscās.* —— **mēcum** (*mē* + *cum*), *mē* is the abl. sing. of *ego;* obj. of *cum.* *Cum* is the prep., governing the abl. case *mē.* *Cum* is usually enclitic (appended to the word it governs) when the object is a personal, relative, or reflexive pronoun; it is always enclitic with a personal pron., but not always with the rel. pronoun. A. & G. 99, *e,* and 104, *e;* B. 142, 4; G. 413, REM. 1; H. 184, 6, and 187, 2.

LINE 11. **licet**, 3d pers. sing. pres. ind. act. of the impersonal verb *licet, licēre, licuit* or *licitum est,* 2 (root *rik* = *lic* = *to leave free,* cf. Greek λείπω = *I leave;* and Latin *linquō,* supine *lic-tum, liceō* = *I am for sale,* etc.); *quae recōgnōscās* may be regarded as the ultimate subj., but in origin at least *licet* is absolutely independent. —— **recōgnōscās**, 2d pers. sing. pres. subjunct. act. of *recōgnōscō, -ere, recōgnōvī, recōgnitum,* 3 (*re* = *again* + *cōgnōscō, cōgnōscō* being a compound of *con* + *nōscō,* from root *gna* = *to know,* cf. γνώμη = *opinion, gnārus* = *knowing*); agrees with the implied subj. *tū.* The subjunctive is independent of *licet,* at least in origin (though in course of time the combination became common, and *ut* was even introduced with the subjunct.), and is a hortatory or jussive subjunctive, e.g. *you may review* (or as a command, *review*); *it is allowed.* Thus it is incorrect to say that *ut* has been omitted here, in spite of the tendency of two such independent clauses to combine. Observe that this subjunct. is jussive, a development of the simple subjunct. of *desire* (*volitive*). When, however, *licet* is used in concessive clauses = *although,* the subjunct. is not *volitive,* but *potential.* A. & G. 331, *i,* and *f,* REM.; B. 295, 6 and 8; G. 607 (esp. the first example given); H. 515, III, and footnote 2. —— **Meministine** (*meministī* + *ne*), *meministī* is 2d pers. sing. perf. ind. of the defective verb *meminī, meminisse,* no pres. or supine; the subj. is *tū* implied in the personal ending. *Meminī* is a perfect form, but has the meaning of the present = *I remember,* cf. *ōdī* = *I hate;* the perfect-stem tenses are regular, e.g. *meminerō, memineram,* etc.; the imperative has *mementō, mementōte.* A. & G. 143, *c;* B. 133; G. 175, 5, *b;* H. 297, I. *Ne* is the enclitic interrogative particle, used in questions simply asking for information; *nōnne* expects an affirmative reply, *num* a negative. Sometimes *ne* has the force of *nōnne,* especially when added to the verb; see *sēnsistīne,* l. 36. —— **mē**, acc. sing. of *ego;* subj.-acc. of *dīcere* in indirect discourse after *meministī.*

12	ante	diem	XII	Kalendās	Novembrēs	dīcere	how I said in the
	before	*the day*	*twelfth*	*the Kalends*	*of November*	*to say*	Senate on the twenty-
13	in	senātū,		fore	in	armīs	certō	first day of October
	in	*the senate*		*(that) would be*	*in*	*arms*	*fixed*	that on an appointed

LINE 12. **ante**, prep. with the acc. ; apparently gov. *diem*, but the use of *ante* in dates is phraseological, and *ante diem* XII (= *duodecimum*) *Kalendās Novembrēs* = *diē* (abl. of time *when*) *duodecimō ante Kalendās Novembrēs.* Such phrases are frequently abbreviated, as A. D. XII, *Kal. Nov.;* and may even be governed by another prep., e.g. *in* or *ex*, as *differre rem in a. d.* XII, *Kal. Nov.* For this phrase, consult A. & G. 259, *e* ; B. 371, esp. 4–7 ; G. APPENDIX, p. 491 ; H. 642, esp. III. On the Roman Calendar and system of dating, see A. & G. 376 ; B. 371, 372 ; G. pp. 491, 492 ; H. 641–645. —— **diem**, acc. sing. of *diēs, dieī,* m. 5th ; phraseological acc., apparent obj. of *ante ;* the phrase probably arose from a transposition of *ante*, for the change from *ante diē duodecimō*, etc., to *ante diem duodecimum* (and the like) is readily understood. —— **duodecimum** (in Roman figures xii), acc. sing. of the ordinal numeral *duodecimus, -a, -um*, the adjectival form of the cardinal *duodecim* (*duo* + *decem*); agrees with *diem.* The Romans reckoned inclusively in dating ; thus this date is the 12th day from and including the first day of November = Oct. 21st. —— **Kalendās**, acc. of the plur. noun *Kalendae, -ārum,* f. 1st (abbreviated *Kal.;* from the root *kal* = *to call*, cf. *calō, clā-mō, classis,* καλ-έω); the real obj. of *ante.* The Kalends = the 1st day of a month, on which the priests proclaimed the order of the days, festivals, etc. ; it was also a day on which debts were commonly called in (also on the Ides and Nones), hence *Kalendārium* or *Calendārium* = the interest-book of a money-lender ; hence our word *Calendar.* The two other days up to which the Romans reckoned dates are the *Idūs* (-*uum*, f. 4th plur.), and the *Nōnae* (-*ārum*), f. 1st, from *nōnus* = 9th, which fell respectively on the 13th and 5th of the month, except in March, May, July, and October, when they fell on the 15th and 7th respectively. —— **Novembrēs**, acc. plur. of the adj. *November, -bris, -bre*, 3d (like *ācer ;* from *novem* = 9, because November is the 9th month, reckoning March as the first of the year, as the early Romans did); agrees with *Kalendās ;* the names of all the months were originally adjectives, *mensis* being expressed or understood. —— **dīcere**, pres. inf. act. of *dīcō, -ere, dīxī, dictum,* 3 ; agrees with the subj.-acc. *mē* in object-dependence on *meministī.* The present inf., instead of the usual perf., is often found with *meminī*, and denotes a recollection which is both *personal*, and *very vivid ;* if the recollection be regarded as something over and done with, even if personal, the perf. inf. is used.

LINE 13. **in**, prep. ; gov. the abl. *senātū.* —— **senātū**, abl. sing. of *senātus, -ūs,* m. 4th ; obj. of the prep. *in ; senātū* again = a meeting of the Senate. On Oct. 21st Cicero summoned the Senate, and reported the existence of a conspiracy, and called on Catiline to defend himself ; Catiline boldly likened the Senate to a weak body with a weak head, and the people to a strong body without a head at all, but added that he would be its head, thus associating himself with the popular leaders, e.g. Caesar, Crassus; see the Introduction. —— **fore**, fut. inf. of *sum ;* agrees with the subj.-acc. *Mānlium,* in indirect discourse after the leading verb of saying *dīcere. Fore* is a form lacking inflections, instead of the periphrastic *futūrum esse.* The order is : *mē dīcere in senātū C. Mānlium, audāciae tuae satellitem atque administrum, fore in armīs certō diē*, etc. —— **in**, prep. ; gov. the abl. *armīs ; in armīs* = *under arms*, is a phrase, as it is in English ; *in armīs* is predicative with *fore.* —— **armīs**, abl. of the plur. noun *arma, -ōrum,* n. 2d (root *or* = *to fit* (something) *closely* to oneself); obj. of the prep. *in. Arma* = all kinds of warlike accoutrements, offensive and defensive. —— **certō**, abl. sing. m. of the adj. *certus, -a, -um* (old part. of *cernō*); agrees with *diē. Certus* = *certain, fixed, sure ;* distinguish *certain* here from *certain* indef. (*quīdam*).

day, to wit, the	diē,	quī	diēs	futūrus esset	ante 14
twenty-seventh day	*on a day,*	*which*	*day*	*would be*	*before*
of October, Gaius	diem	VI	Kalendās	Novembrēs,	C. 15
Manlius, your crea-	*the day*	*sixth*	*the Kalends*	*of November,*	*Gaius*
ture and accomplice	Manlium,		audāciae	satellitem	atque 16
in insolence, would	*Manlius,*		*of your boldness*	*the attendant*	*and*

LINE 14. **diē**, abl. sing. of *diēs, diēī*, m. 5th ; abl. of time *when;* extending the pred. *fore in armīs* of the indirect discourse. A. & G. 256 ; B. 230 ; G. 393 ; H. 429. —— **quī**, nom. sing. m. of the rel. pron. *quī, quae, quod;* agrees with its antecedent *diē*, which is repeated as subj.-nom. *diēs* in the rel. clause ; see note on *quō*, Chap. II, l. 19. —— **diēs**, nom. sing. ; subj. of *futūrus esset* in the rel. clause. —— **futūrus esset**, 3d pers. sing. imperf. subjunct. of the active periphrastic fut. conjugation of *sum, esse, fuī;* agrees with the subj. *quī diēs;* the imperf. subjunct. is used instead of the pres. *futūrus sit*, because *dicere* with *meministī* is in the place of *dīxisse*, i.e. the leading verb is strictly = to the inf. of the perf. indef. (historic), and requires historic sequence in subordinate clauses ; the mood is subjunct. instead of ind., because the rel. clause is subordinate to *dīcere*, and is part of the indirect discourse, representing what Cicero said in the Senate. Turned into *Ōrātiō Recta*, Cicero's words were : *C. Mānlius* (+ appositives) *erit in armīs certō diē, quī diēs erit ante diem*, etc. On the active periphrastic conjunction, consult A. &. G. 129 ; B. 115 ; G. 129, and 247 ; H. 233, and 466, NOTE. For subjunct. mood, A. & G. 336, 2 ; B. 314, 1 ; G. 650 ; H. 524. —— **ante**, prep. + acc. ; apparently gov. *diem*, but really *Kalendās* below ; see *ante*, l. 12 above, for this phrase. This passage shows how the whole phrase is considered as one single notion, *ante diem . . . Novembrēs* being the complement of *futūrus esset* in the pred. ; cf. the governing of the whole phrase by a prep., e.g. *ex, in*, etc. Reconstructed according to probable origin, the passage would read : *quī diēs futūrus esset diēs sextus ante Kalendās Novembrēs*.

LINE 15. **diem**, acc. sing. of *diēs, diēī*, m. 5th ; phraseological acc. with *ante*. —— **sextum** (in figures = vi), acc. sing. m. of the ordinal numeral *sextus, -a, -um* (cardinal *sex*) ; agrees with *diem*. The 6th day (inclusive) before the 1st of November, = Oct. 27th ; but the MSS. vary between VI and IX, so the date may be *ante diem nōnum* = Oct. 24th. —— **Kalendās**, acc. of *Kalendae, -ārum*, f. 1st ; real obj. of *ante;* see *Kalendās*, l. 12 above. —— **Novembrēs**, acc. plur. f. of the adj. *November, -bris, -bre*, 3d ; agrees with *Kalendās*. This and other months are often abbreviated, e.g. *Kal. Nov., Kal. Dec., Kal. Mart.*, etc. —— **Gāium** (= C.), acc. sing. of *Gāius, -ī*, m. 2d ; *praenōmen* of *Mānlius*, and subj.-acc. of *fore* in indirect discourse. With the abbreviation *C*, compare *Cn. = Gnaeus*.

LINE 16. **Mānlium** (probably not of the patrician *gēns Mānlia*), acc. sing. of *Mānlius, -ī*, m. 2d ; subj.-acc. of *fore* in indirect discourse after *dicere*. C. Mānlius was a veteran soldier, who became a centurion under Sulla. He was enriched by Sulla, but when his fortune was spent he tried to regain wealth by joining Catiline's conspiracy. In Catiline's absence he was in command of the revolutionists, and fortified the camp at Faesulae. In the battle which ensued, Manlius led the right wing, and died fighting desperately. —— **audāciae**, gen. sing. of *audācia*, f. 1st ; poss. gen., limiting *satellitem* and *administrum; audāciae* might almost be regarded as objective, as *satellitem* implies agency. For synonyms, consult the note on *virtūs*, Chap. I, l. 39. —— **satellitem**, acc. sing. m. of *satelles; satellitis*, m. and f. 3d (etymology unknown) ; appos. of *Mānlium; satellitem* implies a baser kind of service than *administrum*. Observe how the less common term is defined by a synonym, *administrum*. —— **atque**, cop. conj. ; joins *satellitem* and *administrum*, and (as often) = *and also*.

17	administrum	tuae?	Num	mē	fefellit,	appear under arms?
	helper	*your?*	*Surely not*	*me*	*did escape,*	Was I at all mis-

17 administrum tuae? / Num mē (fefellit, | appear under arms?
   helper   *your?* // *Surely not* *me* (*did escape,* | Was I at all mis-
                                                             | taken, Catiline, not
18 Catilīna, nōn modo rēs tanta, tam atrōx | in the fact merely,
   Catiline, *not* *only* *a matter so great,* *so* *savage* | — most momentous,
                                                             | terrible, and incredi-
19 tamque incrēdibilis, vērum, id quod multō | ble as it was, — but,
   and so *incredible,* *but,* *that* *which* *by much* | what is far more re-

---

LINE 17. **administrum,** acc. sing. of *administer, administrī,* m. 2d (*ad + minister*); appos. of *Mānlium;* joined by *atque* to *satellitem.* —— **tuae,** gen. sing. f. of the poss. adj. *tuus, -a, -um;* agrees with *audāciae.* —— **Num,** interrog. adv., expecting a negative answer. —— **mē,** acc. sing. of *ego;* direct obj. of *fefellit.* —— **fefellit,** 3d pers. sing. perf. ind. act. of *fallō, -ere, fefellī, falsum,* 3 (root *spal* or *sphal = to deceive,* cf. σφάλλω = *I mislead*); agrees with the subj. *rēs.* *Fallit* and *fefellit* are often used impersonally, = *it escapes my notice;* the pass. *fallor = I am deceived,* or *I deceive myself.*

LINE 18. **Catilīna,** voc. sing. of *Catilīna, -ae,* m. 1st; the case of address. —— **nōn,** neg. adv., in the combination *nōn modo . . . vērum = not only . . . but.* Similar combinations are *nōn sōlum,* or *nōn tantum* in the first clause, followed by *sed, vērum, sed etiam, vērum etiam, sed quoque* in the second. Of these *nōn tantum* is not found in Caesar or Sallust, and not often in Cicero; *sed* alone is more common in Livy than in Cicero. A. & G. 149, *e*; B. 343, 2; G. 482, 5, and NOTE 1; H. 554, I, 5. —— **modo,** adv., modifying, *rēs fefellit.* —— **rēs,** gen. *reī,* f. 5th; nom. sing., subj. of *fefellit; rēs* is euphemistic, instead of the offensive word which would describe Catiline's crime against the State. *Rēs* and *ratiō* are indefinite words, both much used in Latin, and the former far outnumbers any other noun in its occurrences. —— **tanta,** nom. sing. f. of the demonstr. adj. *tantus, -a, -um;* agrees with *rēs.* —— **tam,** demonstr. adv., modifies *atrōx. Tam* is often the correlative of *quam, tam . . . quam = so . . . as.* —— **atrōx,** adj. gen. *atrōcis,* 3d; nom. sing. f., agrees with *rēs.*

LINE 19. **tamque** (*tam + que*), *tam,* adv., modifying *incrēdibilis. Que,* enclitic cop. conj., joining *tam atrōx* and *tam incrēdibilis.* —— **incrēdibilis** (*in = not,* + *crēdibilis = believable,* verbal adj. from *crēdō,* cf. *amābilis* from *amō*); agrees with *rēs.* —— **vērum,** adversative conj., connecting *rēs* and *diēs.* —— **id,** acc. sing. n. of the demonstr. pron. *is, ea, id;* in appos. with (*num*) *diēs* (*fefellit*). It is plain that *id* is not in appos. with *diēs,* for it is nonsense to say that the day of the uprising was in itself more remarkable than the uprising (*diēs* more *admīranda* than *rēs*). The whole phrase *id quod . . . admīrandum* is in apposition with the whole idea conveyed in *num diēs mē fefellit,* for it was the fact that Cicero got news of the date, which was more wonderful than the fact that he knew of the conspiracy. Some assign the appositive to the nom. case, but it is better to regard it in all cases as the acc. case; the construction is Greek in origin, cf. Sophocles' *Electra,* l. 130, ἥκετ', ἐμῶν καμάτων παραμύθιον = *you have come,* (your coming being) *a solace to my pain.* Thence the Latin poets derive such expressions as *miserābile vīsū = piteous to see,* explanatory of a whole clause. The prose use of *id quod,* etc., in apposition or explanation is very common; not infrequently *quae rēs,* etc., or *quod,* etc. (without antecedent *id*), occur in similar construction, when *quae rēs* may be explained as *rem quae,* etc., by attraction of the antecedent into the rel. clause. For examples, etc., see A. & G. 200, *e*; B. 247, 1, *b*; G. 324; 333, NOTE 2; 614, REM. 2; H. 363, 5. —— **quod,** nom. sing. n. of the rel. pron. *quī, quae, quod;* agrees with the antecedent *id* in the phrase *id quod,* etc., and is subj. of *est.* —— **multō,** abl. sing. n. of the adj. *multus, -a, -um;* used substantively and = *by much,* the abl. expressing *degree of difference.* This abl. is used with comparatives or expressions which imply comparison, *dīmideō minor = smaller by half,* and is most common with the ablatives *quantō . . . tantō, quō . . . eō* (*by how*

markable, in the day?	magis	est	admīrandum,	diēs ?	Dīxī	ego	20
It was I, too, who	the more	is	to be wondered at,	the day?	Said	I	
declared in the Sen-	idem		in	senātū,		caedem	21
ate that you had ap-	the same (person)	in		the senate,		(that) the murder	
pointed the massacre	tē	optimātium		contulisse			in	22
of the aristocrats to	you	of the aristocrats		had (lit. to have) assigned			for

much . . . by so much), e.g. quantō (quō) longiōrēs, tantō (eō) crēbriōrēs epistulae fiunt = as your letters grow in length, so (in proportion) they grow in frequency. A. & G. 250; B. 223; G. 403; H. 423. These ablatives have an adverbial force; hence multō (with several others) is often described simply as an adverb in -ō, cf. subitō.

LINE 20. **magis**, comparative adv., modifying admīrandum. Magis has no pos. proper, but măgnopere or măgnō opere may be considered such; superl. măximē. Magis is an exception to the ordinary rule that compar. adverbs = the acc. sing. n. of the compar. adj. The root of magis is mag = great, cf. măgnus, magister, and Greek μέγας = great. A. & G. 92; B. 76, 2, and 77, 1; G. 93; H. 306. Synonyms: (1) magis = more, qualitative, denoting a higher grade; (2) plūs, compar. of multum = more, quantitative; (3) amplius = more, in regard to extent or area, or denoting something added; (4) potius = more, more willingly, expressing choice; (5) in English "more" + a neg., is expressed very often by iam + a neg., e.g. I no more desire = nōn iam volō, nothing more = nihil iam.——**est**, 3d pers. sing. pres. ind. of sum; agrees with the subj. quod.——**admīrandum**, nom. sing. n. of admīrandus, -a, -um, gerundive of admīror, ārī, -ātus sum, 1 (ad + mīror), adjectival as often, agrees with the subj. quod in the parenthesis id quod multō magis est admīrandum.——**diēs**, gen. diēī, m. 5th; nom. subj. of fefellit understood from the coördinate clause above.——**Dīxī**, 1st pers. sing. perf. ind. act. of dīcō, -ere, dīxī, dictum, 3 (root dak = to show, cf. indicō, and δείκνυμι = I show); agrees with the subj. ego.——**ego**, nom. sing. of 1st personal pron.; subj. of dīxī; very emphatic, to impress Catiline with the extent of his information.

LINE 21. **idem**, nom. sing. m. of īdem (= is + dem), eadem, idem (= id + dem), determinative pron.; agrees with and intensifies ego. Īdem is declined like is, but m changes to n before d, e.g. acc. m. eundem (eum + dem).——**in**, prep.; gov. the abl. senātū.——**senātū**, abl. sing. of senātus, -ūs, m. 4th; obj. of prep. in = meeting of the Senate, viz. Oct. 21st. It should be remembered that it is doubtful whether the cōnsultum ultimum was passed on the 21st, or, as Dion Cassius says, on the 22d.——**caedem**, acc. sing. of caedēs, -is, f. 3d (caedō = I cut down, I slay); direct obj. of contulisse in the indirect discourse after dīxī; the indirect tē caedem opt. contulisse = direct caedem opt. contulistī.

LINE 22. **tē**, acc. sing. of tū; subj.-acc. of contulisse in indirect speech introduced by dīxī.——**optimātium**, gen. plur. of optimās, -ātis, adj., and m. or f. noun, 3d decl. (optimus); poss. gen., limiting caedem; proper names excepted, optimātēs is the only one of words with the gen. -ātis which makes its gen. plur. in -ium. The optimātēs = the bonī (see note on bonōrum, Chap. I, l. 7), i.e. the aristocratic party, being composed of senators and nōbilēs (i.e. descendants of curule magistrates), and aiming at keeping the chief power in the hands of the few. Their opponents = the populārēs, or democratic party, whose aim was to extend the power of the people; this party was mainly composed of ignōbilēs, and the proletariat in general. Optimātēs (like bonī) does not indicate rank necessarily, for the chief leaders of the populārēs were nōbilēs, e.g. the two Gracchī, and some were even patricians, e.g. Iulius Caesar.——**contulisse**, perf. inf. act. of cōnferō, cōnferre, contulī, collātum, irreg. (con + ferō); agrees with the subj.-acc. tē; contulisse probably = assigned, but might be rendered postponed, if regarded as relative to

28 ante diem V Kalendās Novembrēs, tum cum
  before the day fifth the Kalends of November, then when

24 multī prīncipēs cīvitātis Rōmā nōn tam
  many leading men of the state from Rome not so much

| take place on the 28th of October — the day on which many of the leading men of the state fled |

ll. 13-15. —— **in**, prep. ; gov. the whole phrase *ante diem V Kalendās Novembrēs* as if it were a single word in the acc. case. With regard to *time, in = for ;* see references under *ante,* l. 12. For the general uses of the prep. *in* with the acc. and abl. cases consult A. & G. 153; B. 143; G. 418, 1 ; H. 435, 1.

LINE 23. **ante**, prep. ; originally gov. not *diem* but the date up to which time is reckoned, e.g. *Kalendās ;* see *ante,* l. 12. —— **diem,** acc. sing. of *diēs, dieī,* m. (less often f. in sing.) 5th ; phraseological acc., apparent obj. of *ante ;* this phrase = *contulisse in diem quintum ante Kalendās Novembrēs.* —— **quintum** (= V in figures), acc. sing. m. of the ordinal numeral *quintus, -a, -um* (cardinal *quinque,* cf. πέντε = 5, πέμπτος = 5th); agrees with *diem ;* the day for the massacre in Rome was the 28th of October, i.e. one day after the raising of the standard of revolt at Faesulae. —— **Kalendās,** acc. of *Kalendae, -arum,* f. 1st ; phraseological acc., real obj. of *ante.* For derivation, etc., refer to the note on *Kalendās,* l. 12. —— **Novembrēs,** acc. plur. of the adj. *November, -bris, -bre,* 3d ; agrees with *Kalendās.* —— **tum,** temporal adv. ; the demonstr. antecedent of the rel. *cum ; tum cum . . . profūgērunt* defines the date given above in a way that would bring the events vividly before the minds of the orator's audience. Observe that the *cum* clause following is exactly like any other rel. clause, and therefore the verb *profūgērunt* is indicative ; *cum = quō tempore.* —— **cum** (*quum,* old forms *quom,* rarely *qum = quem,* adverbial use of acc. of rel. *quī*), temporal conj. ; introducing the clause *prīncipēs . . . profūgērunt,* relatively to *tum.* The ind. is regular with *cum* and other temporal conjunctions ; but if the time of the *cum* clause is considered as depending on the time of the main clause, as usually happens in past time, the subjunct. mood is used. Hence *cum* takes the imperf. and pluperf. subjunct., but the ind. of other tenses. But *cum* takes the ind. of past tenses: (1) when it = *as often as* (frequentative), e.g. *cum haec dīxerat, manūs tollēbat = as often as he said these words, he raised his hands ;* (2) when the main and temporal clauses are contemporaneous (with *tum* often added in main clause); e.g. *vōs pāruistis cum pāruit nēmō* (Cic.) = *you were obedient at the time when no one else was obedient ;* (3) when *cum* is used like a rel. = *et* + demonstr. ad *tum* (cf. *quae = et haec*), e.g. *castra ibi posita, cum subitō advēnēre legiōnēs = the camp had been pitched there, when the legions suddenly came up.* A. & G. 325 ; B. 288; G. 580-585; H. 521. Other uses of *cum* are: (a) *causal = since, as,* with the subjunct. of all tenses ; (b) *concessive = although, though,* with the subjunct. of all tenses.

LINE 24. **multī,** nom. plur. m. of *multus, -a, -um ;* agrees with *prīncipēs.* —— **prīncipēs,** nom. plur. of the noun *prīnceps, prīncipis,* m. 3d, strictly m. of adj. *prīnceps* (*prīmus + capiō*); subj. of *profūgērunt ; prīncipēs* here = *leaders, leading men.* Sometimes *prīnceps* is a title, e.g. *prīnceps senātūs.* —— **cīvitātis,** gen. sing. of *cīvitās,* f. 3d (*cīvis*); poss. gen., limiting *prīncipēs.* Synonyms : (1) *cīvitās = state,* as a community of *cīvēs ;* often it = *franchise, right of citizenship ;* (2) *rēs pūblica = state, commonwealth,* with reference to its constitution. —— **Rōmā,** abl. sing. of *Rōma, -ae,* f. 1st ; expressing *place from which,* with a verb of motion. *Motion from* is denoted by the abl. with the prep. *ab, ex,* or *dē ;* but in the case of the *names* of towns or small islands, the abl. is used without the prep. If an appositive is added, the prep. is required, e.g. *ab urbe Rōmā.* The abl. alone is used with a few other words, e.g. *rūre, domō ;* the poets use the abl. without a prep. very freely. Compare the acc. *Rōmam* of limit of motion. A. & G. 258, *a ;* B. 229, 1, *a* and *b :* G. 391 ; 390, 2; H. 412, II, 1. —— **nōn,** neg. adv.; modifies *suī cōnservandī causā.* —— **tam,** adv., antecedent of *quam* below.

from Rome, with the	suī	cōnservandī	quam	tuōrum 25
purpose not so much	*themselves*	*of saving*	*as (for the sake)*	*your*
of ensuring their own				
safety as of putting	cōnsiliōrum	reprimendōrum	causā	profūgērunt. 26
a check on your de-	*plans*	*of repressing*	*for the sake*	*fled.*

LINE 25. **suī**, gen. of the reflexive pron. *sē;* in the gerundive-attraction construction with *conservandī;* the gen. case is governed by the prep. *causā.* *Suī cōnservandī* = *of saving themselves;* we might have expected *suī cōnservandōrum* (as *suī* refers to the *prīncipēs*, plural), or the gerund *sē cōnservandī.* The construction in the gen. as in this passage is idiomatic, and is explained as follows : the gen. *suī* is in origin the gen. sing. n. of the poss. adj. *suus, -a, -um,* supplying a case-deficiency, and its use with the gerundive in the gen. sing. is a survival of its origin ; similar are the genitives *meī* (of *ego*), *nostrī* (of *nōs*), *tuī*, etc., all of which are neut. genitives sing. borrowed from the poss. pronouns. For the ordinary gerundive construction, refer to the note on *habendī*, Chap. I, l. 8. A. & G. 298, *a*; B. 339, 5; G. 428, REM. 1, and NOTE 1; H. 542, I, NOTE 1. —— **cōnservandī**, gen. sing. n. of *cōnservandus, -a, -um,* gerundive of *cōnservō, -āre, -āvī, -ātum,* 1 (*con + servō*); agrees with *suī* as an original neut. sing. in the construction of gerundive attraction. The grammarians differ in their explanation of *cōnservandī* and like verbal genitives ; some consider it a survival of an intermediate stage between the gerund and the gerundive, and the gerund as the earlier form out of which the gerundive (and its peculiar construction) was developed. We certainly find the gen. of the gerund used with the gen. plur. of nouns (a very rare construction), e.g. Cicero, Philippics, V, *facultās agrōrum condōnandī* = *the power of presenting estates;* but when used with the personal pronouns, e.g. *meī, suī, nostrī*, etc., the verbal gen. is preferably considered the gerundive ; see the references on *suī* above. Other explanations of inferior merit are : (1) that *cōnservandī* = *cōnservandōrum.* the sing. form being used to avoid the ending in -*ōrum;* but Cicero uses the ending in -*ōrum* as in l. 26, when he might have said *tua cōnsilia reprimendī* (gerund) if he had disliked the long sounds ; (2) that *cōnservandī* is the gerund gen. used as a noun = *cōnservātiōnis,* and *suī* as objective gen. limiting *cōnservandī,* = *for the sake of the preservation of themselves;* this explanation seems entirely inadmissible. —— **quam**, rel. adv., corresponding to *tam* above ; *nōn tam . . . quam* represents the ideas *suī cōnservandī causā* and *tuōrum cōnsiliōrum reprimendōrum causā* in strong contrast. Cicero would have offended his aristocratic audience if he had accused them of running away from danger ; hence he puts it down to definite policy taken to defeat Catiline. We have no other information on this incident. —— **tuōrum**, gen. plur. n. of the poss. adj. *tuus, -a, -um;* agrees with *cōnsiliōrum;* *tuōrum* = *your*, i.e. Catiline's.

LINE 26. **cōnsiliōrum**, gen. plur. of *cōnsilium, -ī*, n. 2d ; objective gen. dependent on the abl. *causā* used as a preposition ; gen. in the gerundive-attraction construction with *reprimendōrum.* —— **reprimendōrum**, gen. plur. n. of *reprimendus, -a, -um,* the gerundive of *reprimō, -ere, repressī, repressum,* 3 (*re = back, + premō = I press*); agrees in gerundial attraction with *cōnsiliōrum* (the obj. *cōnsilia* of the gerund *reprimendī*). —— **causā**, quasi-prep., adverbial abl. of *causa, -ae,* f. 1s (cf. *grātiā,* adverbial abl. of *grātia, -ae,* f. 1st = *for the sake*); gov. the gen. *cōnsiliōrum reprimendōrum.* *Causā* and *grātiā* usually stand after the gen., e.g. *exemplī causā;* .*causā* + the gen. of the gerund or gerundive is a favorite way of expressing purpose, as in the present passage. In nearly every case the abl. f. of the poss. pron. agreeing with *causā* (less common with *grātiā*) is preferred to the objective gen. of the personal pron., e.g. *tuā senātūsque causā* = *for your sake and the Senate's.* —— **profūgērunt**, 3d pers. plural. perf. ind. act. of *profugiō, -ere, profūgī,* no supine, 3 intrans. (*prō + fugiō*); agrees with the subj. *prīncipēs;* the mood is ind. because the clause is relative, and because it is explanatory of the date

27 Num   īnfitiārī   potes   tē   illō   ipsō
   Surely not   *to deny*   *you are able*   *(that) you*   *that*   *very*

28 diē   meīs   praesidiīs,   meā   dīligentiā
   on day   *my*   *by guards,*   *my*   *by carefulness*

29 circumclūsum   commovēre   tē   contrā
   enclosed about   *to set in motion*   *yourself*   *against*

30 rem pūblicam   nōn   potuisse,   cum
   the commonwealth   *not*   *(lit. to have been) were able,*   *when*

signs. Can you deny that on that very date you were hedged in by my guards and my watchful precautions and unable to make any move against the state, saying all the

ante . . . *Novembrēs* and not included in the indirect discourse *tē contulisse*, etc., after *dīxī*.

LINE 27. **Num**, interrog. adv. ; introducing the question *īnfitiārī potes*, etc., to which a neg. answer is expected (see *num*, Chap. II, l. 11); hence the question = a neg. statement, e.g. *īnfitiārī nōn potes*, etc. —— **īnfitiārī**, pres. inf. of the deponent verb *īnfitior, -ārī, -ātus sum*, 1 (*in* = *not* + *fateor*, 2 = *I confess;* observe the change of conjugation in composition); complementary inf. + *potes*. Synonyms: (1) *negō* = *I deny*, either = *contradicting* as opposed to *affirming*, or = *refusing* as opposed to *granting;* (2) *īnfitior* = *I deny* = *refuse to admit.* —— **potes**, 2d pers. sing. pres. ind. of *possum, posse, potuī*, irreg. (*potis* + *sum*); the subj. *tū* is implied. —— **tē**, acc. sing. of *tū ;* subj.-acc. of *nōn potuisse* below in indirect discourse after *īnfitiārī ; tē* is reflexive. —— **illō**, abl. sing. m. of the demonstr. pron. *ille, illa, illud;* agrees with *diē.* —— **ipsō**, abl. sing. m. of the intensive pron. *ipse, ipsa, ipsum ;* agrees with and emphasizes *diē.*

LINE 28. **diē**, abl. sing. of *diēs, dieī*, m. 5th ; abl. of *time when ;* see *diē*, l. 14. —— **meīs**, abl. plur. n. of the poss. pron. adj. *meus, -a, -um ;* agrees with *praesidiīs.* —— **praesidiīs**, abl. plur. of *praesidium, -ī*, n. 2d ; abl. of the means, modifying *circumclūsum ; praesidiīs* = *guards, protections*, including the men employed by Cicero, and the general precautions taken by him to protect the state. —— **meā**, abl. sing. f. of the poss. pron. *meus, -a, -um ;* agrees with *dīligentiā ;* observe the emphasis on *meīs* and *meā*, which is heightened by the omission of a cop. conj. connecting *praesidiīs* and *dīligentiā* (*asyndeton*). —— **dīligentiā**, abl. sing. of *dīligentia, -ae*, f. 1st (*dīligēns*): abl. of the means, modifying *circumclūsum.*

LINE 29. **circumclūsum**, acc. sing. m. of *circumclūsus, -a, -um*, perf. part. pass. of *circumclūdō, -ere, circumclūsī, circumclūsum*, 3 (*circum* = *around* + *claudō* = *I shut;* root *sklu* = *to fasten;* cf. *clā-vis* = *a key*, κλείς = *a key*, κλείω = *I shut*, and *claustra* = *a bolt*); agrees with the subj.-acc. *tē*, of which *meīs . . . circumclūsum* is a participial enlargement. —— **commovēre**, pres. inf. act. of *commoveō, -ēre, commōvī, commōtum*, 3 (*con* + *moveō*); *complementary* or *prolative* inf. dependent on *potuisse* below; *commovēre* + its obj. *tē* (immediately following) = the medial or reflexive pass. *commovērī*, i.e. *to move*, intrans., or in other words *to make a move* against the state. The whole sentence from l. 27-l. 30 is rather involved ; in the English order it would be : *num īnfitiārī potes tē* (*meīs praesidiīs, meā dīligentiā circumclūsum*) *contrā rem pūblicam nōn potuisse tē commovēre illō ipsō diē* (=*tum*) *cum*, etc. —— **tē**, acc. sing. of *tū ;* direct. obj. (reflexive) of *commovēre.* —— **contrā**, prep. with the acc. ; gov. *rem pūblicam.*

LINE 30. **rem**, acc. sing. of *rēs, reī*, f. 5th ; obj. of the prep. *contrā.* —— **pūblicam**, acc. sing. f. of the adj. *pūblicus, -a, -um ;* agrees with *rem.* —— **nōn**, neg. adv.; modifies *potuisse.* —— **potuisse**, perf. inf. act. of *possum, posse, potuī*, irreg. ; agrees with the subj.-acc. *tē* (l. 27) in indirect discourse after *īnfitiārī ;* all that follows the words *num īnfitiārī potes* stands as object of *īnfitiārī.* —— **cum**, temporal conj., introducing the clause *tū discessū . . . dīcēbas ;* this *cum* clause is not subordinate to *potuisse* in the indirect discourse, for if it were the verb would be *dīcerēs* instead of *dīcēbas ;* the clause

time that as the rest	tū	discessū	cēterōrum	nostrā	tamen,	31
had gone away you	*you*	*at the departure*	*of the rest*	*our* (= *of us*)	*yet*	
were satisfied at any	quī	·	remānsissēmus,	caede	tē	32
rate with the murder	*who*		*had remained,*	*with the murder*	*yourself*	

is a relative one and defines parenthetically the antecedent *illō ipsō diē* (*cum* = *quō diē* etc., in parenthesis). Observe that the subjunct. mood would be necessary if the *cum* clause were not a parenthesis which the speaker brings in to define his own meaning. A. & G. 336, 2; B. 314, 1; G. 650; H. 524.

LINE 31. **tū**, nom. sing of the 2d personal pron.; subj. of *dīcēbas* in the *cum* clause. *Tu* is not particularly emphatic, but is expressed because of some affinity which pronouns seem to have for one another; it is in contrast with *nostrā*; *tū, cēterī*, and *nōs* sums up the whole Roman people. —— **discessū**, abl. sing. of *discessus, -ūs*, m. 4th (from *discēdō* = *I withdraw*); idiomatic abl. of *time when*; this abl. and similar ablatives of nouns derived from verbs may be used in the place of the abl. absolute construction to define a point of time. Ordinarily the abl. of *time when* is rarely found without an adjectival attribute, except in the common and time-sanctioned instances, e.g. *aestāte, hieme*, etc. A. & G. 256; B. 230; G. 393; H. 429. —— **cēterōrum**, gen. plur. m. of the adj. (*cēterus*), *cētera, -um* (akin to *iterum* = *again*): poss. gen., limiting *discessū*. *Cēterī, -ōrum*, m., and *cētera, -ōrum*, n., are very common as substantives. The adj. is rare in the sing., and does not occur more than four times in Cicero; the nom. m. was never used at all. Synonyms: (1) *cēterī* = *others, the rest*, in contrast or comparison, e.g. *cēterīs praestāre* = *to excel the rest*; (2) *reliquī*, = *the rest*, regarded as a remainder in counting (from *relinquō* = *I leave*, hence *those left over*), e.g. *reliquī decem* = *the remaining ten men, the ten others*; occasionally *the others* is rendered by *cēterī et reliquī*, and in post-Augustan prose little or no distinction is made between the meanings of the two words; (3) *aliī* = *others*, not in exhaustive but merely partitive distribution; (4) *alterī*, with a plural noun, = *the other*, of two; e.g. *altera castra* = (*the one*, or) *the other of the two camps*; though the plural is rarely used, the singular is common, = *the other*, of two, opposed to *alius* = *other*, of many. —— **nostrā**, abl. sing. f. of the poss. pron. *noster, nostra, nostrum* (*nōs*); agrees with *caede* below; the adj. *nostrā* = the subjective gen. *nostrī* of *nōs*. *Nostrā, our* = the death of the *two* consuls, but Cicero alone was Catiline's real object of attack. —— **tamen**, adv., with adversative force (hence often adversative conj. = *sed*) throws emphasis on *nostrā*, as distinguished from *cēterōrum*.

LINE 32. **quī**, nom. plur. m. of the rel. pron. *quī, quae, quod*; *quī* agrees in gender and number with the antecedent personal pron. *nos* which is implied in the poss. *nostrā*, and is subj. in its own clause *quī remānsissēmus*. A. & G. 197, *f*, and 199, *b*, NOTE; B. 251, 2; G. no def. example, but cf. 321, REM. 2; H. 445, 6. —— **remānsissē-mus**, 1st pers. plur. pluperf. subjunct. act. *remaneō, -ēre, remānsī*, no supine, 2 (*re* = *back, behind*, + *maneō* = *I remain*); agrees with the subj. *quī* in number, and with the antecedent *nostrā* = *nostrī* in person; the subjunct. mood is necessary as the rel. clause is subordinate in the indirect discourse after *cum dīcēbas*; the pluperf. tense is in historic sequence (the perf. subjunct. after a primary verb of saying, e.g. *dīcis tē contentum esse caede eōrum quī remānserint*). Catiline's words in *ōrātiō recta* = *eōrum quī remān-sērunt caede contentus sum*. —— **caede**, abl. sing. of *caedes*, = *is*, f. 3d; abl. governed by *contentus*. This abl. is sometimes of *cause*, and sometimes of the *means*, and with it is combined a certain *locative* notion; hence some call it a *locative* abl., but abl. of *cause* perhaps defines it better. It is used with such verbs as *laetor, fīdō, glōrior*, etc., and with the adjectives *contentus* and *frētus*. A. & G. 254, *b*; B. 219; G. 401, NOTE 6; H. 425, 1. —— **tē**, acc. sing. of *tū*; subj.-acc. of the pred. *contentum esse* in the acc. and inf. construction after *dīcēbas*.

33 contentum	esse	dīcēbas?	Quid?	Cum
satisfied	*to be*	*said?*	*What?*	*Although*

34 tē	Praeneste		Kalendīs	ipsīs
yourself	*Praeneste*		*on the Kalends*	*very*

35 Novembribus	occupātūrum	nocturnō	impetū
of November	*likely to seize*	*nocturnal*	*by an attack*

36 esse	cōnfīderēs,	sēnsistīne	illam	colōniam
to be	*you trusted,*	*did you not perceive*	*that*	*colony*

of us who had stayed behind? Again, though you felt certain that you would take possession of Praeneste on the very first day of November by a night attack, did you not discover that that col-

LINE. 33. **contentum**, acc. sing. m. of the adj. *contentus, -a, -um* (originally perf. part. pass. of *contineō, -ere, -uī, contentum*, 2); predicative with *esse;* agrees with the subj.-acc. *tĕ.* —— **esse**, pres. inf. of *sum;* agrees with the subj.-acc. *tĕ.* —— **dīcēbas**, 2d pers. sing. imperf. ind. act. of *dīcō, -ere, dīxī, dictum*, 3; agrees with the subj. *tū*, l. 31; the mood is ind. because the *cum* clause is merely explanatory of the single word *dĭc.* On the phases of meaning conveyed by the imperf. tense, consult A. & G. 277; B. 260; G. 231-234; H. 468, 469. —— **Quid**, acc. sing. n. of the interrog. pron. *quis, quae, quid,* used adverbially. *Quid* is here and elsewhere (cf. *quid vērō?* Chap. VI, l. 14) used as a particle denoting transition, and may be rendered *again.* —— **Cum**, concessive conj., taking the subjunct. *cōnfīderēs.* A. & G. 326; B. 309, 3; G. 587; H. 515, III.

LINE 34. **tē**, acc. sing. of *tū;* subj.-acc. of *occupātūrum esse* in the object acc. and inf. clause dependent on the idea of *thinking* or *declaring* implied by *cōnfīderēs.* —— **Praeneste**, acc. sing. of *Praeneste, -is*, n. and f. 3d; direct obj. of *occupātūrum esse.* Praeneste (now Palestrina) was an ancient town of Latium, twenty-three miles to the southeast of Rome. It was famed for its nuts, roses, and especially its temple of Fortune, with its oracle. The younger Marius held out there till the end against Sulla, but in 81 B.C. Sulla took it and made it a *colōnia.* Strabo refers to the strong and commanding nature of its citadel. —— **Kalendīs**, abl. of *Kalendae, -ārum*, f. 1st; abl. of *time when.* —— **ipsīs**, abl. plur. f. of the intensive pron. *ipse, -a, -um;* agrees with *Kalendīs.*

LINE 35. **Novembribus**, abl. plur. f. of the adj. *November, -bris, -bre*, 3d (*novem =* nine; hence the 9th month, March being the 1st month of the year with the early Romans); agrees with *Kalendīs.* —— **occupātūrum**, acc. sing. m. of *occupātūrus, -a, -um*, fut. part. act. of *occupō, -āre, -āvī, -ātum*, 1 (*ob + capiō*); agrees with the subj.-acc. *tĕ*, l. 34; *esse* from below makes with *occupātūrum* the combinate form *occupātūrum esse*, i.e. the fut. inf. act. of *occupō.* *Occupō = I seize*, consistently with its etymology, and in no way = the English *occupy* (*teneō, obtineō*). —— **nocturnō**, abl. sing. m. of the adj. *nocturnus, -a, -um* (from *nox, noctis*); agrees with *impetū.* —— **impetū**, abl. sing. of *impetus, -ūs*, m. 4th (*in = against + petō = I fall upon, attack;* root *pat = to move quickly,* hence *to fly, to fall,* e.g. πέτομαι *= I fly,* πτέρον and *penna* (*= pet-na*) *= a feather, wing*); abl. of the means, extending *occupātūrum esse.*

LINE 36. **esse**, pres. inf. of *sum*, making the combinate fut. inf. *occupātūrum esse;* agrees with the subj.-acc. *tĕ.* —— **cōnfīderēs**, 2d pers. sing. imperf. subjunct. of *cōnfīdō, -ere, cōnfīsus sum*, 3, semi-deponent (*cōn + fīdō*); the subj. *tū* is implied in the personal ending; the subjunct. is necessary after *cum = although.* —— **sēnsistīne** (*sēnsistī + ne*): *sēnsistī* is the 2d pers. sing. perf. ind. act. of *sentiō, -īre, sēnsī, sēnsum*, 4; the subj. *tū* is implied in the termination. *Ne* is the enclitic interrog. particle, usually employed to ask a question without suggesting whether the reply will be neg. or affirmative; in this instance *ne* has the force of *nōnne.* A. & G. 210, *d*; B. 162, 2, *c*; G. 454, REM. 2 and NOTE 5; H. no reference. —— **illam**, acc. sing. f. of the demonstr. pron. of the 3d pers. *ille, illa, illud;* agrees with *colōniam.* —— **colōniam**, acc. sing. of *colōnia, -ae*, f. 1st (from *colōnus = a settler*, cf. *colō = I cultivate*); subj.-acc. of *esse mūnītam* in the acc.

ony had been secured at my command by guards, sentinels, and watchmen? There is nothing you do, nothing you plot, nothing you think about, that I do not	meō	iussū	meīs	praesidiīs,
	my	*by order*	*my*	*with garrisons,*

custōdiīs, 37
with guards,

meō iussū meīs praesidiīs, custōdiīs, 37
my   *by order*   *my*   *with garrisons,*   *with guards,*

vigiliīs   esse   mūnītam?   Nihil 38
with watches to have been   *fortified?*   *Nothing*

agis,   nihil   mōlīris,   nihil   cōgitās,   quod 39
you do,   *nothing*   *you contrive,*   *nothing*   *you meditate,*   *which*

and inf. construction after *sēnsistī*. A Roman *colōnia* only in part = the modern idea of a *colony;* for the former, especially in Italy, was established rather to keep Rome's Italian enemies in check than to relieve the surplus population of Rome, though the latter object was also gained. Moreover in the majority of cases the *colōnia* existed as a town, and it was unnecessary to build dwellings, etc. While most *colōniae* were intended as *praesidia*, some of the most commanding towns were specially fortified and became *colōniae militārēs*. *Colōniae*: (1) *cīvium Rōmānōrum*, adopted by full citizens as their home, the colonists retaining all the rights of citizens; such were the *colōniae maritimae*, and all Rome's earliest colonies; (2) *colōniae Latīnae*, composed partly of Roman citizens and partly of Latins; the former lost part of the full franchise (*cīvitās*), viz. the *suffrāgium* = right of voting. The *colōniae* managed their own internal affairs, and in their government imitated closely the Roman arrangement.

LINE 37. **meō**, abl. sing. m. of the poss. pron. *meus, -a, -um;* agrees with *iussū*.——
iussū, abl. sing. of *iussus, -ūs*, m. 4th (only the abl. *iussū* in use; from *iubeō*, cf. *iussum, -ī*, n. 2d); abl. of cause; the verbal ablatives of cause *iussū, rogātū*, etc., become phraseological in combinations, cf. *meō arbitrātū, iussū cīvium, auctōritāte senātūs*, etc.——
meīs, abl. plur. n. of *meus, -a, -um;* agrees with the nearest substantive *praesidiīs*, and understood in the fem. with *custōdiīs* and *vigiliīs*. A. & G. 187; B. 235, B, 2, *b*); G. 286, 1; H. 439, 2. Some editors regard *meīs* as interpolated; but Cicero is never too modest to give himself praise, and moreover he wants to frighten Catiline by the proofs of his vigilance and executive activity.—— **praesidiīs**, abl. plur. of *praesidium, -ī*, n. 2d; abl. of the means, with *esse mūnītam*.—— **custōdiīs**, abl. plur. of *custōdia, -ae*, f. 1st (here in a concrete sense; from *custōs, custōdis*, m. 3d = *cud-tos*, root *kudh* = *to cover*, cf. κεύθω = *I cover, hide*); abl. of the means, with *esse mūnītam;* observe the impressiveness which the *asyndeton* adds to the various precautions taken.

LINE 38. **vigiliīs**, abl. plur. of *vigilia, -ae*, f. 1st (in concrete sense = *watches*, i.e. watchmen); abl. of the means, with *esse mūnītam*.—— **esse mūnītam**, combinate perf. inf. pass. (the part. *mūnītam* agreeing in gender and number with *colōniam*) of *mūniō, -īre, -īvī, -ītum*, 4 (akin to *moenia*); agrees with the subj.-acc. *colōniam*, in the acc. and inf. construction dependent on *sēnsistī*.—— **nihil**, indecl. n. (contracted *nīl;* from *ne* + *hilum* = *not a trifle*, cf. the form *nihilum* or *nīlum, -ī*, n. 2d); direct obj. of *agis*. *Nihil* in the acc. often = *not at all*, adverbially, as in ll. 4–9 of Chap. I.

LINE 39. **agis**, 2d pers. sing. pres. ind. act. of *agō, -ere, ēgī, actum*, 3 (root *ag* = *drive, lead*, etc.); the subj. is *tū* understood.—— **nihil**, acc. sing. (as above); direct obj. of *mōlīris;* observe the *anaphora*, i.e. the repetition of *nihil* at the beginning of each sentence, and the *asyndeton*, i.e. omission of cop. conjunctions.—— **mōlīris**, 2d pers. sing. pres. ind. of the deponent verb *mōlior, -īrī, -ītus sum*, 4 (from *mōlēs* = (1) *a mass*, (2) *difficulty*); the subj. *tū* is implied in the ending; *mōlīrī* = *to undertake, scheme*, etc., something requiring much physical or mental exertion.—— **nihil**, acc. sing. (as above); direct obj. of *cōgitās*.—— **cōgitās**, 2d pers. sing. pres. ind. act. of *cōgitō, -āre, -āvī, -ātum*, 1 (*cum* + *agitō*); the subj. *tū* is implied. Note the climax which is reached in *cōgitās;* Cicero says he knows all that Catiline *does*, all he *plots* with his fellow-conspirators, all he even *thinks* about.—— **quod**, acc. sing. n. of the rel. pron. *quī, quae, quod;*

40 nōn	ego	nōn	modo	audiam,	sed	only hear of, but
not	*I*	*not*	*only*	*hear,*	*but*	actually see as well
41 etiam	videam	plānēque	sentiam.			and distinctly dis-
(which) even	*I see*	*and openly*	*observe.*			cern.

1	IV.	Recōgnōsce	(tandem)	mēcum	noctem	IV. However, re-
		Look over again	*at length*	*with me*	*night*	view with me that

agrees with the antecedent *nihil,* and is direct obj. of *audiam* (also of *videam* and *sentiam*) in the rel. clause ; *quod* is here the *characteristic* rel. = *tāle ut,* hence the consecutive subjunct. *videam,* etc. A. & G. 319, 2, and *ff.* ; B. 284, 2 and 3 ; G. 552, 1, and 556 ; H. 500, 1, and 504, 2.   The reading here is somewhat doubtful : (1) *quod nōn ego nōn modo,* etc., as here adopted is the reading of Halm, who inserts the first *nōn ;* (2) the MSS. read *quod ego nōn modo,* etc., which obviously requires emendation, for the first neg. *nihil* needs another in the rel. clause to cancel it = a strong affirmative ; thus Halm's *nihil quod nōn . . . audiam = omnia audiō ;* (3) Madvig reads *quin ego* instead of *quod nōn ego ; quin* is often used in consecutive clauses, and is almost as good as *quod nōn (quin = qui,* old adverbial abl. + *ne = not = that not*) ; *quin* is very common in result clauses after verbs of *hindering* and the like, and also after neg. verbs or expressions denoting doubt, e.g. *nōn dubitō ;* (4) some editors adapt the passage in a free way, e.g. *quod ego nōn modō nōn audiam, sed etiam nōn videam,* inserting *nōn* before *videam* without authority ; see note on *videam* below.

LINE 40.   **nōn,** neg. adv. ; limits *audiam ;* understood also with *videam* (= nothing which I not only do *not* hear, but do *not* also see and observe). —— **ego,** gen. *meī ;* nom. sing. of the 1st personal pron., subj. of *audiam.* —— **nōn,** neg. adv., limiting *modo* in the correlative expression *nōn modo . . . sed etiam ;* see note on *nōn,* l. 18. —— **modo,** adv. ; see l. 18. —— **audiam,** 1st pers. sing. pres. subjunct. act. of *audiō, -īre, -īvī,* or *-iī, -ītum,* 4 (root *av = to hear ;* cf. *dīω = dϝίω = I hear*) ; agrees with the subj. *ego ;* the subjunct. mood is consecutive after *quod characteristic.* —— **sed,** adversative conj. ; *sed* is opposed to *nōn modo.*

LINE 41.   **etiam** (*et + iam*), adv., intensifying the adversative notion which *sed* introduces. —— **videam,** 1st pers. sing. pres. subjunct. act. of *videō, -ēre, vīdī, vīsum,* 2 (root *vid = to see,* cf. *εἶδον = ἔϝιδον = I saw*) ; the subject *ego* is understood.   See *vidēs,* Chap. I, l. 13, for synonyms.   Observe that *nōn,* the first word of l. 40, extends its force to *videam ; nōn* need not be understood with *sentiam,* because *videam* and *sentiam* here scarcely differ in meaning and are united so closely by *-que* as to form a single idea. —— **plānēque** (*plānē + que*), *plānē* (for *placnē*) is the adv. formed from the adj. *plānus, -a, -um* (*plac-nus,* from root *plak = spread out ;* cf. πλακ-οῦς = *a flat cake, planca,* and English *plank*) ; modifies *sentiam.   Que* is the enclitic cop. conj., closely connecting *videam* and *sentiam.* —— **sentiam,** 1st pers. sing. pres. subjunct. act. of *sentiō, -īre, sensī, sensum,* 4 ; the subj. *ego* is understood ; *sentiam* is joined by *que* to *videam,* and both verbs are in the consecutive subjunct. like *audiam* above.   *Sentiō* is commonly used of intellectual perception, but lit. it = *I perceive,* i.e. by any of the senses, e.g. *hearing, sight, smell, taste,* or *touch ;* joined closely by *que* to *videam, sentiam* became practically synonymous with it.

LINE 1.   **Recōgnōsce,** 2d pers. sing. pres. imperative act. of *recōgnōscō, -ere, recōgnōvī, recōgnitum,* 3 (*re = again + cōgnōscō = I examine*) ; the subj. *tū* is implied in the personal ending. —— **tandem** (*tam + dem*), adv. ; see Chap. I, l. 1, and references.   *Tandem* is not so much temporal here (*at length*), as transitional (*however*), passing to a new

night before last;	illam	superiōrem:	iam intellegēs multō 2
and you will at once	*that*	*next before last:*	*now you will understand by much*
perceive that I keep	mē	vigilāre ācrius ad	salūtem quam tē 3
sharper watch for the	*me*	*to watch more sharply for*	*the safety than you*
state's safety than	ad	perniciem reī pūblicae.	Dīcō tē 4
you do for its de-	*for*	*the destruction of the commonwealth.*	*I declare you*
struction. I say that			

subject from an old one, as if the latter had been thrashed out completely. —— **mēcum** (*mē + cum*), *mē* is the abl. sing. of *ego;* obj. of *cum. Cum* is the prep. with the abla-tive; governs *mē. Cum* is enclitic (appended to end of the word it governs) when its object is a personal, reflexive, or relative pronoun. —— **noctem,** acc. sing. of *nox, noctis,* f. 3d; direct obj. of *recōgnōsce.*

LINE 2. **illam,** acc. sing. f. of the demonstr. pron. *ille, illa, illud;* agrees with *noctem;* observe that *illam,* by following *noctem,* throws emphasis upon it. —— **superiō-rem,** acc. sing. f. of the adj. *superior, -ius* (comparative of rare *superus, -a, -um;* superl. *suprēmus* and *summus;* see note on *superiōre,* Chap. I, l. 13): agrees with *noctem;* as in Chap. I, l. 13, *superior nox = the night before last,* i.e. the night of Nov. 6th–7th, as opposed to *haec nox* or *proxima nox = last night.* The same night, viz. of Nov. 6th–7th, is referred to as *priōre nocte,* l. 5 below, *priōre* being used to avoid a repetition of the adj. *superior* in this line. Of course the allusion is to the meeting of the conspirators held at the house of Laeca (see Introduction). —— **iam,** temporal adv., with *intellegēs. Iam* marks something as being present in the future, the past, or the present, according to the tense of the verb which *iam* modifies. *Iam* is frequently used in combinations, e.g. *iam tunc, iam prīdem, iam diū,* etc. —— **intellegēs,** 2d pers. sing. fut. ind. act. of *intellegō, -ere, intellēxī, intellectum,* 3 (*inter + legō*); the personal ending *-ēs* implies the subj. *tū.* Remember that *intelligēs* would be an incorrect form, though it is to be found in numerous editions of the classics; so *neglegō,* not *negligō.* For synonyms, etc., refer to the note on *intellegit,* Chap. I, l. 17. Observe that, whereas we should in English couple the imperative and the future by the conj. *and,* e.g. *review with me that night, the night before last,* AND *you will comprehend,* etc., Cicero invariably omits the conjunc-tion, no matter if the future be modified by *iam,* etc., or not. Later writers, e.g. esp. Seneca, connect by *et,* as in a very similar passage, *recōgnōsce et intellegēs,* Seneca. —— **multō,** adverbial abl. n. (cf. *multum,* adverbial acc.) of *multus, -a, -um,* or, better, abl. sing. n. of *multus,* marking the *measure of difference;* modifies *ācrius.* A. & G. 250; B. 223; G. 403; H. 423.

LINE 3. **mē,** acc. sing. of *ego;* subj.-acc. of *vigilāre* in the acc. and inf. construction after *intellegēs* (a *verbum sentiendī*). —— **vigilāre,** pres. inf. act. of *vigilō, -āre, -āvī, -ātum,* 1 (through adj. *vigil = watchful,* from root *vag = to be awake, to be active* or *strong;* cf. *vigeō = I am lively, augeō = I make lively,* hence *increase,* ὑγιής = *healthy,* etc.); agrees with the subj.-acc. *mē* in the object-clause after *intellegēs.* —— **ācrius,** com-parative adv.; modifies *vigilāre. Ācrius* is the compar. of *ācriter,* superl. *ācerrimē;* all are formed regularly from the adj. *ācer, ācris, ācre,* 3d, compar. *ācrior,* superl. *ācerrimus.* A. & G. 148, *b, c;* 92; B. 76, and 77, 1; G. 92, 1 and 2; 93; H. 304, 306. —— **ad,** prep. + the acc.; gov. *salūtem; ad = with a view to, with regard to.* —— **salutem,** acc. sing. of *salūs, -ūtis,* f. 3d (akin to *salvus*); governed by the prep. *ad.* —— **quam,** adv., introducing *tē ad perniciem* in the comparative clause after the compar. adv. *ācrius,* in opposition to *mē ad salūtem;* see note on *quam,* Chap. I, l. 2. —— **tē,** acc. sing. of *tū;* joined to *mē* by the adv. of comparison *quam.*

LINE 4. **ad,** prep. with the acc.; gov. *perniciem; ad* in the same sense as above. —— **perniciem,** acc. sing. of *perniciēs, perniciēī,* f. 5th (*per + nex,* cf. *necō = I kill*);

5 priōre	nocte	vēnisse	inter	you came the night
next before last	*on the night*	*to have come*	*among*	before last into the
				quarter of the Sickle-
6 falcāriōs —	nōn	agam	obscūrē —	makers — I shall
the scythe-makers —	*not*	*I will discuss (it)*	*obscurely —*	speak quite plainly
				— to the house of
7 in	M.	Laecae	domum;	convēnisse	Marcus Laeca; that
into	*Marcus*	*of Laeca*	*the house;*	*to have assembled*	several others, accom-

governed by the prep. *ad;* see synonyms under *pestem*, Chap. I, l. 27. —— **reī**, gen. sing. of *rēs, reī*, f. 5th; objective gen., limiting *salūtem* and *perniciem;* this gen. might be considered subjective so far as it limits *salūtem*, e.g. *the state's safety*, but it is better to take it as objective, e.g. *with a view to the saving of the state.* —— **pūblicae**, gen. sing. f. of the adj. *pūblicus, -a, -um* (akin to *populus*); qualifies *reī*. —— **Dīcō**, 1st pers. sing. pres. ind. act. of *dīcō, -ere, dīxī, dictum*, 3; the subj. *ego* is implied. Observe the emphatic position of *dīcō;* Cicero abruptly passes from rhetorical harangue to undisguised denunciation and accusation (cf. *nōn agam obscūrē* below). —— **tē**, acc. sing. of *tū;* subj.-acc. of *venisse* in the indirect discourse introduced by *dīcō.*

LINE 5. **priōre**, abl. sing. f. of the compar. adj. *prior, prius;* agrees with *nocte; priōre = superiōre*, i.e. *on the night before last*, Nov. 6th-7th. *Prior* and *prīmus* are the compar. and superl. adj. respectively formed from the prep. or adv. *prō;* no positive; cf. *propior* and *prōximus* from prep. *prope.* Some comparative adjectives formed from adverbs or prepositions have a positive, e.g. (*suprā*, adv. and prep.) pos. *superus* (rare), compar. *superior*, superl. *suprēmus* and *summus.* —— **nocte**, abl. sing. of *nox, noctis*, f. 3d; abl. of *time when*, with *venisse.*—— **vēnisse**, perf. inf. act. of *veniō, -īre, vēnī, ventum*, 4 (root *ga, gva*, or *gvan* = Latin *ven;* cf. Greek βα in βαίνω = *I go*); agrees with the subj.-acc. *tē* in *ōrātiō oblīqua* after *dīcō;* the direct thought of Cicero was *tū vēnistī inter falcāriōs.* The perf. inf. is due to the fact that the action expressed by *vēnisse* was prior in time to that expressed by the leading verb *dīcō;* the rule is that the tenses of the inf. in direct discourse are pres., perf. = past, or future relatively to the leading verb. A. & G. 336; B. 317; G. 530, 531; H. 537.—— **inter**, prep. with the acc.; gov. *falcāriōs.*

LINE 6. **falcāriōs**, acc. plur. of *falcārius, -ī*, m. 2d (from *falx, falcis*, f. 3d = *a scythe;* the root idea is *crookedness*, cf. *flectō* = *I bend*, and φάλκης = *a bent piece of ship-timber, a ship's rib*); governed by the prep. *inter; inter falcāriōs* is an idiomatic expression, = lit. *among the sickle-makers*, hence, as the followers of certain occupations in Rome often occupied a certain neighborhood, *in the Sickle-makers' Quarter;* cf. *the Latin Quarter* of Paris, and Harley St., the great London doctors' street. Livy has a similar expression, *inter līgnāriōs* = *on Carpenter Street.* —— **nōn**, neg. adv.; limits *agam; nōn agam obscūrē* is in parenthesis, and signifies that Cicero does not intend to indicate the mere neighborhood where the conspirators met, but to name the actual house, viz. that of M. Laeca. —— **agam**, 1st pers. sing. fut. ind. act. of *agō, -ere, ēgī, actum*, 3; the subj. is *ego* understood; *agam* = *I will deal with the matter (treat of it, discuss it)*, a common meaning of this verb of many senses; the object is *rem*, or some such word understood, or we may regard *agam* as used absolutely. —— **obscūrē**, adv. (formed from the adj. *obscūrus, -a, -um, ob* + root *sku* = *to cover*, cf. *scūtum* = a *covering* thing, hence in war, *a shield*); modifies *agam; obscūrē* is opposed to *apertē*, hence the parenthesis = *agam apertē, I will speak openly.*

LINE 7. **in**, prep.; governs the acc. *domum*, expressing motion. —— **Marcī** (abbreviated M.), gen. sing. of *Marcus*, m. 2d; *praenōmen* of Laeca; poss. gen. limiting *domum.* —— **Laecae**, gen. sing. of *Laeca*, m. 1st; the *cōgnōmen* or family name of Marcus; pass. gen., limiting *domum.* This man belonged to the *gēns Porcia*, hence his full name is *Marcus Porcius Laeca.* He was a senator of good ancestry, and took a prominent part

| plices in the same mad crime, gathered in the same place. Dare you deny it? Why are you silent? I shall prove your guilt, if you are try- | eōdem (complūrēs) ēiusdem (āmentiae) 8
 in the same place several same of the madness
 scelerisque sociōs. Num negāre audēs? 9
 and of crime partners. Surely not to deny (it) you dare?
 quid tacēs? convincam, sī negās; 10
 why are you silent? I shall convict (you) if you deny (it); |

in Catiline's conspiracy, as may be gathered from the fact that Cicero's death was resolved upon in his house (see Introduction). —— **domum**, acc. sing. of *domus, -ūs,* f. 4th (also some 2d decl. forms); governed by the prep. *in.* —— **convēnisse**, perf. inf. act. of *conveniō, -īre, convēnī, conventum,* 4 (*con + veniō*); agrees with the subj.-acc. *sociōs* in indirect discourse after *dīcō,* l. 4 ; the same effect is gained in Latin, by omitting *et* between the two object-clauses *tē vēnisse* and *sociōs convēnisse,* as in English.

LINE 8. **eōdem** (*eō +* suffix *-dem*), adv., formed from the determinate pron. *īdem, eadem, idem,* exactly as *eō* from *is, ea, id;* modifies *convēnisse* and = *in M. Laecae domum.* —— **complūrēs**, acc. of the plur. adj. *complūrēs,* neut. *complūra* or *complūria,* gen. *complūrium* (*con + plūrēs, plūrēs* being the plur. of *plus,* the compar. of *multus*); agrees with the subj.-acc. *sociōs,* or may be regarded as substantival and the subj.-acc. of *convēnisse.* Sallust gives the names and rank of the conspirators who attended the meeting mentioned here. —— **ēiusdem**, gen. sing. f. of the determinative pron. *īdem, eadem, idem* (*is + dem*); agrees with *āmentiae,* and understood in the neut. with *sceleris.* —— **āmentiae**, gen. sing. of *āmentia,* f. 1st (from adj. *āmēns = out of one's mind; ā* marking separation, *+ mēns = mind*); objective gen., with *sociōs;* this gen. is usual with adjectives signifying *participation* (as *socius*), *fulness, knowledge, power,* etc. A. & G. 218, *a;* B. 204, 1; G. 374; H. 399, I. *Amentiae scelerisque = criminal madness,* and is an example of the figure *hendiadys,* i.e. the use of two nouns to express an idea that might be conveyed by a single noun + a modifier : cf. the well-known Vergilian example, *paterīs lībāmus et aurō = we pour libations from bowls and gold,* i.e. *from golden bowls.*

LINE 9. **scelerisque** (*sceleris + que*), *sceleris* is the gen. sing. of *scelus,* n. 3d; objective gen. with *sociōs,* like *āmentiae,* to which it is joined by *que.* Synonyms : (1) *facinus* (from *faciō*) = *a deed,* generally in a bad sense = *misdeed,* unless remarked in some way as commendable, e.g. by an adj., as in Sallust, *praeclārī facinoris;* (2) *maleficium* (*malus + faciō*) = *misdeed,* the generic term; (3) *flāgitium = misdeed,* esp. of one done in the heat of passion; root *bharg =* Latin *flag = to burn; flāgitium* and *facinus* imply a less degree of moral guilt than *scelus;* (4) *scelus = a crime;* (5) *nefās* (*ne + fās,* something not to be spoken of) = *a crime* against the gods; (6) *parricīdium* (*pater + caedō,* hence lit. *the murder of one's father*) = *a horrible crime,* esp. *treason* and *revolution;* this is the worst form of guilt, except *nefās.* —— **sociōs**, acc. plur. m. of the adj. *socius, -a, -um* (akin to *sequor*); may be regarded (1) as a noun and subj.-acc. of *convēnisse,* or (2) as an adj. modifying *complūrēs,* in which case *complūrēs* must be substantival and subj.-acc. of *convēnisse.* —— **Num**, interrog. particle, introducing a question and implying an answer in the negative. —— **negāre**, pres. inf. act. of *negō, -āre, -āvī, -ātum,* 1; objective complementary inf. with *audēs. Negō* is always used instead of *dīcō . . . nōn,* in making a negative indirect statement. —— **audēs**, 2d pers. sing. pres. ind. of the semi-deponent verb *audeō, -ēre, ausus sum,* 2 ; the subj. *tū* is implied. Remember that a semi-deponent is a verb with active meaning and active present-stem tenses, but which lacks an active perf. stem and supplies these tenses in the passive form like a deponent ; whence the name semi-deponent.

LINE 10. **quid**, acc. sing. n. of the interrog. pron. *quis, quae, quid;* adverbial acc. = *why ?* This acc. may be classed under the wide head of accusatives of the *inner*

11	vīdeō	enim	esse	hīc	in	senātū	quōsdam,	ing to deny it; for I
	I see	*for*	*to be*	*here*	*in*	*the senate*	*certain men,*	see that there are

here in the Senate

12	quī	tēcum	ūnā	fuērunt.	Ō	dī	some who were pres-
	who	*with you*	*together*	*were.*	*Oh*	*gods*	ent with you. Ye

object, to which the *cognate* acc. belongs; it is very common with neuter adjectives and pronouns. A. & G. 238; 240, *a*; B. 176, esp. 3; G. 333; H. 378. —— **tacēs**, 2d pers. sing. pres. ind. act. of *taceō, -ēre, -uī, -itum*, 2; the subj. *tū* is understood. Synonyms: (1) *tacēre = to be silent, not to speak*, as opposed to *loquī*; (2) *silēre = to be silent or quiet*, cf. *silentium*, as opposed to *strepere = to make a noise*. —— **convincam**, 1st pers. sing. fut. ind. act. of *convincō, -ere, convīcī, convictum*, 3 (*con + vincō*); the subj. implied is *ego*. *Convincam* is the fut., and not the pres. subjunct., which would require *negēs* instead of *negās* and = *I should prove it, if you were to deny it:* the condition, however, is a logical one, hence the ind. in *protasis* and *apodosis = I shall prove it, if you are denying it now*, i.e. denying it by your silence, expression, and general bearing. A. & G. 306; B. 302; G. 595; H. 508. —— **sī**, conditional conj., introducing the *protasis*, *sī negās*. —— **negās**, 2d pers. sing. pres. ind. act. of *negō, -āre, -āvī, -ātum*, 1; the subj. implied is *tū*.

LINE 11. **vīdeō**, 1st pers. sing. pres. ind. act. of *vīdeō, -ēre, vīdī, vīsum*, 2; the subj. is *ego*, i.e. Cicero, understood. —— **enim**, causal conj. (see note on *enim*, Chap. II, l. 17); connects its own clause with the preceding one, in order to explain it. Cicero's meaning is that he will cross-question some of the senators who attended the meeting at Laeca's house, and by their evidence prove (*convincam*) Catiline's guilt, if he is trying to deny it (*sī negās*). —— **esse**, pres. inf. of *sum, esse, fuī*, the copula; agrees with the subj.-acc. *quōsdam* in the acc. and inf. construction dependent on *vīdeō*. —— **hīc**, adv. of place; = *here*, and modifies *esse* predicatively; *hīc* is further defined by *in senātū*. Many adverbs are formed from the demonstr. pronouns, cf. *hūc = hither, illim, illinc, hinc*, etc. —— **in**, prep.; gov. the abl. *senātū*, marking *place in which*. —— **senātū**, abl. sing. of *senātus, -ūs*, m. 4th; governed by the prep. *in*. —— **quōsdam**, acc. plur. m. of the indef. pron. *quīdam, quaedam, quiddam* (adjectival neut. *quoddam; quī + dam*); substantival, = *certain men;* subj.-acc. of *esse* in the acc. and inf. construction after *vīdeō*. *Quōsdam = certain men*, whom I know but whose names I need not divulge. Sallust gives us the names of eleven patrician and four equestrian accomplices of Catiline, and Cicero must have been as well informed as Sallust, especially as he obtained his information from a conspirator, through Fulvia.

LINE 12. **quī**, nom. plur. m. of the rel. pron. *quī, quae, quod;* agrees with the antecedent *quōsdam* in gender and number, and is subj. of *fuērunt* in its own clause. —— **tēcum** (*tē + cum*), *tē* is the abl. sing. of the 2d personal pron. *tū;* governed by *cum. Cum* is the prep. + the abl.; governing *tē*, and enclitic, as it always is with the personal, reflexive, and relative pronouns, cf. *sēcum, quibuscum*. —— **ūnā**, adv., = *together, at the same time;* modifies *fuērunt. Ūnā* is teh abl. f. sing.; cf. other adverbs, e.g. *quā = where, aliquā = somewhere*, etc. —— **fuērunt**, 3d pers. plur. perf. ind. of *sum;* agrees with the subj. *quī. Fuērunt* is the historical perf. or perf. indefinite (*aorist*), stating past action without reference to its duration. —— **Ō**, interjection; expressing indignation, with the voc. *dī. Ō* is an exclamation of joy, astonishment, sorrow, desire, etc., according to the context; it is conjoined with the nom., acc., and even gen. cases, as well as the voc., and is used with particles, e.g. *ō sī, ō utinam*, in wishes. —— **dī**, voc. plur. of *deus, -ī*, m. 2d (root *dyn = to shine;* akin to Ζεύς, δῖος, diēs, Iovis, dīvus, etc.); addressed in exclamation. The declension of *deus* is noteworthy: the voc. sing. is *deus;* in the plur. additional forms are found, e.g. nom. and voc., *deī, diī*, or *dī;* gen. *deōrum* and *deūm;* dat. and abl. *deīs, diīs*, and *dīs*.

deathless' gods! | immortālēs! | ubinam gentium sumus? 13
where on earth are | *immortal!* | *where of nations (= on earth) are we?*
we? in what city are | in quā urbe | vīvimus? quam rem pūblicam 14
we living? what is | *in what city* | *do we live? what commonwealth*
the government we | habēmus? | Hīc, hīc sunt in nostrō 15
have? Here, here, | *have we?* | *Here, here there are in our*
among our own |

LINE 13. **immortālēs**, voc. plur. m. of the adj. *immortālis, -e*, 3d (*in* = *not*, + *mortalis* = *mortal*, from *mors*, *death*); agrees with *dī*. —— **ubinam** (*ubi* + *nam*), interrog. adv. = *where on earth*; introduces the question. *Nam* is not uncommonly appended to interrog. particles and lends an air of surprise to the questions they introduce, just as γάρ = *for* does in Greek, cf. *quisnam;* the force of *nam* is just the same in the question if the interrog. and *nam* be separated from one another (*tmesis*). A. & G. 210, *f*; B. 90, 2, *d*; G. 498, NOTE 5; H. 351, 4. —— **gentium**, gen. plur. of *gēns, gentis*, f. 3d (root *gan* = Latin *gen* = *to beget;* cf. *gīgnō, genus*, γίγνομαι and γένος); partitive gen., after *ubinam*. This partitive gen. is idiomatic, cf. *ubi terrārum, id temporis*, etc., and is developed from the simple partitive gen. The adverbs with this gen. express *place* as *ubi*, *extent* and *quantity* as *eō arrogantiae* = *to such a degree of presumption*. This gen. is common with neuter adjectives and pronouns, cf. *quid consilī*, Chap. I, l. 15, and in poetry and late prose (esp. Tacitus) in such expressions as *strāta viārum* = *paved streets* (Virgil) and *tacita suspīciōnum* = *silent suspicions* (Tacitus). A. & G. 216, *a*, 4; B. 201, 3; G. 372, NOTE 3; H. 397, 4. For synonyms, see note on *populī*, Chap. I, l. 6. *Gentēs* = *the nations*, i.e. *the world*, as in the phrase *iūs gentium;* for the distinction between *gēns, nātiō, populus*, etc., refer to the note on *populī*, Chap. I, l. 6. A special meaning of *gēns* is *clan*, or *house* (not *family*), each *gēns* embracing several *familiae* which traced back descent to a common ancestor and were in reference to each other *gentīlēs;* the gentile name was the *nōmen* and terminated in *-ius*, e.g. *Pūblius Cornēlius Scīpiō*, and the family name was the *cōgnōmen*, as *Scīpiō* above. —— **sumus**, 1st pers. plur. pres. ind. of *sum, esse, fuī;* the subj. *nōs* is implied by the personal ending.

LINE 14. **in**, prep.; gov. the abl. *urbe*. —— **quā**, abl. sing. f. of the interrog. pron. and adj. *quis, quae, quid;* agrees with *urbe*. —— **urbe**, abl. sing. of *urbs, urbis*, f. 3d; governed by the prep. *in*. —— **vīvimus**, 1st pers. plur. pres. ind. act. of *vīvō, -ere, vīxī, victum*, 3; the subj. *nōs* is implied. —— **quam**, acc. sing. f. of the interrog. pron. *quis, quae, quid;* agrees with *urbem*. One editor remarks that *quā* and *quam* almost = the abl. and acc. f. of *quālis* = *what sort of* (i.e. taking *quā* and *quam* as abl. and acc. of interrog. *quī, quae, quod* = *what sort of*); but this is not the meaning. Cicero rhetorically represents himself as dazed by the guilt of Catiline and the other senators, and asks where in the world he is, — can the city be Rome, can the state be the Roman state, for such crime to exist in it? —— **rem**, acc. sing. of *rēs, reī*, f. 5th; direct obj. of *habēmus*. —— **pūblicam**, acc. sing. f. of the adj. *pūblicus, -a, -um;* agrees with *rem;* as usual *rem pūblicam* = *the state*.

LINE 15. **habēmus**, 1st pers. plur. pres. ind. act. of *habeō, -ēre, -uī, -itum*, 2; the implied subj. is *nōs*, i.e. the speaker and his audience. —— **Hīc** (formed from the demonstr. pron. *hīc, haec, hōc*), demonstr. adv. of place; modifies *sunt*. —— **hīc**, adv. (as above); repeated for emphasis, and expressive of intense indignation and sorrow. —— **sunt**, 3d pers. plur. pres. ind. of *sum;* the subj. understood is an indef. pron. *quidam* or *nōnnūllī*, antecedent of *quī characteristic*, l. 18. —— **in**, prep.; gov. the abl. *numerō*. —— **nostrō**, abl. sing. m. of the poss. pron. *noster, nostra, nostrum* (*nōs*) of the 1st pers. plur.; agrees with *numerō*.

16	numerō,	patrēs	cōnscrīptī,	in	hōc	orbis
	number,	*fathers*	*enrolled,*	*in*	*this*	*of the circle*

17	terrae	sānctissimō	gravissimōque	cōnsiliō,
	of the earth	*most reverend*	*and most dignified*	*council,*

18	quī	dē	nostrō	omnium	interitū,
	(men) who	*about*	*our (= of us)*	*all*	*the overthrow,*

number, Conscript Fathers, in this the most venerable and eminent council of the whole world there are men who are plotting for the destruction of one

LINE 16. **numerō**, abl. sing. of *numerus, -ī*, m. 2d (root *nam = to allot, to number ;* cf. *nummus = a coin*, and *νέμω = I distribute*), governed by the prep. *in*.——**patrēs**, voc. plur. of *pater, patris*, m. 3d (root *pa = to nourish*, cf. πατήρ); the case of address. For note on *patrēs = senators*, etc., and the phrase *patrēs cōnscrīptī*, refer to the notes on these words in ll. 23 and 24 of Chap. II.—— **cōnscrīptī**, voc. plur. m. of *cōnscrīptus, -a, -um*, perf. part. pass. of *cōnscrībō, -ere, cōnscrīpsī, cōnscrīptum*, 3 (*con + scrībō*); qualifies *patrēs*.—— **in**, prep.; gov. the abl. *cōnsiliō*.—— **hōc**, abl. sing. n. of the demonstr. pron. *hīc, haec, hōc ;* agrees with *cōnsiliō*. Observe how Cicero emphasizes the dignity and sanctity of the Senate, and heightens it by placing *cōnsiliō* at the end of the clause and its attributes between the prep. and its object.—— **orbis**, gen. sing. of *orbis*, m. 3d ; poss. gen., limiting *cōnsiliō*. *Orbis terrae* or more commonly *orbis terrārum = the world, the whole earth ; mundus, -ī*, m. 2d = *the universe*.

LINE 17. **terrae**, gen. sing. of *terra*, f. 1st (root *tars = to be dry ;* hence *terra = dry land ;* cf. *torreō = I dry or burn*); subjective gen., limiting *orbis*. Synonyms: (1) *terra = a country ; land*, as opposed to water ; (2) *tellūs = the globe* (poetical, but once in Cic.); (3) *humus = the ground*, the surface of earth (*humilis = low*); (4) *solum = the soil, the ground*, upon which men walk (root *sol = to go*); (5) *ager = land* under cultivation ; (6) *rūs = the country*, as opposed to urban life.—— **sānctissimō**, abl. sing. n. of *sānctissimus, -a, -um*, superl. of the adj. *sanctus, -a, -um* (perf. part. pass. of *sānçiō, -īre, sānxī, sānctum*, 4 = *I consecrate ;* root *sa = whole and sound*, cf. *sānus*, and Greek σαός or σῶς); agrees with *cōnsiliō*. Synonyms: (1) *sacer = sacred*, i.e. consecrated to some deity, and is generally applied to inanimate things, e.g. *sacra āra, sacer lūcus ;* sometimes used of persons in reference to their office, e.g. *sacer vatēs ;* (2) *sacrōsānctus = consecrated*, hence inviolable, applied to what has by a public decree and a solemn oath been declared sacred, e.g. *sacrōsānctus tribūnus, sacrōsānctum foedus ;* (3) *sānctus* is the generic word, and all things are *sāncta* which are *sacra* or *sacrōsāncta*, but not vice versa ; thus *dīvīna* are *sāncta*, but *hūmāna* are *sacra* or *sacrōsāncta*.—— **gravissimōque** (*gravissimō + que*), *gravissimō* is the abl. sing. n. of *gravissimus, -a, -um*, the superl. of the adj. *gravis, -e*, 3d (Latin root *gar = Greek βαρ ;* so *gravis = gar-uis*, cf. *βαρύς = heavy*); agrees with *cōnsiliō ;* joined by *que* to *sānctissimō*. *Gravis* is directly opposed to *levis*, not only in the literal sense = *heavy*, of weight (*levis = light*), but in all its extended and figurative meanings, some of which are (1) *difficult, severe*, (2) *important, serious*, (3) *dignified, venerable, seriously-minded*. *Que* is the enclitic cop. conj., connecting *sānctissimō* and *gravissimō*, the two attributes of *cōnsiliō*.—— **cōnsiliō**, abl. sing. of *cōnsilium, -ī*, n. 2d (akin to verb *cōnsulō*, 3 = *I deliberate*); governed by the prep. *in ;* by *cōnsiliō* is meant the Senate, cf. the 4th Philippic, in which Cicero calls the Senate *orbis terrae consilium*. The root of *cōnsilium* is stated by Wilkins to be *sel* or *sol*, as in *solium = a throne*, and akin to *sed* in *sēdēs ; cōnsilium* denotes a chosen body of counsellors (other meanings are (1) *plan*, (2) *advice*); *concilium, -ī*, n. 2d only has the concrete sense of "a large general meeting" of people called together, root *kal = to call*, as in Greek *καλέω = I call*.

LINE 18. **quī**, nom. plur. m. of the rel. pron. *quī, quae, quod ;* agrees with an indef. antecedent understood as subj. of *sunt*, e.g. *quīdam*, and is the subj. of *cōgitent* in the

and all of us, for the	quī	dē	hūius	urbis	atque	adeō	dē 19
ruin of this city and	*who*	*about*	*this*	*of city*	*and*	*further*	*about*
even for the ruin of	orbis		terrārum		exitiō	cōgitent. 20	
the whole world. I,	*of the circle*		*of lands*		*the ruin*	*are scheming.*	
the consul, see these	Hōs	ego	videō		cōnsul	et	dē 21
men and ask their	*These men*	*I*	*see*		*the consul*	*and*	*about*

rel. clause. The subjunct. *cōgitent* is consecutive, because *quī* expresses a general characteristic; the ind. may be used, in a statement of actual fact, *nōnnūllī sunt quī audent = some there are who dare*, e.g. but never in a statement of tendency; *est quī* and *sunt quī* can very rarely be used with the ind., as the phrase is a recognized expression of general characteristic. A. & G. 320, *a*; B. 283, 2; G. 631, 2; H. 503, I.—— **dē**, prep. with the abl.; gov. *interitū.*—— **nostrō**, abl. sing. m. of the poss. pron. *noster, nostra, nostrum;* agrees with *interitū.*—— **omnium**, gen. plur. m. of the adj. *omnis, -e,* 3d; idiomatic gen., agreeing by *synesis* with the gen. *nostrī* (of *nōs*) which is implied by the poss. *nostrō = dē nostrī omnium interitū;* in other words the poss. pron. represents a gen., and the gen. adj. is in apposition. We may compare Chap. III, l. 31, *nostrā quī remānsissēmus caede = caede nostrī quī remānsissēmus,* for the poss. pron. implying the gen. of the personal pronoun. In Ovid we even find *nostrōs . . . flentis ocellōs = ocellōs meī flentis,* i.e. *nostrōs* is poetical for *meōs,* representing *meī,* with which *flentis* agrees in number. A. & G. 197, *e*; B. 243, 3; G. 321, REM. 2; H. 363, 4, I. Synonyms: (1) *omnis = all,* opposed to *nēmō,* and indicates the *particulars,* as distinguished from (2) *tōtus = all, the whole,* considered *collectively;* (3) *cūnctus* (through *coiūnctus*) = *all,* i.e. together and in one mass (*coacervātim,* as Apulēius puts it); (4) *ūniversus = all,* esp. of all the parts brought into unity (*ūnus + vertō*), cf. *ūniversum = the universe;* hence the meaning *unanimous,* of the coinciding opinions of all the individuals; (5) *integer = all,* esp. *uninjured, untouched* (*in = not + tangō = I touch*).—— **interitū**, abl. sing. of *interitus, -ūs,* m. 4th; governed by the prep. *dē.*

LINE 19. **quī**, nom. plur. m. of the rel. pron.; repeated rhetorically from *quī* above (*anaphora*); more effective than the cop. conjunction *et* (or *atque*) whose place it fills, connecting *dē interitū* with *dē exitiō.*—— **dē**, prep.; gov. the abl. *exitiō* understood from *dē orbis terrārum exitiō* in the next line.—— **hūius**, gen. sing. f. of the demonstr. pron. *hīc, haec, hōc;* agrees with *urbis.*—— **urbis**, gen. sing. of *urbs,* f. 3d; poss. gen., limiting *exitiō* understood; see note on *dē* just above; *hūius urbis = Rōmae.*—— **atque**, cop. conj.; connects *dē hūius urbis* (*exitiō*) with *dē orbis terrārum exitiō.* Observe that *atque* introduces something of importance; it often adds a third member to a series. A. & G. 156, *a*; B. 341; G. 475-477; H. 554, I.—— **adeō** (*ad + eō*), adv., intensifying the addition made in *dē orbis terrārum exitiō. Adeō = so far so; usque adeō = even so far; atque adeō = and further.*—— **dē**, prep.; gov. the abl. *exitiō.* Observe that *dē* need not have been repeated from above, but Cicero prefers to repeat the prep. if he adds a new object with *atque adeō.*

LINE 20. **orbis**, gen. sing. of *orbis,* m. 3d; poss. gen., limiting *exitiō; orbis terrārum = the world,* cf. l. 16.—— **terrārum**, gen. plur. of *terra, -ae,* f. 1st; poss. gen., limiting *orbis = lit. circle of lands,* hence *the whole earth.*—— **exitiō**, abl. sing. of *exitium, -ī,* n. 2d (*ex + eō*); governed by the prep. *dē.*—— **cōgitent**, 3d pers. plur. subjunct. act. of *cōgitō, -āre, -āvī, -ātum,* I (*co = con + agitō = I turn over and over in my mind,* hence *consider thoroughly*); agrees with the subj. *quī;* the subjunct. is consecutive, with *quī* expressing characteristic.

LINE 21. **Hōs**, acc. plur. m. of the demonstr. pron. *hīc, haec, hōc;* direct obj. of *videō; hōs =* the conspirators referred to in *sunt quī cōgitent,* etc. Observe the em-

22 rē pūblicā   sententiam   rogō,   et   quōs | advice   on   matters
the commonwealth   their opinion   I ask (them),   and   whom | touching the public welfare, and as yet

phatic position of *hōs;* as Cicero spoke, he probably turned to face the guilty senators. ——**ego**, nom. sing. of the 1st personal pron. ; subj. of *videō*. *Ego* is emphatic, and in the light of the context implies self-censure ; moreover, Cicero wishes to avoid the 3d person *cōnsul videt*, and the nom. *ego* enables him to use the appositive *cōnsul.* —— **videō**, 1st pers. sing. pres. ind. act. of *videō, -ēre, vīdī, vīsum*, 2 ; agrees with the subj. *ego.* ——**cōnsul**, gen. *cōnsulis*, m. 3d ; nom. sing., in apposition with *ego.* ——**et**, cop. conj. ; connects the clauses of the verbs *videō* and *rogō.* —— **dē**, prep. ; gov. *rē pūblicā.* A. & G. 153; B. 142; G. 417, 5; H. 434, 1.

LINE 22. **rē**, abl. sing. of *rēs, reī*, f. 5th ; governed by the prep. *dē.* ——**pūblicā**, abl. sing. f. of the adj. *pūblicus, -a, -um ;* agrees with *rē*. In the phrase *dē rē pūblicā sententiam rogō* we see the original meaning of *rēs pūblica = the commonwealth*, i.e. *common weal*, the welfare of the community : the development of *rēs pūblica* into a practical synonym of *cīvitās = state* follows naturally ; *rēs pūblica = the state*, with reference to its constitution, *cīvitās = the state*, considered as a community of *cīvēs.* ——**sententiam**, acc. sing. of *sententia, -ae*, f. 1st (from verb *sentiō*, = (1) *opinion*, (2) *declared opinion*, (3) *sentence, decision*) ; acc. of the secondary obj. ; obj. of *rogō.* Verbs of *asking* and *teaching* may govern two accusatives, (1) of the person, the direct obj., (2) of the thing, the secondary object ; this construction is most common with *doceō, rogō, poscō*, but used also sometimes with *interrogō ōrō, pōstulō, flāgitō*, and a few others. Thus in *hōs sententiam rogō, hōs* is the direct, *sententiam* the secondary obj. of *rogō.* With *rogō* we do not find a noun (except *sententiam*) as secondary object nearly so often as we find a neut. pronoun, e.g. *mē eadem rogāvit.* When the verb of asking is passive, the direct obj. of the active verb becomes subj., and the secondary object is retained in the acc. (esp. with *rogō ;* less common with other verbs), e.g. *hī sententiam rogantur = these men are asked their opinion.* The double acc. of inner and outer object is found also with *cēlō = I hide*, e.g. *hōc tē cēlō = I hide this from you.* Other verbs of asking prefer the abl. with a prep. to the acc. of the person (direct obj.), e.g. *ā tē hōc petō (quaerō, postulō*, etc.) *= I ask (demand) this* (direct obj. here) *of you.* A. & G. 239, *c* ; B. 178 ; G. 339 ; H. 374. Synonyms : *opinion* = (1) *sententia*, if well grounded and the result of reflection ; (2) *opīniō*, if mere subjective fancy : *to vote* = (1) *sententiam dīcere*, of senators and judges ; (2) *suffrāgium ferre*, of the people at the *comitia.* —— **rogō**, 1st pers. sing. pres. ind. act. of *rogō, -āre, -āvī, -ātum*, 1 ; joined by *et* to *videō ;* the subj. implied is *ego.* Cicero represents himself as indignant that he, the consul. should consult in the Senate touching the safety of the state men who ought to have been executed for conspiring to overthrow it. *Rogō sententiam* was the formula used by the consul or presiding magistrate in the Senate in asking individual opinions ; any one who spoke on a subject was said *dīcere sententiam* or *cēnsēre.* A certain rule of precedence was adhered to by the magistrate who called the meeting ; he first asked the opinion of the consul elect, then that of the *princeps senātūs*, then that of particular *cōnsūlārēs, praetōriī*, etc. Synonyms : *I ask, request* = (1) *rogō* (perhaps same root as ὀρέγειν = *to reach out for*), the common word ; (2) *petō = I demand ;* akin to *impetus ;* (3) *ōrō (ōs* = the *mouth*) *= I ask*, with formal language ; (4) *obsecrō = I adjure, beseech*, by something holy ; (5) *implorō = I beseech*, esp. *deōs*, in sorrow ; (6) *supplicō = I supplicate* (*sub + plicō*, hence *bending the knee*) ; (7) *precārī = to pray (prēx = a prayer).* ——**et**, cop. conj., connecting the clauses whose verbs are *rogō* and *vulnerō.* —— **quōs**, acc. plur. m. of the rel. pron. *quī, quae, quod ;* agrees in gender and number with its logical antecedent *eōs* in the main clause ; *quōs* may be called the direct obj. of *oportēbat* or, better, the subj.-acc. of the inf. *trucīdārī* in dependence on *oportēbat.*

I do not stab with the words of my mouth those who ought to have been mercilessly slain with the sword. To resume, Catiline,—you attended that night at Laeca's house ;	ferrō	trucīdārī	oportēbat,	eōs 28
	with the sword	*to be slaughtered*	*it behoved*	*them*
	nōndum	vōce	vulnerō. Fuistī	igitur 24
	not yet	*with my voice*	*I wound.* *You were*	*so*
	apud	Laecam	illā	nocte, 25
	at (the house of)	*Laeca*	*that*	*on night,*

LINE 23. **ferrō**, abl. sing. of *ferrum, -ī*, n. 2d ; abl. of the means or instrument, with *trucīdārī. Ferrum* = lit. *iron*, hence by *metonymy* of an *iron* weapon, esp. *a sword.* A. & G. 386 ; B. no ref. ; G. no ref. ; H. 637, III. The axe (*securis*) was carried by the lictors of the kings of Rome and later of the consuls (when outside Rome) as a sign of *imperium* and power of life and death ; but a sword or axe was rarely used as the weapon of execution of condemned criminals. Instead, the condemned man was strangled, *laqueō* = *with a noose*, e.g. Lentulus, and Cethēgus. —— **trucīdārī**, pres. inf. pass. of *trucīdō, -āre, -āvī, -ātuni*, 1 (*trux* = *savage* + *caedō* = *I kill*); agrees with the subj.-acc. *quōs* in the object-clause of *oportēbat.* For synonyms, refer to the note on *occīdit,* Chap. I, l. 38. Observe that the pres. inf. is used (the ordinary construction) instead of the perf. part. pass. + *esse ;* see the note on *interfectum,* Chap. II, l. 20. **oportēbat**, 3d pers. sing. imperf. ind. act. of the impersonal verb *oportet, oportēre, oportuit,* 2 ; the object clause *quōs trucīdārī* is really the subj. of *oportēbat.* The imperf. tense denotes that the necessity for the execution of the conspirators was not momentary in the past, but continuous, i.e. all the actions of the conspirators called for their execution. This tense, then, represents some action as regarded in progress ; not infrequently it may regard the action as begun (inceptive imperf.) or intended (conative imperfect). A. & G. 277 ; B. 260 ; G. 231–234 ; H. 468, 469. —— **eōs**, acc. plur. m. of the demonstr. pron. *is, ea, id ;* direct obj. of *vulnerō ; is* is preferred to the other demonstr. pronouns as the antecedent of *quī*, when the rel. describes the otherwise undescribed antecedent.

LINE 24. **nōndum** (*nōn* + *dum*), temporal adv. ; limits *vulnerō.* —— **vōce**, abl. sing. of *vōx, vōcis*, f. 3d (root *vak* = *to speak, call ;* cf. Greek root ϝεπ, as in ἔπος = ϝέπος = *a word*, and ὄψ = ϝόψ = *voice*) ; abl. of the means, with *vulnerō ; vōce* = here *verbō* or *nōminātim*, i.e. Cicero did not proceed against them yet either by naming them or by bringing them to trial. Synonyms : *word* = (1) *verbum*, as a portion of speech ; (2) *vōx* and *vocābulum*, as *spoken ;* (3) *aīctum* = *an apt saying.* —— **vulnerō**, 1st pers. sing. pres. ind. act. of *vulnerō, -āre, -āvī, -ātum*, 1 (*vulnus* = *a wound*) ; the subj. *ego* is implied. —— **Fuistī**, 2d pers. sing. perf. ind. of *sum, esse, fuī ;* the subj. *tū* is understood. —— **igitur**, illative conj. ; resuming the subject, *num negāre audēs ?* l. 9, where it was interrupted by the digression ll. 12–24. *Igitur* is always post-positive in Cicero. Most of the illative particles, i.e. which represent something as a consequence or sum up an argument, are prae-positive, e.g. *itaque, hīnc, inde, proptereā, quōcircā*, etc., but *ergō* may be either prae-positive or post-positive.

LINE 25. **apud**, prep. with the acc. ; gov. *Laecam. Apud* is used chiefly with persons, and has the three following senses : (1) *at the house of*, as here, (2) *in the presence of*, e.g. *apud iūdicēs*, (3) *in*, i.e. *in the writings of*, e.g. *apud Virgilium* = *in the works of Virgil ; apud* is also used (4) of place, = *at, near*, like *ad* + the acc. or *in* + the abl., and (5) in phrases, e.g. *apud mē sum* = *I am in my senses.* —— **Laecam**, acc. sing. of *Laeca, -ae*, m. 1st ; governed by the prep. *apud.* —— **illā**, abl. sing. f. of the demonstr. pron. *ille, illa, illud ;* agrees with *nocte ; illā nocte* = *priōre nocte*, l. 5, and *noctem, illam superiōrem*, l. 1, i.e. the night of Nov. 6th–7th. —— **nocte**, abl. sing. of *nox, noctis*, f. 3d ; abl. of *time when*, modifying *fuistī.*

26 Catilīna;   distribuistī   partēs   Ītaliae;   statuistī
   Catiline;   *you distributed*   *the parts*   *of Italy;*   *you arranged*

27 quō   quemque   proficīscī   placēret,
   whither   *(that) each man*   *(to) set out*   *it should be agreed;*

28 dēlēgistī   quōs   Rōmae   relinquerēs,   quōs
   you chose   *whom*   *at Rome*   *you should leave,*   *whom*

you divided off Italy into districts; you arranged where it would be best for every man to go; you picked out whom you should leave be-

---

LINE 26. **Catilīna**, voc. sing. of *Catilīna, -ae,* m. 1st; the case of address.——**distribuistī**, 2d pers. sing. perf. ind. act. of *distribuō, -ere, -uī, -ūtum,* 3 (*dis + tribuō*); the subj. *tū* is understood. We learn from Sallust, Chap. 27, that C. Mānlius was sent to Faesulae and the adjacent parts of Etrūria, A. Septimius to the Pīcēne territory, C. Jūlius to Apūlia, and others to other districts.—— **partēs**, acc. plur. of *pars, partis,* f. 3d; direct obj. of *distribuistī.*——**Ītaliae**, gen. sing. of *Ītalia,* f. 1st; partitive gen., limiting *partēs.* The name *Ītalia* is derived in popular fashion by Vergil and other Romans from a legendary hero *Ītalus,* who came from Arcadia and settled in Māgna Graecia (southern Italy). Others derive from Greek ἰταλός = Ϝιταλός = Latin *vitulus, a calf* (Oscan *vitlu*), hence *the cattle land.* More probably *Ītalia* (or *Vītalia*) = the country of the *Italī* or *Vītalī,* an ancient race probably identical with the *Siculī* (mentioned by Thūcȳdidēs in his account of Sicily). Italy proper included the following territorial divisions: Etrūria, Umbria, Pīcēnum, Samnium, Latium, Campānia, Apūlia, Lūcānia, and Bruttium.—— **statuistī**, 2d pers. sing. perf. ind. act. of *statuō, -ere, -uī, -ūtum,* 2 (*status,* from *stō = I stand,* hence *statuō = I make to stand, set up*); the subj. *tū* is understood.

LINE 27. **quō**, interrog. adv., introducing an indirect question, hence the subjunct. *placēret.* *Quō* is the adverbial abl. of *quī,* and is used: (1) interrogative, = *whither,* in direct and indirect questions; (2) relative, = *whither,* corresponding to the demonstr. adv. *eō = thither;* (3) as a final conj., when the purpose clause contains a comparative adj. or ad., e.g. *quō haec facilius faceret = in order that he might do this more easily.* —— **quemque**, acc. sing. m. of the indef. (distributive) pron. *quisque, quaeque, quidque* (adjectival neut. *quodque*); subj.-acc. of the inf. *proficīscī* in the clause of *placēret.* See the note on *quemque,* Chap. I, l. 22.—— **proficīscī**, pres. inf. of the deponent verb *proficīscor, -ī, profectus sum,* 3 (*prō = forward +* root *fac* (*fic* in many compounds, e.g. *efficiō = ex + faciō*) *= to make,* i.e. *to put,* hence *I put myself forward, I set out*) agrees with the subj.-acc. *quemque; quemque proficīscī* is the virtual subj. of the impersonal *placēret.*—— **placēret**, 3d pers. sing. imperf. subjunct. act. of *placet, placēre, placuit* or *placitum est,* 2, the impersonal verb from *placeō, -ēre, -uī, -itum,* 2; an impersonal verb has no subj.-nom., but its clause is its real subj., as *quemque proficīscī* of *placēret.* The subjunct. mood is due to the indirect question with *quō.* A. & G. 334; B. 300; G. 467; H. 528, 2; 529, I. Observe that there is an underneath idea of purpose or design in *quō placēret* as in *quōs relinquerēs,* but the latter subjunct. is due to the *adjectival* clause of design. The construction of *placet* is: (1) *ut* with the subjunct., e.g. *placitum est ut dūcerem;* (2) the acc. and inf., as in this passage; (3) if the person who forms the *resolve* is expressed, it is put in the dat. (as being the indirect obj.), e.g. *senātuī placuit.* *Placet* is often used of the decisions of official bodies.

LINE 28. **dēlēgistī**, 2d pers. sing. perf. ind. act. of *dēligō, -ere, dēlēgī, dēlectum,* 3 (*dē + legō*); the subj. implied is *tū.*—— **quōs**, acc. plur. m. of the rel. pron. *quī, quae, quod;* direct obj. of *relinquerēs.* *Quōs* is final, = *ut eōs.*—— **Rōmae**, locative case of *Rōma, -ae,* f. 1st sing.; denotes *place where,* and modifies *relinquerēs.* *Place where* is expressed by the abl. with *in,* or by the acc. with *ad* or *apud;* but in the case of the names of towns and small islands *place where* is denoted by a special case, the locative. The termination of this case in singular nouns is: *-ae* (1st decl.), *-ī* (2d decl.), *-ī* or *-e*

hind at Rome, whom	tēcum	ēdūcerēs,	dīscrīpsistī	urbis 29
you should take away	*with you*	*you should lead forth;*	*you assigned*	*of the city*
with you; you por-	partēs	ad	incendia,	cōnfīrmāstī	tē	ipsum 30
tioned out sections	*the parts*	*for*	*burning;*	*you asserted*	*you*	*(your)self*
of the city for confla-	iam	esse	exitūrum,	dīxistī	paulum	tibi 31
grations; you made	*now*	*to be*	*about to go forth;*	*you stated*	*a little*	*to you*
a definite statement						

(3d decl.); of plural names, *-īs* (1st and 2d decl.), *-ibus* (3d decl.), cf. *Corinthī = at Corinth, Gādibus = at Cadiz,* etc. The locative also survives in ordinary words, e.g. *domī = at home, humī = on the ground, vesperī = in the evening,* and a limited number of other nouns. A. & G. 258, *c*, 2 ; B. 232 ; G. 411 ; H. 48, 4 ; 51, 8 ; and 66, 4.——'relinquerēs, 2d pers. sing. imperf. subjunct. act. of *relinquō, -ere, relīquī, relīctum,* 3 (*re = behind + linquō = I leave*); agrees with the subj. *tū* understood. The subjunctives *relinquerēs* and *ēdūcerēs* are final, expressing purpose in rel. sentences of design ; *dēlēgistī quōs = dēlēgistī (virōs) ut eōs.* A. & G. 317 ; B. 282, 2 ; G. 630 ; H. 497, I. Sallust (Chap. 43) gives us interesting details, viz. that when Catiline reached Faesulae, Bestia, a tribune of the *plēbs,* was to make a speech representing Cicero as the cause of the war ; Cethēgus was to attack Cicero, and others were to murder prominent citizens in the confusion caused by the immense conflagrations which Statilius and Gabīnius were intended to start in twelve different parts of Rome. Plutarch adds that Lentulus was to be the conspirators' chief in Rome, and was directed to hold Pompey's children as hostages in case Pompey returned with his army.——quōs, acc. plur. m. of the rel. pron. *quī, quae, quod;* direct obj. of *ēdūcerēs; quōs* is final, = *ut eōs,* as above.

LINE 29. tēcum (*tē + cum*), *tē* is the abl. sing. of the 2d pers. pron. *tū; ;* governed by *cum. Cum* is the prep. with the ablative, enclitic because its object is a personal pronoun.——ēdūcerēs, 2d pers. sing. imperf. subjunct. act. of *ēdūcō, -ere, ēdūxī, ēdūctum,* 3 (*ē+dūcō*); the subj. is *tū* understood. At the meeting at Laeca's house Catiline expressed his impatient desire to join the revolutionary camp, and stated that the only hindrance to his departure was that Cicero remained alive; whereupon Cicero's murder was resolved upon at once.——dīscrīpsistī, 2d pers. sing. perf. ind. act. of *dīscrībō, -ere, dīscrīpsī, dīscrīptum,* 3 (*dī = dis + scrībō*); the subj. is *tū* implied. *Dēscrībō* (*dē + scrībō*) *= I copy off, draw, designate; dīscrībō = I assign, apportion, divide off,* and differs from *dēscrībō* by implying division; *dīscrībō* is practically a synonym of *distribuō.*——urbis, gen. sing. of *urbs,* f. 3d ; partitive gen., limiting *partēs.*

LINE 30. partēs, acc. plur. of *pars, partis,* f. 3d ; direct obj. of *dīscrīpsistī.* Sallust says Catiline divided Rome into twelve parts, in each of which a conflagration was to be started ; Plutarch in his characteristic style speaks of 100 parts, each to be fired at one and the same time.——ad, prep. with the acc. ; gov. *incendia.*——incendia, acc. plur. of *incendium, -ī,* n. 2d (*incendō*), governed by the prep. *ad.*——cōnfīrmāstī, 2d pers. sing. perf. ind. act. of *cōnfīrmō, -āre, -āvī, -ātum,* 1 (*con + firmō*); the subj. *tū* is implied. *Cōnfīrmāstī* is the contracted or syncopated form of *cōnfīrmāvistī.* The perfects in *-āvī, -ēvī* may drop the *v* before *s* and *r,* and the perf. in *-īvī* may drop the *v* before *s ;* the vowels are then contracted into one long vowel, e.g. *audīvissent = audīssent, dēlēvērunt = dēlērunt,* etc. A. & G. 128, *a,* 1 ; B. 116, 1 ; G. 131, 1 ; H. 235.——tē, acc. sing. of *tū; ;* subj.-acc. of *esse exitūrum* in the acc. and inf. object clause of *cōnfīrmāstī.* —— ipsum, acc. sing. m. of the demonstr. pron. *ipse, ipsa, ipsum; ;* agrees with and intensifies *tē.*

LINE 31. iam, temporal adv. ; modifies *esse exitūrum; iam* with the future depicts something as *on the very point* of being done.——esse exitūrum, fut. inf. act. of *exeō, exīre, exiī, exitum,* irreg. (*ex + eō*); agrees with the subj.-acc. *tē* in the acc. and inf.

82 **esse etiam nunc morae, quod ego vīverem.**
　to be　even　now　of delay, because　I　was alive.

that you were your-self on the point of departure; you said

83 **Repertī sunt duo equitēs Rōmānī, quī tē istā**
　There were found two　knights　Roman,　who you that

that even at this time you were only a lit-tle delayed, because I

construction. A. & G. 110, *d*; B. 115; G. 246, *ff*; H. 248.——**dīxistī**, 2d pers. sing. perf. ind. act. of *dīcō, -ere, dīxī, dīctum,* 3; the subj. *tū* is implied. Observe how in ll. 24-32 Cicero hurls his accusations at Catiline in short, simple sentences, each sentence following the preceding one without the connecting link of a conjunction. This is a good instance of *asyndeton,* i.e. the omission of a conjunction; cf. Caesar's well-known message from the field of war, *vēnī, vīdī, vīcī.* A. & G. 208, *b*; B. 346; G. 473, REM.; H. 636, I, 1.——**paulum,** acc. sing. of *paulum, -ī,* n. 2d = *a little, a trifle* (the sub-stantival neut. of the adj. *paulus, -a, -um*); subj.-acc. of *esse* in the acc. and inf. con-struction after *dīxistī. Paulus* is derived from *paur + los;* thus *paullus* would be the earlier spelling, though *paulus* is preferred in the MSS. (adapted from the note of Wilkins, quoting Brugman as authority).——**tibi,** dat. sing. of *tū;* dat. of the indirect obj. after *paulum esse morae;* the dat. is that of the possessor, esp. common with *sum.*

LINE 32. **esse,** pres. inf. of *sum;* agrees with the subj.-acc. *paulum* in indirect speech after *dīxistī.*——**etiam** (*et + iam*), adv., intensifying *nunc; etiam = even, still,* and its temporal force shows up in combination with other temporal adverbs.——**nunc,** tem-poral adv., modifying *esse.* The time expressed by adverbs and other words is thrown back as a rule in indirect discourse after a past tense of the leading verb, e.g. *hīc* of direct speech = *ille* of indirect, *nunc* of direct = *tum* of indirect; *nunc* is here retained (instead of giving place to *tum*) from the direct *paulum mihi est etiam nunc morae* for the sake of vividness, and perhaps Cicero is quoting Catiline's very words.——**morae,** gen. sing. of *mora,* f. 1st (akin to *memor,* root *smar = to keep in mind;* the idea in *mora* is of one lingering and being engrossed in thought); partitive gen., limiting *paulum,* cf. *nihil novī,* etc.——**quod** (in origin acc. sing. n. of the rel. *quī*), causal conj., introducing a clause explaining *paulum esse morae.* The causal conjunctions are *quod, quia, quoniam,* and *quandō,* and are followed by the ind. mood in direct discourse, but by the subjunc-tive in indirect, because the reason given in the direct is incorporated as a subordinate clause when changed to the indirect speech. Even in direct speech *quod* must be fol-lowed by the subjunct. if the reason given is not on the speaker's but on another's authority, e.g. *rediit quod amīcum nōn vīdisset = he returned because he had not seen his friend* (the reason not being the speaker's, but that put forward by the other to explain his return). A. & G. 321; B. 286, 1; G. 538-541; H. 516. Cicero distinguishes between *quod* and *quia,* stating that *quia* alone is strictly causal. Indeed *quod* is very common as = *that, the fact that, seeing that,* being used in substantival clauses, etc. A reason which is not accepted is introduced by *nōn quod . . . sed,* though *nōn quia* is met with in Livy and after. *Quod* is more common than *quia* in classical prose, and Caesar only uses *quia* once.——**ego,** nom. sing. of the 1st personal pron.; subj. of *vīverem; ego* is very emphatic.——**vīverem,** 1st pers. sing. imperf. subjunct. act. of *vīvō, -ere, vīxī, vīctum,* 3; agrees with the subj. *ego;* the mood is subjunct. because *quod* introduces a reported reason. A. &. G. 336, 2; B. 314, 1; G. 650; H. 524.

LINE 33. **Repertī sunt,** 3d pers. plur. perf. ind. pass. of *reperiō, -īre, repperī (reperī), repertum,* 4; agrees with the subj. *equitēs.*——**duo,** nom. m. of the cardinal numeral *duo* (Greek δύο or δύω); agrees with *equitēs. Duo* is declined thus: nom. *duo, duae, duo;* acc. *duōs* or *duo, duās, duo;* gen. *duōrum, duārum, duōrum;* dat. and abl. *duōbus, duābus, duōbus:* the gen. *duum* is found occasionally. From four to one hundred the cardinal numerals are indeclinable.——**equitēs,** nom. plur. of *eques, equitis,* m. 3d

was yet alive. Two	cūrā	līberārent	et	sēsē	illā	ipsā	nocte 34
Roman knights were	*from care*	*set free*	*and*	*themselves*	*that*	*very*	*on night*
found to relieve you							
of that anxiety and	paulō	ante	lūcem	mē	in	meō	lectulō 35
voluntarily offer to	*shortly*	*before*	*daylight*	*me*	*in*	*my*	*bed*

(*equus*); subj. of *reperti sunt.* The names of these two men are given by Sallust (Chap. 28), viz. C. Cornēlius, and L. Vargunteius, but Sallust describes the latter as a senator, not a knight. Vargunteius was probably a senator who had been degraded for electoral bribery by the Censors. The *ōrdō equestris* of Cicero's time ranked next to the senatorial order, and consisted of well-to-do merchants, contractors, *pūblicānī,* i.e. tax-farmers, and the like who possessed wealth to the extent of four hundred thousand sesterces. They were distributed through all the towns of Italy, and lent Cicero, who arose from their ranks, their political support at this period, and it was the *equites* who secured his return to Rome from exile, B.C. 57. Cicero's ideal was to foster and secure political sympathy between the knights and the Senate, and he succeeded for a time ; but Caesar eventually won them over by advantageous offers. The *equites,* first formed into a definite order by C. Gracchus (who gave them the sole judicial authority, B.C. 122), were very different from the *equites equō publicō* of the Servian constitution. The latter formed eighteen centuries, were always wealthy citizens, and served as cavalry ; but in course of time the allies furnished the cavalry of the Roman army, and the *equites equō publicō* (also *equō prīvātō,* i.e. cavalry volunteers, not furnished with a horse by the state) completely disappeared as a distinct class.——**Rōmānī,** nom. plur. m. of the adj. *Rōmānus, -a, -um ;* agrees with *equites.*——**quī,** nom. plur. m. of the rel. pron. *quī, quae, quod ;* agrees with the antecedent *equites : quī* expresses characteristic = *tālēs ut.*——**tē,** acc. sing. of *tū ;* direct obj. of *līberārent.*——**istā,** abl. sing. f. of the demonstr. pron. *iste, ista, istud ;* agrees with *curā.*

LINE 34. **cūrā,** abl. sing. of *cūra, -ae,* f. 1st ; abl. of separation, with *līberārent.* Separation is expressed by the abl. with a prep., e.g. *ā* or *ab, dē, ē* or *ex,* often in connection with a verb compounded with that prep., e.g. *ex urbe exiit ;* but the abl. alone is used after a few verbs = *to set free, to deprive.* The simple ablative is also very often used after a verb compounded with *ab,* etc., particularly when figurative. A. & G. 243, *a* ; B. 214, 1 ; G. 390, 2, and NOTE 2 ; H. 414.——**līberārent,** 3d pers. plur. imperf. subjunct. act. of *līberō, -āre, -āvī, -ātum,* 1 (*liber* = *free*) ; agrees with the subj. *quī ;* the subjunct. is consecutive after *quī* characteristic.——**et,** cop. conj., connecting the clauses whose verbs are *līberārent* and *pollicērentur.*——**sēsē,** acc. plur. m. of the reflexive pron. of the 3d pers., acc. and abl. *sē* or *sēsē,* gen. *suī,* dat. *sibi ;* subj.-acc. of the inf. *interfectūrōs esse* in the acc. and inf. construction following the leading verb *pollicērentur ; sēsē* refers back to the subj. *quī.* Observe that, although English idiom omits the subj. of the inf. after verbs of *promising,* e.g. *I promise to do this,* Latin idiom requires it to be expressed.—— **illā,** abl. sing. f. of the demonstr. pron. *ille, illa, illud ;* agrees with *nocte,* i.e. Nov. 6th-7th. It is open to question whether Cicero's murder was attempted in the early morning of the 7th or postponed till the morning of the 8th ; see the notes on ll. 13 and 14 of Chap. I, and the Introduction.——**ipsā,** abl. sing. f. of the demonstr. pron. *ipse, ipsa, ipsum ;* agrees with and strongly emphasizes *illā nocte.*——**nocte,** abl. sing. of *nox, noctis,* f. 3d ; abl. of *time when,* modifying *interfectūrōs esse.* Observe that if *illā ipsā nocte* stood next to and modified *pollicērentur* (instead of being in the object clause of *pollicērentur*), Mommsen's view that the murder was attempted on Nov. 8th would be immensely strengthened.

LINE 35. **paulō,** adv. of degree modifying *ante. Paulō* is the abl. n. sing. of *paulus, -a, -um,* expressing the measure of difference. This abl. is used with comparative adjectives and adverbs, and words implying comparison, e.g. *paulō ante, paulō post.* A. & G.

86 interfectūrōs　esse　pollicērentur.　　Haec　ego
　　about to kill　　*to be*　　*promised.*　　*These things I*

87 omnia,　　vixdum　　etiam　　coetū　　vestrō
　　all,　　*scarcely yet,*　　*even*　　*gathering*　　*your*

88 dīmissō,　　　comperī;　　domum　　meam
　　having been dismissed,　*(I) found out;*　*house*　　*my*

murder me in my
bed that very night
shortly before dawn.
I ascertained all
these arrangements
when your meeting

250; B. 223; G. 403; H. 423.——**ante,** prep. with the acc.; gov. *lūcem.* All prepositions were originally adverbs, and the cases following them had definite significations of their own, of which we see survivals in the locative *domī,* and the acc. *domum. Ante* is often an adverb, e.g. *paulō ante* = *a short time ago, ante . . . quam.*——**lūcem,** acc. sing. of *lūx, lūcis,* f. 3d; governed by *ante.* It was the regular custom in Rome for citizens of wealth and high rank or station to hold early morning levees, which were attended on the one hand by personal friends and those who desired to show their respect for the individual, and on the other hand by *clientēs,* obsequious citizens, and *libertīnī* who repaid the protection they did or might receive from the levee-holder with coarse flattery and cringing attentions. The usual hour was sunrise, cf. the expressions *salūtātiō mātūtīna, officia antelūcāna,* etc.——**mē,** acc. sing. of *ego;* direct obj. of *interfectūrōs esse.*——**in,** prep.; gov. the abl. *lectulō.*——**meō,** abl. sing. m. of the poss. pron. *meus, mea, meum;* agrees with *lectulō.*——**lectulō,** abl. sing. of *lectulus, -ī,* m. 2d (diminutive of *lectus, -ī,* m. 2d, cf. *rīvulus* = *a brooklet,* from *rīvus*); governed by the prep. *in.* The root of *lectus* is often wrongly given as *leg* in *lĕgō,* hence *bed,* as if of something *gathered together.* The Ind.-Eur. root is *lagh* = Greek λεχ = Latin *lec* = English *to lie* (*recline*); cf. λέχος, and λέκτρον = *a bed,* and *lectīca* = *a litter* or *sedan chair.* The levee-holder remained in bed while his clients paid their morning call; cf. the similar custom in France under Louis XIV and successors, and in England under the Georges.

　　LINE 36. **interfectūrōs esse,** fut. inf. act. (the part. agreeing with the subj. acc. *sēsē* in gender, number, and case) of *interficiō, -ere, interfēcī, interfectum,* 3 (*inter* + *faciō*); agrees with the subj.-acc. *sēsē.*——**pollicērentur,** 3d pers. plur. imperf. subjunct. of the deponent verb *polliceor, -ērī, pollicitus sum,* 2 (for *port* + *liceor* = lit. *I bid largely,* hence *promise; port* is an old Latin prep., and becomes the inseparable prep. *po* in composition, denoting power or possession or else emphasizing the meaning of the verb; cf. *pōnō,* for *pōsnō,* for *pōsinō,* for *port* + *sinō*); agrees with the subj. *quī; pollicērentur* is joined by *et* to *līberārent,* and is in similar construction. Synonyms: (1) *prōmittere* = lit. *to send forth* from the mouth, hence *to hold out, to promise;* this is the generic word, denoting every kind of promise; (2) *pollicērī* = *to proffer, to voluntarily pledge oneself* (opposed to *abnuere*); (3) *recipere* = *to pledge oneself,* implying that the risks and results are both guaranteed; cf. Cicero, *de aestāte pollicēris vel potius recipis.*——**Haec,** acc. plur. n. of the demonstr. pron. *hīc, haec, hōc;* direct obj. of *comperī; haec* refers to the details of Catiline's proceedings mentioned in ll. 24-36.——**ego,** nom. sing. of the 1st personal pron.; subj. of *comperī; ego* is again emphatic.

　　LINE 37. **omnia,** acc. plur. n. of the adj. *omnis, -e,* 3d; agrees with *haec.*——**vixdum** (*vix* + *dum*), temporal adv., modifying *dīmissō. Vixdum . . . dīmissō* is an adverbial modifier of the pred. *comperī,* and = a temporal or concessive clause with *cum.*——**etiam** (*et* + *iam*), adv., intensifying *vixdum,* cf. *etiam nunc, quam diū etiam,* and the like.——**coetū,** abl. sing. of *coetus, -ūs,* m. 4th (*co* = *con,* + *eō*); abl. in the abl. abs. construction with *dīmissō;* see note below.——**vestrō,** abl. sing. m. of the poss. pron. *vester, vestra, vestrum;* agrees with *coetū.*

　　LINE 38. **dīmissō,** abl. sing. m. of *dīmissus, -a, -um,* perf. part. pass. of *dīmittō, -ere, dīmīsī, dīmissum,* 3 (*dī* = *dis* + *mittō, I send away*); agrees with *coetū* in the

had scarcely even broken up. I protected and secured my house with stronger guards. I	māiōribus	praesidiīs	mūnīvī	atque	firmāvī; 39
	greater	*with guards*	*I protected*	*and*	*I strengthened;*
	exclūsī	eōs,	quōs	tū	ad mē	salūtātum 40
	I shut out	*those men*	*whom*	*you*	*to me*	*to salute (me)*

abl. abs. construction. This construction is used to define the time or circumstances of an action, and is therefore equivalent to a subordinate clause, temporal, conditional, causal, or concessive, as the case may be. It is grammatically independent of the rest of the sentence, and may take the following forms : (1) a noun or pron. in the abl., with a participle in agreement, e.g. *bellō confectō rediit; hīs cōgnitīs castra posuit; Crassō regente* (the pres. part. act. not very common); (2) a noun or pron. in the abl. with a pred. noun in agreement ; e.g. *Caesare et Pompēiō cōnsulibus; Teucrō dūce; hīs ipsīs cōnsulibus :* in these cases a participle of *sum* is understood, the pred. abl. *cōnsulibus* and *dūce* being really the complement; (3) a noun with an adj. in predicative agreement, e.g. *laxīs laterum compāgibus omnēs accipiunt inimīcum imbrem,* = *all (the ships) let in the fatal flood, the joints of the sides having become loose;* here too a part. of *sum* is understood. Note the following points : (*a*) the noun in the abl. abs. can never be the same as the subject or object of the main clause ; e.g. *Crassus having been defeated, the enemy killed him* = *Crassum victum hostēs interfēcērunt;* (*b*) the abl. abs. is used to supply the want of a perf. part. active (possessed by Greek verbs); e.g. *the general, having pitched his camp, awaited the enemy* = *dūx castrīs positīs hostēs exspectābat;* (*c*) the abl. abs. not only stands in place of a clause, but often in place of two coördinate sentences, e.g. *dūx castrīs positīs hostēs exspectābat* may be rendered, *the general, after (when, although, etc.) he had pitched his camp, awaited the enemy,* or, *the general pitched his camp and awaited the enemy.* A. & G. 255 ; B. 227 ; G. 409, 410 ; H. 431. —— **comperī,** 1st pers. sing. perf. ind. act. of *comperiō, -īre, comperī, compertum, 4;* agrees with the subj. *ego.* Synonyms : (1) *invenīre (in + veniō)* = lit. *to come upon* something, hence *to find,* generally implying chance ; *invenīre* is distinguished from *reperīre* by being usable absolutely ; (2) *reperīre* and *comperīre* (compounds of *re* and *cum* with *pariō* = *I make*) = *to find,* i.e. by search ; they are never found except relatively, i.e. with an object expressed or implied. We learn from Cicero's Letters that his constant use of the verb *comperīre* excited the mockery and taunts of his enemies ; thus in one letter Cicero says of some information he has gained, *audīvī, nam comperisse mē nōn audeō dīcere* = *I have heard (for I dare not say I have "ascertained").* Prof. Wilkins quotes the historian Merivale : "this was the phrase by which the consul was wont to indicate his knowledge of facts when he refrained from revealing his sources of information." —— **domum,** acc. sing. of *domus, -ūs,* f. 4th (some 2d decl. forms ; see note on *domus,* Chap. III, l. 4); direct obj. of *mūnīvī.* When Clodius secured Cicero's banishment in 58 B.C., his Roman mansion was demolished, but was rebuilt at the state's expense after his return in B.C. 57. —— **meam,** acc. sing. f. of the poss. pron. *meus, -a, -um ;* agrees with *domum.*

     LINE 39. **māiōribus,** abl. plur. n. of *māior, māius* (compar. of the adj. *māgnus, -a, -um ;* superl. *māximus*); agrees with *praesidiīs.* —— **praesidiīs,** abl. plur. of *praesidium, -ī,* n. 2d ; abl. of the means, with *mūnīvī.* —— **mūnīvī,** 1st pers. sing. perf. ind. act. of *muniō, -īre, -īvī* or *-iī, -ītum,* 4 (akin to *moenia*); the subj. *ego* is implied. —— **atque,** cop. conj. ; connects *mūnīvī* and *firmāvī. Atque* often = *and also,* introducing a new idea of importance ; here we see its rhetorical use, viz. to connect two sonorous words which are practically synonyms. —— **firmāvī,** 1st pers. sing. perf. ind. act. of *firmō, -āre, -āvī, -ātum,* 1 (*firmus*); the subj. *ego* is implied.

     LINE 40. **exclūsī,** 1st pers. sing. perf. ind. act. of *exclūdō, -ere, exclūsī, exclūsum,* 3 (*ex* = *out* + *claudō* = *I shut*); *ego* is understood as subject. —— **eōs,** acc. plur. m. of the

41 māne	mīserās,		cum		illī	shut out those whom
in the morning	*you had sent,*		*since*		*those*	you had sent to call upon me in the morn-

42 ipsī	vēnissent,	quōs	ego	iam	multīs	ac	ing at my reception,
very men	*had come,*	*whom*	*I*	*already*	*many*	*and*	inasmuch as those very men had come

o h vee

43 summīs	virīs	ad	mē	id		temporis	whose intended visit
very exalted	*to men*	*to*	*me*	*that*		*of time (= at that time)*	at that time I had

demonstr. pron. *is, ea, id;* direct obj. of *exclūsī. Is* is the regular antecedent of *quī,* when the subj. is otherwise undefined. —— **quōs,** acc. plur. m. of the rel. pron. *quī, quae, quod;* agrees with the antecedent *eōs;* direct obj. of *mīserās* in the rel. clause. —— **tū,** nom. sing. of the 2d personal pron.; subj. of *mīserās; tū* is very emphatic. The meaning *tū* conveys is that the person really guilty of the attempted murder was Catiline, not the accomplices sent to do the act. —— **ad,** prep.; gov. the acc. *mē.* —— **mē,** acc. sing. of *ego;* governed by the prep. *ad.* —— **salūtātum,** supine of *salūtō, -āre, -āvī, -ātum,* 1 (*salūs, -ūtis,* f. 3d); expresses purpose after *mīserās.* The acc. supine in *-um* denotes end of motion; that in *-ū* is probably an abl. of specification, though some call it dat. of purpose; both are verbal abstracts of 4th decl. form. The supine in *-um* is used (1) after verbs of motion to express purpose (hence = *ut* + subjunct., e.g. *ut salūtārent*), and may govern a direct object; (2) in the periphrastic fut. inf. pass., with *īrī* (old form from *eō*). A. & G. 302; B. 340, 1; G. 435; H. 546.

LINE 41. **māne** (from old adj. *mānus = good,* cf. *Mānēs = the good spirits;* root *ma (men) = to measure*), adv. of time, modifying *salūtātum. Māne, in the early morning =* lit. *in good season.* —— **mīserās,** 2d pers. sing. pluperf. ind. act. of *mittō, -ere, mīsī, missum,* 3; agrees with the subj. *tū* in the rel. clause. —— **cum,** causal conj. introducing an adverbial clause explaining *exclūsī. Cum* (causal) *= since, as,* invariably takes the subjunct. mood, and so does *cum* (concessive) *= although.* For *cum* temporal, see the note on Chap. III, l. 23. A. & G. 326; B. 286, 2; G. 586; H. 517.—— **illī,** nom. plur. m. of the demonstr. pron. *ille, illa, illud;* subj. of *vēnissent; illī =* the *duo equitēs,* l. 33.

LINE 42. **ipsī,** nom. plur. m. of the demonstr. pron. *ipse, ipsa, ipsum;* agrees with and emphasizes *illī.* —— **vēnissent,** 3d pers. plur. pluperf. subjunct. act. of *veniō, -īre, vēnī, ventum,* 4; agrees with the subj. *illī;* the subjunct. mood follows *cum* causal. —— **quōs,** acc. plur. m. of the rel. pron. *quī, quae, quod;* agrees with the antecedent *illī;* subj.-acc. of *ventūrōs esse* in the indirect discourse dependent on *praedīxeram,* leading verb in the rel. clause. —— **ego,** nom. sing. of the 1st personal pron.; subj. of *praedīxeram.* —— **iam,** temporal adv.; modifies *praedīxeram.* It is difficult to understand how Cicero could have been able to inform others of the plot to murder him, if the attempt was made on Nov. 7th, directly after the meeting at Laeca's house; for it must have been hard for Cicero's informants to get the news to Cicero himself in time to save him. This passage then strongly supports Mommsen's view that the murder was attempted on the morning of the 8th, not long before the Senate met. However, this passage is balanced by *illā ipsā nocte,* l. 34, and the question remains open. —— **multīs,** dat. plur. m. of the adj. *multus, -a, -um;* agrees with *virīs.* —— **ac** (abbreviation of *atque; ac* is used before consonants, except *c, g,* and *qu*), cop. conj., connecting *multīs* and *summīs.* Adjectives expressive of different ideas are commonly connected by a conjunction, and when *multus* is one of two attributes it is always so joined to the other.

LINE 43. **summīs,** dat. plur. m. of the adj. *summus, -a, -um;* agrees with *virīs; summīs = very high* in rank or official position. *Summus* is the superl. of *superus* (rarely used, except *Superī = the gods above*); compar. *superior;* another form of the superl. is *suprēmus.* All are really formed from the adv. *super;* cf. *prior* and *prīmus*

already foretold to many men of the highest position.	ventūrōs *about to come*	esse *to be*	praedīxeram. 44 *(I) had foretold.*
V. Since the facts are so, Catiline, continue in the path which you have begun to follow; depart at length from the	V. Quae cum ita sint, Catilīna, perge 1 *Which things since so are, Catiline, go on* quō coepistī, ēgredere aliquandō ex 2 *whither you have begun, go out some time or other from*		

from *prō.* —— **virīs**, dat. plur. of *vir, virī*, m. 2d ; dat. of the indirect obj., governed by *praedīxeram.* —— **ad**, prep. ; gov. the acc. *mē.* —— **mē**, acc. sing. of *ego ;* governed by the prep. *ad.* —— **id**, acc. sing. n. of the demonstr. pron. *is, ea, id ;* adverbial acc. in the idiom *id temporis ;* cf. *id aetātis = at that age, id genus = of that kind, quod sī = but* (lit. *as to which*) *if*, etc. The adverbial acc. is very common with the sing. neut. of adjectives and pronouns, and is not unlike the cognate acc. and the Greek acc. of respect. A. & G. 240, *b* ; B. 185, 2 ; G. 336, NOTE 2 ; H. 378, 2. Observe that the acc. does not here denote duration of time, but has lost all meaning, for *id temporis = eō tempore.* —— **temporis**, gen. sing. of *tempus*, n. 3d (root *tam = to cut*, hence *tempus = a section* or *portion* of time ; cf. *templum = a space marked out* for consecration, *a temple,* τέμνω = *I cut*) ; partitive gen. (cf. *nihil novī*), limiting *id* in the adverbial phrase *id temporis.*

LINE 44. **ventūrōs esse**, fut. inf. act. (*ventūrōs* agreeing adjectively with *quōs*) of *veniō, -īre, vēnī, ventum*, 4 ; agrees with the subj.-acc. *quōs* in the object clause (indirect discourse) of *praedīxeram.* —— **praedīxeram**, 1st pers. sing. pluperf. ind. act. of *prae-dīcō, -ere, praedīxī, praedīctum*, 3 (*prae = before + dīcō = I tell, foretell*) ; agrees with the subj. *ego* in the rel. clause. *Praedīcō*, 3d conjug., and *praedīcō*, 1st conjug., are etymologically related, being from *prae +* the root *dak = to show*, cf. δείκνυμι ; their meanings must be distinguished ; *praedīcō = I foretell*, sometimes *I warn*, but *praedīcō = I proclaim*, and often *I praise.*

LINE 1. **Quae**, nom. plur. n. of the rel. pron. *quī, quae, quod ;* subj. of *sint ; quae* refers to Catiline's conspiracy as proved in Chap. IV. The relative pronoun or a rel. adverb very commonly stands at the beginning of an independent sentence to connect it with what has preceded, and this occurs even if there be another relative in the clause, e.g. *quae quī vīdērunt = and those who saw these things.* Cicero uses the phrase *quae cum ita sint* when he wishes to have a certain topic regarded as proved (e.g. Catiline's treason) or thoroughly thrashed out, and proceed on to a new subject. A. & G. 180, *f ;* 201, *e* ; B. 251, 6 ; G. 610, and REM. 1 ; H. 453. —— **cum**, causal conj., taking the subjunct. *sint.* —— **ita**, adv., modifying *sint. Ita* is often used correlatively, e.g. *ut . . . ita, = as . . . so; ita* modifies verbs, and *tam* adjectives and other adverbs. —— **sint**, 3d pers. plur. pres. subjunct. of *sum, esse, fuī ;* agrees with the subj. *quae ;* the mood is subjunct. after *cum* causal. —— **Catilīna**, voc. sing. of *Catilīna, -ae*, m. 1st ; case of address. —— **perge**, 2d pers. sing. pres. imperative of *pergō, -ere, perrēxī, perrēctum*, 3 (*per + regō*) ; the personal ending implies the subj. *tū.* Observe the following *asyndeta* (*ēgredere, patent, proficīscere*).

LINE 2. **quō**, rel. adv. = *whither ; quō coepistī* is the rel. clause, and *quō* corresponds to the demonstr. *eō* understood as antecedent in the main clause with *perge.* The rel. pron. is similarly used in statements of fact with the antecedent omitted, e.g. *quae effēcerat (= ea quae effēcerat) narrāvit.* Other uses of *quō* are: (1) interrog. = *whither*, in

3 urbe ; patent portae : proficīscere.   Nimium │ city; the gates are
the city ; are open   the gates :   *march forth.*   *Too* │ open; go forth. Too

direct and indirect questions ; (2) as abl. of measure of difference in correlative clauses,
e.g. *quō diligentius . . . eō melius ;* (3) as final conj., in clauses of purpose containing a
comparative adjective or adv. ; hence followed by the subjunct. mood. —— **coepisti,** 2d
pers. sing. perf. ind. act. of the defective verb (*coepiō, -ere*), *coepī, coeptum,* 3 (no pres.
stem tenses found in classical Latin ; inf. *coepisse,* fut. part. *coeptūrus,* perf. part. **pass.**
coeptus); agrees with the subj. *tū* understood.   *Coepiō* is probably derived from *co =
con* + root *ap* in *apīscor = I seize ;* the pres. is supplied by *incipiō ;* the perf. pass *coeptus sum* is used with a pass. inf., e.g. *appelārī coeptus sum.* A. & G. 143, *a* ; B. 133;
G. 175, 5, *a* ; H. 297, I. Synonyms: *I begin =* (1) *incipiō* (perf. *coepī*), as opposed to
dēsinō = I cease ; (2) *inchoō,* as opposed to *absolvō = I finish ; inchoō* implies com-
mencement without a following completion, hence *inchoātus* may = *incomplete ;*
(3) *ordīrī* (lit. *to weave*) of a long and complicated process ; *ordīrī* always = *to begin*
at the very first link, but *coepisse = to begin,* anywhere in a series. —— **ēgredere,** 2d pers.
sing. pres. imperative of the deponent verb *ēgredior, ēgredī, ēgressus sum,* 3 (*ē + gradior*);
the implied subj. is *tū.* —— **aliquandō** (*alius + quandō*), temporal adv., modifying
ēgredere. Aliquandō here = *tandem aliquandō, at length ;* lit. it = *at some time or
other,* either of the past (hence sometimes *once*) or the future (hence *hereafter*); cf.
ōlim, used of past and future time. *Aliquandō* frequently accompanies imperatives, and
implies that the time has come for some action ; cf. Greek τοτε. —— **ex** (*ē* or *ex* before
consonants ; *ex* before vowels and *h*), prep. ; gov. the abl. *urbe.* Consult A. & G. 152,
b ; B. 142, 2; G. 417; H. 434.

 LINE 3. **urbe,** abl. sing. of *urbs, urbis,* f. 3d ; abl. of *place from which,* governed by
the prep. *ex.* —— **patent,** 3d pers. plur. pres. ind. act. of *pateō, -ēre, -uī,* no supine, 2 ;
agrees with the subj. *portae.* —— **portae,** nom. plur. of *porta, -ae,* f. 1st (root *par = por*
= *to go over, carry over,* cf. *porticus = a colonnade,* and πόρ-θμος = *a ferry*); subj. of
patent. Synonyms: (1) *porta = a gate,* in the wall of a city, camp, or fortified town ;
(2) *iānua = the entrance door* of a house ; (3) *ostium =* any *entrance* (*ōs, ōris,* n. 3d =
mouth) to an enclosed space ; often *the entrance* of a house (= *iānua*), near which a
slave (*ostiārius* or *iānitor*) kept watch, in a small lodge, over those who passed through ;
(3) *foris* (usually plur. *forēs,* since house-doors were doubled and folded into one another)
= *the door* between compartments in a house ; (4) *valvae = folding-doors* in temples
and important buildings ; some think that *forēs* and *valvae* may = *the gate* of a *porta,
porta* indicating the whole structure, and *forēs* the part whereby one passed through.
From the gates of Rome roads branched out, some of which extended all the northern
or southern length of Italy, e.g. *via Flāminia* into Gaul, and *via Appia* to Brindisi.
It is impossible to ascertain the exact number of *portae,* but Pliny says there were thirty-
seven in the reign of Vespasian. Catiline had the choice of three roads to reach the
north of Italy: (1) *via Flāminia,* the northeastern road, on the Adriatic side ; this
started from the *porta Ratumena ;* (2) *via Aurēlia,* running along the Mediterranean
coast to Pisa ; Catiline eventually went by this, on the pretence of going to exile in
Massilia, and took a branch road in Etrūria to Faesulae ; (3) *via Cassia,* lying between
the other two, and the most direct road to Faesulae. —— **proficīscere,** 2d pers. sing. pres.
imperative of the deponent verb *proficīscor, -ī, profectus sum,* 3 ; understand the subj.
tū. —— **Nimium,** adv., modifying *diū. Nimium* is the adverbial acc. sing. neut. of the
adj. *nimius, -a, -um = excessive,* which in turn is derived from the adv. *nimis = too
much* (*ni = ne = not,* + root *ma = to measure,* hence *beyond measure*). The neut.
nimium is sometimes substantival = *too much, excess ;* cf. *multum,* adv. and noun.
Nimium diū . . . dēsīderant expresses two ideas, viz. that Manlius was in fact hourly
expecting Catiline, and that Catiline's departure could not be too soon to suit Cicero.

diū	tē	imperātōrem	tua	illa	Manliāna 4
long	*you*	*the general*	*your*	*that*	*Manlian*
castra	dēsīderant.		Ēdūc	tēcum	etiam 5
camp	*misses.*		*Lead out*	*with you*	*also*
omnēs	tuōs,	sī	minus,	quam	plūrimōs ; 6
all	*your (party)*	*if*	*less (= not),*	*as*	*many (as you can) ;*

long already have you kept that camp of yours under Manlius waiting for its general. Take away with you also all your partizans, or if not all of them, as many as pos-

LINE 4. **diū** (akin to *diēs*), adv. of time ; *nimium diū* limits *dēsīderant*. —— **tē**, acc. sing. of *tū ;* direct obj. of *dēsīderant*. —— **imperātōrem**, acc. sing. of *imperātor, -ōris*, m. 3d (*imperō*) ; in apposition with *tē*. See note on *imperātōrem*, Chap. II, l. 31. —— **tua**, nom. plur. n. of the poss. pron. *tuus, -a, -um ;* agrees with *castra*. —— **illa**, nom. plur. n. of the demonstr. pron. *ille, illa, illud ;* agrees with *castra*. —— **Mānliāna**, nom. plur. n. of the adj. *Mānliānus, -a, -um (of or pertaining to Mānlius) ;* agrees with *castra ;* the poss. gen. *Mānlī* would be more usual. Adjectives derived from proper names were freely invented by Roman writers, cf. *Sullāna tempora = the Sullan age*, and *Herculean labor*. A. & G. 214, *a*, 2 ; B. 354, 4 ; G. 182, 5 ; H. 395, NOTE 2.

LINE 5. **castra**, gen. *castrōrum*, plur. noun n. 2d = *camp* (*castrum, -ī*, n. 2d = *a fortress*) ; nom. plur., subj. of *dēsīderant*. The number of camps is denoted by the distributive numerals, e.g. *bīna castra ; duo castra = two fortresses*. The camp of a consular force of two legions was always laid out on a symmetrical plan ; it was square, being marked out and protected by a *vallum* or rampart of earth, and had gates in each of the four walls ; the general's and officers' quarters were near the gate that faced the enemy. —— **dēsīderant**, 3d pers. plur. pres. ind. act. of *dēsīderō, -āre, -āvī, -ātum*, 1 ; agrees with the personified subj. *castra = iī quī in castrīs sunt*. *Dēsīderāre* does not = *to desire*, but *to miss* or *regret* something which is not possessed ; for this difference and synonyms see the note on *cupientem*, Chap. I, l. 34. The *historic* present *dēsīderant + nimium diū* expresses the continuation into the present of an action begun in the past ; in narrative descriptions the imperf. tense may be similarly used ; the modifying adverbs are *diū, iam diū, dūdum, iam dūdum*, and a few variations, as *nimium diū*. A. & G. 276, *a ;* B. 259, 4 ; G. 230 ; H. 467, III, 2. —— **Ēdūc**, 2d pers. sing. pres. imperative act. of *ēdūcō, -ere, ēdūxī, ēdūctum*, 3 (*ē + dūcō*) ; the subj. *tū* is implied. Four verbs, *dīcō, dūcō, faciō*, and *ferō*, have the shortened imperatives, *dīc, dūc, fāc*, and *fer ; dīce, dūce*, and *fāc* (but not *fere*) are found in early Latin. The abbreviated form is retained in compounds, except those of *faciō*, which are regular, e.g. *perficiō* makes *perfice*. A. & G. 128, *c ;* B. 116, 3 ; G. 130, 5 ; H. 238. —— **tēcum** (*tē + cum*) : *tē* is the abl. of *tū ;* governed by *cum*. *Cum* is the prep. + the abl. ; gov. *tē ;* enclitic because used with a personal pronoun. —— **etiam** (*et + iam*), adv., modifying *ēdūc*.

LINE 6. **omnēs**, acc. plur. m. of the adj. *omnis, -e*, 3d ; agrees with *tuōs*. —— **tuōs**, acc. plur. m. (substantival) of the poss. pron. *tuus, -a, -um ;* direct obj. of *ēdūc*. *Meī, tuī, suī* often = *my (your, his* or *their) friends, relatives*, or *party*. —— **sī**, conditional conj., introducing a *protasis* in which the verb or predicate is supplied from the context. *Ēdūc . . . plūrimōs* comprises two conditions excluding one another, the first condition being understood. In such conditions *sī* is used with the first, and *sīn* (often + *autem, vērō, minus*, or *aliter*) with the second, i.e. when the predicate is expressed ; but when the predicate is understood, *sī minus = if less (if not)*, or *sīn minus, sīn aliter* (rarely *sī nōn) = if otherwise*, introduces the second *protasis*. The passage, with ellipses supplied, = *ēdūc tēcum etiam omnēs tuōs, (sī omnēs ēdūcere poteris) ; sī minus (omnēs ēdūcere poteris), (ēdūc) quam plūrimōs*. —— **minus**, adv. (= *nōn*) ; modifying a predicate understood from *ēdūc*. *Minor, minimus*, and *minus, minimē* are the compar. and superl. degrees of the adj. *parvus* and the kindred adv. *parum* respectively. —— **quam**,

7 pūrgā   urbem.   Māgnō   mē   metū   līberābis,
  cleanse   *the city.*   *Great*   *me*   *from fear* *you will free,*

8 modo   inter   mē   atque   tē
  provided   *between*   *me*   *and*   *you*

9 mūrus   intersit.   Nōbīscum   versārī
  the wall (of the city) *intervene.*   *With us*   *to move about*

sible: purify the city of them. You will set me free from a great anxiety, so soon as the city-wall is between you and me. You cannot abide among us any longer

---

rel. adv.; strengthens the superl. *plūrimōs* idiomatically. *Quam* + a superl. adj. or adv. = *as* (adj. or adv.) *as possible;* strictly speaking, the construction is elliptical, e.g. *ēdūc (tam) plūrimōs quam (poteris).* —— plūrimōs, acc. plur. of *plūrimus, -a, -um* (superl. of *multus, -a, -um;* compar. *plus*); the acc. is idiomatic, strictly being governed by the inf. (supplied with a part of *possum*) of the main verb; but as *quam plūrimī* is a pure idiom, *quam plūrimōs* is the direct obj. of *ēdūc* (understood from *ēdūc* in the first conditional clause).

LINE 7. pūrgā, 2d pers. sing. pres. imperative act. of *pūrgō, -āre, -āvī, -ātum,* 1 (for *pūrigō, pūrus + agō*); the subj. *tū* is implied; *cleanse the city*, i.e. by going away and taking your associates. —— urbem, acc. sing. of *urbs, urbis,* f. 3d; direct obj. of *pūrgā.* —— Māgnō, abl. sing. m. of the adj. *māgnus, -a, -um;* agrees with *metū.* —— mē, acc. sing. of *ego;* direct obj. of *līberābis.* —— metū, abl. sing. of *metus, -ūs,* m. 4th; abl. of separation, with *līberābis;* a prep. *ab* or *ex* is not required after *līberō, prīvō,* and a few other verbs, though necessary after most verbs implying separation; see the note, etc., on *cūrā,* Chap. IV, l. 34. For the signification of *metus, timor,* and other synonyms, refer to the note on *timor,* Chap. I, l. 6. —— līberābis, 2d pers. sing. fut. ind. act. of *līberō, -āre, -āvī, -ātum,* 1; *tū* is understood as subject.

LINE 8. modo, conj. introducing a proviso *modo . . . intersit,* limiting the main clause *māgnō mē metū līberābis.* *Modo* is often conjoined with *dum, = dummodo;* the provisional conjunctions are *dum, dummodo, modo,* and *tantum,* followed by the subjunct. mood. A negative proviso is introduced by *dum, modo,* etc., + *nē,* e.g. *modo nē sit peregrīnus, ingrediātur = provided only he be not a foreigner, let him enter;* in post-classical Latin *nōn* occasionally replaces *nē.* Sometimes a proviso is expressed by the subjunct. mood without any particle, e.g. *sint mīlitēs fīrmī et cōnstantēs, facilis erit trāiectus.* Observe this subjunct. and the subjunct. with *modo* is *hortatory,* while the subjunct. with *dum* or *dummodo* is developed from the temporal construction of *dum* + the subjunct.; A. & G. well compare the English "*so long as*" in colloquial language. A. & G. 314; B. 310; G. 573; H. 513, I.—— inter, prep. with the acc.; gov. *mē* and *tē.*—— mē, acc. sing. of *ego;* governed by the prep. *inter.*—— atque, cop. conj.; connects the two objects of *inter, mē* and *tē.*—— tē, acc. sing. of *tū;* joined by *atque* to *mē;* obj. of the prep. *inter.* English idiom or politeness places the 2d personal pron. before the first, e.g. *you and I;* but in Latin the 1st person precedes the 2d, and the 2d the 3d, e.g. *ego et tū; tū et ille.*

LINE 9. mūrus, gen. *mūrī,* m. 2d; nom. sing., subj. of *intersit.* For synonyms, see note on *moenia,* Chap. II, l. 32. —— intersit, 3d pers. sing. pres. subjunct. of *intersum, interesse, interfuī,* no supine, irreg. (*inter + sum*); agrees with the subj. *mūrus;* the subjunct. is *hortatory,* and expresses a proviso with *modo.* —— Nōbīscum (*nōbīs + cum*): *nōbīs* is the abl. of *nōs* (plur. of the 1st personal pron. *ego*); governed by the prep. *cum.* *Cum* is the prep + the abl.; governs *nōbīs;* enclitic always with the personal, reflexive, and relative pronouns. A. & G. 99, *e;* 104, *e;* B. 142, 4; G. 413, REM. 1; H. 184, 6; 187, 2. —— versārī, pres. inf. of the deponent verb *versor, -ārī, -ātus sum,* 1; complementary inf. with *potes.* *Versor* is strictly the medial or reflexive use of the passive form of *versō, -āre, -āvī, -ātum,* 1 (frequentative of *vertō = I turn*), hence = lit. *I keep turn-*

now: I will not en-dure it or submit to it, I will not allow it.	iam	diūtius	nōn	potes :	nōn 10
	now	*longer*	*not*	*you are able :*	*not*
	feram,	nōn	patiar,	nōn	sinam. 11
	I will endure (it), not		*I will suffer (it),*		*not I will allow (it).*
Deep is our debt of gratitude to the im-	Māgna	dīs	immortālibus	habenda	est 12
	Great	*to the gods*	*immortal*	*to be held (= paid)*	*is*

ing or moving myself about, hence of everyday life = *I dwell, remain;* applied to occupations *versārī* = *to be employed (engaged) in*, e.g. *in rē pūblicā versārī* = *to be a politician* or *statesman.*

LINE 10. **iam**, temporal adv. ; strengthened by *diūtius*, modifies *nōn potes*. In negative sentences *iam* alone, or with *diūtius* = *no longer*.——**diūtius**, adv., defining *iam* more precisely. *Diūtius* is the compar. degree of the adv. *diū*.——**nōn**, neg. adverb ; limits *potes*. *Nōn* (*ne* + *ūnum*) is the common negative ; *haud* is rarely used with verbs (except *sciō* and a few others), but modifies adjectives and adverbs. —— **potes**, 2d pers. sing. pres. ind. of *possum, posse, potuī*, no supine, irreg. (*potis* = *able* + *sum* = *I am*, through *potsum*) ; the subj. *tū* is implied by the personal ending.——**nōn**, neg. adv. ; limits *feram*.

LINE 11. **feram**, 1st pers. sing. fut. ind. act. of *ferō, ferre, tulī, lātum*, irreg. ; the subj. *ego* is implied. Observe (1) the *anaphora*, i.e. the repetition of *nōn* at the beginning of each successive clause ; (2) the *asyndeta*, i.e. omissions of conjunctions ; (3) the use of three synonymous verbs. By these means Cicero puts the greatest emphasis he can on the impossibility of tamely allowing Catiline to attack the constitution. One editor elaborates as follows : Cicero says he will not *bear* it (as a man), *endure* it (as a good citizen), *allow* it (as a magistrate). For a comparison of *ferō, patior, sinō*, and other synonyms, refer to the note on *patimur*, Chap. II, l. 15.——**nōn**, neg. adv., limiting *patiar*.——**patiar**, 1st pers. sing. fut. ind. of the deponent verb *patior, patī, passus sum*, 3 (hence English *passive*) ; the subj. *ego* is implied by the personal ending.—— **nōn**, neg. adv. ; limits *sinam*.——**sinam**, 1st pers. sing. fut. ind. act. of *sinō, -ere, sīvī, situm*, 3 ; the subj. *ego* is understood. The above, from *nōn feram* on, is an excellent example of *anaphora* and *asyndeton*.

LINE 12. **Māgna**, nom. sing. f. of the adj. *māgnus, -a, -um* ; agrees with the subj. *grātia*. Observe how far the modifier *māgna* is separated from the noun it modifies, *grātia;* the order is as follows : *māgna grātia habenda est dīs immortālibus atque huic*, etc. Words which are naturally closely connected, e.g. a noun and its adjective, or a noun and its limiting genitive, are sometimes separated in order to throw particular emphasis on a particular word. A very common and simple method of emphasizing is : (1) to put the subject last, instead of in its usual first place ; (2) to place the verb first, instead of last (as usual) ; (3) to put the object or any important word first or last, instead of between the subject (which begins the clause) and the verb (which ends the clause). A. & G. 344, *e;* B. 348, 349 ; G. 674, and NOTE ; H. 561, III.——**dīs**, dat. plur. of *deus, -ī*, m. 2d ; dat. of the indirect obj., with *habenda est*. *Dīs* is the contracted form of *diīs*, variant of *deīs*, as the nom. *diī* (contracted *dī*) of *deī*.——**immortālibus**, dat. plur. m. of the adj. *immortālis, -e*, 3d (*in* = *not* + *mortālis* = *mortal; mors*) ; agrees with *dīs*. —— **habenda est**, 3d pers. sing. pres. ind. of the passive periphrastic conjugation of *habeō, -ēre, -uī, -itum*, 2 ; agrees with the subj. *grātia*. The periphrastic conjug. passive consists of the gerundive or verbal adj. in *-ndus* + parts of the verb *sum;* it expresses obligation, necessity, or duty ; cf. the active periphrastic conj., viz. parts of *sum* + the fut. part. act., e.g. *habitūrus sum*. If the verb is transitive, the gerundive must agree with the subj. in gender, number, and case, e.g. *grātia habenda est;* but if the verb

13 atque   huic   ipsī   Iovī   Statōrī,
   and   *this*   *very*   *to Jupiter the Establisher,*
14 antīquissimō   custōdī   hūius   urbis,   grātia,
   most ancient *(to) the guardian* *this* *of city,* *gratitude,*

mortal gods and particularly to Juppiter the Stayer here with us, of earliest time this city's guardian,

is intrans., the gerundive is nom. sing. neut. and the construction impersonal, e.g. *lēgibus parendum est.* A. & G. 113, *d* ; B. 337, 7, *b*, 1 ; G. 251 ; H. 234 ; 466, NOTE.

LINE 13.   **atque**, cop. conj., connecting the general *dīs immortālibus* with the particular *huic ipsī Iovī.* Greek and Latin poetry frequently describes the individual by coördinate reference to the class ; cf. Vergil, *quī . . . Italiam fātō profugus Lāvīniaque vēnit lītora = who came, an exile of fate, to Italy and the shores of Lāvīnium.* —— **huic**, dat. sing. m. of the demonstr. pron. *hīc, haec, hōc ;* agrees with *Iovī ; huic* is deictic, as the Senate was assembled in the temple of *Juppiter Stator.* —— **ipsī**, dat. sing. m. of the demonstr. pron. *ipse, ipsa, ipsum ;* agrees with and intensifies *Iovī.* —— **Iovī**, dat. sing. of *Iuppiter (Iupiter),* gen. *Iovis,* m. 3d ; dat. of the indirect obj. with *habenda est ;* joined by *atque* to *dīs. Iuppiter* was called *Diovis* (collateral form of *Iovis,* old nom. for the later *Iuppiter*) by the ancient Romans ; from the root *di* or *dyu = to be bright.* The Greek god *Zeús,* gen. *Διός,* is etymologically akin, and so are the following: *diēs, Diāna, dīvus, deus, δῖος, δῆλος.* Thus *Iuppiter = Diovis pater* or *Diēspiter,* i.e. *the lord* or *father of heaven (brightness).* Jupiter became the supreme ruler of the gods when his father Saturn died ; he kept heaven as his own kingdom, and gave the rule of the sea to his brother Neptune, and the rule of the underworld to his brother Plūtō. —— **Statōrī**, dat. sing. of *stator, statōris,* m. 3d (from *sistō = I cause to stand ;* cf. *stō = I stand ;* root *sta ;* cf. Greek *ἵστημι = I make to stand*) ; personified, agreeing as an appositive with *Iovī.* The allusion in *Statōrī* is to the legend narrated by Livy of the interposition of Jupiter in answer to Rōmulus' vow to build a temple if the god would *stay* the Romans' flight. The battle was against the Sabines, who were eventually overcome, and Jupiter was given the title of *Supporter,* or *Stayer* (i.e. of flight). Plutarch renders *Stator* by *Στήσιος,* and Diō Cassius by *Ὀρθώσιος.* In spite of the vow of Rōmulus, the temple was not erected till B.C. 294. The temple was on the Palatine ; it must not be confused with that of *Juppiter Capitolīnus ;* the latter was dedicated to the worship of *Iuppiter Optimus Māximus,* conjointly with *Iūnō* and *Minerva.*

LINE 14.   **antīquissimō**, dat. sing. m. of *antīquissimus, -a, -um* (superl. of the adj. *antīquus, -a, -um* (akin to *ante*)) ; agrees with *custōdī.* Synonyms : (1) *antīquus = old,* usually of what was in ancient time but no longer exists ; in this passage *antīquissimō = prīmō* ; (2) *vetus = old,* of what has been for a long time and continues to exist, e.g. *vetus amīcitia = a friendship of old standing ;* (3) *vetustus = old,* of something long used and by implication superior, e.g. *vetusta disciplīna* ; (4) *prīscus = old,* implying a claim to reverence, e.g. *prīsca sevēritās ;* (5) *pristīnus = old, earlier,* of a former state in opposition to *presēns ;* (6) *obsolētus = old, out of use,* e.g. *verba obsolēta.* —— **custōdī**, dat. sing. of *custōs, custōdis,* m. (and f.) 3d ; in apposition with *Iovī ; antīquissimō custōdī* refers to the same incident as *Statōrī,* viz. the stayed flight of the Romans. —— **hūius**, gen. sing. f. of the demonstr. pron. *hīc, haec, hōc ;* agrees with *urbis.* —— **urbis**, gen. sing. of *urbs,* f. 3d ; poss. gen., limiting *custōdī.* —— **grātia**, gen. *grātiae,* f. 1st (root *ghar* or *ghra = to glow, to be glad ;* cf. *grātus, χάρις = grace, χαίρω = I rejoice*) ; nom. sing., subj. of *habenda est.* Note : (1) that *grātia* = the emotion, *gratitude,* whereas the plur. *grātiae* = the expression of the emotion, *thanks ;* (2) *grātiam habēre = to feel gratitude* (in the heart), while *grātiam referre = to show gratitude* for something by deed ; *to thank = grātiās* (or *grātēs*) *agere, to owe thanks = grātiam dēbēre, to deserve thanks = grātiam merērī.* The kindred plural noun *grātēs,* f. 3d is not in use except in the nom. and acc. cases, but Tacitus has *grātibus.*

forasmuch as we have	quod	hanc	tam	taetram,	tam	horribilem 15
escaped already so	*because*	*this*	*so*	*foul,*	*so*	*horrible*
often this pest, so	tamque	īnfestam	reī	pūblicae		pestem 16
foul, so dreadful, and	*and so*	*hostile*	*to the commonwealth*			*plague*
so deadly to the state.	totiēns	iam	effūgimus.	Nōn	est	saepius 17
The safety of the state	*so often*	*already*	*we have escaped.*	*Not*	*is*	*more often*
must not too often be	in	ūnō	homine	summa	salūs	perīclitanda 18
imperilled in its en-	*in*	*one*	*man*	*highest*	*the safety*	*to be endangered*

LINE 15. **quod**, conj. ; its clause *quod ... effūgimus* is a statement of fact explaining *grātia habenda est,* hence the indicative mood in the verb ; refer to the note on *quod,* Chap. IV, l. 32. —— **hanc**, acc. sing. f. of the dem. pron. *hīc, haec, hōc;* agrees with *pestem.* —— **tam**, dem. adv., modifying *taetram.* —— **taetram**, acc. sing. f. of the adj. *taeter, taetra, taetrum;* agrees with *pestem.* —— **tam**, dem. adv. ; modifies *horribilem.* —— **horribilem**, acc. sing. f. of the adj. *horribilis, -e,* 3d (from *horreō = I shudder*); agrees with *pestem.*

LINE 16. **tamque** (*tam = que*): *tam* is the dem. adv. ; modifies *īnfestam. Que* is the enclitic cop. conj., joining *tam horribilem* and *tam īnfestam.* —— **īnfestam**, acc. sing. f. of the adj. *īnfestus, -a, -um* (derived from *in* = root *ghan = fend,* through the obsolete verb *fendō = I strike,* which is only found in the compounds *dēfendō = I ward off* a blow, *offendō = I aim a blow at,* etc. ; cf. *infensus = hostile,* and θείνω = *I strike*); agrees with *pestem.* Synonyms : *hostile* = (1) *hostīlis,* i.e. pertaining to a *hostis;* used of *hostile* thought ; (2) *īnfestus,* used (*a*) actively, = *malevolent,* e.g. *gēns īnfesta Rōmānīs,* (*b*) passively, = *disturbed, unsafe,* e.g. *iter;* (3) *īnfensus* (akin to *īnfestus*) = *enraged.* —— **reī**, dat. sing. of *rēs, reī,* f. 5th; dat. of the indirect obj. with *īnfestam.* —— **pūblicae**, dat. sing. f. of the adj. *pūblicus, -a, -um;* agrees with *reī.* —— **pestem**, acc. sing. of *pestis, -is,* f. 3d; direct obj. of *effūgimus.* For *pestis* and synonyms, refer to the note on *pestem,* Chap. I, l. 27.

LINE 17. **totiēns**, numeral adv. (from numeral adj. *tot = so many*); modifies *effūgimus.* The ending in *-iēs* is more usual than that in *-iēns* in numeral adverbs, but *-iēns* is the older. The forms *totiēns* and *quotiēns* are preferred to *totiēs* and *quotiēs.* —— **iam**, temporal adv. ; modifies *effūgimus.* —— **effūgimus**, 1st pers. plur. perf. ind. act. of *effugiō, -ere, effūgī,* no supine, 3 (*ex + fugiō*); understand the subj. *nōs.* The allusion in *totiēns iam effūgimus* is to Catiline's first and quickly frustrated conspiracy (see Introduction) and to his repeated failures to secure election. —— **Nōn**, neg. adv., limiting *est perīclitanda.* —— **est**, 3d pers. sing. pres. ind. of *sum;* agrees with the subj. *salūs; est* and *perīclitanda* form the passive periphrastic conjugation. —— **saepius**, adv., modifying *est perīclitanda. Saepius* is the comparative of the adv. *saepe;* superl. *saepissimē.* The comparative *saepius* expresses an excessive degree, so *nōn saepius = not too often,* or better *not more often* (*than can be helped*). A. & G. 93, *a* ; B. 240, 1 ; G. 297, 2 ; 298; H. 444, 1.

LINE 18. **in**, prep. with the abl. and acc. ; gov. the abl. *homine. In ūnō homine* is a Graecism = *in the person of a single individual,* cf. Thuc. μὴ ἐν ἑνὶ ἀνδρὶ πολλῶν ἀρετὰς κινδυνεύεσθαι. —— **ūnō**, abl. sing. m. of the numeral adj. *ūnus, -a, -um* (gen. *ūnīus,* dat. *ūnī*); agrees with *homine.* —— **homine**, abl. sing. of *homō, hominis,* m. 3d; governed by the prep. *in. Vir = man, husband,* or *hero,* and is never found modified by an adj. expressing any kind of disapproval, i.e. we may have *vir bonus* but not *vir malus; vir = a man,* as distinguished from *fēmina. Homō = a man,* with no implied praise or censure, hence may be modified by either kind of qualifier ; *homō = a man,* as distinguished from a god or another species of animal. —— **summa**, nom. sing. f. of the adj.

19 reī pūblicae.   Quam   diū   mihi,   cōnsulī | tirety in the person
   of the commonwealth.   As   long (as) against me, the consul | of a single man. As
                                                          | long, Catiline, as you
20 dēsīgnātō, Catilīna, īnsidiātus es, nōn pūblicō | laid your plots against
   elect,   Catiline,   you plotted,   not   public | me when I was consul-

summus, -a, -um (superl. of rare positive *superus*, formed from the adv. *super;* compar. *superior*); qualifies and agrees with *salūs. Summa* here = *whole, complete,* and its force is practically adverbial, = *the safety of the state must not be risked in its entirety.* A. & G. 191 ; B. 239 ; 241, 2 ; G. 325, REM. 6 ; H. 443. —— **salūs**, gen. *salūtis,* f. 3d ; nom. sing., subj. of *est perīclitanda.* —— **perīclitanda**, nom. sing. f. of *perīclitandus, -a, -um,* gerundive of *perīclitor, -ārī, -ātus sum,* I deponent (*perīculum*); agrees with the subj. *salūs; est* (from above) + *perīclitanda* = the 3d pers. sing. pres. ind. of the passive periphrastic conjugation of *perīclitor,* agreeing with the subj. *salūs.* Observe that deponents may retain the passive signification of the passive form in the gerundive, and often in the perf. part., e.g. *comitātus* = *accompanied* (from *comitor* = *I accompany*). A. & G. 135; B. 112; G. 113, 220; H. 231. This passage is interpreted in two ways : (1) *The safety of the state must not be risked in the person of one individual.* Some think this *individual* (*ūnō homine*) = Catiline ; but the sentence would then be very pointless and unnecessary ; (2) it is better to regard *in ūnō homine* = Cicero, i.e. the state's safety should not be allowed to depend on one man, whose peril would mean its peril and whose death would cause its overthrow.

LINE 19. **reī**, gen. sing. of *rēs,* f. 5th ; pass. gen., limiting *salūs.* —— **pūblicae**, gen. sing. f. of the adj. *pūblicus, -a, -um;* agrees with *reī.* —— **Quam**, adv. : *quam diū* (*quamdiū*) = *as long as,* being used like the temporal conjunctions *dum, dōnec,* and *quoad. Quam diū* is only used in temporal sentences in which the action of the main verb and that of the verb in the temporal clause is contemporaneous in extent, = *so long as, while.* Cicero was the first to use *quam diū* in temporal clauses ; *tam diū* may be used correlatively in the main clause. The mood of the verb following *quam diū* is ind., whatever the tense (except in indirect discourse, where all subordinate verbs are subjunctive). —— **diū**, adv. of time ; + *quam* = the temporal conj. *quamdiū.* —— **mihi**, dat. sing. of *ego;* obj. of *īnsidiātus es.* Many compounds of *ante, post, prae, ad, con, in, ob,* etc., govern the dat. of the indirect object. A. & G. 228 ; B. 187, III ; G. 347 ; H. 386. —— **cōnsulī**, dat. sing. of *cōnsul, -is,* m. 3d ; appositive of *mihi; cōnsulī dēsīgnātō* = a clause *cum essem cōnsul dēsīgnātus.*

LINE 20. **dēsīgnātō**, dat. sing. m. of *dēsīgnātus, -a, -um,* perf. part. pass. of *dēsīgnō, -āre, -āvī, -ātum,* I (*dē + sīgnō*); agrees attributively with *cōnsulī.* A magistrate who had been duly elected at the *comitia* was styled *dēsīgnātus* (*cōnsul, praetor,* etc.) from the day of election up to the day on which he actually entered upon the duties of his office ; thus Cicero was *dēsīgnātus* from about the end of July, 64 B.C. to Jan. 1st, 63 B.C. A magistrate *elect* (*dēsīgnātus*) could only be deprived of his office if the auspices and omens were found to have been wrongly taken at the election, or if he were proved to have resorted to electoral bribery. —— **Catilīna**, voc. sing. of *Catilīna, -ae,* m. 1st ; the case of address. —— **īnsidiātus es**, 2d pers. sing. perf. ind. of the deponent verb *īnsidior, -ārī, -ātus sum,* I (*in + sedeō,* through the noun *īnsidiae* = *ambush*); the subj. *tū* is implied ; the ind. mood is required with *quam diū.* We know of no particular attack made upon Cicero by Catiline in 64 B.C., but Catiline was a defeated candidate at the consular elections of that year and attributed his failure to Cicero's efforts. Sallust speaks of Catiline's constant attempts to attack Cicero (*īnsidiās parāvit*). —— **nōn**, neg. adv., modifying *dēfendī.* —— **pūblicō**, abl. sing. n. of the adj. *pūblicus, -a, -um;* agrees with *praesidiō. Pūblicus* is a contracted form of *populicus* = pertaining to the *populus, people,* root *pal = ple, to fill.*

elect, I protected myself not by a state-provided guard, but by my own personal watchfulness. When at the last consular elections your intention was to kill me,	mē *myself*	praesidiō, *with a guard,*	sed *but*	prīvātā *private*	dīligentiā 21 *by carefulness*
	dēfendī. *I defended.*	Cum *When*	proximīs *nearest (= last)*	comitiīs 22 *at the elections*
	cōnsulāribus *consular*	mē *me*	cōnsulem *the consul*	in 23 *in*

LINE 21. **mē**, acc. sing. of *ego;* direct obj. (reflexive) of *dēfendī.* —— **praesidiō**, abl. sing. of *praesidium, -ī,* n. 2d ; abl. of the means, enlarging the pred. *dēfendī.* —— **sed**, adversative conj.; joins *pūblicō praesidiō* and *prīvātā dīligentiā,* and presents the latter in contrast with the former. —— **prīvātā**, abl. sing. f. of the adj. *prīvātus, -a, um;* agrees with *dīligentiā.* For the general aspect of the contrast involved in this statement, refer to the note on *pūblicā,* Chap. I, l. 20. —— **dīligentiā**, abl. sing. of *dīligentia, -ae,* f. 1st (from adj. *dīligēns*); abl. of the means with *dēfendī;* joined by *sed* to *praesidiō.* The precaution on which Cicero relied most was a body-guard of friends and dependents; even during his consulship he trusted to this safeguard alone, cf. l. 26–29, esp. *per mē tibi obstitī.* As a matter of fact the state could not help Cicero against Catiline, unless the latter were convicted in court of law, and Cicero was well aware that a public prosecution of Catiline would only drive him to bolder schemes for assassination.

LINE 22. **dēfendī**, 1st pers. sing. perf. ind. act. of *dēfendō, -ere, dēfendī, dēfensum* 3, (*dē* + obsolete verb *fendō,* = *I ward off a blow*); the subj. *ego* is implied by the personal termination. —— **Cum**, temporal conj. followed by the perf. ind. *voluistī,* because *cum* = *quō tempore;* see the note on *cum,* Chap. III, l. 23. —— **proximīs**, abl. plur. n. of the superl. adj. *proximus, -a, -um* (compar. *propior;* no positive ; formed from the adv. *prope*); agrees with *comitiīs; proximīs* here = *last* or *recent,* i.e. the elections held in 63 B.C. to appoint the consuls for the year 62 B.C. The date of this election is disputed; the historian Shuckburgh gives Sept. 21st as the date, apparently on his own authority. Many editors variously assign the elections to Oct. 20th or a little later, but this rests on the supposition that Cicero did not attack Catiline before Oct. 20th, and it is known that the elections were postponed by the Senate a few days, to enable Cicero to acquaint the Senate with Catiline's treasonable doings. But there is no evidence at all to show that the elections were not due as usual about the end of July, when Cicero first denounced Catiline, and secured the postponement of the elections for a few days till he should have rendered Catiline's candidature hopeless by rousing public indignation against him. From July to November Catiline, desperate by reason of his defeat, made preparations for revolution. The above view of the question is simple and probable, and presents Catiline's motives and treasonable progress in proper perspective. —— **comitiīs**, abl. plur. of *comitium, -ī,* n. 2d (*cum* + *eō,* hence *a place of meeting*); abl. of time when, enlarging the pred. *interficere voluistī. Comitium* in the sing. = *a meeting-place,* esp. the *Comitium,* an open space north of the *Forum;* the plur. *comitia* = (1) *an assembly of the people,* e.g. *centuriāta* = *by centuries* (military), *tribūta* = *by tribes,* etc.; (2) *an assembly of the people* for electing magistrates, hence *elections.* For the *comitia,* see the Introduction.

LINE 23. **cōnsulāribus**, abl. plur. n. of *cōnsulāris, -e,* adj. 3d (*cōnsul*); agrees with *comitiīs.* The consuls were elected by the *comitia centuriāta* about the end of July; the praetors were elected a few days later, though at first on the same day as the consuls. —— **mē**, acc. sing. of *ego;* direct obj. of *interficere.* —— **cōnsulem**, acc. sing. of *cōnsul, -is,* m. 3d ; appositive of *mē; cōnsulem* is emphatic and expresses indignation. As consul Cicero probably presided over the *comitia centuriāta* on this occasion ; he was present at all events. —— **in**, prep.; gov. the abl. *campō.*

campō	et	competītōrēs		tuōs
the Campus (Martius) and		*competitors*		*your*

interficere	voluistī,	compressī	cōnātūs	tuōs
to kill	*you wished,*	*I checked*	*attempts*	*your*

nefāriōs	amīcōrum	praesidiō	et	cōpiīs,
dastardly	*of (my) friends*	*by the guard*	*and by the forces,*	

nūllō	tumultū	pūblicē	concitātō ;	
no	*civil strife*	*publicly having been aroused ;*		

the consul, and the candidates who opposed you in the Campus Martius, I crushed your abominable attempts by means of the body-guard and forces furnished by my friends, and no uproar involving the state was

LINE 24. **campō**, abl. sing. of *campus, -ī*, m. 2d (root *skap = to dig ;* cf. κῆπος = *a garden*); governed by the prep. *in. Campus = Campus Mártius*, a large meadow on the northwest of Rome, adjoining the Tiber, and outside the *pōmoerium* (i.e. open space extending round the city proper and enclosing the city auspices). It was used for two purposes : (1) military games and reviews ; (2) the meetings of the *comitia centuriāta*. The *comitia centuriāta* was originally a military classification of the Roman people, and at first they met under arms ; even in Cicero's time the military theory survived, and because the army could never assemble in Rome the *comitia* were held outside the city limits.—— **et**, cop. conj., joining *mē* and *competītōrēs*, the two objects of *interficere*.—— **competītōrēs**, acc. plur. of *competītor, -ōris*, m. 3d (*competō*); direct obj. of *interficere*. Catiline's rivals were *Decimus Iūnius Sīlānus* (the step-father of M. Brūtus who murdered Caesar) and *Lūcius Licinius Mūrēna* (afterwards accused of bribery and defended by Cicero); Sīlānus and Mūrēna were the successful candidates. Another unsuccessful candidate was *Servius Sulpicius*, the renowned jurist, who was *praetor* in 65 B.C. and eventually gained the consulship in B.C. 51.—— **tuōs**, acc. plur. m. of the poss. pron. *tuus, -a, -um ;* agrees with *competītōrēs*.

LINE 25. **interficere**, pres. inf. act. of *interficiō, -ere, interfēcī, interfectum*, 3 (*inter + faciō*); complementary inf. with *voluistī*.—— **voluistī**, 2d pers. sing. perf. ind. act. of *volō, velle, voluī*, no supine, irreg. ; the subj. *tū* is implied by the personal ending.—— **compressī**, 1st pers. sing. perf. ind. act. of *comprimō, -ere, compressī, compressum*, 3 (*con + premō*); the subj. *ego* is understood.—— **cōnātūs**, acc. plur. of *cōnātus, -ūs*, m. 4th (*cōnor, -ārī, -ātus sum*, 1 = *I attempt*); direct obj. of *compressī*.—— **tuōs**, acc. plur. m. of the poss. pron. *tuus, -a, -um ;* agrees with *cōnātūs*.

LINE 26. **nefāriōs**, acc. plur. m. of the adj. *nefārius, -a, -um* (from indecl. noun *nefās, ne = not + fās = right by divine law*, Latin root *fa = to speak*, cf. *fārī ;* hence *nefārius* and *nefandus* are related); agrees with *cōnātūs*.—— **amīcōrum**, gen. plur. of *amīcus, -ī*, m. 2d ; gen. of specification, denoting the substance or material ; limits *praesidiō*. A. & G. 214, *e ;* B. 197 ; G. 361 ; H. 395.—— **praesidiō**, abl. sing. of *praesidium, -ī*, n. 2d ; abl. of the means, with *compressī*. In his speech for Mūrēna, Cicero tells us that he wore a bright cuirass on this occasion, not so much to ward off dagger-thrusts from the body as to draw the attention of the people to the scandalous fact that the consul's life was in danger, and to incite them to close around and protect him.—— **et**, cop. conj. ; joins *praesidiō* and *cōpiīs*.—— **cōpiīs**, abl. plur. of *cōpia, -ae*, f. 1st (= *co-opia*, i.e. *con + ops*, hence in sing. = *abundance ;* the plur. *cōpiae* = (1) *forces, troops*, as here, (2) *resources, riches*); abl. of the means, with *compressī ;* joined by *et* to *praesidiō*.

LINE 27. **nūllō**, abl. sing. m. of the adj. *nūllus, -a, -um* (*ne + ūllus*); agrees with *tumultū*.—— **tumultū**, abl. sing. of *tumultus, -ūs*, m. 4th (from *tumeō = I swell ;* root *tu = to swell*, cf. τύλη = *a swelling, tumulus = a mound ;* hence *tumultus = swelling*, i.e. *excited disturbance*); abl. in the abl. abs. construction with *concitātō. Tumultus* is the

excited. In short, as often as I was the one whom you attacked, I thwarted you by the aid of my resources, although I	dēnique	quotiēnscumque	mē	petistī,	per 28
	finally	*as often as*	*me*	*you aimed at,*	*by*
	mē	tibi	obstitī,	quamquam	vidēbam 29
	myself	*you*	*I stood against,*	*although*	*I saw*

regular word for any armed rising or insurrection in Italy ; *bellum = war* against a foreign enemy or invader. —— pŭblicē, adv. (from adj. *pŭblicus*); modifies *concitātō ; pŭblicē =* in which assistance from the government was necessary. Cicero lays emphasis on his saving the state from burdens and anxiety by finding himself the means to protect his own life. Distinguish the following : (1) *palam* (akin to *plānus*) = *publicly*, i.e. before the eyes of all ; opposed to *clam = secretly ;* (2) *apertē = openly*, e.g. *dīcam aperte ;* opposed to *obscūrē ;* (3) *pŭblicē = publicly*, i.e. involving the state, e.g. *sepelīrī pŭblicē = to have a state funeral ;* opposed to *prīvātim = privately*, i.e. as an ordinary citizen. —— concitātō, abl. sing. m. of *concitātus, -a, -um*, perf. part. pass. of *concitō, -āre, -āvi, -ātum*, 1 (frequentative of *concieō* or *conciō, -īre, -īvī, -ītum = I rouse*); agrees with *tumultū* in the abl. abs. construction ; refer to the note *dīmissō*, Chap. IV, l. 38. For the formation of frequentatives, see the note on *iactābit*, Chap. I, l. 4. A. & G. 167, *b* ; B. 155, 2 ; G. 191, 1 ; H. 336.

LINE 28. dēnique, adv. ; sums up all the particular facts in a general statement. Synonyms : *finally =* (1) *postrēmō*, of that which is last in the order of a series ; (2) *tandem*, of what takes place after long deferment and expectation ; (3) *dēmum* (often following *tum*), of an action which is late in taking place and which might have occurred earlier ; (4) *dēnique*, generally sums up an argument or enumeration, the preceding points of which may have been led by the adverbs *prīmum* (= *firstly*), *deinde* (= *secondly*, or *next*), *tum* (*then*) ; *postrēmum* or *postrēmō* may take the place of *deinde* (*a*) if a new argument is made in the last division, or (*b*) if the speaker wishes to emphasize the fact that he closes finally a particular line of discussion. —— quotiēnscumque (*quotiēns* + the suffix *-cumque*), adv., followed by the ind. of fact *petīstī. Quotiēns* is the numeral adv. of *quot* (*how many*) ; cf. the correl. *totiēns* (from *tot*), and see note on *totiēns*, l. 17. *Quotiēns* may be used interrogatively = *how often ?*, or relatively = *as often as.* The adverbial suffix *-cumque* gives a relative an universal force, cf. *quīcumque = whosoever*, i.e. every single person who ; so *quotiēnscumque = just as often as*, i.e. on every occasion that, etc. A. & G. 105, *a* ; B. 91, 8 ; G. 111, 2 ; H. 187, 3, FOOTNOTE 3. —— mē, acc. sing. of *ego ;* direct obj. of *petīstī.* —— petisti (contracted from *petiistī*), 2d pers. sing. perf. ind. act. of *petō, -ere, -īvī* or *-iī, -ītum*, 3 ; the subj. *tū* is implied by the personal ending. Two vowels which come together are often contracted into one long vowel, so *petiistī = petīstī*, cf. *obīt = obiit, nīl = nihil*, and the gen. of 2 ddecl. nouns in *-ius* and *-ium.* —— per, prep. + the acc. ; gov. *mē ; per mē = meīs cōpiis*, as opposed to *pūblicīs cōpiis.*

LINE 29. mē, acc. sing. of *ego ;* governed by the prep. *per.* —— tibi, dat. sing. of *tū ;* dat. of the indirect obj. governed by *obstitī.* The dat. of the indirect obj. follows compounds of *in, ob, prae, con, ante*, etc. —— obstitī, 1st pers. sing. perf. ind. act. of *obstō, -āre, obstitī, obstātum*, 1 (*ob =* in the way of + *stō = I stand*) ; understand *ego* as subject. —— quamquam (*quam* + *quam*), conj., introducing a concessive clause. Duplicated relative words like *quamquam, quisquis, quotquot* are called generic relatives ; to the same class belong all relatives to which *-cumque* is added. In English we use the subjunct. mood after them, e.g. *quotquot venient = no matter how many may come*, but Cicero and the best writers invariably employ the indicative. *Quamquam* and *etsī* are often merely connective = *and yet, however.* In concessive clauses *quamquam = to what extent soever* (= *although*); the concessive particles *etsī, etiamsī*, and *tametsī* take the ind. or

80	perniciem	meam	cum	māgnā	calamitāte	saw throughout that
	destruction	*my*	*with*	*great*	*disaster*	my overthrow necessarily involved great
81	reī pūblicae	esse		coniūnctam.	Nunc iam	disaster to the state.
	of the commonwealth to be			*united.*	*At this time now*	But now at last you are undisguisedly at-
82	apertē	rem pūblicam		ūniversam	petis ;	tacking the whole constitution; the
	openly	*the commonwealth*		*entire*	*you aim at ;*	
83	templa	deōrum		immortālium,	tēcta	temples of the im-
	the temples	*of the gods*		*immortal,*	*the houses*	mortal gods, the

subjunct. in obedience to the same laws that govern *sī ; licet, quamvīs, cum,* and *ut* (neg. *nē*) all take the subjunct. mood. A. & G. 313, *e* ; B. 309, 2 ; G. 605 ; H. 515, I. ——vidēbam, 1st pers. sing. imperf. ind. act. of *videō, -ēre, vīdī, vīsum,* 2 ; the implied subj. is *ego ;* the imperf. expresses continuation in the past, i.e. Cicero *saw from the beginning* that his own destruction would involve the state in great misfortunes.

LINE 30. perniciem, acc. sing. of *perniciēs, pernicicī,* f. 5th (*per + nex*); subj.-acc. of *esse* in the acc. and inf. construction after *vidēbam (verbum sentiendī).* ——meam, acc. sing. f. of the poss. pron. *meus, -a, -um ;* agrees with *perniciem.* ——cum, prep. ; gov. the abl. *calamitāte.* ——māgnā, abl. sing. f. of the adj. *māgnus, -a, -um ;* agrees with *calamitāte.* ——calamitāte, abl. sing. of *calamitās, calamitātis,* f. 3d ; governed by the prep. *cum.* Synonyms : (1) *calamitās = damage,* originally damage suffered by the crops (*calamus = straw*) from blight or hail-storms ; *calamitās* may be used of an individual's as well as of a people's misfortune ; (2) *damnum = damage,* for which one's self is to be blamed ; esp. *loss* of property or possessions ; (3) *fraus = damage* caused by treachery ; (4) *iactūra* (*iaciō, -ĕre,* 3) = lit. *the throwing away* of something to avoid greater loss or to gain an advantage ; (5) *dētrīmentum* (from *dēterō = I rub away*) = *damage* caused by another.

LINE 31. reī, gen. sing. of *rēs,* f. 5th ; subjective gen., limiting *calamitāte.* ——pūblicae, gen. sing. f. of the adj. *pūblicus, -a, -um ;* qualifies *reī.* ——esse, pres. inf. of *sum, esse, fuī* (the copula); agrees with the subj.-acc. *perniciem* in the acc. and inf. construction ; the pres. inf. denotes that the action of the leading verb and of the verb in the object clause (acc. and inf.) is coextensive in time. ——coniūnctam, acc. sing. f. of the adj. *coniūnctus, -a, -um* (strictly the perf. part. pass. of *coniūngō* (*con + iūngō*), *-ere, coniunxī, coniūnctum,* 3); in the pred. with *esse ;* agrees with the subj.-acc. *perniciem* adjectively. ——Nunc (*num,* cf. Greek νῦν = *now* + the demonstrative suffix *ce ;* cf. *tunc = tum + ce*), temporal adv., limiting *petis ; nunc iam* is emphatic ; the point which the orator makes is that the present attacks of Catiline differ from the past in this, viz. that he is now attacking not the consul but the whole state. ——iam, temporal adv. ; strengthens *nunc.*

LINE 32. apertē (opposed to *obscūrē*), adv. (from the adj. *apertus*); limits the pred. *petis.* ——rem, acc. sing. of *rēs, reī,* f. 5th ; direct obj. of *petis.* ——pūblicam, acc. sing. f. of the adj. *pūblicus, -a, -um ;* agrees with *rem.* ——ūniversam, acc. sing. f. of the adj. *ūniversus, -a, -um* (*ūnus + vertō,* hence *entire, turned into one*); agrees with *rem pūblicam.* For a comparison of *ūniversus, omnis, tōtus,* etc., refer to the note on *omnium,* Chap. IV, l. 18.——petis, 2d pers. sing pres. ind. act. of *petō, -ere, -īvī* or *-iī, -ītum,* 3 ; the implied subj. is *tū. Petere* is a word applied to a blow aimed by a gladiator in combat ; its use here and in l. 28 above suggests the likeness of Catiline to one who risks his own life in trying to take another's.

LINE 33. templa, acc. plur. n. of *templum, -ī,* n. 2d (root *tam = to cut ;* cf. τέμνω = *I cut,* and *ton-deō = I clip*); direct obj. of *vocās. Templum =* (1) a section of the heavens in which the flight of birds was observed for the purpose of taking omens ; (2) any space of ground or any building which had been consecrated by auspices ; esp. of a build-

houses of the city, the lives of all the citizens, the whole of Italy you designate for destruction and devastation. Wherefore, as I cannot yet venture to	**urbis,** *of the city,* **tōtam** *(the) whole (of)* **vocās.** *you call.*	**vītam** *the life* **ad** *to* **Quārē** *Wherefore*	**omnium** *all* **exitium** *ruin* **quoniam** *because*	**cīvium,** *of the citizens,* **et** *and* **id,** *that*	**Italiam** 34 *Italy* **vāstitātem** 35 *devastation* **quod est** 36 *which is*

ing devoted to the worship of a particular deity. The temples at Rome were very numerous; they were erected for the worship not only of indigenous Roman deities, but also of gods and goddesses adopted from the pantheistic systems of foreign nations, e.g. Cybele. Even moral virtues were personified, e.g. *Fidēs,* and had temples of their own. —— **deōrum,** gen. plur. of *deus, -ī,* m. 2d (gen. plur. sometimes *deūm;* nom. plur. *deī, diī,* or *dī;* dat. and abl. *deīs, diīs,* or *dīs;* voc. sing. *deus*); poss. gen., limiting *templa.* ——**immortālium,** gen. plur. m. of the adj. *immortālis, -e,* 3d (*in + mortālis*); qualifies and agrees with *deōrum.* —— **tēcta,** acc. plur. of *tectum, -ī,* n. 2d (*tegō = I cover,* hence *roof, house*); direct obj. of *vocās.* Observe that the objects of *vocās* are enumerated one after another without a single conjunction (*asyndeton*); Latin idiom prefers this or else joins all the members each to the one next it by a cop. conj., e.g. *Pompēius, Caesar, Crassus;* or (*et*) *Pompēius et Caesar et Crassus,* whereas in English we connect only the last two members, e.g. *Pompey, Caesar, and Crassus.*

LINE 34. **urbis,** gen. sing. of *urbs,* f. 3d; poss. gen., limiting *tecta.* —— **vītam,** acc. sing. of *vīta, -ae,* f. 1st; direct obj. of *vocās.* —— **omnium,** gen. plur. of the adj. *omnis, e,* 3d; agrees with *cīvium.* —— **cīvium,** gen. plur. of *cīvis, -is,* m. 3d; poss. gen., limiting *vītam.* —— **Italiam,** acc. sing. of *Italia, -ae,* f. 1st; direct obj. of *vocās;* refer to the note on *Italiae,* Chap. IV, l. 26.

LINE 35. **tōtam,** acc. f. of the adj. *tōtus, -a, -um;* agrees with *Italiam.* —— **ad,** prep. with the acc.; gov. *exitium.* —— **exitium,** acc. sing. of *exitium, -ī,* n. 2d (*ex + eō*); governed by the prep. *ad.* —— **et,** cop. conj., connecting *exitium* and *vāstitātem.* —— **vāstitātem,** acc. sing. of *vāstitās, -ātis,* f. 3d (formed from the adj. *vāstus = waste, desolate*); obj. of the prep. *ad;* joined by *et* to *exitium.*

LINE 36. **vocās,** 2d pers. sing. pres. ind. act. of *vocō, -āre, -āvī, -ātum,* 1 (root *vak = voc = to sound, speak, call,* cf. *vōx;* Greek root ϝεπ, cf. ἔπος = ϝέπος = *a word*); the implied subj. is *tū. Templa . . . tecta . . . vītam . . . Italiam ad exitium . . . vocās* is a variation for the usual matter-of-fact *ēvertere māchināris templa,* etc.; but *vītam* is somewhat strange as an obj. of *ad exitium vocās* in a prose writer. Distinguish the following: (1) *vocāre* = (a) *to name,* like the verbs following, (b) *to summon,* e.g. *vocāre ad arma* (*exitium,* etc.); (2) *nōmināre* (*nōmen = a name,* cf. *nōscō*) = *to call* by name, sometimes *to appoint* by name, e.g. *nōminātus est cōnsul;* (3) *appellāre* = (a) *to name* by an appropriate title, e.g. *imperātōrem,* (b) *to address, appeal to,* e.g. *quem alium appellem* (Cic.) = *whom else can I invoke for assistance?* (4) *nuncupāre = to name,* esp. *to give a name* to something hitherto unnamed. —— **Quārē** (= *quā + rē, quā* being the abl. sing. f. of the rel. *quī,* agreeing with the abl. *rē* = lit. *by which thing*), adv., with the force of an illative conj., cf. *quamobrem, quōcircā,* etc. A. & G. 155, *c;* 156, *e;* B. 344; G. 499, B; 500–503; H. 310, 4; 554, IV. —— **quoniam** (*quom,* acc. of *quī,* old form of *cum + iam*), causal conj., taking the ind. *audeō.* The ind. is used after *quod, quia, quoniam* or *quandō* causal, if the reason given rests on the speaker's own authority; the subjunct., if the reason is another's. *Quoniam* was originally a temporal particle (e.g. in Plautus); as a causal conj., it is used of a reason evident in itself. A. & G. 321; B. 286, 1; G. 538–541; H. 516. —— **id,** acc. sing. n. of the dem. pron. *is, ea, id;* direct obj. of *facere; id* signifies the execution of Catiline. —— **quod,** nom. sing. n. of the rel.

87 prīmum	et	quod	hūius	take that course
first (in importance)	*and*	*which*	*this*	which is obvious and
88 imperī	disciplīnaeque		māiōrum	which is in conform-
of (consular) authority and of the custom			*of (our) ancestors*	ance with the author-

pron. *quī, quae, quod;* agrees with the antecedent *id;* subj. of *est prīmum.* Consult A. & G. 198; B. 250, 1; G. 614; H. 445.——est, 3d pers. sing. pres. ind. of *sum;* agrees with the subj. *quod.*

LINE 37. **prīmum,** nom. sing. n. of the adj. *prīmus, -a, -um* (superl. formed from adv. *prō;* compar. *prior*); in the pred. with *est;* agrees with the subj. *quod. Prīmum* = *the first thing,* i.e. to be done, *the obvious thing.*——et, cop. conj., connecting the following rel. clause with the preceding one. For *et, que,* and *atque* (*ac*), see the note on *que.* Chap. I, l. 9.——quod, nom. sing. n. of the rel. pron. *quī, quae, quod; quod* is repeated from *quod* above ; subj. of *proprium est.*——hūius, gen. sing. n. of the dem. pron. *hīc, haec, hōc;* agrees with *imperī.*

LINE 38. **imperī,** gen. sing. (contracted from *imperii*) of *imperium,* n. 2d ; sub- jective gen., limiting *proprium,* which is substantival. The gen. following adjectives, e.g. *memor,* is in most cases objective, but the gen. is poss. when it limits *proprius* or *commūnis.* This subjective gen. is used after (1) adjectives used substantively, e.g. *amīcissimus cōnsulis* = *the dearest friend of the consul; aequālis Cicerōnis* = *Cicero's contempo- rary;* (2) *similis, proprius, commūnis,* and a few others expressing *likeness, suitability,* or the reverse. Some grammarians consider that *proprius* and *commūnis* are *substanti- val* when used with the gen., but normally adjectival when used with the dative. A. & G. 218; esp. 234, *d*; B. 204, 2; G. 374; esp. 359, REM. 1; H. 399; esp. 391, II, 4. For the contraction in *-ī,* see note on *Palātī,* Chap. I, l. 5. *Hūius imperī proprium* = *the peculiar privilege of the authority I hold* (as proved by the precedents mentioned in the first two chapters); one editor gives *imperī* a meaning it cannot possibly have, ren- dering (*which*) *is in strict accordance with the principles of this government.* Under the emperors the empire was often spoken of as *imperium,* but the form of government was not so described, at least by the early emperors. *Imperī* is indeed used here in a sense a little beyond the strict one (viz. of a consul's or praetor's authority as general of an army *outside the city*), and evidently includes the *cōnsulāris potestās* within Rome and the special (quasi-dictatorial) powers conveyed by the Senate (the Senate's authority to do so is disputed) in the *cōnsultum ultimum* of Oct. 21st or 22d. Synonyms: (1) *impe- rium* = *chief rule,* i.e. military, with power of life or death while the army on service is concerned; (2) *rēgnum* = *sovereignty* of a king, or *unlimited power* such as a king has; (3) *domīnātiō* or *domīnātus* = *arbitrary* (and by implication *tyrannical*) *rule;* (4) *prin- cipātus* = *the rule* of the *princeps,* i.e. first citizen; preferred by the first emperors as a description of their position; (5) *potestās* = *civil power* of the consul, etc., conferred by the *comitia tribūta* or *centuriāta;* opposed to *imperium* conferred solemnly by *comitia cūriāta;* as a general word = *power,* i.e. rightful power as opposed to *potentia;* (6) *potentia* = *power* (i.e. seized and used), generally implying injustice.——disciplī- naeque (*disciplīnae + que*): *disciplīnae* is the gen. sing. of *disciplīna,* f. 1st (= *discipu- līna,* from *discipulus,* i.e. *discō* + the root of *puer*); subjective gen., limiting *proprium,* like *imperī* with which it is connected by *que.* The meaning here is *practice, custom;* other common meanings are: (1) *training, instruction;* (2) *learning, science, culture;* (3) *discipline. Que* is the enclitic cop. conj.; connects *imperī* and *disciplīnae.*—— māiōrum, gen. plur. of *māior, māius,* compar. of the adj. *magnus, -a, -um* (the substan- tival mas. plur. *māiōrēs, -um* = *ancestors*); poss. gen., limiting *disciplīnae;* the allusion is to precedents previously cited, viz. the violent deaths of Spurius Maelius, Tiberius Gracchus, Gāius Gracchus, Sāturnīnus, and Flaccus. See Chapters I and II.

ity I exercise and the	proprium	est,	facere	nōndum	audeō, 89

ity I exercise and the | **proprium** *the particular (duty) is,* | **est,** | **facere** *to do* | **nōndum** *not yet* | **audeō,** 39 *I dare,*
traditional practice of our ancestors, I will take a course which is less rigid in | **faciam** *I will do* | **id,** *that* | **quod** *which* | **est** *is* | **ad** *as regards* | **sevēritātem** 40 *severity*
point of severity but more advantageous for the general wel- | **lēnius** *milder* | **et** *and* | **ad** *as regards* | **commūnem** *common* | **salūtem** 41 *the safety*
fare. For if I order you to be executed, | **ūtilius.** *more useful.* | **Nam** *For* | **sī** *if* | **tē** *you* | **interficī** 42 *to be killed*
the rest of the band of conspirators will | **iusserō,** *I shall order (lit. have ordered)* | | **residēbit** *will remain behind* | | **in** 43 *in*

LINE 39. **proprium**, nom. sing. n. of the adj. *proprius, -a, -um*; agrees with the subj. *quod*.——**est**, 3d pers. sing. pres. ind. of *sum*, agrees with the subj. *quod*.—— **facere**, pres. inf. act. of *faciō, -ere, fēcī, factum*, 3 (*fīō* used as passive); complementary inf. with *audeō*.—— **nōndum** (*nōn + dum*), adv. of time; limits *audeō*.—— **audeō**, 1st pers. sing. pres. ind. of the semi-deponent verb *audeō, -ēre, ausus sum*, 2; the subj. *ego* is implied by the personal ending. A. & G. 136; B. 114, 1; G. 167, 1; H. 268, 3; 465, 2, NOTE 2.

LINE 40. **faciam**, 1st pers. sing. fut. ind. act. of *faciō, -ere, fēcī, factum*, 3; understand the subj. *ego*.—— **id**, acc. sing. n. of the demonstr. pron. *is, ea, id;* direct obj. of *faciam*.—— **quod**, nom. sing. n. of the rel. pron. *quī, quae, quod;* agrees with the antecedent and is subj. of *est* in its own clause.—— **est**, 3d pers. sing. pres. ind. of *sum;* agrees with the subj. *quod*.—— **ad**, prep. with the acc.; gov. *sevēritātem; ad* here = *in point of, touching, with regard to*, like the Greek πρός.—— **sevēritātem**, acc. sing. of *sevēritās, -ātis*, f. 3d (formed from the adj. *sevērus*); governed by the prep. *ad*.

LINE 41. **lēnius**, nom. sing. n. of *lēnior, lēnius*, 3d (compar. of the adj. *lēnis, -e*, 3d); agrees with the subj. *quod; lēnius* is complement of *est* in the predicate.—— **et**, cop. conj.; joins *lēnius* and *ūtilius*.—— **ad**, prep. with the acc.; gov. *salūtem;* used in the same sense as above.—— **commūnem**, acc. sing. f. of the adj. *commūnis, -e*, 3d (*con + mūnis = serving together*, hence *common*); agrees with *salūtem*.—— **salūtem**, acc. sing. of *salūs, -ūtis*, f. 3d (akin to *salvus*); governed by the prep. *ad*.

LINE 42. **ūtilius**, nom. sing. n. of *ūtilior, ūtilius*, compar. of the adj. *ūtilis, -e*, 3d (*ūtor = I use*); joined by *et* to *lēnius;* agrees predicatively with the subj. *quod*.—— **Nam**, causal conj. (prepositive); introduces a reason for the preceding statement. For the use of *nam*, see the note on Chap. I, l. 34; for the causal conjunctions in general, see the note on *enim*, Chap. II, l. 17.—— **sī**, conditional particle, here introducing a logical condition respecting the future, and therefore followed by the ind. mood.—— **tē**, acc. sing. of *tū;* direct of *iusserō*, or rather subj.-acc. of the inf. *interficī* in the object-clause of *iusserō*.—— **interficī**, pres. inf. pass. of *interficiō, -ere, interfēcī, interfectum*, 3 (*inter + faciō*); agrees with the subj.-acc. *tē; tē interficī* is the obj. of *iusserō*. Synonyms: (1) *interficere = to kill*, in general; (2) *necāre = to kill* in a horrible manner, e.g. by scourging; (3) *caedere* and its compound *occīdere* (*ob + caedere*) = *to cut down*, in fight; (4) *trucīdāre = to kill* savagely (*trux, trucis*, adj. 3d = *savage + caedō*), *to butcher;* (5) *percutere* (= *per + quatere*) = *to strike dead; secūrī percutere = to execute;* (6) *iugulare = to kill* by cutting the throat (*iugulum*); hence *to kill treacherously*, as a brigand might; (7) *interimere* (*inter + emere*) = *to put out of the way;* (8) *perimere = to destroy, annihilate.*

LINE 43. **iusserō**, 1st pers. sing. fut. perf. ind. act. of *iubeō, -ēre, iussī, iussum*, 2 (perhaps *ius + hibeō*); understand the subj. *ego*. Synonyms: (1) *iubēre = to command*,

44 rē pūblicā   reliqua   coniūrātōrum   manus; | yet remain within the
the commonwealth (*the*) *rest* (*of*) *of conspirators*   *the band*; | state. But if you
45 sīn   tū,   quod   tē   iam   dūdum   hortor, | leave Rome, as I
but if *you,* *which thing you* *already for a long time* *I urge,* | have long been urg-
46 exieris,   exhauriētur   ex   urbe | ing you to do, all the
will go (lit. *have gone*)*, will be drained off* *from* *the city* | harmful off-scourings

in general ; (2) *imperāre = to command* by right of high authority (e.g. *imperium* of the general) ; (3) *ēdīcere = to command* by official proclamation, e.g. the praetor's *edict* which was law during his year of office or until he himself repealed it ; (4) *mandāre = to enjoin, command, commit* to some one as a charge (*manūs + dō*) ; (5) *praecipere = to enjoin* by right of higher position or knowledge, e.g. as a teacher. Remember that *iubeō* is always followed by an acc. and inf. object clause, whereas *imperō* takes the dat. of the person with a final substantival clause (*ut* or *nē +* the subjunctive).——**residēbit**, 3d pers. sing. fut. ind. act. of *resideō, -ēre, resēdī*, no supine, 2 (*re = behind, back + sedeō*) ; agrees with the subj. *manus. Residēbit =will settle* (i.e. the dregs), in the same metaphor as *sentīna exhauriētur*.——**in**, prep. ; gov the abl. *rē pūblicā.*

LINE 44. **rē**, abl. sing. of *rēs, reī*, f. 5th ; governed by the prep. *in.*——**pūblicā**, abl. sing. f. of the adj. *pūblicus, -a, -um ;* agrees with *rē.*——**reliqua**, nom. sing. f. of — the adj. *reliquus, -a, -um* (akin to *relinquō*) ; agrees with *manus. The rest = (1) reliquus*, regarded as the remainder numerically ; (2) *cēterus*, if contrast or comparison is specially intended.——**coniūrātōrum**, gen. plur. m. of *coniūrātus, -a, -um*, perf. part. pass. of *coniūrō, -āre, -āvī, -ātum*, 1 (*con + iūrō ;* the mas. plur. *coniūrātī, -ōrum*, is used as a noun = *those bound together by oath*, hence *conspirators*) ; gen. of the substance or material, defining *manus*, cf. *argentī pondus = a weight of silver.*——**manus**, gen. *manūs*, f. 4th ; nom. sing., subj. of *residēbit. Manus = (1) the hand*, etymologically as *the measuring thing* from root *ma = to measure ;* (2) *a band* or *company*, in a military sense.

LINE 45. **sīn** (*sī + nē = but if*), conditional conj. If two suppositions are made, the second of which opposes the first, *sī* introduces the *protasis* of the first (as in l. 42), and *sīn* the *protasis* of the second ; sometimes *sīn* is strengthened by an adv., e.g. *vērō, minus.* See the note on *sī*, l. 6.——**tū**, nom. sing. of the 2d personal pron. ; subj. of *exieris.*——**quod**, acc. sing. n. of the rel. pron. *quī, quae, quod ;* adverbial acc. of specification, of the inner object. *Quod* here = *id quod*, i.e. agrees in gender and number with *id* understood ; *id* would be the acc. sing. n. of *is, ea, id*, in apposition with the clause *sīn tū exieris* (= *but if you leave Rome, as* (lit. *that thing which*) *I have long been urging you to do*). *Id quod* and *quod* alone are used as above parenthetically, i.e. independently of the rest of the sentence. A. & G. 200, *e* ; B. 247, I, *b* ; G. 614, REM. 2 ; 324 ; 333, NOTE 2 ; H. 363, 5. For the acc. *id*, see the note and references under *id*, Chap. III, l. 19.——**tē**, acc. sing. of *tū ;* direct obj. of *hortor.*——**iam**, temporal adv., strengthens *dūdum ;* cf. *iam prīdem ;* in such combinations *iam* indicates that the point of view is the present, and *dūdum, diū*, etc., that the range of view is backwards into the past.——**dūdum** (akin to *diū*, and *diēs*), adv. ; *iam dūdum* limits *hortor.*——**hortor**, 1st pers. sing. pres. ind. of the deponent verb *hortor, -ārī, -ātus sum*, 1 ; the implied subj. is *ego. Hortor* is the *historical* present, which is regularly used with *iam diū* and *iam dūdum* to represent an act as begun in past time and continuing into the present. In descriptions, etc., of the past, the imperf. is sometimes similarly used with *iam diū*, cf. Vergil, *iam dūdum ērumpere nūbem ardēbant = they were long since eager to burst through the cloud* (i.e. *they had been eager and were still*). A. & G. 276, *a* ; B. 259, 4 ; G. 230 ; H. 467, III, 2.

LINE 46. **exieris**, 2d pers. sing. fut. perf. ind. act. of *exeō, -īre, -iī, -itum*, irreg. (*ex + eō*) ; agrees with the subj. *tū ;* the ind. is used because the condition is a logical

of the state (which describes your companions) will be drained away from the city. How now, Catiline? Can you possibly hesitate to do at my command

tuŏrum	comitum	māgna	et	perniciōsa 47
your	*of companions*	*great*	*and*	*ruinous*

sentīna	reī pūblicae.	Quid	est, 48
the off-scouring of the commonwealth.	*What (= how) is (it),*		

Catilīna?	num	dubitas	id	mē	imperante 49
Catiline?	*surely not*	*you do hesitate*	*that*	*me*	*commanding*

one, i.e. does not consider possibility or probability, but simply represents that under such and such circumstances a conclusion of a certain kind will follow. In such conditions the mood of the *protasis* is ind., and that of the *apodosis* the ind., the imperative, or the subjunct. in one of its independent uses. A. & G. 306; B. 302; G. 595; H. 508, and 4. The fut. perf. is often employed in conditions where in English the fut. simple would be used; the point of view is extended further into the future, e.g. *sin exieris* = *but if you will have gone away;* strictly speaking, the fut. perf. of the *apodosis* should follow, e.g. *exhausta erit* = *will have been drained away,* but the fut. simple is common in Cicero. —— **exhaurietur,** 3d pers. sing. fut. ind. pass. of *exhauriō, -īre, exhausī, exhaustum,* 4 (*ex = out of + hauriō = I drain*): agrees with the subj. *sentīna.* —— ex, prep.; gov. the abl. *urbe.* —— **urbe,** abl. sing. of *urbs, urbis,* f. 3d; governed by the prep. *ex.* It is regular for the prep. with which a verb implying *separation* is compounded to be repeated with the ablative.

LINE 47. **tuŏrum,** gen. plur. m. of the poss. pron. *tuus, -a, -um;* agrees with *comitum.* —— **comitum,** gen. plur. of *comes, comitis,* m. (and f.) 3d (*com = cum, + eō*); gen. defining *sentīna reī pūblicae.* This kind of gen. is variously called *adnominal, epexegetical, appositional,* and *gen. of specification.* We may call it here *epexegetical* or *appositional,* for it explains of what class of men *the dregs of the state* are made up, and is = to an appositive; cf. *nōmen amīcitiae* = *the name (of) friendship.* A. & G. 214, *f;* B. 202; G. 361; H. 395.—— **magna,** nom. sing. f. of the adj. *māgnus, -a, -um;* agrees with *sentīna; māgna = large,* in point of number.—— **et,** cop. conj.; connects the two epithets *māgna* and *perniciōsa.* —— **perniciōsa,** nom. sing. f. of the adj. *perniciōsus, -a, -um (perniciēs);* agrees with *sentīna.*

LINE 48. **sentīna,** gen. *sentīnae,* f. 1st; nom. sing., subj. of *exhaurietur.* Cicero speaks metaphorically of the *bilge-water* of the state, as we do of the *refuse, off-scourings,* or *dregs* of the community. *Sentīna* = (1) *the bilge* of a ship, (2) *the bilge-water* which *residet,* i.e. collects there (cf. *residēbit,* l. 43); (3) metaphorically = *the dregs.* Observe that *sentīna* is limited by two genitives, *comitum* and *reī pūblicae,* as frequently occurs in Greek; *reī pūblicae* goes so closely with *sentīna* as to form a single notion, viz. *the state's-refuse,* and this notion is explained by *comitum.* —— **reī,** gen. sing. of *rēs,* f. 5th; poss. gen., limiting *sentīna.* —— **pūblicae,** gen. sing. f. of the adj. *pūblicus, -a, -um;* agrees with *reī.* Ernesti suspects that *reī pūblicae* is an interpolation, as *ex urbe* sufficiently shows where *the dregs* were. But an unusual expression like *sentīna* would require explanation for a Roman audience, especially as it is used in metaphor and not in simile. One editor rashly mishandles the text, e.g. transposes *sentīna* and *reī pūblicae,* and calls *reī pūblicae* a dat. of the indirect obj. after *perniciōsa = dangerous to the state;* he explains that a copyist may once have written *sentīna reīpūblicae* instead of *reīpūblicae sentīna,* the error remaining uncorrected by subsequent clerks. —— **Quid,** nom. sing. n. of the interrog. pron. *quis, quae, quid;* subj. of *est; quid est* is a colloquialism = *how now?* —— **est,** 3d pers. sing. pres. ind. of *sum, esse, fuī;* agrees with the subj. *quid.*

LINE 49. **Catilīna,** voc. sing. of *Catilīna, -ae,* m. 1st; the case of address.—— **num,** interrogative particle, expecting a negative reply. —— **dubitās,** 2d pers. sing. pres. ind. act. of *dubitō, -āre, -āvī, -ātum,* 1 (for *duhibitō,* frequentative from *duhibeō,* i.e. *duo*

facere,	quod	iam	tuā	sponte	
to do,	*which*	*just now*	*your*	*by own free-will*	
faciēbās?		Exīre	ex	urbe	
you were (on the point of) doing?		*To go out*	*from*	*the city*	
iubet cōnsul hostem.		Interrogās	mē:	num	
orders the consul the enemy.		*You question*	*me:*	*surely not*	

what you were just now wanting to do of your own accord? The consul is bidding the public enemy to leave the city. "Surely not into ex-

+ *habeō*, hence *I waver* between two alternatives, *hesitate;* cf. *dubius* for *duhibius*, and *bellum* = *duellum* = *war* between two (*duo*) nations); the subj. *tū* is implied.——**id**, acc. sing. n. of the dem. pron. *is, ea, id;* direct obj. of *facere*, and antecedent of *quod* following; *id* is explained by *ēxīre ex urbe iubet cōnsul hostem.*——**mē**, abl. sing. of *ego;* abl. in the abl. abs. construction with the part. *imperante; mē imperante* = *meō iussū.*——**imperante**, abl. sing. m. of *imperāns, -antis*, pres. part. act. of *imperō, -āre, -āvī, -ātum*, 1; agrees with *mē* in the abl. abs. construction; see the note on *dīmissō*, Chap. IV, l. 38.

Line 50. **facere**, pres. inf. ct. of *faciō, -ere, fēcī, factum*, 3; objective complementary inf. with *dubitās*. The inf. is used with *dubitō* (and *nōn dubitō*) = *I hesitate;* the two other constructions of *dubitō* are (1) in the phrase *dubitō an* = *I doubt whether* (= *I am inclined to think*), followed by the deliberative subjunctive; cf. *haud sciō an;* (2) with a neg. followed by *quīn*, e.g. *nōn dubitō quīn haec vēra sint.*——**quod**, acc. sing. n. of the rel. pron. *quī, quae, quod;* agrees with the antecedent *id;* direct obj. of *faciēbās.*——**iam**, adv. of time; limits *faciēbās; iam* here = *just now*, and refers to Catiline's statement at Laeca's house that he was anxious to get away to Faesulae.——**tuā**, abl. sing. f. of the poss. adj. *tuus, -a, -um;* agrees with *sponte.*——**sponte**, abl. sing. of *spons*, f. 3d (akin to *spondeō;* only the abl. sing. is found in Latin); abl. of manner, limiting *faciēbās*. *Sponte* is always modified by a poss. pron., e.g. *tuā, meā, suā*, in classical Latin, and thus conforms to the rule that manner may be expressed by the abl. without *cum*, if the noun in the abl. is modified by an adjective.

Line 51. **faciēbās**, 2d pers. sing. imperf. ind. act. of *faciō, -ere, fēcī, factum*, 3; the subj. *tū* is understood. The imperf. *faciēbās* expresses intention, = *you were on the point of doing.* A. & G. 277, *c;* B. 260, 3; G. 231–234; H. 469, 1.——**Exīre**, pres. inf. act. of *ēxeō, -īre, -iī, -itum*, irreg. (*ēx* + *eō*); inner obj. of *iubet. Iubeō, vetō*, and *sinō* are followed by the direct obj. of the person, and the inf. of the inner object.——**ex**, prep.; gov. the abl. *urbe.*——**urbe**, abl. sing. of *urbs, urbis*, f. 3d; governed by the prep. *ex.*

Line 52. **iubet**, 3d pers. sing. pres. ind. act. of *iubeō, -ēre, iussī, iussum*, 2; agrees with the subj. *consul.* Note the impersonal form of address, which is more formal and authoritative than would be the direct *ego iubeō tē.*——**cōnsul**, gen. *cōnsulis*, m. 3d; nom. sing., subj. of *iubet.* The juxtaposition of *cōnsul* and *hostem* is rhetorically effective.——**hostem**, acc. sing. of *hostis, -is*, m. 3d; direct obj. of *iubet.*——**Interrogās**, 2d pers. sing. pres. ind. act. of *interrogō, -āre, -āvī, -ātum*, 1 (*inter* + *rogō; inter*, = *between*, implies interruption (i.e. for replies) between the questions); understand the subj. *tū.* The startling command to leave Rome must have aroused Catiline into interrupting Cicero for an explanation, or at least it caused him to look perplexed; hence *interrogās mē*, i.e. either in words or by expression of face. Synonyms: (1) *rogō* = *I ask*, submissively; esp. of official questions, e.g. *rogō sententiam* (of a magistrate requesting a senator's opinion), *rogātiō* (of a *bill* under consideration, not yet become *lēx*); (2) *petō* = *I ask, seek*, generally as a favor, or in submission, e.g. *pācem petere;* (3) *interrogō* = *I ask*, expecting a reply; (4) *poscō*, = *I ask*, earnestly; (5) *postulō* = *I demand*, by right of superior power or claim; (6) *quaerō* = *I ask, seek*, either by questions, or by scientific or judicial investigations; (7) *flāgitō* = *I ask, demand*, esp. with importunate solicita-

ile?" you ask of me. This I do not command, but if you ask my advice, I recommend it.	**in exsilium?** *into exile?* **suādeō.** *I advise (it).*	**Nōn iubeō, sed sī mē cōnsulis,** 53 *Not I do order, but if me you consult,* 54

---

tions; (8) *percontārī = to inquire about*, so as to gain a thorough knowledge.——**mē**, acc. sing. of *ego;* direct obj. of *interrogās. Interrogō* (like *rogō*) occasionally governs two acc. objects, viz. the direct obj. of the person, and the secondary obj. of the thing; here the clause *num in exsilium* is the secondary obj. of *interrogās.*——**num**, interrog. particle, introducing a question to which a negative reply is expected. *Num in exsilium? = surely not into exile? ;* the question with the verb, etc., filled in would be after this fashion : *num (mē ēxīre ex urbe iubēs) in exsilium?*

LINE 53.   **in**, prep.; gov. the acc. *exsilium.*——**exsilium**, acc. sing. of *exsilium, -ī*, n. 2d (from *exsul;* probably the root is *sad =* Latin *sed, sol, = to go,* + *ex;* cf. *solum = the ground; exsul* is therefore more correct than the form *exul*, and *exsilium* than *exilium;* others derive from root *sar = sal = to leap,* cf. *saltō = I dance, praesul = a dancer before* the public, ἅλλομαι *= I spring*); governed by the prep. *in,* expressing *motion to* after *exīre* understood from l. 51. Cicero ordered Catiline to *leave Rome* (*ēxīre ex urbe*), but did not dare to *order* him to go *in exsilium;* this he merely *advises* (*suādeō*). In one of his speeches Cicero distinctly says that *exsilium* is not a punishment (*supplicium*) but a means of refuge (*perfugium*) from punishment; he also derives from root *sol,* for he says that exiles *solum vertunt, hōc est, sēdem ac locum mūtant.* Note the following points : (1) *exsilium* was *voluntary* on the part of an accused citizen, and was allowed by law; thus citizens (as Cic. tells us) often withdrew *in colōniās Latīnās* to escape fines; when the charge was a grave one, e.g. scandalous misgovernment (as Verrēs), or the putting to death of Roman citizens illegally (as Cicero), the accused always retired to a foreign country; (2) the continued absence of the exile was made compulsory afterwards by *interdīctiō aquā et ïgnï = prohibition from water and fire,* necessaries of life, i.e. no citizen or Latin might harbor the exile; (3) exile implied loss of property left behind, and loss of political privileges; but the exile remained a *cīvis* unless he attached himself to a foreign ruler; on return to Rome, his property might be restored by special grant (e.g. to Cicero); (4) an exile could be recalled (*revocārī*), and resume his station as a full citizen, e.g. Cicero in B.C. 57. Under the empire exiles used to take away with them all their wealth, of which fact Seneca complains. The emperors employed two other kinds of banishment, both of which differ from *exsilium,* inasmuch as they were not voluntary but enforced : (a) *relēgatiō = banishment* to a certain distance from Rome. The man *relēgātus* did not lose his *cīvitās,* nor yet his property. Apparently he could choose his place of abode, provided it was far enough from Rome, and not within certain well-known limits. Thus, as Ovid remarks, *relēgatiō* was not such a hardship as *exsilium:* (b) *dēportātiō = transportation* to a definite place, generally some barren and rocky island used as a state-prison; those who were *dēportātī* were often afterwards executed by the emperor's command. —— **Nōn,** adv.; limits *iubeō.*——**iubeō,** 1st pers. sing. pres. ind. act. of *iubeō, -ēre, iussī, iussum,* 2 ; understand the subj. *ego.*——**sed,** adversative conj.; joins *iubeō* and *suādeō.*——**sī,** conditional particle; *sī mē cōnsulis = if you now consult me.*——**mē,** acc. of *ego;* direct obj. of *cōnsulis.*——**cōnsulis,** 2d pers. sing. pres. ind. act. of *cōnsulō, -ere, -uī, cōnsultum,* 3 ; the implied subj. is *tū. Cōnsulō +* the acc. e.g. *aliquem, = I consult some one; cōnsulō +* the dat. e.g. *alicuī = I consult for* (the interests of) *some one.*

LINE 54.   **suādeō,** 1st pers. sing. pres. ind. act. of *suādeō, -ēre, suāsī, suāsum,* 2 (root *svad = to taste good, please;* cf. *suāvis* for *suadvis;* Greek root ἁδ *= σϝαδ,* e.g. ἕαδον from ἁνδάνω *= I please*); understand the subj. *ego.*

1 **VI. Quid est enim, Catilīna, quod tē**
What is there for, Catiline, which you

2 **iam in hāc urbe dēlectāre possit? in quā**
now in this city to delight can be able? in which

3 **nēmō est extrā istam coniūrātiōnem**
no one there is outside that of yours conspiracy

4 **perditōrum hominum quī tē nōn metuat, nēmō**
abandoned of men who you not fears, no one

VI. For what is there in this city, Catiline, that can give you pleasure any longer? There is not one man in the city, outside your degraded circle of conspiracy, but dreads you; not one

LINE 1. **Quid**, nom. sing. n. of the interrog. pron. *quis, quae, quid;* subj. of *est.* —— **est**, 3d pers. sing. pres. ind. of *sum, esse, fuī;* agrees with the subj. *quid.* The question *quid est quod dēlectāre possit* = an emphatic neg. *nihil iam amplius dēlectāre potest.* —— **enim**, causal conj., connecting this sentence with the one preceding, and explaining why Cicero advised Catiline to leave Rome, viz. because he is hated by all good citizens. —— **Catilīna**, voc. sing. of *Catilīna, -ae,* m. 1st ; the case of address. —— **quod**, nom. sing. n. of the rel. pron. *quī, quae, quod;* agrees with the antecedent *quid* in gender and number, and is subj. of *possit* in its own clause ; *quod* expresses characteristic, = *of such a kind as.* —— **tē**, acc. sing. of *tū ;* direct obj. of *dēlectāre.*

LINE 2. **iam**, temporal adv. ; modifies *dēlectāre possit. Iam* in negative clauses = *iam amplius (any longer);* see note on *est* above. —— **in**, prep. ; gov. the abl. *urbe.* —— **hāc**, abl. sing. f. of the dem. pron. *hīc, haec, hōc;* agrees with *urbe.* —— **urbe**, abl. sing. of *urbs, urbis,* f. 3d ; governed by the prep. *in.* —— **dēlectāre**, pres. inf. act. of *dēlectō, -āre, -āvī, -ātum,* 1 (root *vlak* or *lak* = Greek ϝελκ and Latin *lac,* = *to draw, allure ;* cf. *laciō* = *I entice,* esp. in compounds, e.g. *illiciō* = *in* + *laciō, laqueus* = *a snare,* and ἕλκω = *I draw);* complementary inf. with *possit.* A. & G. 271 ; B. 326 ; G. 423 ; H. 533. —— **possit**, 3d pers. sing. pres. subjunct. of *possum, posse, potuī,* no supine, irreg. (*potis,* = *able,* + *sum);* agrees with the subj. *quod;* the subjunct. is consecutive in the rel. clause of characteristic. Consult the note and references under *quī,* Chap. II, l. 47. —— **in**, prep. ; gov. the abl. *quā.* —— **quā**, abl. sing. f. of the rel. pron. *quī, quae, quod;* agrees with the antecedent *urbe;* abl. case governed by the prep. *in. In quā* illustrates the use of the rel. pron. in combining two coördinate clauses, and = *nam in eā* etc., explanatory of the sentence *quid . . . possit.* A. & G. 180, *f;* B. 251, 6; G. 610; H. 453.

LINE 3. **nēmō** (*ne* + *homō*), gen. *nūllīus,* acc. *nēminem* or *nūllum, -am,* dat. *nūllī* or *nēminī,* abl. *nūllō, -ā,* m. and f. sing., defective (cases wanting are supplied from *nūllus, ne* + *ūllus);* nom. sing., subj. of *est* following. *Nēmō . . . nōn = no one . . . not,* i.e. *every one; nōn nēmō = not nobody,* i.e. *some one.* —— **est**, 3d pers. sing. pres. ind. of *sum, esse, fuī;* agrees with its subj. *nēmō.* —— **extrā** (for *exterā,* abl. f. of *exter* or *exterus;* supply *parte = on the outside*), adv. and prep. ; as a prep. gov. the acc. *coniūrātiōnem.* —— **istam**, acc. sing. f. of the demonstr. pron. of the 2d person *iste, ista, istud* (gen. *istīus,* dat. *istī);* qualifies *coniūrātiōnem. Istam = that of yours,* spoken in tones expressing scorn and disgust. Refer to the note etc. on *iste,* Chap. I, l. 3. —— **coniūrātiōnem**, acc. sing. of *coniūrātiō, -ōnis,* f. 3d (*coniūrō,* i.e. *con* + *iūrō);* governed by the prep. *extrā ; coniūrātiōnem* is concrete = *band of conspirators;* cf. *servitium* = (1) *slavery,* (2) *a band of slaves.* See the note on *vōcēs coniūrātiōnis = vōcēs coniūrātōrum,* Chap. III, l. 5.

LINE 4. **perditōrum**, gen. plur. m. of the adj. *perditus, -a, -um* (perf. part. pass. of *perdō, -ere, perdidī, perditum,* 3); agrees with *hominum.* —— **hominum**, gen. plur. of *homō, hominis,* m. 3d ; subjective gen., of the kind called *generic,* i.e. denoting the component parts of that which the gen. limits (a branch of the partitive genitive). —— **quī,**

man but hates you. With what brand of family scandal is your life not scorched?	quī nōn ōderit. Quae nota domesticae 5 who not does hate. What mark domestic turpitūdinis nōn inūsta vītae tuae est? quod 6 of dishonor not branded upon life your is? what

nom. sing. m. of the rel. pron. *quī, quae, quod;* agrees in gender and number with the antecedent *nēmō,* and is subj. of *metuat* in the rel. clause of characteristic. Cicero shows a preference for *quī nōn* over *quīn;* when *quīn* is used it approximates to *ut nōn* (consecutive) rather than to *quī nōn.* Study the examples in the following: A. & G. 319, 2, *ff;* 319, *d;* B. 284, 2 and 3; G. 552, 1; 556; H. 500, 1; 504, 2. —— **tē,** acc. sing. of *tū ;* direct obj. of *metuat.* —— **nōn,** negative adv. ; limits *metuat.* —— **metuat,** 3d pers. sing. pres. subjunct. act. of *metuō, -ere, metuī, metūtum,* 3 (*metus*); agrees with the subj. *quī;* the subjunct. is consecutive of tendency with *quī.* The same differences of meaning that are found in the nouns *timor, metus,* etc., exist with the verbs of corresponding form; see under *timor,* Chap. I, l. 6. —— **nēmō,** nom. sing. (subj. of *est* understood from *est,* l. 8); repeated (by *anaphora*) rhetorically from *nēmō* above. A. & G. 344, *f;* B. 350, 11, *b ;* G. 636, NOTE 4 ; H. 636, III, 3.

LINE 5. **quī,** nom. sing. m. of the rel. pron. *quī, quae, quod;* agrees with the antecedent, and is subj. of *ōderet* in the clause of characteristic. —— **nōn,** negative adv. ; limits *ōderit.* —— **ōderit,** 3d pers. sing. of the defective verb *ōdī* (perf.), inf. *ōdisse,* fut. part. *ōsūrus* (no pres. stem tenses); agrees with the subj. *quī;* consecutive subjunct. of general tendency. *Odī* is probably from root *vadh* (Greek *όθ,* Latin *oa*) = *to thrust, strike,* cf. *ώθέω = I thrust;* others say *ōdī* stands for *hōdī,* which is represented as akin to *hostis,* ἔχθος, and the German *hass.* —— **Quae,** nom. sing. f. of the interrog. pron. and adj. *quis, quae, quid* (or interrog. *quī, quae, quod*); agrees with *nota.* **nota,** gen. *notae,* f. 1st (cf. *nōscō,* perf. part. *nōtus*); nom. sing., subj. of *inusta est. Nota* = *a mark* by which something is recognized, hence (1) *the brand* burnt upon the forehead of a runaway and recaptured slave, (2) *the mark* of disgrace accompanied by lowering of rank (e.g. from *senator* to *equēs*), when the censor proceeded against a citizen for immoral conduct. —— **domesticae,** gen. sing. of the adj. *domesticus, -a, -um* (*domus*); agrees with *turpitūdinis. Domesticae* refers to scandals touching Catiline's family life, e.g. (1) that Catiline has caused his own brother's inclusion in the lists of those who were murdered during the Sullan proscriptions, (2) that his relations with an illegitimate daughter violated all decency, (3) that he murdered his wife in order that he might marry the beautiful but profligate Aurēlia Orestilla, (4) that he murdered his son so that no encumbrances might hinder this crime-bought marriage. Cicero alone mentions the murder of his wife (3); Sallust confirms the story of his son's murder.

LINE 6. **turpitūdinis,** gen. sing. of *turpitūdō,* f. 3d (from the adj. *turpis ;* cf. *fortis* and *fortitūdō*); poss. gen., limiting *nota.* —— **nōn,** neg. adv. ; limits *inusta est.* —— **inūsta est** (*est* being transposed from the end of the sentence), 3d pers. sing. of the combinate perf. tense pass. of *inūrō, -ere, inussī, inūstum,* 3 (*in + ūrō* = *ūso,* root *us* = *to burn;* akin to *aὔ = I kindle*); agrees with the subj. *nota.* —— **vītae,** dat. sing. of *vīta, -ae,* f. 1st ; dat. of the indirect obj. dependent on *inusta est.* Compounds (whether trans. or intrans.) of the prepositions *in, ad, ob, sub, prae, con, ante, inter,* etc., govern the dat. of the indirect object. A. & G. 228 ; B. 187, III ; G. 347 ; H. 386. —— **tuae,** dat. sing. f. of the poss. pron. *tuus, -a, -um ;* agrees with *vītae.* —— **(est),** 3d pers. sing. pres. ind. of *sum;* agrees with the subj. *nota,* as also does the participle *inūsta,* with which *est* forms the perf. ind. pass. of *inūrō.* —— **quod,** nom. sing. n. of the interrog. adj. *quī, quae, quod;* agrees with *dēdecus.* Remember that the neut. sing. *quid* of interrog. *quis* is never used adjectively; some indeed assert that *quis* is never adjectival, and explain *vir* as an appositive in *quis vir.*

7 prīvātārum   rērum   dēdecus   nōn   haeret
  private   *of (= in) matters*   *disgrace*   *not*   *does stick*

8 in   fāmā?   quae   libīdō   ab   oculīs,
  in (your) reputation?   *what*   *wantonness*   *from*   *(your) eyes,*

9 quod facinus ā manibus umquam tuīs, quod
  what   *misdeed*   *from*   *hands*   *ever*   *your,*   *what*

10 flāgitium   ā   tōtō   corpore   āfuit?
  villany   *from*   *whole*   *(your) body*   *has been absent?*

What dishonor in your private affairs does not cling to your reputation? What form of lust was ever away from your gaze? what crime from your hands? what shameful vice from the whole of your body?

LINE 7. **prīvātārum**, gen. plur. f. of the adj. *prīvātus, -a, -um* (originally perf. part. pass. of *prīvō*); agrees with *rērum*. *Prīvātārum rērum dēdecus* refers to scandals in connection with Catiline's habits and actions in ordinary life, apart from his family life on the one hand and from politics on the other; this threefold distinction is preserved in ll. 24-29, *illa quae pertinent* (1) *ad prīvātam īgnōminiam*, (2) *ad domesticam . . . turpitūdinem*, (3) *ad summam rem pūblicam*. —— **rērum**, gen. plur. of *rēs, reī*, f. 5th; poss. gen., limiting *dēdecus*. —— **dēdecus**, gen. *dēdecoris*, n. 3d (*dē + decus; decus = ornament, glory*, from root *dak = to esteem* or *to be esteemed;* cf. *decet = it is proper, dignus = dic-nus*, and δοκέω); nom. sing., subj. of *haeret*. —— **nōn**, neg. adv., limiting *haeret*. —— **haeret**, 3d pers. sing. pres. ind. act. of *haereō, -ēre, haesī, haesum*, 2; agrees with the subj. *dēdecus*.

LINE 8. **in**, prep.; gov. the abl. *fāmā*. —— **fāmā**, abl. sing. of *fāma, -ae*, f. 1st (root *bha = fa = to make known*, hence *fāma = report, reputation;* akin to *fārī = to speak*, φήμη *= a voice, report*, etc., etc.); governed by the prep. *in*. —— **quae**, nom. sing. f. of the interrog. *quis, quae, quid*, or *quī, quae, quod;* agrees with *libīdō*. —— **libīdō**, gen. *libīdinis*, f. 3d (root *lubh =* Greek λιφ *=* Latin *lub, lib, to desire;* cf. λίπτομαι *= I am eager*, *libet* or *lubet = it pleases, līber = doing as one desires, i.e. free*); nom. sing., subj. of *āfuit*. Observe that the verb *āfuit* is expressed only with one of the coördinate subjects, viz. *flāgitium*, and is understood with the rest, viz. *libīdō* and *facinus*. This is very common in Latin; the verb might have been plur., *āfuērunt* agreeing with the plurality of subjects. —— **ab**, prep.; gov. the abl. *oculīs;* the prep. *ab* is repeated after *āfuit*. —— **oculīs**, abl. plur. of *oculus, -ī*, m. 2d (root *ak = ὀπ = oc, to see;* cf. ὀφθαλμὸς *= eye*); governed by the prep. *ab*.

LINE 9. **quod**, nom. sing. n. of the interrog. adj. *quī, quae, quod;* agrees with *facinus*. —— **facinus**, gen. *facinoris*, n. 3d (*faciō*); nom. sing., subj. of *āfuit* understood from the next sentence; *facinus* here = *misdeed, crime*, though the root idea of the word implies neither praise nor blame. Refer to the list of synonyms in the note on *sceleris*, Chap. IV, l. 9. —— **ā** (*ab* before vowels and *h; ā* or *ab* before consonants), prep.; gov. the abl. *manibus; ā* is repeated from *āfuit*, and *ab oculīs, ā manibus, ā corpore* express separation. —— **manibus**, abl. plur. of *manus, -ūs*, f. 4th (root *ma = to measure*); gov. by the prep. *ā*. —— **umquam** (sometimes written *unquam*), adv. of time; modifies *āfuit* understood in this clause as the pred. of *quod facinus*. —— **tuīs**, abl. plur. f. of the poss. pron. *tuus, -a, -um;* agrees with *manibus*. —— **quod**, nom. sing. n. of the interrog. adj. *quī, quae, quod;* agrees with *flāgitium*. Observe the *asyndeta* in ll. 8-10.

LINE 10. **flāgitium**, gen. *flagit-iī* or *-ī*, n. 2d (root *bharg =* φλεγ *= flag* or *fulg, to burn, to shine;* cf. *flāgrō, fulgeō*, and φλέγω *= I blaze;* hence *flāgitium =* (1) *a crime* done in the heat of passion, (2) *an eager demand*, cf. *flāgitō = I importune*); nom. sing., subj. of *āfuit*. For synonyms, refer to the note on *sceleris*, Chap. IV, l. 9. —— **ā**, prep.; gov. the abl. *corpore*. —— **tōtō**, abl. sing. n. of the adj. *tōtus, -a, -um;* agrees with *corpore*.

To what weak lad,	cui	tū	adulēscentulō,	quem	corruptēlārum	11
ensnared at last by	*what*	*you*	*to young lad,*	*whom*	*of your enticements*	
the fascination of	illecebrīs		irrētīssēs,		nōn aut ad	12
your allurements, did	*by the allurements*		*you had ensnared,*		*not either for*	

—— **corpore**, abl. sing. of *corpus, corporis,* n. 3d ; governed by the prep. *ā*. —— **āfuit**, 3d pers. sing. perf. ind. of *absum, abesse, āfui,* no supine (*ab* + *sum*), agrees with the nearest subj. *flāgitium,* and is understood with each of the preceding subjects. Sallust gives a similar picture of Catiline's pursuits, describing him as endowed with vigorous physical and mental powers, as rash, licentious, extravagant, and as delighting in civil strife, murder, and rapine.

LINE 11. **cui**, dat. sing. m. of the interrog. pron. and adj. *quis, quae, quid,* or *quī, quae, quod;* agrees with *adulēscentulō*. —— **tū**, nom. sing. of the 2d personal pron. ; subj. of *praetulistī.* —— **adulēscentulō**, dat. sing. of *adulēscentulus, -ī,* m. 2d (diminutive of *adulēscēns;* cf. *rīvulus* of *rīvus, parvulus* of *parvus*); dat. of the indirect obj. with *praetulistī.* Diminutives often signify affection, and are used as terms of endearment; but sometimes express scorn, as in this passage. *Adulēscentulus,* however, frequently implies neither emotion, and practically = *adulēscēns.* Gradations of age are expressed by : *īnfantulus, īnfāns, puerulus, puer, adulēscentulus, adulēscēns, iunior, iuvenis, senior* or *grandior nātū, senex.* Of these the chief divisions are *puer, adulēscēns, iuvenis,* and *senex,* and some hold that each period includes 15 years, i.e. *puer* = up to 15 years of age, *adulēscēns* = 16–30, *iuvenis* = 31–45, and *senex* from 46 years of age onwards. This calculation will serve roughly, but *pueritia* and *adulescentia* each mark a distinct period, whereas *iuventūs* is often used in a general way and including *pueritia* and *adulescentia.* The periods overlap one another, e.g. a child is *puer* till about 16–18 years of age, becomes *adulēscens* (and *vir*) when he dons the *toga virīlis* and remains so till about the age of 30, *iuvenis* from 25 or 30 up to 45 or 50 (any one of age to serve in the army must be *iuvenis,* in early times from 17 years to 46), finally *senex.* Although *adulēscēns* and *adulēscentulus* are formed from *adolēscō* (inceptive of *adoleō*), root *al* = *to grow, to nourish* (cf. *alō* = *I support*), yet the form *adolēscēns* is very far inferior to *adulēscēns* in all the best writers and MSS. ; Ritschel in his *Prolegomena* says *vix umquam bonī librī sine discrepantiā formam* (*adolēscēns*) *agnōscunt.* —— **quem**, acc. sing. m. of the rel. pron. *quī, quae, quod;* agrees with the antecedent *adulēscentulō;* direct obj. of *irrētīssēs* in the rel. clause. Observe that the antecedent of *quem* does not refer to any particular person, but is indefinite ; hence *quem* is generic, i.e. represents a class or type, and is accordingly followed by the consecutive subjunctive.—— **corruptēlārum**, gen. plur. of *corruptēla, -ae,* f. 1st (formed from *corruptus,* the perf. part. pass. of *corrumpō* = *I corrupt,* hence = *corruption, seduction*) ; poss. gen., limiting *illecebrīs.*

LINE 12. **illecebrīs**, abl. plur. of *illecebra, -ae,* f. 1st (*in* + root *lak* = *lac, to allure;* cf. *laciō* = *I entice,* esp. in compounds, *dēliciōsus, laqueus* = *a snare,* etc.); abl. of the means, modifying *irrētīssēs.* —— **irrētīssēs** (*inrētīssēs*), 2d pers. sing. pluperf. subjunct. act. of *irrētiō* (*inrētiō*), *-īre, -īvī, -ītum,* 4 (*in* = *into* + *rēte* = *a net; rēte* is for *srē-te,* from root *sar* = *to put together,* cf. *serō* = *I bind together, entwine*) ; the subj. *tū* is implied by the personal ending ; the subjunct. is consecutive, with *quem* characteristic. *Irrētīssēs* is a contracted form of *irrētīvissēs.* In the perf.-stem tenses active, the *v* often disappears, and the two vowels between which it originally stood contract into one long vowel — this is the rule for perfects in *-āvī, -ēvī,* and *-ōvī* (cf. *cōnfīrmāstī* for *cōnfīrmāvistī,* Chap. IV, l. 30); but while perfects in *-īvī* often drop the *v,* the vowels do not as a rule contract except before *st,* e.g. *audīstī* for *audīvistī,* and *ss,* e.g. *irrētīssēs;* thus we may have *audīverat* or *audierat,* but not *audīrat.* Sallust remarks on the power which Cati-

audāciam	ferrum	aut	ad	libīdinem	facem
his audacity	*a sword*	*or*	*for*	*his lust*	*a torch*

praetulistī?	Quid	vērō?	nūper,	cum
did hold forth?	*What*	*indeed?*	*lately,*	*when*

morte	superiōris	ūxōris	novīs	nūptiīs
by the death	*former*	*of your wife*	*new*	*for nuptials*

you not reach forth a sword for his violence or a torch for his lust? And again, a short time ago, after you had emptied your house for a fresh

---

line held over the minds of young Romanus, and upholds Cicero's charges.——**nōn**, neg. adv., limiting *praetulistī*.——**aut**, disjunctive conj., used correlatively with *aut* below = *either . . . or*. The other disjunctive correlatives are *vel . . . vel; sīve (seu) . . . sīve (seu)*; cf. *et . . . et = both . . . and, neque . . . neque = neither . . . nor*. ——**ad**, prep. with the acc.; gov. *audāciam*; *ad* here and in the next line = *for, with a view to, for the purpose of*.

LINE 13. **audāciam**, acc. sing. of *audācia, -ae*, f. 1st (formed from the adj. *audāx, -ācis*, 3d; *audeō = I dare*); governed by the prep. *ad*.——**ferrum**, acc. sing. of *ferrum, ī-*, n. 2d; direct obj. of *praetulistī*.——*Ferrum* = lit. *iron*, and by metonymy *an iron* or *steel weapon*, esp. *a sword*. *Ferrum ad audāciam* = *a sword for bold*, i.e. *violent, deeds*, rather than *a sword to give him (adulēscentulus) boldness*.——**aut**, disjunctive conj.; connects *ferrum* and *facem;* used correlatively with *aut* above = *either . . . or*. Of the disjunctive conjunctions *vel* (probably an old imperative of *volō*) and its shortened enclitic form *ve* give a choice between two alternatives; *sīve* offers a choice between two names of the same thing; *aut* is used when each alternative excludes the other. A. & G. 156, *c*; B. 342; G. 493–496, esp. 493; H. 554, II.——**ad**, prep.; gov. the acc. *libīdinem;* used in the same sense as in l. 12.——**libīdinem**, acc. sing. of *libīdō, libīdinis*, f. 3d; governed by the prep. *ad*.——**facem**, acc. sing. of *fax, facis*, f. 3d (Latin root *fa-c* = root *bha, to bring to light;* akin to *faciēs;* the root *fac* is allied to root *fa* of *fārī (to speak)*, root *fas* of *nefās*, root *fat* of *fateor*, etc.); direct obj. of *praetulistī*, joined by *aut* to *ferrum*. The metaphor is taken from the custom of slaves lighting their masters home by a torch; Catiline's metaphorical torch was to guide the young men in the pursuit of their lusts, and perhaps there is the further idea of his fanning the flame of their passions.

LINE 14. **praetulistī**, 2d pers. sing. perf. ind. act. of *praeferō, praeferre, praetulī, praelātum*, irreg. (*prae = in front + ferō = I carry*); agrees with the subj. *tū*, l. 11.—— Quid, acc. sing. n. of the interrog. pron. *quis, quae, quid;* idiomatic adverbial acc. = *quid dīcam aē hōc*. *Quid* or *quid vērō* is used by Cicero to mark a transition; in this passage it is made more emphatic by *vērō*, and leads up to a charge of more definite crime.——**vērō**, adverbial abl. of *vērus, -a, -um;* used both as an adv. and as an adversative conjunction. A. & G. 156, *b*; B. 343, 1; G. 483–491; H. 554, III.——**nūper** (*novum + per*), adv. of time (superl. *nūperrimē*); modifies *cumulāstī*.——**cum**, temporal conj.; followed by the subjunct. *vacuēfēcissēs*. *Cum*, like the other temporal conjunctions, usually takes the ind., esp. in the pres. and perf. tenses, but is generally followed by the imperf. and pluperf. subjunct., because in these tenses the time is *described* by the circumstances which also have some causal or concessive force, i.e. the imperf. and pluperf. do not *define* the time so much as *describe* it. A. & G. 325; B. 288; G. 580–585; H. 521.

LINE 15. **morte**, abl. sing. of *mors, mortis*, f. 3d; *morte = nece, by the murder* (expressed euphemistically by Cicero; cf. his announcement to the people, after the strangling of Lentulus and the other four conspirators, *"they have lived their life" = they are dead*), and therefore is an abl. of the means, modifying *vacuēfēcissēs*.——**superiōris**, gen. sing. f. of the adj. *superior, -ius* (compar. of *superus, -a, -um*, from adv. *super;* superl. *suprēmus* or *summus*); agrees with *ūxōris*.——**ūxōris**, gen. sing. of *ūxor*, f. 3d

| marriage by the murder of your first wife, did you not surmount this crime with yet another one over- | domum _your house_ incrēdibilī _incredible_ | vacuēfēcissēs, _you had made vacant,_ scelere _by crime_ | nōnne _not_ hōc _this_ | etiam _also_ scelus _crime_ | aliō _another_ cumulāstī? _did you augment?_ | 16 17 |

(all attempts to trace the etymology of _ūxor_ are fanciful); poss. gen., limiting _morte_. Synonyms: (1) _ūxor_ = _the wife_, as distinguished from _vir_ = _the husband;_ (2) _coniunx_ (_con_ + _iungō_) = usually _wife_, as the partner of her husband's life; sometimes = _husband;_ (3) _marīta_ = _wife_, as opposed to _marītus_ = _husband_ (_mās, maris_ = _male, one of the male sex_). —— **novīs**, dat. plur. f. of _novus, -a, -um;_ agrees with _nūptiīs_. The _new marriage_ was with Aurēlia Orestilla, of whom Sallust says that _praeter formam nihil umquam bonus laudāvit_. Cicero is the only writer who records the charge of wife-murder against Catiline. —— **nūptiīs**, dat. of the plur. noun _nūptiae, -ārum_, f. 1st (from _nūpta_ = _a bride;_ root _nabh_ = _νεφ_ = _neb, nub, to veil;_ cf. _νέφος_ and _nūbēs_ = _a cloud, nebula_ = _a mist_, and _nūbō, -ere, nūpsī, nūptum_, 3 = _I veil myself, I marry_, i.e. as the female participator in the marriage ceremony); dat. of the object for which, or, as it is often called, dat. of purpose. Distinguish between the following: (1) _dūcō_ or _dūcō ūxōrem_ = _I marry_, of the husband; _dūcō_ = _dūcō domum;_ (2) _nūbō_ = _I marry_, of the wife, followed by the dat., e.g. _Catilīnae nūpsit_ = lit. _she veiled herself for Catiline_, i.e. _married Catiline;_ (3) the pass. _mātrimōniō iungor_ is used of either the husband or the wife. _Nūptiae_ were of four kinds: (1) _iūstae_, i.e. between a man or woman, each of whom is a _cīvis_, or between a _cīvis_ and a Latin enjoying the right of _connūbium_ with Rome; (2) _iniūstae_, when one of the parties did not have the _iūs connūbī;_ the children took the status of the less privileged parent, except when the father was a _cīvis_ and the mother had _iūs connūbī;_ in this case the children were _optimō iūre_ citizens; (3) _cum conventiōne in manum_, i.e. when the woman passed from the control (_potestās_) of her father or guardian into her husband's control; (4) _sine conventiōne in manum_, i.e. the wife remained under her father's control, or else was _suī iūris;_ if she was _suī iūris_, she retained the disposition of her own property, but not otherwise. The law recognized three forms of marriage: (a) _cōnfarreātiō_, a religious ceremony at the bride's house, when a sacred cake of meal (_far_) was broken, and other rites observed; (b) _coemptiō_, a fictitious sale of the bride by her father to the husband; (c) _ūsus_, i.e. when the wife stayed at her husband's house for one complete year without being absent three consecutive nights, the marriage was regarded as legally = to one made as in (a) or (b). The bride invariably brought a _dōs_ (cf. French _dot_) according to her means. Marriages _cum conventiōne_ became rare, and laxness generally crept into the ceremony, so that divorces became very common and very easy to obtain. Some say that a marriage by _cōnfarreātiō_ was indissoluble, but probably it could be dissolved by going through a religious ceremony called _diffareātiō_.

LINE 16. **domum**, acc. sing. of _domus, -ūs_, f. 4th (2d decl. forms also); direct obj. of _vacuēfēcissēs_. —— **vacuēfēcissēs**, 2d pers. sing. pluperf. subjunct. act. of _vacuēfaciō, -ere, vacuēfēcī, vacuēfactum_, 3 (_vacuus_ = _empty_ + _faciō_ = _I make_); the implied subj. is _tū;_ for the mood, see the note _cum_ above, l. 14. —— **nōnne** (_nōn_ + _ne_), interrog. particle, the use of which implies that an affirmative reply is expected. Refer to the note on _ne_, Chap. 1, l. 4. —— **etiam** (_et_ + _iam_), adv., modifying _cumulāstī_. —— **aliō**, abl. sing. n. of the adj. _alius, -a, -ud_ (gen. contracts from _ali-īus_ to _alīus_, dat. _aliī;_ _alius_ is akin to ἄλλος); agrees with _scelere_.

LINE 17. **incrēdibilī**, abl. sing. n. of the adj. _incrēdibilis, -e_, 3d (_in_ = _not_ + _crēdibilis_, from _crēdō_); agrees with _scelere_. —— **scelere**, abl. sing. of _scelus, sceleris_, n. 3d; abl. of the means, with _cumulāstī_. —— **hōc**, acc. sing. n. of the dem. pron. _hīc, haec, hōc;_ agrees with _scelus_, i.e. wife-murder (_morte superiōris ūxōris_). —— **scelus**, gen. _sceleris_, n. 3d; acc. sing., direct obj. of _cumulāstī_. —— **cumulāstī**, 2d pers. sing.

18	quod	ego	praetermittō	et	facile	patior
	(which	*I*	*pass over*	*and*	*readily*	*allow*
19	silērī,		nē	in	hāc	cīvitāte	tantī
	to be kept silent,		*lest*	*in*	*this*	*state*	*so great*
20	facinoris	immānitās	aut	exstitisse	aut
	of an outrage	*the monstrosity*	*either*	*to have existed*	*or*

passing belief? But I let this pass, and readily suffer it to be sunk in silence, that it may not seem possible for wickedness of such enormity to have displayed itself

---

perf. ind. act. of *cumulō, -āre, āvī, -ātum,* 1 (*cumulus = a heap;* probably from root *ku = to swell,* cf. κῦμα = *a wave, the swell* of the sea, *cavus = hollow,* κυέω = *I am pregnant,* etc.); the subj. *tū* is understood. *Cumulāstī* is a contraction of *cumulāvistī; v* is frequently dropped in the perf.-stem tenses, and in verbs of the 1st, 2d, and 3d conjugations, the vowels between which it originally stood contract and form one long vowel; cf. *cōnfīrmāstī,* Chap. IV, l. 30, and note. The allusion in this sentence is to the charge which Sallust (*Catilīna,* XV) expressly confirms, viz. that Catiline killed his son in order to marry Orestilla, *quod ea nūbere illī dubitābat timēns prīvīgnum adultum aetāte = because she, fearful of a grown-up step-son, hesitated to marry him;* cf. Sallust in the same passage, *prō certō crēditur necātō fīliō vacuam domum scelestīs nūptiīs fēcisse = he* (Catiline) *is believed for a fact to have murdered his son and to have cleared his house for the criminal marriage.*

LINE 18. **quod,** acc. sing. n. of the rel. pron. *quī, quae, quod;* direct obj. of *praetermittō; quod* may be taken either as referring to and agreeing with the antecedent *scelere,* or better as referring to the whole of the previous clause = *et hōc.*——**ego,** nom. sing. of the 1st personal pron.; subj. of *praetermittō; ego* is emphatic, = *I for my part.* ——**praetermittō,** 1st pers. sing. pres. ind. act. of *praetermittō, -ere, praetermīsī, praetermissum,* 3 (*praeter = beyond, by + mittō = I send,* hence *I let pass, overlook*); agrees with the subj. *ego.* Synonyms: (1) *neglegō = I omit, do not mind,* implying indifference; (2) *omittō = I omit* or *take no notice of,* knowingly and intentionally; (3) *praetermittō = I omit, overlook,* generally from lack of attention; (4) *dīmittō = I omit, give up,* voluntarily.——**et,** cop. conj.; connects *praetermittō* and *patior.*——**facile,** adv. (the adverbial acc. n. of *facilis*); modifying *patior.*——**patior,** 1st pers. sing. pres. ind. of the deponent verb *patior, patī, passus sum,* 3; the subj. is *ego* understood; joined by *et* to *praetermittō. Patior = I suffer,* i.e. I do not actively interfere so as to make the story public. For synonyms, consult the note on *patimur,* Chap. II, l. 15.

LINE 19. **silērī,** pres. inf. pass. of *sileō, -ēre, -uī,* no supine, 2, trans. and intrans.; secondary obj. of *patior,* i.e. *silērī* agrees with *quod* in the obj.-clause of *patior.* For the distinction between *tacēre* and *silēre,* see the note on *tacēs,* Chap. IV, l. 10.——**nē,** negative final conj., = *in order that . . . not;* followed by the subjunct. of purpose *videātur. Nē* is the regular negative in all final clauses (*ut* in affirmative clauses), whether pure or substantival, e.g. after verbs of fearing; it also regularly introduces negative commands and negative wishes, e.g. *utinam nē.* Refer to note on *nē,* Chap. II, l. 2.——**in,** prep.; gov. the abl. *cīvitāte.*——**hāc,** abl. sing. f. of the dem. pron. *hīc, haec, hōc;* agrees with *cīvitāte.*——**cīvitāte,** abl. sing. of *cīvitās, -ātis,* f. 3d (*cīvis*); governed by the prep. *in. Cīvitās = the state,* as being a community of *cīvēs; rēs pūblica = the state,* in reference to its government.——**tantī,** gen. sing. n. of the dem. adj. *tantus, -a, -um;* agrees with *facinoris.*

LINE 20. **facinoris,** gen. sing. of *facinus,* n. 3d (*faciō,* hence *deed;* usually as here in a bad sense, *misdeed, crime*); poss. gen., limiting *immānitās. Tantī facinoris immānitās,* so great a crime's enormity is a variation for the ordinary *facinus tantae immānitātis* (gen. of quality, i.e. descriptive) = *a crime of such enormity.*——**immānitās,** gen. *immānitātis,* f. 3d (from adj. *immānis, -e,* 3d = *monstrous, huge; in = not +*

in this state, or, at least, to have gone unpunished. I pass over the complete bankruptcy of your estate — for you will	nōn	vindicāta esse	videātur.	Praetermittō 21
	not	*to have been avenged*	*may seem.*)	*I pass over*
	ruīnās	fortūnārum	tuārum,	quās	omnēs 22
	the downfall	*of fortunes*	*your*	*which*	*all*

root *ma = to measure*, hence *immeasurable;* cf. the old adj. *mānus = good*, from the same root); nom. sing., subj. of *videātur.*——**aut**, disjunctive conj., used correlatively with *aut* below, = *either . . . or.*——**exstitisse**, perf. inf. act. of *exsistō, -ere, exstiti, exstitum,* 3 (*ex + sistō*); complementary predicative inf., with the copulative verb *videātur.*——**aut**, disjunctive conj. (refer to the notes on *aut*, ll. 12 and 13); connects *exstitisse* and *nōn vindicāta esse.*

LINE 21. **nōn**, neg. adv.; limits *vindicāta esse.*——**vindicāta**, perf. part. pass. of *vindicō, -āre, -āvī, -ātum,* 1 (from *vindex = defender, avenger;* some derive from *venus = sale + dīcō*, others from *vīs = violence + dīcō*, but neither is probable); adjectival complement in the pred. of the copulative *esse, videātur;* agrees in gender, number, and case with the subj. *immānitās;* understand *sī exstiterit* before *nōn vindicāta esse.* A noun or adj. which refers to the subject and is complement of a copulative verb agrees and is put in the same case with the subject. A. & G. 271, *c;* B. 328, 2; G. 205, 206; A. 536, 2. Roman criminal law required that some one must prosecute whenever a crime was committed; if no one did so, the magistrates could not bring the guilty person to justice, nor could they enforce punishment or take any official notice of the crime. The fact that Catiline was not prosecuted for his son's murder may either be considered to prove how low the moral life of Rome had become (and it was undoubtedly very bad, and became much worse later on), or else to show that this rumor was a mere scandal, unsupported by any sort of evidence upon which legal action might be taken.——**esse**, pres. inf. of *sum;* complementary inf. with *videātur. Vindicāta + esse* = the combinate perf. inf. pass. of *vindicō*, corresponding to the coördinate perf. inf. *exstitisse.*——**videātur**, 3d pers. sing. pres. subjunct. pass. of *videō, -ēre, vīdī, vīsum,* 2 (the pass. *videor*, as here, commonly = *I seem*, followed by an inf. or by a pred. adj. or noun with *esse* expressed or understood); agrees with the subj. *immānitās;* the subjunct. is final, expressing purpose after *nē*, l. 19. Prof. Wilkins remarks that *esse videātur* "became a commonplace of rhetoric," and quotes Quintilian, "*esse videātur,*" *iam nimis frequēns.* From this it is clear that there were stock phrases and expressions in ancient rhetoric just as there are in modern; cf. Cicero's pet verb *comperīre*, to which his enemies so much objected. Whereas *esse videātur* is common, *esse vidētur* is avoided in prose, especially at the end of a sentence, because it constitutes two feet, dactyl and trochee (*ĕssĕ vĭdētŭr*), which conclude a hexametric verse in poetry (the conclusion may also be dactyl and spondee, i.e. _ ∪ ∪ followed by _ _).——**Praetermittō**, 1st pers. sing. pres. ind. act. of *praetermittō, -ere, praetermīsī, praetermissum,* 3 (*praeter + mittō*); the subj. *ego* is implied by the personal ending.

LINE 22. **ruīnās**, acc. plur. of *ruīna, -ae,* f. 1st (from *ruō = I rush down, fall down,* = *srovō*, from root *sru = to break forth;* cf. *ῥέω = I flow, Rumo* (an old name for the Tiber), *Rōma = Srouma = the stream-town*, i.e. Rome); direct obj. of *praetermittō.*——**fortūnārum**, gen. plur. of *fortūna, -ae,* f. 1st (lengthened from *fors = chance*, lit. *whatever brings itself*, root *bhar = fer = to bear;* cf. *ferō, φέρω*); poss. gen., limiting *ruīnās. Fortūna = fortune*, either good (*prosperity*) or bad (*misfortune*); personified *Fortūna* is the goddess of fortune, worshipped more by the Romans than the Greeks, and especially at Antium and Praeneste; the plur. *fortūnae = possessions, property*, by metonymy. Catiline had been praetor in B.C. 68, and as propraetor governed the province of Africa in 67. On his return to Rome he sued for election as consul, but his candidature was

23 prōximīs	Īdibus	tibi	impendēre
next	*on the Ides*	*over you*	*to hang*
24 sentiēs :	ad illa	veniō,	quae nōn
you will perceive:	*to those things*	*I come,*	*which not*
25 ad prīvātam	īgnōminiam	vitiōrum	tuōrum,
to private	*the shame*	*of vices*	*your,*

see on the 13th of this month that your bankruptcy is imminent: I proceed not to matters which reflect the shame of your private vices or

withdrawn as he was prosecuted by P. Clōdius Pulcher (Cicero's bitter enemy later on) for extortion. Cicero thought of defending him, but considered the evidence too strong against him, cf. the letter to Atticus in which he says he may be acquitted *sī iūdicātum erit merīdiē nōn lūcēre* = *if it will be decided that the sun does not shine at noon.* Catiline bought his acquittal by giving ruinous bribes to the jury, and so shortly after this we hear of him being completely overwhelmed with debt. —— **tuārum**, gen. plur. f. of the poss. pron. *tuus, -a, -um ;* agrees with *fortūnārum.* —— **quās**, acc. plur. f. of the rel. pron. *quī, quae, quod ;* agrees with the antecedent *ruīnās ;* subj.-acc. of *impendēre* in the acc. and inf. construction dependent on *sentiēs.* —— **omnēs**, acc. plur. f. of the adj. *omnis, -e,* 3d ; stands as a modifier of *quās* in the rel. clause, but really modifies *ruīnās* in the main clause. An emphatic adj. is often placed in the rel. clause in Latin, especially superlative adjectives, e.g. *I will send the most reliable soldiers I have with me* = *mīlitēs quōs fīdissimōs mēcum habeō mittam.*

LINE 23. **prōximīs**, abl. plur. f. of the adj. *prōximus, -a, -um* (superl. formed from the adv. or prep. *prope ;* compar. *propior ;* no positive ; cf. *ulterior* and *ultimus,* from adv. *ultrā*) ; agrees with *Īdibus.* The Ides of November fall on the 13th day ; they fall on the 15th in the months March, May, July, and October. The Kalends (1st day of the month), the Ides, and to a smaller degree the Nones (the 5th day of the month, except in March, May, July, and October, when it was the 7th) were special days on which money-lenders and estate-buyers called in the money due to them or the interest on mortgages, or lent out money which they had collected on previous settling days. Cicero means that the exposure of Catiline's schemes and the certainty of their ultimate failure will cause the creditors of the latter to put such pressure on him on Nov. 13th that he will recognize (*sentiēs*) that the following Kalends (the great settling-day) will complete his financial ruin. —— **Īdibus**, abl. of the plur. n. *Īdūs, -uum,* f. 4th (abbreviated = Id. ; the grammarian Macrobius derives from Etruscan *iduo,* hence *division*); abl. of time when, modified by *prōximīs.* Except with a few words, e.g. *aestāte* = *in summer,* the noun in the abl. always has a modifier. A. & G. 256 ; B. 230 ; G. 393 ; H. 429. —— **tibi**, dat. sing. of *tū ;* indirect obj. of the intrans. verb *impendēre* as a compound of *in.* A. & G. 228 ; B. 187, III ; G. 347 ; H. 386. —— **impendēre**, pres. inf. act. of *impendeō, -ēre,* no perf., no supine, 2 (*in* + *pendeō*) ; agrees with the sub.-acc. *quās* in the (acc. and inf.) object clause of *sentiēs.*

LINE 24. **sentiēs**, 2d pers. sing. fut. ind. act. of *sentiō, -īre, sensī, sensum,* 4 ; the implied subj. is *tū.* —— **ad**, prep. ; gov. the acc. *illa.* —— **illa**, acc. plur. n. of the dem. pron. *ille, illa, illud ;* governed by the prep. *ad.* —— **veniō**, 1st pers. sing. pres. ind. act. of *veniō, -īre, vēnī, ventum,* 4 ; the subj. implied by the personal ending is *ego.* —— **quae**, nom. plur. n. of the rel. pron. *quī, quae, quod ;* agrees with the antecedent *illa,* and is subj. of *pertinent,* l. 29. —— **nōn**, neg. adv., limiting the clause (*quae*) *ad prīvātam īgnōminiam* (*pertinent*).

LINE 25. **ad**, prep. ; gov. the acc. *īgnōminiam.* —— **prīvātam**, acc. sing. f. of the adj. *prīvātus, -a, -um ;* agrees with *īgnōminiam ;* the *prīvāta īgnōminia* was referred to in ll. 7–14. —— **īgnōminiam**, acc. sing. of *īgnōminia, -ae,* f. 1st (*in* + *nōmen,* root *gno* = *to know*) ; governed by the prep. *ad.* —— **vitiōrum**, gen. plur. of *vitium, -ī,* n. 2d (*defect,*

the embarrassments	nōn	ad	domesticam	tuam	difficultātem	ac 26
and dishonor of your	*not*	*to*	*domestic*	*your*	*difficulty*	*and*
home life, but to	turpitūdinem,		sed	ad	summam	rem 27
other matters which	*baseness,*		*but*	*to*	*utmost*	*the weal*
affect the highest	pūblicam	atque	ad	omnium	nostrum	vītam 28
welfare of the state	*common*	*and*	*to*	*all*	*of us*	*the life*
and the life and	salūtemque		pertinent.	Potestne	tibi	haec 29
safety of every one	*and the safety*		*appertain.*	*Is able*	*to you*	*this*
of us. Can this light						

vice, lit. *a twist,* root *vi* = *to entwine, plant;* cf. *vīmen = a pliant twig, vieō = I plait,* and *lτέα = a willow*); subjective gen., limiting *ĭgnōminiam.* —— **tuōrum,** gen. plur. n. of the poss. pron. *tuus, -a, -um;* agrees with *vitiōrum.*

LINE 26. **nōn,** neg. adv., limiting the clause (*quae*) *ad domesticam difficultātem et turpitūdinem* (*pertinent*). *Nōn . . . nōn* is much more emphatic than the correlatives *neque . . . neque,* and strengthens the contrast introduced by *sed.* —— **ad,** prep.; gov. the accusatives *difficultātem* and *turpitūdinem.* —— **domesticam,** acc. sing. f. of the adj. *domesticus, -a, -um;* agrees with the nearest substantive *difficultātem* and is understood with *turpitūdinem.* —— **tuam,** acc. sing. f. of the poss. pron. *tuus, -a, -um;* agrees with *difficultātem* and is understood with *turpitūdinem.* —— **difficultātem,** acc. sing. of *difficultās, -ātis,* f. 3d (*difficilis*); governed by the prep. *ad;* the pecuniary embarrassments of Catiline were touched upon in ll. 21-24. —— **ac** (shortened form of *atque; ac* is used before consonants except *c, g,* and *qu; atque* is used before *c, g, qu,* and vowels), cop. conj., connecting two important ideas. See the note on *que,* Chap. I, l. 9.

LINE 27. **turpitūdinem,** acc. sing. of *turpitūdō, -inis,* f. 3d (from the adj. *turpis, -e,* 3d); governed by the prep. *ad;* joined by *ac* to *difficultātem.* The immorality of Catiline's family life meets more than slight (if short) notice in ll. 5 and 6, and 14-21. —— **sed,** adversative conj.; joins and opposes *ad summam rem pūblicam* to *ad prīvatam . . . turpitūdinem.* —— **ad,** prep.; gov. the accusatives *rem pūblicam* and *vītam salūtemque.* —— **summam,** acc. sing. f. of *summus, -a, -um* (*summus* and *suprēmus* are superl. of the rare pos. *superus,* from adv. *super; compar. superior*); agrees with *rem pūblicam.* —— **rem,** acc. sing. of *rēs, reī,* f. 5th; governed by the prep. *ad; rem pūblicam = public welfare,* rather than *state,* in this passage. Catiline's political crimes are treated after his crimes in his family and in his private life, because the former are more important and bear more directly on the occasion of this meeting of the Senate.

LINE 28. **pūblicam,** acc. sing. f. of the adj. *pūblicus, -a, -um;* agrees with *rem.* —— **atque,** cop. conj.; connects *ad rem pūblicam* and *ad vītam.* —— **ad,** prep.; gov. the accusatives *vītam* and *salūtem.* —— **omnium,** gen. plur. m. of the adj. *omnis, -e,* 3d; agrees with *nostrum.* —— **nostrum,** gen. plur. of the 2d personal pron. *nōs;* poss. gen., limiting *vītam salūtemque.* The personal pronouns have a gen. in *-ī,* which is in nearly all cases used *objectively,* and also a gen. in *-um,* which nearly always is used *partitively,* e.g. *quem nostrum = whom of us?* Chap. I, l. 16. But when *omnium* is used, the gen. *nostrum* or *vestrum* regularly takes the place of *nostrī* or *vestrī,* and in such cases it is not used partitively; *all of us* can only be *nōs omnes,* never *omnēs nostrum.* A. & G. 194, *b;* B. 241, 2; G. 364, REM., and NOTE 2; H. 446, NOTE 3. —— **vītam,** acc. sing. of *vīta, -ae,* f. 1st; governed by the prep. *ad.*

LINE 29. **salūtemque** (*salūtem* + *que*), *salūtem* is the acc. sing. of *salūs, -ūtis,* f. 3d (akin to *salvus*); governed by the prep. *ad;* joined closely by *que* to *vītam,* with which it forms a single idea. *Que* is the enclitic cop. conj.; connects *vītam* and *salūtem.* —— **pertinent,** 3d pers. plur. pres. ind. act. of *pertineō, -ēre, -uī,* no supine, 2 (*per* + *teneō*); agrees with the subj. *quae,* l. 24. —— **Potestne** (*potest* + *ne*), *potest* is 3d pers. sing. pres.

30 lūx,	Catilīna,	aut	hūius	caelī	of day or this air of
daylight,	*Catiline,*	*or*	*this*	*of sky*	heaven afford you
31 spīritus	esse	iūcundus,	cum	sciās	pleasure, Catiline,
the breath (= air)	*to be*	*pleasant,*	*seeing that*	*you know*	seeing that you know there is not one mem-
32 esse	hōrum	nēminem	quī	nesciat	ber of this gathering
to be	*of these (senators)*	*no one*	*who*	*does not know*	ignorant of these

ind. of *possum, posse, potuī,* no supine, irreg. (*potis + sum*); agrees with subj. *lūx. Ne* is the enclitic interrog. particle, used in introducing questions simply for the sake of extracting information, and not with the expectation that the reply will be affirmative or the reverse. See note on *ne,* Chap. I, l. 4.——**tibi,** dat. sing. of *tū;* dat. of the indirect obj., dependent on *esse iūcundus.*——**haec,** nom. sing. f. of the dem. pron. *hīc, haec, hōc;* agrees with *lūx.* A few old editions read *hūius vītae lūx,* instead of *haec lūx,* preferring (with little or no authority) a phrase which balances *hūius caelī spīritus* following.

LINE 30. **lūx,** gen. *lūcis,* f. 3d (root *ruk, luk = to shine,* cf. *lūceō, lūna = lucna, lūmen = lucmen, λύχνος = a lamp*); nom. sing., subj. of *potest.* Synonyms : *lūmen = the light-giving body,* and *lūx = the light* which streams from the *lūmen;* but this distinction is frequently omitted, and *lūmen* is used generally, e.g. for *the light* of a lamp, while *lūx* constantly = *daylight.*——**Catilīna,** -ae, voc. sing. of *Catilīna, -ae,* m. 1st; the case of address.——**aut,** disjunctive conj.; connects the subjects *lūx* and *spīritus.*——**hūius,** gen. sing. n. of the dem. pron. *hīc, haec, hōc;* agrees with *caelī.*——**caelī,** gen. sing. of *caelum (coelum* less correct), n. 2d (root *ku = to swell, be hollow;* cf. κοῖλος and *cavus = hollow; caelum* stands for *cavilum*); poss. gen., limiting *spīritus.*

LINE 31. **spīritus,** gen. *spīritūs,* m. 4th (lit. = *breath, breathing,* from *spīrō = I breathe;* hence by metonymy = *air* (as in this passage), *inspiration,* i.e. as the breath of a god, *breath of life,* i.e. *life (courage* or *pride*); nom. sing., subject of *potest* understood from the clause preceding; joined by *aut* to *lūx.*——**esse,** pres. inf. of *sum;* complementary inf. of *potest.*——**iūcundus,** nom. sing. m. of the adj. *iūcundus, -a, um* (probably for *iuvicundus,* from *iuvō = I please*); complement of *esse* in the full pred. *potest esse iūcundus;* observe that *iūcundus* refers as much to *lūx* as to *spīritus,* but agrees in gender only with the latter because it is the nearer noun. A. & G. 176, 187; B. 233, 2 ; 235, B, 2, *b*); G. 205, 206 ; 286, 1 ; H. 360, 439, 2. *Iūcundus = agreeable,* i.e. as causing joy, e.g. *iūcunda narrātiō = an agreeable story; grātus = agreeable,* i.e. *welcome, acceptable;* medicine is *grāta* to an invalid, but it is not therefore *iūcunda.*——**cum,** causal conj., hence followed by the subjunct. mood. A. & G. 326; B. 286, 2; G. 586; H. 517.——**sciās,** 2d pers. sing. pres. subjunct. act. of *sciō, -īre, scīvī, scītum,* 4 (root *ski = to split, sever, distinguish;* cf. κεδ̓ζω = *I split*); the implied subj. is *tū;* the subjunct. mood depends on *cum* causal. Synonyms : (1) *sciō* (neg. *nesciō*) = *I know* facts or truths as the objects of *conviction,* e.g. *sciō quis sit = I know who he is;* (2) *nōscō = I know* things or attributes as the objects of *perception,* e.g. *nōvī hominem = I know the man;* (3) *cōgnōscō = I know, recognize, ascertain;* (4) *intellegō = I perceive* by the senses or the understanding.

LINE 32. **esse,** pres. inf. of *sum;* agrees with the subj.-acc. *nēminem* in the object-clause (acc. and inf. construction) of *sciās.*——**hōrum,** gen. plur. m. of the dem. pron. *hīc, haec, hōc;* partitive gen., limiting *nēminem ; hōrum* is deictic, and = *of the senators here present.*——**nēminem,** acc. sing. of *nēmō,* m. and f. 3d (= *ne + homō,* dat. *nēminī;* gen. *nūllīus* and abl. *nūllō, -a,* are borrowed from *nūllus, -a, -um*); subj.-acc. of *esse* in the acc. and inf. object-clause of *sciās.*——**quī,** nom. sing. m. of the rel. pron. *quī, quae, quod;* agrees with the indef. antecedent *nēminem ; quī* is characteristic; see the note on *quī,* Chap. II, l. 47.——**nesciat,** 3d pers. sing. pres. subjunct. act. of *nesciō,*

| facts: that on the 31st of December, in the consulship of Lepidus and Tullus, you stood armed with | tē *you* | prīdiē *on the day before* | Kalendās *the Kalends* | Iānuāriās *of January,* | Lepidō 33 *Lepidus* |
| | et *and* | Tullō *Tullus* | cōnsulibus (*being*) *consuls,* | stetisse *to have stood* | in *in* | comitiō 34 *the Comitium* |

-īre, -īvī, or -iī, -ītum, 4 (*ne* + *sciō*); agrees with the subj. *quī;* the subjunct. mood is consecutive, after *quī*, which is generic, i.e. stands for a class.

LINE 33. **tē**, acc. sing. of *tū;* subj.-acc. of the inf. *stetisse* in the object clause of *nesciat* (a *verbum sentiendī*).—— **prīdiē** (abbreviated = *pr.* or *prīd.;* root *pri* in *prior* + *diē*, the abl. of *diēs*), adv., construed as a prep. + the acc.; gov. the acc. *Kalendās*. *Prīdiē, postrīdiē, usque, propius,* and *proxime* may be used either as adverbs or as prepositions with the acc. case, e.g. *proximē Pompēium sedēbam* = *I sat next to Pompey;* sometimes the adjectives *propior* and *proximus* are used, like the adverbs, with the acc., e.g. *proximus Pompēium sedēbam.* *Prīdiē* and *postrīdiē* are also found with the gen. (subjective), e.g. *prīdiē* (*postrīdiē*) *comitiōrum* = *on the day before* (*after*) *the elections;* and *propior, propius, proximus,* and *proximē* are very common with the dat., as might be expected. A. & G. 261, *a*; B. 144, 2; G. APPENDIX, page 491; H. 437.—— **Kalendās**, acc. of the plur. n. *Kalendae, -ārum,* f. 1st (see *Kalendās,* Chap. III, l. 12); governed by the adv. (prepositional) *prīdiē.* *Prīdiē . . . cōnsulibus* = the last day of the year in which Lepidus and Tullus were consuls, i.e. Dec. 31st, B.C. 66.—— **Iānuāriās**, acc. plur. f. of the adj. *Iānuārius, -a, -um* (= belonging to *Iānus,* to whom the first day of each month and the beginning of all things were sacred); agrees with *Kalendās.* *Iānus = Diānus,* from the same root as *diēs, Iuppiter,* etc. Jānus was the porter of heaven, and is represented with two heads (*bifrons*) because he was the guardian deity of gates, and gates face in two directions. A certain arcade near the Forum was sacred to Jānus (it is often wrongly styled a *temple*), and the gate of this was kept shut in times of peace, and left open only in war to signify that Jānus had gone forth to help Rome. The first day of the new year was especially sacred to Jānus.—— **Lepidō**, abl. sing. of the cōgnōmen *Lepidus, -ī,* m. 2d (*lepidus = elegant, charming; Lepidus* was the family name of a distinguished branch of the *gēns Aemilia*); abl. in the abl. abs. construction; *Lepidō* + *Tullō* = a plur. idea with which *cōnsulibus* agrees. The full name of this man was Mānius Aemilius Lepidus, who was colleague of Gāius Volcātius Tullus in the consulship B.C. 66, belonged to the aristocratic party, but retired from politics when civil war broke out between Pompey and Caesar.

LINE 34. **et**, cop. conj., connects *Lepidō* and *Tullō.*—— **Tullō**, abl. sing. of *Tullus, -ī,* m. 2d (the cognōmen of a branch of the *gēns Volcātia*); joined by *et* to *Lepidō;* in the abl. abs. construction with *cōnsulibus.* The *nōmen* of this man was *Volcātius;* his *praenōmen* is given by some as Gāius, by others as Lūcius.—— **cōnsulibus**, abl. plur. of *cōnsul, -is,* m. 3d; predicative in the abl. abs. construction, referring to the composite plur. abl. *Lepidō et Tullō.* Refer to the note on *dīmissō,* Chap. IV, l. 38, for this form of the abl. abs. construction. Observe that the particular year is indicated by the names of the consuls then in office; later on Romans began to reckon from 753 B.C., the assumed date of the foundation of Rome, e.g. Cicero's birth-year B.C. 106 = 648 A.U.C. (A.U.C. = *ab urbe conditā* or *annō urbis conditae*).—— **stetisse**, perf. inf. act. of *stō, stāre, stetī, statum,* 1 (root *sta* + *to stand;* cf. *sistō, statuō,* = *I make to stand,* ἵστημι, etc.); agrees with the subj.-acc. *tē* in the (acc. and inf.) object clause of *nesciat.* In the elections for the consulship held in 66 B.C. Antrōnius and Sulla had defeated Cotta and Torquātus (see Introduction), but later on were convicted of bribery, and the latter pair was appointed. Whereupon Antrōnius, a bold and factious young noble named Pīsō, and Catiline formed a plot to murder the new consuls on the 1st of January, B.C. 65, but as these facts leaked out, the murder was postponed

85 cum   tēlō,   manum   cōnsulum   et | a dagger in the Place
with   a weapon,   a band   of the consuls   and | of Assembly;   that

86 prīncipum   cīvitātis   interficiendōrum | you had collected a
of the leading men   of the state   to be killed (see note) | gang to slaughter the
| consuls and the lead-

87 causā   parāvisse?   scelerī   ac | ing men of the state;
for the sake   to have prepared?   (that) wickedness   and | that your guilty rage

---

till Feb. 5th, when it failed again owing to Catiline's impatience in giving the signal too early. Such is Sallust's account of the first Conspiracy (*Cat.* XVIII). But Suētōnius in his Life of Jūlius Caesar, IX, adds that Caesar and Crassus also took part in this plot, and quotes contemporary writers as his authorities, e.g. Tanūsius Geminus, M. Bibulus, and C. Cūriō. Suētōnius states that Crassus was to become dictator, and Caesar his *magister equitum,* and they would then reorganize the constitution on democratic lines. Tanūsius is quoted as writing that the attempt at murder was not made on Jan. 1st, because Crassus "either from penitence or fear" failed to appear. Suētōnius adds that Pīsō, who was in Spain (and was afterward killed by partizans of Pompey), was to raise an army and march south on Rome. —— **in,** prep.; gov. the abl. *comitiō.* —— **comitiō,** abl. sing. of *comitium, -ī,* n. 2d (*con + eō;* the sing. *the meeting-place; comitia, -ōrum,* = (1) *assembly of the people,* e.g. by centuries, *centuriāta,* (2) *elections*); governed by the prep. *in.* The comitium was a space at the north east of the Forum, from which it was distinguished by being consecrated by the augurs. It was triangular in shape and faced the Cūria or Senate-house. It was in the earliest times the centre of Roman political life. The *comitia cūriāta* regularly met in the *comitium,* and so frequently did the *comitia tribūta;* the *comitia centuriāta* held their meetings as a rule in the *campus Mārtius.*

LINE 35. **cum,** prep.; gov. the abl. *tēlō.* —— **tēlō,** abl. sing. of *tēlum, -ī,* n. 2d (for *tec-lum,* root *tak = to hit*); governed by the prep. *cum.* It was illegal for a citizen to carry arms in Rome. —— **manum,** acc. sing. of *manus, -ūs,* f. 4th; direct obj. of *parāvisse;* observe that the clause (*tē*) *manum . . . parāvisse* is direct obj. of *nesciat,* l. 32, and is coördinate with the clause *tē . . . stetisse . . . cum tēlō,* though it is not connected with it by a conjunction (*asyndeton*). —— **cōnsulum,** gen. plur. of *cōnsul, -is,* m. 3d; in the gerundial-attraction construction with *interficiendōrum,* the gen. case being dependent on the prep. *causā* below. Had Cicero used the gerund the phrase would have been *cōnsulēs et prīncipēs cīvitātis interficiendī causā,* i.e. *cōnsulēs* and *prīncipēs,* both direct objects of *interficiendī;* the gerundial-attraction consists in the objects being attracted into the case of the gerund (here the gen. with *causā*), and the gerundive which agrees with the objects in gender and number being substituted for the gerund. See the note and references given under *habendī,* Chap. I, l. 8. The consuls whose lives Catiline threatened on Jan. 1st, and especially Feb. 5th, B.C. 65, were Lūcius Aurēlius Cotta and Lūcius Mānlius Torquātus. —— **et,** cop. conj., joining *cōnsulum* and *prīncipum.*

LINE 36. **prīncipum,** gen. plur. of *prīnceps, prīncipis,* m. 3d (substantival use of the adj. *prīnceps, prīmus + capiō*); in the construction of gerundival attraction with *cōnsulum,* like *cōnsulum* which is connected with *prīncipum* by *et.* —— **cīvitātis,** gen. sing. of *cīvitās, -ātis,* f. 3d; poss. gen., limiting *prīncipum.* —— **interficiendōrum,** gen. plur. m. of *interficiendus, -a, -um,* gerundive of *interficiō, -ere, interfēcī, interfectum,* 3 (*inter + faciō*); agrees with *cōnsulum* and *prīncipum* by attraction in the gerundial construction; the gen. case is governed by the prep. *causā.*

LINE 37. **causā** (originally abl. of *causa, -ae,* f. 1st; cf. *grātiā,* abl. of *grātia*), prep.; gov. the gen. in the gerundial construction, expressing purpose. *Causā* and *grātiā* commonly

was frustrated not by	furōrī	tuō	nōn	mentem	aliquam	aut 88
panic or any sort of	*frenzy*	*your*	*not*	*purpose (of yours)*	*any*	*or*
reflection on your	timōrem	tuum,	sed	fortūnam	populī 89
part, but by the good	*fear*	*of yours,*	*but*	*the fortune*	*of the people*

follow the gen. case; in the case of the personal pronouns, the corresponding poss. pron. agrees with *causā* instead of the personal pron. being used in the gen., e.g. *tuā causā*, instead of *tuī causā*. —— **parāvisse**, perf. inf. act. of *parō, -āre, -āvī, -ātum*, 1 ; coördinate with *stetisse* above, and like it agreeing with the subj.-acc. *tē*, l. 33, in the acc. and inf. construction dependent on the leading verb of *perception, nesciat*, l. 32. A. & G. 272, and REM. ; 336 ; B. 330, 331 ; G. 527 ; H. 534, 535. —— **scelerī**, dat. sing. of *scelus, sceleris*, n. 3d ; dat. of the indirect governed by *obstitisse*. Intrans. compounds of *ob* usually govern the dat. case, but *obīre* is used with the accusative. —— **ac**, cop. conj. ; joins the two objects *scelerī* and *furōrī*.

LINE 38. **furōrī**, dat. sing. of *furor, -ōris*, m. 3d (*from furō = I rage*); indirect object of *obstitisse;* joined by *ac* to *scelerī*. To Cicero any form of attack upon the constitution appeared in the light of absolute madness, cf. the combination in Chap. IV, l. 8, *āmentiae scelerisque*. —— **tuō**, dat. sing. m. of the poss. pron. *tuus, -a, -um ;* agrees with *furōrī* and is understood with *scelerī*. —— **nōn**, neg. adv., limiting the idea *mentem aut timōrem obstitisse*. —— **mentem**, acc. sing. of *mēns, mentis*, f. 3d ; subj.-acc. of *obstitisse* understood from the adversative clause following ; the whole clause *scelerī . . . obstitisse* is dependent on *nesciat*, l. 32, and is coördinate with the object-clause *tē . . . parāvisse* above. *Potestne tibi . . . nesciat*, ll. 29–32, may be understood immediately before this clause, when the interconnection of the entire sentence (ll. 29–40) will be at once apparent. *Mentem* is by some arbitrarily rendered *change of mind*, but it cannot have this meaning literally ; Cicero evidently intends to contrast *mentem* with *furōrī* (i.e. revolution = madness, to give up revolutionary ideas = sanity restored), but as it is scarcely applicable in its literal sense makes it vague by the addition of *aliquam*. *Aliquis* and *quīdam* are frequently employed to hint at something indefinitely, or, as it were, to apologize for the use of an expression ; cf. *quādam dēclīnātiōne*, l. 47. —— **aliquam**, acc. sing. f. of the indef. pron. *aliquis, aliqua, aliquid* (adjectival neut. is *aliquod; alius + quis*); agrees with *mentem*, which is thereby toned down and apologized for. For the indef. pronouns, consult the note on *quāsdam*, Chap. II, l. 4. —— **aut**, disjunctive conj. ; joins *mentem* and *timōrem*. *Aut* is used when the alternatives offered are mutually exclusive, e.g. the two motives which might have led Catiline to desist from revolution are distinctly opposed to one another, viz. *repentance*, which implies a moral reformation, and *fear*, which implies no such reformation, but only dread of the consequences. A. & G. 156, *c* ; B. 342 ; G. 493–496 ; H. 554, II.

LINE 39. **timōrem**, acc. sing. of *timor, -ōris*, m. 3d (*timeō = I fear*); joined by *aut* to *mentem;* a subj.-acc. of *obstitisse* in the object-clause of *nesciat*. For synonyms, refer to the note on *timor*, Chap. I, l. 6. —— **tuum**, acc. sing. m. of the poss. pron. *tuus, -a, -um;* agrees with *timōrem*, as being the nearest noun, but *tuam* is also understood from *tuum* in agreement with *mentem* above. A. & G. 187 ; B. 235 (B, 2, *b*); G. 286, 1 ; H. 439, 2. —— **sed**, adversative conj.; joins and strongly opposes *fortūnam* to *mentem aliquam aut timōrem*. *Sed* is the strongest of the adversative conjunctions, as it may introduce something in direct contradiction ; it is often strengthened by the addition of *tamen, autem, vērō*, or *enim*. Of the other particles *tamen* alone is really adversative ; it is prepositive except when it emphasizes a particular word. *Vērum* and *vērō* are really adverbs (from adj. *vērus*), but are used as = to *sed, verum* standing first and *vērō* second word in its sentence. *At* introduces a new and lively objection, and so does its intensified form *atquī;* these are most common in subjects which are being discussed

40 Rōmānī	obstitisse?	Ac	iam	illa
Roman	*(lit. to have) opposed?*	*And*	*now*	*those things*

41 omittō—	neque	enim	sunt	aut	obscūra	aut
I omit—	*neither*	*for*	*are*	*either*	*obscure*	*or*

fortune of the Roman People. And now I will say no more of those events, for there are later misdeeds to your account

argumentatively. The weakest of all the adversatives is *autem*, which is little more than connective. A. & G. 156, *b*; B. 343, 1; G. 485; H. 554, III.——**fortūnam**, acc. sing. of *fortūna, -ae*, f. 1st (cf. *fors*); subj.-acc. of *obstitisse* in the acc. and inf. object-clause of *nesciat*, l. 32. The allusion is to Catiline's mistake in giving the signal for murder (Feb. 5th, B.C. 65) before enough conspirators had assembled. Cicero attributes this to the *Fortune of the Roman People;* cf. Sallust (*Cat.* Chap. 41), *tandem vīcit fortūna reī pūblicae*. *Fortūnam* here is almost the personification of *chance*, viz. the goddess Fortūna, who had several temples in Rome, and was much worshipped throughout Italy, especially at Antium and Praeneste.——**populī**, gen. sing. of *populus*, m. 2d (old form *poplus;* akin to *plebs, pleō*, from root *pal = ple = to fill*, cf. πλέος = *full, manipulus = a handful, a small company of soldiers;* the consonant *p* is reduplicated, cf. *pependī*, perf. of *pendō;* others less probably derive from *polpolus*, as if a reduplication of πολύς = *much, many*); poss. gen., limiting *fortūnam*.

LINE 40. **Rōmānī**, gen. sing. m. of the adj. *Rōmānus, -a, -um* (*Rōma*); agrees with *populī*. All those who possessed the Roman franchise were collectively called *populus Rōmānus*, or when special stress was laid on their peaceful enjoyment of civic rights *Quirītēs;* in more formal language their title was *populus Rōmānus Quirītium* (or *Quirītēs*). The abbreviations P. R. (= *populus Rōmānus*) and S. P. Q. R. (= *senātus populusque Rōmānus*) are common in inscriptions and in MSS. of the classics.—— **obstitisse**, perf. inf. act. of *obstō, -āre, obstitī, obstātum*, 1 (*ob + stō*); agrees with the subj.-acc. *fortūnam* and is understood with the subj.-accusatives *mentem* and *timōrem* above, in the second acc. and inf. object-clause (ll. 37-40, *scelerī . . . obstitisse*) of the verb of *perception, nesciat*, l. 32.——**Ac** (short form of *atque; ac* used before all consonants except *c, g, qu*); connects the sentence and subject-matter which follows with what has preceded.——**iam**, adv. of time; modifies *omittō*.——**illa**, acc. plur. n. of the dem. pron. of the 3d pers. *ille, illa, illud;* direct obj. of *omittō*. *Illa = those acts of the past*, in contrast with later misdeeds (*commissa posteā*).

LINE 41. **omittō**, 1st pers. sing. pres. ind. act. of *omittō, -ere, omīsī, omissum*, 3 (*ob + mittō*); the subj. *ego* is understood. For synonyms, see the note on *praetermittō*, Chap. VI, l. 18. Observe that Cicero's "*I pass over*" is of the usual rhetorician's kind of omission, viz. a pretence at sparing which does as much damage to the opponent as a sustained charge. Cicero in ll. 43-48 passes on to later misdeeds, and hints that again and again he barely escaped with his life from Catiline's increasing attempts to murder him, though this is certainly an exaggeration. Some historians throw great doubt on the question whether Cicero's life was ever threatened at all, even after the meeting at Laeca's house, but we may safely accept that Catiline did attempt to get rid of Cicero, when he saw that it was Cicero who was wrecking his revolutionary hopes.——**neque** (*ne + que = and . . . not*), cop. conj., connecting the parenthetic clause *neque . . . posteā* with the main statement *illa omittō*. Note that *neque* negatively limits not only *obscūra* (*neque obscūra = aperta*), but also *nōn multa* (*neque nōn multa = permulta*). When a negative word limits another negative word, the result is a very emphatic affirmation, cf. *haud ignōrō = I am not ignorant of*, i.e. *I know very well*, and *nōn sine nūmine dīvum = not without the will* (i.e. *by the express direction*) *of the gods* (Vergil). Sometimes the word or phrase limited by a negative is not negative itself, e.g. *nōn similis = dissimillimus;* cf. an excellent example in Greek from Plato's *Apology*,

which are not only numerous but well known. How often you tried to murder me when I was	nōn *not*	multa *many*	commissa *the (deeds) committed*	posteā — : 42 *afterwards—:*
	quotiēns *how often*	tū *you*	mē　dēsīgnātum, *me (as consul) elect,*	quotiēns 43 *how often*

17, B, ὁμολογοίην ἂν ἔγωγε οὐ κατὰ τούτους εἶναι ῥήτωρ = *I would confess that I am not an orator of their stamp,* i.e. that I am far superior to them. This figure, common in Latin and in Greek, is called *lītotēs* or *meiōsis* (*understatement*). A. & G. 386; 209, *c*; B. 375, 1; G. 700; H. 637, VIII.——**enim**, causal conj.; indicating that the parenthesis, as usual, is explanatory of something preceding it. *Enim* usually stands second in its clause, sometimes third, e.g. after a noun with a prep.; *nam* generally stands first. See note on *enim*, Chap. II, l. 17.——**sunt**, 3d pers. plur. pres. ind. of *sum, esse, fuī;* agrees with the subj. *commissa.*——**aut**, disjunctive conj., correlatively with *aut* following, = *either . . . or.*——**obscūra**, nom. plur. n. of the adj. *obscūrus, -a, -um* (*ob* + root *sku* = *to cover*, cf. *scūtum*, σκεύη; cf. also kindred root *ska* = *to cover*, whence σκιά = *shadow, caecus,* etc.); agrees with the subj. *commissa.*——**aut**, disjunctive cop. conj., connecting *obscūra* and *nōn multa.* For the disjunctive conjunctions and their use correlatively, see A. & G. 156, *c*; B. 342; G. 493-496; H. 554, II.

Line 42. **nōn**, adv., limiting the adj. *multa*, *nōn multa = permulta;* see note on *neque* above. *Nōn* modifying an adj. or adv. emphasizes the negation; it is the regular neg. modifier of verbs.' *Haud* is little used with verbs, being found only with some six or seven verbs in Cicero, e.g. *haud ignōrō, haud sciō an;* but it is common with adverbs and adjectives.——**multa**, nom. plur. n. of the adj. *multus, -a, -um;* joined by *aut* to *obscūra;* agrees with the subj. *commissa.*——**commissa**, nom. plur. of *commissum, -ī,* n. 2d (the substantival neut. of *commissus, -a, -um,* perf. part. pass. of *committō, -ere, commīsī, commissum,* 3 (*con* + *mittō*); subj. of *sunt.* It is possible to understand a vague subject in the neut. plur., e.g. *alia*, and to take *commissa sunt* as perf. ind. pass. in the 3d pers. plur., agreeing with this subject. Synonyms: (1) *factum = a deed, a thing done*, in general; (2) *rēs = a fact, a thing,* but *rēs gestae = deeds,* esp. in historical chronicles, hence usually *exploits,* such as battles fought, etc.; (3) *commissum* and *facinus = deed,* usually in a bad sense, unless a modifier expresses a contrary notion; *facinus* is modified by an adj., but *commissum* by reason of its verbal nature by an adverb, e.g. *bonum facinus, bene commissum,* and esp. *commissa posteā* in this passage.——**posteā** (*post* + *eā*, abl. sing. f. of *is*, or as some think *post* + *ea*, neut. acc. plur. of *is*), adv., modifying *commissa.* With *posteā* compare *anteā, praetereā,* etc.; in early Latin the adverbs *post, ante,* etc., may have been used with the abl. case; their use with the acc. as prepositions is merely a growth from a constant combination of the adverb and the accusative's own case signification.

Line 43. **quotiēns** (from *quot;* cf. *totiēns* from *tot*), adv., modifying *cōnātus es. Quotiēns . . . effūgī,* l. 48, is explanatory of *illa;* Cicero uses the more vivid direct exclamation instead of the indirect exclamation *omittō quotiēns . . . cōnātus sīs.* The forms *quotiēns* and *totiēns* are preferred to *quotiēs* and *totiēs,* but the termination in *-ēs* is much more common than that in *-ēns* in other numeral adverbs.——**tū**, nom. sing. of the 2d personal pron.; subj. of *cōnātus es;* the juxtaposition of *tū* and *mē* is for effect.—— **mē**, acc. sing. of *ego;* direct obj. of *interficere cōnātus es* understood from the next clause.——**dēsīgnātum**, acc. sing. n. of *dēsīgnātus, -a, -um,* perf. part. pass. of *dēsīgnō, -āre, -āvī, -ātum,* 1 (*dē* + *sīgnō*); agrees with *mē*, and = *dēsīgnātum cōnsulem.* A consul was called *dēsīgnātus* from the day of his election to the day (Jan. 1st of the next year) on which he actually entered upon his duties as consul.——**quotiēns**, adv., modifying *cōnātus es. Quotiēns* is repeated by *anaphora* from above, and is more forcible than would be a cop. conj. connecting the two coördinate clauses.

44 vērō   cōnsulem   interficere   cōnātus es !
   actually   *(me) as consul*   *to kill*   *you endeavored!*

45 quot   ego   tuās   petītiōnēs   ita
   how many   *I*   *of yours*   *blows,*   *so*

46 cōniectās,   ut   vītārī   posse   nōn
   aimed   *that*   *to be avoided*   *to be able*   *not*

47 vidērentur,   parvā   quādam   dēclīnātiōne   et,
   they seemed,   *slight*   *certain*   *by a bending aside*   *and,*

consul-elect, and again when I was actually consul! From how many of your thrusts, so aimed that they seemed impossible to escape, have I slipped away by just a little swerve

LINE 44. **vērō** (abl. neut. sing. of *vērus, -a, -um;* cf. *vērum,* the adverbial acc. sing. n.), adv., emphasizing the whole clause. *Vērum* and *vērō* are often used as adversative conjunctions.——**cōnsulem,** acc. sing. of *cōnsul, -is,* m. 3d ; in appos. with *mē* understood from *mē* above as the direct obj. of *interficere.*——**interficere,** pres. inf. act. of *interficiō, -ere, interfēcī, interfectum,* 3 (*inter + faciō*); objective complementary inf. with *cōnātus es.*——**cōnātus es,** 2d pers. sing. perf. ind. of the deponent verb *cōnor, -ārī, -ātus sum,* 1 ; agrees with the subj. *tū.*

LINE 45. **quot,** indecl. adj., qualifying *petītiōnēs. Quot* is used (1) interrogatively, in direct and indirect questions, = *how many?* (2) in exclamations, as in this passage, (3) correlatively with *tot, tot . . . quot=so many, as many . . . as.*——**ego,** nom. sing. of the 1st personal pron. ; subj. of *effūgī;* observe the rhetorical proximity of *ego* and *tuās,* and cf. *tū mē* in l. 43.——**tuās,** acc. plur. f. of the poss. pron. *tuus, -a, -um* ; agrees with *petītiōnēs.*——**petītiōnēs,** acc. plur. of *petītiō, -ōnis,* f. 3d (from *petō = I thrust, attack*); direct obj. of *effūgī.* Cicero uses in this passage terms borrowed from the contests of gladiators, e.g. *petītiō, dēclīnātiō,* and *corpore effugere.* Catiline is likened to a gladiator, desperately seeking an opening for a thrust ; cf. Chap. XI of Oration II, *ad init.; et prīmum gladiātōrī illī cōnfectō et sanciō cōnsulēs imperātōrēsque vestrōs oppōnite.*——**ita,** adv., modifying *coniectās. Ita* and *sīc* modify verbs, and *tam* adjectives and adverbs. The combination *ita . . . ut* is frequent in consecutive sentences, and especially when a restriction is intended, e.g. *ita fruī volunt voluptātibus ut nūllī propter eās cōnsequantur dolōrēs = they wish to enjoy their pleasures without any pain ensuing on account of them. Ita . . . ut* sometimes (but rarely) is found in final sentences, e.g. *ita mē gessī nē tibi pudōrī essem = I behaved myself so as not to be a disgrace to you. Ita . . . ut* is common within clauses, = *so . . . as,* e.g. *ut hī virī . . . ita illī, = as these men, . . . so those.*

LINE 46. **coniectās,** acc. plur. f. of *coniectus, -a, -um,* perf. part. pass. of *coniciō -ere, coniēcī, coniectum,* 3 (*con + iaciō*); agrees with *petītiōnēs; ita coniectās = quae ita coniectae sunt.*——**ut,** consecutive conj. = *so that,* followed by the subjunct. *vidērentur.* For the various uses of *ut* see note on *ut,* Chap. I, l. 39.——**vītārī,** pres. inf. pass. of *vītō, -āre, -āvī, ātum,* 1 ; complementary inf., supplementing *posse;* see note on *invenīrī,* Chap. II, l. 44.——**posse,** pres. inf. of *possum, posse, potuī,* no supine, irreg. (*potis + sum*); complementary inf., supplementing *vidērentur.* A. & G. 271 ; B. 326 ; G. 423 ; H. 533.——**nōn,** neg. adv., limiting *vidērentur.*

LINE 47. **vidērentur,** 3d pers. plur. imperf. subjunct. pass. of *videō, -ere, vīdī, vīsum,* 2 (the pass. *videor, -ērī, vīsus sum,* commonly = *I seem,* as here); understand as subj. a pron. in the nom. plur. f. referring to *petītiōnēs;* the subjunct. mood is consecutive, expressing *result* after *ut.* Observe the personal construction of this verb, which is regular in Latin, while English idiom prefers the impersonal *it seems, it seemed. Vidētur, vidēbātur,* and *vīsum est,* etc., are used impersonally in the sense *it seems (seemed) best,* and are followed by an *ut* clause. The general rule in Latin is that the personal construction is required with passive forms of *dīcō, iubeō,* and *vetō,* and with *videor = I seem.* A. & G. 330, *b* ; B. 332 ; G. 528 ; H. 534, I, and NOTES. The per-

to one side, and " by	ut	āiunt,	corpore	effūgī!	Nihil	agis, 48
the body," as people	*as*	*they say,*	*with the body*	*I escaped!*	*Nothing*	*you do,*

sonal construction is preferred always in simple tenses of verbs of *saying, showing, believing,* and *perceiving,* e.g. *it was heard that Bibulus was in Syria = Bibulus audiē-bātur esse in Syriā,* but the impersonal in compound tenses, e.g. *trāditum est rēgēs fuisse;* but if a dat. is combined with the verb of *saying,* the impersonal construction must be used, e.g. *narrātur mihi mercātōrēs abiisse.* —— **parvā,** abl. sing. f. of the adj. *parvus, -a, -um;* agrees with *dēclīnātiōne.* —— **quādam,** abl. sing. f. of the indef. pron. *quidam, quaedam, quiddam* (adjectival neut. *quoddam; quī +* suffix *-dam*); agrees with *dēclīnā-tiōne;* its force is to soften down the metaphor. Refer to the note on *quāsdam,* Chap. II, l. 4. —— **dēclīnātiōne,** abl. sing. of *dēclīnātiō, -ōnis,* f. 3d (from *dēclīnō = I turn away, dē +* root *kli = to lean;* cf. κλίνω *= I make to bend,* κλιτύς *and clīvus = hill-side*); abl. of manner, modifying *effūgī.* —— **et,** cop. conj., joining *dēclīnātiōne* and *corpore.*

LINE 48. **ut,** adv. *= as,* and followed by the ind. mood. *Ut* takes the ind. when used: (1) as an adv. of manner, *= as;* (2) in exclamations, *= how!* (3) as an adv. of time, *as, since.* As a subordinate temporal conj., *ut* is usually followed by the indicative. —— **āiunt,** 3d pers. plur. pres. ind. act. of the defective verb *āiō,* 3; as the subj. under-stand some such word as *hominēs,* = the French indef. pron. *on* (e.g. *on dit = they say, men say*). The only ind. tenses which are found are the imperf. *āiēbam* (complete); the pres. in the following persons, 1st *āiō,* 2d *ais,* 3d *ait,* 3d plur. *āiunt;* the perf., 3d sing. *ait.* In the subjunct. pres. we find 2d *āiās,* 3d *āiat,* 3d plur. *āiant;* 2d pers. sing. imperative *= aī;* pres. part. *= āiēns,* used adjectively *= affirmative.* A. & G. 144, *a;* B. 135; G. 175, 1; H. 297, II, 1. In poetry *āiō* is used like *dīcō,* and may introduce an indirect statement; but in prose it is little used, and only as a rule in parentheses, as in this phrase *ut āiunt.* Synonyms: (1) *āiō = I affirm, say yes;* (2) *fārī = to utter,* i.e. intelligible sounds, hence *to speak,* cf. φημί; (3) *loquī = to speak,* i.e. to put thoughts into word-form; (4) *dīcō = I say,* in reference to a statement's form, and esp. of an orator; (5) *inquam = I say,* and is always used within quotations which are stated in direct form, e.g. *"haec enim," inquit, "omnia fēcī," = "for all these things," said he, "have I done."* *Ut āiunt,* like *quādam,* tones down the force of the metaphor, and by its position before *corpore* marks out *corpore* as a colloquial expression describing one of the means by which a gladiator avoided his antagonist's blows. —— **corpore,** abl. sing. of *corpus, corporis,* n. 3d; abl. of the means, modifying *effūgī;* joined by *et* to *dēclīnā-tiōne.* *Corpore* shows rather *how* the blows were escaped, than *with what;* for gram-matical purposes it is easier to regard it as abl. of means, but many nouns so used are hard to distinguish from idiomatic ablatives of manner. An excellent example of a sim-ilar usage in another author is afforded by Vergil, *Aen.* V, 437, *Stat gravis Entellus, nīsūque immōtus eōdem Corpore tēla modo atque oculīs vigilantibus exit,* = *Entellus stands heavily, and unmoved and tense escapes the blows only by* (inclination of) *his body and by his watchfulness of eye.* From the above account of a boxing match, it is clear that *corpore = by movement of the body,* and not that blows were parried by the body, as they might be by a shield. Many editors run *dēclīnātiōne* and *corpore* together as an instance of *hendiadys;* this simplifies the passage, but the position of *ut āiunt* and its evident reference to the particular word *corpore* are then ignored. A. & G. 385; B. 374, 4; G. 698; H. 636, III, 2. —— **effūgī,** 1st pers. sing. perf. ind. act. of *effugiō, -ere, effūgī, effugitum,* 3 (*ex + fugiō;* root *bhug = fug = to turn one's self,* cf. φυγή *= flight, fugō = I put to flight*); agrees with the subj. *ego,* l. 45. —— **Nihil** (sometimes abbreviated *nīl*), acc. sing. of the neut. indecl. noun *nihil* (apocopated form of *nihilum, -ī,* n. 2d, *ne + hilum = not a trifle*); direct obj. of *agis.* Some editions omit *nihil agis.* —— **agis,** 2d pers. sing. pres. ind. act. of *agō, -ere, ēgī, āctum,* 3; the subj. implied is *tū.*

49 nihil	adsequeris,	neque	tamen	cōnārī	ac
nothing	*you attain,*	*and not*	*yet*	*to attempt*	*and*
50 velle	dēsistis.	Quotiēns	tibi		iam
to wish	*you cease.*	*How often*	*for (=from) you*		*already*

say. You effect nothing, you gain nothing — yet you do not abandon your attempts or your purpose. How many

LINE 49. **nihil**, acc. sing. (as above); direct obj. of *adsequeris;* observe the *asyndeton* and *anaphora.* —— **adsequeris**, 2d pers. sing. pres. ind. of the deponent verb *adsequor, -ī, adsecūtus sum,* 3 (*ad + sequor*) ; the implied subj. is *tū.* Synonyms : (1) *adsequī* and *consequī = to obtain,* i.e. by effort; (2) *potīrī = to obtain, get possession of,* forcibly ; (3) *nancīscī = to obtain,* by chance ; (4) *adipīscī* (*ad + apīscī*) = *to obtain,* something worth obtaining, e.g. *victōriam, glōriam;* (5) *impetrāre = to obtain,* something in answer to a petition. Note the different signification which the following prepositions give to *sequor* in composition : (a) *sequor = I follow;* (b) *consequor* or *adsequor = I overtake,* hence *obtain;* (c) *persequor = I follow constantly,* generally with hostile intent, hence *I persecute;* (d) *īnsequī = to follow closely,* e.g. a defeated enemy ; (e) *obsequor = I follow* another's opinion, hence *I agree with,* + dat. case; cf. English *obsequious;* (f) *subsequī = to follow immediately,* cf. English *subsequent;* (g) *prosequī = to follow* as a mark of honor or respect, hence *to escort.* —— **neque** (*ne + que = and . . . not*), cop. coördinating conj., connecting the clauses of *adsequeris* and *dēsistis.* *Et nōn* is avoided, except when a single word is negatived; cf. *negō eum haec fēcisse,* not *dīcō eum haec nōn fēcisse.* The simple sentences *nihil agis . . . dēsistis* are more after English idiom than Latin ; we should rather have expected something like *nihil cum (although) agās, nihil cum adsequāris, nōn tamen cōnārī ac velle dēsistis.* —— **tamen**, adversative adv., indicating that the clause is opposed to the preceding clause. —— **cōnārī**, pres. inf. of the deponent verb *cōnor, -ārī, -ātus sum,* 1 ; objective complementary inf. with *dēsistis; cōnārī* is here absolute and = *cōnātūs facere.* —— **ac**, cop. conj. ; joins the two object-infinitives *cōnārī* and *velle.*

LINE 50. **velle**, pres. inf. of *volō, velle, voluī,* no supine, irreg. ; objective complementary inf. with *dēsistis;* like *cōnārī, velle* is used absolutely, = *to entertain desires.* —— **dēsistis**, 2d pers. sing. pres. ind. act. of *dēsistō, -ere, dēstitī, dēstitum,* 3 (*dē + sistō*) ; the implied subj. is *tū.* *Dēsistō = I leave off,* and it is used either absolutely or with the abl. of separation (sometimes the gen. in poetry); in Cicero it is often followed by a complementary inf. such as follows verbs signifying *continuance, ending, wishing, being able, resolving,* etc. For references, see note on *posse,* l. 46. —— **Quotiēns** (see l. 43), adv., modifying *extorta est.* —— **tibi**, dat. sing. of *tū;* dat. instead of the abl. of separation, which (esp. of persons) may follow compounds of *ab, ex, dē,* and in some instances *ad;* the dative marks the action as *done* to the object, involving advantage or disadvantage, and so is more vivid than the abl. of separation with a preposition. Not seldom the dat. of the person is followed by the abl. (with *ab, dē, ex*) of the particular thing, both dat. and abl. dependent on the same compound verb, as *tibi dē manibus* here. A. & G. 229, and *c* ; B. 188, 2, *d*; G. 345, REM. 1 ; H. 385, 4, 2. For the simple dat. of reference (advantage or disadvantage), to which class this dat. belongs, consult A. & G. 235 ; B. 188, 1 ; G. 350 ; H. 384, 1, 2. Some editors prefer to regard *tibi* as an ethic dat., = *how often have you seen that dagger wrested from your hands;* this dat. is a special kind of dat. of reference, almost invariably used of personal pronouns, and signifying the interest which is felt by the individual meant; cf. two stock examples, *quid mihi Celsus agit? = tell me, what is Celsus doing?,* and *pulset mihi lictōrem = let me see him strike the lictor* (lit. *let him strike the lictor for me*). A. & G. 236 ; B. 188, 2, *b*; G. 351 ; H. 389. —— **iam**, temporal adv.; modifies *extorta est.* *Iam* is used in many ways and with many senses, e.g. *now, already, immediately, no doubt, indeed, moreover,* etc.

times already has	extorta est	ista	sīca	dē	manibus! 51
that dagger of yours	*has been torn away*	*that*	*dagger*	*from*	*your hands!*
been wrested from					
your grasp! How	quotiēns	excidit	cāsū	aliquō	et 52
often has it slipped	*how often*	*has it dropped*	*by chance*	*some*	*and*
by some chance from					
your fingers, and	ēlapsa est!	quae	quidem	quibus	abs 53
fallen to the ground!	*has slipped!*	*which (dagger)*	*indeed*	*what*	*by*
As for the dagger in-					
deed, I know not to	tē	initiāta	sacrīs		ac 54
what sacred mission	*you*	*(it) has been dedicated*	*to sacred rites*		*and*

LINE 51. **extorta est**, 3d pers. sing. perf. ind. pass. of *extorqueō, -ēre, extorsī, extortum,* 2 (*ex + torqueō;* root *tark = τραχ = torc* or *torqu,* i.e. *to turn, wind;* cf. τρέπω = *I turn*); agrees with the subj. *sīca.* —— **ista**, nom. sing. f. of the dem. pron. *iste, ista, istud;* agrees with *sīca;* implies scorn and disgust, cf. *iste,* Chap. I, l. 3. —— **sīca**, gen. *sīcae,* f. 1st (perhaps akin to *secō = I cut,* from root *sak = sec, to split;* cf. κε-δζω = *I split,* and κέ-αρνον = *a carpenter's axe*); nom. sing., subj. of *extorta est.* The *sīca* was a curved dagger with a sharp point, and was the national weapon of Thracians, hence its use by "Thracian" gladiators. To a Roman the *sīca* seemed the weapon of a murderous ruffian, and thus it signifies Cicero's scornful opinion of Catiline. —— **dē**, prep. with the abl.; gov. *manibus.* —— **manibus**, abl. plur. of *manus, manūs,* f. 4th ; governed by the prep. *dē.*

LINE 52. **quotiēns**, adv. ; modifies *excidit.* —— **excidit**, 3d pers. sing. perf. ind. act. of *excidō, -ere, excīdī,* no supine, 3 (*ex = out of + cadō = I fall*); understand as subj. *illa* referring to *sīca;* *excidit = excidit ē tuīs manibus.* —— **cāsū**, abl. sing. of *cāsus, -ūs,* m. 4th (from verb *cadō,* hence lit. *a falling-out, chance*); abl. of manner, with the modifier *aliquō,* hence *cum* is not required ; modifies *excidit.* *Cāsū* and some other ablatives, e.g. *lēge, fraude, vī, numerō, pedibus, ratiōne,* etc., may express manner without the addition either of *cum* or of a modifier. —— **aliquō**, abl. sing. m. of the indef. pron. *aliquis, aliqua, aliquid* (neut. adjectival *aliquod; alius + quis*); agrees with *cāsū,* which it renders vague. —— **et**, cop. conj. ; joins *excidit* and *ēlapsa est.*

LINE 53. **ēlapsa est**, 3d pers. sing. perf. ind. of the deponent verb *ēlābor, -ī, ēlapsus sum,* 3 (*ē = ex + lābor*); agrees with the subj. *illa* (or some other pron.) referring to *sīca;* joined by *et* to *excidit.* —— **quae**, nom. sing. f. of the rel. pron. *quī, quae, quod;* agrees with *sīca,* l. 51, the antecedent, and is subj. of *initiāta (sit)* and of *dēvōta sit.* Observe that *quae* is connective, and = *et haec (sīca).* A. & G. 180, *f*; B. 251, 6; G. 610; H. 453. The sentence may be simplified thus: *et quidem nesciō quibus sacrīs (haec sīca) abs tē initiāta (sit) ac dēvōta sit, quod necesse esse eam in cōnsulis corpore dēfīgere putās.* —— **quidem**, adv., modifying *nesciō,* or rather the whole clause. —— **quibus**, dat. plur. n. of the interrog. pron. (adjectival) *quis, quae* [*quid,* only substantival in nom. and acc.], or of the interrog. adj. *quī, quae, quod* (see note on *quem,* Chap. I, l. 3); agrees with *sacrīs,* and introduces an indirect question after *nesciō,* hence the subjunct. mood in *initiāta ac dēvōta sit;* the direct form of the question would be *quibus sacrīs initiāta ac dēvōta est?* —— **abs** (akin to English *of, off,* and to Greek ἀπό = *from*), prep. with the abl.; gov. *tē.* *Abs* is an antiquated form of *ab,* and is rare in classical prose except with *tē;* it is used in composition, e.g. the prep. *absque* (*abs + que*), *abstineō* (*abs + teneō*).

LINE 54. **tē**, abl. sing. of *tū;* governed by the prep. *abs,* expressing agency after the passives *initiāta ac dēvōta sit.* —— **initiāta**, nom. sing. f. of *initiātus, -a, -um,* perf. part. pass. of *initiō, -āre, -āvī, -ātum,* 1 (*initium = a beginning; in = into + root i = to go;* cf. *īmus = we go* (from *eō*), and ἴμεν = *we go* (from εἶμι)); agrees with the subj. *quae*

55 dēvōta sit,	nesciō,	quod	eam	you have consecrated
(it) has been vowed,	*I know not,*	*because (= that)*	*it*	it and vowed it, that
56 necesse	putās	esse	in	cōnsulis	you think it a binding
necessary	*you think (it)*	*to be*	*in*	*of the consul*	obligation upon you
57 corpore	dēfīgere.				to plunge it in the
the body	*to fix.*				consul's body.

(*sīca*); supply *sit* from *dēvōta sit* = the 3d pers. sing. perf. subjunct. pass., coördinate with *dēvōta sit* (where see note). —— **sacrīs**, dat. plur. n. of the adj. *sacer, sacra, sacrum* (the neut. is here substantival = *rites, ceremonies;* elsewhere *sacrum* = *a sacred place, sanctuary*); dat. of the indirect obj. after *dēvōta sit.* Some regard *quibus sacrīs* as an abl. of the means = *by what rites it has been consecrated and set apart, and see an allusion to the charge* made by Sallust (*Cat.* XXII) that Catiline bound his confederates together by an oath, which each made as he drank from a goblet containing human blood. There seems to have been a general supposition that the conspirators swore fidelity by participating in a human sacrifice, for Dio Cassius and Plutarch tell a similar tale, the latter stating that the flesh of the human victim was eaten. —— **ac**, cop. conj. ; connecting *initiāta (sit)* and *dēvōta sit.*

LINE 55. **dēvōta sit**, 3d pers. sing. perf. subjunct. pass. of *dēvoveō, -ēre, dēvōvī, dēvōtum,* 2 (*dē* + *voveō*); agrees with the subj. *quae;* the mood is subjunct. in the indirect question introduced by *quibus* above. A. & G. 334; B. 300; G. 467; H. 528, 2, and 529, I. The allusion in *initiāta ac dēvōta sit* is to the practice of dedicating a special memento of some important event to a particular deity; thus Horace represents the sailor as hanging up his dripping garments in a temple in gratitude for escaping death in a shipwreck, and similarly one recovered from sickness dedicated appropriate offerings in the temple of Aesculapius. Tacitus even speaks of the dedication of weapons with which important murders had been perpetrated. *Initiātus* is the technical term for one *initiated* into sacred mysteries, and *dēvōtus* of one whose life is *vowed* to a definite object; here the dagger is supposed to be set apart for a special purpose, and after its mission was fulfilled it was to be no longer used but dedicated in some patron divinity's temple. —— **nesciō**, 1st pers. sing. pres. ind. act. of *nesciō, -īre, -īvī or -ī̆ī, -ītum,* 4 (*ne* = *not* + *sciō* = *I know*); the implied subj. is *ego.* *Nesciō* is used in phrases, e.g. *nesciō an* = *perhaps* (lit. *I know not whether*); in combination with *quis* = an indef. pron., e.g. *nesciō quis* = *some one or other.* —— **quod** (acc. neut. of *quī*), conj. = *that, seeing that, inasmuch as,* followed by the ind. *putās.* *Quod* does not = *because,* i.e. is not a pure causal conj. like *quia;* the *quod* clause in this passage is a substantival phrase, and is employed as a kind of accusative of reference; consult the note on *quod,* Chap. IV, l. 32. —— **eam**, acc. sing. f. of the dem. pron. *is, ea, id;* direct obj. of *dēfīgere; eam* = *sīcam.*

LINE 56. **necesse**, acc. sing. of the indecl. neut. adj. *necesse* (*ne* = *not* + *cēdō* = *I yield,* hence *inevitable*); predicative with *esse,* agreeing with the subj.-acc. (verbal noun) *dēfīgere,* in the acc. and inf. construction dependent on *putās.* —— **putās**, 2d pers. sing. pres. ind. act. of *putō, -āre, -āvī, -ātum,* 1 ; the subj. *tū* is implied. For synonyms, refer to the note on *arbitrāris,* Chap. I, l. 16. —— **esse**, pres. inf. of *sum;* agrees with the (inf. as verbal noun) subj.-acc. *dēfīgere,* in the acc. and inf. construction following *putās.* —— **in**, prep. ; gov. the abl. *corpore.* —— **cōnsulis**, gen. sing. of *cōnsul, -is,* m. 3d ; poss. gen., limiting *corpore.* Observe that *cōnsulis* precedes the noun it limits ; the gen. is frequently placed between the noun it limits and a prep., or between the limited noun and its adjective.

LINE 57. **corpore**, abl. sing. of *corpus, corporis,* n. 3d ; governed by the prep. *in.* —— **dēfīgere**, pres. inf. act. of *dēfīgō, -ēre, dēfīxī, dēfīxum,* 3 (*dē* + *fīgō*); the inf. is

| VII. Tell me now, what kind of life is that life of yours? I shall talk with you now in such a way | **VII.** Nunc vērō quae tua est ista vīta? 1
Now indeed what of yours is that life?
Sīc enim iam tēcum loquar, nōn ut 2
So for now with you I will speak not that |

here substantival, and the verbal phrase *dēfīgere eam in cōnsulis corpore* acts as the subj.-acc. of *necesse esse* in the object-clause of *putās;* the direct thought would be *necesse est aēfīgere eam in cōnsulis corpore.* The inf. mood exercises both verbal and substantival functions: as a verb (1) it admits of different tenses, (2) is modified by adverbs, (3) and may govern an object (e.g. *dēfīgere eam* here); as a neuter noun, it can stand as the subj. or obj. of a sentence. As a noun, the inf. may be nom.-subj. of *est, fuit,* etc. + a neut. adj., of an impersonal verb, or of a verb used impersonally; e.g. *turpe est mentīrī = lying is disgraceful;* or it may be subj.-acc. in indirect speech, e.g. *dīxit turpe esse mentīrī.* The other cases of the verbal noun are supplied by the gerund; the acc. of the gerund is only used with prepositions, which may never be used with the actual infinitive. A. & G. 270; B. 326–328; G. 280; H. 532, 538.

LINE 1. **Nunc**, temporal adv., modifying *est.* *Nunc* is used, rather than *iam,* when an emphatic contrast is to be drawn between the present and the past.——**vērō**, adv., with the force of an adversative conj.; connects and contrasts the topics discussed in this and the previous chapter.——**quae**, nom. sing. f. of the interrog. adj. *quī, quae, quod;* agrees with *vīta.* The difference between the interrogative words *quī* and *quis* is that *quis = which, what,* while *quī = what, of what kind,* i.e. *quī* approximates to *quālis.*——**tua**, nom. sing. f. of the poss. pron. *tuus, -a, -um;* agrees with *vīta.* In the combination *ista tua, tua* denotes the person referred to (as possessor), and *ista,* while preserving its demonstrative signification, also expresses the scorn and disgust felt by the speaker.——**est**, 3d pers. sing. pres. ind. of *sum, esse, fuī;* agrees with the subj. *vīta.*——**ista**, nom. sing. f. of *iste, ista, istud,* dem. adj. and pron. of the 2d person; agrees with *vīta.* *Iste = is +* suffix *te;* cf. the suffix δε in ὅδε. As an adj. *iste* may imply praise or censure, according to the context; but in the law courts, when the defendant is referred to, it always expresses contempt. A. & G. 102, *c;* B. 87, and 246, 4; G. 306, and NOTE; H. 450, 1, and NOTE.——**vīta**, gen. *vītae,* f. 1st; nom. sing., subj. of *est;* *vīta* here = *ratiō vīvendī.*

LINE 2. **Sīc** (*sī + ce;* refer to the note on *hūius,* Chap. II, l. 17), adv., modifying *loquar.*——**enim**, causal conj.; connecting the sentence above with the explanatory discussion which follows.——**iam**, adv. of time; limits *loquar.*——**tēcum** (*tē + cum*): *te* is the abl. sing. of *tē;* governed by the prep. *cum.* *Cum* is the prep. + the abl.; gov. *tē.* *Cum* is enclitic, i.e. is appended to the abl. which it governs, when its object is a personal, relative, or reflexive pron., cf. *quibuscum, sēcum.*——**loquar**, 1st pers. sing. fut. ind. of the deponent verb *loquor, loquī, locūtus sum,* 3 (root *lak = to sound, speak;* cf. Greek ἔλακον *= I shouted,* λακερός *= talkative*); the implied subj. is *ego.* For synonyms, *dīcō, āiō,* etc., refer to the note on *āiunt,* Chap. VI, l. 48.——**nōn**, neg. adv.; limits *videar; nōn* at the beginning of a clause, indicating what *is not* the case, is often followed by another clause introduced by an adversative conj., e.g. *sed,* indicating what *is* the case.——**ut**, consecutive conj., expressing result, and taking the subjunct. *videar.* *Ut* consecutive *= that, so that;* its neg. is *ut nōn;* the clause to which the *ut* clause is subordinate frequently contains some dem. word, e.g. *ita, sīc, tantus, tālis, tam,* etc., which is a kind of antecedent to *ut.* Distinguish *ut* consecutive from *ut* final, *= that, in order that,* expressing purpose; neg. *nē;* also governs the subjunct. mood. Refer to the note on *ut,* Chap. I, l. 39. A. & G. 319; B. 284; G. 552; H. 500. *Ut,* meaning *as, when, how,* is followed by the ind. mood.

Latin	English gloss	Right column
3 odiō　　permōtus　esse　videar,　quō　dēbeō,	by the hatred　moved　　to be　I may seem　by which　I ought,	as to make myself appear influenced not
4 sed　　　　ut　　　　misericordiā,　　　　quae	but that (I may seem to be moved)　by pity,　　which	by hatred as I ought to be, but by pity
5 tibi　　nūlla　　dēbētur.　　　Vēnistī　　paulō	to you none (= not at all)　is due.　　You came　a little	which is in no way due to you. A short

LINE 3. **odiō**, abl. sing. of *odium, -ī,* n. 2d (root *vadh = to thrust,* cf. ὠθέω; akin to ὀαἴ); abl. of the cause, with *permōtus esse.*——**permōtus esse**, perf. inf. pass. of *permoveō, -ēre, permōvī, permōtum,* 2 (*per,* intensive, + *moveō*); prolative inf., supplementing the predication with *videar;* the perf. inf. is used instead of the pres. *permovērī,* because Cicero is thinking of the judgment of posterity, and so say *that I may seem to have been influenced,* not *to be influenced.* Note that *permōtus* agrees with *ego,* the implied subj. of *videar.* For the inf., see note on *facere,* Chap. I, l. 23.——**videar**, 1st pers. sing. pres. subjunct. of *videor, -ērī, vīsus sum,* 2 = *I seem* (the deponent use of the pass. of *videō, -ēre, vīdī, vīsum,* 2) ; the implied subj. is *ego;* the subjunct. mood expresses result, after *ut* above.——**quō**, abl. sing. n. of the rel. pron. *quī, quae, quod;* agrees in gender and number with the antecedent *odiō,* and is abl. of cause, with *permōtus esse* understood as the complementary inf. of *dēbeō* from the preceding clause *ut permōtus esse videar.* The moving cause is frequently expressed by the abl. + a part., e.g. *īrā adductus (commōtus, incēnsus, impulsus,* and the like), and the abl. usually precedes the participle. A. & G. 245 ; B. 219 ; G. 408, and NOTE 2 ; H. 416.——**dēbeō**, 1st pers. sing. pres. ind. act. of *dēbeō, -ēre, -uī, -itum,* 2 (for *dēhibeō = dē + habeō = I keep back,* hence *I owe;* hence of duty, *I ought, must*); the subj. *ego* is implied by the personal ending; understand with *dēbeō* the complementary inf. *permōtus esse.* Synonyms : (1) *dēbeō = I ought,* signifying that the duty is a moral one, suggested by the conscience (subjective); (2) *oportet mē = I ought,* the duty resting on external grounds (objective); (3) *necesse est* signifies that the action is obligatory by natural law, and hence unavoidable ; (4) *cōgī = to be obliged,* of necessity due to external circumstances ; (5) the gerundive *-ndum est,* or *-ndus, -a, -um est* marks a purely circumstantial obligation.

LINE 4. **sed**, adversative conj. connecting the clause *nōn ut . . . dēbeō* (which is rejected by the speaker) with the clause *ut . . . dēbētur* (which is accepted).——**ut**, consecutive conj. (see *ut,* l. 2); the clause following is elliptical, and after *ut* we must understand the verb of the preceding *ut* clause, = *ut (permōtus esse videar) misericordiā.* A verb (especially parts of *sum*) or verbal phrase is often omitted in a sentence closely connected (or coördinate) with another sentence which contains the verb or verbal phrase, when the omission can be readily supplied from the context.——**misericordiā**, abl. sing. of *misericordia, -ae,* f. 1st (through the adj. *misericors,* from *misereor = I pity* + *cor = the heart*); abl. of the cause, with *permōtus esse* (understood ; see note on *ut* above).——**quae**, nom. sing. f. of the rel. pron. *quī, quae, quod;* agrees in gender and number with the antecedent *misericordiā,* and is subj. to *dēbētur.*

LINE 5. **tibi**, dat. sing. of *tū;* indirect obj. of *dēbētur.*——**nūlla**, nom. sing. f. of *nūllus, -a, -um (ne + ūllus);* agrees with the subj. *quae = quae misericordiā)* in the rel. clause, and modifies *dēbētur* adverbially. Many adjectives may have adverbial force, e.g. *laetī vēnērunt = they came gladly,* but the most common are *prior, prīmus, ultimus, postrēmus, volēns, tōtus, ūnus,* and *sōlus.* A. & G. 191 ; B. 239, and 241, 2 ; G. 325, REM. 6; H. 443. *Nūlla* here is much more emphatic than *nōn, = which is in no sense due to you;* the simple thought would be *misericordia nūlla tibi dēbētur.* Prof. Wilkins points out that *nūllus* is used by Cicero in his letters and dialogues instead of *nōn,* which is a colloquial idiom met with in comic writers, and quotes *Sextus ab armis*

while ago you came into the Senate. Who in this throng-ing assembly, who of all your friends and connections, gave you greeting? Seeing	ante in senātum. *before into the senate.* frequentiā, tot *concourse, so many* necessāriīs salūtāvit? *connections saluted?*	Quis tē ēx hāc tantā 6 *Who you out of this (so) great* ēx tuīs amīcīs ac 7 *out of of yours friends and* Sī hōc post hominum 8 *If this since of men*

nūllus discēdit; but this idiom does not occur in the speeches of Cicero. —— **dēbĕtur,** 3d pers. sing. pres. ind. pass. of *dēbeō, -ēre, -uī, -itum,* 2 (*dē = habeō*); agrees with the subj. *quae.* —— **Vēnistī,** 2d pers. sing. perf. ind. act. of *veniō, -īre, venī, ventum,* 4 ; the subj. *tū* is implied. —— **paulō,** adverbial abl. sing. n. of the adj. *paulus, -a, -um* (root *pava = pau = little;* cf. *paucus, pauper;* the form *paullus* has no good authority); abl. of the measure of difference, limiting *ante.* This abl. is used with comparative adjectives and adverbs, e.g. *dīmidiō minor = smaller by half,* and with words implying comparison, e.g. *post* and *ante.* A. & G. 250; B. 223; G. 403; H. 423. There is little doubt that *paullus* was the earlier form, but the MSS. support *paulus.*

LINE 6. **ante,** adv., used here of time (often prep. + acc.); modifies *vēnistī.* —— **in,** prep.; expresses *motion into* with the acc. *senātum.* —— **senātum,** acc. sing. of *senātus, -ūs,* m. 4th; governed by the prep. *in; senātum = the meeting of the Senate.* —— **Quis,** nom. sing. m. of the interrog. pron. *quis, quae, quid;* subj. of *salūtāvit;* the question *quis salūtāvit* = a negation, *nēmō salūtāvit.* —— **tē,** acc. sing. of *tū;* direct obj. of *salūtāvit.* —— **ex,** prep. (*ē* or *ex* before consonants, *ex* before vowels and *h*); gov. the abl. *frequentiā; ex* + the abl. is frequently a variant for the partitive genitive. —— **hāc,** abl. sing. f. of the dem pron. *hīc, haec, hōc;* agrees with *frequentiā.* —— **tantā,** abl. sing. f. of the adj. *tantus, -a, -um;* agrees with *frequentiā.*

LINE 7. **frequentiā,** abl. sing. of *frequentia, -ae,* f. 1st (through the adj. *frequēns,* root *bhrak = φρακ = frequ* or *farc, to shut up fast, to cram;* cf. *φράσσω = I fence in, cōnferciō = I stuff together*); governed by the prep. *ex.* The allusion is, of course, to the very large attendance of senators at the meeting. —— **tot,** indecl. adj.; qualifies *amīcīs.* —— **ex,** prep.; gov. the abl. *amīcīs* and also the abl. *necessāriīs.* —— **tuīs,** abl. plur. m. of the poss. pron. *tuus, -a, -um;* agrees with *amīcīs.* —— **amīcīs,** abl. plur. of *amīcus, -ī,* m. 2d (originally the substantival mas. of the adj. *amīcus, -a, -um*); governed by the prep. *ex,* denoting partition. —— **ac,** cop. conj.; joins *amīcīs* and *necessāriīs. Ac* is a shortened form of *atque.*

LINE 8. **necessāriīs,** abl. plur. of *necessārius, -ī,* m. 2d (strictly the substantival mas. of the adj. *necessārius, -a, -um;* from *necesse*); governed by the prep. *ex;* joined by *ac* to *amīcīs.* Synonyms: (1) *necessārius = a relative,* or one who is closely bound to another person by friendship, business relations, etc.; (2) *propinquus (prope) = a relative,* the general word; (3) *affīnis = a relation* or *connection,* by marriage; (4) *consānguineus* and *cōgnātus = a blood relative.* A list of relatives would include the following: *proavus, avus, parentēs, pater, māter, soror, frāter, vir, marītus, uxor, con-iūnx, fīlius, fīlia, nepōs,* etc. —— **salūtāvit,** 3d pers. sing. perf. ind. act. of *salūtō, -āre, -āvī, -ātum,* 1; agrees with the subj. *quis.* —— **Sī,** conditional particle, introducing a logical condition with the ind. *contigit.* —— **hōc,** nom. sing. n. of the dem. pron. *hīc, haec, hōc;* subj. of *contigit; hōc* refers to the fact that the senators avoided greeting Catiline when he entered the assembly. —— **post,** prep.; gov. the acc. *memoriam; post hominum memoriam = lit. after (since) the memory of men,* i.e. *within the memory of man.* —— **hominum,** gen. plur. of *homō, -inis,* m. 3d; poss. gen., limiting *memoriam. Hominēs,* not *virī,* is always used when the allusion is to *men* or *mankind* in general, as in this passage.

9 memoriam	contigit	nēminī,	vōcis	that no one else has
the memory	has happened	to no one,	of the voice	ever within the memory of man been
10 exspectās	contuméliam,		cum	treated in such a fashion, do you wait
do you wait for	the reproach		seeing that	for the voicing of
11 sīs	gravissimō		iūdiciō	the Senate's scorn,
you have been (lit. are)	severest		judgment	crushed as you have

LINE 9. **memoriam**, acc. sing. of *memoria, -ae*, f. 1st (from the adj. *memor*); governed by the prep. *post*.——**contigit**, 3d pers. sing. perf. ind. act. of *contingō, -ere, contigī, contāctum*, 3 (*con + tangō*); agrees with the subj. *hŏc*. When *contingō* or *obtingō* have the meaning *happen*, the supine is not found. Synonyms: (1) *fierī = to happen*, in general; (2) *ēvenīre* (*ē = out + venīre = to come*) = *to turn out*, i.e. well or ill, according to antecedent circumstances; hence *ēventus = result*; (3) *ūsū venīre = to happen in one's experience*; (4) *contingere* and *obtingere* = lit. *to take hold of*, hence *to happen*, denoting a certain propriety of connection between the event and the person affected by the event. Thus it is commonly used in a good sense, of fortunate occurrences; cf. Seneca, (*scīs*) *plura mala contingere nōbīs quam accidere*, which Prof. Mayor renders *misfortunes are oftener a blessing than a curse*. But *contingere* not infrequently implies misfortune, as does *contigit* in this passage; (5) *accidere* (*ad + cadō = I fall*) = *to happen*, of any casual or unforeseen happening. As in the above example from Seneca, *accidere* usually implies that the occurrence is unlucky; cf. the English word *accident*.——**nēminī**, dat. sing. of *nēmō*, m. and f. 3d (*ne + homō*; the gen. and abl., *nēminis* and *nēmine*, are not found, and the gen. *nūllīus* and the abl. *nūllō, -a*, of *nūllus, -a, -um*, take their place); dat. of the indirect obj. with *contigit*.——**vōcis**, gen. sing. of *vōx*, f. 3d; subjective gen. (of material), limiting and explaining *contuméliam*.

LINE 10. **exspectās**, 2d pers. sing. pres. ind. act. of *exspectō, -āre, -āvī, -ātum*, 1 (*ex + spectō = I look out for*); the implied subj. is *tū*. Questions in Latin are usually introduced by an interrog. word, e.g. *quis, quantus, quō*, or by an interrog. particle, *ne, nōnne, num*; but occasionally, as here, the fact that a question is asked is expressed only by the tone of the speaker's voice and the nature of the context. A. & G. 210, *b*; B. 162, 2, *d*; G. 453; H. 351, 3.——**contuméliam**, acc. sing. of *contumélia, -ae*, f. 1st (*con + tumeō*); direct obj. of *exspectās*.——**cum**, concessive conj. = *although*; taking the subjunct. mood *oppressus sīs*. A. & G. 326; B. 309, 3; G. 587; H. 515, III. For *cum* temporal, see *cum*, Chap. III, l. 23; for *cum* causal, see *cum*, Chap. IV, l. 41. *Cum* causal and concessive always take the subjunct.; *cum* temporal takes the ind., except imperf. and pluperf. subjunct.

LINE 11. **sīs**, 2d pers. sing. pres. subjunct. of *sum, esse, fuī*; agrees with the implied subj. *tū*. See *oppressus* below.——**gravissimō**, abl. sing. n. of *gravissimus, -a, -um*, superl. of the adj. *gravis, -e*, 3d; agrees with *iūdiciō*.——**iūdiciō**, abl. sing. of *iūdicium, -ī*, n. 2d (from *iūdex, -icis*, m. 3d = *a judge*; akin to *iūs, iūngō, iūrō*, etc., from root *yu = to bind, join*); abl. of the means, with *oppressus sīs*. There is, however, little to distinguish this abl. from (1) an abl. of cause, like *odiō permōtus esse videar quō dēbeō*, l. 3, or (2) an abl. of manner, with *cum* omitted, as frequently when the noun is modified by an adjective. *Iūdicium* = (1) *decision, opinion*, in general, (2) *verdict, sentence*, i.e. of *iūdicēs* in a law court, (3) *a trial*. In the plur. *iūdicia = trials*, which were conducted exclusively by senators (as *iūdicēs*, i.e. jury) until C. Gracchus appointed the *equitēs* as sole *iūdicēs*. Sulla restored the *iūdicia* to the senators, but the *lēx Aurēlia* of B.C. 70 created three decuries of *iūdicēs*, viz. of senators, knights, and tribunes of the treasury, and this last arrangement held good till B.C. 55, when Pompey limited the choice of *iūdicēs* to the richest of these three orders.

been by the over-whelming sentence of its silence? What of this again? with what feelings, pray, do you suppose you will have to submit to this fact, that at your approach the seats near you were

taciturnitātis	oppressus?	Quid?	quod 12
of silence	*overwhelmed?*	*What (of this)?*	*that*
adventū	tuō	ista	subsellia 13
at approach	*your*	*those near you*	*seats*
vacuēfacta sunt,	quod	omnēs	cōnsulārēs, 14
were vacated;	*that*	*all (members)*	*of consular rank*
quī tibi persaepe ad caedem			cōnstitūtī 15
who by you very often for murder			*appointed*

LINE 12. **taciturnitātis**, gen. sing. of *taciturnitās*, f. 3d (from the adj. *taciturnus;* *taceō = I keep silence*); gen. of material, limiting *iūdiciō;* cf. *vōcis* above. —— **oppressus**, nom. sing. m. of *oppressus, -a, -um*, perf. part. pass. of *opprimō, -ere, oppressī, oppressum*, 3 (*ob + premō*); agrees with the subj. *tū* understood. *Oppressus + sīs* (above) = the 2d pers. sing. perf. subjunct. pass. of *opprimō*, and the subjunct. mood follows *cum* concessive. —— **Quid**, idiomatic acc. of the interrog. pron. *quis, quae, quid;* the construction is elliptical = *quid dīcam dē hoc, quod*, etc., *what shall I say of the fact that*, etc.; cf. *quid*, Chap. III, l. 33. Cicero often uses *quid quod* in quick transition from one point in an argument to a new one. —— **quod** (adverbial acc. of *quī*), conj. = *that, the fact that* (*not* causal). The clause following *quod*, l. 12, and the clause following *quod*, l. 14, are substantival, and are equivalent to accusatives of reference, for they are summed up in *hōc*, l. 19 (the subj.-acc. of *ferendum* (*esse*) in the obj. clause of *putās*). A. & G. 333, *a;* B. 299, 2; G. 525, 2; H. 516, 2, NOTE.

LINE 13. **adventū**, abl. sing. of *adventus, -ūs*, m. 4th (*adveniō, ad + veniō*); abl. of *time when*, with the modifier *tuō*. The abl. of time is always accompanied by an attribute, except in some common expressions, e.g. *hieme, aestāte*, etc. —— **tuō**, abl. sing. m. of the poss. pron, *tuus, -a, -um;* agrees with *adventū*. —— **ista**, nom. plur. n. of the dem. pron. of the 2d pers. *iste, ista, istud;* agrees with *subsellia*. *Ista* here has, not its contemptuous forensic sense, but its original demonstrative force = *those near you.* —— **subsellia**, nom. plur. of *subsellium, -ī*, n. 2d (*sub + sella; sella = sedla*, from *sedeō = I sit*, root *sad;* cf. *sēdes = a seat, solium = a chair of state, ἕδος = a seat*, etc.); subj. of *vacuēfacta sunt* in the *quod* clause. *Subsellium* = strictly *a law bench* or *seat, the seat* of an ordinary senator, as distinguished from the *sellae* of curule magistrates. The *sellae curūlēs* were probably on a raised platform; cf. the *subsellia* in the law-court, which are distinguished from the raised *sella curūlis* of the presiding praetor. Certain seats in the theatre, circus, etc., were also called *subsellia*.

LINE 14. **vacuēfacta sunt**, 3d pers. plur. perf. ind. pass. of *vacuēfaciō, -ere, vacuēfēcī, vacuēfactum*, 3 (*vacuus + faciō*); agrees (the participial component in gender and number) with the subj. *subsellia*. —— **quod**, conj. like *quod*, l. 12); introducing the substantival clause *omnēs cōnsulārēs . . . relīquērunt*, l. 18, the whole *quod* clause being = to an acc. of reference. —— **omnēs**, nom. plur. m. of the adj. *omnis, -e*, 3d; agrees with *cōnsulārēs*. Synonyms: (1) *omnēs = all*, in detail and wherever situated; (2) *cunctī = all*, together and in a heap. —— **cōnsulārēs**, nom plur. of *cōnsulāris, -is*, m. 3d (the substantival mas. of the adj. *cōnsulāris, -e*, 3d, formed from the noun *cōnsul*); subj. of *relīquērunt*, l. 18, in the *quod* clause. The *cōnsulārēs = ex-consuls*, who had special seats in the Senate-house, as also had *praetōriī = ex-praetors.*

LINE 15. **quī**, nom. plur. m. of the rel. pron. *quī, quae, quod;* agrees with the antecedent *cōnsulārēs*, and is subj. of *cōnstitūtī fuērunt*. —— **tibi**, dat. sing. of *tū;* dat. of the agent, with *cōnstitūtī fuērunt*. The so-called dat. of the agent is regularly used after a gerund or gerundive, e.g. *hōc tibi faciendum est = this must be done by you*. It is also often found with perf. pass. participles, and combinate tenses formed with such

16 fuērunt,	simul	atque	adsēdistī,	forsaken and all the senators of consular rank, men again and
have been,	*at the same time*	*as* (lit. *and*)	*you sat down,*	

participles, but in prose this dat. is rare except with the personal pronouns. As a matter of fact the dat. is not so much one of the agent, as of the person interested in or affected by the action ; therefore *tibi* may be rendered "appointed for murder *in your mind.*" Observe how nearly the dat. of the agent approaches the ethic dat., for which see references under *tibi*, Chap. VI, l. 50.   While prose writers only use the dat. of the agent of personal pronouns, and following participles of certain verbs, the Latin poets make a free use of this dative, cf. Horace, *bellaque mātribus dētestāta ;* Vergil, *Aen.* I, l. 440, *neque cernitur ūllī = and he is seen by no one.*   The dative of the agent, in prose or poetry, is imitated from the Greek construction, e.g. τὰ μοὶ πεπραγμένα = *the things done by me.* The participle *cōnstitūtus* is accompanied by the dat. of the agent in several different passages ; as a rule in Cicero the signification of the participle is one of *intention, provision,* or *agreement ;* cf. Chap. IX, l. 41, *cuī sciam pactam et cōnstitūtam cum Mānliō diem.*   A. & G. 232, *a* ; B. 189, 2 ; G. 354 ; H. 388. —— **persaepe** (*per = very* in composition with adjectives or adverbs, + *saepe ;* cf. *permultus, perfacilis,* etc.); adv., modifying *cōnstitūtī fuērunt.*   Cicero exaggerates if he wishes his audience to believe that Catiline formed several different plans at different times to murder prominent Romans. —— **ad,** prep. ; gov. the acc. *caedem ;* *ad* here expresses purpose, = *for, with a view to.* —— **caedem,** acc. sing. of *caedēs, -is,* f. 3d (cf. *caedō = I cut down*); governed by the prep. *ad.* —— **cōnstitūtī,** nom. plur. m. of *cōnstitūtus, -a, -um,* perf. part. pass. of *cōnstituō, -ere, -uī, -ūtum,* 3 (*con + statuō*), agrees with the subj. *quī.* See note on *fuērunt* following.

LINE 16.   **fuērunt,** 3d pers. plur. perf. ind. of *sum, esse, fuī ;* agrees with the subj. *quī.   Cōnstitūtī + fuērunt =* the 3d pers. plur. perf. ind. (periphrastic tense) pass. of *cōnstituō,* agreeing with the subj. *quī.* The perf. pass. part. + *fuī* (instead of with *sum*) is used : (1) when the participle has a quasi-adjectival force, e.g. *convīvium exōrnātum fuit = the banquet was furnished forth ;* (2) when a *past state* is indicated, as in this passage, for *cōnstitūtī fuērunt* signifies that the persons were once destined for murder, but that the peril no longer exists ; the ordinary perf. pass. *cōnstitūtī sunt* would either stand for a *past act,* = *were destined,* or for a *present state,* = *have been destined.* —— **simul,** adv. = *at the same time* (akin to *similis, simplex,* etc., and to Greek ἅμα). *Simul . . . simul = partly . . . partly, not only . . . but also. Simul* alone or + *atque* (*ac*) = *as soon as,* and is used as a temporal conj.   In historical narrative, *simul* or *simul ac* takes a similar construction to other temporal clauses, e.g. with *ubi, ut, ut prīmum, cum prīmum,* and *postquam,* and is commonly followed by the historical perf. (as in this passage, *adsēdistī*) or the historical present in the ind. mood.   Less commonly the imperf. or pluperf. ind. follows these particles, the imperf. follows *simul* only once in Sallust, but never in Cicero or Caesar, and the pluperf. only once in Cicero and never in Caesar.   A. & G. 324 ; B. 287 ; G. 561, *ff* ; H. 518. —— **atque,** cop. conj. ; here forms a temporal particle with *simul.* The origin of the combination of *simul* and *atque* as a single temporal conjunction is apparent ; instead of *simul atque* introducing a subordinate clause, there are really two coördinate clauses connected by *atque,* and *simul* is included in the first and understood in the second, e.g. *cōnsulārēs simul relīquērunt, atque* (*simul*) *adsēdistī = at the same time the senators of consular rank left* (*that part of the seats empty*) *and* (*at the same time*) *you sat down,* i.e. *as soon as you sat down, the senators left your part of the seats empty.* —— **adsēdistī,** 2d pers. sing. perf. ind. act. of *adsīdō, -ere, adsēdī,* no supine, 3 (*ad + sīdō,* akin to *sedeō*); the subj. *tū* is implied by the personal ending ; the perf. is historical, after *simul atque.*   Catiline, an ex-praetor, was entitled to a special seat above those of ordinary senators.

again picked out in	partem	istam	subselliōrum	nūdam	atque	17
your mind for mur-	*part*	*that (= your)*	*of the seats*	*bare*	*and*	
der, as soon as you	inānem	reliquērunt,	quō	tandem	animō	18
took your seat, left	*empty*	*left,*	*what*	*finally*	*with mind*	
that part of the	hōc	tibi	ferendum	putās ?	Servī	19
benches bare and	*(that) this*	*by you*	*(is) to be borne*	*do you think?*	*Slaves*	

LINE 17. **partem**, acc. sing. of *pars, partis,* f. 3d; direct obj. of *reliquērunt.* —— **istam**, acc. sing. f. of the dem. pron. *iste, ista, istud;* agrees with *partem;* used like *ista,* l. 13. —— **subselliōrum**, gen. plu. of *subsellium, -ī,* n. 2d; partitive gen., limiting *partem.* For etymology, etc., refer to the note on *subsellia,* l. 13. —— **nūdam**, acc. sing., f. of the adj. *nūdus, -a, -um* (probably akin to Sanskrit root *nadsh = to feel shame);* agrees with *partem.* Observe that *nūdam* and *inānem* are *proleptic,* i.e. express the result of the action of the verb, and in anticipation represent it as completed; cf. the well-known Vergilian example of this figure in *Aen.* III, l. 237, *scūta latentia condunt* = lit. *they conceal their hidden shields* (i.e. their shields *in hiding* or *so as to be hidden*), and cf. also such expressions as *I hurled him prostrate.* A. & G. 385; B. 374, 5; G. no reference, but cf. 325, at beginning; H. 636, IV, 3. *Nūdus = naked, bare,* and here is almost synonymous with *inānem;* as applied to persons, *nūdus* may = (1) *naked,* i.e. entirely unclad, or (2) *lightly-clad,* denoting, like the Greek adj. γυμνός, a special form of dress worn by men engaged in laborious physical work, e.g. by ploughmen. *Vacuus* is the general word for *empty; inānis = empty,* in censure, about that which should be full, cf. the figurative *inānia verba = empty,* i.e. *meaningless words.* —— **atque**, cop. conj.; joins *nūdam* and *inānem.*

LINE 18. **inānem**, acc. sing. f. of the adj. *inānis, -e,* 3d; agrees with *partem; inānem,* like *nūdam,* is *proleptic.* —— **reliquērunt**, 3d pers. plur. perf. ind. act. of *relinquō, -ere, relīquī, relictum,* 3 (*re = behind + linquō = I leave;* root *rik = liqu, lic, to leave;* cf. λείπω from Greek root λιπ); agrees with the subj *cōnsulārēs.* —— **quō,** abl. sing. m. of the interrog. adj. *quī, quae, quod;* agrees with the abl. *animō.* —— **tandem** (*tam* + suffix *-dem*), adv.; emphasizes the question with *quō animō. Tandem* = *at length,* but is better rendered *pray, I ask,* etc., when it strengthens questions or commands; cf. the Greek δή in questions, e.g. ποῖ δή ἡ ὁδός ἄγει; = *whither exactly does the road lead?* and cf. Chap. IV, l. 1, *Recognōsce tandem = review, pray,* etc. —— **animō,** abl. sing. of *animus, -ī,* m. 2d (root *an = to breathe;* cf. *anima = breath, life, the animal principle of life, animal,* ἄνεμος = *wind,* etc.); abl. of manner, without *cum,* because the abl. has the modifier *quō.* Synonyms : (1) *animus = the mind, the soul,* in opposition to *corpus = the body* and to *anima = physical life; animus = mind,* especially as the seat of the emotions, hence *animus* sometimes = *courage;* (2) *anima = the soul,* as the supporter of life; cf. *animam ēdere = to give up the ghost;* lit. *anima = breath,* cf. *animam dūcere = to draw breath;* (3) *mens = the mind,* especially as *the intellect;* but *mens* is sometimes used with *animus* as a synonym ; (4) *ingenium* (*in* + *gignō*) = *mind,* or rather *inborn ability,* especially in regard to creative power.

LINE 19. **hōc,** acc. sing. of the dem. pron. *hīc, haec, hōc;* subj.-acc. of *ferendum (esse)* in the acc. and inf. construction dependent on *putās. Hōc* refers to and summarizes the state of things mentioned in the *quod* clause, ll. 12–14, and in the *quod* clause, ll. 14–18. Some editors omit *hōc* and read *quō tandem animō tibi ferendum putās?* In this case the substantival *quod* clauses act as direct subj.-acc. of *ferendum (esse),* and the gerundive is singular partly because *ferendum (esse)* is quasi-impersonal (= *how do you think it is to be endured that at your approach,* etc.) and partly because the *quod* clauses, though two in number, express one single idea, viz., that Catiline was treated

20 mēhercule	meī	sī	mē	istō	pactō	empty? In the name of Hercules, if even
by Hercules	*my*	*if*	*me*	*that*	*in manner*	my slaves feared me

as an outcast by the senators.——tibi, dat. sing. of *tū ;* dat. of the agent after the gerundive *ferendum* (*esse*). The agent is always put in the dat. after a gerund or gerundive, except when the gerundive belongs to a verb which takes a dat. of the indirect obj. in the act., and is therefore only used impersonally in the pass., e.g. *persuādendum est tibi ā mē* (*ā mē* expresses the agent); in such cases the agent is expressed by the abl. with *ā* or *ab*, because *persuādendum est tibi mihi* would leave it doubtful whether *tibi* was agent and *mihi* indirect obj., or vice-versa. Refer to the note on *mihi*, Chap. II, l. 36.—— **ferendum**, acc. sing. n. of *ferendus, -a, -um*, gerundive of *ferō, ferre, tulī, lātum*, irreg. (cf. Greek φέρω); agrees with the subj.-acc. *hōc* in the acc. and inf. object clause of *putās* (as a *verbum sentiendī*); supply *esse* with *ferendum*. Parts of *sum*, especially *esse* and *est*, are very commonly omitted in Latin, but in all such cases the necessary part of *sum* can easily be supplied in the light of the context. For synonyms, see the note on *patimur*, Chap. II, l. 15.—— **putās**, 2d pers. sing. pres. ind. act. of *putō, -āre, -āvī, -ātum*, 1 (root *pu = to cleanse*, hence *putō* has a rare sense = *to cleanse, to prune ;* hence *to set in order* one's intellect, *to reckon, consider*); the implied subj. is *tū*. For synonyms, refer to the note on *arbitrāris*, Chap. I, l. 16.—— **Servī**, nom. plur. of *servus, -ī*, m. 2d ; subj. of *metuerunt*. Observe the emphatic position of *servī ; servī . . . arbitrāris*, l. 24, is an excellent example of *a fortiori* argument. "The Greeks call this method of argument ἐνθύμημα in the narrower sense, i.e. a rhetorical conclusion, which is drawn from a contrast " (quoted from Prof. Wilkins *in locō*). Roman slaves were of three kinds : (1) *captīvī =* prisoners of war, who remained the property of the captor, or else were employed or sold at auction by the state ; (2) *servī* by birth, for the children of *servī* or of a female slave were considered slaves by law ; cf. the American law on slavery, which recognized as a slave any person born of a slave mother, although the negro taint might be only 1 in 16, or 1 in 32 ; slaves born in a Roman master's house were called *vernae ;* (3) *servī* by judicial sentence, i.e. former *cīvēs* who had suffered degradation (*aēminūtiō capitis māxima*) for such military offences as desertion from the army, refusal to answer to one's name when a levy was made, mutilation of oneself to escape service, or for such civil offences as avoiding enrolment in the censor's lists with the intent of escaping taxation, and (by the XII tables, though the law was afterwards repealed) insolvency. Slaves had absolutely no political rights, and the master might torture or kill them as he pleased. They were generally known by foreign names, e.g. the country they came from, etc. They could not legally marry, but might cohabit (*contubernium*), and their children became *vernae*. They could not hold any property, even what they acquired honestly, unless the master refused to exercise his right to take it ; such property as they were permitted to keep was called *pecūlium*. Slave-trading and selling in market was a regular thing in Rome. A slave might be set free : (a) *vindictā*, a ceremony conducted before a magistrate ; (b) *censū = by enrolment in the census by the censor, at the master's request ; (c) *testāmentō = by will*, after which the liberated slave owed certain duties to his master's heirs or executors as his *patrōnī*. In early Rome slaves were very few, but the foreign wars of Rome (esp. in the time of Scīpiō Asiaticus) brought thousands of slaves to Italy, and this greatly aggravated the agrarian difficulties. In the time of Horace, ten slaves was considered an extremely small *familia*, and two hundred slaves a large one. Under the emperors a few wealthy men had as many as four thousand slaves each. The price of an ordinary slave was from eighty dollars upwards.

LINE 20. **mēhercule**, exclamation, = *by heaven, by Herculēs. Mēhercule* is a compound of *mē*, adverbial or exclamatory acc. of *ego*, and *hercule*. Corrsen regards *Hercule*

in such a fashion as all your fellow-citizens fear you, I	metuerent, ut tē metuunt omnēs cīvēs 21
	feared, as you fear all fellow-citizens

as vocative, with the final *s* lost, of *Herculēs*, gen. *Hercul -is* or *-ī*, m. (Etruscan *Hercle*); but many others prefer to consider *Hercule* a clipped form of the nom. *Herculēs;* possibly the original expression was *mē Herculēs iūvet* (optative subjunct.) = *may Hercules help me !* The name of the hero occurs in the following exclamatory forms : *Herculēs, mĕherculēs* or *mē Herculēs, Hercule, mĕhercule* or *mē Hercule, Hercle* (syncopated), *mĕhercle* or *mē Hercle* (syncopated). In the speeches of Cicero *mĕhercule* occurs thirty-two times, whereas *mĕherculēs* is only found five times. Herculēs was worshipped as a god by the early Italians, but it is doubtful how far the later Roman accounts and worship of this hero were native and how far borrowed from the Greek hero Hēraclēs (ʿΗρακλῆς), whose worship was prevalent throughout Greece and esp. among the Dorians. Herculēs was the son of Jupiter (Zeus) and Alcmēnē, and was renowned for his marvellous strength, his twelve prodigious labors, and numerous other feats and adventures (for details, consult a classical dictionary). After his death Herculēs was deified, and in Greece he was worshipped both as a god and as a hero. The best of many statues representing him is the Farnese Herculēs, preserved in Naples. —— meī, nom. plur. m. of the poss. adj. *meus, -a, -um ;* agrees with *servī*. —— sī, conditional particle ; followed by the imperf. subjunct. *metuerent*, of an impossible supposition in the present. —— mē, acc. sing. of the 1st personal pron. *ego ;* direct obj. of *metuerent*. —— istō, abl. sing. n. of the dem. pron. *iste, ista, istud ;* agrees with *pactō ; istō* here is both scornful and demonstrative, and by itself would = *in the same way as* YOU *are feared*, but for further clearness Cicero adds *ut tē metuunt omnēs cīvēs tuī.* Consequently *istō pactō* is an adverbial phrase = *ita*, and is used correlatively with *ut* following ; cf. *nūllō pactō = nēquāquam, not at all.* —— pactō, abl. sing. of *pactum, -ī*, n. 2d (= (1) *agreement, bargain*, (2) as here, *manner, fashion ;* originally the neut. of *pactus, -a, -um*, perf. part. pass. of *pangō, -ere*, perf. *panxī, pēgī,* or *pepigī, pactum,* 3, from root *pag = to bind fast*, cf. πήγνυμι); abl. of manner, without *cum*, as *istō* modifies the ablative.

LINE 21. **metuerent**, 3d pers. plur. imperf. subjunct. act. of *metuō, -ere, -uī, -ūtum,* 3 (*metus*); agrees with the subj. *servī* in the *protasis* with *sī ;* the imperf. subjunct. is used in conditions when some act or occurrence is represented hypothetically as taking place in the present time (though it does not do so in reality). Conditions may be divided into two kinds: (A) Logical conditions, which merely state something according to a formula, and are not concerned with the possibility or reality of the supposition, as — *if this is (was, or will be) so, then that is (was, or will be) so*, e.g. *if men are immortal, they are equal to the gods ;* in such conditions the *protasis* (or clause with *sī, nisi* or *sī nōn*) has its verb in the ind. mood and the verb of the *apodosis* (so-called conclusion) is either ind., imperative, or the subjunct. in one of its independent constructions. (B) Ideal or imaginary conditions. These may be (1) of the future, when the verbs of *protasis* and *apodosis* are both in the pres. subjunct. ; e.g. *if men were to become immortal, they would be like the gods ;* cf. Chap. VIII, ll. 1 and 2, *sī tēcum . . . patria loquātur.* Often all notion of time disappears, and the pres. subjunct. presents an imaginary case purely as a vague hypothesis, e.g. *if giants were to appear on the earth,* in which supposition there is little or no consideration of time, and none of the possibility ; (2) of the present time, when the verb in both clauses is in the imperf. subjunct.; the condition is unreal and unfulfilled in the present ; (3) of past time, when both verbs are in the pluperf. subjunct., e.g. *if he had had a shield, he would have escaped death ;* here again the condition is unreal, and is opposed to actual fact of the past. Sometimes (2) and (3) are combined in one condition, e.g. *sī pecuniam habērēs, domum ēmissēs* = *if you had had money* (but you had not, as you have not now), *you would have bought the*

22 tuī,   domum   meam   relinquendam   putārem :
   your, (that) house   my   (ought) to be left   I should think:

23 tū   tibi   urbem   nōn
   you   by you (that) the city (should be left)   not

24 arbitrāris?   et   sī   mē   meīs   cīvibus
   do (you) think?   And   if   myself   my   to fellow-citizens

should think it my
duty to leave my own
house: do you, then,
not judge it to be
your duty to leave
the city? And if I
saw myself even un-

house. For conditional sentences in general consult A. & G. 304-309; B. 301-304; G. 589 *ff*; H. 507-512. For the imperf. subjunct. see especially A. & G. 308; B. 304; G. 597; H. 510.——**ut,** adv., = *as;* the *ut* clause is explanatory of *istō pactō.*——**tē,** acc. sing. of *tū;* direct obj. of *metuunt.*——**metuunt,** 3d pers. plur. pres. ind. act. of *metuō, -ere, -uī, -ūtum,* 3; agrees with the subj. *cīvēs.* The same distinctions are to be drawn between the verbs *timeō, metuō,* etc., as between the nouns *timor, metus,* etc.; refer to the note on *timor,* Chap. I, l. 6.——**omnēs,** nom. plur. m. of the adj. *omnis, -e,* 3d; agrees with *cīvēs.* The statement that *all* Catiline's fellow-citizens feared him implies that those who did not fear him, i.e. his followers, were not any longer to be considered *cīvēs.* Cicero, on the strength of *ultimum cōnsultum* and the powers (whether recognized by the people or not) which it gave him, claims the right of degrading those who attacked the state; cf. Chap. XI, ll. 25-28. *At numquam in hāc urbe, quī ā rē pūblicā dēfēcērunt, cīvium iūra tenuērunt.*——**cīvēs,** nom. plur. of *cīvis, -is,* m. or f. 3d; subj. of *metuunt.*

LINE 22. **tuī,** nom. plur. m. of the poss. pron. *tuus, -a, -um;* agrees with *cīvēs.*—— **domum,** acc. sing. of *domus, -ūs,* f. 4th (with some forms in the 2d decl., e.g. *domō, domōs, domōrum*); subj.-acc. of the inf. *relinquendam (esse)* in the acc. and inf. object clause dependent on *putārem* as leading verb.——**meam,** acc. sing. of the poss. pron. *meus, -a, -um;* agrees with *domum.*——**relinquendam,** acc. sing. f. of *relinquendus, -a, -um,* gerundive of *relinquō, -ere, relīquī, relīctum,* 3 (*re + linquō*); *esse* must be supplied with *relinquendam,* = the pres. inf. of the periphrastic pass. conjugation of *relinquō,* agreeing with the subj.-acc. *domum.* The direct thought = *domus mea relinquenda est.* A. & G. 129; B. 337, 7, *b*), 1); G. 251; H. 234, and 266, NOTE.—— **putārem,** 1st pers. sing. imperf. subjunct. act. of *putō, -āre, -āvī, -ātum,* 1 (see *putās,* l. 19); the implied subj. is *ego;* the tense and mood correspond with those of *metuerent* in the *protasis* (where see note), and show that an unreal case is imagined in the present time, the impossibility of which is disregarded for the sake of argument. Note that *arbitrāris* is used in l. 24, and for synonyms refer to the note on *arbitrāris,* Chap. I, l. 16.

LINE 23. **tū,** gen. *tuī* (borrowed from *tuus;* cf. *meī,* gen. of *ego,* borrowed from *meus,* etc.); nom. sing., subj. of *arbitrāris.* Observe (1) the emphatic position of *tū;* the personal pronouns, when in the nom. case, are not usually expressed except when emphasis or contrast is intended; (2) that the question is not introduced by an interrog. particle; *ne* may be supplied with *nōn,* = *nōnne,* which is used when an affirmative reply is expected, as in this passage; however, the question is rhetorical, and = *surely you think you ought to leave the city.* See the note on *sentīs,* Chap. I, l. 11; (3) that in the sentence *tū . . . arbitrāris* we must supply *relinquendam (esse)* (agreeing with the subj.-acc. *urbem*) from the previous sentence, with which this sentence is logically connected.——**tibi,** dat. sing. of *tū;* dat. of the agent, with *relinquendam esse* supplied, cf. *tibi ferendum,* l. 19.——**urbem,** acc. sing. of *urbs, urbis,* f. 3d; sub.-acc. of *relinquendam esse* (to be supplied from *relinquendam,* l. 22) in the object-clause of *arbitrāris* (a verb of *thinking*).——**nōn,** neg. adv.; limits *arbitrāris.* *Nōn* here = *nōnne.*

LINE 24. **arbitrāris,** 2d pers. sing. pres. ind. of the deponent verb *arbitror, -ārī, -ātus sum,* 1 (from the noun *arbiter = an umpire* in a dispute, lit. *ar = ad + bītō = I*

deservedly an object	iniūriā	suspectum	tam	graviter 25
of such serious sus-	*by wrong*(= *wrongfully*)	*suspected*	*so*	*seriously*
picion and disgust to				
my fellow-citizens, I	atque	offēnsum	vidērem,	carēre	mē 26
should prefer to with-	*and*	*offensive*	*I saw,*	*to abstain*	*myself*
draw out of their sight	aspectū	cīvium	quam	īnfēstīs	omnium 27
rather than be re-	*from the sight of the citizens*	*than*		*hostile*	*of (them) all*

go, akin to *veniō*, hence, *one who goes to inquire into something*); agrees with the subj. *tū*. —— **et**, cop. conj.; connects the sentence following with the one preceding. —— **sī**, conditional particle; followed by the imperf. subjunct. of an unreal supposition respecting present time. —— **mē**, acc. sing. of *ego ;* subj.-acc. of *esse* understood (*suspectum* and *offensum* are predicative with *esse*) in the object-clause of *vidērem*. —— **meīs**, dat. plur. m. of the poss. pron. *meus, -a, -um;* agrees with *cīvibus.* —— **cīvibus**, dat. plur. of *cīvis, -is*, m. or f. 3d; dat. of the indirect obj. dependent on *suspectum* and *offensum*. The dat. of the indirect obj. follows *offensum* naturally, but *suspectum* + this dat. is a little strained unless we render *suspectum* as *as an object of suspicion* (*to my fellow-citizens*). Possibly *meīs cīvibus* is a dat. of *personal interest* (advantage or disadvantage) = *in the eyes of my fellow-citizens*. A. & G. 235; B. 188, 1; G. 350; H. 384, 1, 2.

LINE 25. **iniūriā**, abl. sing. of *iniūria, -ae*, f. 1st (*in* = *not* + *iūs* = *right*); idiomatic abl. of manner, modifying *suspectum*. *Cum* is required with the abl. of manner, unless the noun in the abl. be modified by an attributive, e.g. *cum cūrā*, or *māgnā cūrā* or *māgnā cum cūrā*. But *inūriā* (= *wrongfully*) and a few other simple ablatives have acquired the force of adverbs, and are used without *cum;* cf. *vī* = *by force, silentiō, cāsū, lēge*, etc. A. & G. 248; B. 220; G. 399; H. 419, III. —— **suspectum**, acc. sing. m. of the adj. *suspectus, -a, -um* (properly the perf. part. pass. of *suspiciō, -ere, suspēxī, suspectum*, 3, from *sub* + *speciō* = *I look at from beneath*, i.e. from under frowning eyebrows; cf. ὑποπτεύω); complement of *esse* understood in the predicate; agrees with the subj.-acc. *mē*. —— **tam**, adv.; limits *graviter*. —— **graviter** (from the adj. *gravis, -e*, 3d), adv.; limits *suspectum* and *offēnsum*.

LINE 26. **atque**, cop. conj.; joins *suspectum* and *offensum*. —— **offēnsum**, acc. sing. m. of *offēnsus, -a, -um*, adj. (properly perf. part. pass. of *offendō, -ere, offendī, offēnsum*, 3, *ob* + obsolete *fendō*, which only occurs in compounds, cf. *dēfendō;* root *ghan* = *fend, to strike*); agrees with the subj.-acc. *mē; offensum* is predicative, like *suspectum*, to which it is joined by *atque*. —— **vidērem**, 1st pers. sing. imperf. subjunct. act. of *videō, -ēre, vīdī, vīsum*, 2; the implied subj. is *ego ;* the imperf. subjunct. after *sī* expresses an unreal condition in present time. —— **carēre**, pres. inf. act. of *careō, -ēre, -uī, (-itum)*, fut. part. *caritūrus*, 2; agrees with the subj.-acc. *mē* in the acc. and inf. object-clause of *māllem*. Observe that *carēre* governs the abl. *aspectū ;* the rule is that verbs of *plenty* or *want* take the abl., but *egeō* and *indigeō* very often take the gen. case. A. & G. 243, *f;* 223, NOTE; B. 214, 1; G. 405; H. 414, I, and 410, V, 1. —— **mē**, acc. sing. of *ego ;* subj.-acc. of *carēre* after *māllem* as leading verb; see note on *māllem* below.

LINE 27. **aspectū**, abl. sing. of *aspectus, -ūs*, m. 4th (from *aspiciō, ad* + *speciō*); governed by *carēre*. —— **cīvium**, gen. plur. of *cīvis, -is*, m. or f. 3d; poss. gen., limiting *aspectū*. —— **quam**, adv., introducing the comparative clause (*mē*) *īnfēstīs . . . cōnspicī* after the comparative adv. *magis* incorporated in *māllem* of the main clause (*māllem* = *magis vellem*). —— **īnfēstīs**, abl. plur. m. of the adj. *īnfēstus, -a, -um* (some say = *īnfēnstus*, from *in* + *fendō*, and so another form of *īnfēnsus* from the same root; others derive from *in* + *feriō* = *I strike* (*fendō* also = *I strike*), thinking it unlikely that two synonymous adjectives would be derived from the same root); agrees with *oculīs*. Synonyms: (1) *hostīlis* = *hostile*, pertaining to a *hostis*, i.e. public enemy in the field; (2) *īnfēnsus* (*in* + *fendō*) = *hostile, exasperated;* (3) *īnfēstus* (*in* + *feriō*) = *hostile*,

28 oculīs	cōnspicī	māllem :	tū	cum	garded with eyes of
by the eyes to be regarded	*I should prefer:*	*you*	*since*	hatred by them all.
29 cōnscientiā	scelerum	tuōrum	āgnōscās	As you with the knowledge of your
with the knowledge	*of crimes*	*your*	*(you) recognize*	own guilt recognize

and is used either actively, of persons, e.g. *gēns īnfēsta Rōmānīs* = *a race hostile* (*danger-ous, malevolent*) *to the Romans*, or passively of things, e.g. *iter īnfēstum* = *an unsafe* (*dangerous*) *route.*—— **omnium**, gen. plur. m. (substantival) of the adj. *omnis, -e*, 3d; poss. gen., limiting *oculīs; omnium*, i.e. *cīvium.*

LINE 28. **oculīs**, abl. plur. of *oculus, -ī*, m. 2d; abl. of the means, with *cōnspicī.*—— **cōnspicī**, pres. inf. pass. of *cōnspiciō, -ere, cōnspēxī, cōnspectum*, 3 (*con + speciō*); coör-dinate with *carēre*, to which it is joined by *quam*, and like *carēre* agrees with the subj.-acc. *mē.*—— **māllem**, 1st pers. sing. imperf. subjunct. act. of *mālō, mālle, māluī*, no supine, irreg. (*magis* = *more, rather + volō* = *I wish;* hence *I prefer*); the subj. *ego* is implied by the personal ending; the imperf. subjunct. in the main clause or *apodosis* (as in the *protasis*, or *if* clause) shows the condition to be unreal in present time. Note the construction with *māllem* here, viz. the acc. and inf. *mē carēre, mē cōnspicī*. A verb of *wishing* (*volō, cupiō, mālō*, etc.) is followed as a rule by the *complementary* inf., e.g. *mālō carēre*, when the subj. of each is the same, but sometimes by the acc. and inf., as in this passage; cf. Chap. II, ll. 23 and 24, *cupiō mē esse clēmentem;* when the subj. of the inf. is different from that of the verb of wishing, two constructions may be used, (1) the acc. and inf. (preferably after *volō* and *cupiō*), e.g. *cupiunt tē dare operam ut* = *they wish you to take pains that*, etc., (2) the subjunct., with *ut* expressed or understood, e.g. *māllem (ut) bona redderentur* = *I would rather the goods were restored.* A. & G. 331, *b*, and NOTE; B. 331, IV, *a*; G. 532, REM. 2; H. 535, II.—— **tū**, gen. *tuī;* nom. sing., subj. of *āgnōscās; tū* is emphatic, and for this reason stands first in the clause, though it is com-mon for the subject of the *cum* clause to precede *cum* when the same noun or pronoun is also subj. of the main clause. Cicero here urges upon Catiline the line of conduct which he has just said he would himself pursue under similar conditions.—— **cum**, causal conj.; followed by the subjunct. *āgnōscās;* see *cum*, Chap. IV, l. 41.

LINE 29. **cōnscientiā**, abl. sing. of *cōnscientia, -ae*, f. 1st (*con + sciō*, cf. *scientia*, hence *common knowledge;* root *ski* = *sci, to see, to split, to distinguish;* cf. *secō*); abl. of cause, with *āgnōscās. Cōnscientia* does not = *conscience*, but rather *feeling, consciousness*, often to be rendered *sense of right* or *sense of guilt*, according to the context, cf. the adj. *cōnscius*, e.g. *mēns sibi cōnscia rēctī.*—— **scelerum**, gen. plur. of *scelus, sceleris*, n. 3d (see note on *sceleris*, Chap. IV, l. 9); objective gen., limiting *cōnscientiā.* The objective gen. is regular with adjectives expressing *knowledge, power, memory*, etc., and also fol-lows nouns which retain the verbal notion of the verbs from which they are formed; cf. *aurī amor* = *love of gold.* A. & G. 217; B. 200; G. 363, 2; H. 396, III. Distinguish the subjective and objective genitives as follows: *amor deī* = *the love of God*, which, if subjective, = *the love which God has for us*, but, if objective, = *the love which we feel for God.*—— **tuōrum**, gen. plur. m. of the poss. pron. *tuus, -a, -um;* agrees with *scelerum.*—— **āgnōscās**, 2d pers. sing. pres. subjunct. act. of *āgnōscō, -ere, āgnōvī, āgnitum*, 3 (*ad + (g)nōscō:* root *gna* = *gno* = *to know*, cf. γνῶσις = *knowledge*); agrees with the subj. *tū;* the subjunct. mood is dependent on *cum* causal; the tense is pres. in regular sequence with the pres. *dubitās* in the main clause. A. & G. 286; B. 267, 268; G. 509, *ff;* H. 491. Note the following: (1) *nōscō* = *I come to know;* (2) *cōgnōscō* = *I learn about, ascertain*, e.g. *hīs rēbus cōgnitīs;* (3) *recōgnōscō* = *I recollect, ascertain anew, revise;* (4) *āgnōscō* = (a) *I recognize*, e.g. a person, (b) *I recognize* something in its true char-acter; (5) *ignōscō* (*in* = *not + gnōscō* = *I search into*) = *I pardon*, of offences, and is followed by the dative of the person.

the justice and the	odium	omnium	iūstum	et	iam 30
long-standing meet-	*the hatred*	*of all*	*(to be) just*	*and*	*already*
ness of their universal	diū	tibi	dēbitum,	dubitās,	quōrum 31
hatred of you, can you	*for a long time*	*to you*	*owed,*	*do you hesitate*	*of whom*
hesitate to shun the	mentēs	sēnsūsque	vulnerās,	eōrum 32
sight and presence of	*the minds*	*and the feelings*	*you wound,*	*of those (men)*
the men whose minds	aspectum	praesentiamque	vītāre?	Sī tē 33
and feelings you are	*the sight*	*and the presence*	*to shun?*	*If you*
wounding? Suppos-				

LINE 30. **odium**, acc. sing. of *odium, -ī*, n. 2d (cf. *ōdī = I hate*, hence *odium =* (1) *hate*, (2) *ill-will*); subj.-acc. of *iūstum (esse)* and of *dēbitum (esse)* in the acc. and inf. construction following *āgnōscās* (as a verb of *feeling* or *perception*). —— **omnium**, gen. plur. m. of the adj. *omnis, -e*, 3d; subjective gen., limiting *odium ; omnium* is substantival, and *odium omnium = the hatred felt by all men* or *by all the citizens.* —— **iūstum**, acc. sing. n. of the adj. *iūstus, -a, -um (iūs = right)*; agrees predicatively with *odium*, being the complement of *esse* understood. —— **et**, cop. conj.; joins the two predicate adjectives *iūstum* and *dēbitum.* —— **iam**, adv. of time; strengthens *diū.*

LINE 31. **diū** (root *dyu = to shine ;* cf. *diēs, dūdum*, etc.), adv. of time; modifies *dēbitus.* The *historic* present accompanies *iam diū*, and signifies that an action begun in the past is continued into the present. The direct form would be *odium omnium iūstum et iam diū dēbitum (est).* —— **tibi**, dat. sing. of *tū ;* dat. of the indirect obj. with *dēbitum.* —— **dēbitum**, acc. sing. n. of the adj. *dēbitus, -a, -um* (perf. part. pass. of *dēbeō* (for *dēhibeō, dē + habeō*), *-ēre, -uī, -itum*, 2); agrees with the subj.-acc. *odium ;* complement of *esse*, which is to be supplied. —— **dubitās**, 2d pers. sing. pres. ind. act. of *dubitō, -āre, -āvī, -ātum*, 1 (for *duhibitō*, frequentative form of *duhibeō*, i.e. *duo + habeō*); the subj. *tū* is implied by the personal ending. Observe that the question has no introductory interrog. particle; this is sometimes the case, esp. when the main clause is preceded by a number of subordinate clauses. When *dubitō = I hesitate*, it may be followed by a complementary (epexegetic, prolative, or explanatory) infinitive, as in this passage *dubitās . . . vītāre.* Note: (1) *dubitō an = I doubt whether = I am inclined to think ;* (2) *nōn dubitō quīn = I do not doubt that (but)*, etc. + subjunct. mood. —— **quōrum**, gen. plur. m. of the rel. pron. *quī, quae, quod ;* agrees with the logical antecedent *eōrum*, l. 32; poss. gen., limiting *mentēs* and *sensūs.* The relative clause should naturally follow its correlative, but when special emphasis is thrown upon the correlative the relative clause may precede; the order simplified = *dubitās vītāre aspectum praesentiamque eōrum quōrum . . . vulnerās.*

LINE 32. **mentēs**, acc. plur. of *mēns, mentis*, f. 3d; direct obj. of *vulnerās* in the rel. clause. —— **sēnsūsque** (*sēnsūs + que*), *sēnsūs* is the acc. plur. of *sēnsus, -ūs*, m. 4th (from *sentiō = I feel*); direct obj. of *vulnerās ;* joined by *que* to *mentēs. Que* is the enclitic cop. conj. (Greek τε enclitic), used to join two words or ideas between which there is a close internal connexion. Refer to the note on *que*, Chap. I, l. 9. —— **vulnerās**, 2d pers. sing. pres. ind. act. of *vulnerō, -āre, -āvī, -ātum*, 1 (*vulnus = a wound*, Sanskrit *vran*); the subj. *tū* is implied by the personal ending. *Vulnerās* is here used figuratively; cf. Chap. IV, l. 24, *eōs nōndum vōce vulnerō.* —— **eōrum**, gen. plur. m. of the dem. pron. *is, ea, id;* poss. gen., limiting *aspectum* and *praesentiam. Is* and not *ille* is the common antecedent of *quī*, when the person or thing to which the rel. refers is not defined otherwise than by the rel. pron., e.g. *eī quī haec facere solent malī sunt.*

LINE 33. **aspectum**, acc. sing. of *aspectus, -ūs*, m. 4th (from *aspiciō*); direct obj. of *vītāre.* —— **praesentiamque** (*presentiam + que*), *praesentiam* is the acc. sing. of *praesentia, -ae*, f. 1st (formed through *praesēns*, adj. and pres. part. of *praesum ;* of

| 84 | parentēs | timērent | atque | ōdissent | tuī | nec | ing that your parents |
| | *parents* | *feared* | *and* | *hated* | *your and not* | | feared and hated you |

ing that your parents feared and hated you and you could not by any means at all conciliate them, you

| 85 | eōs | ūllā | ratiōne | plācāre | possēs, | ut | opīnor, |
| | *them* | *any* | *by means* | *to soothe you were able,* | | *as* | *I think,* |

absēns from *absum ;* the original verb *sum* has no pres. part.); direct obj. of *vītāre ;* joined by *que* to *aspectum. Que* is the enclitic cop. conj., connecting *aspectum* and *praesentiam.* —— **vītāre**, pres. inf. act. of *vītō, -āre, -āvī, -ātum,* I (= *vic-i-tō,* from root *vik* = ικ = *vic, to yield ;* cf. *vicis = change, alternation*); complementary inf. in close dependence on the principal verb *dubitās.* See the note on *invenīrī,* Chap. II, l. 44. —— **Sī**, conditional particle, followed by the imperf. subjunct. *timērent* of an unreal supposition in present time. —— **tē**, acc. sing. of *tu ;* direct obj. of *timērent* and of *ōdissent.*

LINE 34. **parentēs**, nom. plur. of *parēns, -entis,* m. or f. 3d (*pariō = I bring forth,* sometimes *I beget*); subj. of *timērent.* —— **timērent**, 3d pers. plur. imperf. subjunct. act. of *timeō, -ēre, -uī,* no supine, 2 ; agrees with the subj. *parentēs ;* the imperf. subjunct. signifies that the condition, assumed of the present time, is contrary to fact, but imagined as taking place for the sake of argument. —— **atque**, cop. conj., joins *timērent* and *ōdissent. Atque* very often joins a word or idea of a forcible description to a preceding word or idea which is less forcible ; cf. *nūdam atque inānem,* l. 17, and Chap. IV, l. 39, *mūnīvī atque fīrmāvī* (*mūnīvī =* simply *I fortified,* not necessarily implying that the precautionary measures were sufficient, whereas *fīrmāvī = I made strong* (*firmus*) against any and every attack). —— **ōdissent**, 3d pers. plur. pluperf. subjunct. act. of the defective verb *ōdī, ōdisse,* fut. part. *ōsūrus* (no pres. tense and no pres. stem tenses); agrees with the subj. *parentēs ; ōdissent* is joined by *atque* to *timērent,* and relates to pres. and not to past time, for, as the perf. form *ōdī = I hate* (not *I hated*), the pluperf. *ōderam* (subjunct. *ōdissem*) = an imperf., i.e. *I hated* (not *I had hated*). —— **tuī**, nom. plur. m. of the poss. pron. *tuus, -a, -um ;* agrees with the subj. *parentēs.* Observe the strange position of *tuī ;* when two important and emphatic words or ideas are closely connected (as *parentēs* and *timērent atque ōdissent*), they are given a prominent position usually at the beginning of a sentence, and the less important parts of the sentence follow after ; cf. *haec rēs ūnius est propria Caesaris = this exploit belongs to Caesar alone.* A. & G. 344, *e ;* B. 348, 349 ; G. 671 ; 672, *a ;* 676 ; H. 561, III. —— **nec** (shortened form of *neque, ne + que = and . ∴ not*), cop. conj., connects the coördinate clauses *parentēs . . . ōdissent* and (*tū*) *possēs,* each of which belongs to the *protasis,* i.e. the subordinate part with *sī.*

LINE 35. **eōs**, acc. plur. m. of the dem. pron. *is, ea, id ;* direct obj. of *plācāre ; eōs* refers to *parentēs.* Observe that though *parentēs = pater et māter,* they are referred to in *eōs* in the mas. ; it is the regular rule in Latin for the masculine gender to take precedence over the feminine ; so *hominēs = mankind* (men and women) is masculine. —— **ūllā**, abl. sing. of the adj. *ūllus, -a, -um ;* agrees with *ratiōne. Quisquam = any one* (at all) and *ūllus = any* (at all) are mainly used in negative sentences (cf. *nec ūllā* here), in sentences implying negation, e.g. *quis* (= *nēmō*) *ex hīs rēbus ūllum gaudium capere potest?,* and in sweeping statements, e.g. *sōlis candor illustrior est quam ūllīus īgnis = the brilliancy of the sun is brighter than that of any fire.* —— **ratiōne**, abl. sing. of *ratiō, -ōnis,* f. 3d ; *ratiōne +* the attribute *ūllā* is the abl. of manner. *Ratiōne* is one of the few ablatives that may express manner without the addition of *cum* or an epithet. —— **plācāre**, pres. inf. act. of *plācō, -āre, -āvī, -ātum,* I (akin to *placeō* and φιλέω); complementary inf., predicative with *possēs.* —— **possēs**, 2d pers. sing. imperf. subjunct. of *possum, posse, potuī,* no supine, irreg. (*potis = able + sum*); coördinate and in the same construction with *timērent atque ōdissent* above, to which it is joined by *nec ;* agrees

| would retire, I believe, to some place or other out of their view. As the case stands, your native land, the common | ab　　eōrum　oculīs　aliquō　　　　concēderēs : ₃ *from of them (= their) eyes　somewhither you would withdraw:*

nunc　tē　patria,　quae　commūnis　est　parēns ₃ *now　you your country which　common　is the parent* |

with the subj. *tū* understood in the second *sī* clause. —— **ut**, adv. = *as ; ut opīnor* is parenthetic, and refers to the statement in the next line. Several editions read *tū* instead of *ut :* in this case *opīnor* stands parenthetically by itself, and *tū* is subj. of *concēderēs*. The reading *ut* is adopted by the German editor Halm, who is followed in this text throughout. —— **opīnor**, 1st pers. sing. pres. ind. of the deponent verb *opīnor, -ārī, -ātus sum*, 1 (adj. *opīnus* in compounds ; perhaps akin to Greek οἴομαι = *I think ;* the act. *opīnō, -āre, -āvī, -ātum*, 1, is found in Cicero) ; the implied subj. is *ego*. Synonyms : (1) *opīnārī* = *to fancy, think,* i.e. with no certain knowledge, cf. Cic. *sapiēns nihil opīnātur* = *the wise man* (of the Stoics) *never forms opinions* = he never has doubts (in sarcasm) ; (2) *crēdere* = *to think, believe,* from conviction ; (3) *putāre* (root *pu* = *to cleanse*) = *to think,* after clear reflection ; (4) *existimāre* (*ex + aestimāre*) = *to think,* after logical consideration of all the facts ; (5) *iūdicāre* = *to think, judge, decide ;* (6) *censēre* = *to think,* esp. of official opinions, e.g. in the Senate ; (7) *rērī* = *to think,* after a prearranged consideration ; (8) *arbitrārī* = *to think,* sometimes like *opīnor,* but often in restricted etymological sense (*arbiter* = *an umpire, ar* = *ad + bītō* = *I go,* hence *one who goes to inquire*) = *to judge, decide.*

LINE 36. **ab** (*ab* before vowels or *h, ā* or *ab* before consonants), prep. ; gov. the abl. *oculīs,* expressing separation. —— **eōrum**, gen. plur. m. of the dem. pron. *is, ea, id ;* poss. gen., limiting *oculīs ; eōrum* refers to *parentēs,* l. 34. —— **oculīs**, abl. plur. of *oculus, -ī,* m. 2d ; governed by the prep. *ab.* —— **aliquō** (adverbial abl. n. sing. of the indef. pronominal adj. *aliquī, aliqua, aliquod, alius + quī ;* cf. *quō, eō*), adv. = *somewhither,* cf. Chap. VIII, l. 27, *in aliquās terrās ;* modifies *concēderēs.* The adverbial abl. n. of pronouns commonly denotes *place to which,* cf. *quō* = *whither, eō* = *thither ;* whereas the abl. f. sing. = *place where,* cf. *aliquā, eā, quā.* —— **concēderēs**, 2d pers. sing. imperf. subjunct. act. of *concēdō, -ere, concessī, concessum,* 3 (*con + cēdō*) ; the implied subj. is *tū ; concēderēs* is the verb of the *apodosis* (principal sentence) in the condition introduced by *sī,* l. 33. The imperfect tense signifies that the supposition is made regarding the present time ; see the note on *metuerent,* Chap. VII, l. 21.

LINE 37. **nunc** (*num + ce*), adv. ; *nunc* is here transitional, = the Greek νῦν δέ = *but now, but as the facts are ;* the orator passes from merely hypothetical cases to the actual facts which must be considered. —— **tē**, acc. sing. of *tū ;* direct obj. of *ōdit* and of *metuit.* —— **patria**, gen. *patriae,* f. 1st (noun formed from the adj. *patrius, -a, -um,* = belonging to one's *father,* hence *fatherland ;* cf. *pater,* πατήρ, πατριά = *lineage* or *clan,* root *pa* = *to nourish*) ; nom. sing., subj. of *ōdit.* The natural order would be for the subj. to precede the object, but *tē* is emphatic and therefore stands prominently first, and moreover the subj. is somewhat long, owing to the adjectival enlargement *quae . . . nostrum.* —— **quae**, nom. sing. f. of the rel. pron. *quī, quae, quod ;* agrees with the antecedent *patria,* and is subj. of *est.* —— **commūnis**, nom. sing. f. of the adj. *commūnis, -e,* 3d (*con + mūnis* = *ready to be of service,* hence *commūnis* = lit. *serving together, common ;* root *mu* = *to enclose, protect,* cf. *mūnus* = *a service, moenia, mūrus,* ἄμυνα = *defence,* etc.) ; agrees with *parēns.* —— **est**, 3d pers. sing. pres. ind. of *sum, esse, fuī ;* agrees with the subj. *quae.* —— **parēns** (akin to *pariō*), gen. *parentis,* m. and f. 3d ; nom. sing., *complement* of *est* in the pred., hence in the same case as the subj. *quae.* A. & G. 176 ; B. 167, 168 ; G. 205, 206 ; H. 360. As a conspirer against this *parēns,* Catiline is called *parricīda ;* cf. Chap. XII, l. 13.

38 omnium	nostrum,	ōdit	ac	metuit	et	iam	mother of us all,
all	*of us,*	*hates*	*and*	*fears*		*and already*	hates you and fears
							you and has long
39 diū	nihil	tē	iūdicat		nisi	dē	since judged you as
for a long time nothing	*you*	*judges*			*unless respecting*		one who thinks about

LINE 38. **omnium**, gen. plur. m. of the adj. *omnis, -e*, 3d; agrees with *nostrum.*
—— **nostrum**, gen. of the 2d personal pron. plur. *nōs* (sing. *ego*); poss. gen., limiting
parēns. The gen. of the personal pronouns in *-um* (*nostrum, vestrum*) is usually partitive, and the form in *-ī* objective (*nostrī, vestrī*); but Cicero always uses the form in
-um instead of that in *-ī* when *omnium* precedes. When a personal pron. is possessor,
the possession is regularly marked by the poss. pron. corresponding, instead of by the
gen. of the personal pron., e.g. *mea māter* not *māter meī;* but Cicero uses *omnium
nostrum,* or *omnium vestrum* (i.e. when *omnium* precedes), especially when the limited
noun is also modified by an adj. (as *parēns* is by *commūnis*). When there is no such
adj., we often use expressions such as *quae est nostra omnium parēns,* in which the poss.
adj. must stand before *omnium,* and *omnium* is idiomatic (agreeing as it seems with the
gen. *nostrī,* denoting possession, whose place the poss. *nostra,* agreeing with *parēns,*
takes).—— **ōdit**, 3d pers. sing. perf. ind. of the defective verb *ōdī* (perf. form. with pres.
meaning), inf. *ōdisse,* fut. part. *ōsūrus;* agrees with the subj. *pătria.* That *ōdit* refers to
pres. time and not to past is clear, for the pres. tense following *metuit* is coördinate.——
ac (*ac* before consonants, except *c, g, qu;* *atque* before *c, g, qu,* and vowels), cop. conj.;
joins *ōdit* and *metuit.*—— **metuit**, 3d pers. sing. pres. ind. act. of *metuō, -ere, -uī, -ūtum,*
3; coördinate with *ōdit,* and agrees with the same subj. *pătria.*—— **et**, cop. conj.; connects the previous sentences *patria . . . ōdit ac metuit* with the sentence following *iam
. . . iūdicat . . . cōgitāre.*—— **iam**, adv. of time; strengthens *diū.* Refer to the note
on *iam,* Chap. I, l. 11.
LINE 39. **diū** (cf. *diēs, dūdum,* etc.), adv. of time; modifies *iūdicat.*—— **nihil**
(apocopated form of *nihilum, -ī,* n. 2d, *ne = not + hilum = a trifle*), acc. sing. of the
indecl. noun *nihil;* direct obj. of *cōgitāre* in the acc. and inf. object-clause of *iūdicat.*
The order simplified = (*pătria*) *iam diū iūdicat tē nihil cōgitāre nisi ae parricīdiō suō.*
—— **tē**, acc. sing of *tū;* subj.-acc. of *cōgitāre* in the acc. and inf. construction dependent
on *iūdicat.*—— **iūdicat**, 3d pers. sing. pres. ind. act. of *iūdicō, -āre, -āvī, -ātum,* 1 (cf.
iūdex; probably *iūs + dīcō*); understand as subj. a pron. in the nom. case referring to
pătria; iūdicat = pronounces judicially (as a *iūdex*), and the idea is that Catiline's country
has held court over his habits and actions and pronounces him guilty of treason. *Iūdicat*
is the *historic* present (used in vivid narration) which is regular after *iam diū,* or *iam
dūdum = pronounces now and has for a long time been pronouncing,* i.e. expresses past
action continued into the present. Continued action in the past is similarly expressed
by the *historic* imperf. + *iam diū* (*dūdum*), e.g. *iam diū iūdicābat* would = *had for a
long time been pronouncing.* A. & G. 276, *a;* B. 259, 4; G. 230; H. 467, III, 2.——
nisi (*nē + sī = if not*), conj., in elliptical construction after the neg. word *nihil,* and =
but, except, besides; cf. the similar use of εἰ μή with no verb following. The full idea is,
you plan nothing except (= *unless you plan*) *for the country's destruction.* As a conj.,
nisi differs in use from *sī nōn; nōn* (in *sī nōn*) limits a single word, and so an opposing
positive is expected; the *ni* of *nīsi* limits the main clause, which is not accepted if the
conditional clause be accepted; e.g. *nisi fallor, Rōmānus erat* = either *he was a Roman,
if I am not mistaken* or *he was not a Roman, if I am mistaken.* A. & G. 315, *a;* B. 306;
G. 591; H. 507, and 3, NOTE 3.—— **dē**, prep. with the abl.; gov. *parricīdiō.* The two
common meanings of *dē* are (1) of place, or separation, *from, down from;* (2) of reference, *about, concerning.* *Dē* may also express *source,* after verbs of receiving. A. & G.
153; B. 142; G. 417, 5; H. 434, I.

nothing but her de-	parricīdiō	suō	cōgitāre :	hūius	tū 40
struction. Will you	*impious ruin*	*her own*	*to meditate :*	*of this (country) you*	
not show respect for	neque	auctōritātem		verēbere	nec 41
her authority and	*neither*	*the authority*		*will (you) reverence*	*nor*

LINE 40. **parricīdiō**, abl. sing. of *parrīcīdium, -ī*, n. 2d (through *parricīda* from *pater + caedō*); governed by the prep. *dē. Parricīdium* = lit. *the murder of one's father*, and is particularly suitable here, as *patria* is personified (*parēns omnium nostrum*); hence it is practically a synonym of *interitus* or *exitium ;* but even when there is no personification, *parricīda* often = *a horrible criminal*, i.e. without implying the murder of a parent in literal fact, and *parricīdium* similarly = *a horrible crime*, especially *treachery* to one's benefactor, and *treason* against one's country.   The older forms are *paricīda* and *paricīdium*, and so the grammarian Roby derives from *pār = like*, on the ground that there are no other examples of *patri-* becoming assimilated to *parri-;* but it appears that Cicero once uses a form *patricīda*, which proves that he accepts the derivation from *pater* and *caedō*. —— **suō**, abl. sing. n. of the poss. pron. reflexive *suus, -a, -um* (cf. *sē*, and Greek *ἕ = σϝε, οὗ, οἷ* ; and *ἑός, σφός* adjectival); agrees with *parricīdiō ;* the reflexive *suō* refers back to the subj. *patria ; suō* takes the place of the gen. *suī*, objective with *parricīdiō*. —— **cōgitāre**, pres. inf. act. of *cōgitō, -āre, -āvī, -ātum*, I (*con + agitō = to turn over and over together* in one's mind, hence *to ponder upon, to scheme* in a bad sense); agrees with the subj.-acc. *tē* in the acc. and inf. construction dependent on the leading verb *iūdicat. Cōgitō* may either be followed by a direct obj. or *dē +*the abl. ; in this passage we find both, viz. *nihil = dē nūllā rē*, and *aē parricīdiō. Cōgitō*, as a *verbum sentienaī*, may also take the acc. and inf. —— **hūius**, gen. sing. f. of the dem. pron. *hīc, haec, hōc ;* poss. gen., limiting *auctōritātem ; hūius* is emphatic, and limits not only *auctōritātem*, but also the objects in the coördinate clauses following, viz. *iūdicium* and *vim*, hence it stands first in the sentence. —— **tū**, nom. sing. of the 2d personal pron.|; subj. of *verēbere ; tū* is emphatic.   When two pronouns (or two poss. adjectives, or a poss. adj. and a pron.) occur in contrast or any kind of close connection in the same sentence, Latin favors their juxtaposition, as *hūius tū* here (i.e. Catiline's country on the one hand and Catiline himself on the other); cf. *nōbīs tua*, Chap. III, l. 9; *mē tibi*, Chap. V, l. 29; and *meī sī mē istō*, l. 20 of this Chapter.   So also any words strongly contrasted may stand together, cf. *iubet cōnsul hostem*, Chap. V, l. 52.

LINE 41. **neque** (*ne + que*), cop. conj., used correlatively with *nec* following ; *neque . . . nec . . . nec = neither . . . nor . . . nor;* the *ne* of *neque* limits *verēbere*.   Refer to the note, etc., on *neque*, Chap. III, l. 1. —— **auctōritātem**, acc. sing. of *auctōritās, -ātis*, f. 3d (from *auctor ;* cf. *augeō, augustus*); direct obj. of *verēbere*. —— **verēbere** (another form of *verēberis*), 2d pers. sing. fut. ind. of the deponent verb *vereor, -ērī, -itus sum*, 2 (= *I hold in reverential awe*, from root *var = to be wary ;* cf. *verēcundus = modest*); agrees with the subj. *tū*.   Observe : (1) the ending in *-re*, which occurs seven times in the fut. ind. in this speech, twice in the pres. subjunct., and not at all in the pres. ind. ; whereas the ending in *-ris* is found six times in the pres. ind., once in the pres. subjunct., and not at all in the future.   Other writers support the generalization which may be made from these tenses and figures, except as regards the fut. ind., for the ending in *-ris* is very common in this tense outside Cicero.   (2) The question has no particle to distinguish it as such, and may only be understood as a question by the tones of the speaker's voice or by the interrogation mark in writing ; see note on *exspectās*, l. 10.   (3) No conj. connects the clause *hūius tū*, etc., with the preceding clause *patria . . . iūdicat*, etc. ; the latter really stands in a causal relation to the former, and the logical form is as a rule observed in Latin, e.g. *nunc cum tē patria . . . ōderit ac metuat et . . . iūdicet, hūius tū*, etc. ?   But Cicero purposely avoids the logical subordination

42 iūdicium	sequĕre	nec	vim	obedience to her
(her) judgment	*will you follow*	*nor*	*her violence*	

43 **pertimēscēs?**   .   Quae   tēcum,   Catilīna,   sīc
will you fear?   *Which (country) with you,*   *Catiline,*   *thus*

44 agit   et   quōdam   modō   tacita   loquitur :
treats and   *certain*   *in a fashion (though) silent*   *speaks:*

obedience to her judgment? Will you not fear her power? For in this way, Catiline, as it were, your country pleads with you with silent elo-

when he wishes to make an impressive point, and uses instead short and vigorous simple sentences, placing the sentence which contains the pith of the argument last and allowing a pause for rhetorical effect (with *asyndeton*, as here). —— nec, cop. conj., connecting the clauses of *verēbere* and *sequĕre*.

LINE 42. **iūdicium**, acc. sing. of *iūdicium, -ī,* n. 2d (*iūdex*); direct obj. of *sequĕre;* *iūdicium* is quasi-legal, and = *sententiam,* the official *decision* or *verdict* of the *patria* as *iūdex.* Supply *hūius* with *iūdicium,* like *hūius auctōritātem* above. —— **sequĕre** (another form of *sequĕris*), 2d pers. sing. fut. ind. of the deponent verb *sequor, -ī, secūtus sum,* 3; the implied subj. is *tū.* **Sequĕre** is here figurative = *will you follow,* i.e. *obey, act in accordance with.* —— nec, cop. conj.; joins the clauses of *sequĕre* and *pertimēscēs.* —— vim, acc. sing. of *vīs,* acc. vim, abl. *vī,* f. 3d (other cases in sing. very rare; the plur. is *vīrēs, -ium,* etc. = *vīrēs;* cf. *violentus,* and *Īs = strength, ἴφιος = strong,* etc.); direct obj. of *pertimēscēs.* The proper meaning of *vīs* in the sing. is *force, violence,* but sometimes it = *energy, quantity, number;* the plur. *vīrēs = strength,* and sometimes *military forces, troops.* Supply *hūius,* as above, with *vim.*

LINE 43. **pertimēscēs**, 2d pers. sing. fut. ind. act. of *pertimēscō, -ere, pertimuī,* no supine, 3 (*per* intensive + *timēscō,* inceptive form of *timeō;* see note on *hebēscere,* Chap. II, l. 15); the implied subj. is *tū.* *Pertimēscēs* is more forcible than the simple verb *timēbis;* for the distinction between *verēbere* and *pertimēscēs,* consult the synonymous nouns (which have corresponding verbs) in the note on *timor,* Chap. I, l. 6. —— **Quae,** nom. sing. f. of the rel. pron. *quī, quae, quod;* agrees with the antecedent *pătria,* l. 37, but is here merely connective = *patria enim.* The rel. at the beginning of a new sentence = a dem. pron. + a causal, adversative, or cop. conj. (as the context may require), and is due to a desire to mark the unity and interconnection of sentences in extended argument or narration; cf. the common phrase *quae cum ita sint.* A. & G. 180, *f;* 201, *e;* B. 251, 6; G. 610, and REM. 1; H. 453. —— **tēcum** (*tē + cum*), *tē* is the abl. sing. of *tū;* governed by the prep. *cum.* *Cum* is the prep. (enclitic with the personal, reflexive, and rel. pronouns); gov. the abl. *tē.* —— **Catilīna,** voc. sing. of *Catilīna, -ae,* m. 1st; the case of address. —— **sīc** (*sī +* dem. suffix *-ce*), adv. of manner; modifies *agit,* and refers to what follows in ll. 45-63.

LINE 44. **agit**, 3d pers. sing. pres. ind. act. of *agō, -ere, ēgī, actum,* 3; agrees with the subj. *quae. Agere cum +* the abl. = *to treat, confer, plead with. Agere* has more different meanings probably than any other Latin verb, e.g. (1) *set in motion, drive,* (2) *direct, guide,* (3) *spend, pass,* of time, (4) *do, perform, manage,* etc., (5) *incite, urge,* (6) *drive away,* of plunder, hence *rob,* (7) *pursue,* etc., etc. It is also used in many idioms, e.g. *grā-tiās agere = to return thanks;* the imperative *age = come!* as an interjection; *actum est de +* the abl. = *it is all over* or *up with,* etc. Martial devotes an epigram to the illustration of some of these uses. —— **et,** cop. conj.; connects the clauses of *agit* and *loquitur.* —— **quōdam,** abl. sing. m. of the indef. pron. *quīdam, quaedam, quiddam* (*quoddam* is adjectival; see the note on *quāsdam,* Chap. II, l. 4); agrees with *modō.* As often, *quōdam* softens the violence of the figure by which words are, so to speak, put into the mouth of Catiline's native country; *quōdam modō* may be rendered *so to speak;* cf. Chap. VI, l. 47, *quādam dēclīnātiōne,* and cf. the similar use of *aliquis,* and see the note on *aliquam*

quence: "For some years past there has been no crime except devised by you, no shameful deed but had your help; in

"Nūllum iam aliquot annīs facinus exstitit 45
" No　　　　now　　some　within years misdeed has occurred

nisi per tē, nūllum flāgitium sine tē; 46
except through you,　　no　　villany　　without you;

---

mentem, Chap. VI, l. 38. —— **modō**, abl. sing. of *modus, -ī*, m. 2d; abl. of manner, with which *cum* is not required, as *mōdō* is qualified by the attribute *quōdam*. —— **tacita**, nom. sing. f. of the adj. *tacitus, -a, -um* (in origin perf. part. pass. of *taceō, -ēre, -uī, -itum*, 2, trans. and intrans., hence *tacitus* = passively *silent, passed in silence, hidden, secret*, actively *silent, still*); agrees with the subj. *quae* (= *patria*) *tacita* = (*though*) *silent*, actively. Observe: (1) *tacita* is practically adverbial = *tacitē*. A. & G. 191; B. 239; G. 325, REM. 6; H. 443. (2) *tacita loquitur* is a good instance of the figure called *oxymōron* (ὀξύμωρον, neut. of ὀξύμωρος = *pointedly foolish*, from ὀξύς = *sharp, keen* + μωρός = *dull, sluggish, foolish*), i.e. the usage in one phrase of expressions which contradict one another. This figure is met with in both Greek and Latin, cf. Chap. VIII, l. 51, *cum tacent, clāmant*, and Sophocles, *Antigone*, l. 74, ὅσια πανουργήσασα = *having wrought a holy crime*. Other examples well known are *insāniēntis sapientiae* = *of foolish wisdom*, *strenua inertia* = *vigorous idleness*, *splendidē mendāx* = *magnificently lying*. Tennyson (speaking of Lancelot) affords us an excellent English example: *His honor rooted in dishonor stood, And faith unfaithful kept him falsely true*. A. & G. 386; B. 375, 2; G. 694; H. 637, XI, 6. —— **loquitur**, 3d pers. sing. pres. ind. of the deponent verb *loquor, -ī, locūtus sum*, 3; joined by *et* to *agit*, and agrees with the subj. *quae*. The figure by which lifeless objects or abstractions are represented as *persōnae* (= *characters*, as in a play, hence endowed with human qualities, e.g. reasoning power, speech, emotions, and the like) is called in Greek προσωποποιΐα (*personification*).

LINE 45. **Nūllum**, nom. sing. n. of the adj. *nūllus, -a, -um* (*ne* + *ūllus*); agrees with *facinus*. —— **iam**, adv. of time; modifies the adverbial phrase *aliquot annīs*. —— **aliquot**, indecl. numeral adj. (*alius* + *quot*); agrees with *annīs*. —— **annīs**, abl. plur. of *annus, -ī*, m. 2d (for *am-nus* = *that which goes round*, hence *a year*, cf. Vergil, *volvenda diēs*; cf. the inseparable prepositions *ambi, amb-, am-*, e.g. *amplus* = lit. *full all round*, hence *large*; cf. also ἀμφί = *on both sides round about*); abl. of *time within which*. *Time how long* is expressed by the acc., e.g. *trēs diēs morātus est* = *he lingered for three days; time when* is expressed by the abl. alone, e.g. *prīmā lūce* = *at dawn; time within which* is expressed (a) by the abl. alone, e.g. *hīs decem annīs nihil scripsit* = *he has written nothing within these ten years*, or (b) by the abl. with *in*, e.g. *in brevī spatiō* = *within a brief period* of time. —— **facinus**, gen. *facinoris*, n. 3d (*faciō*); nom. sing., subj. of *exstitit*. See note on *sceleris*, Chap. IV, l. 9, for synonyms. —— **exstitit**, 3d pers. sing. perf. ind. act. of *exsistō, -ere, exstitī, exstitum*, 3 (*ex* = *forth* + *sistō*, used intransitively = *I appear*, esp. of one who appears in court on a fixed day; *sistō*, trans. = *I make to stand;* cf. *stō*, ἵστημι trans., ἕστην intrans.); agrees with the subj. *facinus*.

LINE 46. **nisi** (*nē* + *sī*), conditional conj.; here = *unless, except*, in elliptical construction. Refer to the note on *nisi*, l. 39. —— **per**, prep.; gov. the acc. *tē*. *Per* + the acc. often expresses agency, especially when the agent is the ultimate source of an action and not the actual doer; *per* + the acc. is necessary here, partly because *abs tē* may only follow a passive verb and partly because Catiline hired others to do some of the violent deeds which are hinted at. *Nūllum . . . per tē* refers generally to the crimes which stained Catiline's career from the time when he was quaestor in Sulla's army to the time when he conspired against Rome. —— **tē**, acc. sing. of *tū;* governed by the prep. *per*. —— **nūllum**, nom. sing. n. of *nullus, -a, -um;* agrees with *flāgitium*. —— **flāgitium**, gen. *flagit-iī* or *-ī*, n. 2d (akin to *flagrō* and φλέγω = *I burn;* hence *flāgitium* = *a dis-*

47 tibi	ūnī	multōrum	cīvium	necēs,	your case only has
for you	*alone*	*many*	*of citizens*	*the deaths,*	the assassination of
48 tibi	vēxātiō	dīreptiōque	sociōrum		many citizens, the
for you	*the harassing*	*and the pillaging*	*of (our) allies*		harassing and plun-
					dering of the allies,

graceful act done in the heat of passion); nom. sing., subj. of *exstitit* understood from the preceding sentence. The allusion is to Catiline's crimes of immorality, e.g. against the vestal virgin Fabia, who was a sister of Cicero's wife Terentia (for this crime Catiline was accused in B.C. 73, but escaped condemnation by the intercession of Q. Lutātius Catulus); cf. also Q. Cicero, (*Catilīna*) *ēducātus in sorōris stupris.* —— **sine**, prep. with the abl.; gov. *tē.* —— **tē**, abl. sing. of *tū;* governed by the prep. *sine.*

LINE 47. **tibi**, dat. sing. of *tū;* dat. of *personal interest* or *reference,* indicating the person to whose interest or advantage (or the reverse) an action takes place. A. & G. 235; B. 188, 1; G. 350, 352; H. 384, 1 and 2. —— **ūnī**, dat. sing. m. of the numeral adj. *ūnus, -a, -um;* agrees with *tibi; ūnī = sōlī.* —— **multōrum**, gen. plur. m. of the adj. *multus, -a, -um;* agrees with *cīvium.* —— **cīvium**, gen. plur. of *cīvis, -is,* m. (some-times f.) 3d; objective gen. with *necēs.* The objective gen. is common with nouns derived from verbs, such as *nex* from *necō, amor* from *amō,* etc. Refer to the note on *scelerum,* l. 29. —— **necēs**, nom. plur. of *nex, necis,* f. 3d (root *nak = to perish, destroy;* cf. *necō = I kill, noxa = injury, noceō, perniciēs,* and νέκυς and νεκρός = *corpse*); the pred. *impūnītae fuērunt ac līberae* must be understood from the next sentence. It is common in Latin for a verb to be expressed in one clause (agreeing with the subj. of that clause), and to be understood in the coördinate clauses; a similar principle is exempli-fied in the agreement of an adj. with the nearest of several substantives which it modi-fies. The plur. form *necēs* is rare; *nex* = (1) *a violent death,* (2) *murder, slaughter;* cf. the synonyms under *pestem,* Chap. I, l. 27. The allusion here is to the part taken by Catiline in the Sullan proscriptions. He is said to have been in his element when mur-dering the proscribed, whether at Sulla's orders, or because they were his personal ene-mies. He caused his own brother's name to be placed on the proscription list, because he had previously murdered him and feared trial. Catiline, at the head of some Gallic soldiery, killed many of the *equitēs,* and among them his brother-in-law Caecilius, and a relation of Cicero whose name was M. Marius Grātidiānus.

LINE 48. **tibi**, dat. sing. of *tū;* dat. of *reference* (the person affected by the action), like *tibi* above. —— **vēxātiō**, gen. *vēxātiōnes,* f. 3d (from verb *vēxō* = lit. *I move violently,* hence *I harass;* root *vagh* = ϝεχ or ἐχ = *veh, to move,* trans.; cf. ὄχος = *a carriage, vehō = I carry; vēxō* is frequentative of *vehō*); nom. sing., subj. of *fuit. Vēxātiō . . . sociōrum* refers to Catiline's oppression in the province of Africa which he governed as prō-praetor, B.C. 67. Even before Catiline left Africa in B.C. 66 to sue for the consulship, a deputation came to Rome from Africa to complain of the terrible extortion and misgovernment to which they had had to submit. Consequently Catiline was prosecuted in the court *de repetundīs,* and retired from his candidature. In B.C. 65 P. Clōdius Pulcher was allowed to bring the trial on, but Catiline bribed him and the *iūdicēs,* and escaped condemnation (but only narrowly, for the senators on the jury con-demned him, while the *equitēs* and *tribūnī aerāriī* acquitted). —— **dīreptiōque** (*dīreptiō + que*), *dīreptiō* is the nom. sing. of *dīreptiō, -ōnis,* f. 3d (from the verb *dīripiō, dis + rapiō,* = *I plunder*); joined by *que* to *vēxātiō,* with which it expresses one idea, viz. oppression. *Que* is the enclitic cop. conj.; joins *vēxātiō* and *dīreptiō; que* here, as gen-erally, joins two words which have a close internal connection. —— **sociōrum**, gen. plur. of *socius, -ī,* m. 2d (substantival masc. of the adj. *socius, -a, -um,* = lit. *following to share,* hence *ally, partner;* root *sak = to follow,* cf. *sequor*); objective gen., limiting *vēxātiō* and *dīreptiō.* Up to the time of the Social War, *Sociī* was the technical name for all

been unpunished and	impūnīta	fuit	ac	lībera ;	tū	nōn	sōlum 49
unrestrained. You	*unpunished*	*has been*	*and*	*unrestrained ; you*		*not*	*only*
have succeeded not	ad	neglegendās	lēgēs	et	quaestiōnēs, 50
only in disregarding					
laws and law-courts,	*to*	*neglect* [see NOTE]	*the laws*	*and*	*investigations,*

citizens of Italian communities which did not possess the full Roman franchise ; these were sometimes distinguished from the *Latīnī* (members of the Latin league, to whom Rome gave greater privileges than to other *sociī ;* their name was *Sociī Latīnī,* or *nōmen Latīnum,* or *Sociī Latīnī nōminis*). But in the field of war the *sociī* and the *nōmen Latīnum* were distinguished from *Rōmānī mīlitēs ;* in the period preceding the Social War, the *sociī* had to equip and pay infantry equal in number to what Rome furnished, and twice as many cavalry troops ; the *sociī* fought on the wings (*alae*), and provided the general's special body-guard. In B.C. 89, after the Social War, the full Roman *cīvitās* was reluctantly given to all the Italian communities, and thenceforward the subjects of Rome in foreign provinces were called *sociī* (e.g. those in the province of Africa, here mentioned). Jūlius Caesar granted the Roman franchise freely to many peoples, and not very long afterwards all Roman subjects became Roman citizens also.

LINE 49. **impūnīta,** nom. sing. f. of the adj. *impūnītus, -a, -um* (*in = not + pūnītus = punished,* perf. part. pass. of *pūniō*) ; agrees with *vēxātiō ;* the adj. is sing. because *vēxātiō* and *dīreptiō* are almost synonymous and express one idea. Catiline was in fact prosecuted in B.C. 64 by L. Luccius for the murders committed during the Sullan proscriptions, but Caesar, leader of the democrats, presided at the trial, and apparently for private reasons, and because he hoped to make political use of Catiline, secured a verdict of acquittal. Catiline's magnetic influence over good men and bad is exemplified by the fact that several *cōnsulārēs* testified favorably respecting his character at this trial (or, as others think, at the trial *aē repetundīs*).—**fuit,** 3d pers. sing. perf. ind. act. of *sum, esse, fuī ;* agrees with the subj. *vēxātiō* (which *dīreptiō* merely amplifies, without adding any essentially new idea).—**ac,** cop. conj. ; joins the two predicate adjectives *impūnīta* and *lībera.*—**lībera,** nom. sing. f. of the adj. *līber, lībera, līberum* (akin to *libet,* hence *doing as one pleases, free*) ; agrees with the subj. *vēxātiō ; lībera* signifies that nothing hampered Catiline in his desire to oppress, and that he escaped the unpleasant consequences which would have befallen other men.—**tū,** nom. sing. of the 2d personal pron. ; subj. of *valuistī. Tū* is very emphatic ; cf. *tibi ūnī* above.— **nōn,** neg. adv. ; limits *sōlum,* or we may regard both *nōn* and *sōlum* as limiting *valuistī* understood in the first clause *tū . . . quaestiōnēs.* The phrase *nōn sōlum* (*nōn modo* or *nōn tantum*) . . . *vērum etiam* (*vērum quoque, sed etiam*) is employed when special emphasis is to be thrown on one of two words or ideas, the emphatic word or idea being that which follows the adversative conjunction. Cicero often used *nōn modo* and *nōn sōlum,* but very seldom *nōn tantum.* A. & G. 149, *e ;* B. 343, 2 ; G. 482, 5 ; H. 554, I, 5.—**sōlum** (acc. n. sing. of *sōlus, -a, -um ;* cf. adv. *multum, facile,* etc.), adv. ; modifies *valuistī* understood (from below) in the clause *tū . . . quaestiōnēs.*

LINE 50. **ad,** prep. ; gov. *neglegendās lēgēs,* expressing purpose. *Ad +* the acc. gerund or gerundive (attraction), like *causā* or *grātiā +* the gen. of the gerund or gerundive, = *ut* final + the subjunctive.—**neglegendās,** acc. plur. f. of *neglegendus, -a, -um,* gerundive of *neglegō, -ere, neglēxī, neglēctum,* 3 (*nec + legō ;* the form *negligō,* etc., is incorrect) ; agrees with *lēgēs* in the construction of gerundival attraction. The gerundive is always used after a prep. with the acc., and not the acc. gerund + a direct object ; but the gen. of the gerund is preferred to the gen. of the gerundive when the obj. of the gerund is a neut. pronoun, e.g. *haec perficiendī causā.* A. & G. 296–301 ; B. 337, 7 ; 339 ; G. 115, 3 ; 427–433 ; H. 543, 544. Refer to the note on *habendī,*

51	vērum	etiam	ad	ēvertendās	perfringendāsque	but also in over-
but	*even*	*to*	*overthrow*	*and break through (them)*	throwing and break-

Chap. I, l. 8.——lēgēs, acc. plur. of *lēx*, *lēgis*, f. 3d ; acc. in the gerundial construction with *neglegendās*, governed by the prep. *ad*. The etymology of *lēx* is doubtful : (1) root *leg*, of *legō = I read*, hence of a resolution put in writing and read to the people so that they may sanction it and make it law ; (2) root *lagh = lec, to lie*, denoting something *laid down ;* this is improbable ; (3) root *lig = to bind*, cf. *ligō, obligation, lictor*, etc., this appears the most likely derivation. A bill proposed to the people, but not yet sanctioned by them, was called, *rogātiō*, and the people were said *iubēre* or *antīquāre rogātiōnem* according as they accepted or rejected it ; as soon as a *rogātiō* was formally passed (*lāta est*) it was *lēx*. Note the following phrases : (a) *lēgem abrogāre = to repeal a law ;* (b) *aliquid lēgī dērogāre = to repeal part of a law ;* (c) *aliquid lēgī subrogāre = to add new clauses to a law*. Roman law consists of the following : (1) the Twelve Tables, drafted in B.C. 450 at the earnest desire of the people, and comprising all that was important in early traditional law ; (2) *lēgēs* passed in *comitia centuriāta* with the sanction of the Senate (*senātūs auctōritās*); (3) *plēbiscīta*, i.e. laws passed in *comitia tribūta ;* these were originally binding only on plebeians, but after the *lēx Hortensia*, B.C. 287, were binding without restriction on all Roman *cīvēs ;* (4) *senātūs cōnsulta* became practically *lēgēs*, if they were accepted, i.e. if they were not made null by *intercessiō ;* these were common during the supremacy of the Senate, but their authority was disputed if they ran counter to any law passed in *comitia* (e.g. the *cōnsultum ūltimum*); (5) *ēdīcta* of magistrates had the force of law during the year of office in which they were issued. The *lēgēs cūriātae*, passed by the *comitia cūriāta*, were merely part of formal ceremony.——et, cop. conj. ; joins *lēgēs* and *quaestiōnēs*.——quaestiōnēs, acc. plur. of *quaestiō*, *-ōnis*, f. 3d (from *quaerō = I investigate*); acc. in the gerundial construction with *neglegendās ;* joined by *et* to *lēgēs ; quaestiōnēs = law-courts*, or *criminal trials*. The two praetors presided at private or civil trials, while the national assembly, *comitia centuriāta*, judged criminal trials. In specially grave cases the people appointed a *quaesītor* or *quaestor* (a special officer, not the annually elected treasury official) to preside ; the first of these was appointed in 413 B.C. Such a court was called *quaestiō extraordināria*. As crime increased with population, and the *comitia* grew less and less able to deal with complicated offences, the special commissions (*quaestiōnēs*) became the rule for trying serious crimes, until in time *quaestiōnēs perpetuae* were established, i.e. courts set apart for particular kinds of crime. The first of these was established in 149 B.C., viz. *quaestiō dē repetundīs* (*of restitution*), devoted to the trial of provincial governors. Other *quaestiōnēs perpetuae* followed in course, viz. *dē pecūlātū, dē ambitū, dē māiestāte*. The president of the court was always one of the praetors (exclusive of the *praetor urbānus*, who tried civil suits between *cīvēs*, and the *praetor peregrīnus*, who tried civil suits between foreigners, or between foreigners and Romans) or else an officer called *iūdex quaestiōnis*. This officer merely sat as president, for the *iūdicēs* and not he brought in the verdict. Sulla reorganized the criminal law system of Rome, and appointed two new praetors (eight in full number) to deal with the *quaestiōnēs* which he added, e.g. *dē falsō* (*of forgery* of wills, etc.). The praetors were further increased by Jūlius Caesar to sixteen. Yet the people sometimes judged in *comitia* or appointed commissioners to judge (*extrā ōrdinem quaerere*) crimes affecting religion or the lives of citizens, e.g. the profanation of the mysteries of the *Bona Dea* by Clōdius, and the murder of Clōdius by Milō's armed gang of adherents.

　　LINE 51. **vērum** (adverbial acc. sing. n. of *vērus*, *-a*, *-um*), adversative conj., joining the preceding clause with the one following.——etiam (*et + iam*), adv., modifying *valuistī* and emphasizing the whole clause.——ad, prep. ; gov. the acc. *ēvertendās perfringendāsque* (sc. *lēgēs et quaestiōnēs*); the construction is exactly similar to that of

ing through them.	valuistī.	Superiōra	illa,	quamquam 52
Those earlier mis-	*you have had power.*	*Earlier*	*those (offences),*	*although*
deeds of yours,				
although they were	ferenda	nōn	fuērunt,	tamen, ut 53
unendurable, I nev-	*to be borne*	*not*	*they were,*	*nevertheless,* *as*
ertheless did endure				
as well as I could.	potuī,	tulī :	nunc	vērō mē tōtam 54
But now it is insuf-	*I could*	*I endured :*	*now*	*however (that) I wholly*

ad neglegendās lēgēs, etc., above. —— **ēvertendās**, acc. plur. f. of *ēvertendus, -a, -um*, gerundive of *ēvertō, -ere, ēvertī, ēversum*, 3 (*ē* + *vertō* = *I overturn*); agrees in the construction of gerundival attraction with *lēgēs et quaestiōnēs* which must be supplied from the coördinate clause above. This reading is only found in one MS., but is adopted by Halm, the great German authority on Cicero's speeches. *Ēvincendās* and *vincendās* (in similar grammatical construction), the gerundives of *ēvincō* and *vincō* respectively, both have good MS. authority, and are frequently used with the sense of winning safely through difficulties. —— **perfringendāsque** (*perfringendās* + *que*), *perfringendās* is the acc. plur. f. of *perfringendus, -a, -um*, gerundive of *perfringō, -ere, perfrēgī, perfractum*, 3 (*per* = *through* + *frangō* = *I break*, root *bhrag* = *to break*, cf. ῥήγνυμι); joined by *que* to *ēvertendās* and in the same grammatical construction. The metaphor is that of *breaking through* the laws and courts as one might *break through* or *out of* fetters. The allusion is to Catiline's evasion of condemnation when accused of assault upon a vestal virgin, and also when accused of extortion in Africa. *Que* is the enclitic cop. conj.; joins *ēvertendās* and *perfringendās*.

LINE 52. **valuistī**, 2d pers. sing. perf. ind. act. of *valeō, -ēre, -uī, -itum*, 2; agrees with the subj. *tū*. —— **Superiōra**, acc. plur. n. of *superior, -ius*, adj. 3d (compar. of rare pos. *superus*, formed from the adv. *super ;* superl. *summus* and *suprēmus*); agrees with the pron. *illa*. —— **illa**, acc. plur. n. of the dem. pron. *ille, illa, illud ;* direct obj. of *tulī*. —— **quamquam** (*quam* + *quam*), concessive conj., followed by the ind. *fuērunt*. For the construction, etc., of *quamquam*, refer to the note and references given under *quamquam*, Chap. V, l. 29.

LINE 53. **ferenda**, nom. plur. n. of *ferendus, -a, -um*, gerundive of *ferō, ferre, tulī, lātum*, irreg. (φέρω); agrees with *illa* understood as subj. of *fuērunt*. The gerundive *ferenda* is here adjectival in personal construction (see note on *habendī*, Chap. I, l. 8); *ferenda* + *fuērunt* = the 3d pers. plur. perf. ind. of the periphrastic pass. conjugation of *ferō*. See the note and references under *habenda est*, Chap. V, l. 12. —— **nōn**, neg. adv. ; limits *fuērunt*. —— **tamen**, adv., with adversative force. The adv. *tamen* frequently stands in the main clause after a concessive clause introduced by *quamquam*, *etsī*, or *quamvīs*, i.e. *tamen* and a concessive particle are used correlatively. *Tamen* is also common as an adversative conj.; see note on *tamen*, Chap. I, l. 18. —— **ut**, adv., followed by the ind. *potuī*. *Ut*, meaning *as, when, how*, is followed by the ind. ; *ut* meaning *in order that* (of purpose), or *so that* (of result), or *that* (in final or consecutive substantival clauses) is followed by the subjunctive. See note on *ut*, Chap. I, l. 39.

LINE 54. **potuī**, 1st pers. sing. perf. ind. of *possum, posse, potuī*, no supine, irreg. (*potis* + *sum*); the subj. *ego* is implied by the personal ending. —— **tulī**, 1st pers. sing. perf. ind. act. of *ferō, ferre, tulī, lātum*, irreg. ; the subj. *ego* is implied by the personal ending. The perf. *tulī* is from the root *tal* = *to lift, bear ;* cf. the ante-classical *tulō*, perf. *tetulī*, which is a collateral form of *ferō ;* cf. also *tollō, tolerō*, and τλῆναι = *to endure*. *Lātus* likewise is from root *tal* = *ilātus*. For a full list of synonyms, see the note on *patimur*, Chap. II, l. 15. —— **nunc**, adv. of time ; modifies *est ferendum*. *Nunc* emphatically contrasts the present circumstances with the past. —— **vērō**, adv. used as

55 esse	in	metū	propter	ūnum	tē,
(am) to be in		*fear*	*on account of*	*alone*	*you,*

56 quidquid		increpuerit		Catilīnam
(that) whatever (thing)		*has made a noise*		*Catiline*

57 timērī,		nūllum	vidērī		contrā
(is) to be feared,	*(that) no*	*seems (lit. to seem)*		*against*

ferable that I should be in a state of utter apprehension through just you alone; that, if a rumor, no matter of what, spreads abroad, 'Catiline' is

conj. with adversative force; joins the preceding sentence with the sentence *nunc . . . nōn est ferendum.* —— **mē**, acc. sing. of *ego;* subj.-acc. of the inf. *esse.* The acc. and inf. *mē esse in metū* is a substantival phrase and a subj. of *ferendum est;* similar subject phrases are *Catilīnam timērī*, and *nūllum cōnsilium vidērī*, etc., following. Observe that the inf. is properly a verbal noun, and may be used with or without a subj.-acc. as the subj. or object of a sentence; e.g. subj. *mentīrī turpe est* = *lying is disgraceful*, or *tē mentīrī turpe est* = *that you are lying is disgraceful;* obj. *pūgnāre māvult* = *he prefers fighting.* A. & G. 270; B. 326–328; G. 280; H. 532, 538. —— **tōtam** (adverbial acc. sing. f. of the adj. *tōtus, -a, -um*), adv., modifying *esse in metū.* The adj. *tōtum*, agreeing with *mē*, might have been used with similar meaning.

LINE 55. **esse**, pres. inf. of *sum, esse, fuī;* agrees with the subj.-acc. *mē; in metū* is predicative with *esse*, = *metuere.* —— **in**, prep. with the abl.; gov. *metū.* —— **metū**, abl. sing. of *metus, metūs*, m. 4th; governed by the prep. *in.* —— **propter** (contraction from *propiter*, from *prope*, adv. or prep. = *near*, hence *propter* as adverb and sometimes as prep. = *near, close to*, but usually as prep. = *on account of*), prep. with the acc.; gov. *tē.* —— **ūnum**, acc. sing. m. of the numeral adj. *ūnus, -a, -um* (gen. *ūnīus*, dat. *ūnī*); agrees with *tē; ūnum* = *sōlum.* —— **tē**, acc. sing. of *tū;* gov. by the prep. *propter.*

LINE 56. **quidquid** (another spelling *quicquid*), nom. sing. n. of the indef. rel. pron. *quisquis*, no fem., *quidquid* (*quodquod* is the adjectival neut.); subj. of *increpuerit.* The adjectival form proper of this pron. is *quīquī, quaequae, quodquod*, of which the m. and f. forms are not used. *Quisquis* (like the interrog. *quis*) may sometimes be used adjectively, but only rarely in classical Latin. Though English idiom often employs the subjunct. with general relatives, such as *quīcumque, quisquis, quotquot*, e.g. *quisquis est* = *no matter who he is* (or *may be*), the verb is ind. in Latin, except for special reasons, e.g. subordination in indirect discourse, or attraction of mood. —— **increpuerit**, 3d pers. sing. perf. subjunct. act. of *increpō, -āre, -uī, -itum*, 1 (*in + crepō*); agrees with the subj. *quidquid;* the subjunct. mood is used because the construction of the main clause to which *quidquid* is subordinate is oblique, i.e. acc. and inf. with the quasi-impersonal *nōn ferendum est* = *it is not to be endured that*, etc. A. & G. 336, 2; B. 314, 1; G. 650; H. 524. The perf. tense is in primary sequence with the inf. *timērī*, relatively to which it expresses past action. A. & G. 336, B; B. 318; G. 516–518; H. 525. *Quidquid increpuerit* (= lit. *no matter what has made a noise*) is a kind of disguised condition, = *if any rumor* or *whenever any rumor has arisen.* —— **Catilīnam**, acc. sing. of *Catilīna, -ae*, m. 1st; subj.-acc. of *timērī;* like *mē esse in metū* above, *Catilīnam timērī* is a substantival phrase standing as subj. of the quasi-impersonal *ferendum est.*

LINE 57. **timērī**, pres. inf. pass. of *timeō, -ēre, -uī*, no supine, 2; agrees with the subj.-acc. *Catilīnam.* These acc. and inf. phrases = substantival *quod* clauses, e.g. *quod Catilīna timētur* = *the fact that Catiline is feared.* —— **nūllum**, acc. sing. n. of the adj. *nūllus, -a, -um* (*ne + ūllus;* gen. *nūllīus*, dat. *nūllī*); agrees with *cōnsilium.* Observe the *asyndeta*, i.e. absence of coördination conjunctions between the subj.-infinitives *esse in metū, timērī*, and *vidērī.* —— **vidērī**, pres. inf. pass. of *videō, -ēre, vīdī, vīsum*, 2 (in the deponent use of the pass. = *I seem*); agrees with the subj. acc. *cōnsilium.* The

| the word of dread; | mē | cōnsilium | inīrī | posse, | quod | ā 58 |
| that apparently no | *me* | *design* | *to be initiated* | *to be able* | *which* | *from* |
| plot can be set in |
| motion against me | tuō | scelere | abhorreat, | nōn | est | ferendum. 59 |
| that is not aided by | *your* | *wickedness* | *shrinks away,* | *not* | *is* | *to be endured.* |
| your villainy. Where- |
| fore get you gone, | Quam | ob | rem | discēde | atque | hunc 60 |
| and root this terror | *Which* | *on account of* | *thing* | *go away* | *and* | *this* |

inf. is in personal construction (not as in English, *it seems that,* etc.), but *vidētur, vīsum est,* etc., may be impersonal with the sense, *it seems best.* The logical order of the infinitives in this passage is *vidērī posse inīrī* (= *seems to be able to be entered upon*), i.e. *posse* is explanatory of *vidērī,* and *inīrī* of *posse.* —— **contrā,** prep.; gov. the acc. *mē.* Like most prepositions, *contrā* is often adverbial = *opposite, on the contrary, in reply.*

LINE 58. **mē,** acc. sing. of *ego;* governed by the prep. *contrā.* —— **cōnsilium,** acc. sing. of *cōnsilium, -ī,* n. 2d; subj.-acc. of *vidērī;* like the subj.-infinitives above, *cōnsilium vidērī* is subj. of *ferendum est.* —— **inīrī,** pres. inf. pass. of *ineō, inīre, inīvī* or *iniī, initum,* irreg. (*in* + *eō*); complementary or epexegetical inf. supplementing *posse.* —— **posse,** pres. inf. of *possum, posse, potuī,* no supine, irreg.; complementary or epexegetical inf. supplementing *vidērī.* —— **quod,** nom. sing. n. of the rel. pron. *quī, quae, quod;* agrees with the antecedent *cōnsilium* and is subj. of *abhorreat.* —— **ā,** prep. with the abl.; gov. *scelere,* expressing separation.

LINE 59. **tuō,** abl. sing. n. of the poss. pron. *tuus, -a, -um;* agrees with *scelere.* —— **scelere,** abl. sing. of *scelus, -eris,* n. 3d; governed by the prep. *ā.* Separation is regularly expressed by the abl. with a prep. (*ā, ab, dē, ē, ex*), usually with a verb compounded with the prep., as in this passage. The abl. without a prep. is used after verbs of *wanting, setting free,* and *depriving.* —— **abhorreat,** 3d pers. sing. pres. subjunct. act. of *abhorreō, -ēre, -uī,* no supine, 2 (*ab* + *horreō,* hence = lit. *I shrink back from*); agrees with the subj. *quod;* the subjunct. mood is consecutive after *quod* characteristic; but even if *quod* were not generic, the subjunct. would be required as in *increpuerit.* The verb *abhorrēre* often has no sense of repulsiveness or fear (implied by the literal meaning), but = *to be averse to, to be inconsistent with.* So here *abhorreat* simply = *absit;* we should rather have expected *ā quō tuum scelus abhorreat,* but Cicero has added liveliness to Latin literature by originating many such inversions and elegant methods of expression. —— **nōn,** neg. adv.; limits *ferendum est.* —— **est ferendum,** 3d pers. sing. pres. ind. of the periphrastic pass. conjugation of *ferō, ferre, tulī, lātum,* irreg.; *est ferendum* is quasi-impersonal, = *it is not to be endured that,* etc., and (as in the case of many impersonal verbs) the clause that follows in the English is the real subject; thus the infinitives *mē esse in metū,* etc., are subject, and *est ferendum* = *is not a thing to be endured.*

LINE 60. **Quam,** acc. sing. f. of the rel. pron. *quī, quae, quod;* agrees with *rem; quam* is connective. *Quam ob rem (quamobrem), quōcircā, quā rē (quārē),* etc., are classed among the illative conjunctions. A. & G. 155, *c;* 156, *e;* B. 344; G. 449, B; 500–503; H. 310, 4; 554, IV. —— **ob** (old form *obs;* akin to *apud,* and ἐπί = *upon, to, toward*), prep. + the acc.; gov. *rem.* *Ob* is commonly used like *propter* = *on account of.* In composition, *ob* has the meaning *against, towards, before, at,* e.g. *obeō* = *I go towards,* i.e. *to meet, obiciō* (*ob* + *iaciō*) = *I throw before* or *in the way of.* The *b* is usually assimilated before *f, g, p,* and *c,* e.g. *occīdō* (*ob* + *caedō*), *offerō* (*ob* + *ferō*). —— **rem,** acc. sing. of *rēs, reī,* f. 5th; governed by the prep. *ob.* —— **discēde,** 2d pers. sing. pres. imperative act. of *discēdō, -ere, discessī, discessum,* 3 (*dis* = *apart, away,* + *cēdō* = *I go*); the subj. *tū* is implied by the personal ending. Cicero returns to the advice which is the main subject of Chap. V, cf. ll. 1–3, l. 51, etc. —— **atque,** cop. conj.;

61 mihi　timōrem　ēripe,　sī　est　vērus,
　from me　*fear*　*snatch away,*—*if (the fear) is*　*true*

62 nē　opprimar,　sin　falsus,　ut　tandem
　lest　*I be crushed,*　*but if (it is)*　*false,*　*that*　*at length*

63 aliquandō　timēre　dēsinam."
　sometime　*to fear*　*I may cease."*

1　VIII.　Haec　sī　tēcum,　ut　dīxi,
　　　These things if　*with you,*　*as I have stated,*

from my mind, so that, if it be well founded, I may escape overthrow, but if it be groundless, that sometime hereafter I may finally cease to be afraid."

VIII. If your country were to address you with words

joins *discēde* and *ēripe*. —— **hunc**, acc. sing. m. of the dem. pron. *hĭc, haec, hōc;* agrees with *timōrem; hŭnc* refers to ll. 54–59.

LINE 61.　**mihi**, dat. sing. of *ego;* indirect obj. of *ēripe*. Verbs of *taking away, prohibiting,* and the like may take the dat. of the indirect obj., but as a rule the abl. of separation with a prep. is preferred in prose, unless there is an emphatic notion of *personal interest* present, as there is in *mihi*. This dative is common in poetry and also in late prose. A. & G. 229, and *c*; B. 188, 2, *d*; G. 345, REM. 1; 347, 5; H. 385, 2 and 4, 2). —— **ēripe**, 2d pers. sing. pres. imperative act. of *ēripiō, -ere, -uī, ēreptum,* 3 (*ē + rapiō*); the subj. *tū* is implied by the personal ending. —— **sī**, conditional conj., followed by the ind. of logical condition. Observe that the *sī* clause does not depend on the main clause with *ēripe*, but on the clause *nē opprimar*. —— **est**, 3d pers. sing. pres. ind. act. of *sum, esse, fuī;* understood as subj. *timor* or a pron. referring to *timor*. —— **vērus**, nom. sing. m. of the adj. *vērus, -a, -um;* predicative with *est*, and agrees with the subj. of *est*, viz. *timor* understood (from *timōrem*).

LINE 62.　**nē**, negative final conj., followed by the subjunct. of purpose *opprimar*. For the uses of *nē*, refer to the note on *nē*, Chap. II, l. 2. —— **opprimar**, 1st pers. sing. pres. subjunct. pass. of *opprimō, -ere, oppressī, oppressum,* 3 (*ob + premō*); the subj. *ego* is implied by the personal ending. —— **sin** (*sī + nē*), conditional conj.; supply *est* from *vērus est* above. When two conditions are mutually exclusive, *sī* is used with the first, and *sin* with the second; *sin = if not* or *but if,* and is often strengthened by the addition of *minus, secus,* or *aliter*. It is common for *sin* to be used without a verb, when the verb can easily be supplied, as in this passage. —— **falsus**, nom. sing. m. of the adj. *falsus, -a, -um;* agrees with *timor* understood, and is predicative with *est* understood. We may supply omissions thus: *ēripe,* — *sī (timor) est vērus, nē opprimar, sin (timor est) falsus, ut,* etc. *Fallō, falsus, fallāx,* σφάλλω + *I mislead,* are akin, from root *spal* or *sphal* = *to deceive, disappoint.* —— **ut**, final conj., taking the subjunct. of purpose *dēsinam*. A. & G. 317; B. 282; G. 545; H. 497. —— **tandem** (*tam +* suffix *-dem*), adv. of time, modifies *dēsinam*.

LINE 63.　**aliquandō** (*alius + quandō*), adv.; in combination with *tandem* renders the point of time more indefinite. —— **timēre**, pres. inf. act. of *timeō, -ēre, -uī,* no supine, 2; complementary inf. with *dēsinam; timēre* absolute = *timōrem habēre*. —— **dēsinam**, 1st pers. sing. pres. subjunct. act. of *dēsinō, -ere, desīvī* or more common *dēsiī, dēsitum,* 3 (*dē + sinō*); the subj. *ego* is implied by the personal ending.

LINE 1.　**Haec**, acc. plur. n. of the dem. pron. *hĭc, haec, hōc;* direct obj. of *loquātur*. —— **sī**, conditional particle; followed by the subjunct. *loquātur*. —— **tēcum** (*tē + cum*), *tē* is the abl. sing. of *tū;* governed by the prep. *cum. Cum* is the prep. + the abl.; gov. *tē*. —— **ut**, adv. = *as,* hence followed by the ind. *dīxī*. —— **dīxī**, 1st pers. sing. perf. ind. act. of *dūcō, -ere, dīxī, dīctum,* 3; the subj. *ego* is implied by the personal ending.

such as I have de-	patria	loquātur,	nōnne	impetrāre 2
scribed, ought she	*your country*	*should speak,*	*not*	*to obtain (her wish)*
not to gain her de-	dēbeat,	etiam	sī	vim	adhibēre	nōn 8
sire, even though she	*ought she,*	*even*	*if*	*violence*	*to apply*	*not*
could not employ	possit ?	Quid,	quod	tū	tē 4
force? What shall	*she may be able ?*	*What (of the fact) that*		*you yourself*
I say of your vol-				

LINE 2. **patria**, gen. *patriae*, f. 1st ; nom. sing., subj. of *loquātur*.——**loquātur**, 3d pers. sing. pres. subjunct. of the deponent verb *loquor, loquī, locūtus sum*, 3 ; agrees with the subj. *patria*. In the previous Chapter, ll. 44–63, the utterances of the personified *patria* are given in direct form ; here the pres. subjunct. shows that such a conversation is an imaginary supposition, which is possible as a conception of the mind, no matter whether it be in fact possible or impossible. Conditions with the pres. or perf. subjunct. in *protasis* and in *apodosis* are best called *future ideal* (though the idea of time is some-times scarcely present at all, and no other idea except that of the conceivability of the supposition). Contrast with the imperf. subjunct., *metuerent*, Chap. VII, l. 21. A. & G. 307, *b*, *c* ; B. 303 ; G. 596, 1 ; H. 509.——**nōnne** (*nōn* + *ne*), interrog. adv., intro-ducing the question *dēbeat impetrāre*, to which an affirmative reply is expected.——**im-petrāre**, pres. inf. act. of *impetrō, -āre, -āvī, -ātum*, 1 (*in* + *patrō* = *I accomplish*) ; complementary inf., with *dēbeat*. The regular meaning of *impetrāre* is *to obtain*, as the result of a petition.

LINE 3. **dēbeat**, 3d pers. sing. pres. subjunct. act. of *aĕbeō, -ēre, -uī, -itum*, 2 (for *dēhibeō = dē + habeō*) ; understand as subj. a nom. f. sing. pron. *ea* or *illa* referring to *patria*. *Dēbeat* is subjunct., like *loquātur* above, in *ideal future* condition.——**etiam** (*et* + *iam*), adv., modifying the condition with *sī*.——**sī**, conditional particle, followed by the concessive subjunct. *possit*. *Etiam sī (etiamsī), even now if*, is used as a conces-sive conjunction ; cf. other combinations of *sī, etsī (et + sī, even if), tametsī (for tamen etsī = yet even if)*. The general rule is that the above particles are followed by the ind. or subjunct. moods, according to the general principles which govern the use of *sī*. How-ever, the ind. is commoner than the subjunct., particularly after *etsī* ; *etiam sī* is an excep-tion, for it takes the subjunct. more often than the ind. mood. Observe that whereas *etsī* and *quamquam* may simply connect = *and yet, however* (limiting the entire sentence preceding), *etiam sī* is not so used, nor does it appear to be found except in conditional sentences. A. & G. 313, *c* ; B. 309, 2 ; G. 604 ; H. 515, II. For other conditional par-ticles, refer to the note on *quamquam*, Chap. V, l. 29.——**vim**, acc. sing. of *vis*, f. 3d (abl. *vī* ; gen. and dat. very rare ; plur.= *vīrēs*, for *vīsēs, -ium*, etc.) ; direct obj. of *adhibēre*.——**adhibēre**, pres. inf. act. of *adhibeō, -ēre, -uī, -itum*, 2 (*ad* + *habeō*) ; com-plementary inf., with *possit*.——**nōn**, negative adv. ; limits *possit*. *Nōn* is preferred with verbs ; but *nōn* or *haud* with adjectives and adverbs.

LINE 4. **possit**, 3d pers. sing. pres. subjunct. of *possum, posse, potuī*, no supine, irreg. (*potis* + *sum*, through *pot-sum*) ; agrees with a pron. *ea* or *illa* understood, referring to *patria*.——**Quid**, acc. sing. n. of the interrog. pron. *quis, quae, quid* ; idiomatic acc. in the phrase *quid quod = what of the fact that*, etc. ; the construction is elliptical, and some verb may be understood governing *quid*, e.g. *quid dīcam aĕ hōc quod*, etc. *Quid*, when used alone (= *again*), and when followed by *quod*, marks a transition to a new idea.——**quod**, conj. = *that*, in the idiom *quid quod*, followed by the ind. *dedistī*. See the note on *quod*, Chap. IV, l. 32.——**tū**, nom. sing. of the 2d personal pron. ; subj. of *dedistī*. Observe the emphasis on *tū*, which is intensified by the juxtaposition of *tē* and the addition of *ipse*.——**tē**, acc. sing. of *tū* ; direct obj. of *dedistī* ; *tē* is reflexive, i.e. refers back to the subj. *tū*.

5 ipse	in	custōdiam	dedistī ?	quod	untary offer to put
yourself	*into*	*custody*	*have given?*	*that*	yourself under sur-

veillance? what of

6 vītandae	suspīciōnis	causā	ad	your statement, made
to be avoided	*of suspicion*	*for the sake*	*at (= with)*	with the object of es-

caping suspicion, that

7 M'.	Lepidum	tē	habitāre	velle	dīxistī ?	you were ready to
Manius	*Lepidus*	*yourself*	*to live*	*to wish*	*you stated?*	take up your quarters

LINE 5. **ipse**, nom. sing. m. of the dem. pron. *ipse, ipsa, ipsum (is + pse* for *pte,* cf. *suōpte = suō + pte*); agrees with and intensifies *tū. Ipse* must be distinguished from *sē ; sē* is always a pure pron. and is reflexive (i.e. denotes the same person or thing as the subj. of the sentence), whereas *ipse* is adjectival, and emphasizes a noun or pron. expressed or understood, e.g. *tū tē dedistī = you gave yourself,* but *tū ipse dedistī = you yourself gave. Ipse* is often better rendered *actually, very, in person, voluntarily,* etc. ——in, prep. ; gov. the acc. *custōdiam.* —— **custōdiam**, acc. sing. of *custōdia, -ae,* f. 1st (from *custōs*); governed by the prep. *in ; in custōdiam* here = *in custōdiam līberam. Custōdia lībera* (the φυλακή ἄδεσμος of Dion Cassius) = *surveillance without imprisonment,* and was ordered by the Senate or magistrates when a Roman of high position was accused of a crime (e.g. against the state) which seemed to call for severer notice than an ordinary offence, for which bail was as a rule accepted. The defendant, pending his trial, was put in the safe-keeping of some distinguished citizen, who thereby became responsible for the prisoner's appearance on the day of trial. When an accused person offered to go *in custōdiam,* it was considered a sign that he was confident of honorable acquittal. Catiline's action was a bold attempt to avert suspicion and excite sympathy. Cicero's allusion is to the accusation which L. Aemilius Paullus had made (under the *lex Plautia dē vī*) against Catiline of inciting to riot ; this accusation was led up to by Cicero's disclosures before the Senate, Oct. 21st and 22d, and especially by the news that Mānlius had taken up arms against the state on Oct. 27th. As Catiline's plans were not yet fully matured, his offer of *lībera custōdia* was simply a blind. Catiline's trial never took place, for he presently joined the camp of Mānlius. As regards the principle of *lībera custōdia,* the student should note that after 461 B.C. no Roman citizen was imprisoned pending trial, for such imprisonment would have been inconsistent with the acknowledged right of a citizen to withdraw into voluntary exile at any time before an actual verdict was given against him. —— **dedistī,** 2d pers. sing. perf. ind. act. of *dō, dare, dedī, datum,* 1 ; agrees with the subj. *tū.* —— **quod,** conj., repeated from *quid quod* above, and followed in the new clause by the ind. *dīxistī.*

LINE 6. **vītandae,** gen. sing. f. of *vītandus, -a, -um,* gerundive of *vītō, -āre, -āvī, -ātum,* 1 (for *vicitō,* root *vic = to yield*); agrees with *suspīciōnis* in the construction of gerundival attraction ; the gen. is dependent on *causā.* —— **suspīciōnis,** gen. sing. of *suspīciō,* f. 3d ; gen. in the gerundial construction (instead of the gerund *vītandī +* the direct obj. *suspīciōnem ;* the gerund is rarely used except absolutely or with neut. pron. as object); the gen. depends on *causā.* —— **causā,** abl. sing. of *causa, -ae,* f. 1st, used as a prep + the gen. (cf. *grātiā*); gov. *vītandae suspīciōnis,* expressing purpose. See the note on *causā,* Chap. III, l. 26. —— **ad,** prep. gov. the acc. *M'.* (= *Mānium*) *Lepidum. Ad* is here used like *apud,* = *with, at the house of.*

LINE 7. **M'.** (= **Manium**), acc. sing. of *Mānius, -ī,* m. 2d ; *praenōmen* of *Lepidum.* —— **Lepidum,** acc. sing. of *Lepidus, -ī,* m. 2d ; governed by the prep. *ad.* See the note on *Lepidō,* Chap. VI, l. 33. —— **tē,** acc. sing. of *tū ;* subj.-acc. of *velle* in the acc. and inf. construction dependent on the verb of *saying, dīxistī.* —— **habitāre,** pres. inf. act. of *habitō, -āre, -āvī, -ātum,* 1 (frequentative of *habeō,* hence *I occupy continually, dwell,* trans. and intrans.); *complementary* inf. with *velle.* Synonyms: (1) *incolere = to in-*

| with Manius Lepidus? And yet, when you were not received in by him, you actually dared to come to me and asked me to hold you in charge in my house. When you | ā
by
mē
me
tē
you | quō
whom
venīre
to come
adservārem
I should keep | nōn
not
ausus es
you dared
rogāstī.
you asked. | receptus
having been received
atque
and
Cum
When | etiam
even
ut
that
ā
from | ad
to
domī
at home
mē
me | 8

meae 9
my
quoque 10
also |

habit, dwell in, of a body of people ; (2) *commorārī = to sojourn*, of temporary, not fixed abode ; (3) *habitāre +* acc., or with prep. *in, apud, cum, = to dwell in*, of individuals ; *habitārī = to be inhabited*, may be used of the place.——**velle**, pres. inf. of *volō, velle, voluī*, no supine, irreg. ; agrees with the subj.-acc. *tē.*——**dīxistī**, 2d pers. sing. perf. ind. act. of *dīcō, -ere, dīxī, dictum*, 3 ; the subj. *tū* is implied by the personal ending.

LINE 8. **ā**, prep. + the abl. ; gov. *quō*, expressing the agency after *receptus; ā quō* illustrates the connective use of the rel. pron., i.e. = *et ab eō.*——**quō**, abl. sing. m. of the rel. pron. *quī, quae, quod;* agrees with the antecedent *Lepidum* in gender and number, and is abl. of the agent governed by the prep. *ā.*——**nōn**, negative adv. ; limits *receptus.*——**receptus**, nom. sing. m. of *receptus, -a, -um*, perf. part. pass. of *recipiō, -ere, recēpī, receptum*, 3 (*re + capiō*) ; agrees with *tū*, the implied subj. of *ausus es.* *Ā quō . . . receptus* is equivalent to a clause with *cum.*——**etiam** (*et + iam*), adv. ; modifies *ausus es.*——**ad**, prep. ; gov. the acc. *mē.*

LINE 9. **mē**, acc. sing. of *ego;* governed by the prep. *ad.*——**venīre**, pres. inf. act. of *veniō, -īre, vēnī, ventum*, 4 ; *complementary* or *epexegetical* inf. with *ausus es.* A. & G. 271 ; B. 326 ; G. 423 ; H. 533.——**ausus es**, 2d pers. sing. perf. ind. of the semideponent verb *audeō, -ēre, ausus sum*, 2 ; the subj. *tū* is implied. Refer to the note on *audeat*, Chap. II, l. 47.——**atque**, cop. conj. ; joins the clauses of *ausus es* and *rogāstī.* ——**ut**, final conj., introducing the complementary substantival final clause *ut . . . adservārem* in dependence on the leading verb of *asking, rogāstī.* Substantival final clauses follow (1) verbs of *willing, warning, urging, resolving, endeavoring*, and *demanding*, as with *rogāstī* in this passage ; (2) verbs of *hindering;* (3) verbs of *fearing.* The negative particle is *nē*, sometimes *ut nē*. A. & G. 331 ; B. 295, 296 ; G. 546 ; H. 498. ——**domī**, locative case of *domus, -ūs*, f. 4th (see note on *domus*, Chap. III, l. 4) ; *domī meae = at my home* is an adverbial extension of the pred. *adservārem.* Observe that *domī = at home*, but *in the house* is *in domō*, not *domī.* A classical variant for the usual locative *domī* is *domuī.* When a poss. pron. accompanies *domī* or *domuī* the case is regarded as gen. in form, and the pron. is therefore gen. in agreement, e.g. *domī meae = at my house.* The locative case denotes *place where*, and is used with the names of towns and small islands ; it survives in a few general words, e.g. *domī, humī = on the ground, mīlitiae = in the field* (of war), *vesperī = in the evening*, etc. A. & G. 258, *d* ; B. 232, 2 ; G. 411, esp. REM. 4 ; H. 426, 2.——**meae**, gen. sing. f. of the poss. pron. *meus, -a, -um;* agrees with *domī.*

LINE 10. **tē**, acc. sing. of *tū;* direct obj. of *adservārem.*——**adservārem**, 1st pers. sing. imperf. subjunct. act. of *adservō, -āre, -āvī, -ātum*, 1 (*ad + servō*) ; the subj. *ego* is implied by the personal ending ; the subjunct. is final after *ut*, and the *ut* clause stands as object of *rogāstī.*——**rogāstī** (contracted for *rogāvistī*), 2d pers. sing. perf. ind. act. of *rogō, -āre, -āvī, -ātum*, 1 ; the subj. *tū* is implied by the personal ending. For the contraction, see the note on *cōnfīrmāstī*, Chap. IV, l. 30 ; and for synonyms, etc., see the note on *rogō*, Chap. IV, l. 22.——**Cum**, temporal conj. ; followed by the subjunct. *tulissēs.*——**ā**, prep. ; gov. the abl. *mē*, denoting separation.——**mē**, abl. sing. of *ego;* governed by the prep. *ā.*——**quoque**, adv. or cop. conj. ; as usual, its position is directly

11	id	respōnsum	tulissēs,	mē	nūllō	modō
	that	*answer*	*you had gained, (that) I*		*no*	*in way*

12	posse		īsdem	parietibus		tūtō
	was (lit. *to be*) *able*		*same*	*within the house-walls*		*in safety*

18	esse	tēcum,	quī	magnō	in	perīculō
	to be	*with you, who* (= *since I*)		*great*	*in*	*danger*

had obtained your answer from me also, namely, that it was quite impossible for me to live in security within the same walls with you, seeing that I was already exposed

after the emphatic word. *Quoque* is less strong than *etiam* ; *quoque* never begins a sentence. A. & G. 151, *a* ; 345, *b* ; B. 347, 1 ; G. 479 ; H. 554. I, 4.

LINE 11.   **id**, acc. sing. n. of the dem. pron. *is, ea, id;* agrees with *respōnsum; id respōnsum* is explained by the acc. and. inf. *mē nūllō modō posse . . . continērēmur* below. —— **respōnsum**, acc. sing. of *respōnsum, -ī,* n. 2d (in origin the substantival neut. of *respōnsus,* perf. part. pass. of *respondeō, re* + *spondeō*) ; direct obj. of *tulissēs.* —— **tulissēs**, 2d pers. sing. pluperf. subjunct. act. of *ferō, ferre, tulī, lātum,* irreg. ; the implied subj. is *tū;* the subjunct. mood in the pluperf. and imperf. tenses follows *cum* temporal, the ind. in other tenses. See note on *cum,* Chap. III, l. 23. —— **mē**, acc. sing. of *ego;* subj.-acc. of *posse* in the acc. and inf. construction dependent on *respōnsum tulissēs,* = *cum respondissem* or *cum ā mē audīvissēs.* —— **nūllō**, abl. sing. m. of the adj. *nūllus, -a, -um (ne* + *ūllus;* gen. *nūllīus,* dat. *nūllī*) ; agrees with *modō.* —— **modō**, abl. sing. of *modus, -ī,* m. 2d ; abl. of manner, with which *cum* is not required, as *nūllō* modifies *modō.*

LINE 12.   **posse**, pres. inf. of *possum, posse, potuī,* irreg. ; agrees with the subj.-acc. *mē.* —— **īsdem**, abl. plur. m. of the determinative pron. *īdem, eadem, idem (is* + suffix *-dem*) ; agrees with *parietibus.* In the declension notice that *m* changes to *n* before *d;* e.g. *eundem = eum + dem.* A. & G. 101, and *c;* B. 87 ; G. 103, 2 ; H. 186, VI, and FOOTNOTE C on page 73. —— **parietibus**, abl. plur. of *pariēs, -etis,* m. 3d ; abl. of the means, with *tūtō esse* = lit. *be safe by means of the same walls;* render *within the same walls. Pariēs* = properly a *party-wall; moenia* = *city-wall; mūrus* is often used like *moenia,* but is also the general word for *wall.* —— **tūtō** (adverbial abl. sing. n. of the adj. *tūtus, -a, -um*), adv. ; predicative with *esse;* the adj. *tūtum,* predicative, agreeing with *mē* would have had the same meaning. The superl. of *tūtō* is *tūtissimō.* Many adverbs are adverbial ablatives of adjectives, cf. *vērō, subitō, citō;* cf. also the abl. of pronouns and nouns, e.g. *quō, eō, quā, forte, cāsū,* etc. A. & G. 148, *e;* B. 77, 2 ; G. 91, *c, d;* H. 304, II.

LINE 13.   **esse**, pres. inf. of *sum;* agrees with the subj.-acc. *mē* above. —— **tēcum** (*tē* + *cum*), *tē* is the abl. sing. of *tū;* governed by *cum. Cum* is the prep. + the abl., governing *tē,* and appended to *tē,* as regularly when its obj. is a personal, reflexive, or rel. pronoun. —— **quī**, nom. sing. m. of the rel. pron. *quī, quae, quod;* agrees with the antecedent *mē,* and is subj. of *essem.* The rel. here has a causal sense, = *cum ego,* although it is not grammatically necessary to suppose so in order to account for the subjunct. *essem,* inasmuch as the clause following *respōnsum tulissēs* is indirect in form (*mē . . . posse*) and *essem* is the verb of the subordinate rel. clause. A. & G. 336, 2 ; B. 314, 1 ; G. 650 ; H. 524. Cicero's direct reply to Catiline may have been *ego nūllō modō possum īsdem parietibus tūtō esse tēcum, quī magnō in perīculō* SUM, *quod īsdem moenibus continēmur,* but the wide separation of the rel. *quī* from the antecedent *ego,* and the natural expectation that a reason for the statement in the main clause would follow, makes it almost a certainty that the direct form of the rel. clause was *quī magnō in perīculō* SIM. The rel. pron. is often used + the subjunct. when *cause* or *concession* is to be expressed, cf. *virum simplicem quī nōs nihil cēlet* = *guileless man, not to hide anything from us!* (i.e. since he does not hide) ; *illī quī obsidēs in castra misissent, tamen*

to great danger, ow-ing to the fact that we were shut in to-gether by the same city-walls, you went to the praetor Quin-tus Metellus. By	essem,	quod	īsdem	moenibus	continērēmur, 14
	was	*because*	*same*	*by the city-walls*	*we were enclosed,*
	ad	Q.	Metellum	praetōrem	vēnistī : ā 15
	to	*Quintus*	*Metellus*	*the praetor*	*you came :* *by*

arma dēpōnere nolēbant = though they had sent hostages to the camp, they were yet unwill-ing to lay down their arms. Whereas the ind. + *quī* states a fact, the subjunct. states *why* or *in spite of what* the action of the principal sentence takes place. When *quī* is causal, it is frequently conjoined with the particles *ut, utpote,* or *quippe ;* there is only a slight difference between *quī* causal or concessive and *quī* characteristic. A. & G. 320, *e* ; B. 283, 3 ; 633, 634 ; H. 517 ; 515, III, and NOTE 4.——**mágnō**, abl. sing. n. of the adj. *mágnus, -a, -um ;* agrees with *perīculō.*——**in,** prep. ; gov. the abl. *perīculō.* ——**perīculō,** abl. sing. of *perīculum, -ī,* n. 2d ; governed by the prep. *in.*

LINE 14. **essem,** 1st pers. sing. imperf. subjunct. of *sum, esse, fúī ;* agrees with the subj. *quī = cum ego.* The verb in the rel. clause regularly takes the person of the ante-cedent, *ego quī fēcī, tū quī fēcistī, is quī fēcit,* etc. The imperf. *essem* is in *historic* sequence, after the *historic* leading verb *tulissēs.*——**quod,** conj., giving a reason ; followed by the subjunct. *continērēmur* because the clause is subordinate in indirect discourse. *Quod* causal, in direct discourse, is followed by the ind. if the reason given is that of the speaker, but by the subjunct. if the reason be adopted on another's authority. A. & G. 321 ; B. 286, 1 ; G. 538-541 ; H. 516.——**īsdem,** abl. plur. n. of the determinative pron. *īdem, eadem, idem* (*is* + *dem, ea* + *dem, id* + *dem*) ; agrees with *moenibus.*——**moenibus,** abl. of the plur. noun *moenia, -ium,* n. 3d (see note on *moe-nia,* Chap. II, l. 32) ; abl. of the means, modifying *continērēmur.*——**continērēmur,** 1st pers. plur. imperf. subjunct. pass of *contineō, -ēre, -uī, contentum,* 2 (*con* + *teneō*) ; the subj. implied by the personal ending is *nōs,* i.e. *ego et tū.* In Latin, when two or more personal pronouns are subj. of one verb, the pron. of the 1st person is expressed before the 2d, and that of the 2d person before the 3d ; the verb is plur., and the verb is in the person of the first of the pronouns, e.g. *et ego et tū audīmus ; et tū et ille audītis.* The subjunct. mood of the verb here is due to the subordination of the clause in a sen-tence of indirect form, *mē posse,* etc., and the tense is in *historic* sequence with the *his-toric tulissēs.* Had the leading verb been *primary,* e.g. *respōnsum fers,* the subordinate verbs would have been *primary* also, i.e. (*quī*) *sim,* and (*quod*) *continēmur.* A. & G. 336, B ; B. 318 ; G. 516-518 ; H. 525.

LINE 15. **ad,** prep. ; gov. the acc. *Q.* (= *Quintum*) *Metellum.*——**Q.** (abbreviation for *Quintum*), acc. sing. of *Quintus, -ī,* m. 2d ; *praenōmen* of *Metellum.*——**Metel-lum,** acc. sing. of *Metellus, -ī,* m. 2d ; governed by the prep. *ad. Metellus* was the *cog-nōmen* or *family-name* of a distinguished branch of the *gēns Caecilia.* The person referred to is *Quintus Caecilius Metellus Celer,* who was praetor in B.C. 63, and consul in B.C. 60. He was a zealous supporter of the aristocratic party. He was sent to raise forces against Catiline in the Gallic and Picene districts, and by cutting off all retreat in the direction of the Alps, he forced Catiline to give battle to M. Petreius at Pistōria. Metellus died in B.C. 59. Distinguish him from his younger brother of the same name (except that his *āgnōmen* was *Nepos,* not *Celer*), who was tribune in 62 B.C. and consul in 57 B.C., and supported Pompey against the aristocratic party. The younger brother was not praetor till B.C. 60.——**praetōrem,** acc. sing. of *praetor, -ōris,* m. 3d (for *praei-tor,* from *prae* + *eō*) ; acc. in appos. with *Metellum.*——**vēnistī,** 2d pers. sing. perf. ind. act. of *veniō, -īre, vēnī, ventum,* 4 ; the subj. *tū* is implied by the personal ending.——**ā,** prep. ; gov. the abl. *quō.*

16 quō	repudiātus	ad	sodālem	tuum,	him, too, you were
whom	*having been refused*	*to*	*associate*	*your,*	rejected, and off you went to your boon-
17 virum	optimum,	M.	Metellum	· dēmigrāstī,	companion, the ad-
a man	*very good,*	*Marcus*	*Metellus*	*you went off,*	mirable Marcus Metellus; you
18 quem	tū	vidēlicet	et	ad	custōdiendum	thought, of course,
whom	*you*	*clearly*	*both*	*as to*	*guarding*	that he would be

LINE 16. **quŏ**, abl. sing. m. of the rel. pron. *quī, quae, quod;* agrees with the antecedent *Metellum*, and is governed by the prep. *ā* (abl. of the agent, with *repudiātus*). —— **repudiātus**, nom. sing. m. of *repudiātus, -a, -um*, perf. part. pass. of *repudiō, -āre, -āvī, -ātum*, 1 (from the noun *repudium*, perhaps *re + pudeō*); agrees with *tū*, the implied subj. of *dēmigrāstī*. The part. is in common usage, taking the place of a coördinate sentence, e.g. *ā quō* (= *et ab eō repudiātus es . . . et . . . dēmigrāstī*). A. & G. 292, REM.; B. 336, 3; 337, 2; G. 437; H. 549, 5.—— **ad**, prep.; gov. the acc. *M. Metellum.*—— **sodālem**, acc. sing. of *sodālis, -is*, m. (and f.), 3d (substantival use of the adj. *sodālis, -e*, 3d; from stem *ἑθ*, cf. *ἔθος = custom*, *suescō, cōnsuētūdō*, hence *sodālis = a regular* or *boon companion*); acc. in appos. with *M. Metellum.*—— **tuum**, acc. sing. m. of the poss. pron. *tuus, -a, -um;* agrees with *sodālem.*

LINE 17. **virum**, acc. sing. of *vir, virī*, m. 2d; acc. in appos. with *sodālem* or *Metellum.*—— **optimum**, acc. sing. of *optimus, -a, -um*, adj. (superl. of *bonus;* compar. *melior*); agrees with *virum*. *Virum optimum* is ironical, as is clearly shown by the remarks following *quem tū vidēlicet . . . putāstī*. Attributes are never added to proper names in Latin, so *the excellent Metellus* of English idiom = in Latin *Metellus, vir optimus.*—— **M.** (abbreviation for *Marcum*), acc. sing. of *Marcus, -ī*, m. 2d; *praenōmen* of *Metellum.*—— **Metellum**, acc. sing. of *Metellus, -ī*, m. 2d; governed by the prep. *ad.* There is much doubt as to the correct reading in this passage; many MSS. read *M. Marcellum*. But the reading *Metellum* occurs in the MSS. of Quintilian, who quotes the passage, and in three MSS. of Cicero; moreover, Dion Cassius seems to have confused the praetor Metellus and some other Roman of the same name. A certain M. Metellus was praetor in B.C. 69, and presided at the trial of *Verrēs*, but the man mentioned here can hardly be he, for Cicero's ironical praise proves him to be a person of very little worth. If *Marcellum* be adopted, distinguish from the Marcellus mentioned in l. 46. . . . There were two men, father and son, each named Marcellus, who took part in the conspiracy of Catiline. —— **dēmigrāstī**, 2d pers. sing. perf. ind. act. of *aēmigrō, -āre, -āvī, -ātum*, 1 (*aē + migrō*); the implied subj. is *tū*. *Dēmigrāstī* is contracted from *dēmigrāvistī;* see the note on *cōnfīrmāstī*, Chap. IV, l. 30.

LINE 18. **quem**, acc. sing. m. of the rel. pron. *quī, quae, quod;* agrees with the antecedent *Metellum*, and is subj.-acc. of *fore* in the acc. and inf. object-clause of *putāstī*. —— **tū**, nom. sing. of the 2d personal pron.; subj. of *putāstī*. —— **vidēlicet** (contracted from *vidēre licit = it is permitted to see*), adv., modifying *putāstī*. *Vidēlicet = it is evident, clearly, forsooth, of course*, and, as often, is here ironical, thereby showing that Metellus really lacked in a marked degree the good qualities sarcastically ascribed to him. Compare the adv. *scilicet*, similarly formed = *scīre licet*, and similar in meaning. —— **et**, cop. conj.; used correlatively with *et* following; *et . . . et = both . . . and.* —— **ad**, prep.; gov. the acc. *custōdiendum. Ad +* the acc. of the gerund or gerundive expresses purpose; cf. the gen. with *causā*. After adjectives expressing *suitability* and like ideas, *ad +* the acc. gerund, etc., is common. —— **custōdiendum**, acc. sing. of *custōdiendum, -ī* (no. nom.; dat. and abl. *custōdiendō*), gerund of *custōdiō, -īre, -īvī, -ītum*, 4; governed by the prep. *ad.* The gerund is the verbal noun, and supplements the inf. as such; thus the inf. may stand as subj. (nom.) or obj. (acc.) in a sentence. The gerund supplies the other

| very careful in keep-
ing watch over you,
very shrewd to sus-
pect, and very reso-
lute in bringing to
punishment! But
how far away, in your
opinion, ought a man
to be from the prison- | **dīligentissimum**　　　　et　　　ad　　　**suspicandum** 19
most careful　　　　　　*and*　　*as to*　　　　*suspecting*
sagācissimum　et　ad　vindicandum　fortissimum 20
most shrewd　　*and as to*　　*punishing*　　　*most resolute*
fore　　　　putāstī.　　　Sed　　　quam　　　longē 21
to be likely to be　you thought.　　*But*　　*how*　　　*far*
vidētur　ā　carcere　atque　ā　vinculīs 22
does he seem　from　prison　and　from　bonds |

cases of the verbal noun, viz. acc. governed by a prep., gen., dat., and abl. A. & G. 295 ; B. 338 ; G. 425, *ff* ; H. 541, 542.

LINE 19. **dīligentissimum**, acc. sing. m. of the adj. *dīligentissimus, -a, -um,* superl. of *dīligēns,* adj. 3d (strictly pres. part. act. of *dīligō*) ; agrees with the subj.-acc. *quem,* and is a complement of *fore* in the predicate. Observe that *ad custōdiendum* is dependent on *dīligentissimum*. In spite of all surveillance Catiline found no one able to prevent him from proceeding with his schemes and attending treasonable meetings, e.g. at Laeca's house.——**et,** cop. conj. ; joins *dīligentissimum* and *sagācissimum*.——**ad,** prep. ; gov. the acc. *suspicandum ; ad suspicandum* expresses purpose, and depends on *sagācissimum*.—— **suspicandum,** acc. sing. of the gerund of *suspicor, -ārī, -ātus sum,* I deponent (cf. *suspiciō ; sub + speciō*) ; governed by the prep. *ad.*

LINE 20. **sagācissimum,** acc. sing. m. of *sagācissimus, -a, -um,* superl. of *sagāx, -ācis,* adj. 3d of one termination (compar. *sagācior, -ius*) ; agrees with the subj. -acc. *quem* and is complement of *fore* in the predicate, like *dīligentissimum* above.——**et,** cop. conj. ; joins *sagācissimum* and *fortissimum*.——**ad,** prep. ; gov. the acc. *vindicandum ; ad vindicandum* expresses purpose and depends on the adj. *fortissimum*.——**vindicandum,** acc. sing. of the gerund of *vindicō, -āre, -āvī, -ātum,* I (from *vindex, vindicis,* m. 3d) ; governed by the prep. *ad.* —— **fortissimum,** acc. sing. m. of *fortissimus, -a, -um,* superl. of the adj. *fortis, -e,* 3d (akin to *fīrmus*) ; agrees with the subj.-acc. *quem* and is complement of *fore* in the predicate.

LINE 21. **fore,** fut. inf. of *sum, esse, fuī ;* agrees with the subj.-acc. *quem,* in the acc. and inf. construction dependent on *putāstī. Sum* also has the usual kind of inf. consisting of the fut. part. + the pres. inf., *futūrus esse ;* so we occasionally find the imperf. subjunct. *forem = essem.*——**putāstī,** 2d pers. sing. perf. ind. act. of *putō, -āre, -āvī, -ātum,* I ; the implied subj. is *tū ; putāstī* is contracted from *putāvistī,* like *dēmigrāstī,* l. 17 above.——**Sed,** adversative conj. ; connects its own sentence with the sentences preceding, and introduces an idea in opposition to what has gone before.——**quam,** adv., interrog. ; modifies *longē.* See note on *quam,* Chap. I, l. 2.——**longē** (compar. *longius ;* superl. *longissimē ;* formed from the adj. *longus*), adv., modifying the pred. *vidētur dēbēre abesse.*

LINE 22. **vidētur,** 3d pers. sing. pres. ind. pass. of *videō, -ēre, vīdī, vīsum,* 2 (*videor* in the sense *I seem,* not as pass. of *videō*) ; the subj. implied by the personal ending is a pron., e.g. *is,* which is the antecedent of *quī.* Observe that *vidētur* is not impersonal here ; the verb *videor* is regularly used personally, except with the particular meaning *it seems best (vidētur,* etc.).——**ā,** prep. ; gov. the abl. *carcere,* expressing separation. A prep. is generally found with the abl. even when the verb expressing separation is compounded with a prep., viz. *ā, ab, aē, ē* or *ex ;* but the abl. alone is used after verbs signifying *to set free, deprive,* or *want.*——**carcere,** abl. sing. of *carcer, -is,* m. 3d ; gov. by the prep. *ā. Carcer* here = what is now known as the Mamertine Prison (*carcer Mamertīnus,* a name for which there is no classical authority), viz. the *Tulliānum* or state prison situated on one slope of the Capitoline hill. This was at first a fountain with a strong

23	abesse	dēbēre,	quī	sē	ipse	iam	cell and prison-
	to be away	*to owe (it)*	*who*	*himself*	*in person*	*already*	fetters, when his own
							lips have already
24	dīgnum	custōdiā	iūdicārit?			Quae	pronounced him as
	worthy	*of surveillance*	*has judged?*			*Which things*	deserving of private

jet of water (*tullus*), and was made a prison by Ancus Martius. To it was added a dungeon underneath, where condemned criminals were executed. Both parts survive to-day, but have been turned into chapels. The *Tulliānum* was never used for penal imprisonment, a form of punishment scarcely known to the ancient Romans; but condemned criminals were detained there for short times, pending their execution, which took place there also. After execution, the bodies of the victims were displayed on the *Scālae Gemōniae*, a flight of steps opposite the gate, and finally cast into the Tiber. In the *Tulliānum* several enemies of Rome were strangled, e.g. Jugurtha, Lentulus, Cethēgus, etc. *Carcer* (akin to *arceō* and ἕρκος, hence *a barrier, prison*), and esp. the plur. *carcerēs*, is used of *the barriers* or *starting-places* in the arena from which competitors in foot and chariot races set off. —— atque, cop. conj.; joins *ā carcere* and *ā vinculīs*. —— ā, prep.; gov. the abl. *vinculīs*, expressing separation. —— vinculīs, abl. plur. of *vinculum, -ī*, n. 2d (from *vinciō* = *I bind*); governed by the prep. *ā*. *Vinculum* is sometimes contracted to *vinclum;* cf. *pōculum* and *pōclum*. *Vincula* is the usual term for *imprisonment*. In his 4th oration Cicero, commenting on Caesar's proposal that Lentulus, etc., be imprisoned for life, expresses the opinion that such a punishment would be infinitely more exquisite and severe than death.

LINE 23. **abesse**, pres. inf. of *absum, abesse, āfuī*, irreg. (*ab + sum*); complementary inf. logically following *dēbēre*. —— **dēbēre**, pres. inf. act. of *dēbeō, -ēre, -uī, -ītum*, 2; complementary inf. with *vidētur*. Refer to the note on *dēbeō*, Chap. VII, l. 3. —— **quī**, nom. sing. m. of the rel. pron. *quī, quae, quod;* subject of *iūdicārit;* the antecedent of *quī* is the unexpressed subj. of *vidētur*, viz. a pron. *is* or *ille*, referring to Catiline. —— **sē**, acc. sing. of the reflexive pron. of the 3d pers. sing. or plur., *sē* or *sēsē* (gen. *suī*, dat. *sibi*, abl. *sē* or *sēsē*); subj.-acc. of *dīgnum* (*esse*) in the object clause of *iūdicārit*. —— **ipse**, nom. sing. m. of the dem. pron. *ipse, ipsa, ipsum;* agrees with and intensifies the subj. *quī; ipse* may be rendered *of his own accord*. *Sē* and *ipse* are emphasized by their conjunction. —— **iam**, adv. of time; limiting *iūdicārit*.

LINE 24. **dīgnum**, acc. sing. m. of the adj. *dīgnus, -a, -um* (for *dicnus*, root *dak* = *dic, to be esteemed*, hence *worthy;* cf. *decet*, δοκέω, etc.); agrees with the subj.-acc. *sē*, and is predicative with *esse* understood (parts of *sum* are frequently omitted, esp. the pres. ind. and pres. inf.). Cicero attempts to combat Catiline's appeal *ad misericordiam* (when he offered to go under house-arrest) by mockingly arguing that a man must deserve strict imprisonment in the state-prison if with his own mouth he declares himself a fit subject for house-arrest. —— **custōdiā**, abl. sing. of *custōdia, -ae*, f. 1st; dependent on *dīgnum*. The adjectives *dīgnus, indīgnus, frētus*, and a few others are followed by the abl. case. —— **iūdicārit**, 3d pers. sing. perf. subjunct. act. of *iūdicō, -āre, -āvī, -ātum*, 1; agrees with the subj. *quī; iūdicārit* is contracted from *iūdicāverit*. The subjunct. admits of two explanations: (1) that the *quī* clause gives a reason for the main clause, i.e. *quī* is causal = *cum is;* see the note on *quī*, l. 13; (2) that *quī*, which has no definite expressed antecedent, stands for a class, i.e. is the generic or characteristic rel., = *tālis ut*, followed by the consecutive subjunctive. A. & G. 320, *a;* B. 283; G. 631, 2; H. 503, I. The tense is perf. in sequence with the leading verb *vidētur*, which is primary. —— **Quae**, nom. plur. n. of the rel. pron. *quī, quae, quod;* subj. of *sint; quae* is connective, = *et haec*, and the clause sums up the facts previously stated. The phrase *quae cum ita sint* is a favorite with Cicero; cf. Chap. V, l. I, and the references there given under *quae*.

custody? As this is the case, Catiline, if you cannot die with a calm mind, do you hesitate to depart to some other part of the world and sur-	cum *since*	ita *so*	sint, *are,*	Catilīna, *Catiline,*	dubitās, *do you hesitate,*	sī ēmorī 25 *if to die*
	aequō *even*	animō *with mind*	nōn *not*	potes, *you are able,*	abīre *to go away*	in 26 *to*
	aliquās *some (other)*	terrās *lands*	et *and*	vītam *life*	istam, *that,*	multīs 27 *many*

LINE 25. **cum**, causal conj., taking the subjunct. *sint;* cf. Chap. V, L 1. —— **ita**, adv.; modifies *sint.* —— **sint**, 3d pers. plur. pres. subjunct. of *sum, esse, fuī;* agrees with the subj. *quae*, and is subjunct. following *cum* causal. —— **Catilīna**, voc. sing. of *Catilīna, -ae*, m. 1st; the case of address. —— **dubitās**, 2d pers. sing. pres. ind. act. of *dubitō, -āre, -āvī, -ātum*, 1; the subj. *tū* is implied by the personal ending. Observe (1) that *dubitō* = *I hesitate* is followed by an epexegetical or complementary inf. (*abīre*), (2) that the question is not marked by an interrog. particle, but is expressed by the tone of voice (spoken) or a punctuation sign (written); *num* might have been used, as a reply in the negative is expected. —— **sī**, conditional conj.; the ind. mood *potes* follows, i.e. the condition is logical, not ideal; *sī* here practically introduces a reason, = *seeing that.* —— **ēmorī**, pres. inf. of the deponent verb *ēmorior, ēmorī*, no perf., 3 (*ē + morior*); complementary inf. with *potes; ēmorī* = *to die outright*, and it seems that suicide is suggested. The idea is this, that if Catiline cannot bring himself to commit suicide or confess his treason and submit to execution, he ought at least to have no hesitation about signing his own political death-sentence by retiring into exile. The old reading *morārī* = *to remain* (i.e. in Rome and among enemies) has been discarded by all the best modern editors.

LINE 26. **aequō**, abl. sing. m. of the adj. *aequus, -a, -um;* agrees with *animō* = *with a calm mind, with equanimity. Aequus* has several different meanings: (1) *plain, level*, cf. *aequor* = *a plain surface*, hence *the sea* (poetical) in its quiet state; (2) *equal*, cf. *aequālis* = *contemporary;* (3) *fair, just;* (4) *calm, resigned*, esp. + *animus;* (5) *favorable, kind;* (6) *aequum est* = *it is fair* or *reasonable.* —— **animō**, abl. sing. of *animus, -ī*, m. 2d; abl. of manner, with the modifier *aequō.* —— **nōn**, neg. adv.; limits *potes.* —— **potes**, 2d pers. sing. pres. ind. of *possum, posse, potuī;* the subj. *tū* is implied by the personal ending. —— **abīre**, pres. inf. act. of *abeō, abīre, abiī, abitum*, irreg. (*ab + eō*); complementary inf., following *dubitās.* —— **in**, prep.; gov. the acc. *terrās.*

LINE 27. **aliquās**, acc. plur. f. of the indef. pronominal adj. *aliquī, aliqua, aliquod* (*alius + quī*); agrees with *terrās; aliquās* practically = *nesciō quās;* cf. *aliquō*, Chap. VII, l. 36. The adj. *aliquī* has the same indefinite force as the pron. *aliquis;* it appears that *aliquis* is not used adjectively. —— **terrās**, acc. plur. of *terra, -ae*, f. 1st (see the note on *terrae*, Chap. I, l. 32, for synonyms, etc.); governed by the prep. *in;* as the plur. *terrās* can hardly have the special sense of *terra*, i.e. *country*, we may translate *to some other part of the globe.* —— **et**, cop. conj.; connects the two object complementary infinitives of *dubitās*, viz. *abīre* and *mandāre.* —— **vītam**, acc. sing. of *vīta, -ae*, f. 1st; direct obj. of *mandāre. Vītam fugae sōlitūdinīque mandāre* illustrates the literary refinements of elegance which Cicero was the first to impart to Latin prose; Caesar would have prepared a direct concrete expression, such as *tē fugae, etc., mandāre.* —— **istam**, acc. sing. f. of the dem. adj. of the 2d pers. *iste, ista, istud;* agrees with *vītam; istam* as usual implies contempt. —— **multīs**, abl. plur. n. of the adj. *multus, -a, -um;* agrees with *suppliciīs; multīs* refers to those offences for which Catiline was prosecuted but secured acquittal, and to others for which he was not, but ought to have been tried and punished.

28 suppliciīs　　　iūstīs　　　dēbitīsque　　　ēreptam, | render your miser-
　　from punishments　*just*　　　　*and due*　　　*snatched,* | able life, snatched
　　　　　　　　　　　　　　　　　　　　　　　　　　　| into safety from many
29 fugae sōlitūdinīque mandāre?　　　　　　　"Refer" | a punishment justly
　　to flight and to solitude　*to commit?*　"Refer" *(the question),* | d ue, to exile and
　　　　　　　　　　　　　　　　　　　　　　　　　　　| solitude? "Put the

LINE 28. **suppliciīs**, abl. plur. of *supplicium, -ī*, n. 2d (from *supplex, supplicis,*
adj. 3d, *sub = plicō*, hence *bending the knee*, (1) in entreaty, (2) as here, for punishment); abl. of separation, with *ēreptam.* The prep. with which the verb denoting
separation is compounded usually accompanies the ablative, but is often omitted after
verbs of *removing, excluding*, etc., and in a large number of technical expressions.
A. & G. 243, *b*; B. 214, 2 and 3; G. 390, 1, and 2, NOTE 3; H. 413. It is, however,
quite likely that *suppliciīs* is the dat. of separation which follows several compounds of
ab, dē, or *ex*, and indeed *ēripiō* appears to be common with this dative. But the dat. of
separation is not very common in classical prose (though frequent in poetry and late
prose) except when there is a strong notion of personal interest, and when the word in
the dat. indicates a *person* (as opposed to *things*). A. & G. 229, and *c*; B. 188, 2, *d*;
G. 345, REM. 1; H. 385, 2, and 4, 2). —— **iūstīs**, abl. plur. n. of the adj. *iustus, -a, -um*
(from *iūs*); agrees with *suppliciīs.* When *multus* is one of *two* adjectives which modify
a noun, the adjectives are connected by a cop. conj. (usually *et*); but when there are
more than two adjectives, *multus* stands first and is not connected by *et* with the second.
—— **dēbitīsque** (*dēbitīs + que*), *dēbitīs* is the abl. plur. n. of the adj. *dēbitus, -a, -um*
(prop. perf. part. pass. of *dēbeō, -ēre, -uī, -itum*, 2); agrees with *suppliciīs. Que* is the
enclitic cop. conj.; connects *ustīs* and *dēbitīs.* —— **ēreptam**, acc. sing. f. of *ēreptus, -a,
-um ;* perf. part. pass. of *ēripiō, -ere, ēripuī, ēreptum*, 3 (*ē = out of + rapiō = I snatch*);
agrees with *vītam ;* the participial extension *ēreptam =* a rel. clause *quae (vīta)* . . .
ērepta est. Synonyms : (2) *sūmō* (*= sub + emō*; the original meaning of *emō* is *I
take ;* later, *I buy*) = *I take*, so as to make use of, e.g. *togam, cibum ;* (2) *dēmō*
(*dē + emō*) = *I take away*, i.e. some part from the whole, in opposition to *addere ;* (3)
adimō (*ad + emō*) = *I take away* (*something* from *some one*), hence *I deprive* some one
of a possession ; (4) *ēripiō = I take* or *tear away* something from some one, implying
violence in the agent and reluctance to yield in the person acted upon ; (5) *auferō*
(*ab + ferō*) = *I take away*, by force and with selfish motives.
　　LINE 29. **fugae**, dat. sing. of *fuga, -ae*, f. 1st (cf. φυγή, φεύγω, *fugiō, fugō*, etc. ;
root *bhug = φυγ = fug, = to bend* or *turn around*, i.e. oneself in flight); dat. of the
indirect obj. dependent on *mandāre.* —— **sōlitūdinīque** (*sōlitūdinī + que*), *sōlitūdinī* is
the dat. sing. of *sōlitūdō, -inis*, f. 3d (from the adj. *sōlus ;* cf. *cōnsuētūdō* from *cōnsuētus*);
dat. of the indirect obj. dependent on *mandāre. Que* is the enclitic cop. conj., connecting *fugae* and *sōlitūdinī.* —— **mandāre**, pres. inf. act. of *mandō, -āre, -āvī, -ātum*, 1
(*manus + dō*, hence *I put into the hands of* some one, *I commit*); like *abīre*, to which
et (l. 27) joins it, *mandāre* is a complementary inf. with *dubitās*, l. 25. —— **Refer**, 2d
pers. sing. pres. imperative act. of *referō, referre, rettulī, relātum*, irreg. (*re + ferō*); the
implied subject is *tū*, referring to Cicero. *Dīcō* and *ferō*, and their compounds, omit the
final *ĕ* in the 2d pers. sing. of the pres. imperative act., and retain the long quantity
of the 1st syllable of the simple verb, e.g. *aīc, dūc, ēdūc ; faciō* also makes *fac*, but the
compounds are regular, e.g. *perficiō* makes *perfice : ferō* makes *fer* in the simple verb
and as the final syllable of compounds. A. & G. 128, *c*; B. 116, 3; G. 130, 5; H. 238.
Referre ad senātum is the regular technical phrase for *laying a matter* before the Senate
for discussion. The magistrate who had called the meeting and presided at it (the
consul or consuls jointly, or another curule magistrate) first communicated any intelligence he might have to make (*rem ad senātum dēferre*), and then he put any question

question," say you,	inquis	"ad	senātum";	id	enim	postulās,	et, 30
"to the Senate"—	you say,	"to	the senate";	that	for	you demand, and,
this is what you ask,						
and you say that, if	sī	hīc	ōrdō	sibi		placēre 31
this council decrees	if	this	order (= Senate)	to itself		to seem good

requiring discussion before the house (*rem referre*). This could not be done by a senator not holding office, but only by a magistrate entitled to summon a meeting. The putting of the subject forward was called *relātiō*. After this the magistrate was said *cōnsulere senātum* = to ask the opinion of the Senate, and this he did by asking individual senators for their views. It was usual to ask the magistrates elect to speak first in their order of precedence, then the *cōnsulārēs*, *praetōrī*, etc., in order. Sometimes a division arose (*discessiō*) and the senators voted (*pedibus ībant*); but if a quick decision was required, the votes might be taken without discussion (*senātus cōnsultum per relātiōnem*).

Line 30. **inquis**, 2d pers. sing. pres. ind. act. of the defective verb *inquam*, irreg.; the subj. *tū* is implied by the personal ending. This verb is always post-positive, i.e. stands alone or with its subj. within the quotation which it introduces; cf. *quoth he*. The pres. ind. tense is complete, *inqu-am, -is, -it, -imus, -itis* (rare), *-iunt;* in the imperf. the only survival is *inquiēbat;* fut. *inquiēs, inquiet;* perf. *inquistī, inquit;* imperative, *inque, inquitō*. A. & G. 144, *b*; B. 134; G. 175, 2; H. 297, II, 2. For synonyms, see the note on *āiunt*, Chap. VI, l. 48. Possibly Catiline interrupted Cicero in his speech, and demanded that the Senate be asked whether it favored his exile or not; or else Cicero puts into words the thought which he imagined was running through Catiline's mind. At any rate *refer ad senātum* seems to show that Catiline believed the Senate would not be resolute enough to vote for his exile, and that Cicero was aware of this. —— **ad**, prep.; gov. the acc. *senātum*. —— **senātum**, acc. sing. of *senātus, -ūs*, m. 4th; governed by the prep. *ad*. —— **id**. acc. sing. n. of the dem. pron. *is, ea, id;* direct obj. of *postulās; id* refers to the quotation *refer ad senātum*. —— **enim**, causal conj.; introduces the sentence in which it stands as parenthetically explanatory of *refer ad senātum*. —— **postulās**, 2d pers. sing. pres. ind. act. of *postulō, -āre, -āvī, -ātum*, 1 (connected with *poscō*); the subj. *tū* is implied by the personal ending. For synonyms, see the list given under *rogō*, Chap. IV, l. 22. —— **et**, cop. conj.; joins *postulās* and *dīcis*.

Line 31. **sī**, conditional particle, followed by the subjunct. *dēcrēverit*. The condition is really a logical one, and the ind. would be used were it not for the fact that the *sī* clause is included in the indirect discourse dependent on *dīcis;* the condition is a reported one, and the verb of the *apodosis* is *obtemperātūrum esse* (not *dīcis*). The direct form = *sī hīc ōrdō sibi placēre dēcrēverit* (fut. perf. ind., not perf. subjunct. as it is in Cicero's words) *mē īre in exsilium, obtemperābō*. Observe that the *apodosis* or main clause of a conditional sentence in indirect discourse has its verb in the inf., except when in direct discourse it is an imperative or when the apodosis is interrog., in which cases in indirect discourse the verb must be subjunctive. A. & G. 337, 1 and 2; B. 319, A, B; G. 657; H. 527, I. Observe that the fut. perf. of the direct *protasis* becomes perf. subjunct. after a primary leading verb (as *dīcis* in this passage) in indirect speech; after an historic leading verb it would be pluperf. subj. (e.g. *dīxistī sī hīc ōrdō dēcrēvisset*, etc., *tē obtemperātūrum esse*). From the following model sentences it will be seen that in reported conditions of the logical type the tense in the *protasis*, and not the tense of the inf. (*apodosis*) is affected by the tense of the leading verb. (A) Present: dir. *sī mē cōnsulis, suādeō* = indir. *dīcō (dīxī), sī mē cōnsulās (cōnsulerēs), mē suādēre;* (B) Future: dir. *sī mē cōnsulās, suādēbō* = ind. *dīcō (dīxī), sī mē cōnsulās (cōnsulerēs), mē suāsūrum esse;* (C) Fut.-Perfect in Protasis: dir. *sī mē cōnsulueris, suādēbō* = ind. *dīcō (dīxī), sī mē cōnsulueris*, i.e. perf. subjunct. (*cōnsuluissēs*), *mē suāsūrum esse;* (D) Imperf. or Aorist

32 dēcrēverit		tē	īre	in	that its decision is
shall decree (lit. *have decreed*)		*(that) you*	*should* (lit. *to*) *go*	*into*	that you should go
33 exsilium,	obtemperātūrum		tē	esse	into exile, you will
exile,	*about to submit*		*you are* (lit. *to be*)		submit. I will not
34 dīcis.	Nōn	referam,	id	quod	put the question, for
you say.	*Not*	*I will refer (it),*	*that* (= *a thing*)	*which*	such a proceeding is
					repugnant to my prin-

Perfect: dir. *sī mē cōnsulēbās* (or *cōnsuluistī*, aorist), *suāsī* = ind. *dīcō* (*dīxī*), *sī mē cōn-suleres* (*cōnsulerēs*), *mē suāsisse*. —— **hīc**, nom. sing. m. of the dem. pron. *hīc, haec, hōc;* agrees with *ōrdō*. —— **ōrdō**, gen. *ordinis*, m. 3d ; nom. sing., subj. of *dēcrēverit*. Cicero frequently uses *hīc ōrdō* as = to *senātus;* in Livy *ōrdō* sometimes has a very different meaning = *centuria, a century* (of which there were sixty in every legion). —— **sibi**, dat. sing. m. of the reflexive pron. *sē, suī,* etc. ; refers back to the subj. *hīc ōrdō*, and is dat. of the indir. obj. governed by *placēre*. A. & G. 226; B. 187, II, and *a* ; G. 346 ; H. 384, I ; 385, I, II. —— **placēre**, pres. inf. act. of the impersonal construction *placet, placēre, placuit* or *placitum est*, of the verb *placeō, -ēre, -uī, -itum,* 2 ; *sibi placēre* is the obj. of *dēcrēverit;* the real subj. in acc. and inf. construction (following *dēcrēverit*) of *placēre* is the inf. clause *tē īre in exsilium*. Remember that though an impersonal verb appears to have no subject, the clause dependent on the impersonal verb is its logical subject. So here the literal sense is : *if this order shall decree that your going into exile pleases it,* = *if it shall decree that it is resolved upon your going into exile.*

LINE 32. **dēcrēverit**, 3d pers. sing. perf. subjunct. act. of *dēcernō, -ere, dēcrēvī, dēcrētum,* 3 (*dē + cernō*) ; agrees with the subj. *hīc ōrdō;* for the tense and mood, see the note on *sī* above. —— **tē**, acc. sing. of *tū;* subj.-acc. of *īre; tē īre* is a substantival phrase, acting as logical subj. of the impersonal inf. *placēre* in the indir. object-clause of *dēcrēverit*. —— **īre**, pres. inf. act. of *eō, īre, īvī* or *iī, itum,* irreg. ; agrees with the subj.-acc. *tē; īre* acts as subj. of *placēre* after *dēcrēverit*. —— **in**, prep. ; gov. the acc. *exsilium.*

LINE 33. **exsilium**, acc. sing. of *exsilium, -ī,* n. 2d ; governed by the prep. *in.* Refer to the discussion of exile in the note on *exsilium*, Chap. V, l. 53. —— **obtemperā-tūrum**, acc. sing. m. of *obtemperātūrus, -a, -um,* fut. part. act. of *obtemperō, -āre, -āvī, -ātum,* 1 (*ob + temperō*) ; *obtemperātūrum + esse* (following) = the fut. inf. act. of *obtem-perō*, agreeing with the sub.-acc. *tē* in the acc. and inf. object-clause of *dīcis. Tē obtem-perātūrum esse* is the *apodosis* or principal clause of the conditional sentence introduced by *sī* above ; see the note on *sī* above. Synonyms : (1) *pārēre* = *to obey*, and denotes an obedience to necessity or the will of one whose superiority is admitted ; (2) *oboedīre* (*ob + audīre* = *to obey*, the generic verb, denoting obedience from whatever motive, neces-sity or choice ; whereas *pārēre* implies subjection or inferiority (cf. *pārentēs* = *imperiō subiectī*, i.e. *subjects*), *oboedīre* implies nothing ; (3) *obtemperāre* = lit. *to restrain one's self towards* some one else, hence *to comply with the wishes of, to obey*, implying delibera-tion and self-restraint ; (4) *dictō* (*aliquem*) *audientem esse* = *to obey orders*, in military reference ; (5) *obsequī* (*ob + sequor*) = *to obey*, voluntarily. —— **tē**, acc. sing. of *tū;* subj.-acc. (reflexive) of the inf. *obtemperātūrum esse* in the object-clause of *dīcis.* —— **esse**, pres. inf. of *sum, esse, fuī;* *esse + obtemperātūrum* = the compound fut. inf. act. *obtemperō.*

LINE 34. **dīcis**, 2d pers. sing. pres. ind. act. of *dīcō, -ere, dīxī, dictum,* 3 ; the subj. *tū* is implied by the personal ending. It seems probable that Catiline had received private assurance from senators of the aristocratic party that they would not proceed against the members of the conspiracy if Catiline retired voluntarily into exile. —— **Nōn**, neg. adv. ; limits *referam*. —— **referam**, 1st pers. sing. fut. ind. act. of *referō, referre, rettulī, relā-*

ciples; nevertheless I	abhorret	ā	meīs	mōribus,	et	tamen	35
will let you see what	*shrinks aloof*	*from*	*my*	*character,*	*and*	*yet*	
the members of this	faciam	ut	intellegās,		quid	hī	36
Senate think about	*I will contrive*	*that*	*you may understand*		*what*	*these men*	
you. (*A pause.*) Go	dē	tē	sentiant.	Egredere	ex	urbe,	37
forth from the city,	*about*	*you*	*feel.*	*Go out*	*from*	*the city,*	

tum, irreg.; the subj. implied is *ego*. It would have been illegal for Cicero to put a motion involving exile before the Senate, for exile was not inflicted as a punishment but was by universal consent recognized as a means whereby an accused citizen might of his own free will escape condemnation and its penalties; moreover, the Senate was not a judicial court, and so could not pass sentence on Catiline. —— **id**, acc. sing. n. of the dem. pron. *is, ea, id;* *id* is an idiomatic appositional acc., in apposition not with the full sentence *non referam*, but with the idea conveyed by the verb *referam;* we may render *I shall not put the question, for such an action is repugnant to my character.* See the references under *id*, Chap. III, l. 19. —— **quod**, nom. sing. n. of the rel. pron. *qui, quae, quod;* agrees with the antecedent *id*, and is subj. of *abhorret.* In parenthetic explanations like this *quod* is often used without an antecedent *id.*

LINK 35. **abhorret**, 3d pers. sing. pres. ind. act. of *abhorreō, -ēre, -uī,* no supine, 2 (*ab + horreō*); agrees with the subj. *quod.* —— **ā**, prep.; gov. the abl. *mōribus,* expressing separation in conjunction with the verb *abhorret.* —— **meīs**, abl. plur. m. of the poss. pron. *meus, -a, -um;* agrees with *mōribus.* —— **mōribus**, abl. plur. of *mōs, mōris,* m. 3d (in the sing. = *way, manner;* in the plur. = *manners, character*); governed by the prep. *ā;* in ll. 34–37 Cicero accounts for his refusal to comply with Catiline's suggestion on the ground of natural mildness of character and leniency, implying that if the motion of banishment were submitted, Catiline's condemnation was inevitable. —— **et**, cop. conj.; joins the sentences *non referam* and *faciam*, etc. —— **tamen**, adversative adv. (or conj.); signifies that the sentence contains an idea in opposition to what has preceded.

LINE 36. **faciam**, 1st pers. sing. fut. ind. act. of *faciō, -ere, fēcī, factum,* 3 (*fīo* is used as the passive); the subj. *ego* is implied. *Facere, efficere, perficere, cōnsequī,* and other verbs of *effecting*, are followed by *ut* + the subjunct.; the subjunct. is sometimes final, sometimes consecutive, hence the neg. may be *ut nōn* or *nē;* but in a large majority of cases the subjunct. is that of result, and *ut nōn* is the rule in classical prose. Observe that the *ut* clause is substantival, and is obj. of an active verb of *effecting* (as in this passage), and subj. of a passive verb. A. & G. 332; B. 297, 1; G. 553; H. 501, II. —— **ut**, consecutive conj.; introduces the substantival clause of result *ut intellegās . . . sentiant;* the *ut* clause is object of *faciam.* —— **intellegās**, 2d pers. sing. pres. subjunct. act. of *intellegō, -ere, intellēxī, intellectum,* 3 (*inter + legō;* often incorrectly written *intelligō*); the subj. *tū* is implied. Refer to the note and synonyms under *intellegit,* Chap. I, l. 17. —— **quid**, acc. sing. n. of the interrog. pron. *quis, quae, quid;* direct obj. of *sentiant; quid . . . sentiant* is an indirect question in objective dependence on *intellegās.* See the note on *ēgeris,* Chap. I, l. 14. —— **hī**, nom. plur. m. of the dem. pron. *hīc, haec, hōc;* subj. of *sentiant; hī = senātōrēs quī hīc adsunt.*

LINK 37. **dē**, prep.; gov. the abl. *tē = concerning you.* —— **tē**, abl. sing. of *tū;* governed by the prep. *dē.* —— **sentiant**, 3d pers. plur. pres. subjunct. acc. of *sentiō, -īre, sēnsī, sēnsum,* 4; agrees with the subj. *hī;* the mood is subjunct. because *quid* introduces an indirect question (the direct = *quid hī dē tē sentiunt?*) in dependence on *intellegās.* A. & G. 334; B. 300; G. 467; H. 528, 2; 529, I. —— **Egredere**, 2d pers. sing. pres. imperative of the deponent verb *ēgredior, ēgredī, ēgressus sum,* 3 (*ē + gradior*); the subj. *tū* is implied by the personal ending. —— **ex**, prep. + the abl. (*ē* or *ex* before consonants,

38 **Catilīna,　lībérā　rem pūblicam　metū;　in**
　Catiline;　free　the commonwealth　from fear; into

39 **exsilium, sī hanc vōcem exspectās, proficīscere.**
　exile,　if　this　word　you wait for,　set off.

40 **Quid　est,　Catilīna?　ecquid　attendis,**
　What　is (it),　Catiline?　at all　do you give heed,

Catiline; set the state free from fear; depart into exile, if exile is the word for which you are waiting. (*A pause.*) How now, Catiline? Are you taking any notice, do

---

ex before vowels and *h*); gov. *urbe.* It is usual to express separation by the abl. + a prep. (*ā, ab, de, ē, ex*), esp. + a verb. compounded with the preposition.——**urbe**, abl. sing. of *urbs, urbis,* f. 3d; governed by the prep. *ex.*

LINE 38. **Catilīna**, voc. sing. of *Catilīna, -ae,* m. 1st; the case of address.—— **lībérā**, 2d pers. sing. pres. imperative act. of *liberō, -āre, -āvī, -ātum,* 1; the subj. *tū* is implied. Observe the *asyndeta;* cf. the well known *vēnī, vidī, vicī.* A. & G. 208, *b*; B. 346; G. 473, REM.; H. 636, I, 1.—— **rem**, acc. sing. of *rēs, reī,* f. 5th; direct obj. of *lībérā.*—— **pūblicam**, acc. sing. f. of the adj. *pūblicus, -a, -um;* agrees with *rem.*—— **metū**, abl. sing. of *metus, -ūs,* m. 4th; abl. of separation, with *lībérā.* Note that a few verbs meaning *to set free, deprive, want,* are followed by the abl. of separation without a preposition. Synonyms: (1) *metus = anxiety, apprehension,* esp. *fear of imminent evil;* (2) *timor = fear,* caused by timidity or cowardice; the generic word; (3) *formīdō = terror* (Cic. says it = *metus permanēns*); (4) *pavor = distracting fear* (= *metus locō movēns mentem,* Cic.); (5) *verēcundia = reverential fear, awe;* (6) *horror = shuddering fear,* cf. *horrescō = I shiver;* (7) *trepidātiō = consternation;* cf. *trepidō = I hurry about in agitation.*—— in, prep.; gov. the acc. *exsilium,* expressing *motion to.*

LINE 39. **exsilium**, acc. sing. of *exsilium, -ī,* n. 2d; governed by the prep. *in.*—— **sī**, conditional particle; followed by the ind. *expectās.*—— **hanc**, acc. sing. f. of the dem. pron. *hīc, haec, hōc;* agrees with *vōcem; hanc* is here emphatic, = *if this is the word you are waiting for* (referring to *exsilium*).—— **vōcem**, acc. sing. of *vōx, vōcis,* f. 3d; direct obj. of *exspectās.*—— **expectās**, 2d pers. sing. pres. ind. act. of *exspectō, -āre, -āvī, -ātum,* 1 (*ex + spectō*); the subj. *tū* is implied by the personal ending.—— **profi- cīscere**, 2d pers. sing. pres. imperative of the deponent verb *proficīscor, proficīscī, pro- fectus sum,* 3 (inceptive form of *prōficiō, prō = before + root fac (fic) = to place,* hence lit. *I put myself forward,* i.e. *set out*); the subj. *tū* is implied by the personal ending. Here again Cicero returns to the object of his desire in delivering this speech, viz. that Catiline should leave Rome; whether he really went into exile or joined the camp of Mānlius was not a matter of much account to the orator. The exhortations *ēgredere ... proficīscere* were doubtless made with great solemnity of manner, and Cicero paused to let his words take effect. Complete silence held the meeting, and Cicero proceeds to point the lesson which the silence conveys (*Quid est,* etc.).

LINE 40. **Quid**, nom. sing. n. of the interrog. pron. *quis, quae, quid;* subj. of *est.* *Quid est* = the colloquial *how now!*—— **est**, 3d pers sing. pres. ind. of *sum, esse, fuī;* agrees with the subj. *quid. Quid est* draws attention to the fact that no one protested when Cicero told Catiline to go into exile. Yet Catiline had friends among the senators present; cf. Chap. XII, ll. 19-28; but these had been crushed into silence by Cicero's scathing remarks, cf. Chap. IV, ll. 12-24.—— **Catilīna**, voc. sing. of *Catilīna, -ae,* m. 1st; the case of address.—— **ecquid**, adv. = *at all;* modifies *attendis. Ecquid* is strictly the acc. neut. sing. of the interrog. pron. *ecquis,* no fem. form, *ecquid;* cf. the adj. *ecquī, ecqua* (*ecquae* rare), *ecquod.* Like *quid* in questions, *ecquid* is properly a kind of cognate acc. (of respect) with *attendis = are you paying any attention at all? Ecquis* is a strong interrog.; sometimes it combines with *nam,* e.g. *ecquaenam, ecquōs- nam;* the abl. *ecquō* is used adverbially.—— **attendis**, 2d pers. sing. pres. ind. act. of

you at all observe the	ecquid	animadvertis	hōrum	silentium ? 41
members' silence ?	*at all*	*do you observe*	*of these (men)*	*the silence?*
They are submissive,	Patiuntur,	tacent.	Quid	exspectās 42
they are silent. Why	*They let (it pass),*	*they are silent.*	*Why*	*do you wait for*
do you wait for their				
expressed authoriza-	auctōritātem	loquentium,	quōrum	voluntātem 43
tion, when you	*the command*	*of (them) speaking,*	*of whom*	*the desire*

attendō, -ere, attendī, attentum, 3 (*ad* + *tendō* = lit. *I direct,* i.e. *my mind, to;* hence with or without *animum* = *I pay heed, observe*); the subject *tū* is implied.

LINE 41. **ecquid,** adv., modifying *animadvertis.* —— **animadvertis,** 2d pers. sing. pres. ind. act. of *animadvertō, -ere, animadvertī, animadversum,* 3 (*animum* + *advertō* = *I direct attention to, I notice;* cf. *animum attendere*); the subj. *tū* is implied. Synonyms : (1) *videō* = *I see,* the generic word ; (2) *cernō* = *I see clearly,* so as to discriminate ; (3) *aspicere* (*ad* + *speciō*) = *to look at,* whether with or without intent ; (4) *spectāre* = *to look at steadily,* e.g. at the movement of the heavenly bodies ; (5) *intuērī* = *to gaze upon;* (6) *animadvertere* = *to see, notice,* as opposed to *overlooking* with the eyes. *Animadvertere* in this and many other passages implies not mere sensual perception but mental perception, = *to notice, pay attention to.* In this relation distinguish between : (1) *animadvertere* = *to notice* mentally, as opposed to *overlooking* (cf. above) ; (2) *notāre* = *to note, mark, observe,* so as to impress upon the memory (*ut memoriae haereat,* Dumesnil) ; (3) *observāre* = *to observe narrowly, to watch,* implying conscious effort and a desire to form a judgment about something (*ut iūdicium ferāmus,* Dumesnil). Note the phrase *animadvertere in aliquem* = *to punish any one* (by an ellipse of *suppliciō*). —— **hōrum,** gen. plur. m. of the dem. pron. *hīc, haec, hōc;* poss. gen., limiting *silentium; hōrum,* sc. *senātōrum,* cf. *hī,* l. 36. —— **silentium,** acc. sing. of *silentium, -ī,* n. 2d (from *silēns,* pres. part. act. of *sileō, -ēre, -uī,* no supine, 2 ; etymology doubtful); direct obj. of *animadvertis,* and probably also of *attendis,* though we may take *ecquid attendis* absolutely, i.e. *are you paying any attention?*

LINE 42. **Patiuntur,** 3d pers. plur. pres. ind. of the deponent verb *patior, patī, passus sum,* 3 ; understand as subj. *hī* (referring to the senators); *patiuntur* implies non-interference, and so is strictly appropriate here. See the synonyms under *patimur,* Chap. II, l. 15. —— **tacent,** 3d pers. plur. pres. ind. act. of *taceō, -ēre, -uī, -itum,* 2 ; understand the subj. *hī. Silēre* = *to keep quiet* (as opposed to *strepere,* or *sonāre* = *to make a noise*), cf. *silentium* above ; *tacēre* = *to be silent,* i.e. not to speak. Cicero takes full advantage of the opportunity which the prevailing silence gives him of creating a dramatic scene ; observe the impressive effect produced by the simple means of omitting a cop. conj. between *patiuntur* and *tacent,* and substituting a pause in the delivery of the words. —— **Quid,** adverbial acc. neut. sing. of the interrog. pron. *quis, quae, quid,* = *why?* ; introduces a question. Originally, as used with simple verbs, *quid* was an acc. similar to the *cognate* acc. ; in longer and more involved sentences *quid* practically = *cūr.* —— **exspectās,** 2d pers. sing. pres. ind. act. of *exspectō, -āre, -āvī, -ātum,* 1 (*ex* + *spectō*); the subj. *tū* is implied.

LINE 43. **auctōritātem,** acc. sing. of *auctōritās, -ātis,* f. 3d (from *auctor;* cf. *augeō*); direct obj. of *expectās. Auctōritātem* is here concrete, = *the expressed request,* with allusion to *sī hīc ōrdō dēcrēverit,* etc., in ll. 31–33 above. As a technical term *auctōritās* (sc. *senātūs*) = a resolution which has received the approving sanction of a majority in the Senate and which would have become a *senātūs cōnsultum* but for the *intercessiō* which invalidates it. —— **loquentium,** gen. plur. m. of *loquēns, -entis,* pres. part. of the deponent verb *loquor, -ī, locūtus sum,* 3 ; sc. *eōrum,* as antecedent of *quōrum,* and consider *loquentium* as agreeing with *eōrum;* the gen. is poss., limiting

44 tacitōrum	perspicis?	At	sī	hōc	idem	clearly perceive their
(being) silent	*you perceive?*	*But*	*if*	*this same thing*		unspoken desire?

Yet if I had deliv-

45 huic	adulēscentī	optimō,	P.	Sēstiō,	sī	ered the same mes-
this	*to young man*	*excellent,*	*Publius*	*Sestius,*	*if*	sage to this worthy

young man, Publius

auctōritātem. —— **quōrum**, gen. plur. m. of the rel. pron. *quī, quae, quod;* agrees with the antecedent *loquentium* (substantival, or *eōrum* understood); poss. gen., limiting *voluntātem.* —— **voluntātem**, acc. sing. of *voluntās, -ātis,* f. 3d (Ind.-Eur. root *var* or *val* = Greek βουλ, βολ = *vol, to will, choose;* cf. βούλομαι and *volō* = *I will, wish,* and Homeric ἐβόλοντο for ἐβούλοντο); direct object of *perspicis.* Note the emphatic antithesis between *auctōritātem loquentium* (the expressed recommendation) and *voluntātem tacitōrum* (the unexpressed desire); also observe that classical Latin (more so in Caesar than in Cicero) prefers concrete attribution wherever possible.

LINE 44. **tacitōrum**, gen. plur. m. of the adj. *tacitus, -a, -um* (*taceō*); agrees with *quōrum;* emphatic. —— **perspicis**, 2d pers. sing. pres. ind. act. of *perspiciō, -ere, perspēxī, perspectum,* 3 (*per + speciō* = lit. *I look through,* hence *I see plainly*); the subj. *tū* is implied by the personal ending. —— **At**, adversative conj.; introducing a lively objection, which adds to the force of the argument. *At* is used : (1) to introduce a contrast, especially in argumentative sentences, = *but yet, but on the other hand;* (2) to make a qualification after a neg., or *sī, etsī,* etc., = *but yet, however, at least;* (3) to make a direct contradiction, = *but on the contrary. Atquī* is a stronger form of *at.* For a comparison of *at* and other adversative conjunctions, refer to the note on *tamen,* Chap. I, l. 18. —— **sī**, conditional particle ; introducing an unreal supposition respecting past time, and therefore followed by the pluperf. subjunct. both in the *protasis* (*dīxissem*) and in the *apodosis* (*intulisset*); cf. the use of the pluperf. subjunct. in unreal wishes for the past, e.g. *utinam adfuissem* = *would that I had been present!* (but I was not present). A. & G. 308 ; B. 304 ; G. 597 ; H. 510. —— **hōc**, acc. sing. n. of the dem. pron. *hīc, haec, hōc ;* direct obj. of *dīxissem; hōc* refers to *in exsilium proficīscere* above. —— **idem**, acc. sing. n. of the determinative pron. *īdem, eadem, idem* (for *is-dem, ea-dem, id-dem*); agrees with and emphasizes *hōc. Idem* is often used with a force similar to that of *ipse,* cf. *hōc ipsum;* but sometimes it adds an adverbial force, = *also, besides,* e.g. *īdem parāvī commeātūs* = *I also got together stores of provisions.*

LINE 45. **huic**, dat. sing. m. of the dem. pron. *hīc, haec, hōc;* agrees with *adulēscentī.* —— **adulēscentī**, dat. sing. of *adulēscēns, -entis,* m. (or f.) 3d (strictly = *adolēscēns,* pres. part. act. of *adolēscō;* as a noun or adj. the form *adulēscēns,* not *adolēscēns,* was preferred by classical writers); dat. in apposition with *Pūbliō Sēstiō.* Refer to the note on *adulēscentulō,* Chap. VI, l. 11. —— **optimō**, dat. sing. m. of the adj. *optimus, -a, -um* (superl. of *bonus;* compar. *melior*); agrees with *adulēscentī.* —— **Pūbliō** (abbreviated = P.), dat. sing. of *Pūblius, -ī,* m. 2d ; *praenōmen* of *Sēstiō.* —— **Sēstiō**, dat. sing. of *Sēstius, -ī* (*Sēxtius, -ī,* is another form), m. 2d ; dat. of the indirect obj., dependent on *dīxissem.* Pūblius Sēstius was quaestor of Cicero's colleague C. Antōnius in this year (63 B.C.). He became tribune of the people in B.C. 58, and during his year of office (B.C. 57) he exerted himself to secure Cicero's recall from exile, and thereby secured the great orator's gratitude ; this was manifested in the year 56 B.C. when Sēstius was accused (*dē vī*) of violent behavior during his tribunate, for, like *Milō,* he had kept an armed body-guard about his person to oppose Clōdius and his riotous partizans. Cicero came forward to defend Sēstius (the speech still survives), and his oration and the influence of Pompey procured a verdict of acquittal. When the civil war broke out, Sēstius first of all sided with Pompey, but later became a partizan of Caesar. —— **sī**, conditional particle ; repeated from above for effect ; the repetition of a

Sestius, or to the brave Marcus Marcellus, ere now and with the best justification the Senate would have laid violent hands upon me, consul as I am, even	fortissimō	virō	M.	Mārcellō	dīxissem,	iam 46
	very brave	*to a man*	*Marcus*	*to Marcellus*	*I had said,*	*already*
	mihi	cōnsulī	hōc	ipsō	in	templō	senātus 47
	upon me	*the consul*	*this*	*very*	*in*	*temple*	*the senate*
	iūre	optimō		vim	et	manūs 48
	with the right	*best*		*violence*	*and*	*hands*

word at the beginning of a new clause is called *anaphora*. Observe that the repeated word often takes the place of a conj. (so *sī* here takes the place of a disjunctive conj. *or*). A. & G. 344, *f*; B. 350, 11, *b*; G. 636, NOTE 4; H. 636, III, 3.

LINE 46. **fortissimō**, dat. sing. m. of the adj. *fortissimus, -a, -um* (superl. of *fortis, -e*, 3d; compar. *fortior*); agrees with *virō*. *Fortissimō virō* and the like are stereotyped compliments, common in deliberative bodies, cf. the modern complimentary terms, *the honorable member*, etc. —— **virō**, dat. sing. of *vir, -ī*, m. 2d; appositive of *Marcō Marcellō*. —— **Marcō** (abbreviated = M.), dat. sing. of *Marcus, -ī*, m. 2d; *praenōmen* of *Marcellō*. —— **Marcellō**, dat. sing. of *Marcellus, -ī*, m. 2d; dat. of the indirect obj. with *dīxissem*. If *M. Marcellum* be read in l. 17 above, do not confuse with the Marcellus mentioned here. Marcus Claudius Marcellus was consul in B.C. 51, and must be carefully distinguished from (1) his cousin Gāius Claudius Marcellus, consul in B.C. 50, and (2) from his brother Gāius Claudius Marcellus, consul in B.C. 49. The Marcellus of this passage was an intimate friend of Cicero and a bitter opponent of Jūlius Caesar; e g. he proposed in the Senate that Caesar's province be taken from him and given to some one else. When Pompey was driven from Italy, Marcellus went with him, and after the battle of Pharsālus (48 B.C.) retired into exile to Mytilēnē, where he studied philosophy. Cicero addressed several letters to him, advising him to return to Rome and demand political pardon. In 46 B.C. Caesar, at the earnest request of Gāius Marcellus and many senators, reluctantly pardoned Marcus, whereupon Cicero delivered his speech of thanks (which is now extant). Marcellus set out to return to Rome, but was murdered at Athens, and was buried in the Academy with high honors by the Athenians. Marcellus was noted for his ability as an orator and as a thinker, and for his strength of character. —— **dīxissem**, 1st pers. sing. pluperf. subjunct. act. of *dīcō, -ere, dīxī, dīctum*, 3; the implied subject is *ego;* for the mood, see the note on *sī*, l. 44. —— **iam**, adv. of time; modifies *intulisset*.

LINE 47. **mihi**, dat. sing. of *ego;* dat. of the indirect obj., dependent on *intulisset*. Many trans. and intrans. compounds of *in, con, prae*, etc., govern a dat. of the indirect object. A. & G. 228; B. 187, III; G. 347; H. 386. —— **cōnsulī**, dat. sing. of *cōnsul, -is*, m. 3d; appositive of *mihi;* *cōnsulī* = a concessive clause, *although I am consul*, cf. *hōc ipsō in templō*, which signifies that even fear of irreverence towards the gods would not have restrained the Senate from doing violence to his person. —— **hōc**, abl. sing. n. of the dem. pron. *hīc, haec, hōc;* agrees with *templō*. —— **ipsō**, abl. sing. n. of the dem. pron. *ipse, ipsa, ipsum;* agrees with *templō;* emphatic. —— **in**, prep.; gov. the abl. *templō*, expressing *place where*. —— **templō**, abl. sing. of *templum, -ī*, n. 2d; governed by the prep. *in*. *Templum* = properly *a section marked out*, esp. for religious observances; hence *templum = the section* of the heavens observed by the augurs for omens; esp. *the section* of ground marked out for a building dedicated to worship of the gods, then of the building itself; cf. *tempus = a section* of time, *tondeō = I shear*, τέμνω = *I cut* (root *tam = to cut*). —— **senātus**, gen. *senātūs*, m. 4th (*senex = old*); nom. sing., subj. of *intulisset; senātus* is here collective, = *senātōrēs*.

LINE 48. **iūre**, abl. sing. of *iūs, iūris*, n. 3d (root *yu = to bind;* cf. *iungō*); abl. of manner, with the attribute *optimō*. *Iūre* is one of a limited number of ablatives that

49 intulisset.   Dē tē autem, Catilīna, cum | in this very temple.
   would have directed. About you   but,   Catiline,   when | But in regard to you,

50 quiēscunt,   probant;   cum   patiuntur, | Catiline, their still-
   they are quiet,   they approve;   when   they suffer, | ness means approval,
                                                            | their acquiescence is

51 dēcernunt;   cum   tacent,   clāmant: neque | their vote, their si-
   they decree;   when they are silent, they cry out: and not | lence is a shout. And

---

express manner adverbially without *cum*. —— **optimō**, abl. sing. n. of *optimus, -a, -um* (superl. of *bonus*); agrees with *iūre*. —— **vim**, acc. sing. of *vīs* (abl. *vī:* gen. and dat. very rare; plur. *vīrēs, -ium,* for *vīsēs;* sing. = *violence,* plur. = *strength*); direct obj. of *intulisset*. Observe that *vim et manūs intulisset = would have laid violence and hands,* i.e. *violent hands;* the expression of a single idea, ordinarily requiring a noun + an adj. or a limiting gen., by two nouns connected by a cop. conj. is called *hendiadys* (ἕν διὰ δυοῖν = *one thing by means of two;* cf. the stock example from Vergil, *pateris libāmus et durō = we pour libations from bowls and gold,* i.e. *from golden bowls.* A. & G. 385; B. 347, 4; G. 698; H. 636, III, 2. —— **et**, cop. conj.; joins *vim* and *manūs*. —— **manūs**, acc. plur. of *manus, -ūs,* f. 4th; direct obj. of *intulisset;* joined by *et* to *vim*.

LINE 49. **intulisset**, 3d pers. sing. pluperf. subjunct. act. of *inferō, īnferre, intulī, illātum,* irreg. (*in + ferō*); agrees with the subj. *senātus;* for the mood, refer to the note on *sī,* l. 44. —— **Dē**, prep.; gov. the abl. *tē.* —— **tē**, abl. sing. of *tū;* governed by the preposition *dē.* —— **autem**, adversative conj.; connects this sentence with the preceding one, and introduces a contrast. —— **Catilīna**, voc. sing. of *Catilīna, -ae,* m. 1st; the case of address. —— **cum**, temporal conj.; followed by the pres. ind. *quiēscunt. Cum,* like all temporal particles, usually takes the ind. mood, but in the imperf. and pluperf. tenses takes the subjunct., because the time of the temporal clause depends on the time of the main clause. When the action in both clauses is coincident, *cum* takes the ind. in all tenses, and *tum* is often added in the principal clause; here the action of *quiēscunt* and *probant* is contemporaneous; cf. below *patiuntur, dēcernunt; tacent, clāmant.* A. & G. 325; B. 288; G. 580-585; H. 521.

LINE 50. **quiēscunt**, 3d pers. plur. pres. ind. act. of *quiēscō, -ere, quiēvī, quiētum,* 2 (inceptive, formed from noun *quiēs = rest, quiet;* root *ki = to lie quiet;* cf. *cīvis,* κεῖμαι = *I lie down*); understand as subj. *eī* or *illī,* referring to *senātus* (= the plur. *senātōrēs*), l. 47. —— **probant**, 3d pers. plur. pres. ind. act. of *probō, -āre, -āvī, -ātum,* 1 (from adj. *probus = good,* hence *I think good, I approve*); understand *illī* or *senātōrēs* as subject. —— **cum**, temporal conj.; with the ind. *patiuntur.* —— **patiuntur**, 3d pers. plur. pres. ind. of the deponent verb *patior, patī, passus sum,* 3; the subject understood is the same as must be supplied with *quiēscunt,* viz. *senātōrēs;* the same subj. is understood with the verbs following.

LINE 51. **dēcernunt**, 3d pers. plur. pres. ind. act. of *dēcernō, -ere, dēcrēvī, dēcrētum,* 3 (*dē + cernō*); understand the subj. *illī,* referring to *senātōrēs* (supplied with *patiuntur*). —— **cum**, temporal conj.; with the ind. *tacent.* —— **tacent**, 3d pers. plur. pres. ind. act. of *taceō, -ēre, -uī, -itum,* 2; understand *senātōrēs* as subject. —— **clāmant**, 3d pers. plur. pres. ind. act. of *clāmō, -āre, -āvī, -ātum,* 1 (root *kal* or *kla = to call;* cf. *calō = I summon,* καλέω = *I call,* κλῆσις = *a call, con-cil-ium,* etc.); understand as subj. *eī* or *illī* referring to *senātōrēs* (the supplied subj. of *tacent*). *Cum tacent, clāmant* is a good example of *oxymoron,* for which consult the note and references under *tacita loquitur,* Chap. VII, l. 44. Observe the climax to which the three *cum* clauses lead: *they approve* of your exile, *they decree it, they shout* to proclaim it. —— **neque** (*ne + que*), copulative coördinating conj.; *que* connects the sentence with the one preceding, and *ne* negatives *hī; neque hī sōlum = et nōn sōlum hī* (*clāmant*).

so it is not only with the senators (whose authority is forsooth so precious to you, though their lives are of no value) but also with yonder noble and respected gen-	hī	sōlum,	quōrum	tibi	auctōritās	est 52
	these men	*only,*	*whose*	*to you*	*authority*	*is*
	vidēlicet	cāra,	vīta	vīlissima,		sed 53
	forsooth	*dear*	*(and whose) life*	*most cheap,*		*but*
	etiam	illī	equitēs	Rōmānī,	honestissimī	atque 54
	also	*those*	*knights*	*Roman,*	*most worthy*	*and*

LINE 52. **hĭ**, nom. plur. m. of the dem. pron. *hĭc, haec, hŏc;* subj. of *clămant* (readily supplied from the context); *hĭ* (*hŏs, hŏrum,* etc.) in this speech = *the senators,* and here there is a contrast between *hĭ* and *equitēs.* —— **sōlum**, adv. (adverbial acc. sing. of *sōlus*); modifies *hĭ*, to which *equitēs* is opposed by *sed etiam* following. See the note on *nŏn*, Chap. VII, l. 49. —— **quōrum**, gen. plur. m. of the rel. pron. *quī, quae, quod;* poss. gen., limiting *auctōritās* and *vīta.* —— **tibi**, dat. sing. of *tū;* dat. of the indirect obj., with *cāra est;* if *tibi* be understood in the clause (*quōrum*) *vīta vīlissima* (*est*), it may be classed as a dat. of personal interest = *in your eyes.* —— **auctōritās**, gen. *auctōritātis*, f. 3d (*auctor*); nom. sing., subj. of *est cāra* in the rel. clause; *auctōritās* = here either *authority* in general, or *authorization*, in allusion to ll. 31–33. —— **est**, 3d pers. sing. pres. ind. of *sum, esse, fuī;* agrees with the subj. *auctōritās; est* must be understood in the next clause with *vīta.*

LINE 53. **vidēlicet**, adv. (for *vidēre licet;* see the note on *vidēlicet,* l. 18); modifies the pred. *cāra est,* and is ironical. Cicero ironically contrasts Catiline's assumed respect for the dignity and authority of the Senate (see ll. 31–33) and his desire to massacre its prominent members (see Chap. I, ll. 19–24). —— **cāra**, nom. sing. f. of the adj. *cārus, -a, -um;* agrees with the subj. *auctōritās,* and is predicative with *est.* —— **vīta**, gen. *vītae*, f. 1st; nom. sing., subj. of the rel. clause (*quōrum*) *vīta vīlissima* (*est*), which is coördinate with the previous clause *quōrum auctōritās . . . est cāra.* Observe the absence of a cop. conj., connecting the two clauses (*asyndeton*), and also the mode of expressing contrast by arranging the principal words of the contrasted clauses in similar order (*anaphora*). A. & G. 344, *f,* I ; B. 350, II, *b* ; G. 682 ; H. no reference. —— **vīlissima**, nom. sing. f. of the adj. *vīlissimus, -a, -um* (superl. of *vīlis, -e,* adj. 3d = *cheap, of small price,* hence sometimes *poor, mean*); agrees with the subj. *vīta* (in the second rel. clause introduced by *quōrum*) and is predicative with *est* (supplied from the first rel. clause *quōrum auctōritās est cāra*). —— **sed**, adversative conj.; joins its own clause with the one preceding. *Nōn sōlum* (*modo* or *tantum*) with one member is regularly followed by an adversative conj., esp. *sed* and *vērum,* + *etiam* or *quoque.* Various combinations are to be found, but *nōn sōlum . . . sed etiam* is by far the most common.

LINE 54. **etiam** (*et + iam*), adv.; *sed etiam* introduces a qualification, esp. after *nōn sōlum* and similar expressions. —— **illī**, nom. plur. m. of the dem. pron. *ille, illa, illud;* agrees with *equitēs; illī* is deictic, and = *the knights yonder,* to whose numbers, as they thronged about the temple-door, Cicero probably drew attention by a gesture. —— **equitēs**, nom. plur. of *eques, -itis,* m. 3d (*equus*); a similar pred. must be supplied with the subj. *equitēs* as with *hĭ* above, viz. any one or all of the principal verbs *probant, dēcernunt, clāmant,* in ll. 50 and 51. Omissions are frequent in Latin, just as they are in most languages, when the word or words missing can be easily supplied from or suggested by the context. —— **Rōmānī**, nom. plur. m. of the adj. *Rōmānus, -a, -um* (*Rōma*); agrees with *equitēs.* —— **honestissimī**, nom. plur. m. of the adj. *honestissimus, -a, -um* (superl. of *honestus, -a, -um,* from *honōs*); agrees with *virī.* Synonyms: *noble* = (I) *nōbilis,* or *generōsus,* with reference to birth; (2) *bonus, honestus, ingenuus, līberālis, generōsus,* with reference to character. —— **atque**, cop. conj.; joins the attributes *honestissimī* and *optimī.*

						tlemen, the Roman knights, and all our other brave fellow-citizens, who surround this assembly — you yourself can see their throning masses, you can note their enthusiasm, and

55 optimī   virī,   cēterīque   fortissimī   cīvēs,
   excellent   *men,*   *and the rest (of the) very brave   citizens*

56 quī   circumstant   senātum,   quōrum   tū   et
   who   *stand around*   *the senate,*   *of whom*   *you both*

57 frequentiam   vidēre   et   studia   perspicere   et
   the throning   *to see*   *and the eagerness   to perceive   and*

LINE 55. **optimī**, nom. plur. m. of the adj. *optimus, -a, -um* (superl. of *bonus*); agrees with *virī*.——**virī**, nom. plur. of *vir, -ī*, m. 2d; appositive of *equitēs*.—— **cēterīque** (*cēterī + que*) : *cēterī* is the nom. plur. m. of the adj. *cēterus, -a, -um* (nom. m. sing. is not used; usually the plur. is found); agrees with *cīvēs*. *Cēterī cīvēs* = the 3d division of the Roman people, as distinguished from the *ōrdinēs* of senators and knights. Synonyms: (1) *cēterī = the others*, implying contrast or comparison ; (2) *reliquī* (*relinquō*) = *the rest*, i.e. those remaining over from an enumeration, e.g. *reliquī decem* = *the remaining ten*; (3) *aliī = others*, but never *the others*. *Cēterus* appears to be derived from the dem. particle *ce* + a pron. corresponding to the Sanskrit *itara = the other ;* cf. Greek ἕτερος. *Que* is the enclitic cop. conj. ; connects *equitēs* and *cīvēs*, which are coördinate in the same construction.—— **fortissimī**, nom. plur. m. of the adj. *fortissimus, -a, -um* (superl. of *fortis, -e*, adj. 3d); agrees with *cīvēs*. *Fortissimī* is a kind of eulogistic commonplace ; cf. *honestissimī atque optimī virī* above.—— **cīvēs**, nom. plur. of *cīvis, -is*, m. and f. 3d (root *ki = ci = to lie*, hence of members of a community engaged in the ordinary routine of undisturbed civic life); joined by *que* to *equitēs ;* a subj. of *probant* (*dēcernunt, clāmant*) understood from above.

LINE 56. **quī**, nom. plur. m. of the rel. pron. *quī, quae, quod;* agrees with the antecedent nouns *equitēs . . . cēterīque cīvēs*, and is subj. of *circumstant*. The temple of Juppiter, it will be remembered, was surrounded by a dense multitude of *equitēs* and loyal citizens, whose intention was to protect the consul and the Senate from harm, if (as seemed probable) the conspirators made an armed attack upon the meeting; cf. Chap. I, l. 8, *hīc mūnītissimus habendī senātūs locus.*—— **circumstant**, 3d pers. plur. pres. ind. act. of *circumstō, -āre, circumstetī*, no supine, 1 (*circum = around* + *stō = I stand*); agrees with the subj. *quī*. Many intrans. verbs (like *stō, eō*, etc.), when compounded with *ad, ante, ob, circum, trāns*, etc., become trans., and may be used either absolutely or with a direct obj. in the acc. case; cf. *illa . . . praetereō*, Chap. I, l. 35. A. & G. 228, *a* ; B. 175, 2, *a* ; G. 331 ; H. 372.—— **senātum**, acc. sing. of *senātus, -ūs*, m. 4th; direct obj. of *circumstant; senātum* here = the place of meeting.—— **quōrum**, gen. plur. m. of the rel. pron. *quī, quae, quod;* agrees with the antecedents *equitēs cīvēsque*, and is a poss. gen. limiting *frequentiam, studia*, and *vōcēs*. Observe that in Latin (as in English), two coördinate rel. clauses preferably stand unconnected by a cop. conjunction ; so the clauses of *quī* and *quōrum* in this passage.—— **tū**, gen. *tuī ;* nom. sing., subj. of *potuistī ; tū* is emphatic.—— **et**, cop. conj. ; used correlatively with *et* below ; *et . . . et = both . . . and.*

LINE 57. **frequentiam**, acc. sing. of *frequentia, -ae*, f. 1st (root *bhark*, or *bhrak* = φρακ = *farc, frequ, to cram, to shut in fast;* cf. φράσσω = *I fence in, farciō = I stuff, cōnfertus* and *frequēns = crowded*); direct obj of *vidēre*.—— **vidēre**, pres. inf. act. of *videō, -ēre, vīdī, vīsum*, 2 ; complementary inf., completing the predication with *potuistī*, or with the pres. *potes* (understood from *potuistī*).—— **et**, cop. conj. ; connects the objective complementary infinitives *vidēre* and *perspicere*.—— **studia**, acc. plur. of *studium, -ī*, n. 2d (*studeō*); direct obj. of *perspicere*.—— **perspicere**, pres. inf. act. of *perspiciō, -ere, perspēxī, perspectum*, 3 (*per + speciō*, hence *I see clearly*); complementary inf.,

a short while ago you yourself could distinctly hear their voices. These same men, whose hands and weapons I have for a long time scarcely been able to keep off from you, I	vōcēs *the voices*	paulō *a little*	ante *before*	exaudīre *to hear clearly*	potuistī. 58 *(you) were able.*
	Quōrum *Whose*	ego *I*	vix *scarcely*	abs *from*	tē iam *you already*	diū 59 *for a long time*
	manūs *hands*	ac *and*	tēla *weapons*	contineō, *(I) am holding back,*	eōsdem 60 *(these) same men*

with *potuistī*, or with the pres. *potes* understood.——**et**, cop. conj. ; connects the objective complementary infinitives *perspicere* and *exaudīre*.

LINE 58. **vōcēs**, acc. plur. of *vōx, vōcis*, f. 3d ; direct obj. of *exaudīre;* the allusion may be to bursts of applause from those knights who caught Cicero's remarks from time to time, e.g. when Cicero bade Catiline retire into exile. —— **paulō**, adverbial abl. neut. sing. of the adj. *paulus, -a, -um* (*paullus*); abl. of measure of difference, modifying *ante*. This abl. is employed with comparative adjectives and adverbs, and with *ante* and *post* (which imply comparison); cf. *dīmidiō minor*. —— **ante**, adv. (cf. *anteā; ante* is more common as a prep. + the acc.); limits *exaudīre*. *Paulō ante* may be a reference to the time when Catiline was on his way to the senate; or it may refer to some dramatic episode in the course of the speech. At any rate a considerable body of citizens, gathered at the open folding-doors of the temple, followed the proceedings and acquainted the rest of the crowd outside with what was occurring within. —— **exaudīre**, pres. inf. act. of *exaudiō, -ire, -īvī, -ītum*, 4 (*ex + audiō*); complementary inf., with *potuistī*. Synonyms : (1) *audīre = to hear*, in general ; *audīre aliquem = to hear some one ; audīre ex* (*ab*) *aliquō = to hear something from some one* ; (2) *exaudīre = to hear plainly*, in spite of the distance of the sound or the low pitch of voice, etc. ; (3) *auscultāre* (probably = *ausicultāre*, from *ausicula = auricula = the external ear*) + dat. *alicuī = to listen attentively to any one*. —— **potuistī**, 2d pers. sing. perf. ind. act. of *possum, posse, potuī*, no supine, irreg. ; agrees with the emphatic subj. *tū*, l. 56 ; *potuistī* is the verb of the rel. clause with *quōrum*. Possibly *potes* is to be supplied with *vidēre* and *perspicere*, while *potuistī* alone goes with *paulō ante exaudīre;* see the marginal translation. *Possum* is a verb which suggests a further action of the same subject, and is therefore assisted in its predication by a complementary or epexegetical inf., e.g. *vidēre, perspicere, exaudīre*.

LINE 59. **Quōrum**, gen. plur. m. of the rel. pron. *quī, quae, quŏd;* agrees with the antecedent *eōsdem*, and is a poss. gen. limiting *manūs* and *tēla*. When special emphasis is to be thrown on the principal sentence, the rel. clause stands out of its logical position and precedes the main clause. —— **ego**, gen. *meī;* nom. sing., subj. of *contineō; ego* is emphatic. —— **vix**, adv. ; limits *contineō*. Distinguish : (1) *vix* is objective and negative, = *almost not, scarcely;* hence may often be used for *nōn*, e.g. *dīcī vix potest = it can scarcely be said;* (2) *aegrē* (adv. from *aeger*) = *scarcely, with trouble*, subjective, i.e. with reference to the person who feels troubled ; e.g. *aegrē ferō = I bear with difficulty, I chafe under; aegrē* is affirmative. —— **abs** (a form of *ā, ab*), prep. ; gov. the abl. *tē*, expressing separation, in dependence on *contineō*. *Abs* is common with *tē;* in composition, *abs* is used before the letters *c, q, t*, and *p*. —— **tē**, abl. sing. of *tū;* governed by the prep. *abs*. —— **iam**, adv. of time ; strengthens *diū;* cf. *iam dūdum, iam nunc*, etc. —— **diū**, adv. of time ; modifies *contineō*.

LINE 60. **manūs**, acc. plur. of *manus, -ūs*, f. 4th; direct obj. of *contineō*. —— **ac**, cop. conj., connects *manūs* and *tēla*. —— **tēla**, acc. plur. of *tēlum, -ī*, n. 2d ; direct obj. of *contineō*. *Tēlum* = lit. *a hitting thing*, hence (1) *a missile*, esp. *spear, dart, arrow*, etc. ; (2) *a weapon, sword*, etc., held in the hand. The old derivation from τῆλε

						shall without difficulty induce to escort you all the way to the city-gates, on condition only that you leave this city and neighborhood which you have long since been eager to bring to ruin.
61 facile	addūcam	ut	tē	haec,		quae	
easily	*I will persuade*	*that*	*you*	*this (neighborhood),*		*which*	
62 vāstāre		iam		prīdem		studēs,	
to ravage		*already*		*long since*		*you are eager,*	
63 relinquentem			ūsque		ad	portās	
leaving (=if you leave)			*as far as*		*to*	*the city-gates*	
64 prōsequantur.							
they attend.							

= *afar* (hence *missile*, i.e. as hurled from afar) is no longer accepted; so some derive from *tendō* (which = *I hurl* in poetry), as if for *tend-lum;* but the most likely derivation is from the Ind.-Eur. root *tak* or *tuk* = (1) *to hit*, (2) *to prepare*, (3) *to generate*, i.e. *tēlum* = *tec-lum*, cf. Greek τόξον = *a bow*. —— **contineō**, 1st pers. sing. pres. ind. act. of *contineō, -ēre, -uī, contentum,* 2 (*con + teneō*); agrees with the subj. *ego. Contineō* is the *historic* pres., regular with *iam diū, iam dūdum,* etc., which is used when action begun in the past continues into the present; see the references under *hortor,* Chap. V, l. 45. The indicatives *contineō* and *addūcam* give a proper balance to the antithesis; otherwise we might have expected a concessive subjunct. *contineam* = *although I am only with difficulty keeping off,* etc. (see the note on *quī,* l. 13). —— **eōsdem**, acc. plur. of *īdem, eadem, idem,* determinative pron.; antecedent of *quōrum* and direct obj. of *addūcam; eōsdem* is more emphatic than *eōs* would be, and marks the antithesis between *vix contineō manūs* and *addūcam ut prōsequantur.*

LINE 61. **facile,** adv. (in origin the acc. sing. n. of the adj. *facilis, -e,* 3d); modifies *addūcam.* —— **addūcam**, 1st pers. sing. fut. ind. act. of *addūcō, -ere, addūxī, adductum,* 3 (*ad + dūcō*); the subj. *ego* is implied by the personal ending. —— **ut,** conj.; followed by the subjunct. *prōsequantur* in the substantive clause of purpose dependent on *addūcam.* Verbs of *willing, desiring, persuading, warning, exhorting,* etc., are followed by the final subjunctive, with *ut* or *nē.* A. & G. 331; B. 295, 1; G. 546, esp. NOTE 1; H. 498, I. —— **tē,** acc. sing. of *tū;* direct obj. of *prōsequantur.* —— **haec,** acc. plur. n. of the dem. pron. *hīc, haec, hōc;* direct obj. of *relinquentem; haec* = *all this,* i.e. Rome and all the neighborhood. —— **quae,** acc. plur. n. of the rel. pron. *quī, quae, quod;* agrees with the antecedent *haec,* and is direct obj. of *vāstāre.*

LINE 62. **vāstāre,** pres. inf. act. of *vāstō, -āre, -āvī, -ātum,* 1 (= to make *vāstus,* i.e. *desolate; vāstus* is akin to *vacuus* = *empty*); complementary inf. with *studēs.* —— **iam,** temporal adv., strengthening *prīdem;* cf. *iam diū,* etc. —— **prīdem** (from a root *pra* = *before;* cf. Greek πρό, πρίν, and Latin *prae, prīmus, princeps*), adv. of time; limits *studēs.* With *iam prīdem +* the *historic* pres. *studēs,* cf. the similar Greek construction πάλαι ἤδη ἐπιθυμεῖ. —— **studēs,** 2d pers. sing. pres. ind. act. of *studeō, -ēre, uī,* no supine, 2; the subj. *tū* is implied by the personal ending.

LINE 63. **relinquentem,** acc. sing. m. of *relinquēns, -entis,* pres. part. act. of *relinquō, -ere, relīquī, relictum,* 3 (*re = behind + linquō = I leave*); agrees with and extends *tē,* the obj. of *prōsequantur.* The part. *relinquentem* represents a disguised condition, = *addūcam ut tē, sī haec, quae vāstāre iam prīdem studēs, relinquere volēs, ūsque ad portās prōsequantur.* A. & G. 310; B. 305; G. 600; H. 507, 1–3. —— **ūsque,** adv. of extent in space (or time); modifies the adverbial phrase *ad portās;* see the note on *ūsque,* Chap. I, l. 1. —— **ad,** prep.; gov. the acc. *portās,* expressing *motion to.* —— **portās,** acc. plur. of *porta, -ae,* f. 1st; governed by the prep. *ad.* For synonyms, and note on the gates of Rome, refer to the note on *portae,* Chap. V, l. 3.

LINE 64. **prōsequantur,** 3d pers. plur. pres. subjunct. of the deponent verb *prōsequor, prōsequī, prōsecūtus sum,* 3 (*prō + sequor*); understand as subj. a pron. *eī* or *illī*

IX. And yet, what	IX.	Quamquam		quid		loquor ? 1
use is there in my		*And yet*		*why*		*do I speak?*
talking? Just imag-						
ine anything forcing	tē		ut	ūlla	rēs	frangat ? 2
you into subjection,	*(is it possible) you*		*that*	*any*	*thing*	*may crush?*

(referring to the persons indicated by *eōsdem*, l. 60). The subjunct. is final with *ut;*
see note on *ut.* See the note on *adsequeris,* Chap. VI, l. 49, for a comparison of the
different means which *sequor* assumes in composition with different prepositions. *Prōsequī = to escort,* usually in a good sense: so here Cicero means that the city will be so
glad to get rid of him that just before he starts off it will be almost friendly to him, and
accord him the honor of an escort (such as a man's friends were accustomed to give him
when departing on a long journey).

LINE 1. **Quamquam** (*quam + quam*), conj., = *and yet;* connects the sentence
with the one preceding, and has the force of an adversative conjunction. Observe that
quamquam (and *etsī* also, but less often) may be used purely as a copulative conj.;
usually it is a subordinate conj., used in concessive clauses, = *although,* and followed by
the ind. mood. See the note on *quamquam,* Chap. V, l. 29. —— **quid,** adverbial acc.
sing. n. of the interrog. pron. *quis, quae, quid;* here and in similar cases *quid* is practically an interrog. adv. = *cūr, why?* Originally the feeling of the case was present to
consciousness, and *quid* was an acc. of the inner object (closely akin to the cognate
acc.), e.g. *quid glōriāris = what* (boasting) *do you boast? = what does your boasting
mean?* or *why do you boast?* —— **loquor,** 1st pers. sing. pres. ind. of the deponent verb
loquor, loquī, locūtus sum, 3; the subj. *ego* is implied by the personal ending.

LINE 2. **tē,** acc. sing. of *tū;* direct obj. of *frangat.* The usual position of the
direct object is between the subject and the verb, e.g. *ut ūlla rēs tē frangat,* but *tē* is
here spoken with great emphasis and scorn. —— **ut,** conj.; introducing the exclamatory
question *tē . . . frangat.* NOTE. The construction *ut* + the subjunct. in exclamatory
questions is variously explained: (1) some think that *ut* is final and the subjunct.
denotes *purpose,* and that the *ut* clause depends on a preceding sentence, e.g. *and yet
why do I speak?* (is it) *in order that anything may crush you?* The interrogative form
of the *ut* clause would thus mark the impossibility of the action suggested; (2) Allen and
Greenough and others regard the construction as elliptical, and regard *ut* as the consecutive
conj. + the consecutive subjunct., in a substantive clause of result dependent on some phrase
or idea which may be supplied, e.g. (*spērandumne sit fore*) *ut ūlla rēs tē frangat? = can
it be expected that anything will crush you?* In the words supplied *sit,* the deliberative
subjunct., seems to be more suitable to the idea of the question than the ind. *est.* The
above may very well be the origin of the construction; (3) some think the question is
an indirect one, dependent on a principal verb understood, e.g. (*I do not know*) *how
anything will ever crush you;* but this explanation of the construction is not satisfactory;
(4) Gildersleeve and Harkness agree in thinking that the construction is not elliptical,
but the former classifies under the head of Consecutive Sentences. Harkness renders *ut*
as *how,* and considers the subjunct. potential, = *how should anything subdue you?* The
last seems to be the preferable explanation. A. & G. 332, *c*; B. 277, *a*; G. 558;
H. 486, II, NOTE. Frequently exclamatory questions with *ut* are accompanied by the
interrog. particle *-ne* (inserted and appended to one of the emphatic words), e.g. *egone
ut mentiar?* (Plautus) = *that I should speak falsely!* Observe that the question asks
not what *is the case,* but what *might be the case,* and that a negative answer is always implied; moreover, the question expresses great indignation or surprise. The force of the
exclamation is exactly like that of the exclamatory acc. and inf., cf. Vergil, *Aen.* I, l. 37,
Mēne inceptō dēsistere victam? = must I retire from my purpose baffled? So here

3 tū	ut	umquam	tē	corrigās?	tū	you ever reforming
you	*that*	*ever*	*yourself*	*may improve?*	*you*	your character, you
4 ut	ūllam	fugam	meditēre?	tū ut	ūllum	giving even so much as a thought to exile
that	*any*	*flight*	*may consider?*	*you that*	*any*	or having any kind
5 exsilium		cōgitēs?	Utinam	tibi	istam	of notion of banish-
exile		*may meditate?*	*Would that*	*to you*	*that*	ment! Ah, if only

Cicero might have said, *tēne ūllam rem frangere = is anything likely to crush you?* A. & G. 274; B. 334; G. 534; H. 539, III.——ūlla, nom. sing. f. of the adj. *ūllus, -a, -um* (gen. *ullīus,* dat. *ūllī*); agrees with *rēs*. *Ullus* is only used in negative sentences, or those implying total negation; cf. the note on *ūllā*, Chap. VII, l. 35. Here *ūlla* is properly used, because the exclamatory question is equivalent to an indignant and emphatic negative statement.——rēs, gen. *reī*, f. 5th; nom. sing., subj. of *frangat*.——frangat, 3d pers. sing. pres. subjunct. act. of *frangō, -ere, frēgī, fractum,* 3 (root *bhrag* = *to break;* cf. root *ϝραγ,* and *ῥήγνυμι = I break*); agrees with the subj. *rēs;* the subjunct. follows *ut* in the idiomatic construction discussed in the note on *ut* above.

LINE 3. tū, gen. *tuī;* nom. sing., subj. of *corrigās*. Like *tē* above, *tū* is very emphatic, YOU *ever reform yourself!*——ut, conj., followed by the subjunct. *corrigās,* in exclamatory question; the construction is similar to that of the line above.——umquam (*unquam*), adv.; modifies *corrigās;* the force of *umquam* in this sentence is parallel to that of *ulla* in the preceding sentence.——tē, acc. sing. of *tū;* direct obj. (reflexive) of *corrigās*.——corrigās, 2d pers. sing. pres. subjunct. act. of *corrigō, -ere, cor-rēxī, corrēctum,* 3 (*cum + regō*); agrees with the subj. *tū;* for the subjunct., see the note on *ut,* l. 2.——tū, nom. sing.; subj. of *meditēre;* emphatic. Observe the repetition of *tū* at the beginning of each question (*anaphora*); the exclamatory questions thus emphasized are far more forcible than would be denunciatory statements, and well illustrate Cicero's mastery of rhetoric and his skill in driving a point home.

LINE 4. ut, conj., introducing an exclamatory question, exactly as above.——ūllam, acc. sing. of the adj. *ūllus, -a, -um;* agrees with *fugam; ūllam* (like *ūlla* above) implies complete negation, *you think of exile indeed!*——fugam, acc. sing. of *fuga, -ae,* f. 1st (root *bhug* = *φυγ* = *fug, to turn one's self, to flee;* cf. *φυγή = flight, exile, fugiō, fugō,* etc.); direct obj. of *meditēre. Fugam* is here a synonym of *exsilium; φυγή* is the regular word for *exile* in Greek literature.——meditēre, 2d pers. sing. pres. subjunct. of the deponent verb *meditor, -ārī, -ātus sum,* 1; agrees with the subj. *tū;* the subjunct. mood is in similar construction with *corrigās* and *frangat* above. In this oration Cicero uses the termination in *-re* twice in the pres. subjunct., and that in *-ris* once; for a comparison with other tenses, refer to the note on *verēbere,* Chap. VII, l. 41.——tū, nom. sing.; subj. of *cōgitēs;* emphatic.——ut, conj., introducing an exclamatory question, exactly as in the sentences above.——ūllum, acc. sing. n. of the adj. *ūllus, -a, -um;* agrees with *exsilium*.

LINE 5. exsilium, acc. sing. of *exsilium, -ī,* n. 2d; direct obj. of *cōgitēs*. See the note on *exsilium,* Chap. V, l. 53.——cōgitēs, 2d pers. sing. pres. subjunct. act. of *cōgitō, -āre, -āvī, -ātum,* 1 (*con + agitō,* hence *to turn over and over in the mind, to ponder upon*); agrees with the subj. *tū;* the subjunct. is in similar construction to *corrigās* and *frangat* above.——Utinam (*utī + nam*), adv. = *oh that! would that!* introduces a wish with the pres. subjunct. *duint* for the future. In wishes the optative or volitive subjunct. is always used, with or without the introductory particles *ut* (*utī*) *ō sī* (rare), *utinam*. The regular negative particle is *nē,* e.g. *nē fiat = may it not happen!* Sometimes a second wish may be added by *neque* (rare in classical Latin, and never in Caesar). *Utinam nē* and *utinam nōn* are both found. The pres. subjunct. of the verb

the immortal gods	mentem	dī	immortālēs	duint !	Tametsī 6
would put such an	*intention*	*the gods*	*immortal*	*may give !*	*Although*
idea into your head !	videō,	sī	meā	vōce	perterritus	īre in 7
Although, if from ter-	*I see,*	*if*	*my*	*by voice*	*frightened*	*to go into*
ror at my words you						

is used when the wish, no matter how extravagant, is for the future; the imperf. sub-junct., when the wish is for the present, and therefore unrealized; the pluperf. subjunct., when the wish is expressed for the past, and consequently also unrealized. A. & G. 267; B. 279; G. 260, 261; H. 483. —— **tibi**, dat. sing. of *tū*; indirect obj. of *duint*. —— **istam**, acc. sing. of *iste, ista, istud*, dem. pron. of the 2d pers.; agrees with *mentem;* observe that *istam* does not have the implication of scorn which *iste* usually has in the orations; see the note on *iste*, Chap. I, l. 3.

LINE 6.   **mentem**, acc. sing. of *mēns, mentis*, f. 3d; direct obj. of *duint*. —— **dī**, nom. plur. of *deus, -ī*, m. 2d (cf. *diēs, Iuppiter*, etc.); subj. of *duint*. The voc. sing. of *deus* is the same as the nom. sing.; in the plur. are found nom. *deī, diī*, and *dī* (con-traction of *diī*), gen. *deōrum* and *deūm*, dat. and abl. *deīs, diīs, dīs*, acc. *deōs*. —— **im-mortālēs**, nom. plur. m. of the adj. *immortālis, -e*, 3d (*in = not + mortālis = mortal*, from *mors*); agrees with *dī*. —— **duint**, 3d pers. plur. pres. subj. act. of an obsolete verb *duō* (perhaps an archaic form of *dō, I give*, but by many referred to some other root); agrees with the subj. *dī;* the subjunct. is optative with *utinam*, and the pres. tense marks the wish as one for the future. *Duim, duis, duit*, and *duint* are archaic survivals, found in solemn oaths or attestations, in legal formulae, and in the comic writers Plautus and Terence. For the letter *i* as the characteristic vowel (instead of the usual *a*), cf. the pres. subjunctives *sim* (of *sum*), *velim* (of *volō*), *nōlim* (of *nōlō*), *mālim* (of *mālō*), *possim* (of *possum*), etc. In ordinary phraseology *dent* (3d pers. plur. pres. subjunct. act. of *dō, dare, dedī, datum*, 1) would have been used. A. & G. 128, *e*; B. 116, 4, *d*; G. 130, 4; H. 240, 3. —— **Tametsī** (for *tamen etsī*), conj., used copulatively; connects the sentence with the one preceding, and adds adversative force to its own clause. Some take *tametsī* as a subordinate conj., = *although*, and introducing the clause *tametsī . . . impendeat* in concessive subordination to the main clause *utinam . . . duint;* but it is better to render *tametsī* as *and yet*, or *however*, connecting two principal sentences; cf. *quamquam* and *etsī*, which must frequently be considered as copulative.

LINE 7.   **videō**, 1st pers. pres. ind. act. of *videō, -ēre, vīdī, vīsum*, 2; the subj. *ego* is implied by the personal ending. —— **sī**, conditional particle, introducing the *protasis* of the condition *sī . . . impendeat*. Observe that the condition is reported in the form of an indirect exclamation dependent on *videō*. The direct form of the hypothesis = *sī . . . animum indūxeris* (fut. perf. ind.), *quanta tempestās . . . impendet = if you (shall) make up your mind*, etc. . . . , *how great a storm . . . threatens*, i.e. the apodo-sis is an exclamation, and so, in dependence on *videō*, may perhaps be better described as an indirect exclamation than an indirect question (the construction being identical in both cases; see the references under *ēgeris*, Chap. I, l. 14). For indirect conditions, see the note and references under *sī*, Chap. VIII, l. 31. —— **meā**, abl. sing. f. of the poss. adj. *meus, -a, -um;* agrees with *vōce*. —— **vōce**, abl. sing. of *vōx, vōcis*, f. 3d; abl. of the means or instrument, with *perterritus*. —— **perterritus**, nom. sing. m. of *perterritus, -a, -um*, perf. part. pass. of *perterreō, -ēre, -uī, -itum*, 2 (*per* intensive + *terreō = I frighten greatly;* cf. *permoveō, perfacilis*, etc.); predicative, agreeing with the implied subj. of *indūxeris*, viz. *tū*. Observe that the part. here takes the place of a clause coördinate with *sī indūxeris* and a cop. conj., e.g. *sī perterritus sīs et . . . animum indūxeris;* in such cases the part. always denotes action prior in time to that of the verb of the clause in which it stands, and serves to weld the sentence closer together in respect of unity and logical subordination. A. & G. 292, REM.; B. 336, 3; 337, 2; G. 437; H. 549, 5. ——

8	exsilium	animum	indūxeris,	quanta	make up your mind
	exile	*your mind*	*you shall make up,*	*how great*	to withdraw into ex-
9	tempestās	invidiae	nōbīs,	sī minus in	ile, I see how violent
	a storm	*of ill-will*	*over us,*	*if less (= not) for*	a storm of ill-will
					threatens to burst
10	praesēns	tempus,	recentī	memoriā scelerum	over me, if not at
	present	*the time,*	*(being) fresh*	*the memory of crimes*	the present moment

īre, pres. inf. act. of *eō, īre, īvī, iī, itum,* irreg.; complementary inf. in the pred. with *animum indūxeris* and expressing the further action of the same subject which *animum indūxeris* implies. Many kinds of verbs imply a further action of the same subject, and are followed by the inf. alone without a subj.-acc., e.g. verbs of *knowing, daring, seeming, learning, beginning, ceasing,* etc. A. & G. 271; B. 326; G. 423; H. 533.——in, prep.; gov. the acc. *exsilium.*

LINE 8. **exsilium,** acc. sing. of *exsilium, -ī,* n. 2d; governed by the prep. *in.*——**animum,** acc. sing. of *animus, -ī,* m. 2d; direct obj. of *indūxeris. Animum indūcere* is an idiom = lit. *to bring one's mind to* something, and may be rendered in English idiom by *to make up one's mind.* The noun *animus* figures in several idiomatic expressions, which may be readily studied in a reliable dictionary. For synonyms, see the note on *animō,* Chap. VII, l. 18.——**indūxeris,** 2d pers. sing. perf. subjunct. act. of *indūcō, -ere, indūxī, inductum,* 3 (*in + dūcō*); the subj. implied is *tū; indūxeris* is subjunct. because the hypothesis is indirect in form and dependent on the leading verb *videō,* and the tense is primary because *video* is primary; see the note on *sī* above.——**quanta,** nom. sing. f. of the adj. *quantus, -a, -um* (used as interrog., and as rel. often with correlative *tantus;* cf. *tam . . . quam, tālis . . . quālis*); agrees with *tempestās* and introduces the *apodosis* of the condition (*quanta . . . impendeat*), which is in the form of an indirect exclamation.

LINE 9. **tempestās,** gen. *tempestātis,* f. 3d (akin to *tempus,* from root *tam = to cut;* so *tempestās = a portion of time, a period,* in respect of its physical qualities, hence *weather, storm,* and figuratively *calamity*); nom. sing., subj. of *impendeat.* The metaphor, *a storm of unpopularity,* is a familiar one in English, as in Latin.——**invidiae,** gen. sing. of *invidia,* f. 1st (from the adj. *invidus,* cf. *invideō = I envy*); gen. of material, explaining of what the *tempestās* consists. A. & G. 214; B. 197, 202; G. 361; H. 395.——**nōbīs,** dat. plur. of *ego* (plur. *nōs*); dat. of the indirect obj., governed by the compound of *in, impendeat.* Intransitive verbs, compounded with *in, con, prae,* and other prepositions, frequently govern a dat. of the indirect object. A. & G. 228; B. 187, III; G. 347; H. 386. Observe that *nōbīs* is used instead of *mihi;* such pluralizing is rhetorical, and begins with Cicero; it is common in English in official references to one's self, cf. the royal or the editorial *we;* an excellent Latin example is the following (from Cicero): *librum ad tē dē senectūte mīsimus = we* (i.e. *I*) *have sent you a treatise on old age.* A. & G. 98, *b;* B. 187, II, *a;* G. 204, NOTE 7; H. 446, NOTE 2.——**sī,** conditional particle; *sī minus* is often used without the verb being expressed, but the omission can always be easily supplied from the context; so here we may supply *impendeat* with *sī minus* (= *impendet* of direct condition). Refer to the notes on *sī minus,* Chap. V, l. 6.——**minus,** adv., practically = *not;* modifies *impendeat,* which may be supplied with *sī. Minus* is the acc. neut. sing. of *minor, minus,* adj. 3d, compar. of *parvus;* superl. *minimus.*——**in,** prep.; gov. the acc. *tempus.*

LINE 10. **praesēns,** acc. sing. n. of *praesēns, -entis,* pres. part. of *praesum;* agrees adjectively with *tempus. Sum* and its compounds have no pres. part., except *praesum* and *absum,* which have *praesēns* and *absēns.*——**tempus,** acc. sing. of *tempus, temporis,* n. 3d (root *tam = to cut,* hence *a section of time;* cf. τέμνω = *I cut*); governed by the

while the recollec-	tuōrum,	at	in	posteritātem	impendeat. 11
tion of your crimes					
is fresh, at all events	your,	however	for	the future time	may overhang.
at a future period.					
But the risk is worth	Sed	est	tantī,	dum modo	ista 12
the price, provided	But	it is	of so much (worth),	provided that	that

prep. *in.* Synonyms: (1) *tempus = time,* in general; the plur. *tempora = the times,* i.e. the circumstances of the time, e.g. *in the time of Augustus = temporibus* (not *tempore*) *Augusti ;* (2) *tempestās = a point* or *a space of time, a period ;* (3) *aevum* (poetical)*= a lifetime, an age, a generation ;* cf. *διών = διϝών, a lifetime,* and the English word *aeon ;* (4) *aetās* (contracted from *aevitās*) *= a period of life, an epoch.*——**recentī,** abl. sing. f. of the adj. *recēns, -entis,* 3d; *recentī* is predicative, and agrees with *memoriā* in the abl. abs. construction; as regularly when an adj. agrees predicatively with a noun or pronoun in this construction, the abl. of the missing pres. part. of *sum* may be mentally understood, i.e. *the memory of your crimes (being) fresh = while the recollection of your crimes is fresh in the mind.*   For a full note on the abl. absolute, see the note on *dimissō,* Chap. IV, l. 38.   Synonyms: (1) *novus* (opposed to *antīquus*)*= new,* in reference to not having been before ; cf. *rēs nova = a novelty ; novus homō = an upstart* politically, i.e. the first of a family to hold curule office ; (2) *recēns* (opposed to *vetus = of old standing*)*= fresh, new,* in reference to recent occurrence for the first time; e.g. *recēns lac = fresh milk ; recentēs cōpiae = fresh troops,* which must be distinguished from *novī mīlitēs = new troops,* i.e. *recruits.*——**memoriā,** abl. sing. of *memoriā, -ae,* f. 1st (from adj. *memor,* root *smar = μερ, μαρ = mor, to keep in mind ;* cf. *μέριμνα = anxious thought, μαρτύρομαι = I call to witness*); agrees with *recentī* in the abl. abs. construction.—— **scelerum,** gen. plur. of *scelus, sceleris,* n. 3d; objective gen., with *memoriā.*   Nouns and adjectives expressing agency often take the gen. case.   A. & G. 217; B. 200; G. 363, 2; H. 396, III.

LINE 11. **tuōrum,** gen. plur. n. of the poss. adj. *tuus, -a, -um ;* agrees with *scelerum.*——**at,** conj.; introduces the qualification *in posteritātem,* in opposition to *in praesēns tempus* in the *sī* clause above.   *At* is here used in the *apodosis* like δέ in the *apodosis* of a Greek sentence.——**in,** prep.; gov. the acc. *posteritātem ; in* + the acc. in reference to time *= for.*——**posteritātem,** acc. sing. of *posteritās, -ātis,* f. 3d; governed by the prep. *in.   In posteritātem = in posterum tempus ; posteritās* (from *posterus,* from *post*) *= (1) future time,* hence (2) *people of a future age, posterity.*——**impendeat,** 3d pers. sing. pres. subjunct. act. of *impendeō, -ēre,* no perf., no supine, 2 (*in = upon + pendeō = I hang,* intrans.); agrees with the subj. *tempestās ;* the verb is subjunct., because *quanta* introduces an indirect exclamation in dependence on *videō.*   Observe that *quanta . . . impendeat* is the *apodosis* of the indirect condition, of which *sī . . . indūxeris* is the *protasis.*

LINE 12. **Sed,** adversative conj.; joins the sentence to the one preceding, and introduces an idea in opposition.——**est,** 3d pers. sing. pres. ind. of *sum, esse, fuī ;* the subj. of *est tantī* is understood, viz. an acc. and inf. clause such as *tempestātem istam invidiae mihi impendēre = it is worth while (that this storm of hatred should threaten me),* if only, etc.——**tantī,** gen. sing. n. of the adj. *tantus, -a, -um ;* *tantī* is predicative with *est,* and is a gen. of value *= it is of so much value,* i.e. *it is worth while.*   When definite value or cost is stated, the abl. is used, e.g. *vīgintī talentīs vēndidit = he sold it for twenty talents ;* the gen. expresses indefinite or general value or cost, and the gen. neut. sing. of several adjectives is found, e.g. *magnī, parvī, nihilī, minimī, plūris,* etc.   A. and G. 252, *a ;* B. 203, 3-5; G. 380; H. 404, 405.   The gen. of value or cost is an extension of the regular gen. of quality.   But observe that *est tantī* is always used with the sense of *operae pretium est = it is worth while ;* cf. a similar passage in II, Chap. VII, *Est mihi tantī,*

13 sit	privāta	calamitās	et	ā	only such disaster be
may be	*private*	*disaster*	*and*	*from*	mine alone and do

14 reī pūblicae	perīculīs	sēiungātur.	Sed
of the commonwealth	*the perils*	*may be divided.*	*But*

not involve the state
in any peril. How-
ever, it is quite out
of the question to

15 tū	ut	vitiīs	tuīs	commoveāre,	ut	lēgum
you	*that*	*by vices*	*your*	*should be startled,*	*that*	*of the laws*

expect you, you, I

Quirītēs, hūius invidiae falsae atque inīquae tempestātem subīre. —— **dum**, conditional conj.; regularly followed by the subjunct. *sit* and *sēiungātur*. A proviso may be introduced by *dum* alone, or by *modo* alone, or by *dum modo* (*dummodo*) in combination; the negative is *dum nē*, or *modo nē*. A. & G. 314; B. 310; G. 573; H. 513, 1. The verb, according to the sense, is either pres. or imperf. subjunctive. —— **modo**, adv. = *only*, in combination with the conj. *dum*. *Modo* is often used alone as a conditional conj.; cf. *modo . . . intersit,* Chap. V, l. 8. —— **ista**, nom. sing. f. of the dem. pron. of the 2d pers. *iste, ista, istud;* agrees with *calamitās = that misfortune* (of which *you* are the cause).

LINE 13. **sit**, 3d pers. sing. pres. subjunct. of *sum, esse, fuī;* agrees with the subj. *ista calamitās;* the subjunct. mood is necessary after *dum modo.* —— **prīvāta**, nom. sing. f. of the adj. *prīvātus, -a, -um* (properly perf. part. pass. of *prīvō*); complement in the pred. with *sit*, and agrees with the subj. *calamitās.* *Prīvāta = personal,* i.e. affecting only Cicero, and that purely as an individual, and not in any way involving the state; cf. the proviso in the following coördinate clause. Refer to the note on *pūblicī,* Chap. I, l. 20. —— **calamitās**, gen. *calamitātis* f. 3d (from *calamus = straw* or *a reed,* hence lit. *damage to the crop,* then *loss, misfortune,* in general); nom. sing., subj. of *sit.* *Calamitās* in Cicero almost invariably expresses *political misfortune* or *ruin,* very seldom *calamity* or *misfortune* in the general sense. See the synonyms given in the note under *calamitāte,* Chap. V, l. 30. It may be here pointed out that *to suffer loss* is expressed in Latin by *damnum facere, iactūram facere, calamitātem accipere* (not by *damnum,* etc., *patī = to submit to loss*), the particular noun being selected according to the nature of the damage, for which see the list of synonyms. —— **et**, cop. conj.; joins *sit prīvāta* and *sēiungātur.* —— **ā**, prep. with the abl.; gov. *perīculīs,* expressing separation in combination with the verb *sēiungātur.*

LINE 14. **reī**, gen. sing. of *rēs,* f. 5th; poss. gen. limiting *perīculīs;* in English we would rather say *peril to the state.* —— **pūblicae**, gen. sing. f. of the adj. *pūblicus, -a, -um* (for derivation, etc., see *pūblicī* and note, Chap. I, l. 20); agrees with *reī; reī pūblicae,* as usual, represents one idea, and = *of the state.* —— **perīculīs**, abl. plur. of *perīculum, -ī,* n. 2d (akin to *porta, experior,* περάω = *I pass through,* etc., from root *par = to go through;* hence, *perīculum = something to be gone through,* with an added notion of difficulty, and so *a trial, danger*); governed by the prep. *ā.* —— **sēiungātur**, 3d pers. sing. pres. subjunct. pass. of *sēiungō, -ere, sēiūnxī, sēiūnctum,* 3 (*sē* or *sēd,* old prep. + the abl. = *apart, without,* only used in composition in classical Latin + *iungō;* cf. *sēcēdō, sēcernō,* etc.); agrees with the subj. *calamitās,* and is subjunct. in similar construction to *sit,* above, with which its clause is connected by the conj. *et.* —— **Sed**, adversative conj.; introduces an oppositional idea, but as a conj. preserves the interconnection of thought between its own and the previous sentence.

LINE 15. **tū**, gen. *tuī;* nom. sing., subj. of *commoveāre* (*pertimescās* and *cēdās*). *Tū* is emphatic by position, and scornful; moreover, it should be remembered that the nom. of the personal pronouns is only expressed for emphasis or contrast. —— **ut**, final conj.; followed by the subjunct. of purpose *commoveāre;* the *ut* clause is a complementary substantival final one, and is part of the subj. of *est postulandum* (the rest of the subj. being completed by the other *ut* clauses following). Final substantival clauses (with *ut* or *nē* +

say, to be startled at	poenās	pertimēscās,	ut	temporibus 16
your misdoings, terrified at the penalties	*the penalties*	*you should dread,*	*that*	*to the times* (= *exigencies*)
of the law, or yield	reī pūblicae	cēdās,	nōn	est 17
to the superior claim	*of the common weal*	*you should yield,*	*not*	*is*

the subjunct.) accompany verbs of *willing, warning, beseeching, urging, demanding, resolving,* etc., and the substantival clause acts as subj. when the verb of *willing,* etc., is pass. (as here), as obj. when the verb of *willing,* etc., is active. It should be noted that the inf. is often used with many verbs of the above classes; it is common with *postulō,* esp. in early Latin, but *rogō, quaesō, flāgitō, pōscō,* and *ōrō* all preferably (and some invariably) take *ut* and the subjunctive. A. & G. 331; B. 295, 296; G. 546, and NOTES 1 and 3; H. 498. —— **vitiīs,** abl. plur. of *vitium, -ī,* n. 2d (root *vi* = *to entwine,* hence *vitium* = lit. *a twist,* hence *fault, offence, vice, defect;* related are *vītis* = *a vine,* *vieō* = *I plait,* ἰτέα = *a willow,* and our word *withe*); abl. of the means, with *commovēre,* or else abl. of the cause. —— **tuīs,** abl. plur. n. of the poss. adj. *tuus, -a, -um;* agrees with *vitiīs.* —— **commovēre,** 2d pers. sing. pres. subjunct. pass. of *commoveō, -ēre, commōvī, commōtum,* 2 (*con* + *moveō*); agrees with the subj. *tū;* the subjunct. is final, following *ut.* Note the ending in *-re* instead of in *-ris,* and note the comparisons in the note on *verēbere,* Chap. VII, l. 41. *Commovēre* and *permovēre* imply greater violence of motion or of agitation than the simple verb *movēre.* —— **ut,** final conj.; followed by *pertimēscās* = a complementary final clause, like the one above. Observe the *asyndeta,* i.e. the absence of conjunctions to connect the coördinate substantival clauses. —— **lēgum,** gen. plur. of *lēx, lēgis,* f. 3d; poss. gen., limiting *poenās; lēgum poenās* = *the penalties ordained by the laws.*

LINE 16. **poenās,** acc. plur. of *poena, -ae,* f. 1st (cf. *pūniō;* similar in form is the connection between *moenia* and *mūniō*); direct obj. of *pertimēscās.* Synonyms: (1) *poena* (ποινή) = originally *punishment* in the shape of a fine, then *punishment* in general; (2) *multa* = *a fine;* (3) *supplicium* (*supplex, sub* + *plicō*) = (a) *bending down* in entreaty, hence *supplication,* (b) *bending down* to receive punishment, hence *execution;* (4) *castīgātiō* (*castum* + *agere* = *to correct,* cf. *pūrgō* for *pūrum agō,* hence) = *correction,* for the purpose of improving, the means used being *verba* or *verbera* (*words* or *lashes*). Similar distinctions exist between the verbs, viz.: (1) *poenā afficere aliquem* or *poenās ab aliquō petere* (*expetere, repetere*); *pūnīre* is less common; (2) *multāre;* (3) *supplicium sūmere;* (4) *castīgāre.* —— **pertimēscās,** 2d pers. sing. pres. subjunct. act. of *pertimēscō, -ere, pertimuī,* no supine, 3 (*per* + *timēscō,* inchoative form of *timeō*); the subj. *tū* is implied; the subjunct. follows *ut* final; cf. *commovēre.* The inceptive verb is specially appropriate here, for it suggests that fear of the law would be a new experience for Catiline. —— **ut,** final conj.; followed by the subjunct. of purpose, *cēdās,* similar in construction to *commovēre* and *pertimēscās.* —— **temporibus,** dat. plur. of *tempus, temporis,* n. 3d; dat. of the indirect obj., with *cēdās.* A. & G. 226; B. 187, II; G. 346; H. 384, I. *Tempora* here = *the needs of the time, the exigencies of the state,* in reference to a political crisis; the meaning is that it is impossible to expect that Catiline would set a higher value on the needs of the state than on his own desires, and sacrifice the latter to the former.

LINE 17. **reī,** gen. sing. of *rēs,* f. 5th; poss. gen., limiting *temporibus.* —— **pūblicae,** gen. sing. f. of the adj. *pūblicus, -a, -um;* agrees with *reī.* —— **cēdās,** 2d pers. sing. pres. subjunct. act. of *cēdō, -ere, cessī, cessum,* 3; the implied subj. is *tū* (expressed with the first verb *commovēre,* and understood with those following in like construction). Cicero uses this verb = *to give way to* in other passages with similar meaning, e.g. *reī pūblicae cēdere* (speech for Sulla). A few editors read *concēdās,* the compound of *cēdō,* and this used to be the popular lection; but now *cēdās* is recognized as the better and more authoritative

18 postulandum.   Neque   enim   is
   to be demanded.   *Neither*   *for that (kind of) man*

19 es,   Catilīna,   ut   tē   aut   pudor   umquam
   you are,   Catiline,   that   you   either   shame   ever

20 ā   turpitūdine   aut   metus   ā   perīculō   aut
   from   baseness   or   fear   from   danger   or

of the state's neces-
sity. For you are
not at all the kind
of man, Catiline, to
be ever reclaimed by
a sense of shame from
the path of dishonor,

---

reading.——**nōn**, neg. adv.; limits *postulandum est.*——**est**, 3d pers. sing. pres. ind. act. of *sum, esse, fuī; est + postulandum* = the 3d pers. sing. pres. ind. of the periphrastic pass. conjugation of *postulō*, and is quasi-impersonal = *it is not to be asked that you should be startled*, etc., etc.; observe that the substantival clauses (*that you should be startled*, etc., etc.) are really the subj. of *postulandum est*, i.e. we may render *that you should be startled*, etc., *is a thing not to be expected.*

LINE 18. **postulandum**, nom. sing. n. of *postulandus, -a, -um*, gerundive of *postulō, -āre, -āvī, -ātum*, 1 (akin to *pōscō*); may be considered impersonal with *est*, hence the neut. sing., or as neut. in agreement with the nearest of the subject-complementary *ut* clauses, and understood with each of the rest. A. & G. 113, *d*; 129; B. 337. 7, *b*), 1); G. 251; H. 234; 466, NOTE. For synonyms, refer to the note on *rogō*, Chap. IV, l. 22. ——**Neque** (*ne + que = and . . . not*), cop. conj.; *neque + enim* connects the sentence with the previous one; *neque* negatives the pred. *is es.*——**enim**, causal conj., which, in combination with *neque*, connects this and the preceding sentence; *neque enim* = καὶ γάρ οὐ in Greek. Remember that *enim* is always post-positive, and that *nam* (in prose) is always pre-positive.——**is**, nom. sing. n. of the dem. pron. *is, ea, id; is* is predicative, and agrees in gender and number with *tū* (the implied subj. of *es*). *Is* here practically = *tālis*, i.e. *you are not the man to*, etc. (*the kind of man*, or *such a man as to*, etc.).

LINE 19. **es**, 2d pers. sing. pres. ind. act. of *sum, esse, fuī;* the subj. implied by the personal ending is *tū.*——**Catilīna**, voc. sing. of *Catilīna, -ae*, m. 1st; the case of address. ——**ut**, consecutive conj.; followed by the subjunct. of result *revocāverit.* This sentence admirably illustrates the kind of subjunct. found in clauses of relative characteristic, for we might very well have had in this passage: *neque enim is es, quem aut pudor . . . revocāverit*, i.e. the character of the verb is identical, whether the consecutive clause be introduced by *quem* or by *ut*. A. & G. 319; B. 284; G. 552; H. 500. ——**tē**, acc. sing. of *tū;* direct obj. of *revocāverit.* ——**aut**, disjunctive conj., used correlatively with *aut* following, = *aut* (*either*) . . . *aut* (*or*) . . . *aut* . . . (*or*). Disjunctives : (1) *aut*, when each alternative excludes the other (as do *pudor* and *metus*, and *metus* and *ratiō*); (2) *sīve* (*seu*) offers a choice between two names of the same thing; (3) *vel* (*ve*) is the weakest conj., and merely gives a choice between two alternatives. Correlatives are *aut . . . aut, sīve . . . sīve*, etc., but not *aut . . . sīve* or other dissimilar combinations. A. & G. 156, *c*; B. 342; G. 494; H. 554, II, 2.—— **pudor**, gen. *pudōris*, m. 3d (from verb *pudeō*); nom. sing., a subj. of *revocāverit.* Synonyms : (1) *pudor = sense of shame, modesty* (in opposition to *impudentia*); (2) *pudīcitia = purity, chastity* (in opposition to *impudīcitia*).——**umquam**, adv. ; limiting *revocāverit. Umquam* was not found in the old common texts, but occurs in Quintilian's quotation of this passage, and is adopted by modern editors of the Catilinarian speeches.

LINE 20. **ā**, prep.; gov. the abl. *turpitūdine*, expressing *separation* with the verb *revocāverit.* Remember that separation is usually expressed by a prep. and the abl. (*ab, dē, ex*), except with a few simple verbs, e.g. *līberō, prīvō*, etc. ——**turpitūdine**, abl. sing. of *turpitūdō, -inis*, f. 3d (from adj. *turpis;* cf. *fortitūdō* from *fortis*); governed by the prep. *ā.* Observe that *pudor* is contrasted with its natural opposite *turpitūdō*, and

from pursuits of dan-	ratiō	ā	furōre	revocāverit.	Quam 21
ger by fear, or from	*reason*	*from*	*madness*	*may have recalled.*	*Which*
madness by reason.					
Wherefore, as I have	ob		rem,	ut	saepe	iam	dīxī, 22
already frequently	*on account of*		*thing,*	*as*	*often*	*already*	*I have said,*

that a similar opposition is felt between *metus* and *perīculum*, and between *ratiō* and *furor;* Prof. Wilkins quotes a very apposite passage from the speech in behalf of Cluentius : *vīcit pudōrem libīdō, timōrem audācia, ratiōnem āmentia.* —— **aut,** disjunctive conj.; joins *pudor* and *metus.* —— **metus,** gen. *metūs,* m. 4th; nom. sing., a subj. of *revocāverit,* which must be supplied from the coördinate clause *ratiō ā furōre revocāverit.* —— **ā,** prep.; gov. the abl. *perīculō,* expressing *separation.* —— **perīculō,** abl. sing. of *perīculum, -ī,* n. 2d; governed by the prep. *ā.* —— **aut,** disjunctive conj.; joins *metus* and *ratiō.*

LINE 21. **ratiō,** gen. *ratiōnis,* f. 3d; nom. sing., subj. of *revocāverit; ratiō* = here *sound reasoning, proper judgment. Ratiō* has many different meanings, of which the most important are : (1) *reckoning, calculation;* (2) *a list, register;* (3) *a sum, number;* (4) *a business affair, transaction;* (5) *relation, reference,* in the abstract ; (6) *respect, regard, concern, consideration,* e.g. *ratiōnem habēre;* (7) *course, conduct, manner;* (8) *condition, sort;* (9) *the reasoning faculty, judgment, reason;* (10) *a motive, reason;* (11) in rhetoric, *an argument,* based on reasoning ; (12) *reasonableness, propriety, rule, order;* (13) *theory, doctrine;* (14) *knowledge,* etc. From the above it may be seen that *ratiō* is a word of frequent occurrence in Latin, esp. in philosophical treatises. —— **ā,** prep.; gov. the abl. *furōre,* expressing *separation.* —— **furōre,** abl. sing. of *furor, -is,* m. 3d (from verb *furō* = *I rage*); governed by the prep. *ā.* —— **revocāverit,** 3d pers. sing. perf. subjunct. act. of *revocō, -āre, -āvī, -ātum,* 1 (*re* = *back* + *vocō* = *I call*); agrees with the subj. *ratiō;* the subjunct. is consecutive with *ut* above. Note that *revocāverit* is sing., and agrees only with the nearest (*ratiō*) of its three subjects, being understood with each of the first two ; frequently it happens that the verb. will be sing. in agreement with the nearest subject, even though one or more subjects of plural number precede the sing. subject. A. & G. 205, *d;* B. 255, 2 and 3 ; G. 285, EXCEPTION 1 ; H. 463, I. Of course, the regular rule is that the verb will be plural if there be more than one subject. Many editors read *revocārit,* the contracted form of *revocāverit;* for references, etc., consult the note on *cōnfīrmāsti,* Chap. IV, l. 30. —— **Quam,** acc. sing. f. of the rel. pron. *quī, quae, quod;* agrees with *rem. Quam ob rem, quā rē,* and other adverbial phrases with the rel., are classed as *illative* conjunctions like *itaque, igitur,* etc.; see the references under *quārē,* Chap. V, l. 36. *Quam ob rem* connects the sentence with the preceding one, and denotes that the statement which it introduces is a logical result of previous argument or discussion.

LINE 22. **ob,** prep.; gov. the acc. *rem.* Synonyms : *because of* = (1) **ob,** as indicating the objective reason; (2) *propter,* stating the subjective reason ; (3) *causā* (following its gen.), stating the purpose in view ; (4) *per,* stating the permitting or the hindering cause, esp. + *licet* or *posse,* e.g. *per tē licet* = *it is allowed so far as you are concerned; per aetātem pūgnāre nōn potest* = *he is unable to fight on account of his age;* (5) *prae* + the abl., stating the hindrance, and only in negative clauses, e.g. *prae lacrimīs loquī nōn possum* = *I am not able to speak for* (*because of*) *my tears.* —— **rem,** acc. sing of *rēs, reī,* f. 5th ; governed by the prep. *ob.* —— **ut,** adv. = *as;* followed by the ind. *dīxī. Ut,* meaning *as* or *when,* is in direct discourse followed by the ind. mood. —— **saepe** (compar. *saepius,* superl. *saepissimē*), adv.; modifies *dīxī.* —— **iam,** adv. of time ; modifies *dīxī.* —— **dīxī,** 1st pers. sing. perf. ind. act. of *dīcō, -ere, dīxī, dictum,* 3 ; the subj. implied by the personal ending is *ego.* "Leave Rome" is the burden of Chap. II, and indeed of the whole oration.

23	proficīscere ;	ac,	sī	mihi	inimīcō,	ut	said, take yourself
	set out ;	*and,*	*if*	*against me*	*enemy,*	*as*	off; and if you want
							to fan the flame of
24	praedicās,	tuō	cōnflāre	vīs	invidiam,		hatred against me, —
	you proclaim,	*your*	*to blow (= excite)*	*you wish*	*ill-will,*		your personal enemy,
							as you openly declare
25	rēctā	perge	in	exsilium :		vix	me, — make haste
	straightway	*proceed*	*into*	*exile :*		*scarcely*	away into exile. If
							you do that, I shall
26	feram	sermōnēs	hominum,	sī		id	find it hard to endure
	I shall bear	*the talk*	*of men,*	*if*		*this*	

LINE 23. **proficīscere**, 2d pers. sing. pres. imperative of the deponent *proficīscor, proficīscī, profectus sum*, 3 (*prō* + root *fac*, in compounds *fic*, with inchoative termination, = lit. *to put one's self forward, to set out*); the subj. implied by the personal ending is *tū*.——**ac**, cop. conj. ; connects the sentence with the previous one.——**sī**, conditional particle, followed by the ind. *vīs*. In logical conditions (i.e. those which assert that *if this is (was, will be) so and so, that is (was, will be) so and so*, without consideration of possibility, probability, and simply as a formula) the verb of the *protasis* is ind., and the verb of the *apodosis* must be either ind., imperative, or subjunct. in one of its independent uses. A. & G. 306; B. 302; G. 595; H. 508, and 4.——**mihi**, dat. sing. of *ego ;* dat. of the indirect obj. with *cōnflāre*. Remember that compounds, trans. and intrans., of *con, ad, ante, ob, prae, in*, etc., take the dat. of the indirect obj., and trans. compounds like *cōnflāre* have also an acc. of the direct obj., e.g. *invidiam* following.——**inimīcō**, dat. sing. of *inimīcus, -ī*, m. 2d (substantival mas. of the adj. *inimīcus, -a, -um*, from *in = not* + *amīcus = friendly*); in apposition with *mihi ; inimīcō* . . . *tuō* = an adjectival enlargement of *mihi, quem inimīcum esse tuum praedicās. Inimīcus = a personal enemy*, whereas *hostis = a public enemy*, i.e. a foreign state.——**ut**, adv. = *as ;* with the ind. *praedicās*.

LINE 24. **praedicās**, 2d pers. sing. pres. ind. act. of *praedicō, -āre, -āvī, -ātum*, I (*prae = before all, openly* + *dicō = I proclaim ;* akin to *dīcō*, from root *dak = to show ;* cf. δείκνυμι); the subj. *tū* is implied by the personal ending. Carefully distinguish *praedicō* (1st conjug.) = *I proclaim*, from *praedīcō* (3d conjug.) = *I foretell, predict*. The adverbial clause *ut praedicās* modifies *inimīcō tuō*, as its position clearly indicates ; see the note on *inimīcō* above.——**tuō**, dat. sing. m. of the poss. adj. *tuus, -a, -um ;* agrees with *inimīcō*.——**cōnflāre**, pres. inf. act. of *cōnflō, -āre, -āvī, -ātum*, I (*con* + *flō = I blow ;* root *bhal, bhla, bhlu = to blow, swell, flow ;* cf. *flōreō = I bloom, blow*, of flowers, *fluō, fleō*, etc.); complementary object-inf. of *vīs*. For the construction of verbs of wishing, see the note on *māllem*, Chap. VII, l. 28. The metaphor is taken from *blowing* the fire of the blacksmith's forge.——**vīs**, 2d pers. sing. pres. ind. act. of the irreg. verb *volō, velle, voluī*, no supine ; the implied subj. is *tū*.——**invidiam**, acc. sing. of *invidia, -ae*, f. 1st (*invideō = I envy, I feel ill-will towards*); direct obj. of *cōnflāre. Invidia* is not so well rendered in English by the kindred word *envy*, as by *hatred, ill-will, odium, unpopularity* (subjective or objective).

LINE 25. **rēctā**, abl. sing. f. of the adj. *rectus, -a, -um*, used adverbially, with *viā* understood, = *straightway ;* modifies *perge*.——**perge**, 2d pers. sing. pres. imperative act. of *pergō, -ere, perrēxī, perrēctum*, 3 trans. and intrans. (*per* + *regō*); the subj. *tū* is implied by the personal ending.——**in**, prep. ; gov. the acc. *exsilium*, expressing *motion to*.——**exsilium**, acc. sing. of *exsilium, -ī*, n. 2d; governed by the prep. *in*.——**vix**, adv., limiting *feram ; vix feram* is idiomatic, = *I shall find it hard to endure ;* cf. *aegrē ferre*, and see the note on *vix*, Chap. VIII, l. 59.

LINE 26. **feram**, 1st pers. sing. fut. ind. act. of the irreg. verb *ferō, ferre, tulī, lātum ;* the subj. *ego* is implied.——**sermōnēs**, acc. plur. of *sermō, ōnis*, m. 3d (akin to

what men will say of	fēceris,	vix	mōlem	istīus 27
me; if you go into	you shall have done;	scarcely	the burden	that
exile at the consul's	invidiae,	sī in	exsilium	iussū	cōnsulis 28
orders, I shall find	of ill-will,	if into	exile	by order	of the consul

serō = *I weave*, from root *svar* = *to arrange, bind together*, hence *words woven together, conversation, discourse;* others derive from root *svar* = *to tune, sound,* cf. *susurrus* = *whispering,* σῦριγξ = *a musical pipe*); direct obj. of *feram.* Cicero here and in some other passages seems to use *sermō* in an uncomplimentary sense, = *the comments, remarks* of censure, cf. *in sermōnem hominum atque vituperātiōnem venīre* (speech *in Verrem*). Synonyms: (1) *sermō* = (a) *conversation* among several, (b) colloquial speech, language, e.g. *sermō cotīdiānus, sermō patrius* = *native speech;* (2) *lingua* = lit. *the tongue,* hence *utterance, language, speech;* (3) *ōrātiō* (from *ōrāre* = originally *to speak,* from *ōs, ōris,* n. 3d = *the mouth*) = (a) *speech,* i.e. the ability to express thoughts in words, e.g. *ferae ōrātiōnis expertēs sunt* = *beasts are devoid of the faculty of speech;* (b) *a speech, oration,* i.e. a discourse artistically arranged and put together ; (c) *style* of expression, e.g. *ōrātiō pūra.* —— *hominum,* gen. plur. of *homō, hominis,* m. 3d (old form *hemō;* akin to *humus* = *the earth*); poss. gen., limiting *sermōnēs; hominum* = *of men,* in general, cf. *omnēs hominēs* = *every one.* Synonyms : (1) *homō, hominēs* = *a man (men, mankind),* as distinguished from the gods on the one side and the lower animals on the other ; (2) *vir* = *a man,* as distinguished from a woman, or *a husband* as distinguished from *a wife;* a special meaning is *hero.* The general word for *men* = *mankind* is *hominēs,* including male and female members of the human race. —— *sī,* conditional particle ; with the ind. *fēceris,* in a logical hypothesis. —— *id,* acc. sing. n. of the dem. pron. *is, ea, id;* direct obj. of *fēceris; sī id fēcerīs* = *sī in exsilium exieris.*

LINE 27. **fēceris,** 2d pers. sing. fut.-perf. ind. act. of *faciō, -ere, fēcī, factum,* 3 ; the implied subj. is *tū; sī id fēceris* is the *protasis* of the condition, while *vix feram,* etc., is the *apodosis,* the usual order of the clauses being reversed. —— **vix,** adv., limiting *sustinēbō.* —— **mōlem,** acc. sing. of *molēs, -is,* f. 3d (etymology uncertain; = (1) *a mass,* hence (2) *a huge structure,* (3) *a dam, mole,* (4) *weight, bulk,* (5) *labor, difficulty,* (6) *a large number, a crowd*); direct obj. of *sustinēbō.* —— **istīus,** gen. sing. of the dem. pron. of the 2d pers. *iste, ista, istud;* agrees with *invidiae; istīus* = *of which you will be cause.*

LINE 28. **invidiae,** gen. sing. of *invidia,* f. 1st ; gen. of the substance or material, explaining *mōlem.* —— **sī,** conditional particle ; with the ind. *ieris,* in a logical condition. —— **in,** prep. ; gov. the acc. *exsilium,* expressing *motion to.* —— **exsilium,** acc. sing. of *exsilium, -ī,* n. 2d (from *exsul;* the forms *exul* and *exilium* are not correct) ; governed by the prep. *in.* —— **iussū,** abl. sing. of *iussus, -ūs,* m. 4th (cf. *iussum, -ī,* n. 2d, from *iubeō;* only the abl. sing. *iussū* is in use); abl. of cause, modifying *ieris. Cause (by reason of which,* or *in accordance with which* anything is said to be or to be done) is usually expressed by the abl. without a prep., esp. in combination with verbs of emotion (e.g. *doleō, laetor, exsultō, gaudeō,* etc.), perf. participles pass. (e.g. *odiō adductus, commōtus,* etc.), or adjectives (e.g. *amōre dignus, ardēns*). It may also be expressed (1) by the abl. with *ab, ā, ex,* or *prae,* e.g. *ex invidiā labōrāre* = *to suffer from unpopularity* (Cic.), (2) by the acc. with *ob, per, propter,* e.g. *propter timōrem fūgērunt* = *on account of their fear they fled.* Observe that a number of ablatives of cause, including *iussū,* are phraseological, and are used in combination with a poss. adj. or a poss. gen., e.g. *cōnsulis* (or *meō, tuō,* etc.) *iussū, missū, rogātū, cōnsiliō, arbitrātū, hortātū, meā auctōritāte,* etc. ; these are all verbals. A. & G. 245; B. 219; G. 408; H. 416.—— **cōnsulis,** gen. sing. of *cōnsul, -is,* m. 3d; poss. gen., limiting *iussū.*

29	ieris,		sustinēbō.		Sīn	autem	it hard to bear up
	you shall have gone,		*I shall support.*		*But if*	*however*	under the burden of the odium which you
30	servīre	meae	laudī	et	glōriae	māvīs,	have excited. If on the other hand you
	to work for	*my*	*(for) glory*	*and*	*renown*	*you prefer,*	would rather promote my credit and
31	ēgredere	cum	importūnā	scelerātōrum	manū,		renown, depart with
	go out	*with*	*savage*	*of criminals*	*your band,*		your savage gang of

LINE 29. **ieris,** 2d pers. sing. fut.-perf. ind. act. of the irreg. verb *eō, īre, īvī* or *iī, itum;* the implied subj. is *tū.* In the condition *sī in exsilium . . . sustinēbō* observe that the verb of the *protasis* is fut.-perf., and that of the *apodosis* fut.-simple; this is a very common variation with Cicero from the fut.-simple in both clauses; the fut.-perf. in both clauses of a future condition is comparatively rare in Cicero. —— **sustinēbō,** 1st pers. sing. fut. ind. act. of *sustineō, -ēre, -uī, sustentum,* 2 (*subs,* old form of *sub,* + *teneō;* from the supine *sustentum* is formed the frequentative verb *sustentō*); the subj. *ego* is implied by the personal ending. *Sustinēre = to sustain, bear, support aloft,* i.e. a burden which presses one down, metaphorically; *sustentāre = to sustain,* in the sense of *to keep, maintain, support,* a very different sense from that of *sustinēre.* For synonyms of *sustinēre,* see the note on *patimur,* Chap. II, l. 15. —— **Sīn** (*Sī + ne*), conditional particle, = *but if, if however;* with the ind. *māvīs,* in a logical hypothesis. When two conditions exclude one another, the first is led by *sī,* and the second by *sīn; sīn* is frequently strengthened by *autem, vērō, minus, secus,* or *aliter* (*sī minus, sīn minus,* and *sīn aliter* are especially common in the sense *if not, if otherwise,* without a verb, which can be supplied from the context). —— **autem,** adversative conj. (always post-positive); connects the clause with the previous one, and adds further oppositional force to *sīn.*

LINE 30. **servīre,** pres. inf. act. of *serviō, -īre, -īvī, -ītum,* 4 (*servus*); objective complementary inf. with *māvīs; servīre* is one of the number of verbs that govern a dat. of the indirect object. —— **meae,** dat. sing. f. of the poss. adj. *meus, -a, -um;* agrees with *lauaī.* —— **laudī,** dat. sing. of *laus, laudis,* f. 3d (for *claus,* so *laudō* for *claudō,* from root *klu = to hear;* cf. *clueō* or *cluō,* and κλύω = *I hear myself called* in some way, *I am called, clārus* and κλυτός = *renowned, glōria,* etc.); dat. of the indirect obj., dependent on *servīre. Laudī* here has the second of the three following meanings of *laus:* (1) *praise;* (2) *glory, fame, renown;* (3) *merit, credit,* as the ground of praise. —— **et,** cop. conj.; joins *laudī* and *glōriae.* —— **glōriae,** dat. sing. of *glōria, -ae,* f. 1st; dat. of the indirect obj., dependent on *servīre;* joined by *et* to *laudī; meae,* expressed with *laudī,* is understood with *glōriae.* —— **māvīs,** 2d pers. sing. pres. ind. act. of *mālō, malle, māluī,* no supine, irreg. (*magis + volō = I wish rather, I prefer*); the subj. *tū* is implied by the personal termination.

LINE 31. **ēgredere,** 2d pers. sing. pres. imperative of the deponent verb *ēgredior, ēgredī, ēgressus sum,* 3 (*ē + gradior*); the subj. *tū* is implied by the personal ending. —— **cum,** prep.; gov. the abl. *manū,* expressing *accompaniment.* —— **importūnā,** abl. sing. f. of the adj. *importūnus, -a, -um;* agrees with *manū.* The original meaning of *importūnus* is *unsuitable, out of place,* hence *harsh, rude, dangerous, outrageous, savage,* etc., according to the nature of the substantive with which it is used. —— **scelerātōrum,** gen. plur. of *scelerātus, -ī,* m. 2d (substantival mas. of *scelerātus, -a, -um,* perf. part. pass. of *scelerō = I pollute,* cf. *scelus*); gen. of the substance or material, explaining of what *manū* consists. *Scelerātī, perditī,* and *latrōnēs* are Cicero's favorite terms for Catiline's associates. —— **manū,** abl. sing. of *manus, -ūs,* f. 4th (root *ma = to measure,* hence *the hand,* as *the measuring thing; band, gang, company* is a later sense); governed by the prep. *cum.*

criminals, betake yourself to Manlius, uprouse the worthless among the citizens, cut yourself off from honest men, make offensive war upon your country, revel in your wicked	cōnfer	tē	ad	Mānlium,	concitā	perditōs 82
	betake	*yourself*	*to*	*Manlius,*	~~rouse up~~	*abandoned*
	cīvēs,	sēcerne	tē	ā		bonis, 83
	the citizens,	*separate*	*yourself*	*from*		*the loyal (men),*
	īnfer	patriae	bellum,		exsultā	impiō 84
	carry in	*upon your country*	*war,*		*exult*	*impious*

LINE 32. **cōnfer**, 2d pers. sing. pres. imperative act. of *cōnferō, cōnferre, contulī, collātum,* irreg. (*cōn* + *ferō*); the subj. *tū* is implied by the personal ending. *Ferō* and its compounds omit the final *e* of the 2d pers. sing. of the above tense; cf. *dīc, fac, dūc, ēdūc,* etc. (but *perfice, cōnfice,* etc., with compounds of *faciō*). *Sē cōnferre* is a common synonym of simple verbs of motion, e.g. *veniō, eō.* —— **tē**, acc. sing. of *tū ;* direct obj. (reflexive) of *cōnfer.* —— **ad**, prep.; gov. the acc. *Mānlium.* —— **Mānlium**, acc. sing. of *Mānlius, -ī,* m. 2d; governed by the prep. *ad.* Refer to the note on *Mānlium,* Chap. III, l. 16. —— **concitā**, 2d pers. sing. pres. imperative act. of *concitō, -āre, -āvī, -ātum,* 1 (frequentative form of *conciō* or *concieō*); the subj. *tū* is implied. Observe the string of imperatives beginning with *ēgredere,* l. 31, and note the crisp directness of the injunctions given through them, which is heightened by the *asyndeton.* —— **perditōs**, acc. plur. m. of the adj. *perditus, -a, -um* (properly perf. part. pass. of *perdō, -ere, perditī, perditum,* 3, from *per* + *dō* = *I make away with, destroy*); agrees with *cīvēs.* Synonyms: (1) *āmittere* (*ā* + *mittō*) = *to lose,* with or without blame; (2) *perdere* = *to lose,* by one's own fault; hence *perditī* = *men morally lost,* i.e. *corrupt, profligate, abandoned.*

LINE 33. **cīvēs**, acc. plur. of *cīvis, -is,* m. (and f.) 3d; direct obj. of *concitā;* the *perditī cīvēs* are contrasted with the *bonī cīvēs* (see the clause following). —— **sēcerne**, 2d pers. sing. pres. imperative act. of *sēcernō, -ere, sēcrēvī, sēcrētum,* 3 (*sē* = *apart* + *cernō* = *I distinguish*); the implied subj. is *tū.* *Cernō,* though its usual meaning is *I see, perceive,* implies *discrimination,* as it is derived from the root *skar* = κρι = *cer,* cf. κρίνω = *I separate, I judge.* —— **tē**, acc. sing. of *tū ;* direct obj. (reflexive) of *sēcerne.* —— **ā**, prep.; gov. the abl. *bonīs,* expressing *separation.* —— **bonīs**, abl. plur. m. of the adj. *bonus, -a, -um* (compar. *melior,* superl. *optimus*); *bonīs* is here substantival, and the abl. is governed by the prep. *ā.* *Bonus* and *bonī,* substantival, are political terms, = *loyal citizens ;* they are frequently applied by Cicero to members of the aristocratic party (*optimātēs*). Refer to the note on *bonōrum,* Chap. I, l. 7.

LINE 34. **īnfer**, 2d pers. sing. pres. imperative act. of *īnferō, īnferre, intulī, illātum,* irreg. (*in* + *ferō*); the implied subj. is *tū.* *Bellum īnferre* + the dat. = *to invade.* —— **patriae**, dat. sing. of *patria, -ae,* f. 1st (= *patria terra,* from the adj. *patrius*); dat. of the indirect obj., governed by *īnfer.* Compounds of *in, ob, prae,* etc., govern a dat. of the indirect obj., and if trans. take also the acc. of the direct obj. —— **bellum**, acc. sing. of *bellum, -ī,* n. 2d (for *duellum* = *war* between two nations, from *duo ;* cf. *perduelliō* = *treason,* and the English word *duel*); direct obj. of *īnfer.* *Bellum* is the regular word used by Latin writers for *war* between Rome and a foreign nation; thus it is implied that Catiline has forfeited all right to be considered a Roman citizen. —— **exsultā**, 2d pers. sing. pres. imperative act. of *exsultō, -āre, -āvī, -ātum,* 1 (frequentative form of *exsiliō,* hence lit. = *leap about, bound,* i.e. *revel, exult*); the implied subj. is *tū.* —— **impiō**, abl. sing. n. of the adj. *impius, -a, -um* (*in* = *not* + *pius* = *reverent, dutiful*); agrees with *latrōciniō.* *Pius* does not = *pious,* but rather *loyal, dutiful,* i.e. displaying proper respect and deference for a higher authority, esp. the authority of one's parents, the gods, or one's country (so in the frequent Vergilian phrase, *pius*

35 latrōciniō,	ut	ā	mē	nōn	ēiectus	ad	brigandage, so that it may be seen that you went forth not into the midst of strangers, as one cast forth by me, but into the midst of friends who had invited you. And yet why should
in brigandage,	*that*	*by*	*me*	*not*	*cast forth*	*to*	
36 aliēnōs,	sed		invītātus		ad	tuōs	
strangers	*but*		*invited*		*to*	*your friends*	
37 īsse		videāris.	Quamquam		quid	ego	
to have gone		*you may seem.*	*And yet*		*why*	*I*	

Aenēās); the neg. *impiō* is therefore appropriate in this passage, as Catiline treats his country, not with dutiful obedience, but with armed hostility.

LINE 35. **latrōciniō**, abl. sing. of *latrōcinium, -ī,* n. 2d (cf. *latrōcinor = I practise highway robbery,* from *latrō = a robber,* brigand; root *lu* or *lav = to get booty;* cf. λεία *= booty,* λατρεύω, ληίζομαι *= I seize booty, lucrum = gain*); abl. of the cause, with the verb of emotion *exsultā.* A. & G. 245; B. 219; G. 408; H. 416. Cicero here uses *latrōcinium* to correct *bellum* above, as the latter was too honorable a word to apply to Catiline's hostile attitude. *Latrō* originally *= a mercenary soldier* (λατρεύων, i.e. fighting for hire); mercenary soldiers have little or no respect for life or property, and so their marauding habits soon earned for them a reputation no better than that of highwaymen. Varrō derives from *latus = the side,* i.e. of the general, as if *latrōnēs* were the body-guard — an amusing instance of ancient etymological inaccuracy. — **ut**, conj.; followed by the subjunct. *videāris.* Observe that *ut . . . videāris* may be regarded as a *purpose* clause (denoting the intention in Cicero's mind in ordering Catiline to leave Rome and take the field), or as a *result* clause (denoting the natural consequence of such action as Cicero would have Catiline take). Both ideas seem to be blended, just as they do in English with *that* introducing the clause. The use of *nōn* in the clause does not guide us, for *nōn* does not limit the verb *videāris* but only the word *ēiectus.* — **ā**, prep.; gov. the abl. *mē,* expressing the *agency.* — **mē**, abl. sing. of *ego;* governed by the prep. *ā.* — **nōn**, neg. adv.; limits *ēiectus.* — **ēiectus**, nom. sing. m. of *ēiectus, -a, -um,* perf. part. pass. of *ēiciō, ēicere, ēiēcī, ēiectum,* 3 (*ē + iaciō*); agrees with *tū* (the implied subj. of *videāris*); the participles *ēiectus* and *invītātus* are predicative, and take the place of infinitives, e.g. *ut ā mē nōn ēiectus esse (et īsse) ad aliēnōs, sed invītātus (esse et) ad tuōs īsse videāris.* See the references under *perterritus,* l. 7. — **ad**, prep.; gov. the acc. *aliēnōs,* expressing *motion to.*

LINE 36. **aliēnōs**, acc. plur. of *aliēnus, -ī,* m. 2d *= a stranger, foreigner* (substantival mas. of the adj. *aliēnus, -a, -um,* formed from *alius,* hence *= belonging to another, strange, foreign, unfriendly,* etc.); governed by the prep. *ad;* with *ad aliēnōs* supply *īsse* from below. — **sed**, adversative conj., connecting *nōn ēiectus ad aliēnōs* (*īsse*) with *invītātus ad tuōs īsse.* — **invītātus**, nom. sing. m. of *invītātus, -a, -um,* perf. part. pass. of *invītō, -āre, -āvī, -ātum,* 1 (for *in-vic-itō = in-vec-itō,* from *in +* root *vak = voc, vec,* i.e. *to sound, speak, call;* akin to *vōx, vocō, ὄψ,* etc.); agrees with *tū,* the implied subj. of *videāris; invītātus* is predicative, and for use see *ēiectus* above. — **ad**, prep.; gov. the acc. *tuōs,* expressing *motion to.* — **tuōs**, acc. plur. of *tuī, -ōrum,* m. 2d (substantival mas. of the poss. adj. *tuus, -a, -um;* cf. the substantival neut. *tua, -ōrum, = your possessions;* so *meī, mea, suī, sua,* etc.); governed by the prep. *ad. Tuī* substantival *= your friends, your party.* The substantival use of adjectives is very common in Latin; see A. & G. 188, 189; B. 236-238; G. 204, NOTES 1-4; H. 441.

LINE 37. **īsse**, perf. inf. act. of *eō, īre, īvī* or *iī, itum,* irreg.; complementary inf. with *videāris. Īsse* is a contracted form of *iisse.* — **videāris**, 2d pers. sing. pres. subjunct. poss. of *videō, -ēre, vīdī, vīsum,* 2 (the pass. *videor* usually *= I seem*); the subj. *tū* is implied by the personal ending. — **Quamquam** (*quam + quam*), conj., *= and*

I urge you, seeing that I know that you have already sent men on to await you under arms at Forum Aurelium — seeing that	tē *you*	invītem, *should invite,*	ā *by*	quō *whom*	iam *already*	sciam 38 *I know*
	esse praemissōs, *(men) to have been sent on,*		quī *who*	tibi *for you*	ad *at*	Forum 39 *Forum*
	Aurēlium *Aurelium*	praestōlārentur *should stand ready*			armātī? *armed?*	cuī 40 *by whom*

yet; connects the sentence with the previous one in oppositional relation. *Quamquam, cum, etsī,* etc., which usually introduce subordinate clauses, not seldom serve as coordinating conjunctions; thus *quamquam* here = *at tamen = but yet.* The meaning of the following passage (to l. 47) is that it is not really necessary to urge Catiline to leave Rome, as it is well known that he has already made independent arrangements to do so as a rebel. —— **quid**, adverbial acc. neut. sing. of the interrog. pron. *quis, quae, quid* (practically = *cūr, why*); introduces the question following. *Quid,* as an acc. of the inner obj., = *with reference to what?;* see the note on *quid,* l. 1. —— **ego**, nom. sing. of the 1st personal pron.; subj. of *invitem.* The subj., though a personal pronoun, is here expressed in order to make a contrast with *tē;* pronouns, personal or poss., frequently stand next to one another in this way.

LINE 38. **tē**, acc. sing. of *tū;* direct obj. of *invītem.* —— **invītem**, 1st pers. sing. pres. subjunct. act. of *invitō, -āre, -āvī, -ātum,* 1 ; agrees with the subj. *ego;* the subjunct. is *deliberative.* The *deliberative* subjunct. is used in questions implying *doubt, indignation,* or else the *impossibility* or *futility* of doing something; *quid invītem* here expresses futility. There is little difference between this and the potential subjunctive. Allen & Greenough regard it as developed from the *hortatory* subjunct., e.g. *quid dīcam = what am I to say,* = *dīcam, quid?,* i.e. *let me say, what?;* when once established in the pres. tense, it might be easily transferred to the past, e.g., *quid dīcerem = what was I to say?* A. & G. 268; B. 277; G. 265; H. 484, V. —— **ā**, prep.; gov. the abl. *quō,* expressing *agency.* —— **quō**, abl. sing. m. of the rel. pron. *qui, quae, quod;* agrees in gender and number with the antecedent *tē,* and is governed by the prep. *ā.* —— **iam**, temporal adv.; modifies either *sciam* or *esse praemissōs.* —— **sciam**, 1st pers. sing. pres. subjunct. act. of *sciō, -īre, scīvī, scītum,* 4 (root *ski = to split, distinguish;* cf. *secō = I cut,* κεᾷω = *I split,* etc.); the implied subj. is *ego;* the subjunct. is causal, i.e. *ā quō iam sciam = cum iam ā tē sciam,* etc., *seeing that I know,* etc. When *quī* is followed by the causal subjunct., *ut, utpote,* or *quippe* frequently accompanies the relative; *quī is* sometimes used with the concessive subjunctive. A. & G. 320, *e;* B. 283, 3; G. 633, 634; H. 517; 515, III, and NOTE 4.

LINE 39. **esse praemissōs**, perf. inf. pass. of *praemittō, -ere, praemisi, praemissum,* 3 (*prae = before + mittō = I send*); *esse praemissōs* is the regular combinate perf. inf. pass., = *esse* + the perf. part. pass.; agrees (*praemissōs* adjectively) with *eōs* or *hominēs* understood as subj.-acc. (being the implied antecedent of the rel. *quī* following) in the acc. and inf. construction (*ā quō . . . armātī*) dependent on the leading verb *sciam.* —— **quī**, nom. plur. m. of the rel. pron. *quī, quae, quod;* agrees with *eōs* or *hominēs* understood as subj.-acc. of *praemissōs esse* and as antecedent of the rel. pronoun; subj. of *praestōlārentur.* —— **tibi**, dat. sing. of *tū;* dat. of the indirect obj., with *praestōlārentur* (as a compound of *prae*). —— **ad**, prep.; gov. the acc. *Forum Aurēlium = at Forum Aurēlium.* —— **Forum**, acc. sing. of *Forum, -ī,* n. 2d; governed by the prep. *ad.*

LINE 40. **Aurēlium**, acc. sing. n. of the adj. *Aurēlius, -a, -um;* agrees with *Forum. Forum Aurēlium* (or *Forum Aurēlī;* cf. *Appī Forum* on the *via Appia,* and *Forum Iūlium* or *Iūlī* in *Gallia Narbonensis*), now called *Montalto,* is a small town in Etruria,

41	sciam	pactam	et	cōnstitūtam	cum	I know you have set-
	I know	*to have been agreed*	*and*	*to have been arranged*	*with*	tled and arranged a

42	Mānliō	diem?	ā	quō	etiam	aquilam	illam	day with Manlius —
	Manlius	*the day?*	*by*	*whom*	*also*	*eagle*	*that*	seeing moreover that

situated on the great *via Aurèlia* (running north from Rome to Pisa); it is called after the road on which it stood, cf. *Forum Appii*. This and other small towns of a similar kind of name were originally settlements made for the comfort of workmen building the roads (e.g. the *via Appia* and the *via Aurèlia*), where they might have shelter at night, store food, and the like. —— **praestōlārentur**, 3d pers. plur. imperf. subjunct. of the deponent verb *praestolor, -āri, -ātus sum*, 1 (*prae* + root *stol = to set, place*, cf. στέλλω = *I set, send*, στόλος = *an expedition*); agrees with the subj. *quī; praestōlārentur* is the *final* subjunct., expressing purpose, for *quī = ut eī*. A. & G. 317; B. 282; G. 545; H. 497. The tense is imperfect, in accordance with the regular rule of tense sequence in subordinate clauses, in dependence on the historic *esse praemissōs*. A. & G. 336, B; B. 318; G. 516-518; H. 525. —— **armāti**, nom. plur. m. of the adj. *armātus, -a, -um* (properly perf. part. pass. of *armō, -āre, -āvī, ātum*, 1 = *I equip with arms* (*arma, -ōrum*, n. 2d)); agrees with and adjectively enlarges the subj. *quī*. Cicero might have said *ā quō iam sciam armātōs praemissōs esse, quī . . . praestōlārentur*, but by using *armāti* in the rel. clause instead of *armātōs* in the main clause, and by placing *armāti* at the end of the *quī* clause, the fact that Catiline's friends bore arms to resist lawful authority is made specially prominent and emphatic. —— **cui**, dat. sing. m. of the rel. pron. *quī, quae, quod*; agrees with the antecedent *tē*, l. 38 (which is also antecedent of *quō*, l. 38, and of *quō*, l. 42); dat. of the agent with the participles (with which supply *esse*) *pāctam* and *cōnstitūtam*. It should be remembered that the dat. of the agent is regular after a gerund or gerundive, and also common after compound passive tenses, and esp. after perf. participles passive. Except with the gerund or gerundive, there is generally a strong idea of personal interest in the so-called dat. of the agent, and the dat. is in most cases a dat. of a personal pronoun; cf. the Greek τὰ μοι πεπραγμένα. This dat. recurs in the 2d Oration, cf. *quem ad modum esset* EI *ratiō belli dēscripta*, and again MIHI *cōnsultum ac prōvīsum est*. A. & G. 232, *a*; B. 189, 2; G. 354; H. 388. Observe that *cui sciam* states a reason, like *ā quō iam sciam* above. All the Mss. read *cum sciam*, but modern editors all read *cui* as preserving the rel. character of the clauses.

LINE 41. **sciam**, 1st pers. sing. pres. subjunct. act. of *sciō, scīre, scīvī, scītum*, 4; the subj. *ego* is implied. *Sciam* is a causal subjunct.; see *sciam*, l. 38. —— **pactam**, acc. sing. f. of *pactus, -a, -um*, perf. part. pass. of *pacīscō, -ere*, no perf., *pactum*, 3, or perhaps the perf. part. (used passively, cf. *comitātus*, etc.) of the more common deponent form *pacīscor, -ī, pactus sum*, 3 (root *pag = παγ = pag*, or *pac, to bind fast*; cf. πήγνυμι (*ἐ-πάγ-ην*) = *I fix, pangō*, etc.); agrees with the subj.-acc. *diem*; with *pactam* supply *esse*, = the perf. inf. pass., agreeing with *diem* in the acc. and inf. construction dependent on *sciam*. —— **et**, cop. conj.; joins *pactam* (*esse*) and *cōnstitūtam* (*esse*). —— **cōnstitūtam**, acc. sing. f. of *cōnstitūtus, -a, -um*, perf. part. pass. of *cōnstituō, -ere, -uī, cōnstitūtum*, 3 (*con* + *statuō = I cause to stand*, from root *sta = to stand;* hence *cōnstituō = I set up, arrange, appoint, establish*); like *pactam* (to which it is joined by *et*), *cōnstitūtam* agrees with the subj.-acc. *diem*, and similarly *esse* must be supplied (= the perf. inf. passive). —— **cum**, prep.; gov. the abl. *Mānliō*.

LINE 42. **Mānliō**, abl. sing. of *Mānlius, -ī*, m. 2d; governed by the prep. *cum*. —— **diem**, acc. sing. of *diēs, -ēī*, m. 5th (*diēs* here has the less common f. gender; in the plur. the gender is regularly m.); subj.-acc. of *pactam* (*esse*) and of *cōnstitūtam* (*esse*) in the acc. and inf. object-clause (indirect discourse) of the leading verb *sciam*. The allusion in *pactam . . . diem* may be to the date of Catiline's departure from Rome, so

I know that you have sent on also that wonderful silver eagle, —	argenteam,	quam	tibi	ac	. tuīs 43
	silver,	*which*	*to you*	*and*	*to your (party)*

that the men sent on to Forum Aurēlium might know exactly when to expect him, or to the date when Mānlius would be in arms, cf. Chap. III, ll. 11-17; possibly, to avoid delay, Catiline's junction with the rebel forces and Mānlius' armed movement were timed for one and the same day. —— **ā**, prep.; gov. the abl. *quō*, expressing *agency.* —— **quō**, abl. sing. m. of the rel. pron. *quī, quae, quod;* agrees with the antecedent *tē*, l. 38 (which is antecedent also of *quo*, l. 38, and of *cuī*, l. 40), and is governed by the prep. *ā.* Observe that *quō*, like the relatives referred to above, is causal, and so the verb *sciam*, l. 46, is subjunctive. This sentence is slightly involved; rearranged it reads *ā quō etiam aquilam illam argenteam praemissam esse sciam; quam . . . futūram* and *cuī . . . fuit* are adjectival enlargements of *aquilam*, and are inserted parenthetically, hence the verb of each clause (viz. *cōnfīdō* in the one, and *cōnstitūtum fuit* in the other) is in the ind. mood, although the clauses are in form subordinate to the acc. and inf. object-clause *aquilam praemissam esse.* ——**etiam** (*et + iam*), adv., modifying either *sciam* or *praemissam esse* below. —— **aquilam**, acc. sing. of *aquila, -ae*, f. 1st (possibly root *ac = swift, sharp;* cf. ὠκύς *= swift*, ὄcιor = *swifter, ācer*, etc.); subj.-acc. of *praemissam esse* (1. 47) in the acc. and inf. construction dependent on *sciam* below. The silver eagle referred to was, according to Sallust, Chap. 59, the one which Marius had had when he overcame the Cimbrī ("*quam bellō Cimbricō C. Marius in exercitū habuisse dīcēbātur*"). NOTE A. It appears that before the time of Marius there had been only one standard for a whole Roman army, and not a particular one for each legion; according to Ovid, this *signum* consisted of a bundle of hay set upon the end of a long pole. According to Pliny, before Marius the eagle was only one of five kinds of standards, the others being a representation in bronze or silver of a wolf, boar, minotaur, and horse. Marius, in his second consulship, fixed the *aquila* (usually of silver, in later times of gold) with outstretched wings as the legionary standard, and it was intrusted to the *prīmipīlus* and carried in the front line (whereas it had been carried in the third line, viz. the *triārii*). While the *aquila* always continued to be the principal standard, there were several other *signa* or *vexilla*, for each cohort and each century had its own standard (some supposing that *signum = the standard* of a *cohors*, and that *vexillum = the standard* of a *centuria*, though this distinction is not strictly kept by Roman writers). The purpose of the standards was to guide the evolutions, etc., of the soldiers, e.g. *signa inferre = to advance, signa convertere = to wheel*, etc. NOTE B. Prof. Beesly and a few other scholars quote Catiline's superstitious care and adoption of the old *aquila* which Marius had used among their reasons for describing Catiline as the accepted leader of the democratic party. Thus Prof. Beesly says, "He was the successor in direct order of the Gracchī, of Sāturnīnus, of Drūsus, of Sulpicius, and of Cinna, and was recognized as such both by friends and enemies." But an overwhelming majority of modern classical authorities maintain that, while Catiline might have taken this position, he lacked the necessary strength and decision of character to do so, and set his own selfish desires before the political necessities of the popular party. Thus Caesar, who had hoped to make political use of him, presently withdrew his support as Catiline's political sponsor, and Catiline became a discontented revolutionist, possessed of no real influence with the better part of the popular party. —— **illam**, acc. sing. f. of the dem. pron. *ille, illa, illud;* agrees with *aquilam; illam* is emphatic. When *ille* follows a noun, it = *that wellknown, that famous*, or *that notorious;* the usual place of the dem. pronouns is before the nouns which they qualify.

LINE 43. **argenteam**, acc. sing. f. of the adj. *argenteus, -a, -um* (from the noun *argentum, -ī*, n. 2d = *silver;* root *arg* = Sanskrit *raj* = Greek ἀργ = Latin *arg, to be*

44 omnibus	cōnfīdō	perniciōsam	ac	fūnestam	the very eagle (which
all	*I trust*	*baleful*	*and*	*fatal*	will, I trust, prove
45 futūram,		cui	domī	tuae	sacrārium	baleful and fatal to
to be about to be,	*for which*	*at house*	*your*	*the shrine*	you and all your con- federates) to whose

bright, to shine; cf. Sanskrit *rajatam = silver*, ἄργυρος *= silver*, *argilla = white clay*, etc.); agrees with *aquilam.* Silver, and sometimes bronze, was the most common metal of which *aquilae* were made; gold *aquilae* became more common later, esp. during the empire.——**quam**, acc. sing. f. of the rel. pron. *quī, quae, quod;* agrees with the antecedent *aquilam*, and is subj.-acc. of *futūram (esse)* in the acc. and inf. object-clause dependent on *cōnfīdō.* Observe: (1) that the *quam* clause by no means defines *aquilam*, but *quam* rather *= et eam;* (2) that *quam* is a subordinate clause in indirect discourse, and yet the verb *cōnfīdō* is ind. ; the reason is that neither the *quam* clause nor the clause of *cui* following is an integral part of the indirect discourse, but is a kind of "aside" comment made parenthetically by the speaker.——**tibi**, dat. sing. of *tū;* dat. of the indirect obj., with *perniciōsam ac fūnestam, futūram.*——**ac**, cop. conj. ; joins *tibi* and *tuīs.*——**tuīs**, dat. plur. of *tui, -ōrum*, m. 2d *= your friends (kinsmen, party*, or other appropriate noun); dat. of the indirect obj., like *tibi* above, to which it is joined by *ac. Tui, -ōrum*, is the mas. plur. of the poss. adj. *tuus, -a, -um*, used substantively; cf. *bona* = lit. *good things*, hence *property, possessions.*

LINE 44. **omnibus**, dat. plur. m. of the adj. *omnis, -e*, 3d; agrees with *tuīs.*—— **cōnfīdō**, 1st pers. sing. pres. ind. of the semi-deponent verb *cōnfīdō, -ere, cōnfīsus sum*, 3 (a perf. *cōnfīdī* is sometimes found; so *diffīdī* and *diffīsus sum* from *diffīdō;* cōn*fīdō* is a compound of *con* and the semi-deponent *fīdō*); the subj. *ego* is implied by the personal ending. For semi-deponents refer to the note on *audeat*, Chap. II, l. 47.—— **perniciōsam**, acc. sing. f. of the adj. *perniciōsus, -a, -um* (from *perniciēs*); agrees with the subj.-acc. *quam ; perniciōsam* is predicative, being a complement of *futūram (esse).* ——**ac** (short form of *atque*), cop. conj. ; connects *perniciōsam* and *fūnestam.*—— **fūnestam**, acc. sing. f. of the adj. *fūnestus, -a, -um* (formed from the noun *fūnus*, *fūneris*, n. 3d = *death, funeral;* hence *fūnestus = fatal*); agrees with the subj.-acc. *quam*, and is predicative like *perniciōsam*, to which it is joined by *ac.*

LINE 45. **futūram**, acc. sing. f. of *futūrus, -a, -um*, fut. part. of *sum, esse, fui;* agrees with the subj.-acc. *quam* in gender and number ; with *futūram* must be supplied *esse =* the fut. inf. of *sum*, agreeing with *quam* in the acc. and inf. object-clause dependent on *cōnfīdō.* —— **cui**, dat. sing. f. of the rel. pron. *quī, quae, quod;* agrees with the antecedent *aquilam.* Observe: (1) that, like the preceding clause *quam . . . futūram*, the clause *cui . . . fuit* is parenthetic, and so, in spite of its being subordinate in indirect speech, the verb remains ind. instead of being subjunct. (for subjunct. it would have to be, if the clause were really a part of the indirect discourse ; see the note on *vitēmus*, Chap. I, l. 24); (2) that the connection of coördinate rel. clauses by a cop. conjunction is avoided in Latin just as it is in English (*asyndeton*); hence the *cui* clause follows the *quam* clause without any connecting word. —— **domī**, locative case of *domus, -ūs*, f. 4th (with several 2d decl. case-forms); denotes *place where*, and modifies the pred. *cōnstitūtum fuit.* For the locative case, consult the note on *Rōmae*, Chap. IV, l. 28 ; and for the cases of *domus*, see the note on *domus*, Chap. III, l. 4. —— **tuae**, gen. sing. f. of the poss. adj. *tuus, -a, -um ;* agrees with *domī* (the locative), which, for purposes of adjectival attribution, is regarded as equivalent to a genitive. —— **sacrārium**, nom. sing. of *sacrārium, -ī*, n. 2d (from adj. *sacer*); subj. of *cōnstitūtum fuit.* Catiline is said to have paid peculiar veneration to the eagle which was Marius' legacy, and to have declared *sacred* a certain room of his house in which he kept the eagle. A parallel is intended between the *sacrārium* of Catiline ("a shrine of crime") and the *sacrārium* or little chapel in which the legionary

service you dedicated	scelerum	[tuōrum]	cōnstitūtum	fuit,	sciam 46
in your own house	of villanies	[your]	established	was	I know
your secret chamber	esse praemissam?		Tū	ut	illā 47
of crime? What an	to have been sent forward?		You	(is it possible) that	that
idea, to suppose that	carēre	diūtius	possīs,	quam	venerāri 48
you could for any	to do without	longer	you may be able,	which	to reverence
length of time do					

eagle was kept in camp; when the army was in camp, the eagles were always kept near the general's headquarters (*praetōrium*) in a spot which the soldiers held *sacrum*. The superstitious Roman soldiers were fearful of anything that might bring ill-luck upon their arms; hence they paid adoration to the eagle as the emblem of their success; cf. Dion Cassius, who speaks of the eagle's repository as νεώς (= *a temple*). The nouns *sacrum*, *sacrārium*, and *sacellum* may be used of a *chapel*, but often they signify a portion of ground made sacred by the presence of an altar, and not necessarily covered over.

LINE 46. **scelerum**, gen. plur. of *scelus, sceleris*, n. 3d; subjective gen., limiting *sacrārium*. Some editors consider *scelerum tuōrum* as an interpolation; *tuōrum* has not very good authority in the Mss., but *scelerum* is well supported. —— **tuōrum**, gen. plur. n. of the poss. adj. *tuus, -a, -um;* agrees with *scelerum*. *Tuōrum* is bracketed, because it should probably be omitted; however, Hahn retains it. —— **cōnstitūtum fuit**, 3d pers. sing. periphrastic perf. tense pass. of *cōnstituō, -ere, -uī, -ūtum*, 3 (= *cōnstitūtum*, nom. sing. n. of the perf. part. pass. of *cōnstituō* + *fuit*, 3d pers. sing. perf. ind. of *sum*); agrees with the subj. *sacrārium;* the verb is ind., because the clause is not ind. in form, but included parenthetically within the ind. object-clause of *sciam*. For the difference between *cōnstitūtum fuit* and the ordinary perf. pass. *cōnstitūtum est*, refer to the note on *cōnstitūtī fuērunt*, Chap. VII, l. 15. —— **sciam**, 1st pers. sing. pres. subjunct. act. of *sciō, -īre, -īvī, -ītum*, 4; the implied subj. is *ego;* the mood is subjunct., because *ā quō* is causal (see note on *sciam*, l. 38).

LINE 47. **esse praemissam**, perf. inf. pass. of *praemittō, -ere, praemīsī, praemissum*, 3 (*prae + mittō*); agrees with the subj.-acc. *aquilam*, l. 42, in the acc. and inf. construction dependent on *sciam;* as is the rule in combinate passive infinitives, the participle agrees adjectively with the subj.-accusative. —— **Tū**, nom. sing. of the 2d personal pron.; subj. of *possīs; tū* is emphatic. —— **ut**, conj., followed by the subjunct. *possīs; tū ut . . . possīs* is the exclamatory idiom explained in the note on *ut*, l. 2. —— **illā**, abl. sing. f. of the dem. pron. *ille, illa, illud; illā* refers to *aquilam*, l. 42; the abl. case is governed by *carēre*. Verbs and adjectives expressing *plenty* or *want* are followed by the abl. of that of which there is abundance or lack; occasionally, however, the gen. case takes the place of the abl., and the gen. is preferred after *egeō* and *indigeō*. A. & G. 243, *f;* 223, NOTE; B. 214, 1; G. 405; H. 414, 1; and 410, V, 1.

LINE 48. **carēre**, pres. inf. act. of *careō, -ēre, -uī*, no supine, 2 (fut. part. *caritūrus;* akin to κείρω = *I shear*); complementary inf., expressing the further action of the same subject which *possīs* suggests. —— **diūtius**, adv.; modifies *carēre possīs; diūtius* is the compar. of *diū*, superl. *diūtissimē*. —— **possīs**, 2d pers. sing. pres. subjunct. of *possum, posse, potuī*, no supine, irreg. (*potis + sum*); agrees with the subj. *tū;* the pres. subjunct. is employed in exactly similar construction to *ut . . . frangat*, l. 2. —— **quam**, acc. sing. f. of the rel. pron. *quī, quae, quod;* agrees with the antecedent *illā*, and is direct obj. of *venerāri*. —— **venerāri**, pres. inf. pass. of *veneror, -ārī, ātus sum*, 1 deponent (cf. Sanskrit root *van* = *to tend, worship;* the act. form *venerō, -āre*, no perf., *venerātum*, 1, is only rarely found); complementary or prolative inf., predicative with *solēbās*. Observe that Cicero puts a bad construction on every action of Catiline, e.g. he calls the *sacrārium*, where he kept the *aquila*, a secret chamber of crime.

49 ad	caedem	proficīscēns	solēbās,	ā
to	*bloodshed*	*going forth*	*you were wont,*	*from*

50 cūius	altāribus	saepe	istam	impiam
of which	*the altars*	*often*	*that of yours*	*impious*

51 dexteram	ad	necem	cīvium	trānstulistī ?
right hand	*to*	*the murder*	*of citizens*	*you transferred ?*

without that eagle, which it was your constant custom to worship when setting forth on an errand of bloodshed, from whose altar you have often turned away your sinful hand to the murder of citizens!

LINE 49. **ad**, prep.; gov. the acc. *caedem ;* *ad* here denotes both *purpose* and *motion.* —— **caedem**, acc. sing. of *caeaēs, -is,* f. 3d (cf. *caedō = I cut, kill ;* root *skidh* = σχιδ = Latin *scid, cid, caed = to cut, cleave ;* cf. σχίζω = *I split*); governed by the prep. *ad.* —— **proficīscēns**, nom. sing. m. of *proficīscēns, -entis,* pres. part. of the deponent verb *proficīscor, -ī, profectus sum,* 3 (*pro* + inceptive form of root *fic* = lit. *I put myself forward,* hence *set out*); agrees with *tū,* the implied subj. of *solēbās.* Participles may be used attributively, like adjectives, or predicatively, in the place of a clause ; *proficīscēns* here = *cum vīs proficīscī.* Observe that, like the pres. ind., the pres. part. may mark *attempted* or *intended* action ; so *proficīscēns = when intending to set out ;* there is little difference between this and the fut. participle. —— **solēbās**, 2d pers. sing. imperf. ind. of the semi-deponent verb *soleō, -ēre, solitus sum,* 2 ; the subj. *tū* is implied by the personal ending. Remember that semi-deponents have active forms of the pres.-stem tenses, but as they lack perf.-active stems, the perf. tenses are supplied in the passive form, but with active meanings. A. & G. 136 ; B. 114, 1 ; G. 167, 1 ; H. 268, 3 ; 465, 2, NOTE 2. —— **ā**, prep.; gov. the abl. *altāribus,* expressing *separation* in combination with *trānstulistī.* Observe : (1) that the rel. word begins a rel. clause, unless it be governed by a prep., in which case the prep. stands first and the rel. second ; (2) that the clause *ā cūius altāribus . . . trānstulistī* is coördinate with the preceding rel. clause *quam venerārī . . . solēbās,* and that they stand together without connection by a cop. conj.; this is preferred in English as well as in Latin.

LINE 50. **cūius**, gen. sing. f. of the rel. pron. *quī, quae, quod ;* agrees with the antecedent *illā* (i.e. *aquilā*), and is poss. gen. limiting *altāribus.* —— **altāribus**, abl. of the plur. noun *altāria, -ium,* n. 3d (from the adj. *altus* = *high*); governed by the prep. *ā.* The regular word for *altar* is *āra, -ae,* f. 1st ; *altāria* (which may be used in plur. sense = *altars,* or in sing. = *an altar*) = properly the upper or higher (*altus*) part of the *āra* upon which the sacrifices were set, but by *synecdoche* commonly signifies the altar itself, cf. *carīna* = lit. *keel,* hence = *nāvis ;* so many other poetical words. A. & G. 386 ; B. no reference ; G. 695 ; H. 637, IV. —— **saepe** (compar. *saepius,* superl. *saepissimē*), adv.; modifies *trānstulistī.* —— **istam**, acc. sing. f. of the dem. pron. *iste, ista, istud ;* agrees with *dexteram.* —— **impiam**, acc. sing. f. of the adj. *impius, -a, -um* (*in* + *pius*); agrees with *dexteram ;* see the note on *impiō,* l. 34.

LINE 51. **dexteram**, acc. sing. of *dextera, -ae,* f. 1st (more often as *dextra, -ae,* f. 1st ; the f. sing. of the adj. *dexter, dextera* or *dextra, dexterum* or *dextrum,* with *manus* supplied, root *dak* = *to take hold of ;* cf. δεξιός = *on the right hand,* ἀμφιδέξιος = *with two right hands,* i.e. using either hand equally well, *dexterous,* etc.); direct obj. of *trānstulistī.* —— **ad**, prep.; gov. the acc. *necem.* —— **necem**, acc. sing. of *nex, necis,* f. 3d (root *nak* = *to destroy ;* cf. *necō = I kill,* νέκυς = *a corpse*); governed by the prep. *ad.* —— **cīvium**, gen. plur. of *cīvis, -is,* m. and f. 3d ; objective gen., following *necem.* **trānstulistī**, 2d pers. sing. perf. ind. act. of *trānsferō, trānsferre, trānstulī, trānslātum,* irreg. (*trāns* + *ferō*); the subj. *tū* is implied by the personal ending.

X. Ere long you	**X.**	**Ībis**	**tandem**	**aliquandō,**	**quō** **tē** 1
will go whither those		*You will go*	*finally*	*some time,*	*whither you*
raging and unbridled	**iam**	**prīdem**	**ista**	**tua**	**cupiditās** **effrēnāta** 2
passions of yours long	*already*	*long ago*	*that*	*of yours*	*desire*	*uncurbed*
since began to hurry	**ac**	**furiōsa**	**rapiēbat.**	**Neque**	**enim** **tibi** 3
you ; for such a	*and*	*raging*	*began to hurry.*	*Neither*	*for*	*to you*

LINE 1. **Ībis,** 2d pers. sing. fut. ind. act. of *eō, īre, īvī* or *iī, itum,* irreg. (compounds make perf. in *-iī*, not in *-īvī*, e.g. *exiī, abiī*); the subj. *tū* is implied by the personal ending. —— **tandem** (*tam* + suffix *-dem*), adv.; modifies *ībis*. —— **aliquandō** (*alius* + *quandō*), adv. ; strengthens *tandem,* cf. the opening words of Oration II. —— **quō** (abl. of *quī*), rel. adv. = *whither ;* introduces the clause *quō . . . rapiēbat. Quō* denotes *place whither,* and *quā* denotes *place where ;* cf. the corresponding dem. adverbs *eō* = *thither,* and *eā* = *there. Quō . . . rapiēbat* = that Catiline will be hurried into civil war. For other uses of *quō,* see the note on *quō,* Chap. V, l. 2. —— **tē,** acc. sing. of *tū ;* direct obj. of *rapiēbat.*

LINE 2. **iam,** adv. of time ; strengthens *prīdem. Iam* frequently combines with and adds force to other adverbs, cf. *iam diū, iam dūdum, iam nunc,* etc. —— **prīdem** (root *pra* = *prī, pro, before,* + suffix *-dem*), adv. of time ; modifies *rapiēbat.* —— **ista,** nom. sing. f. of the dem. pron. *iste, ista, istud ;* agrees with *cupiditās.* Observe that *tua* assigns the possession to the proper person, and *ista* lends it demonstrative emphasis and at the same time expresses the speaker's contempt. —— **tua,** nom. sing. f. of the poss. adj. *tuus, -a, -um ;* agrees with *cupiditās.* For the combination *ista tua,* cf. *furor iste tuus,* Chap. I, l. 3. —— **cupiditās,** gen. *cupiditātis,* f. 3d (from the adj. *cupidus,* formed in turn from the verb *cupiō ;* cf. the Sanskrit root *kup,* which expresses violent emotion, e.g. (1) *to be angry,* (2) *to desire strongly*); nom. sing., subj. of *rapiēbat.* The relation of *cupiditās* to synonyms, e.g. *optiō,* etc., may be gathered from a consideration of the kindred verbs, *cupiō, optō,* etc. ; see the note on *cupientem,* Chap. I, l. 34. —— **effrēnāta,** nom. sing. f. of the adj. *effrēnātus, -a, -um* (*ex* + part. *frēnātus,* of *frēnō ;* or else direct perf. part. pass. of *effrēnō, -āre,* no perf., *effrēnātum,* 1 ; *frēnum* = *a bridle, frēnō* = *I curb, firmus,* and *fortis* are akin, from root *dhara* = *to hold in*); agrees with *cupiditās.* Catiline, at the mercy of his passions, is compared to the driver of a runaway horse ; *furiōsa* and *rapiēbat* following admirably sustain the familiar metaphor.

LINE 3. **ac,** cop. conj. ; joins *effrēnāta* and *furiōsa.* —— **furiōsa,** nom. sing. f. of the adj. *furiōsus, -a, -um* (formed from the noun *furia, -ae,* f. 1st = *rage,* madness ; cf. *furō*); agrees with *cupiditās ;* joined by *ac* to *effrēnāta.* —— **rapiēbat,** 3d pers. sing. imperf. ind. act. of *rapiō, -ere, -uī, raptum,* 3 (root *rap* = *to seize ;* cf. *rapiaus, raptor, rapīnā,* and Greek root ἁρπ, ἁρπάζω = *I seize, plunder,* ἁρπαξ = *grasping,* etc.); agrees with the subj. *cupiditās.* The imperf. tense has particular force, which may be interpreted by either of the following explanations or perhaps by a combination of both : (1) the emphasis may be laid on the gradually accelerated progress of Catiline's defection, and the imperf. is the *historic* imperf. which is used in narrative in close conjunction with *iam diū, iam prīdem,* etc., marking the continuation of an action begun in the past to a period nearer the present ; (2) the emphasis falls on the remoteness in regard to time of Catiline's first tendency towards treason, and the imperf. is *inchoative* (*inceptive*), = *began to hurry.* A. & G. 277 ; B. 260 ; G. 231-234 ; H. 468, 469. —— **Neque** (*ne* + *que*), neg. cop. coördinating conj. = *and not ;* connects the sentence with the preceding one. —— **enim,** causal conj. ; in combination with *neque,* connects the sentence in the light of an explanation with the preceding sentence. *Neque enim cor-*

						course, so far from
₄ haec	rēs	adfert	dolōrem,	sed	quandam	causing you pain, af-
this	*thing*	*does bring*	*sorrow,*	*but*	*certain*	fords you altogether
						inconceivable delight.
₅ incrēdibilem		voluptātem.		Ad	hanc tē	It was for this career
incredible		*a pleasure.*		*For*	*this you*	

responds to the common Greek idiomatic combination καὶ γάρ ὀυ = *and . . . for . . . not;* the explanation is that there is an ellipse of an idea easily supplied after καὶ (*que*), which idea is explained by the clause with γάρ (*enim*) by means of denying a supposition contrary to the one ellipsed ; e.g. in the present passage we may supply as follows : AND (*you will go willingly*), FOR *this revolution does* NOT *cause you pain.* —— **tibi**, dat. sing. of *tū;* dat. of the indirect obj. dependent on *adfert* (a compound of *ad*) ; *tibi* is emphatic by position.

LINE 4. **haec**, nom. sing. f. of the dem. pron. *hīc, haec, hōc;* agrees with *rēs; haec* refers to Cicero's general description of Catiline's attitude, and *haec rēs* signifies not merely his departure to the camp of Manlius (*ībis tandem*, etc.) but the fact of the existence of civil war. —— **rēs**, gen. *rei*, f. 5th ; nom. sing., subj. of *adfert*. —— **adfert**, 3d pers. sing. pres. ind. act. of *adferō (afferō), adferre (afferre), attulī, allātum (adlātum)*, irreg. (*ad + ferō*) ; agrees with the subj. *haec rēs*. —— **dolōrem**, acc. sing. of *dolor, -ōris*, m. 3d (*doleō*) ; direct obj. of *adfert*. Synonyms: *grief, pain* = (1) *aegritūdō*, the generic word, whose application was in Augustan times confined to mental disorder, though afterwards extended to bodily disorder and disease ; cf. Cicero *aegritūdinī subiciuntur angor, maeror, dolor, luctus, aerumna, afflictātiō;* (2) *dolor (aegritūdō cruciāns*, i.e. *torturing grief*, Cic.) = either *pain* of body, or *grief* of mind ; in the latter case it is opposed to *gaudium;* (3) *maeror* (= Cicero's *aegritūdō flēbilis*, i.e. *tearful grief*) = *grief, melancholy*, and its expression by the countenance or by weeping ; (4) *angor* (Cicero's *aegritūdō premēns*) = *sharp pain*, of mind or body ; (5) *luctus* (from *lugeō;* Cicero defines as *aegritūdō ex ēius qui cārus fuit interitū*) = *grief, mourning*, esp. for the death of a relative or dear friend ; it also signifies the outward demonstration of the emotion by means of sombre garb, lamentations, etc., cf. Livy, *senātūs cōnsultō diēbus trīginta luctus est fīnītus* = *by a decree of the senate the mourning was brought to an end in thirty days* ; (6) *maestitia* = *lasting melancholy;* (7) *tristitia* (from adj. *tristis*) = *sadness, sorrow*, which exhibits itself in gloomy looks, as opposed to *laetitia* (= *joy, gladness*, exhibited in the countenance). —— **sed**, adversative conj. ; connects and opposes *neque adfert dolōrem* and *quandam . . . voluptātem (adfert)*. —— **quandam**, acc. sing. f. of the indef. pron. *quīdam, quaedam, quiddam* (adjectival neut. *quoddam*) ; agrees with *voluptātem. Quandam* serves to apologize for so direct an accusation, and softens the violence of *voluptātem* in the reference to treasonable doings. See the note on *quāsdam*, Chap. II, l. 4, for the apologetic force which sometimes attaches to *quīdam* and *aliquis*. Observe that the *m* of *quam-dam* changes to *n* before *d* : so *quendam* for *quemdam, eundem* and *eandem* (from *īdem, is + -dem*), etc.

LINE 5. **incrēdibilem**, acc. sing. f. of the adj. *incrēdibilis, -e*, 3d (*in = not + crēdibilis = believable; crēdō*) ; agrees with *voluptātem*. —— **voluptātem**, acc. sing. of the noun *voluptās, -ātis*, f. 3d (from the adj. and adv. *volup*, shortened for *volupis;* cf. the adjectives *voluptārius* and *voluptuōsus;* the root is *val* = Greek ϝελπ, *to hope, desire*, as ἐλπίζω (for ϝελπίζω) = *I hope*) ; direct obj. of *adfert* (understood after *sed* from *adfert* in the preceding coördinate clause). —— **Ad**, prep. ; gov. the acc. *āmentiam; ad* here expresses purpose or end in view, with reference to each of the coördinate verbs following, *peperit, exercuit*, and *servāvit*. —— **hanc**, acc. sing. f. of the dem. pron. *hīc, haec, hōc;* agrees with *āmentiam*. —— **tē**, acc. sing. of *tū;* direct obj. of *peperit*, and understood as direct obj. of *exercuit* and *servāvit*. Like *tibi* in l. 3, *tē* is rendered emphatic by its position.

of madness that nature brought you into the world, that inclination trained you, that fortune reserved you. Never have you set your heart upon peace, nay more,	āmentiam *madness*	nātūra *nature*	peperit, *brought into life,*	voluntās 6 *your inclination*
	exercuit, *has trained,*	fortūna *fortune*	servāvit. *has preserved.*	Numquam tū 7 *Never you*
	nōn modo *not only (sc. not)*	ōtium, *peace,*	sed nē bellum *but not war*	quidem 8 *even*

LINE 6. **āmentiam**, acc. sing. of *āmentĭa, -ae*, f. 1st (formed from the adj. *āmĕns, = ab + mĕns, out of one's senses, mad*); governed by the prep. *ad*.—**nātūra**, gen. *nātūrae*, f. 1st (from *nātus*, perf. part. of *nāscor*, for *gnascor;* root *gna* or *gan = to beget, bring forth;* cf. *gīgnō*); nom. sing., subj. of *peperit*.—**peperit**, 3d pers. sing. perf. ind. act. of *pariō, -ere, peperī, partum*, 3 (fut. part. *pariturus;* cf. *parturiō, pars, pāreō*, and perhaps *pārō*); agrees with the subj. *nātūra*. Distinguish the parts, conjugation, and meaning of: (1) *parō, -āre, -āvī, -ātum*, 1 = *I make ready, prepare;* (2) *pāreō, -ēre, -uī, -itum;* 2 = *I appear*, or, in different relation, *I obey;* (3) *pariō = I bring forth*, conjugated as described above.—**voluntās**, gen. *voluntātis*, f. 3d (akin to *volō, voluptās*, etc.); nom. sing., subj. of *exercuit;* observe the absence of conjunctions to connect this sentence with the one preceding and the one following (*asyndeton*). *Voluntās* = simply *inclination*, the literal sense, and not *policy*, in the sense of *political inclination*. Sallust states that while a youth Catiline entered upon a career of violence and crime, in which he found extraordinary satisfaction and delight.

LINE 7. **exercuit**, 3d pers. sing. perf. ind. act. of *exerceō, -ēre, -uī, -itum*, 2 (*ex + arceō*); agrees with the subj. *voluntās*.—**fortūna**, gen. *fortūnae*, f. 1st (lengthened from *fors*, akin to *ferō; fors = whatever brings itself*, hence *chance;* cf. *fortasse, fortuitus*, etc.); nom. sing., subj. of *servāvit*. Cicero here takes a fatalistic view, and represents Catiline as a criminal, spared the ordinary punishments which would have fallen to any one but Catiline, in order that he might accomplish a special destiny. Synonyms: (1) *fors = chance, luck;* (2) *fortūna = the fortune* which intermingles with individual lives; often personified, as the goddess of fortune; (3) *fēlīcitās* (root *fe*, cf. *fēcundus*) = *the happy conditions* caused by fortune; (4) *rēs secundae = fortune, prosperity*, lit. *fortunate events*, concrete.—**servāvit**, 3d pers. sing. perf. ind. act. of *servō, -āre, -āvī, -ātum*, 1; agrees with the subject of *fortūna*.—**Numquam** (*ne + unquam*), adv.; limits *concupīstī*.—**tū**, nom. sing. of the 2d personal pron.; subj. of *concupīstī; tū* is emphatic, and as spoken reflects the speaker's contempt.

LINE 8. **nōn**, neg. adv.; in the phrase *nōn modo (nōn)*, which modifies *ōtium concupīstī*, followed by the adversative combinate *sed nē . . . quidem*. Just as an affirmation is made by *nōn modo (sōlum* or *tantum) . . . sed (vērum) etiam (quoque)*, so a negation may be made by *nōn modo (sōlum* or *tantum) nōn . . . sed nē . . . quidem* (or *sed vix*). NOTE. (1) If the two clauses constituting the sentence have each the same verb (e.g. *concupīstī* in this passage) and the verb stands in the second of the clauses with the second member, *nōn modo* usually takes the place of *nōn modo nōn*, i.e. the negation is only actually *expressed* in the second clause (viz. by *nē . . . quidem*) and is understood from it in the first clause (just as *nōn concupīstī* is understood, from *nē . . . quidem concupīstī*, after *nōn modo* in the first clause). Thus our passage practically = the following: *tū nōn modo nōn ōtium nisi nefārium concupīstī, sed nē bellum quidem nisi nefārium concupīstī, = you not only did not desire peace (unless it were wicked), but did not even desire a war, unless it were wicked*. (2) Observe the distribution of the negation, for *nunquam* and *nōn* in the first clause and *nunquam* and *nē* do not cancel one another and make an affirmative; in fact *nōn* and *nē* repeat the

9 **nisi　nefārium　concupīstī.** **Nanctus es　ex** | never upon war, ex-
　unless　heinous　you desired. 　*You obtained　from* | cept its price be
　　　　　　　　　　　　　　　　　　　　　　　　　　crime. You have
10 **perditīs　　atque　ab　omnī　nōn　modo** | raked up a gang of
　abandoned (men) and　by　every　not　only | scoundrels, a gang

negative. This is the regular rule of negative distribution ; Upcott quotes Cicero, *Ea Caesar numquam neque fēcit neque fēcisset = Caesar never did and never would have done those things;* cf. also II, Chap. IV, at the end, *Nēmō nōn modo Rōmae sed nē ūllō quidem in angulō tōtīus Ítaliae oppressus aere aliēnō fuit.* Carefully study the examples in A. & G. 209, *a* ; B. 343, 2 ; G. 482, 5 ; H. 552, 2.—— **modo**, adv. ; in the phrase *nōn modo* (*nōn*), limiting *concupīstī* understood (from the second clause) as governing *ōtium* in the first clause.—— **ōtium**, acc. sing. of *ōtium, -ī*, n. 2d ; direct obj. of *concupīstī* (expressed in the next clause, and understood in this one). Synonyms : (1) *ōtium*, in opposition to *negōtium* = (*a*) *leisure, rest* from business, e.g. *ōtiō fruī = to enjoy leisure,* (*b*) *peace,* as a state or condition of freedom from external enemies ; (2) *pāx* (from stem *pac,* as in *paciscor, pāngō*) = *peace,* as the outcome of diplomatic conference and agreement with an enemy.—— **sed**, adversative conj. ; connects and opposes *nōn modo* (*nōn*) *ōtium* and *nē bellum quidem*.—— **nē**, adv. ; *nē + quidem = not . . . even,* and limits *bellum;* the word or words limited by *nē . . . quidem* always stand between the *nē* and the *quidem*, as *bellum* does in this passage. For the uses of *nē* refer to the note on *nē*, Chap. II, l. 2.—— **bellum**, acc. sing. of *bellum, -ī*, n. 2d (for *duellum,* from *duo;* hence lit. *conflict between two combatants;* cf. *duel*); direct obj. of *concupīstī*.—— **quidem**, adv. ; limits *bellum* in the combination *nē . . . quidem*.

LINE 9. **nisi** (*nē + sī*), conj. ; here used absolutely, with adverbial force, modifying *nefārium*. For this construction of *nisi* without a verb, refer to the note on *nisi*, Chap. VII, l. 39.—— **nefārium**, acc. sing. of the adj. *nefārius, -a, -um* (from the indecl. noun *nefās, ne + fās, = that which is contrary to divine law, heinous crime;* the root is *fa = to speak,* cf. *fārī, fāma,* etc., and *nefandus = lit. not to be spoken,* hence *execrable*); agrees with *bellum*, and is to be supplied with *ōtium* as well.—— **concupīstī**, 2d pers. sing. perf. ind. act. of *concupīscō, -ere, concupīvī, concupītum*, 3 (*con + cupīscō,* an inceptive or inchoative form of *cupiō*); agrees with the subj. *tū* above. *Concupīstī* is a contraction for *concupīvīstī;* such contractions are common before *s* or *r* in the perf. (fut.-perf., or pluperf.) of verbs which make the perf. in *-āvī, -ēvī,* or *-ōvī,* cf. *cōnfīrmāstī,* but only occur before *-st* in perfects in *-īvī;* notice that not only does the *v* disappear, but the two vowels between which it stood in the full form coalesce and combine into one long vowel.—— **Nanctus es**, 2d pers. sing. of the combinate perf. tense ind. of *nancīscor, -ī, nanctus sum*, 3 deponent (*nactus sum* is another form of the perf.; root *nak* = Greek ἔνεκ = *to reach, obtain, carry away,* cf. ἤνεγκον, ἠνέχθην, etc.); agrees (the part. *nanctus* agreeing in gender and number) with *tū*, the subj. understood. Synonyms : (1) *nancīscī = to obtain,* usually implying by chance ; (2) *adsequī* and *cōnsequī = to obtain,* by determined effort ; (3) *adipīscī* (*ad + apīscī = lit. to reach out for something*) = *to obtain,* something worth obtaining, e.g. *victōriam;* (4) *potīrī = to obtain, get possession of,* usually implying by force ; (5) *impetrāre = to obtain,* in answer to a petition.—— **ex**, prep. ; gov. the ablatives *perditīs* and *dērelictīs,* expressing *the source* or *origin.* Note that *ex perditis* and *ex dērelictīs* are adverbial modifiers of *cōnflātam.* This rather involved sentence may be simplified by arranging thus : *nanctus es improbōrum manum cōnflātam ex perditīs atque (ex) dērelictīs nōn modo ab omnī fortūnā vērum etiam (ā) spē.* Observe that *dērelictīs* is coördinate with *perditīs,* and that *dērelictīs* is limited by *nōn modo ab omnī . . . spē.*

LINE 10. **perditīs**, abl. plur. m. of *perditus, -a, -um*, perf. part. pass. (used substantively, = *ex hominibus perditīs*) of *perdō, -ere, perdidī, perditum*, 3 ; governed by the

welded together out of worthless fellows whom fortune and hope alike have abandoned. What gratification you will derive in their company! What de-	fortūnā, vērum etiam spē dērelictīs 11 *fortune but also (by) hope (from men) forsaken* cōnflātam improbōrum manum. Hīc tū 12 *welded together of wicked (associates) a band. Here you* quā laetitiā perfruēre ! quibus gaudiīs 13 *what pleasure (you) will enjoy ! what in delights*

prep. *ex.* —— **atque,** cop. conj. ; connects *ex perditīs* and (*ex*) *dērelictīs.* —— **ab,** prep. ; gov. the abl. *fortūnā,* and must be understood with *spē.* *Ab omnī fortūnā* and (*ab omnī*) *spē* express agency (i.e. *fortūnā* and *spē* are personified) and are modifiers, not of *perditīs,* but of *dērelictīs.* —— **omnī,** abl. sing. f. of the adj. *omnis, -e,* 3d; agrees with *fortūnā.* —— **nōn,** negative adv. ; combined with *modo,* = *not only,* modifying *ab omnī fortūnā.* —— **modo,** adv. ; for *nōn modo* in the first clause, followed by *vērum etiam* in the second, see the note on *nōn,* Chap. III, l. 18.

LINE 11. **fortūnā,** abl. sing. of *fortūna, -ae,* f. 1st (see l. 7); governed by the prep. *ab.* —— **vērum** (adverbial acc. sing. n. of the adj. *vērus, -ā, -um ;* cf. *vērō,* abl. sing. n., used as adv. and conj.), adversative conj., connecting *nōn modo ab omnī fortūnā* with *etiam* (*ab omnī*) *spē.* —— **etiam** (*et* + *iam*), adv. ; modifies *dērelictīs,* with reference to its modifier (*ab omnī*) *spē.* —— **spē,** abl. sing. of *spēs, speī,* f. 5th; governed by *ab,* understood from the coördinate phrase *ab fortūnā* above; *omnī* is also to be supplied from above with *spē.* —— **dērelictīs,** abl. plur. m. of *dērelictus, -a, -um,* perf. part. pass. of *dērelinquō, -ere, dērelīquī, dērelictum,* 3 (*dē* + *relinquo ; relinquō* = *re* + *linquō*); *dērelictīs* is coördinate with *perditīs,* and so is an abl. of *source* or *origin* governed by *ex* (supplied from *ex perditīs*). *Ex dērelictīs ab omnī spē,* etc. = *ex hominibus dērelictīs ab omnī spē* or *ex hominibus quī ab omnī spē,* etc., *dērelictī sunt.*

LINE 12. **cōnflātam,** acc. sing. f. of *cōnflātus, -a, -um,* perf. part. pass. of *cōnflō, āre, -āvī, -ātum,* 1 (*com* + *flō,* = lit. *I blow together, kindle, weld together ;* root *bhla* = *fla, to blow,* cf. *flōreō, flāmen ; fluō, φλύω, fleō,* and φλύω are from kindred roots); *cōnflātam* agrees with *manum,* and is predicative, i.e. = a clause *manum quae cōnflāta est ex perditīs.* *Cōnflātam* = *fused together* or *welded together ;* the metaphor is taken from working in metals, and is common in Cicero; cf. Virgil, Georgics I, l. 508, *falcēs cōnflantur in ensem.* The Greek verb συμφυσᾶν = *cōnflāre,* and is used in similar metaphor. —— **improbōrum,** gen. plur. m. of the adj. *improbus, -a, -um* (*in* = *not* + *probus* = *upright, honest*); gen. of substance or material, defining *manum* and explaining of what *manum* consists ; this gen. is practically identical with the so-called *appositional, epexegetic,* or *adnominal* genitive. Compare: *adnominal,* A. & G. 214, *f ;* B. 202; G. 361; H. 395; and *gen. of material,* A. & G. 214, *e ;* B. 197; G. 361; H. 395. Observe that *improbōrum* is substantival, = *of wicked men ;* the use of adjectives as nouns is very common, cf. *amīcus* = *a friend, bona* = *property.* —— **manum,** acc. sing. of *manus, -ūs,* f. 4th; direct obj. of *nanctus es; manum* here = *band, gang.* —— **Hīc,** demonstr. adv. ; modifies *perfruēre ; hīc* = *inter ēius modī comitēs.* —— **tū,** nom. sing. of the 2d personal pron.; subj. of *perfruēre ; tū* is emphatic, = *you, such a man as you are.*

LINE 13. **quā,** abl. sing. f. of *quī, quae, quod ;* agrees with *laetitiā ;* the sentence is exclamatory. —— **laetitiā,** abl. sing. of *laetitia, -ae,* f. 1st (from the adj. *laetus*); obj. of *perfruēre. Fruor* and its compounds, like *fungor, ūtor, potior,* etc., govern the abl. case. A. & G. 249; B. 218, 1 ; G. 407; H. 421, I. Synonyms: (1) *gaudium* (cf. *gaudeō*) = *joy,* such as is felt inwardly, as opposed to *dolor ;* (2) *laetitia* (cf. *laetor*) = *joy,* which reveals itself in the expression and actions ; *laetitia* is opposed to *tristitia,* and is a stronger term than *gaudium.* —— **perfruēre,** 2d pers. sing. fut. ind. of the deponent verb *perfruor, -ī, perfrūctus sum,* 3 (*per* intensive, = *thoroughly* + *fruor* = *I*

14 exsultābis!	quantā	in	voluptāte	bacchābere,
you will exult!	*how great*	*in*	*pleasure*	*you will revel*
15 cum	in	tantō	numerō	tuōrum	neque
when	*in*	*so great*	*a number of your (friends)*		*neither*
16 audiēs	virum	bonum	quemquam	nec
you will hear	*man*	*good*	*any at all*	*nor*

lights you will run wild in! In what pleasure will you revel, when in all the number of your associates you will neither hear nor see even a single man

enjoy); agrees with the subj. *tū*. Cicero prefers the termination in *-re* to that in *-ris* for the fut. ind. passive, and uses *-re* seven times in this speech and *-ris* not at all. But other writers use *-ris* as much as *-re* in this tense, and, like Cicero, in the pres. ind. and pres. subjunct. passive.—— **quibus**, abl. plur. n. of *quī, quae, quod;* agrees with *gaudiīs; quibus* marks this sentence as exclamatory.—— **gaudiīs**, abl. plur. of *gaudium, -ī,* n. 2d (root *gau = to be glad;* cf. γαῦρος = *exulting, haughty,* and γῆθος = *joy*); abl. of cause, with *exsultābis.* Remember that this abl. is common with verbs expressive of emotion, and esp. with past participles, e.g. *commōtus, incitātus, etc.* Note that *laetitiā* is a more forcible word than *gaudiīs,* but the balance is maintained by adding a stronger verb with *gaudiīs* (than *perfruēre* with *laetitiā*), viz. *exsultābis.*

Line 14. **exsultābis**, 2d. pers. sing. fut. ind. act. of *exsultō, -are, -āvī, -ātum,* 1 (frequentative form of *exsitiō*); agrees with the implied subj. *tū. Exsultābis* etymologically = *you will leap* (*dance*), hence metaphorically *you will riotously delight.* —— **quantā**, abl. sing. f. of the adj. *quantus, -a, -um ;* agrees with *voluptāte. Quantus* may be used: (1) in exclamations, as in this passage, = *how great!;* (2) interrogatively, direct and indirect, *how great?;* (3) relatively, corresponding to dem. *tantus,* = *as great . . . as.* —— **in**, prep. gov. the abl. *voluptāte.* —— **voluptāte**, abl. sing. of *voluptās, -ātis,* f. 3d (see *voluptātem,* l. 5, for derivation, etc.); governed by the prep. *in.* —— **bacchābere**, 2d pers. sing. fut. ind. of the deponent verb *bacchor, -ārī, -ātus sum,* 1 (from the noun *Bacchus*); agrees with the implied subj. *tū ;* observe the *asyndeta. Bacchārī = to revel,* and *bacchātiō = revel,* are derived from the name *Bacchus* (Βάκχος), given both by Greeks and Romans to the god Dionȳsus (Διόνυσος). Bacchus was the god of wine and of riotous enjoyment. He was the son of Jupiter and Semelē, the daughter of Cadmus of Thebes. Hēra (Jūnō) drove him mad, and in this state he wandered through Egypt, Asia, and India, teaching the cultivation of the vine. On his return to Europe he compelled the nations to pay him divine worship. On his travels he was accompanied, first by the Graces, but later by the *Bacchae* or *Bacchantēs* (Βάκχαι), a number of women devoted to his service. The name of *Bacchae* or *Bacchantēs* was also given to those women who in later times kept up his worship, exciting themselves to frenzy by drinking wine. It is from the dithyrambic choruses sung at the festivals of Dionȳsus that the Greek drama was developed.

Line 15. **cum**, temporal conj. ; followed by the ind. *audiēs; cum* here = *quō tempore = nam eō tempore.* The ind. mood is regular with *cum* in primary tenses, and occurs for special reasons in the historic tenses also ; but the subjunct. is the rule with the imperf. and pluperfect. See the note on *cum,* Chap. III, l. 23.—— **in**, prep. ; gov. the abl. *numerō.* —— **tantō**, abl. sing. m. of the dem. adj. *tantus, -a, -um ;* agrees with *numerō.* —— **numerō**, abl. sing. of *numerus, -ī-,* m. 2d (root *nam = to allot;* cf. νέμω = *I distribute,* etc.); governed by the prep. in.—— **tuōrum**, gen. of *tui,* plur. m. 2d (substantival m. of the poss. adj. *tuus, -a, -um ;* so *meī, nostrī* (as in Caesar), *suī, etc.*); not so much a partitive gen. as a descriptive gen., limiting *numerō.* —— **neque** (*ne + que*), negative cop. conj. ; used correlatively with *nec* below, = *neither . . . nor.*

Line 16. **audiēs**, 2d pers. sing. fut. ind. act. of *audiō, -īre, -īvī, -ītum,* 4 (root *av = to hear;* cf. ἀΐω, for ἀϜίω, = *I hear*); agrees with the subj. *tū* implied by the personal

true to his country.	vidēbis.	Ad	hūius	vītae	studium	meditātī	17
It is for the living of	*you will see.*	*For*	*this*	*of life*	*the pursuit*	*studied*	
a life ‚like this that	illī	sunt	quī	feruntur	labōrēs	tuī,	18
your so-called train-	*those have been* (lit. *are*)		*which*	*are called*	*labors*	*your;*	

ending.——**virum**, acc. sing. of *vir, -ī,* m. 2d ; direct object of *audiēs*, and supplied in the coördinate clause following as the direct obj. of *vidēbis. Vir* or *homō* may be used when a complimentary attribute is added (as *bonum* here); but if the attribute be uncomplimentary (e.g. *improbus, malus,* etc.), *homō* and not *vir* is the noun to employ. For further distinctions consult the note on *virī,* Chap. I, l. 23.——**bonum**, acc. sing. m. of the adj. *bonus, -a, -um;* agrees with *virum; bonum = loyal, patriotic,* in a political sense.——**quemquam**, acc. sing. m. of the indef. pron. or adj. *quisquam, quaequam, quidquam* or *quicquam (quis + quam)* ; agrees with *virum. Quisquam* and *ūllus* are rarely used except in negative sentences, or sentences whose import is a negation, e.g. a rhetorical question.——**nec** (abbreviated form of *neque*), cop. conj. ; connects *audiēs* and *vidēbis.* Some editors prefer to read *neque* here. Of the various negative correlative combinations the most common are *neque . . . neque,* and *nec . . . nec;* but *neque . . . nec* is not unusual, though the inverse order *nec . . . neque* is rare. Now and then *et . . . neque,* and *neque . . . et* may be met with, but opportunities for the correlation of an affirmative and negative conjunction are not common. A. & G. 155, *a;* B. 341, 3 ; G. 480, NOTE 3 ; H. 554, I, 5.

LINE 17. **vidēbis**, 2d pers. sing. fut. ind. act. of *video, -ēre, vīdī, vīsum,* **2** ; agrees with the subj. *tū* implied by the personal ending.——**Ad**, prep. ; gov. the acc. *studium,* expressing *purpose* or *end in view* and modifying *meditātī.*——**hūius**, gen. sing. f. of the dem. pron. *hīc, haec, hōc;* agrees with *vītae,* and = *(a life) of this kind,* i.e. comfortless camp-life, with the dregs of Italy for camp-mates.——**vītae**, gen. sing. of *vīta,* f. 1st ; objective gen., with *studium; vītae* here = *modī vīvendī.*——**studium**, acc. sing. of *studium, -ī,* n. 2d (from *studeō; studium =* (1) *inclination, zeal, enthusiasm;* (2) *pursuit, study,* as here ; (3) *devotion, attachment*); governed by the prep. *ad.*——**meditātī**, nom. plur. m. of *meditātus, -a, -um,* perf. part. of the deponent verb *meditor, -ārī, -ātus sum,* 1; agrees with the subj. *illī (labōrēs).* Observe : (1) that *meditātī,* + *sunt* following, = 3d pers. plur. perf. ind. of *meditor,* agreeing with *illī (labōrēs)* as subj.; (2) that, like the perf. participles of some other deponents, *meditātī* has passive force, hence *meditātī sunt = have been studied;* for the passive signification, cf. *comitātus, testātus,* etc., and *meditātum et cōgitātum scelus* (Cic. Philippics). A. & G. 135, *b* and *f*; B. 112 *b*; G. 167, NOTE 2 ; H. 231, 2.

LINE 18. **illī**, nom. plur. m. of the dem. pron. *ille, illa, illud;* subj. of *meditātī sunt;* the full subj. is *illī labōrēs,* but *labōrēs* is emphasized by being included as complement of *feruntur* in the relative clause; see the note on *feruntur.*——**sunt**, 3d pers. plur. pres. ind. of *sum, esse, fuī;* agrees with the subj. *illī; sunt* combines with *meditātī,* forming the perf. tense of *meditor* (see note above).——**quī**, nom. plur. m. of the rel. pron. *quī, quae, quod;* agrees with the subj. *illī.*——**feruntur**, 3d pers. plur. pres. ind. pass. of *ferō, ferre, tulī, lātum,* irreg.; agrees with the subj. *quī.* The sentence *illī quī feruntur labōrēs tuī (meditātī sunt)* admits of two constructions : (1) *those practices which are called your training-exercises;* here *feruntur* is copulative, and *labōrēs tuī* is predicative; we find the mas. *illī* instead of a neut. *illa* (e.g. *illa quae feruntur labōrēs tuī*) by reason of the attraction exerted by the emphatic word *labōrēs;* (2) *those training-exercises of yours which are so much talked about* (*which are matter of common talk*); here *illī labōrēs =* the antecedent of *quī,* and *feruntur* is not copulative, but a full predicate (= *praedicāntur*); the sentence is colloquial, and = οἱ λεγόμενοι πόνοι (so Upcott). The editor of this book has adopted the first construction, but the second is equally good,

19 iacēre	humī	nōn	sōlum	ad	obsidendum	ing has been prac-
(viz.) to lie on the ground	*not*		*only*		*for to be looked out for*	tised — your lying on

the ground, not only
to watch for chances

20 stuprum,	vērum	etiam	ad	facinus	obeundum,	of debauchery, but
debauchery,	*but*	*also*	*for*	*crime*	*to be undertaken;*	also to perpetrate

and finds favor with many; in any case, observe the meaning of *feruntur*, and cf. the common expression *ferunt = men say* (*report, narrate*). —— **labōrēs**, nom. plur. of *labor*, *-ōris*, m. 3d (root *labh* = ἀλφ = *lab, to lay hold of, to work;* cf. ἀλφή, ἄλφημα = *produce, gain*); predicative with *feruntur*, and therefore in the same case as the subj. *quī*. Consultation of a dictionary indicates that there are two forms *labor* and *labos*, and the same is the case with several other nouns, e.g. *honor* (*honos*), *lepor* (*lepos*), *arbor* (*arbos*), *pavor* (*pavos*), *clāmor* (*clāmōs*), etc. It appears that the original ending was in *s*, though Madvig asserts that nouns derived from verbs can only end in *-or*, e.g. *amor* (not *amos*); but Quintilian permits *clāmos* (*clāmor*, from verb *clāmō = I shout*). The change from *s* to *r* began with the oblique cases, and then gradually *s* yielded to *r* in the nominative case also. The change belongs to a period somewhat about 350–300 B.C., as we may gather from Cicero's statement (in one of his letters) that *L. Papīrius Crassus*, who was consul in 336 B.C., was the first of his *gēns* to cease being called *Papīsius* (*quī prīmum Papīsius est vocārī dēsitus*). The Medicean Virgil always reads *arbos, honos*, and *labor* (not *arbor, honor*, and *labos*). However, it is certain that Cicero preferred *labor*, and *honos* and *lepos* are also regularly found in his works. Most monosyllabic words retain *s* in the nominative, with the change to *r* in the oblique cases, e.g. *mās*, gen. *māris;* *aes*, gen. *aeris;* *flōs*, gen. *flōris*. [The substance of the above discussion is taken from Prof. Mayor's note on *honos*, in Chap. VI of Cicero's 2d Philippic Oration.] —— **tuī**, nom. plur. m. of the poss. adj. *tuus, -a, -um;* agrees with *labōrēs*.

LINE 19. **iacēre**, pres. inf. act. of *iaceō, -ēre, -uī*, no supine, 2 (intrans. form of *iaciō;* root *i = to go*, cf. *eō*, εἰμι; just as *iaciō = lit. I make to go*, hence *I throw*, so *iaceō = I am thrown*, hence *I lie*); substantival, and in the nom. case, being an appositive of *labōrēs;* compare *vigilāre* following, which is also an appositive, and note the absence of a connecting conjunction (*asyndeton*). An inf. is a noun, inasmuch as it may be the subj. or obj. of a sentence, e.g. *mentīrī est turpe* (subj.); it is a verbal, inasmuch as it admits of tenses, is modified by adverbs, and governs an object. Consult A. & G. 270; B. 326–328; G. 280; H. 532, 538. —— **humī**, locative case of *humus, -ī*, f. 2d (cf. *homō* (old form *hemō*), χαμαί = *on the ground, hūmānus, humilis*); modifies *iacēre*. *Humus* is one of the few nouns which, apart from the names of towns and small islands (e.g. *Rōmae = at Rome*), retain the old locative case; cf. *domī = at home, rūrī = in the country, mīlitiae = on military service, vesperī = in the evening*. —— **nōn**, neg. adv.; *nōn sōlum* modifies *ad obsidendum stuprum*. —— **sōlum**, adv. (in origin acc. sing. n. of the adj. *sōlus, -a, -um;* cf. *multum, facile*, etc.); in the common combination, *nōn sōlum*, preceding *vērum etiam*, which introduces something still more emphatic. —— **ad**, prep.; gov. the acc. *obsidendum stuprum*, expressing *purpose*. Other ways of expressing purpose are: (1) *causā* or *grātiā* + the gen. of the gerund or gerundive; (2) *ut* (*nē*), or *quō* (if the purpose clause contain a comparative adverb or adjective) + the subjunct. mood; (3) *quī* + the subjunct.; (4) the supine in *-um*, after verbs expressing or implying *motion;* (5) sometimes by the fut. part. in *-rus*. —— **obsidendum**, acc. sing. n. of *obsidendus, -a, -um*, gerundive of *obsideō, -ēre, obsēdī, obsessum*, 2 (*ob + sedeō*); agrees with *stuprum* in the construction of gerundival attraction. See the note on *habendī*, Chap. I, l. 8. In addition to its military sense of *to besiege, to invest, obsidere* often = *to lie in wait for, to be secretly on the watch for*.

LINE 20. **stuprum**, acc. sing. of *stuprum, -ī*, n. 2d; governed by *ad*, and in the gerundival construction with *obsidendum*. There is a low play on the words in the above phrase;

| crimes; your spying by night and secret designs not only upon the husbands' slumbers, but also upon the property of peaceable citizens. You | vigilāre *to watch* somnō *against the sleep* bonīs *against the goods* | nōn *not* marītōrum, *of husbands,* ōtiōsōrum. . *of peaceful men.* | sōlum *only* | īnsidiantem **21** (subj. = *you*) *plotting* vērum *but* Habēs, *You have (a place) where* | etiam **22** *also* ubi **23** |

the meaning is that Catiline cultivated his remarkable physical powers to serve him not only as a soldier in the camp, but also as a libertine in the vicious enterprises of his private life. —— **vērum**, adversative conj. (and adv.; in origin acc. neut. sing. of the adj. *vĕrus;* cf. the abl. sing. n. *vĕrō*, used similarly); connects *ad obsidendum stuprum* and *ad facinus obeundum.* —— **etiam** (*et + iam*), adv.; intensifies *ad facinus obeundum.* —— **ad**, prep.; gov. the acc. *facinus obeundum*, expressing purpose. —— **facinus**, acc. sing. of *facinus, facinoris*, n. 3d (*faciō*, hence lit. = *deed*, but, as a rule, in a bad sense, *misdeed, crime*); governed by *ad*, and in the gerundival construction with *obeundum.* See the synonyms in the note on *sceleris*, Chap. IV, l. 9. —— **obeundum**, acc. sing. n. of *obeundus, -a, -um*, gerundive of *obeō, obīre, obiī, obitum*, irreg. trans. and intrans. (*ob + eō* = lit. *I go to meet*, hence often = *to meet regularly*); agrees with *facinus* in the construction of gerundival attraction. Though *eō* is intrans., *obeō, praetereō*, etc., are trans., as intrans. verbs frequently acquire an active force when compounded with *ad, ante, praeter, ob, trāns*, etc. A. & G. 228, *a;* B. 175, 2, *a;* G. 331; H. 372.

LINE 21. **vigilāre**, pres. inf. act. of *vigilō, -āre, -āvī, -ātum*, 1 (from the adj. *vigil* = *wakeful, watchful;* root *vag* or *aug* = *to be awake, to be active;* cf. ὑγιής = *healthy*, *vigeō, augeō*, etc.); agrees with the subj.-acc. *tē* understood; *vigilāre* is coördinate with *iacĕre*, and like it is an appositive of *labōrēs*. Remember that the inf. may be subj. or obj., no matter if it agrees with an expressed or implied subj.-acc. or not. It is evident that *tē* must be supplied with *vigilāre* as subj.-acc., for the participle *īnsidiantem* refers to and enlarges the subj. of *vigilāre*. —— **nōn**, negative adv.; *nōn sōlum* modifies *īnsidiantem somnō marītōrum*. —— **sōlum**, adv.; in combination with *nōn.* —— **īnsidiantem**, acc. sing. m. of *īnsidiāns, -antis*, pres. part. of *īnsidior, -ārī, ātus sum*, 1 deponent (from *īnsidiae* = *an ambush, in + sedeō;* hence *īnsidiārī* = *to lay an ambush for, to plot against*); agrees with *tē*, the implied subj.-acc. of *vigilāre.*

LINE 22. **somnō**, dat. sing. of *somnus, -ī*, m. 2d (for *sop-nus*, from root *svap* = ὑπ = *sop, to sleep;* cf. ὕπνος, for σύπνος, = *sleep; sopor*, for *svopor; somnium* = a *dream*); dat. of the indirect obj., governed by *īnsidiantem* (as a compound of *in*). —— **marītōrum**, nom. plur. of *marītus, -ī*, m. 2d = *a husband* (in origin the substantival mas. of the adj. *marītus, -a, -um*, from *mās, māris* = *male;* cf. *marīta* = one provided with a *mās*, hence *a wife*); poss. gen., limiting *somnō.* —— **vērum**, adversative conj. (see l. 20); connects *īnsidiantem somnō marītōrum* and (*īnsidiantem*) *bonīs ōtiōsōrum.* —— **etiam**, adv.; intensifies *īnsidiantem bonīs ōtiōsōrum.*

LINE 23. **bonīs**, dat. of *bona, -ōrum*, n. 2d = *property, possessions* (substantival neut. plur. of the adj. *bonus, -a, -um;* cf. *bonum, -ī*, n. 2d = *advantage; bonus* = a *good man; bonī, -orum*, = *the good*, esp. as a political term); dat. of the indirect obj., governed by *īnsidiantem;* joined by *vērum* to *somnō.* —— **ōtiōsōrum**, gen. plur. m. (substantival = *of peaceable men*) of the adj. *ōtiōsus, -a, -um* (from the noun *ōtium*); poss. gen., limiting *bonīs. Ōtiōsī* = citizens of steady and quiet habits, who would be as unlikely to suspect robbery as to have the means at hand to resist it. —— **Habēs**, 2d pers. sing. pres. ind. act. of *habeō, -ēre, -uī, -itum*, 2 ; agrees with the subj. *tū*, which is implied by the personal ending. Observe that the object of *habēs* is the clause *ubi ostentēs patientiam*, etc. —— **ubī**, adv. (for *quo-bi*); introduces the consecutive clause

24 ostentēs　　　tuam　illam　praeclāram　patientiam
you may display of yours　that　famous　endurance

25 famis,　　frīgoris,　　inopiae　　rērum　　omnium,
of hunger,　of cold,　　of lack　of things　all,

26 quibus　　tē　　brevī　　tempore　cōnfectum　esse
by which　yourself　short　in time　overcome　to be

> now have an opportunity of displaying your remarkable power of enduring hunger, cold, and complete destitution, and you will find before long your

ubĭ ostentēs patientiam; habēs ubĭ = habēs locum in quō, the relative word expressing characteristic and consequently followed by the subjunctive mood. The uses of *ubi* are: (1) adv. of place, interrog. or relative, = *where;* (2) adv. of time, interrog. or relative, = *when;* (3) adv. in place of the rel. pron., = *whereby, with whom,* etc.

LINE 24. **ostentēs,** 2d pers. sing. pres. subjunct. act. of *ostentō, -āre, -āvī, -ātum,* I (frequentative of *ostendō, obs + tendō*); agrees with the subj. *tū* implied by the personal ending; the subjunct. is consecutive following *ubĭ,* which expresses *characteristic (you have an opportunity for,* etc.). Synonyms: (1) *monstrō* (akin to *moneō*) = *I point out,* e.g. *viam digitō;* (2) *dēmonstrō = I indicate, I call attention to;* (3) *significō = I make known by signs (signĭs),* e.g. *fraudem;* (4) *indicō = I disclose;* (5) *exhibeō = I hold out to view;* (6) *ostendō = I stretch out to the light, display,* e.g. *potestātem;* (7) *ostentō = I show,* esp. *show off, parade, display.* —— **tuam,** acc. sing. of the poss. adj. *tuus, -a, -um;* agrees with *patientiam.* —— **illam,** acc. sing. f. of the dem. pron. *ille, illa, illud;* agrees with and emphasizes *patientiam.* —— **praeclāram,** acc. sing. f. of the adj. *praeclārus, -a, -um (prae = very + clārus = famous;* the other meaning of *prae* in composition is *before,* cf. *praedīcō = I foretell*); agrees with *patientiam.* —— **patientiam,** acc. sing. of *patientia, -ae,* f. 1st (from *patiēns,* pres. part. of the deponent *patior*); direct obj. of *ostentēs.*

LINE 25. **famis,** gen. sing. of *famēs,* f. 3d; objective gen., dependent on *patientiam.* A. & G. 217; B. 200; G. 363, 2; H. 396, III. —— **frīgoris,** gen. sing. of *frīgus,* n. 3d (cf. ῥῖγος = *frost, cold*); objective gen. dependent on *patientiam* and coördinate with *famis;* note the absence of conjunctions. —— **inopiae,** gen. sing. of *inopia,* f. 1st (from adj. *inops; in + ops*); objective gen., dependent on *patientiam* and coördinate with *famis* and *frīgoris.* —— **rērum,** gen. plur. of *rēs, reī,* f. 5th; subjective gen., defining *inopiae. Omnium rērum = complete,* taking the place of an adjectival attribute; it is found with several nouns, e.g. *cōpia, abundantia,* etc.; cf. II, Chap. XI, *cum omnium rērum dēspērātiōne.* —— **omnium,** gen. plur. f. of the adj. *omnis, -e,* 3d; agrees with *rērum.*

LINE 26. **quibus,** abl. plur. n. of the rel. pron. *quī, quae, quod;* refers (not to *omnium rērum* as antecedent, but) to the antecedents *famis, frīgoris, inopiae;* abl. of the means or instrument, modifying *cōnfectum esse.* Observe that the antecedents of *quibus* are abstract expressions and not all of the same gender, hence the relative *quibus* is neuter = *by which things (agencies, means,* etc.). —— **tē,** acc. sing. of *tū;* subj.-acc. of the inf. *cōnfectum esse* in the object-clause of *sentiēs* (a verb of *perception*). —— **brevī,** abl. sing. n. of the adj. *brevis, -e,* 3d; agrees with *tempore.* —— **tempore,** abl. sing. of *tempus, temporis,* n. 3d; abl. of *time within which.* Distinguish the following: (1) *duration* of time, expressed by the acc., e.g. *duās hōrās = for two hours;* (2) *point* of time, expressed by the abl., e.g. *quartā hōrā = at the fourth hour;* (3) *time within which,* expressed by the abl. and sometimes by the abl. with *in,* e.g. *(in) hĭs decem annīs = within these ten years.* In all of the above the noun usually has a modifier, but remark exceptions like *aestāte = in summer.* —— **cōnfectum,** acc. sing. m. of *cōnfectus, -a, -um,* perf. part. pass. of *cōnficiō, -ere, cōnfēcī, cōnfectum,* 3 (*con + faciō;* most compounds of *faciō* make the passive in *-ficior,* but a few like *faciō,* e.g. *patefaciō, patefīō*);

sentiēs.	Tantum	prōfēcī	tum,	cum	tē 27
you will feel.	*So much*	*I effected*	*then,*	*when*	*you*

ā	cōnsulātū	reppulī,	ut	exsul	potius 28
from the consulship		*I thrust back,*	*that*	*as an exile*	*rather*

temptāre	quam	cōnsul	vexāre	rem pūblicam 29
to attack	*than*	*as consul*	*to harass*	*the commonwealth*

strength consumed by these trials. When I kept you out of the consulship, I accomplished this much at any rate, that though you might assail the state in the character of an exile you could

---

agrees with the subj.-acc. *tē ; cōnfectum + esse =* the perf. inf. pass. of *cōnficiō. Cōnfectum esse = to have been finished (done up,* or *exhausted),* colloquially. —— **esse,** pres. inf. of *sum ;* combines with *cōnfectum,* as described above, and agrees with the subj.-acc. *tē* in the object-clause of *sentiēs.*

LINE 27. **sentiēs,** 2d pers. sing. fut. ind. act. of *sentiō, -īre, sensī, sensum,* 4 ; agrees with the implied subject *tū* in the relative clause. —— **Tantum,** acc. sing. n. of the adj. *tantus, -a, -um ;* direct obj. of *prōfēcī. Tantum prōfēcī = I accomplished only so much,* i.e. *I accomplished so much at any rate ; tantum* is defined by the *ut* clauses following. *Tantum* may be considered an adverbial modifier. —— **prōfēcī,** 1st pers. sing. perf. ind. act. of *prōficiō, -ere, prōfēcī, prōfectum,* 3 (*prō + faciō =* (1) *I succeed,* intrans., (2) *I accomplish,* trans.); agrees with the implied subj. *ego.* —— **tum,** adv. of time ; modifies *prōfēcī ; tum cum reppulī* defines the time of the principal verb *prōfēcī.* Observe that the *cum* clause is exactly like any other rel. clause, for *cum* refers to the antecedent *tum* (*tum cum = eō tempore quō*), and therefore the verb of the *cum* clause is indicative. —— **cum,** temporal conj., correlative of *tum ;* with the ind. *reppulī.* See the note on *cum,* Chap. III, l. 23. —— **tē,** acc. sing. of the 2d pers. pron. *tū ;* direct obj. of *reppulī.*

LINE 28. **ā,** prep., gov. the abl. *cōnsulātū,* expressing *separation* in combination with *reppulī.* —— **cōnsulātū,** abl. sing. of *cōnsulātus, -ūs,* m. 4th (*= the office of cōnsul, consulship*); governed by the prep. *ā.* The substance of the *ut* clauses shows that the allusion in this passage is not to Cicero's defeat of Catiline in the elections held in the year 64 B.C., but to the success of his efforts in securing Catiline's defeat when, at the elections held under Cicero's presidency in 63 B.C., he appeared as a candidate for consular office for 62 B.C. It will be remembered that Cicero prevented intimidation of the voters by appearing with a force of armed friends in the Campus Martius. —— **reppulī,** 1st pers. sing. perf. ind. act. of *repellō, -ere, reppulī, repulsum,* 3 (*re = back + pellō = I drive*); agrees with the subj. *ego* implied by the personal ending. —— **ut,** consecutive conj. ; introduces the objective substantival clause of result *ut . . . possēs ; ut* clauses of this kind are found after any verb of *effecting,* e.g. *prōficiō, efficiō, perficiō,* etc. A. & G. 332; B. 297, 1 ; G. 553, 1 ; H. 501, II. —— **exsul,** gen. *exsulis,* m. (and f.) 3d (probably from root *sad = sed* or *sol, = to go, + ex = out ;* thus *exsul* and not *exul* is the correct form, and *exsilium* (not *exilium*)); nom. sing., in apposition with the implied subj. of *possēs,* viz. *tū.* —— **potius,** comparative adv. *= rather* (adj. indecl. *potis* or *pote ;* compar. *potior ;* superl. *potissimus*); modifies *temptāre.* Synonyms: (1) *potius = more, rather,* of the choice between two things ; (2) *magis = more,* qualitative, in answer to the question 'how greatly ?'; (3) *amplius = more, more widely,* of a growth or an addition ; (4) *plus = more,* quantitative, in answer to the question 'how much ?'.

LINE 29. **temptāre,** pres. inf. act. of *temptō, -āre, -āvī, -ātum,* 1 (intensive of *tendō*); complementary or epexegetical inf., expressing the further action of the subj. of *possēs.* The celebrated scholar Bentley in a note on a passage in Terence remarks that in his study of the most ancient as well as of more recent classical Mss. he has always found either *temptāre* or more rarely *temtāre,* but never the popular form *tentāre ;* ever since the time of Bentley the best scholars have read *temptare, quattuor, scaena,* etc.,

30 possēs,   atque   ut   id,   quod   esset   ā | not harass it as a
  you might be able,   *and*   *that* *that*   *which*   *was*   *by* | consul, and that the
                                     | criminal   enterprise
31 tē   scelerātē   susceptum,   latrōcinium   potius | which you have taken
  you   *wickedly*   *undertaken,*   *brigandage*   *rather* | in hand should better
                                       | merit the name of
32 quam   bellum   nōminārētur. | brigandage than of
  than   *war*   *should be called.* | war.

---

even when in conflict with etymological probabilities (e.g. we should etymologically ex-pect *tentō*), because the mass of the Mss. evidence is in favor of such orthography. —— quam, adv.; introduces an inf. clause of comparison. —— cōnsul, gen. *cōnsulis*, m. 3d ; nom. sing., in apposition with the implied subj. of *possēs,* viz. *tū.* Observe the play on the two contrasted words *exsul* and *cōnsul* (both probably from the same root). —— vexāre, pres. inf. act. of *vexō, -āre, -āvī, -ātum,* I (frequentative of *vehō*); complement-ary inf. with *possēs.* —— rem, acc. sing. of *rēs, reī,* f. 5th ; direct obj. of *vexāre.* —— pūblicam, acc. sing. f. of the adj. *pūblicus, -a, -um;* agrees with *rem.*

LINE 30. possēs, 2d pers. sing. imperf. subjunct. of *possum, posse, potuī,* no supine, irreg. (*potis = able + sum = I am*); agrees with the subj. *tū* implied by the personal ending ; the subjunct. is consecutive following *ut.* —— atque, cop. conj.; joins the coördinate substantival clauses *ut . . . possēs* and *ut id . . . nōminārētur.* —— ut, con-secutive conj.; introduces the substantival clause of result *ut id . . . nōminārētur* as obj. of *prōfēcī.* —— id, nom. sing. n. of the dem. pron. *is, ea, id;* subj. of *nōminārētur.* —— quod, nom. sing. n. of the rel. pron. *quī, quae, quod;* agrees with the antecedent *id* in gender and number, and is subj. of *susceptum esset.* —— esset, 3d pers. sing. im-perf. subj. of *sum, esse, fuī;* agrees with the subj. *quod; esset + susceptum =* the plu-perf. subjunct. pass. of *suscipiō.* It is the regular rule for a verb dependent on a subjunctive (as *possēs*) to be itself subjunctive. Some editors retain the older reading *est ā tē scelerātē susceptum* (*est . . . susceptum =* perf. ind. pass.), and explain the ind. mood on the ground that the *quod* clause is not an integral part of the consecutive sentence, but an addition of the speaker explaining *id;* cf. Chap. VII, ll. 2 and 3, *nōn ut odiō permōtus esse videar, quō* DEBEŌ. —— ā, prep.; gov. the abl. *tē,* expressing *the agent* after the passive verb *susceptum esset.*

LINE 31. tē, abl. sing. of *tū;* governed by the prep. *ā.* —— scelerātē, adv. (formed from *scelerātus,* perf. part. pass. of the verb *scelerō,* I); modifies *susceptum esset.* —— susceptum, nom. sing. n. of *susceptus, -a, -um,* perf. part. pass. of *suscipiō, -ere, suscēpī, susceptum,* 3 (*subs,* old form of *sub, + capiō*); agrees with the subj. *quod; susceptum + esset* (above, where see note) = the 3d pers. sing. pluperf. subjunct. pass. of *suscipiō.* Synonyms: (1) *suscipere,* opposed to *recusāre, = to undertake* a thing or business, in general ; (2) *recipere = to undertake* a matter assigned to one, and to engage to be responsible in oneself for the results and the risks involved. —— latrōcinium, gen. *latrōciniī,* n. 2d (from verb *latrōcinor,* I ; from *latrō*); nom. sing., predicative with the copulative verb *nōminārētur.* See the note on *latrōciniō,* Chap. IX, l. 35. —— potius, comparative adv. ; modifies the pred. *latrōcinium* (*nōminārētur*).

LINE 32. quam, adv.; introduces a clause of comparison after *potius.* —— bellum, gen. *bellī,* n. 2d (for *du-ellum,* from *duo*); nom. sing., predicative with *nōminārētur.* Observe the contrast between *latrōcinium* and *bellum;* if Catiline had been elected consul in 63 B.C., he might have been said in virtue of his office (with military im-perium) to be waging *war.* —— nōminārētur, 3d pers. sing. imperf. subjunct. pass. of *nōminō, -āre, -āvī, -ātum,* I (from *nōmen;* root *gna = to know,* cf. *nōscō,* etc.); agrees with the subj. *id;* the subjunct. is consecutive, in the substantival clause of result intro-duced by *ut* (l. 30) in dependence on the principal verb *prōfēcī.*

XI. Now, Conscript Fathers, to enable me to escape by solemn prayer and entreaty what seems to be an almost justifiable complaint on the part of my country, lend careful at-

XI. Nunc ut ā mē, patrēs cōnscrīptī, 1
Now that from me, fathers enrolled,

quandam prope iūstam patriae querimōniam 2
certain nearly just of my country a complaint

dētester ac dēprecer, percipite, quaesō, 3
I may ward off and plead against, attend to, I beg,

LINE 1. **Nunc**, adv.; with a force not so much temporal as resumptive; = Greek νῦν δέ. —— **ut**, final conj.; followed by the subjunctives *dētester* and *dēprecer*, in a pure clause of purpose. —— **ā** (*ā* or *ab* before consonants, *ab* before words beginning with a vowel or *h*), prep.; gov. the abl. *mē*, expressing *separation* in combination with the verbs *dētester* and *dēprecer*. —— **mē**, abl. sing. of *ego;* governed by the prep. *ā.* —— **patrēs**, voc. plur. of *pater, patris*, m. 3d; the case of address. Not all *patrēs familiās* became *patrēs* in the sense of *senators*, but only such as were chosen by the consul or censor (out of the *patriciī*, descendants of the most ancient *gentēs*), or such as succeeded to a seat in the senate by virtue of having held curule office. —— **cōnscrīptī**, voc. plur. m. of *cōnscrīptus, -a, -um*, perf. part. pass. of *cōnscrībō, -ere, cōnscrīpsī, cōnscrīptum*, 3 (*con + scrībō*); agrees with *patrēs*. *Patrēs cōnscrīptī = enrolled fathers*, the epithet *cōnscrīptī* serving to distinguish those *patrēs* (patrician heads of families) who were senators from those who were not. The old explanation, that the phrase = *patrēs et cōnscrīptī* = (patrician) *senators and enrolled* (plebeians), is no longer accepted.

LINE 2. **quandam**, acc. sing. f. of the indef. pron. and adj. *quīdam, quaedam, quiddam* (adjectival neut. *quoddam; qui + -dam*); agrees with *querimōniam;* as often, this pronoun qualifies or apologizes for something, as in this passage for *prope iūstam = an almost justifiable complaint, so to speak.* Observe that *m* changes to *n* before *d;* thus *quemdam* to *quendam*, and *quamdam* to *quandam*. —— **prope**, adv. (compar. *propius;* superl. *proximē*); limits *iūstam.* Many adverbs in early times acquired prepositional force; cf. *prope* + the acc., *ante* + acc., *palam* + abl., etc. —— **iūstam**, acc. sing. f. of the adj. *iūstus, -a, -um* (from noun *iūs = right, law*, lit. *that which is binding;* root *yu = to bind*); agrees with *querimōniam.* —— **patriae**, gen. sing. of *patria*, f. 1st (in origin f. of adj. *patrius, -a, -um*, with *terra* understood); poss. gen., limiting *querimōniam.* —— **querimōniam**, acc. sing. of *querimōnia, -ae*, f. 1st (from verb *queror = I complain;* root *quer* or *ques*, akin to Sanskrit *cvas = to heave a sigh*); direct obj. of *dētester*, and understood as direct obj. of the coördinate verb *dēprecer.* Synonyms: (1) *questus = complaint* in general; (2) *querimōnia = complaint* about what has in actual fact been suffered; (3) *querēla = complaint* about something suffered in fact or in imagination.

LINE 3. **dētester**, 1st pers. sing. pres. subjunct. of the deponent verb *dētestor, -ārī, -ātus sum* 1 (*dē*, marking separation + *testor*, from *testis = a witness;* hence lit. *I bear witness from, I avert by solemn adjuration*); the implied subj. is *ego;* the subjunct. is final with *ut.* —— **ac** (abbreviated form of *atque*), cop. conj.; connects *dētester* and *dēprecer. Atque* (*ac*) is often used instead of *et* to join two important words or ideas. —— **dēprecer**, 1st pers. sing. pres. subjunct. of the deponent verb *dēprecor, -ārī, -ātus sum*, 1 (*dē*, with force as in *dētester + precor = I pray;* hence *I avert by pleading;* cf. English *I deprecate*); the implied subj. is *ego.* —— **percipite**, 2d pers. plur. pres. imperative act. of *percipiō, -ere, percēpī, perceptum*, 3 (*per + capiō*); the subj. *vōs* is understood. *Percipere =* lit. *to seize completely*, i.e. with the understanding, hence *to hear, to comprehend.* —— **quaesō**, 1st pers. sing. pres. ind. act. of *quaesō, -ere, -īvī* or *-iī*, no supine, 3 (old form of *quaerō;* the 1st pers. plur. is *quaesumus;* etymology doubtful); the subj. is *ego* understood. *Quaeso* is parenthetical = *I pray you; quaesumus* is often similarly used.

4 dīligenter	quae	dīcam,	et	ea
carefully	*(those things) which*	*I shall say,*	*and*	*them*

5 penitus	animīs	vestrīs	mentibusque
deeply	*to minds*	*your*	*and to (your) intellects*

6 mandāte.	Etenim	sī	mēcum	patria,	quae
commit.	*For*	*if*	*with me*	*my country,*	*which*

tention, I beg of you, to the words which I am about to speak, and lay them safely up within your inmost hearts and minds. For imagine my country, which

LINE 4. **dīligenter**, adv. (from adj. *dīligēns; dīligēns* is pres. part. of *dīligō, dis +*
legō = I select apart; hence *dīligenter = carefully, with discrimination*); modifies *per-*
cipite. —— **quae**, acc. plur. n. of the rel. pron. *quī, quae, quod;* agrees in gender and
number with *ea*, understood as direct obj. of *percipite*, i.e. *quae dīcam* is not the interrog.
pron. + pres. subjunct. in indirect interrogation, but the rel. + the fut. ind. (= *ea quae*
dīcam). When the rel. + its verb = a single phrase or idea, the antecedent is frequently
omitted, especially when a part of *is, ea, id;* cf. *quī adsunt audiant = let those present*
listen. —— **dīcam**, 1st pers. sing. fut. ind. act. of *dīcō, -ere, dīxī, dictum,* 3; the subj.
ego is implied by the personal ending; *quae dīcam* practically = *mea verba.* All com-
mentators agree that the following elaborate defence of Cicero's policy in dealing with
the conspirators could not have been a part of the speech as spoken by Cicero in the
senate; it was probably worked up at a later period for publication. Yet Cicero may
very well have given an extempore account of his action to his audience, which account
served as the basis for his exoneration as we now find it. —— **et**, cop. conj.; connects the
imperatives *percipite* and *mandāte.* —— **ea**, acc. plur. n. of the dem. pron. *is, ea, id;*
direct obj. of *mandāte; ea* refers to *quae dīcam* (*my words*).

LINE 5. **penitus** (root *pen = to enter;* cf. *penetrō*), adv.; modifies *mandāte*, or
the adverbial phrase *animīs . . . mentibusque.* —— **animīs**, dat. plur. of *animus, -ī,* m.
2d; indirect obj. of *mandāte. Animīs mentibusque=to your hearts and minds; animus*
and *mēns* are here practically synonymous; when they are distinguished *animus = the*
heart, the mind, as the seat of the emotions (cf. *animus = courage, anger,* etc.), while
mēns = the mind, the intellect, the seat of the reason. —— **vestrīs**, dat. plur. m. of the
poss. adj. *vester, vestra, vestrum* (poss. of the personal pron. plur. *vōs*); agrees with
animīs, and is understood in the fem. with *mentibus.* —— **mentibusque** (*mentibus +*
que), *mentibus* is the dat. plur. of *mēns, mentis,* f. 3d; indirect obj. of *mandāte;* joined
to *animīs* by *que. Que* is the enclitic cop. conj.; connects *animīs* and *mentibus; que,*
as distinguished from the copulative conjunctions, connects two words or ideas which
have in themselves a close internal connection.

LINE 6. **mandāte**, 2d pers. plur. pres. imperative act. of *mandō, -āre, -āvī, -ātum,*
1 (*manus + dō = I put in hand, commit*); the implied subj. is *vōs*, referring to the
patrēs cōnscrīptī (l. 1); coördinate with *percipite* above. —— **Etenim** (*et + enim,* =
for truly, and indeed), causal conj.; connects what follows with what has preceded.
The causal particles are : (1) *nam*, praepositive, except when yielding to metrical needs
in poetry; (2) *enim*, postpositive in classical, but praepositive in ante-classical Latin;
often strengthened by other conjunctions, e.g. *atenim* (*at + enim*), *enimvērō,* etc.;
(3) *namque*, standing first, not very common except in Livy; (4) *etenim*, standing
first, very common in classical and esp. Ciceronian Latin, but rare in ante-classical and
post-classical authors. *Etenim =* the Greek καὶ γάρ, with the ellipse of an idea between
the two; so here *and (it is your duty to listen to me carefully) for if,* etc. A. & G.
156, *d;* B. 345; G. 498; H. 310, 5, and 554, V. —— **sī**, conditional particle; expresses
an ideal conception for the immediate present or the future with the pres. subjunct.
loquātur. Refer to the note and grammatical references under *loquātur*, Chap. VIII,
l. 2, —— **mēcum** (*mē + cum*), *mē* is the abl. of *ego;* governed by *cum. Cum* is the

is far more precious to me than my own life, imagine all Italy and the whole state thus addressing me:	mihi	vītā	meā	multō	est	cārior,	sī	cūncta 7
	to me	*than life*	*my*	*by much*	*is*	*dearer,*	*if*	*entire*
	Italia,	sī	omnis	rēs	pūblica	sīc	loquātur:	8
	Italy,	*if*	*all*	*the commonwealth*		*thus*	*were to speak:*	

prep. + the abl., governing *mē* and appended to it (as regularly with the personal and reflexive pronouns, and usually with the relative; cf. *sēcum, quibuscum*).——**patria,** gen. *patriae*, f. 1st.; nom. sing., subj. of *loquātur*. *Patria* is personified, and imagined as interrogating Cicero; cf. the personification in Chap. VII, l. 44, and Chap. VIII, l. 2. ——**quae,** nom. sing. f. of the rel. pron. *qui, quae, quod;* agrees with the antecedent *patria*, and is subj. of *est* in its own clause.

LINE 7. **mihi,** dat. sing. of *ego;* dat. of the indirect obj., in dependence on *cārior est.*——**vītā,** abl. sing. of *vīta, -ae*, f. 1st.; abl. of comparison (= *quam vītā*), after the comparative *cārior*. When two words are compared, the second may be put in the same case as the first, and be preceded by *quam*, or *quam* may be omitted and the second noun put in the abl. case. But when the first noun is in any case other than the nom. or acc., *quam* is used, and the noun following takes the same case as the first noun. A. & G. 247, and footnote; B. 217; G. 296; H. 417.——**meā,** abl. sing. f. of the poss. adj. *meus, -a, -um;* agrees with *vītā*.——**multō,** adv. (in origin the abl. neut. of *multus* expressing *measure of difference* with the comparative *cārior* = *dearer by much*); modifies *cārior*.——**est,** 3d pers. sing. pres. ind. act. of *sum, esse, fuī;* agrees with the subj. *quae*. Observe that the verb of the subordinate *quae* clause is indicative, in spite of the general rule, viz. that a clause subordinate to a subjunctive clause or an equivalent inf. clause will have its own verb subjunctive; but this rule only holds good when the subordinate clause is an integral part of the subjunctive clause, for when the subordinate clause states *a fact* which is true in itself apart from any statement made in the subjunctive or inf. clause the ind. mood is employed. So here *quae . . . est cārior* is really an addition made by the speaker, and not indissolubly linked with the subjunct. clause *sī patria . . . loquātur*. A. & G. 342; B. 324, 1; G. 629; H. 529, II, NOTE I.—— **cārior,** nom. sing. f. of *cārior, cārius*, compar. degree of the adj. *cārus, -a, -um;* agrees with the subj. *quae; cārior* is predicative with *est*.——**sī,** conditional particle; repeated by *anaphora* from *sī* above. The repetition of *sī* is more effective than the use of a cop. conj., e.g. *sī patria . . . et cūncta Italia . . . et omnis rēs pūblica*. Although the verb of the *protasis* (*loquātur*) is only expressed in the last *sī* clause, it must be understood in each of the preceding clauses introduced by *sī*.——**cūncta,** nom. sing. f. of the adj. *cūnctus, -a, -um* (for *co = con + iūnctus*, perf. part. of *iungō*); agrees with *Italia*. For the distinction between *tōtus, cūnctus*, and *omnis*, refer to the note on *omnium*, Chap. I, l. 11.

LINE 8. **Italia,** gen. *Italiae*, f. 1st (for derivation, see Chap. IV, l. 26); nom. sing., subj. of *loquātur* understood from below.——**sī,** conditional particle; repeated by *anaphora*.——**omnis,** nom. sing. f. of the adj. *omnis, -e*, 3d; agrees with *rēs pūblica*. ——**rēs,** gen. *reī*, f. 5th; nom. sing., subj. of *loquātur*.——**pūblica,** nom. sing. f. of the adj. *pūblicus, -a, -um;* agrees with *rēs*.——**sīc** (*sī* + the dem. suffix *-ce* abbreviated; cf. *hīc*), adv. of manner; modifies *loquātur; sīc* refers to what follows in ll. 9–43.—— **loquātur,** 3d pers. sing. pres. subjunct. of the deponent verb *loquor, loquī, locūtus sum*, 3; agrees with the nearest subject *rēs pūblica*, and is understood with each of the preceding subjects *patria Italia*. The real subject of *loquātur* is *our country*, whether regarded as the *fatherland* (*patria*), a territorial division (*Italia*), or a community of citizens recognizing the same form of government, and united by identity of political interests (*rēs pūblica*). The pres. subjunct. *loquātur* represents an imaginary case purely as a hypothesis, the possibility of which is disregarded for the sake of argument. Observe

9 " M.   Tullī,   quid   agis?   Tūne   eum,
" *Marcus   Tullius,   what   are you doing?   (Will) you   him,*

10 quem   esse   hostem   comperistī,   quem   ducem
whom   to be   an enemy   you have found,   whom   the leader

11 bellī   futūrum   vidēs,   quem   exspectārī
of a war   about to be   you see,   whom   to be awaited

"Marcus Tullius, what are you doing? Will you allow a man who is, as you have discovered, a public enemy, who will be, as you perceive, the leader of a war, who

---

that the condition whose *protasis* is *sī . . . loquātur* lacks a formally expressed *apodosis;* the substance of what the *apodosis* would be is given in the early part of Chap. XII; the absence of the *apodosis* is due to the inordinate length of the *protasis* (l. 6–the end of the chapter). The non-completion or the change of a construction is called *anacolūthon.* A. & G. 385; B. 374, 6; G. 697; H. 636, IV, 6.

LINE 9. **Marce** (abbreviated = *M.*), voc. sing. of *Marcus, -ī,* m. 2d; the case of address. *Marcus* is the *praenomen* of Cicero. —— **Tullī,** voc. sing. of *Tullius, -ī,* m. 2d; the case of address. *Tullius* is the *nōmen,* or gentile name of Cicero. The *nōmen* invariably ended in *-ius,* and daughters were regularly called by the gentile name with the fem. inflexion in *-a,* e.g. *Tullia, Cornēlia.* —— **quid,** acc. sing. n. of the interrog. pron. *quis, quae, quid;* direct obj. of *agis.* —— **agis,** 2d pers. sing. pres. ind. act. of *agō, -ere, ēgī, actum,* 3; the subj. *tū* is implied by the personal ending. —— **Tūne** (*tū + ne*), *tū* is the 2d personal pron. sing.; subj. of *patiēre,* l. 15. *Ne* is the enclitic interrogative particle, appended to the emphatic word *tū; ne* simply asks for information, whereas *nonne* expects an affirmative and *num* a negative reply. Observe how the juxtaposition of *tū* and *eum* heightens the antithesis; it has in several previous cases been remarked that pronouns, especially when contrasted, appear to stand together, as if they exerted and experienced mutual attraction. Though comparatively simple and free from complex subordination, the sentence *tūne . . . videātur* (ll. 9–17) approaches nearer to being a *period* than any which has so far occurred in this speech. A. & G. 346, *a, b;* B. 351, 5; G. 684–687; H. 573. —— **eum,** acc. sing. m. of the dem. pron. *is, ea, id;* direct obj. of *patiēre,* l. 15, and subj.-acc. of *exīre,* l. 15. Note how far the subj. and obj. of *patiēre* are separated from it; this is regular in the structure of the *period,* which is a complex sentence whose main sentence is not completed till the close. *Eum* here = *Catilīnam,* who is described by the qualities stated in the rel. clauses following.

LINE 10. **quem,** acc. sing. m. of the rel. pron. *quī, quae, quod;* subj.-acc. of *esse* in the acc. and inf. object clause of *comperistī.* —— **esse,** pres. inf. of *sum, esse, fuī;* agrees with the subj.-acc. *quem.* —— **hostem,** acc. sing. of *hostis, -is,* m. 3d; is predicative with *esse,* and refers to the subj.-acc. *quem,* therefore taking the same case. The meaning is that Catiline behaved like a *hostis* or public enemy, and deserved that name; he was not in fact officially declared *hostis* till a short time after the delivery of the 2d speech. —— **comperistī,** 2d pers. sing. perf. ind. act. of *comperiō, -īre, comperī, compertum,* 3; agrees with *tū* understood as its subj. in the rel. clause. For synonyms and note on Cicero's fondness for this verb, refer to *comperī,* Chap. IV, l. 38. —— **quem,** acc. sing. of the rel. pron. *quī, quae, quod;* subj.-acc. of *futūrum* (*esse*) in the object clause of *vidēs; quem* agrees in gender and number with the antecedent *eum.* —— **ducem,** acc. sing. of *dux, ducis,* m. 3d (cf. *dūcō = I lead*); predicative with *futūrum* (*esse*), and therefore in the same case as *quem.*

LINE 11. **bellī,** gen. sing. of *bellum,* n. 2d; objective gen., dependent on *ducem.* —— **futūrum,** acc. sing. m. of *futūrus, -a, -um,* fut. part. of *sum, esse, fuī;* agrees with the subj.-acc. *quem;* with *futūrum* supply *esse* = the fut. inf. of *sum,* object of the verb of perception *vidēs.* —— **vidēs,** 2d pers. sing. pres. ind. act. of *videō, -ēre, vīdī, vīsum,* 2; the implied subj. is *tū.* —— **quem,** acc. sing. m. of the rel. pron. *quī, quae, quod;* subj.-

is, to your knowl-edge, awaited as commander in the enemy's camp, a prime source of crime, a ringleader of conspiracy, a re-cruiter of slaves and	imperātōrem	in	castrīs	hostium	sentīs, 12
	as general	*in*	*the camp*	*of the enemy*	*you are aware,*
	auctōrem	sceleris,	prīncipem	coniūrātiōnis, 13
	the author	*of crime,*	*the chief*	*of a conspiracy,*
	ēvocātōrem		servōrum	et	cīvium 14
	the summoner (to revolt)		*of slaves*	*and*	*of citizens*

acc. of *exspectārī* in the acc. and inf. object clause of the verb of *perception, sentīs.* —— **exspectārī**, pres. inf. pass. of *exspectō -āre, -āvī, -ātum,* 1 (*ex* + *spectō*); agrees with the subj.-acc. *quem.* Notice the pres. inf.; this tense shows that the action of the inf. and of the leading verb is contemporaneous. A. & G. 336, A.; B. 270, 1; G. 530, 531; H. 537.

LINE 12. **imperātōrem,** acc. sing. of *imperātor, -ōris,* m. 3d (from verb *imperō*); predicate appositive of *quem,* complementing *exspectārī. Imperātor = the general in chief command; dux = a general,* in high but not chief command. —— **in,** prep.; gov. the abl. *castrīs,* denoting *place where.* —— **castrīs,** abl. of the plur. noun *castra, -ōrum,* n. 2d (the sing. *castrum, -ī,* n. 2d = *a fortress; two camps*=not *duo castra (two fortresses),* but *bīna castra*); governed by the prep. *in.* —— **hostium,** gen. plur. of *hostis, -is,* m. 3d; poss. gen., limiting *castrīs.* Observe that Cicero no longer hesitates to speak of the con-spirators as *hostēs.* —— **sentīs,** 2d pers. sing. pres. ind. act. of *sentiō, -īre, sensī, sensum,* 4; the subj. *tū* is implied by the personal ending.

LINE 13. **auctōrem,** acc. sing. of *auctor, auctōris,* m. 3d (through the perf. part. pass. *auctus,* from *augeō;* hence the form *autor* sometimes found is incorrect); in apposition with the direct obj. *eum,* l. 9. —— **sceleris,** gen. sing. of *scelus,* n. 3d; objective gen., limit-ing *auctōrem,* i.e. if *agency* rather than *state* is expressed by *auctōrem;* but we may consider *sceleris* a poss. gen. = *the crime's originator.* —— **prīncipem,** acc. sing. of *prīnceps, prīncipis,* m. and f. 3d (*prīmus* + *capiō*); acc. in apposition with *eum;* observe that the appositives *auctōrem, prīncipem,* and *ēvocātōrem* stand unconnected by a conj. —— **coniūrātiōnis,** gen. sing. of *coniūrātiō,* f. 3d (*con* + *iūrō,* hence *coniūrātiō = a compact sealed by oath* for evil purposes, *a conspiracy*); poss. gen., limiting *prīncipem.* It is possible but unnecessary to regard *coniūrātiōnis* as concrete, = *coniūrātōrum,* i.e. *the ringleader of conspirators.*

LINE 14. **ēvocātōrem,** acc. sing. of *ēvocātor, -ōris,* m. 3d (from *ēvocō = I summon out, ex* + *vocō*); acc. in apposition with *eum.* From Sallust, Chap. 44, we learn that Catiline refused to call upon the slave population of Italy to join his forces, and Lentulus sent a letter to him at Faesulae expostulating with him for weakening his fighting strength by entertaining scruples that were ridiculous, especially as the Senate had declared him an outlaw. Catiline's real reason for declining slave assistance was that he feared that many citizens who would otherwise join him would be disgusted and incensed if he used the slaves. Those who whitewash Catiline's character contend that he was unwilling, as the leader of the democratic party, forced into war as Marius had been forced, to sully his arms as a Roman citizen fighting for political principles. However, other con-spirators were not so scrupulous, and hoped to stir up a rebellion of slaves on a scale equal to that which Spartacus had led, and there were uprisings of slaves and gladiators at Capua and in Apūlia. —— **servōrum,** gen. plur. of *servus, -ī,* m. 2d; objective gen., limiting *ēvocātōrem.* The number of slaves in Italy was enormous, as we may judge from the fact that in the slave-war in Sicily (B.C. 103–99) a million slaves perished, while 60,000 fell in the last battle fought by Spartacus (71 B.C.). —— **et,** cop. conj.; connects *servōrum* and *cīvium.* —— **cīvium,** gen. plur. of *cīvis* (m. and f.), 3d; objective gen., coördinate with *servōrum.*

15	perditōrum,	exīre	patiēre,	ut	abs	ruined citizens — will
	abandoned,	*to go forth*	*will (you) allow,*	*that*	*by*	you allow such a
						man so to depart
16	tē	nōn	ēmissus	ex	urbe,	sed	inmissus	that men will think
	you	*not*	*sent forth*	*from*	*the city,*	*but*	*hurled*	not that you have
								ejected him from the
17	in	urbem	esse	videātur?	Nōnne	hunc	city but rather that
	against	*the city*	*to be*	*he may seem?*	*Not*	*this (fellow)*	you have hurled him

LINE 15. **perditōrum**, gen. plur. m. of the adj. *perditus, -a, -um* (strictly perf. part. pass. of *perdō = I lose, destroy*); agrees with *cīvium*. *Perditi* in Cicero = men devoid of all honorable instincts, lacking civic virtue and patriotism, and generally bankrupt. —— **exīre**, pres. inf. act. of *exeō, exīre, exīī, exitum*, irreg. (*ex + eō*); agrees with the subj.-acc. *eum*, l. 9, i.e. *eum exīre* is the obj. of the main verb *patiēre;* with *exīre* supply *ex urbe*. —— **patiēre**, 2d pers. sing. fut. ind. of the deponent verb *patior, patī, passus sum*, 3; agrees with the subj. *tū*, l. 9. Note the termination in *-re*, which Cicero in every instance (at least in this speech) uses instead of that in *-ris* for the future; but he always uses *-ris* in this speech for the pres. ind.; for the pres. subjunct. we find *-ris* and *-re*, apparently without particular preference for either. *Patiēre = will you allow*, i.e. passively, without any effort of resistance; *sinō* and *permittō* would not be so expressive of the thought intended; see note on *patimur*, Chap. II, l. 15. —— **ut**, conj.; followed by the subjunct. of result, *videātur*. —— **abs** (old form of *ab*), prep.; gov. the abl. *tē*, expressing *the agent* after the passive inf. *ēmissus (esse)*. *Abs* is little used except with the particular pron. *tē*.

LINE 16. **tē**, abl. sing. of *tū;* governed by the prep. *abs*. —— **nōn**, negative adv.; limits not the verb *videātur*, but the particular word *ēmissus*, as is evident from the opposition of *sed inmissus*. —— **ēmissus**, nom. sing. m. of *ēmissus, -a, -um*, perf. part. pass. of *ēmittō, -ere, ēmīsī, ēmissum*, 3 (*ex + mittō*); agrees with *is* or *ille* understood as subj. of *videātur* (referring to *eum*, i.e. *Catilīnam*, l. 9); with *ēmissus* supply *esse* (from *inmissus esse* below), = the perf. inf. pass. of *ēmittō*, which is complementary or epexegetical with *videātur*. Observe the *paranomasia* or play on the words *ēmissus* and *inmissus*, and cf. Chap. X, l. 28, *exsul . . . cōnsul;* Cicero is fond of this rhetorical device. —— **ex** (*ē* or *ex* before consonants, *ex* before *vowels* or *h*), prep.; gov. the abl. *urbe*, denoting *separation* in combination with *ēmissus*. Whenever possible, the prep. with which a verb implying *separation* is compounded is repeated with the ablative. —— **urbe**, abl. sing. of *urbs, urbis*, f. 3d; governed by the prep. *ex*. —— **sed**, adversative conj.; joins and at the same time opposes *inmissus* to *ēmissus*. —— **inmissus**, nom. sing. m. of *inmissus, -a, -um*, perf. part. pass. of *inmittō, -ere, inmīsī, inmissum*, 3 (*in = into, against, + mittō, I send*); agrees with the implied subj. of *videātur;* with *inmissus* take *esse* following, = the perf. inf. pass., coördinate with *ēmissus (esse)* and complementary with *videātur*. The idea suggested by *ēmissus* is that of the discharge of a suspected person against whom there is not sufficient evidence; *inmissus* suggests the throwing of a dangerous weapon.

LINE 17. **in**, prep.; gov. the acc. *urbem; in* here = *against*. —— **urbem**, acc. sing. of *urbs, urbis*, f. 3d; governed by the prep. *in*. —— **esse**, pres. inf. of *sum; esse* must be combined with each of the participles *ēmissus* and *inmissus*. —— **videātur**, 3d pers. sing. pres. subjunct. pass. of *videō, -ēre, vīdī, vīsum*, 2 (*videor = I seem*); the subj. implied by the personal ending is a pron. referring to *eum*, i.e. *Catilīnam*, l. 9. The subjunctive is dependent on *ut*, and the main idea is that of *result* (consecutive subjunct.), though there is also a slight notion of *purpose* (final subjunct.) as though Cicero's motive in letting Catiline leave Rome was that he might harm the city. The presence of *nōn* is no guide as to the kind of subjunct., for it merely limits the particular word *ēmissus*.

upon it? Will you not order him to be led to prison, to be hurried to his death, to be executed with the severest form of	in	vincla	dūcī,	nōn	ad	mortem	rapī, 18
	into	*bonds*	*to be led,*	*not*	*to*	*death*	*to be hurried,*
	nōn		summō		suppliciō		mactārī 19
	not		*greatest*		*with the punishment*		*to be destroyed*

An exactly similar blending is seen in Chap. IX, ll. 35–37, *ut ā mē nōn ēiectus . . . sed invītātus . . . īsse videāris.* The present tense *videātur* is in primary sequence with the principal verb *patiēre.* —— **Nōnne** (*nōn + ne*), interrog. particle; introduces a question; *nōnne* is used when an affirmative reply is expected, and it usually begins the question. —— **hunc,** acc. sing. m. of the dem. pron. *hīc, haec, hōc;* direct obj. of *imperābis,* in the object clauses *hunc dūcī, (hunc) rapī, (hunc) mactārī.* Observe that an acc. and inf. clause follows *imperābis.* When the verb of the object clause of *imperō* is passive, Caesar and Cicero regularly employ an acc. and inf.; but when the verb is active, the object goes in the dat. and a subjunct. clause with *ut* follows.

LINE 18. **in,** prep.; gov. the acc. *vincla.* —— **vincla,** acc. plur. of *vinclum, -ī,* n. 2d (*vinclum* is an apocopated form of *vinculum,* from *vinciō = I bind;* cf. *pōculum* and *pōclum*); governed by the prep. *in. To put into prison =* in Latin *in vincula dūcere* (not *in carcerem dūcere,* for *carcer =* the *Tulliānum,* i.e. the condemned cell). —— **dūcī,** pres. inf. pass. of *dūcō, -ere, dūxī, ductum,* 3; agrees with its subj.-acc. *hunc, hunc dūcī* being the object of *imperābis.* —— **nōn,** negative adv.; repeated from *nōn* in *nōnne* (*nōn + ne*) above. The repetition of *nōn* at the beginning of each object clause is an instance of *anaphora.* A. & G. 344, *f*; B. 350, 11, *b*; G. 636, NOTE 4; H. 636, III, 3. The repeated words *nōn . . . nōn* take the place of cop. conjunctions, e.g. *et . . . et,* connecting the obj.-infinitives *dūcī . . . rapī . . . mactārī.* —— **ad,** prep.; gov. the acc. *mortem.* —— **mortem,** acc. sing. of *mors, mortis,* f. 3d; governed by the prep. *ad.* —— **rapī,** pres. inf. pass. of *rapiō, -ere, -uī, raptum,* 3 (root *rap = ἁρπ = to seize;* cf. ἁρπάζω *= I seize*); coördinate with *dūcī;* supply *hunc* from the clause preceding.

LINE 19. **nōn,** negative adv.; repeated from *nōn* in *nōnne;* serves to connect the clause with the previous one. —— **summō,** abl. sing. n. of the adj. *summus, -a, -um,* superl. of the rare pos. *superus, -a, -um* (compar. *superior;* another superl. form is *suprēmus; superus* is formed from the adv. *super*); agrees with *suppliciō; summō suppliciō = morte.* —— **suppliciō,** abl. sing. of *supplicium, -ī,* n. 2d (from the adj. *supplex, supplicis; sub + plicō,* implying *bending* of the knee, whether in entreaty or to receive punishment); abl. of the means or instrument, with *mactārī.* —— **mactārī,** pres. inf. pass. of *mactō, -āre, -āvī, -ātum,* 1; coördinate with *rapī* and *dūcī;* supply *hunc* from above. *Mactāre* has the following different meanings: (1) *to kill, slaughter;* (2) *to afflict, punish,* with the abl. of the punishment, as in this passage; (3) *to glorify, to extol;* (4) *to venerate, worship;* (5) *to sacrifice, to immolate* a victim to the gods. There can be little doubt that the primitive meaning was *to kill,* from root *makh =* μαχ *= mac, to slaughter;* cf. *macellum = a meat-market,* μάχομαι *= I fight,* μάχαιρα *= a knife;* but some derive from an obsolete verb *magō,* akin to the Sanskrit root *mah = to venerate,* in which case *macto* would be a frequentative form. Certainly the adj. *mactus, -a, -um = worshipped, extolled;* cf. Horace, *macte esto virtūte.* It is easy to see that the sense *to worship* might have came from *to kill,* i.e. in sacrifice, and vice versa; possibly the ancients were themselves uncertain of the derivation. One commentator says that *mactāre* in its primitive sense *= magis augēre,* i.e. in relation to sacrificial worship, *to consummate* the sacrifice by the slaughter of the victim; hence *mactant honōribus = they advance with honors,* i.e. add new honors to; but of course *magis augēre* is impossible as a derivation.

20 imperābis?	Quid	tandem	tē	impedit?	punishment? Pray
will you order?	*What*	*at length*	*you*	*hinders?*	tell me, what stands in your way? The
21 Mōsne		māiōrum?	At	persaepe	usage of our ances-
(Does) the custom	*of (our) ancestors?*		*But*	*very often*	tors? No, for times without number in
22 etiam	prīvātī	in	hāc	rē pūblicā	this state of ours
even	*private (citizens)*	*in*	*this*	*commonwealth*	even private individ-

LINE 20. **imperābis**, 2d pers. sing. fut. ind. act. of *imperō, -āre, -āvī, -ātum*, 1; the implied subj. is *tū* (i.e. Cicero, whom his country is supposed to be criticising). Synonyms: (1) *iubēre = to command*, in general; construed with the acc. and inf.; (2) *imperāre = to command*, with the authority of higher position, e.g. *imperium;* construed with the dat. and *ut* + the subjunct. act., or with the acc. and the inf. of a verb used *passively;* (3) *ēdīcere = to command*, e.g. by an official ordinance, esp. the praetor's edict; followed by *ut* or *nē* + the subjunct.; (4) *mandāre = to command*, as a trust. —— **Quid**, nom. sing. n. of the interrog. pron. *quis, quae, quid;* subj. of *impedit*. —— **tandem**, adv.; emphasizes the question; *quid tandem = what, pray,* etc.? *Tandem* is often added to interrogative pronouns and adverbs, and sometimes to verbs, esp. imperatives, cf. *recōgnōsce tandem mēcum.* A. & G. 210, *f;* B. no reference; G. no reference; H. 351, 4. *Nam*, enclitic, is similarly used, cf. *ubinam gentium sumus?* —— **tē**, acc. sing. of *tū;* direct obj. of *impedit*. —— **impedit**, 3d pers. sing. pres. ind. act. of *impediō, -īre, -īvī, -ītum*, 4 (for *im-ped-iō*, from *in + pēs, pedis,* m. 3d, hence = lit. *I put* some one's *feet in* some obstruction, hence *I entangle, embarrass, obstruct, hinder;* cf. *compediō = I fetter, expediō = I extricate*); agrees with the subj. *quid*. Synonyms: (1) *impedīre = to hinder*, e.g. *profectiōnem;* cf. *mīles impedītus;* (2) *implicāre* (*in + plicāre*) = lit. *to fold in* something, *to envelop, to entangle;* (3) *prohibēre* (*prō + habēre*) = lit. *to hold before*, i.e. *away from* something, *to prevent* one from doing something, e.g. *prohibēre mīlitēs commeātū;* (4) *irrētīre* (*in + rēte* = *a net*) = *to snare;* (5) *illaqueāre* (*in + laqueus = a noose*) = lit. *to catch in a noose, to entangle.*

LINE 21. **Mōsne** (*mōs + ne*), *mōs* is the nom. sing. of *mōs, mōris,* m. 3d (perhaps from root *ma = to measure*, hence *the measuring* or *guiding rule of life*); understand from the previous sentence the pred. *impedit*, of which *mōs* is the subject. The sing. *mōs = custom, manner, precedent;* the plur. *mōrēs = habits, character.* *Ne* is the enclitic interrog. particle, introducing a question. —— **māiōrum**, gen. of the plur. noun *māiōrēs*, m. 3d = *ancestors;* poss. gen., limiting *mōs.* *Māiōrēs* is the substantival mas. plur. of *māior,* compar. of *māgnus;* cf. *māior nātū = older.* —— **At**, adversative conj.; connects the sentence with the one preceding. *At* is mostly used in argumentative passages, (1) introducing a supposed case which requires rebuttal, = *but, you may say;* (2) or, as here, introducing the refutation of a previously stated objection. —— **persaepe** (*per*, intensive, = *very + saepe = often*) adv.; modifies *multārunt. Persaepe* is an oratorical exaggeration, for Cicero has cited but one case of the kind described, viz. the murder of Tiberius Gracchus by Publius Scīpiō; cf. Chap. I, ll. 28–32.

LINE 22. **etiam**, adv.; intensifies the particular word *prīvātī*, rather than the pred. *multārunt.* —— **prīvātī**, nom. plur. of *prīvātus, -ī*, m. 2d (the part. *prīvātus, -a, -um*, used substantively; cf. *amīcus, aequālis,* etc.); subj. of *multārunt. Prīvātus =* a man who holds no political office; so the adj. *prīvātus, -a, -um = private, personal,* i.e. affecting a man purely in his own person, in opposition to *pūblicus = public,* involving *the state.* It will be remembered that Scīpiō was *pontifex māximus* when he led the riot in which Tiberius Gracchus was killed, but this office was not political, e.g. a man might be *chief priest* and at the same time stand for political office. —— **in**, prep.; gov.

uals have punished
dangerous citizens
with death. Or the
laws which have been
passed concerning the
punishment of Roman
citizens? No, for

perniciōsōs	cīvēs	morte	multārunt.	An 23
dangerous	*citizens*	*with death*	*have punished.*	*Or*
lēgēs,		quae	dē	cīvium 24
(do) the laws (hinder you)		*which*	*about*	*of citizens*
Rōmānōrum		suppliciō	rogātae sunt?	At 25
Roman		*the punishment*	*have been proposed?*	*But*

the abl. *rēpūblicā.* —— **hāc,** abl. sing. f. of the dem. pron. *hīc, haec, hōc;* agrees with *rēpūblicā.* —— **rē,** abl. sing. of *rēs, reī,* f. 5th; governed by the prep. *in.* —— **pūblicā,** abl. sing. f. of the adj. *pūblicus, -a, -um;* agrees with *rē.*

LINE 23. **perniciōsōs,** acc. plur. m. of the adj. *perniciōsus, -a, -um* (from *perniciēs; per + nex*); agrees with *cīvēs.* —— **cīvēs,** acc. plur. of *cīvis, -is,* m. and f. 3d; direct obj. of *multārunt.* —— **morte,** abl. sing. of *mors, mortis,* f. 3d; may be described as abl. of the means, or as abl. of the penalty, limiting *multārunt.* Judicial verbs take the acc. of the person, and the gen. of the *charge,* and the gen. of the *penalty,* if it be indefinite, but the abl. of the *penalty,* when it is specific. —— **multārunt** (for *multāvērunt*), 3d pers. plur. perf. ind. act. of *multō, -āre, -āvī, -ātum,* 1 (from the noun *multa = a fine*); agrees with the subj. *prīvātī.* The etymology of *multō* and *multa* is uncertain; *multa* is said by Festus to be Oscan in origin; some without much authority refer to root *mark = μαρπ = to seize,* and cf. *μάρπτω = I seize.* Observe the omission of the *v* of the perf., and the contraction of the vowels *ā* and *ē* into the single long vowel *ā;* this process is common with perfects in *-āvī, -ēvī,* and *-ōvī,* both before *s* and before *r;* cf. *firmāstī* for *firmāvistī,* and *firmāram* for *firmāveram;* perfects in *-īvī* may drop the *v* before *s* and *r,* but the vowels do not contract except before *s* or *st;* e.g. *audīveram* or *audieram* (but not *audīram*), and *audiissem* (*audissem* rare), and *audīstī* for *audīvistī.* —— **An,** conj.; introduces the second part (*an lēgēs impediunt*) of the direct disjunctive question, of which the first was introduced by *-ne* (*mōsne . . . impedit?*). In direct disjunctive questions, the first part is introduced by *utrum* or *-ne,* or else by no particle at all. For examples, and full note on the use of *an,* refer to *an,* Chap. I, l. 28.

LINE 24. **lēgēs,** nom. plur. of *lēx, lēgis,* f. 3d; subj. of *impediunt,* which must be supplied from *impedit,* l. 20. The laws bearing on the question are the following : (a) the *lēgēs Valeriae,* three in number, and passed in B.C. 509, 449, and 300; these established the right of appeal to the people from a magistrate's sentence to scourging and death, viz. *nē quis magistrātus cīvem Rōmānum adversus provocātiōnem necāret nēve verberāret;* (b) three *lēgēs Porciae,* one of which probably belongs to the year 197 B.C., the other two of unknown date; these reënacted the provisions of the *lēgēs Valeriae,* and added stringent punishment for their violation; (c) the *lēx Semprōnia* of C. Gracchus (122 B.C.) *dē lībertāte cīvium Rōmānōrum;* this again enforced the principle of the Porcian laws. Note that the above laws permitted the people to exercise the right of putting an accused criminal to death. Yet this right was very seldom exercised, for the accused was always allowed to retire into voluntary exile (the exile was not ordained as a *punishment*), and according to Sallust, Chap. LI (*aliae lēgēs . . . exsilium permittī iubent*), the right of the accused to escape execution by exile was established by law. —— **quae,** nom. plur. f. of the rel. pron. *quī, quae, quod;* agrees with the antecedent *lēgēs,* and is subj. of *rogātae sunt.* —— **dē,** prep. = *about concerning;* gov. the abl. *suppliciō.* —— **cīvium,** gen. plur. of *cīvis, -is,* m. and f. 3d; objective gen., limiting *suppliciō.*

LINE 25. **Rōmānōrum,** gen. plur. m. of the adj. *Rōmānus, -a, -um;* agrees with *cīvium.* —— **suppliciō,** abl. sing. of *supplicium, -ī,* n. 2d (see *suppliciō,* l. 19); gov-

26 numquam	in	hāc	urbe,	quī	ā	never in this city have
never	*in*	*this*	*city*	*(those) who*	*from*	those who have
27 rē pūblicā		dēfēcērunt,		cīvium	iūra	proved faithless to the constitution re-
the commonwealth		*have revolted*		*of citizens*	*the rights*	tained the rights of
28 tenuērunt.	An invidiam		posteritātis		timēs?	citizens. Or do you
have held.	*Or the obloquy*		*of posterity*		*do you fear?*	fear the obloquy of

erned by the prep. *dē*. —— **rogātae sunt**, 3d pers. plur. perf. ind. pass. of *rogō, -āre, -āvī, -ātum*, 1 ; agrees (the part. *rogātae*, adjectively in gender, number, and case) with the subj. *quae*. *Rogātae sunt* = properly *were proposed*, i.e. to the *comitia*, and is here loosely used for *lātae sunt* or *perlātae sunt* = *were passed*. The process of law-making was as follows : the people in *comitia* were asked what their will was respecting the measures proposed, with the formula *velītis iubeātis, Quirītēs*. They then voted by ballot ; the ballot tablets bore, one the letters U. R. (= *utī rogās*, approving the pro-posal), and the other the letter A. (= *antīquō*, voting against the proposal). The proposal was called *rogātiō*, but if carried, became *lēx ;* cf. the distinction between the modern *bill* and *law*. —— **At**, adversative conj. ; introducing an argument combating the suggestion of illegality made in the preceding question.

LINE 26. **numquam** (*ne + unquam*), adv. ; modifies *tenuērunt*. The usual posi-tion of an adverb is next to the verb, the verb standing last in the sentence ; *numquam* is therefore strongly emphasized by standing at the beginning of the sentence and far from the verb *tenuērunt*. —— **in**, prep. ; gov. the abl. *urbe*, expressing *place where*. —— **hāc**, abl. sing. f. of the dem. pron. *hīc, haec, hōc ;* agrees with *urbe*. —— **urbe**, abl. sing. of *urbs, urbis*, f. 3d ; governed by the prep. *in*. —— **quī**, nom. plur. m. of the rel. pron. *quī, quae, quod ;* subj. of *dēfēcērunt*. Observe that the antecedent of *quī* is not expressed ; this is not uncommon when the antecedent would be a pronoun not otherwise defined by the relative, cf. l. 4 above, *percipite . . . quae dīcam ;* so here we may supply, as the antecedent of *quī, eī* or *illī* (the implied subj. of the principal verb *tenuērunt*. —— **ā**, prep. ; gov. the abl. *rē pūblicā*, expressing *separation*.

LINE 27. **rē**, abl. sing. of *rēs, reī*, f. 5th ; governed by the prep. *ā*. —— **pūblicā**, abl. sing. f. of the adj. *pūblicus, -a, -um ;* agrees with *rē*. —— **dēfēcērunt**, 3d pers. plur. perf. ind. act. of *dēficiō, -ere, dēfēcī, dēfectum*, 3 (*dē + faciō*) ; agrees with the subj. *quī ; dēfēcērunt* is here intrans. = *have deserted, have revolted*, but sometimes *dēficere* is active, = *to fail* a person. —— **cīvium**, gen. plur. of *cīvis, -is*, m. and f. 3d ; poss. gen., limiting *iūra*. —— **iūra**, acc. plur. of *iūs, iūris*, m. 3d ; direct obj. of *tenuērunt*.

LINE 28. **tenuērunt**, 3d pers. plur. perf. ind. act. of *teneō, -ēre, -uī, tentum*, 2 ; the subj. implied by the personal ending is *eī*, understood as the antecedent of *quī ; tenu-ērunt* here = *retinuērunt*. Cicero's contention is that rebel citizens, in virtue of their treason, cease to be *cīvēs* and become *hostēs ;* so Catiline and his associates were afterward declared by the state. But the argument is not legally sound, for the accused could claim trial and could not be executed except by the expressed will of the people, and even so there was the loophole of voluntary exile. However, Cicero rested his defence for his execution of Lentulus and Cethēgus on the *senātūs cōnsultum ultimum*, and found that the people refused to recognize any senatorial authorization which pretended to suspend even for a time those laws which were the charter of Roman liberty. —— **An**, conj. ; introduces a new alternative in the compound question. It is regular for the second member and any other alternatives in disjunctive questions to be intro-duced by *an*. —— **invidiam**, acc. sing. of *invidia, -ae*, f. 1st ; direct obj. of *timēs*. —— **posteritātis**, gen. sing. of *posteritās*, f. 3d = (1) *future time*, (2) *future genera-tions, posterity* (from adj. *posterus*, from adv. *post*) ; subj. gen., limiting *invidiam*,

future times? Truly noble is the gratitude with which you repay the Roman people, who have uplifted you, a man brought by self into notice,	Praeclāram *Remarkable*	vērō *truly*	populō *to the people*	Rōmānō *Roman*	refers 29 *you return*
	grātiam, *gratitude,*	quī *which*	tē, *you,*	hominem *a man*	per 30 *through*
	tē *yourself (only)*	cōgnitum, *known,*	nūllā *no*	commendātiōne 31 *with recommendation*

i.e. *hatred felt by posterity*. With this concrete sense of *posteritās* Mr. Taylor compares the occasional use of *nōbilitās* = *the nobility;* cf. *servitium* which sometimes = *those who are in a state of slavery, slaves*. —— **timēs**, 2d pers. sing. pres. ind. act. of *timeō, -ēre, -uī*, no supine, 2; the implied subject is *tū*.

LINE 29. **Praeclāram**, acc. sing. f. of the adj. *praeclārus, -a, -um* (*prae* = *very* in composition, + *clārus* = *famous*); agrees with *grātiam; praeclāram refers grātiam* is ironical, for Cicero *means* exactly the opposite of what he *says*. —— **vērō** (abl. sing. n. of the adj. *vērus, -a, -um;* cf. *vērum*, adv. and conj.), adv.; modifies *praeclāram*. —— **populō**, dat. sing. of *populus, -ī*, m. 2d (root *pal* = *ple, to fill;* πλῆθος); dat. of the indirect obj., dependent on *refers*. —— **Rōmānō**, dat. sing. m. of the adj. *Rōmānus, -a, -um;* agrees with *populō*. —— **refers**, 2d pers. sing. pres. ind. act. of *referō, referre, rettulī, relātum*, irreg. (*re* + *ferō*); the subj. *tū* is implied. *Grātiam referre* = *to return gratitude* by deed, *to recompense* some one for something. Note the following: (1) *sē referre* = *to go back, to retire;* (2) *referre ad senātum* = *to put the subject to the senate*, i.e. for discussion.

LINE 30. **grātiam**, acc. sing. of *grātia, -ae*, f. 1st (root *ghar, ghra* = χαρ = *gra, to be glad;* cf. *grātus*, χαίρω, χάρις); direct obj. of *refers*. Note the following : (1) *grātiam alicuī habēre* = *to feel gratitude towards some one;* (2) *grātiās* or *grātēs agere* = *to return thanks*. —— **quī**, nom. sing. m. of the rel. pron. *quī, quae, quod;* agrees with the antecedent *populō*, and is subj. in its own clause of *extulit*, l. 34. —— **tē**, acc. sing. of *tū;* direct obj. of *extulit*. —— **hominem**, acc. sing. of *homō, hominis*, m. 3d; acc. in apposition with *tē*. Observe that *per tē cōgnitum* is intended to appear disparaging, hence *hominem* and not *virum*. —— **per**, prep.; gov. the acc. *tē; per tē cōgnitum* = *become known through your own exertions*, i.e. who, but for what you have achieved, would have been a nobody; cf. *per mē tibi obstitī*, Chap. V, l. 28. Cicero was a *novus homō*, i.e. a citizen whose ancestors had never held curule office, but who had won his own position among the nobility by securing election himself to a curule magistracy. Cicero was very proud of this achievement, so the substance of ll. 30–34 is only very transparently veiled self-praise.

LINE 31. **tē**, acc. sing. of *tū;* governed by the prep. *tē*. —— **cōgnitum**, acc. sing. m. of *cōgnitus, -a, -um*, perf. part. pass. of *cōgnōscō, -ere, cōgnōvī, cōgnitum*, 3 (*con* + *nōscō*, for *gnōscō*, root *gna* = *to know*); predicative, agreeing with *hominem; cōgnitum* = *known*, i.e. as a public character. —— **nūllā**, abl. sing. f. of the adj. *nūllus, -a, -um* (gen. *nūllius*, dat. *nūllī; ne* + *ūllus*); agrees with *commendātiōne*. —— **commendātiōne**, abl. sing. of *commendātiō, -ōnis*, f. 3d (from the verb *commendō*, I, *com* + *mandō*); abl. of quality, often called descriptive abl., modifying the direct obj. *tē; nūllā commendātiōne māiōrum* = a *cum* clause (*though you have no recommendation of ancestry*). The noun in the abl. is always accompanied by an attribute, the noun and attribute describing some other noun or pronoun; the gen. of description is also used, e.g. *vir malī ingenī* = *a man of bad* disposition; cf. Virgil, *Aen.* I, l. 71, *Sunt mihi bis septem praestantī corpore nymphae* = *I have twice seven nymphs of surpassing beauty*. A. & G. 251; B. 224; G. 400; H. 419, II. Thus *a man of great courage* may be expressed, (1) *vir māgnae virtūtis*, (2) *vir māgnā virtūte*.

32 maiōrum,	tam	mātūrē	ad	summum	altogether lacking
of ancestors,	*so*	*early*	*to*	*highest*	recommendations of
33 imperium	per	omnēs	honōrum	gradūs	ancestry, so early
the authority	*through*	*all*	*of offices*	*the steps*	through all the grades of office to
34 extulit,	sī	propter	invidiae	aut	supreme power, if
has raised,	*if*	*on account of*	*of unpopularity*	*or*	through fear of un-

LINE 32. **maiōrum**, gen. of the plur. noun *maiōrēs*, m. 3d = *ancestors* (substantival plur. of the compar. adj. *maior*); subjective gen., limiting *commendātiōne; maiōrum commendātiō = recommendation of ancestors* (i.e. coming to a man or given him by the possession of noble ancestors. —— **tam**, adv.; modifies *mātūrē*. *Tam* never modifies verbs, but is the most common word of its kind with adjectives and adverbs. *Tam* and *quam* are often used correlatively. —— **mātūrē** (from the adj. *mātūrus = ripe, fully grown, seasonable, early;* perhaps akin to Sanskrit root *mah = to grow*), adv.; modifies *extulit.* The *lēx Villia Annālis* (180 B.C.) determined, in reference to each of the higher magistracies, the age at which a man might be eligible for election (*quot annōs nātī quemque magistrātum peterent caperentque*). We are not told what the respective ages were, but the instance of Cicero is some guide, for he was elected to the consulship in his 43d year, and held this and the other offices of the *cursus honōrum* at the earliest possible age (*suō annō* is the idiomatic expression). Cicero was 31 when he held the quaestorship, 37 when curule aedile, 40 when praetor. From other sources it is known that, whatever a man's age, he could not pass on from the aedileship to the praetorship, or from the praetorship to the consulship, until two clear years had intervened. —— **ad**, prep.; gov. the acc. *imperium.* —— **summum**, acc. sing. n. of the adj. *summus, -a, -um* (superl. of *superus*); agrees with *imperium.*

LINE 33. **imperium**, acc. sing. of *imperium, -ī,* n. 2d (*imperō*); governed by the prep. *ad; summum imperium = consulātum,* as the consulship was the highest office in the state, and carried with it the supreme command of the army outside Rome (cf. *imperātor*). —— **per**, prep.; gov. the acc. *gradūs.* —— **omnēs**, acc. plur. of the adj. *omnis, -e,* 3d; agrees with *gradūs.* —— **honōrum**, gen. plur. of *honos, honōris,* m. 3d (the sing. = *esteem, repute, glory;* the plur. = *public dignity, public office*); poss. gen., limiting *gradūs.* —— **gradūs**, acc. plur. of *gradus, gradūs,* m. 4th; governed by the prep. *per.* The *lēx Villia Annālis* probably defined the regular succession of offices; at any rate the *lēgēs annālēs* of Sulla did so; cf. the *lēx Cornēlia dē magistrātibus,* which forbade candidature for the praetorship and consulship to any one who had not previously held the office of quaestor or praetor respectively. The aedileship could apparently be omitted, but this was seldom done, as this office gave opportunity for holding public games, gladiatorial shows, and thus winning the applause and favor of the Roman voters. The need of a law regulating the *cursus honōrum* is very apparent from a glance at the careers of some citizens of earlier times; e.g. (1) Appius Claudius Caecus, censor in B.C. 312, consul in B.C. 307 and again 296, praetor in B.C. 295; (2) Tiberius Gracchus, curule aedile B.C. 216, and consul B.C. 215.

LINE 34. **extulit**, 3d pers. sing. perf. ind. act. of *efferō, efferre, extulī, ēlātum,* irreg. (*ex + ferō = I carry forth, elevate*); agrees with the subj. *quī,* l. 30. —— **sī**, conditional particle; followed by the ind. *neglegis* of a logical condition in pres. time. —— **propter**, prep.; gov. the acc. *metum. Propter* here has the usual meaning *on account of;* sometimes it = *near,* like *prope,* from which it is derived. —— **invidiae**, gen. sing. of *invidia,* f. 1st (from verb *invideō*); objective gen., limiting *metum. Invidia* does not = *envy,* but *odium, hatred, unpopularity.* —— **aut**, disjunctive conj.; connects *invidiae* and *perīculī.* See the note on *aut,* Chap. IX, l. 19.

popularity or of some	alicŭius	perīculī	metum	salūtem 35
possible danger you	*any*	*of danger*	*fear*	*the safety*
disregard the safety				
of your fellow-	cīvium	tuōrum	neglegis.	Sed sī quis 36
countrymen. But if	*of fellow-citizens* *your*		*you neglect.*	*But if any*
there is any fear of	est	invidiae	metus,	num est 37
unpopularity, surely	*there is* *of unpopularity*		*fear,*	*surely not is*

LINE 35. **alicŭius**, gen. sing. n. of the indef. adj. *aliquī, aliqua, aliquod* (cf. the pron. *aliquis, aliqua, aliquid*); agrees with *perīculī*. Refer to the note on *quǎsdam*, Chap. II, l. 4.——**perīculī**, gen. sing. of *perīculum*, n. 2d; objective gen., limiting *metum;* coördinate with *invidiae*.——**metum**, acc. sing. of *metus, metūs*, m. 4th; governed by the prep. *propter*. Synonyms: (1) *metus = fear, anxiety*, due to prevision of imminent calamity; (2) *timor = fear*, due to timidity or cowardice; (3) *pavor = mind-disturbing fear;* (4) *formīdō = terror, dread* (= *metus permanēns*); (5) *trepidātiō = consternation, agitated fear;* (6) *horror = shuddering fear;* (7) *verēcundia = reverential* or *superstitious fear, awe.*——**salūtem**, acc. sing. of *salūs, salūtis*, f. 3d (akin to *salvus*); direct obj. of *neglegis*. When used in epistolary addresses, *salus* or *salūtem* is frequently abbreviated to *Sal.* or simply *S.*

LINE 36. **cīvium**, gen. plur. of *cīvis, -is*, m. (and f.), 3d; poss. gen., limiting *salūtem*. The gender of *cīvis* is mas., except when it refers definitely to a woman.——**tuōrum**, gen. plur. m. of the poss. adj. *tuus, -a, -um;* agrees with *cīvium*.——**neglegis**, 2d pers. sing. pres. ind. act. of *neglegō, -ere, neglēxī, neglectum*, 3 (*nec + legō*); the subj. *tū* is implied by the personal ending; *neglegis* is the verb of the *protasis* with *sī*, while *refers* is the verb of the *apodosis*. Remember that there is absolutely no authority for the forms *negligō* (*negligentia*, etc.), *aequiparō*, or *intelligō* (*intelligentia*), and that the correct forms are *neglegō* (*neglegentia*), *aequeparō*, *intellegō* (*intellegentia*). Synonyms: (1) *neglegō = I neglect, disregard*, implying indifference; (2) *praetermitto = I disregard, overlook*, from lack of attention; (3) *omittō = I omit, disregard*, knowingly and intentionally.——**Sed**, adversative conj.; connects the thought of this sentence with that of the preceding one.——**sī**, conditional particle; followed by the ind. *est* of a logical condition in present time.——**quis**, nom. sing. m. of the indef. pron. and adj. *quis, qua, quid;* used adjectively, agreeing with *metus*. This pronoun (= *any one, any*) is rarely used except in clauses introduced by *sī, nisi, nē,* or *num;* but it occurs in compounds, e.g. *aliquis, quisquam.*

LINE 37. **est**, 3d pers. sing. pres. ind. act. of *sum, esse, fuī;* agrees with the subj. *metus;* the ind. is regular in the *protasis* of conditional sentences which are logical in form, i.e. which make a statement according to a formula, e.g. *if this is (was, will be) true, that is (was, will be) true;* the verb of the *apodosis* may be either ind. (like *pertimēscenda est* here), imperative, or the subjunct. in one of its independent uses as principal verb. A. & G. 306; B. 302; G. 595; H. 508, and 4.——**invidiae**, gen. sing. of *invidia*, f. 1st; objective gen., with *metus*. Distinguish subjective and objective genitives as follows: (a) subjective, *amor deī = the love of God*, i.e. which God feels for us; (b) objective, *amor deī = the love of God*, i.e. which we feel for God.——**metus**, gen. *metūs*, m. 4th; nom. sing., subj. of *est* in the *protasis*.——**num**, interrog. particle; introduces the *apodosis* in the form of a question, and (as distinguished from *nōnne* or *-ne*) implies a negative reply. The question introduced by *num* is rhetorical, and is equivalent to an emphatic negative statement, e.g. unpopularity due to firm conduct *is much less to be feared* than unpopularity due to neglect of duty.——**est**, 3d pers. sing. pres. ind. of *sum, esse, fuī;* agrees with the subj. *invidia; est* must be taken with *pertimēscenda =* the 3d pers. sing. pres. ind. of the periphrastic pass. conjugation of *pertimēscō*.

88 vehementius   sevēritātis   ac   fortitūdinis
more strongly   *of (= due to) severity*   *and*   *due to courage*

89 invidia   quam   inertiae   ac
the unpopularity   *than*   *(that) due to inactivity*   *and*

40 nēquitiae   pertimēscenda.   An   cum   bellō
due to inefficiency   *to be dreaded.*   *Or*   *when*   *by war*

41 vāstābitur   Ītalia,   vexābuntur   urbēs,   tēcta
shall be ravaged   *Italy,*   *shall be harassed*   *cities,*   *houses*

the unpopularity which is earned by stern discipline and resoluteness is not so strongly to be dreaded as that earned by inaction and inefficiency. Or do you not reckon that while Italy is

LINE 38. **vehementius,** adv. in the compar. degree (pos. *vehementer,* superl. *vehementissimē;* formed from the adj. *vehemēns, vĕ + mēns* = lit. *not having mind,* hence *unreasonable, violent, vehement*); modifies *est pertimēscenda.* —— **sevēritātis,** gen. sing. of *sevēritās,* f. 3d (from the adj. *sevērus, -a, -um*); objective gen., with *invidia; invidia sevēritātis = the odium (hatred) of severity,* i.e. which is inspired by and felt for severity. —— **ac** (shortened form of *atque*), cop. conj.; connects *sevēritātis* and *fortitūdinis. Atque* (*ac*) is often used, instead of the commoner *et,* to join important or sonorous words. —— **fortitūdinis,** gen. sing. of *fortitūdō,* f. 3d (from the adj. *fortis;* for termination, cf. *turpitūdō* from adj. *turpis*); objective gen., coördinate with *sevēritātis.*

LINE 39. **invidia,** gen. *invidiae,* f. 1st; nom. sing., subj. of *est pertimēscenda.* —— **quam,** adv.; introduces (*invidia*) *inertiae ac nēquitiae pertimēscenda est* in comparison with *invidia sevēritātis ac fortitūdinis* (*pertimēscenda est*) after the comparative adv. *vehementius.* —— **inertiae,** gen. sing. of *inertia,* f. 1st (from the adj. *iners* = *in, not + ars, skilled in production;* root *ar = to join,* cf. *sollers, arma, ἀρετή,* etc.); objective gen. (like *sevēritātis* above), limiting *invidia,* which must be supplied in the clause following *quam* from *invidia* in the clause preceding *quam.* Synonyms: (1) *inertia = indolence,* originally due to lack of skill; (2) *īgnāvia* (from adj. *īgnāvus, in = not + (g) nāvus = active*) *= idleness, cowardice;* (3) *segnitia* (adj. *segnis*) *= sluggishness;* (4) *dēsidia = sloth,* from *dēsideō = I sit idle;* (5) *pigritia* (from *piger,* cf. *piget = it displeases*) *= apathy, listlessness.* —— **ac,** cop. conj.; connects *inertiae* and *nēquitiae.*

LINE 40. **nēquitiae,** gen. sing. of *nēquitia,* f. 1st (from the indecl. adj. *nēquam = worthless*); objective gen., coördinate with *inertiae.* —— **pertimēscenda,** nom. sing. f. of *pertimēscendus, -a, -um,* gerundive of *pertimēscō, -ere, pertimuī,* no supine, 3 (*per.* intensive = *very much, thoroughly + timēscō,* inceptive of *timeō*); agrees with the subj. *invidia. Pertimēscenda est = ought to be dreaded* or *must be dreaded;* see the note on *est,* above. —— **An,** conj.; introduces another addition to the series of alternatives in the compound question begun in l. 20 (*quid . . . impedit?*), and continued l. 23 (*an leges impediunt?*), l. 28 (*an invidiam timēs?*). —— **cum,** temporal conj.; with the future ind. *vāstābitur* (with *vexābuntur* and *ārdēbunt* coördinate). Observe that the *cum* clause defines *tum,* and that *tum* limits (not *exīstimās*) *cōnflagrātūrum* (*esse*), which is indirect in form; we should therefore expect a subjunctive instead of the fut. ind. with *cum.* But probably Cicero began the sentence in direct form, intending to say in the *apodosis tū nōn invidiae incendiō cōnflagrābis?,* but making the small alteration which we find in the text through an afterthought. —— **bellō,** abl. sing. of *bellum, -ī,* n. 2d; abl. of the means, modifying *vāstābitur.*

LINE 41. **vāstābitur,** 3d pers. sing. fut. ind. pass. of *vāstō, -āre, -āvī, -ātum,* 1 (from the adj. *vāstus; vāstus* is perhaps akin to *vacuus,* and = *desolate,* sometimes *huge;* cf. *vast* and *waste*); agrees with the subj. *Ītalia.* We find the fut. simple *vāstābitur* instead of the more usual fut.-perf. *vāstāta erit,* because the correlation of *tum* and *cum* marks the action of the subordinate verbs and of *cōnflagrātūrum* (= direct *cōnflagrābis*) as coincident. Note that the coördinate clauses, *urbēs vexābuntur* and *tēcta ārdēbunt,* follow

being ravaged, while cities are being wasted and houses are in flames, you yourself will then perish in the conflagration of a nation's hatred?"	ārdēbunt, *shall be in flame,*	tum *then*	tē *yourself*	nōn *not*	existimās 4s *do you think*
	invidiae *of unpopularity*		incendiō *with the blaze*		cōnflagrātūrum?" 48 *likely to be consumed?"*
XII. To these most sacred utterances of the com-	XII. Hīs *These*	ego *I*	sānctissimīs *most sacred*	reī pūblicae 1 *of the commonwealth*	

without the medium of connecting conjunctions (*asyndeton*).——Ītalia, gen. *Italiae*, f. 1st; nom. sing., subj. of *vāstābitur*.——vexābuntur, 3d pers. plur. fut. ind. pass. of *vexō*, *-āre*, *-āvī*, *-ātum*, 1 (frequentative of *vehō*; = lit. *I move violently*, hence *I trouble, harass*); agrees with the subj. *urbēs;* coördinate with *vāstābitur* in dependence on *cum*. —— urbēs, nom. plur. of *urbs*, *urbis*, f. 3d; subj. of *vexābuntur*. —— tēcta, nom. plur. of *tectum*, *-ī*, n. 2d (in origin, neut. sing. of *tectus*, *-a*, *-um*, perf. part. pass. of *tegō = I cover*, hence lit. *the covered thing*, a *house* or *building*, *roof;* root *stag* = Latin *steg* or *teg*, *to cover;* cf. στέγω = *I cover*, *stega* = *the deck of a ship*, *tegmen* = *a covering*, *toga* = *the toga* (lit. the covering garment)); subj. of *ardēbunt*.

LINE 42. **ārdēbunt**, 3d pers. plur. fut. ind. act. of *ārdeō*, *-ēre*, *ārsī*, *ārsum*, 2 intrans.; agrees with the subj. *tēcta;* coördinate with *vexābuntur* and *vāstābitur*. —— tum, dem. adv. of time; modifies *cōnflagrātūrum* (sc. *esse*). —— tē, acc. sing. of *tū;* subj.-acc. (reflexive) of the inf. *cōnflagrātūrum* (sc. *esse*), in the acc. and inf. construction dependent on *existimās* (a *verbum sentiendī*). —— nōn, neg. adv.; modifies *existimās*, as the position shows, and not *cōnflagrātūrum* (*esse*). *Nōn* in questions serves the same purpose as *nōn* in *nōnne*, i.e. implies an affirmative answer. —— existimās, 2d pers. sing. pres. ind. act. of *existimō*, *-āre*, *-āvī*, *-ātum*, 1 (*ex* + *aestimō* = (1) *I reckon*, (2) *consider, think, suppose*); the implied subj. is *tū*. Synonyms: (1) *existimāre = to think, reflect*, after logical consideration; (2) *putāre = to think*, as the result of reflection; (3) *opinārī = to fancy, suppose*, with or without reasonable grounds; (4) *iūdicāre = to think, judge*, after weighing the evidence; (5) *censēre = to think*, esp. *to declare one's official opinion*.

LINE 43. **invidiae**, gen. sing. of *invidia*, f. 1st; gen. of the substance or material, defining *incendiō*. A. & G. 214, *e*; B. 197; G. 361; H. 395. —— incendiō, abl. sing. of *incendium*, *-ī*, n. 2d (from the verb *incendō = I set on fire;* root *can = to burn*, cf. καίω); abl. of the means or instrument, modifying *cōnflagrātūrum* (= *will burn*, intrans., i.e. in passive, *will be consumed*). The metaphor from fire is very frequent in Latin, especially with reference to the passions of love and hate. —— cōnflagrātūrum, acc. sing. m. of *cōnflagrātūrus*, *-a*, *-um*, fut. part. act. of *cōnflagrō*, *-āre*, *-āvī*, *-ātum*, 1 (*con* + *flagrō;* root *bhrag* or *bharg* = φλέγ = Latin *flag* and *fulg, to burn;* cf. φλέγω and *flagrō = I blaze, flamma* for *flag-ma, fulgeō, flāgitium*, etc.); agrees with the subj.-acc. *tē;* with *cōnflagrātūrum* must be supplied *esse*, making the fut. inf. which is required for indirect speech. The pres. ind. and pres. inf. of *sum* are very often omitted when the necessary part is indicated by the context and can be supplied.

LINE 1. **Hīs**, dat. plur. f. of the dem. pron. *hīc, haec, hōc;* agrees with *vōcibus;* *hīs* refers to the criticism put into the mouth of the personified State in ll. 9–43. —— ego, gen. *meī* (borrowed from poss. adj. *meus*); nom. sing., subj. of *respondēbō*. *Ego* is emphatic; note the attraction of pronouns into juxtaposition, which is so frequent in Cicero. —— sānctissimīs, dat. plur. f. of the adj. *sanctissimus*, *-a*, *-um*, superl. of

2 vōcibus   et   eōrum   hominum,   quī   hōc
  to utterances and   _those_   _of men_   _who_   _this_

3 idem   sentiunt,   mentibus   pauca
  same thing   _feel_   _to the minds (=thoughts) a few (words)_

4 respondēbō.   Ego,   sī   hōc   optimum   factū
  (I) will reply.   _I,_   _if this thing   best   to be done_

monwealth, and to
the thoughts of those
who entertain simi-
lar views, I for my
part will make this
brief reply. Had I
thought, Conscript

sanctus, -a, -um ; agrees with _vōcibus._ Cicero considered it the _sacred_ duty of all citizens to respect and safeguard the interests of the state. —— **reī,** gen. sing. of _rēs,_ f. 5th; poss. gen., limiting _vōcibus._ —— **pūblicae,** gen. sing. of the adj. _pūblicus, -a, -um ;_ agrees with _reī._

LINE 2. **vōcibus,** dat. plur. of _vōx, vōcis,_ f. 3d; dat. of the indirect obj., dependent on _responaēbō. Vōcibus = the utterances,_ contrasted with _mentibus_ following, which = _the_ (unexpressed) _thoughts._ —— **et,** cop. conj.; connects _vōcibus_ and _mentibus._ —— **eōrum,** gen. plur. m. of the dem. pron. _is, ea, id ;_ agrees with _hominum._ —— **hominum,** gen. plur. of _homō, hominis,_ m. 3d; dat. of the indirect obj., dependent on _respondēbō ;_ joined by _et_ to _vōcibus._ —— **quī,** nom. plur. m. of the rel. pron. _quī, quae, quod ;_ agrees in gender and number with the antecedent _hominum,_ and is subj. of _sentiunt_ in its own clause. —— **hōc,** acc. sing. n. of the dem. pron. _hīc, haec, hōc ; hōc = hanc sententiam,_ i.e. is a kind of cognate acc. with _sentiunt._ A neuter pronoun or a colorless adjective is often so used. A. & G. 238, _b_ ; B. 176, 2, _a_ ; G. 333, 1 ; H. 378, 2.

LINE 3. **idem,** acc. sing. n. of the dem. pron. _idem, eadem, idem_ (for _is-dem, ea-dem, id-dem,_ i.e. _is_ + suffix _-dem_) ; agrees with _hōc,_ or we might say that _hōc_ agrees with _idem. Idem = the same,_ and is often used like _ipse,_ esp. in reference to another action of the same subj., e.g. _idem fēci — I also did._ —— **sentiunt,** 3d pers. plur. pres. ind. act. of _sentiō, -īre, sensī, sensum,_ 4; agrees with the subj. _quī._ The verb _sentīre_ often has a political meaning = _to think_ with some one, _to hold the same views_ as some one; cf. Chap. XIII, l. 30, _quid dē rē pūblicā sentiat,_ and cf. also the similar use of the Greek verb φροντίζειν. —— **mentibus,** dat. plur. of _mēns, mentis,_ f. 3d; indirect obj. of _respondēbō ;_ coördinate with _vōcibus_ above. _Mentibus_ here = _to the thoughts_ or _feelings._ —— **pauca,** acc. plur. n. of the adj. _paucus, -a, -um_ (root _pava = little ;_ cf. _paulus, pauper, ταῦρος,_ etc.) ; direct obj. of _respondēbō ; pauca_ is used substantively, and = _pauca verba._

LINE 4. **respondēbō,** 1st pers. sing. fut. ind. act. of _respondeō, -ēre, respondī, responsum,_ 2 (_re_ + _spondeō_) ; agrees with the subj. _ego._ —— **Ego,** nom. sing. of the 1st personal pron. ; subj. of _dedissem,_ and implied as subj. of _iūdicārem._ —— **sī,** condi- tional particle; followed by the subjunct. _iūdicārem_ of an ideal condition respecting past time, and therefore necessarily unrealized. See the note on _metuerent,_ Chap. VII, l. 21, and consult A. & G. 304–309 ; B. 301–304 ; G. 589, _ff_ ; H. 507–512. —— **hōc,** acc. sing. of the dem. pron. _hīc, haec, hōc ;_ subj.-acc. in the acc. and inf. construction of _esse,_ which must be supplied in the predicate with _optimum factū,_ in dependence on _iūdicārem_ (a _verbum sentiendī_). _Hōc_ is explained by the oppositional phrase _Catilī- nam morte multārī._ —— **optimum,** acc. sing. n. of _optimus, -a, -um,_ superl. of the adj. _bonus, -a, -um_ (compar. _melior_) ; predicative, agreeing with the subj.-acc. _hōc ;_ the full predicate is (_esse_) _optimum factū,_ i.e. as often, the inf. of _sum_ must be supplied. —— **factū,** supine in _u_ of the verb _faciō, -ere, fēcī, factum,_ 3 (pass. _fīō, fierī, factus sum_) ; defines _in what respect_ the death of Catiline (_hōc_) is _optimum._ The supines are verbal abstracts of the 4th declension ; that in _-um_ is an acc., and is used after verbs of motion to express purpose, e.g. _legātōs misit pācem petītum = he sent ambassa- dors to sue for peace ;_ that in _u_ is probably an abl. of specification, though some gram- marians describe as a dat. of purpose (cf. the old 4th decl. dat. in _-ū,_ for _-uī,_ found

Fathers, that the best thing to be done was for Catiline to be punished with death, I should not have given yon cutthroat the enjoyment of a	iūdicārem, *considered,*	patrēs *fathers*	cōnscrīptī, *enrolled,*	Catilīnam 5 *(that) Catiline*
	morte *with death*	multārī, *(to) be punished,*	ūnius *one*	ūsūram *the enjoyment* hōrae 6 *of hour*
	gladiātōrī *to gladiator*	istī *that*	ad *for*	vīvendum *living* nōn 7 *not*

in Vergil and other poets, e.g. Aen. I, l. 476, *Fertur equīs, currūque haeret resupīnus inānī*). There are only a few supines in *-ū* in use, e.g. *dictū, vīsū, audītū*, and they accompany an adjective (or the nouns *fās, nefās, opus*) to explain its reference; cf. Aen. I, 111, *miserābile vīsū = piteous to see.* A. & G. 303; B. 340, 2; G. 436; H. 547.

LINE 5. **iūdicārem**, 1st pers. sing. imperf. subjunct. act. of *iūdicō, -āre, -āvī, -ātum,* 1 (*iūdex*); the subj. *ego* is implied by the personal ending. Observe the imperf. subjunct. in the *protasis*, and pluperf. in the *apodosis;* it is usual in ideal conditions respecting past time to have the pluperf. subjunct. in both clauses, e.g. *sī jūdicāvissem . . . nōn dedissem = if I had considered . . . I should not have given;* but instead of this we have the imperf. *iūdicārem*, which strictly relates only to present time. The reason for the mixed tenses here is this, that the imperf. *iūdicārem* includes the sense of both *iūdicāvissem* and *iūdicārem*, i.e. denotes that the subject's state of mind in the past is the same as it is *now = if I thought* (as I did then and do now). —— **patrēs**, voc. plur. of *pater, patris*, m. 3d; the case of address. —— **cōnscrīptī**, voc. plur. m. of *cōnscrīptus, -a, -um*, perf. part. pass. of *cōnscrībō, -ere, cōnscrīpsī, cōnscrīptum,* 3 (*con* + *scrībō*); agrees with *patrēs*. For this form of address, consult the notes on *patrēs* and *cōnscrīptī*, Chap. II, ll. 23, 24. —— **Catilīnam**, acc. sing. of *Catilīna, -ae*, m. 1st; subj.-acc. of *multārī; Catilīnam morte multārī* is an acc. substantival phrase in opposition with and explaining *hōc* (the subj.-acc.) of (*esse*) *optimum factū*.

LINE 6. **morte**, abl. sing. of *mors, mortis*, f. 3d; abl. of the means, modifying *multārī*. —— **multārī**, pres. inf. pass. of *multō, -āre, -āvī, -ātum,* 1 (from noun *multa = a fine;* this word is said to be of Oscan origin); agrees with the subj.-acc. *Catilīnam*. —— **ūnius**, gen. sing. f. of the numeral adj. *ūnus, -a, -um* (old forms are *oenus* and *oinos;* cf. *οἴνη = the ace* on dice); agrees with *hōrae*. —— **ūsūram**, acc. sing. of *ūsūra, -ae*, f. 1st (from *ūtor = I use*); direct obj. of *dedissem*. *Ūsūram* is here to be rendered literally, in accordance with its etymology, as *use, enjoyment;* two other derived meanings are very common, (1) *use*, i.e. in a mercantile sense, either of the interest on capital, or of money lent, (2) *interest*, on money lent, usually reckoned by the month, and subject to settlement or renewal on the Nones, Ides, or Kalends, particularly the last. —— **hōrae**, gen. sing. of *hōra*, f. 1st (cf. Greek ὥρα = any limited period of time, whether of a year, month, or day, hence = *season, hour, the fitting time*, etc.); objective gen., with *ūsūram*. In the Roman system of computation of time, *hōra = hour*, i.e. one of the twelve equal periods into which the natural day (from sunrise to sunset) was divided. Thus the Roman *hour* was always varying in length, being shortest at the winter solstice and longest at the summer solstice, and only corresponded with our own *hour* at two points in the year, viz. at the two equinoxes. It should be remembered that the night (from sunset to sunrise) was divided, not into twelve hours, but into four equal *vigiliae* (*watches*), called *prīma, secunda, tertia*, and *quarta vigilia*.

LINE 7. **gladiātōrī**, dat. sing. of *gladiātor, -ōris*, m. 3d (from *gladius = a sword*, hence, lit. *a fighter with a sword*); indirect obj. of *dedissem; gladiātōrī istī = Catilīnae*. At about this period of the republic certain popular leaders, e.g. Clōdius, were beginning to attach to themselves bodyguards of worthless citizens, slaves, and gladiators, with

8 dedissem.　　Etenim　sī　summī　virī　et | single hour to live in.
I would have given.　For　　if　highest　the men　and | For if men in the
9 clārissimī　cīvēs　Sāturnīnī　et　　Gracchōrum | highest position and
most famous　the citizens　of Saturninus and　　of the Gracchi | citizens of the great-
 | est distinction have

---

whose assistance they engaged in street fights with other demagogues; hence the word *gladiātor = footpad*, or *assassin;* see the note on *sīca*, Chap. VI, l. 51. Gladiatorial shows originated in the idea that the *mānēs* or spirits of the dead were appeased by offerings of blood, and so we first hear of them at funeral games. But they soon became a regular public spectacle; the Emperor Trajan at one festival matched as many as ten thousand gladiators to fight. The gladiators were for the most part slaves, though sometimes Roman citizens (even emperors) took part in the combats. There were special *lūdī* or schools, where novices were trained by trainers called *lanistae*. The shows usually took place in special amphitheatres, formerly in the *circus māximus*. For the various types of gladiators, and for the rules observed in combat, consult any dictionary of antiquities. —— **istī**, dat. sing. m. of the dem. pron. *iste, ista, istud;* agrees with *gladiātōrī*. —— **ad**, prep.; gov. the acc. of the gerund *vīvendum*, denoting *purpose*. —— **vīvendum**, gen. *vīvendī* (dat. and abl. *vīvendō;* no nom. case); acc. sing. of the gerund of *vīvō, -ere, vīxī, victum*, 3; governed by the prep. *ad.* The gerundive supplements the inf. as verbal noun by adding to it oblique cases with inflexions; the inf. is the acc. as the direct of verbs, but the gerund in *-dum* is the acc. of the verbal noun as the object of a preposition. A. & G. 295; B. 338; G. 425, *ff;* H. 541, 542. —— **nōn**, negative adv.; limits *dedissem*.

LINE 8. **dedissem**, 1st pers. sing. pluperf. subjunct. act. of *dō, dare, dedī, datum*, 1; agrees with the subj. *ego*, l. 4; *dedissem* is the verb of the *apodosis*, in the unrealized condition respecting past time introduced by *sī* above. —— **Etenim** (*et + enim*), causal conj.; connects the sentence following with the one preceding. *Etenim* = καὶ γάρ, with an idea ellipsed, e.g. *and* (I state this fearlessly), *for if the chief men*, etc. —— **sī**, conditional particle; with the ind. *contāminārunt* and *honestārunt; sī* here = *seeing that*, a meaning which we often give to *if* in English. —— **summī**, nom. plur. m. of the adj. *summus, -a, -um* (superl. of *superus;* compar. *superior*); agrees with *virī. Summī virī = men of the highest position*, esp. politically, i.e. *magistrātūs; clārissimī cīvēs* refers to private citizens, e.g. Pūblius Scīpiō, who slew Tiberius Gracchus. For types of the men here described as *summī*, see Chap. II, *passim*. Observe that the sentence *etenim sī . . . putārem* (ll. 8–18) takes up again and answers the first and third questions of the previous chapter, viz. l. 21, *does the practice of our ancestors hinder you?* and l. 28, *Or do you fear future unpopularity?* The second question (l. 23, *do the laws hinder you?*) remains here unanswered, as Cicero could have no legal support (rather the reverse) in executing Roman citizens. —— **virī**, nom. plur. of *vir, virī*, m. 2d; *virī + cīvēs* = the composite subj. of *contāminārunt* and *honestārunt*. —— **et**, cop. conj.; joins together *virī* and *cīvēs*.

LINE 9. **clārissimī**, nom. plur. m. of *clārissimus, -a, -um*, superl. of the adj. *clārus, -a, -um* (root *klu = to hear*, hence *clārus = heard of, renowned;* cf. κλύω = *I hear*, κλυτός = *renowned, glōria*, etc.); agrees with *cīvēs*. —— **cīvēs**, nom. plur. of *cīvis, -is*, m. 3d; part of the subj. (see *virī* above) of *contāminārunt* and *honestārunt*. —— **Sāturnīnī**, gen. sing. of *Sāturnīnus*, m. 2d; poss. gen., limiting *sanguine*, l. 11. See the note on *Sāturnīnum*, Chap. II, l. 11. —— **et**, cop. conj.; connects *Sāturnīnī* and *Gracchōrum*. —— **Gracchōrum**, gen. of *Gracchī*, m. plur. 2d (*Gracchus* is the *cōgnomen* of a family of the famous *gēns Semprōnia*); poss. gen., limiting *sanguine*, and so coördinate with *Sāturnīnī*. The two great legislators, Tiberius and Gāius Gracchus, are often spoken of together as *Gracchī = the Gracchi;* cf. *Cicerōnēs = Ciceros, men like*

brought upon them-selves not pollution but on the contrary honor by the execu-tion of Saturninus, the Gracchi, Flaccus, and several others of time past, there was	et	Flaccī	et	superiōrum	complūrium 10
	and	*of Flaccus*	*and*	*earlier*	*of several men*
	sanguine	nōn	modo	sē	nōn contāminārunt, 11
	by the blood	*not*	*only*	*themselves*	*not have polluted,*
	sed	etiam	honestārunt,	certē	verendum 12
	but	*even*	*have covered with honor,*	*surely*	*to be feared*

Cicero, or *the Ciceros* (father and son). For Tiberius, see the note on *Gracchum,* Chap. I, l. 30, and for his death, ll. 28–32. For Gāius, see the note on *Gracchus,* Chap. II, l. 5, and for his death, ll. 1–7.

LINE 10. **et,** cop. conj.; connects *Gracchōrum* and *Flaccī.* —— **Flaccī,** gen. sing. of *Flaccus,* m. 2d; poss. gen., limiting *sanguine,* and so coördinate with *Sāturnīnī* and *Gracchōrum* above. *Flaccī = Marcī Fulvī Flaccī,* for whom see the note on *Fulvius,* Chap. II, l. 8. *Flaccus* is the *cōgnomen,* which was often a nickname (cf. *cicerō = chick-pea*), and appears in the name of members of the Fulvian and the Valerian *gentēs;* cf. also Quintus Horātius Flaccus, the great Augustan poet. —— **et,** cop. conj.; connects *Flaccī* and *superiōrum.* —— **superiōrum,** gen. plur. m. of the adj. *superior, -ius,* compar. of *superus* (*superiōrēs* is substantival = *men of earlier times*); poss. gen., limiting *san-guine,* and so coördinate with *Sāturnīnī,* etc., above. For the substantival use of adjec-tives, consult A. & G. 188, 189; B. 236–238; G. 204, NOTES 1–4; H. 441. Cicero has cited one instance of an early date, viz. the death of Spurius Maclius; see Chap. I, ll. 34–38. —— **complūrium,** gen. m. of the plur. adj. *complūrēs,* neut. *complūra* or *complūria,* 3d (*com + plūrēs*); agrees with *superiōrum;* of course *complūrium* is a rhetorical exaggeration.

LINE 11. **sanguine,** abl. sing. of *sanguis, sanguinis,* m. 3d (= (1) *blood,* hence (2) *slaughter,* by metonymy); abl. of the means, modifying *contāminārunt,* and also under-stood as a modifier of *honestārunt.* —— **nōn,** negative adv.; *nōn modo* modifies *nōn contāminārunt.* Here we see the full expression, *nōn modo nōn . . . sed etiam;* when the verb of the two clauses is one and the same, being expressed in the second clause, it is common for the second *nōn* to be omitted and understood. —— **modo,** adv.; in the phrase *nōn modo nōn.* —— **sē,** acc. plur. of the reflexive pron. of the 3d pers., sing. or plur., no nom. gen. *suī,* dat. *sibi,* abl. *sē;* direct obj. of *contāminārunt,* and understood as direct obj. of *honestārunt; sē* refers back to the subj. of the *sī* clause, viz. to *virī et cīvēs.* —— **nōn,** negative adv.; limits *contāminārunt.* Observe that *nōn . . . nōn* cancel and equal an affirmation, while *modo* in the combination leads up to the direct affirma-tion following *sed etiam.* —— **contāminārunt** (contracted form of *contāmināvērunt*) 3d pers. plur. perf. ind. act. of *contāminō, -āre, -āvī, -ātum,* 1 (for *con-tag-minō; con +* root *tag = to touch,* hence *I touch, defile, contaminate;* cf. *tangō, contāgium,* etc.); agrees with the composite subj. *virī et cīvēs.* The omission of the *v* of the perf. act. and the contraction of the enclosing vowels is particularly common in verbs of the 1st conjuga-tion; see the note on *cōnfirmāstī,* Chap. IV, l. 30, and cf. *honestārunt* following.

LINE 12. **sed,** adversative conj.; connects *honestārunt* with *nōn modo nōn contāmi-nārunt.* —— **etiam** (*et + iam*), adv.; adds corroborative emphasis to *honestārunt.* —— **honestārunt** (contracted form of *honestāvērunt*), 3d pers. plur. perf. ind. act. of *honestō, -āre, -āvī, -ātum,* 1 (from *honos,* through the adj. *honestus; honestō = I cause to be hon-estus,* i.e. *I cover with honor*); coördinate with *contāminārunt.* —— **certē,** adv. (formed from the adj. *certus, -a, -um*); modifies *nōn erat verendum.* —— **verendum,** nom. sing. n. of *verendus, -a, -um,* gerundive with passive meaning of the deponent verb *vereor, verērī, veritus sum,* 2 (root *var = ver = to be wary;* cf. Greek root ϝορ, ὀρ, in ὅρομαι = *I watch,* ὁράω = *I see*); *verendum + erat =* the 3d pers. sing. imperf. ind. of the periphrastic pas-

13	mihi	nōn	erat,	nē	quid	hōc	parricīdā	surely no need for
	by me	*not*	*it was,*	*lest*	*anything*	*this*	*murderer*	me to fear that, because I put this
14	cīvium		interfectō		invidiae	mihi	in	murderer of his fellow-countrymen to
	of citizens		*having been killed*		*of unpopularity*	*upon me*	*for*	death, popular re-

sive conjugation of *vereor*, and is impersonal = *it was not to be feared*. The gerundive is used personally in all genders, or impersonally in the neut. sing.; study carefully the note and references under *habendī*, Chap. I, l. 8. Whenever a substantival clause is dependent on an impersonal verb, that clause is its logical subj.; so the logical subj. of *erat verendum* is the clause *nē quid . . . redundāret*.

LINE 13. **mihi**, dat. sing. of *ego;* dat. of the agent. The agent is regularly put in the dat. after a gerund or gerundive, except when ambiguity might arise, i.e. when the verb itself governs a dat., in which case the agent is expressed by the abl. case with *ā* or *ab*. Remember also that the dat. of the agent is found sometimes after passive verbs, esp. after the perf. part. passive, and in poetry even after adjectives. A. & G. 232; B. 189, 1; G. 354, 355; H. 388.——**nōn**, adv.; limits *erat verendum*.——**erat**, 3d pers. sing. imperf. ind. of *sum, esse, fuī;* combines with *verendum*, forming the periphrastic imperf. ind. passive; the point of view is that of the past (cf. *nōn dedissem*), hence the imperfect tense.——**nē**, conj.; introduces the final substantival clause *quid . . . redundāret*, in dependence on the verb of *fearing, erat verendum*. The negative of *nē* in this construction is *ut*, e.g. *vereor nē* = *I fear that* something will happen; *vereor ut* = *I fear that* something will *not* happen. A. & G. 331, *f*; B. 296, 2; G. 550; H. 498, III.——**quid**, nom. sing. n. of the indef. pron. *quis, qua, quid;* subj. of *redundāret*. This pronoun is only used after *nē, nisi, sī*, or *num*. It is to be found in several compounds, e.g. *aliquis, quisquam, quispiam*, etc.——**hōc**, abl. sing. m. of the dem. pron. *hīc, haec, hōc;* agrees with *parricīdā*.——**parricīdā**, abl. sing. of *parricīda, -ae*, m. 1st (for etymology, etc., see the note on *parricīdiō*, Chap. VII, l. 40); abl. in the abl. absolute construction with *interfectō* = a clause *cum hīc parricīda interfectus fuisset*. A full discussion, with grammatical references, of this construction will be found in the note on *dīmissō*, Chap. IV, l. 38. Catiline is called *parricīda*, because he was the murderer of *cīvēs*, i.e. his political brothers, seeing that the *patria* is "*omnium nostrum commūnis părēns*"; *parricīda* may be used of any one guilty of a crime (e.g. murder of a father, of a relative, of a citizen; sacrilege) involving *impietās*.

LINE 14. **cīvium**, gen. plur. of *cīvis, -is*, m. and f. 3d; objective gen., with *parricīdā* = *murderer of citizens*.——**interfectō**, abl. sing. m. of *interfectus, -a, -um*, perf. part. pass. of *interficiō, -ere, interfēcī, interfectum*, 3 (*inter + faciō*); agrees with *parricīdā*, in the abl. absolute construction.——**invidiae**, gen. sing. of *invidia*, f. 1st (*invideō*); partitive gen., limiting *quid* = lit. *anything of unpopularity*, hence *any unpopularity*. The partitive genitive represents the *whole*, of which a *part* is taken, and so is a branch of the common possessive genitive. It is used: (1) with nouns, e.g. *pars mīlitum;* (2) pronouns, e.g. *iī nostrum* = *those of us;* (3) adjectives, esp. numerals, e.g. *multī* or *ūnus mīlitum;* (4) compar. and superl. adjectives, e.g. *fortior* or *fortissimus mīlitum*.= *the braver* or *the bravest of the soldiers;* (5) many neuter adjectives or pronouns, as in this passage, cf. *nihil novī* = lit. *nothing of new, nothing new;* (6) adverbs, e.g. *ubi terrārum* = *where in the world?* A. & G. 216, 3; B. 201, 2; G. 369; H. 397, 3. Compare Chap. II, l. 3, *nē* QUID DĒTRĪMENTI *res pūblica caperet*.——**mihi**, dat. sing. of *ego;* dat. of the indirect obj., dependent on *redundāret*.——**in**, prep.; gov. the acc. *posteritātem*. In relations of time, *in* + the acc. = *for*, from the standpoint of the present, but must often be rendered *in* or *at* in idiomatic English. For this and other uses of *in*, consult A. & G. 153; B. 143; G. 418, 1; H. 435, 1.

| sentiment would over-take me like a flood in the future. But even supposing that such resentment threatened me in all seriousness, neverthe-less I have always been so disposed as | posteritātem | redundāret. | Quodsī | ea | mihi 15 |
| | *the future time* | *should flood over.* | *But if* | *it (= odium)* | *me* |

| | māximē | impendēret, | tamen | hōc | animō 16 |
| | *very greatly* | *threatened,* | *yet* | *this* | *in mind* |

| | fuī | semper, | ut | invidiam | virtūte 17 |
| | *I have been* | *always,* | *that* | *odium* | *by virtue* |

LINE 15. **posteritātem**, acc. sing. of *posteritās, posteritātis,* f. 3d (from the adj. *pos-terus,* which is from the adv. *post*); governed by the prep. *in; in posteritātem = in posterum tempus. Posteritās* is used in two senses: (1) *the future,* (2) *people of the future, posterity.*——**redundāret,** 3d pers. sing. imperf. subjunct. act. of *redundo, -āre, -āvī, -ātum,* 1 (*red = re + undō; =* lit. *I surge back; undō = I rise in waves, I surge,* and *unda = a wave,* are from root *ud* or *und = to wet;* cf. ὕδωρ *= water*); agrees with the subj. *quid;* the subjunct. mood is final, following *nē* in dependence on *erat verendum.* The imperf. tense is required, because the principal verb *erat verendum* is historic, and calls for historic sequence in subordinate clauses. A. & G. 286; B. 267, 268; G. 509, *ff;* H. 491. The metaphor is taken from a stream which has burst its banks, flooding the adjacent country.——**Quodsī,** conj. *= but if;* followed by the imperf. subjunct. *impendē-ret* in the *protasis,* marking the supposition as referring to the present, and therefore un-realized. *Quodsī = quod + sī,* i.e. *sī* introduces the condition, while *quod* is an adverbial acc. of reference, *= as to which,* i.e. *as regards the above.* A. & G. 240, *b;* B. 185, 2; G. 334; H. 453, 6.——**ea,** nom. sing. f. of the dem. pron. *is, ea, id;* subj. of *impendēret; ea = invidia.*——**mihi,** dat. sing. of *ego;* dat. of the indirect obj., dependent on *impendē-ret.* Many compounds of *in* (like *impendēre*), *con, prō,* etc., govern the dative of the indirect object.

LINE 16. **māximē** (formed from *māximus,* superl. of the adj. *magnus*), adv.; modi-fies *impendēret.*——**impendēret,** 3d pers. sing. imperf. subjunct. act. of *impendeo, -ēre,* no perf. no supine, 2 (*in = over, upon, + pendeō = I hang*); agrees with the subj. *ea.* Distinguish *impendēret* from *impendēret* (imperf. subjunct. act. of *impendō, -ere, impendī, impensum,* 3, *= I weigh out, expend, employ,* transitive). Observe that the condition is irregular in form: the imperf. subjunct. of the *protasis* marks the hypothesis as an ideal one respecting the present time, and we should expect the imperf. subjunct. also in the *apodosis.* But the orator changes the form of the *apodosis* by an afterthought, with the direct statement *hōc animō semper fuī.* He might just as well have said *quodsī ea mihi impendēret, tamen invidia virtūte parta glōria, nōn invidia esset (ut semper putāvī) = but if hatred threatened me now, yet hatred earned by virtue would be (as I have always thought it) glory, not hatred.* However, it is not uncommon for the *apodosis* to be altered, esp. by the means employed here, viz. the addition of a principal clause, not found in the original form of the condition, or at least only found as a parenthesis, to which the original *apodosis* is made subordinate by alteration to an acc. and inf. or to a substantival subjunct. object clause.——**tamen,** adv. (used as adversative conj.); strengthens the oppositional force of the statement following. *Tamen* is often used in the *apodosis* of a condition with *quodsī;* cf. ὅμως in the *apodosis* in Greek.——**hōc,** abl. sing. m. of the dem. pron. *hīc, haec, hōc;* agrees with *animō.*——**animō.** abl. sing. of *animus, -ī,* m. 2d; abl. of quality, otherwise called descriptive abl., describing the subj. of *fuī.* A. & G. 251; B. 224; G. 400; H. 419, II.

LINE 17. **fuī,** 1st pers. sing. perf. ind. of *sum, esse, fuī;* the subj. *ego* is implied by the personal ending.——**semper,** adv. of time; modifies the pred. *hōc animō fuī.*——**ut,** conj.; followed by the subjunct. *putārem;* the clause *ut . . . putārem* is explana-

18	partam	glōriam,	nōn	invidiam	putārem.
	acquired	*(to be) glory,*	*not*	*odium*	*I thought.*

19	Quamquam	nōnnūllī	sunt	in	hōc
	And yet	*some*	*there are*	*in*	*this*

20	ōrdine,	quī	aut	ea	quae
	order (= Senate),	*who*	*either*	*those things*	*which*

21	imminent	nōn	videant,	aut	ea	quae
	impend	*not*	*see*	*or those things which*		

to regard unpopularity incurred by manly conduct as glory, and not as unpopularity. And yet there are some in this Council who either do not see the dangers which are imminent or conceal their perception

tory of *hōc animō.* —— **invidiam,** acc. sing. of *invidia, -ae,* f. 1st ; subj.-acc. of *esse,* which must be supplied in the indirect pred. *glōriam esse,* dependent on *putārem* (a *verbum sentiendī*). —— **virtūte,** abl. sing. of *virtūs, virtūtis,* f. 3d (from *vir ;* hence (1) *manliness,* (2) *courage,* cf. ἀνδρία = *courage,* from ἀνήρ, gen. ἀνδρός = *a man,* (3) *virtue*); abl. of the means, modifying *partam.*

LINE 18. **partam,** acc. sing. f. of *partus, -a, -um,* perf. part. pass. of *pariō, -ere, peperī, partum,* fut. part. *pāritūrus,* 3 ; predicate part., agreeing with *invidiam ; invidiam virtūte partam* here = *invidiam quae virtūte parta esset.* —— **glōriam,** acc. sing. *of glōria, -ae,* f. 1st (akin to *clārus*); predicative, complement of *esse* understood. —— **nōn,** negative adv. ; limits *invidiam* (*esse*). —— **invidiam,** acc. sing. of *invidia, -ae,* f. 1st ; predicative, complement of *esse* understood. Observe that the subj. of the indirect statement (dependent on *putārem*) is *invidiam,* l. 17 ; hence the predicate words *glōriam* and *invidiam* (l. 18) take the same case as the subject. A. & G. 176 ; B. 167, 168 ; G. 205, 206 ; H. 360. —— **putārem,** 1st. pers. sing. imperf. subjunct. act. of *putō, -āre, -āvī, -ātum,* 1 ; the subj. *ego* is implied by the personal ending ; the subjunct. is consecutive, with *ut,* explaining *hōc animō* above.

LINE 19. **Quamquam,** (*quam + quam*) conj. = *and yet ;* connects the sentence with the previous one. *Quamquam,* and less commonly *etsī,* which are usually subordinate conjunctions = *although,* may be used to connect coördinately. —— **nōnnūllī,** (*nōn + nūllī*), nom. plur. m. of the adj. *nōnnūllus, -a, -um ; nōnnūllī* is substantival, and subj. of *sunt.* —— **sunt,** 3d pers. plur. pres. ind. of *sum, esse, fuī ;* agrees with the subj. *nōnnūllī.* —— **in,** prep. ; gov. the abl. *ōrdine.* —— **hōc,** abl. sing. m. of the dem. pron. *hīc, haec, hōc ;* agrees with *ōrdine.*

LINE 20. **ōrdine,** abl. sing. of *ōrō, ōrdinis,* m. 3d ; governed by the prep. *in ; in hōc ōrdine* = *in senātū.* —— **quī,** nom. plur. m. of the rel. pron. *quī, quae, quod ;* agrees with the indef. antecedent *nōnnūllī,* and is subj. of *videant ; quī* is *generic,* i.e. represents a class (= *tālēs ut*), hence followed by the subjunct. *videant.* A. & G. 320 ; B. 283 ; G. 631, 2 ; H. 503, I. Distinguish *quī,* as used here, from *quī,* as used in l. 22. —— **aut,** disjunctive conj. ; used correlatively with *aut* below, = *either . . . or.* —— **ea,** acc. plur. n. of the dem. pron. *is, ea, id ;* direct obj. of *videant.* —— **quae,** nom. plur. n. of the rel. pron. *quī, quae, quod ;* agrees with the antecedent *ea,* and is subj. of *imminent.* Observe that when the antecedent of the rel. clause is not otherwise expressly defined than by the statement made in the rel. clause the antecedent is usually a part of *is, ea, id.*

LINE 21. **imminent,** 3d pers. plur. pres. ind. act. of *immineō, -ēre,* no perf., no supine, 2 (*in + minor*); agrees with the subj. *quae.* Note the ind. mood, which is employed instead of the subjunct., because stress is laid on the *fact* of dangers being imminent ; otherwise the rule would require a subjunctive, because the rel. clause is subordinate to the subjunct. in *quī nōn . . . videant.* A. & G. 342 ; B. 324 ; G. 629 ; H. 529, II, NOTE I. —— **nōn,** negative adv. ; limits *videant.* —— **videant,** 3d pers. plur. pres. subjunct. act. of *videō, -ēre, vīdī, vīsum,* 2 ; agrees with the subject *quī* above ;

| of what they do see; and it is these men who have fostered Catiline's hopes by their pacific declara- | **vident** *they see* **mollibus** *mild* | **dissimulent:** *disguise:* **sententiīs** *by views* | **quī** *who* **aluērunt,** *have fostered,* | **spem** *the hope* | **Catilīnae** 22 *of Catiline* **coniūrātiōnemque** 23 *and the conspiracy* |

the subjunct. is *consecutive*, as regularly with *quī generic* or *characteristic; see quī* above. —— **aut,** disjunctive conj.; connects *videant* and *dissimulent.* —— **ea,** acc. plur. n. of the dem. pron. *is, ea, id;* direct obj. of *dissimulent,* or of *vidēre* in *sē vidēre* supplied. —— **quae,** acc. plur. n. of the rel. pron. *quī, quae, quod;* agrees with the antecedent *ea,* and is direct obj. of *vident* following.

LINE 22. **vident,** 3d pers. plur. pres. ind. act. of *videō, -ēre, vīdī, vīsum,* 2; the implied subj. of *vident* is a pron. *eī* or *illī,* referring to *nōnnūllī,* l. 19; the mood is ind. for the same reason as in the case of *imminent* above (where see note). —— **dissimulent,** 3d pers. plur. pres. subjunct. act. of *dissimulō, -āre, -āvī, -ātum,* 1 (for *dissimilō, dis* marking contradiction + *similis = like;* the Latin root is *sim,* Greek ἁμ or ὁμ = *like;* cf. *similis, simul, simulō, semel, semper,* and ἅμα, ὅμοιος, ὁμοῦ); agrees with the subj. *quī* (generic), l. 20; the subjunct. is consecutive and coördinate with *videant.* Synonyms: (1) *simulō* = lit. *I make like, I pretend, I invent,* i.e. that something is which really is not, e.g. (a) + direct obj., *morbum simulāre = to feign sickness,* (b) + acc. and inf., *mē aegrōtum esse simulō;* (2) *dissimulō,* = *I hide, I pretend* that something is not which really is, e.g. (a) + direct obj., *morbum dissimulāre = to hide sickness* (feigning health), (b) + acc. and inf., *mē aegrōtum esse dissimulō.* The distinction may be memorized in the following hexameter: *Quae nōn sunt simulō; quae sunt, ea dissimulantur.* —— **quī,** nom. plur. m. of the rel. pron. *quī, quae, quod;* agrees with the antecedent *nōnnūllī,* and is subj. of *aluērunt* and *corrōborāvērunt.* Observe that *quī* here really begins a new sentence, i.e. the ind. mood of *aluērunt.* A. & G. 180, *f;* B. 251, 6; G. 610; H. 453. —— **spem,** acc. sing. of *spēs, speī,* f. 5th; direct obj. of *aluērunt.* —— **Catilīnae,** gen. sing. of *Catilīna,* m. 1st; poss. gen., limiting *spem.*

LINE 23. **mollibus,** abl. plur. f. of the adj. *mollis, -e,* 3d (probably for *mov-lis =* (1) *easily moved, pliant;* (2) *weak, uncertain;* (3) *delicate, soft;* root *mav =* Latin *mov, to push out of place;* cf. *mōbilis,* and ἀμείβω = *I change*); agrees with *sententiīs.* There is probably no connection between *mollis* and μαλακός. *Mollibus* suggests a rebuke, implying that mild, weak, and conciliatory speeches were made instead of the vigorous and resolute denunciations which the occasion required. It is not necessary to suppose that Cicero suspected treasonable collusion. The reference in *quī spem . . . corrōborāvērunt* is to the time, just before the elections, 63 B.C., when Cicero warned the Senate of danger and when Catiline, called upon to speak, declared that he would lead the people against the infirm Senate. Cicero, in his speech for Mūrēna, laments the Senate's weakness on this occasion, cf. *neque tamen satis sevērē prō reī indignitāte dēcrēvit.* —— **sententiīs,** abl. plur. of *sententia, -ae,* f. 1st (*sentiō*); abl. of the means or instrument, modifying *aluērunt.* *Sententia* is the regular word for the declaration of opinion made by a senator; the speaker was not compelled to adhere to the subject under discussion, but might speak on any subject of a public nature, hence when it was so desired a party might delay the settlement of a particular question by speaking on extraneous subjects the whole day. —— **aluērunt,** 3d pers. plur. perf. ind. act. of *alō, -ere, uī-, altum* or *alitum,* 3 (root *al = to nourish;* cf. *alumnus,* ἄν-αλ-τος = *insatiable,* etc.); agrees with the subj. *quī.* —— **coniūrātiōnemque** (*coniūrātiōnem +* *que*), *coniūrātiōnem* is the acc. sing. of *coniūrātiō, -ōnis,* f. 3d (*con + iūrō*); direct obj. of *corrōborāvērunt.* *Que* is the enclitic cop. conj.; connects the coördinate rel. clauses *quī . . . aluērunt* and (*quī*) *. . . corrōborāvērunt.*

24 nāscentem	nōn	crēdendō	corrōborāvērunt;
growing	*not*	*by believing*	*have strengthened;*

25 quōrum	auctōritāte	multī,	nōn	sōlum
whose	*by authority*	*many men,*	*not*	*only*

26 improbī,	vērum	etiam	imperītī,	sī	in
the dishonest,	*but*	*also*	*the inexperienced,*	*if*	*upon*

tions and strengthened the conspiracy at its birth by refusing to believe in its existence. And guided by their authority many others, not the rogues alone but also the unin-

LINE 24. **nāscentem**, acc. sing. f. of *nāscēns, -entis,* pres. part. of the deponent verb *nāscor, nāscī, nātus sum,* 3; agrees with *coniūrātiōnem* and = a temporal clause like *dum nāscitur.*——**nōn**, negative adv.; limits *crēdendō* (not *corrōborāvērunt*).—— **crēdendō**, abl. of the gerund *crēdendum, -ī,* of the verb *crēdō, -ere, crēdidī, crēditum,* 3 (Sanskrit *çrat* or *çrad = trust* + root *dha = to put;* for root *dha* = Latin *da, fa, fac,* cf. *con-dō, ab-dō,* etc.); abl. of the means, modifying *corrōborāvērunt.* The abl. of the gerund or gerundive expresses: (1) *the means,* as above; (2) *cause;* (3) less often, *manner* or *circumstance.* Study the examples in A. & G. 301; B. 339, 1; G. 431; H. 542.　*Crēdere* is used: (1) intransitively = *to believe,* with the dat., e.g. *crēdō tibi = I believe, trust in you;* with acc. of neuter pronouns, e.g. *id quod volunt crēdunt;* (2) transitively, in the sense *to commit, entrust, lend,* with the acc. and dat. of the direct and indirect objects respectively.——**corrōborāvērunt**, 3d pers. plur. perf. ind. act. of *corrōborō, -āre, -āvī, -ātum,* 1 (*con* + *rōborō,* from noun *rōbur,* gen. *rōboris,* n. 3d = *strength;* probably akin to Greek root ρω in ρώ-ννυμι = *I strengthen*); agrees with the subj. *quī,* and is coördinate with *aluērunt.*

LINE 25. **quōrum**, gen. plur. m. of the rel. pron. *quī, quae, quod;* agrees with the antecedent *nōnnūllī* (l. 19) i.e. *nōnnūllī quī coniūrātiōnem corrōborāvērunt,* and is poss. gen., limiting *auctōritāte.* Like *quī* in l. 22, *quōrum* is here connective and begins a new sentence = *nam hōrum auctōritāte,* etc.——**auctōritāte**, abl. sing. of *auctōritās, -ātis,* f. 3d (from *auctor*); abl. of the cause, modifying *dīcerent.* It is more usual for *the cause* of an action to be expressed by the abl. in conjunction with a perf. part. passive, e.g. *quōrum auctōritāte adductī (impulsī, incitātī,* etc.). A. & G. 245, and 2, *b*; B. 219; G. 408, and NOTE 2; H. 416.　Some editors read *auctōritātem secūtī* for *auctōritāte.*—— *Auctōritāte* here = *on the authority, by the influence;* sometimes *auctōritās* has a special meaning, viz. senatorial *sanction* of a measure which an interposition of veto alone prevented from becoming a *senātūs cōnsultum.*——**multī**, nom. plur. m. (substantival) of the adj. *multus, -a, -um;* subj. of *dīcerent. Multi* here = *multī aliī,* i.e. not members of the Senate.——**nōn**, negative adv.; *nōn sōlum* modifies *improbī.*——**sōlum** (acc. neut. sing. of the adj. *sōlus, -a, -um;* cf. adv. *multum, vērum,* etc.), adv.; combines with *nōn* as an adverbial modifier.

LINE 26. **improbī**, nom. plur. m. of the adj. *improbus, -a, -um (in = not + probus = honest, virtuous*); agrees with *multi = multī, quī sunt improbī,* or we may consider *improbī* as substantival (= *the dishonest*) and appositive of *multī. Improbī,* evidently refers to followers of the senators *quī ea quae vident dissimulent* (l. 21), i.e. corrupt followers of corrupt patrons.——**vērum**, adversative conj.; connects and opposes *improbī* and *imperītī.* See the note and references under *tamen,* Chap. I, l. 18.——**etiam** (*et + iam*), adv.; intensifies *imperītī.*——**imperītī**, nom. plur. m. of the adj. *imperītus, -a, -um (in = not + perītus = experienced, skilled*); agrees with *multī,* or else substantival in apposition. *Imperītī* = the ignorant and politically blind followers of ignorant senators (*quī ea imminent nōn videant,* l. 20).——**sī**, conditional particle; with the pluperf. subjunct. *animadvertissem* of an ideal supposition in regard to past time.—— **in**, prep.; gov. the acc. *hunc.*

formed, would say	hunc	animadvertissem,	crūdēliter	et 27
that I had acted in	this (fellow)	I had inflicted punishment,	cruelly	and
a savage and tyran-				
nical fashion, if I had	rēgiē	factum esse	dīcerent.	Nunc 28
inflicted punishment	tyrannically	(it) to have been done	would say.	Now
on Catiline. Now,				
however, I perceive	intellegō,	sī iste,	quō intendit,	in 29
that if he once ar-	I discern,	if that (fellow)	whither he purposes	to

LINE 27. **hunc**, acc. sing. m. of the dem. pron. *hĭc, haec, hŏc ;* governed by the prep. *in ; hunc = Catilīnam.* —— **animadvertissem**, 1st pers. sing. pluperf. subjunct. act. of *animadvertō, -ere, animadvertī, animadversum,* 3 *(animum + advertō) ;* the subj. *ego* is implied by the personal ending ; in the *protasis* with *sī.* The verb *animadvertō* is often written *animum advertō* and = lit. *I turn my mind (attention) towards, I notice, observe ;* see the note on *animadvertīs,* Chap. VIII, l. 41 ; it is followed by the acc. of the direct object. In a judicial sense *animadvertere* is used with *suppliciō* understood = *to notice with punishment, to punish, to inflict punishment on,* and is followed by (a) the acc. of the direct object, (b) by *in* + the acc., in which case emphasis is laid on the attention which has been bestowed on the circumstances of the offence. —— **crūdēliter** (formed from the 3d decl. adj. *crūaēlis, -e ;* root *kru = to be hard ;* cf. *crūdus = unripe, raw) ;* modifies *factum esse.* —— **et,** cop. conj. ; connects *crūdēliter* and *rēgiē.*

LINE 28. **rēgiē** (from the adj. *rēgius, -a, -um ;* from *rēx, rēgis,* m. 3d), adv. ; modifies *factum esse. Rēgiē* is the Latin equivalent for the Greek τυραννικῶς ; the Romans and Greeks found that *kingship* and the rule of a τύραννος (= *despotic ruler)* were opposed to the principles of freedom. The Tarquins had made the word *rēx* odious to Romans, and the description of an action as *rēgium* was always likely to arouse indignation against it ; this feeling lasted long, and showed itself in many secret organizations and conspiracies in the early empire. Compare II, Chap. VII, line 19, (*mē) crūdēlissimum tyrannum exīstimārī velint.* Cicero was exposed to much criticism for his so-called despotic conduct during his consulship ; he speaks in one of his speeches of this, *quī nōs tyrannōs vocās.* —— **factum esse,** perf. inf. of *fīō, fierī, factus sum,* used as pass. of *faciō, -ere, fēcī, factum,* 3 ; understand as subj.-acc. a pron., e.g. *id,* referring to *sī animadvertissem ; factum esse* is obj. of *dīcerent.* —— **dīcerent,** 3d pers. plur. imperf. subjunct. act. of *dīcō, -ere, dīxī, dictum,* 3 ; agrees with the subj. *multī,* l. 25 ; *dīcerent* is the verb of the *apodosis,* and the imperf. tense expresses continuity of action, i.e. *they would have said* and *they would be saying now.* —— **Nunc,** adv. of time ; used partly in a temporal sense and partly to contrast the present with the past, = *now, as it is.*

LINE 29. **intellegō,** 1st pers. sing. pres. ind. act. of *intellegō, -ere, intellēxī, intellectum,* 3 *(inter + lēgō) ;* the subj. *ego* is implied by the personal ending. See the synonyms and the note under *intellegit,* Chap. I, l. 17. Observe that *intellegō,* as a verb of *perception,* throws the condition following into an indirect form ; hence the *protasis* has the perf. subjunct. *pervēnerit,* and the verb of the *apodosis* is the pres. inf. *fore.* In direct form the condition would be: *sī iste . . . in Manliāna castra pervēnerit* (fut. perf. ind.), *nēmō tam stultus erit (quī,* etc.), *nēmō tam improbus quī nōn fateātur.* A. & G. 337, 1 and 2 ; B. 319, A, B ; G. 657 ; H. 527, I. —— **sī,** conditional particle ; introducing a logical condition respecting the future, and followed by the perf. subjunct. *pervēnerit* (= fut. perf. ind. of direct statement). —— **iste,** nom. sing. m. of the dem. pron. of the 2d pers. *iste, ista, istud ;* subj. of *pervēnerit ; iste* refers to Catiline, and has its usual forensic signification of contempt ; = *that fellow.* See note on *iste,* Chap. I, l. 3. —— **quō** (abl. n. sing. of *quī),* adv., = *eō quō, thither, whither ;* introduces the clause *quō intendit* as an adverbial modifier of *pervēnerit.* —— **intendit,** 3d pers. sing. pres. ind. act. of *intendō, -ere, intendī, intensum* or *intentum,* 3 *(in + tendō = lit. I stretch towards,* hence

30 Manliāna	castra	pervēnerit,	nēminem	tam
of Manlius	*the camp*	*shall come,*	*no one*	*so*

31 stultum	fore	quī	nōn	videat
foolish	*to be likely to be*	*who*	*not*	*can see*

32 coniūrātiōnem	esse	factam,	nēminem	tam
a conspiracy	*to have been*	*made,*	*no one*	*so*

33 improbum	quī	nōn	fateātur.	Hōc
dishonest	*who*	*not*	*may confess (it).*	*This (man)*

rives, as he purposes, at the camp of Manlius, there will be no one so dull as not to see that a conspiracy has been set on foot or so shameless as not to acknowledge the reality of it. Yet,

I aim, purpose, urge, etc.); the implied subj. is *iste*, which is the expressed subj. of *per-vēnerit*. *Quō intendit* is a kind of additional statement made in parenthesis and referring to *in Manliāna castra ;* hence, as it might well be left out without disturbing the sentence, the verb is indicative, though the verb of a subordinate clause in indirect speech is properly in the subjunctive. A. & G. 336, 2 ; B. 314, 1; G. 650; H. 524.——**in,** prep.; gov. the acc. *castra,* expressing *limit of motion.*

LINE 30. **Manliāna,** acc. plur. of the adj. *Manliānus, -a, -um* (formed from the proper noun *Manlius, -ī,* m. 2d ; cf. *Sultānus* from *Sulla*); agrees with *castra.*—— **castra,** acc. of the plur. noun *castra, -ōrum,* n. 2d (*castrum, -ī,* n. 2d = *fortress*); governed by the prep. *in.*—— **pervēnerit,** 3d pers. sing. perf. subjunct. act. of *perveniō, -īre, per-vēnī, perventum,* 4 (*per + veniō*); agrees with the subj. *iste.* For the mood, see the note on *intellegō,* l. 29.—— **nēminem,** acc. sing. of *nēmō,* m. 3d, dat. *nēminī (nē + homō ;* the gen. and abl. are wanting, and are supplied by *nūllīus,* and *nūllō,* from *nūllus, -a, -um*); subj.-acc. of *fore* in the acc. and inf. object clause of *intellegō ; nēminem fore,* etc., is the *apodosis* of the condition introduced by *sī* above. For model sentences and remarks on the form of reported conditions after primary and historic leading verbs, refer to the note on *sī,* Chap. VIII, l. 31.—— **tam,** adv.; modifies *stultum.* *Tam* never modifies verbs, only adverbs and adjectives ; use *ita* and *adeō* with verbs.

LINE 31. **stultum,** acc. sing. m. of the adj. *stultus, -a, -um ;* agrees with the subj.-acc. *nēminem ;* predicative, being the complement of *fore* in the acc. and inf. construction. ——**fore,** fut. inf. of *sum, esse, fuī ;* agrees with the subj.-acc. *nēminem.* The fut. inf. of *sum* is also formed in the familiar way by means of the fut. part. *futūrus, -a, -um + esse.* —— **quī,** nom. sing. m. of the rel. pron. *quī, quae, quod ;* agrees with the antecedent *nēmi-nem,* and is subj. of *videat ; quī* is equivalent to *ut is,* introducing a clause of result.—— **non,** negative adv.; limits *videat.*—— **videat,** 3d pers. sing. pres. subjunct. act. of *videō, ēre, vīdī, vīsum,* 2; agrees with the subj. *quī ;* the subjunct. is consecutive, after *quī = ut is.* A. & G. 319; B. 284; G. 552; H. 500.

LINE 32. **coniūrātiōnem,** acc. sing. of *coniūrātiō, -ōnis,* f. 3d (*con + iūrō*); subj.-acc. of *factum esse,* in dependence on the verb of *perception videat.*——**esse factam,** perf. inf. of *fīō, fierī, factus sum,* used as the passive of *faciō, -ere, fēcī, factum,* 3 (root *dha = fa, fac = to put, place, make,* with a large number of derivatives); agrees (the part. *factam* in gender, number, and case) with the subj.-acc. *coniūrātiōnem.* In composite infinitives and composite ind. and subjunct. tenses it is very common for (1) the part. of *sum* to precede the participle, as in this passage, and (2) for other words, often a large number, to separate the participle from the part. of *sum.*—— **nēminem,** acc. sing. of *nēmō,* m. 3d (see *nēminem,* above); subj.-acc. of *fore tam improbum (fore* being supplied from the preceding coördinate object-clause).—— **tam,** adv.; modifies *improbum.*

LINE 33. **improbum,** acc. sing. m. of the adj. *improbus, -a, -um (in = not + probus = upright, honest*); agrees with the subj.-acc. *nēminem,* l. 32; predicative, being the complement of *fore* understood.—— **quī,** nom. sing. m. of the rel. pron. *quī, quae, quod ;* agrees with the antecedent *nēminem,* and is subj. of *fateātur ; quī* introduces a rel.

| if Catiline alone be put to death, I discern that this disease which is in the state may be repressed for a short time but can- | autem *however* | ūnō *one* | interfectō *having been killed,* | intellegō *I perceive* | hanc *this* 84 |
| | reī pūblicae *of the commonwealth* | pestem *plague* | paulisper *for a little while* | reprimī, *to be checked,* 85 |

clause of result = *ut is.* In sentences of this kind Cicero prefers *quī nōn* to *quīn* (*quī,* old abl., + *nōn*); *quī nōn* marks the tendency, and *quīn* the result (= *ut nōn*).——**nōn,** negative adv.; limits *fateātur.*——**fateātur,** 3d pers. sing. pres. subjunct. of the deponent verb *fateor, fatērī, fossus sum,* 2 (akin to *fārī, fās, fāma,* φημί, φαίνω, etc.); agrees with the subj., *quī;* the subjunct. is consecutive, with *quī = ut is.* The perf. of *fateor* is not very often found; indeed the compound *confiteor* is much more used than *fateor.* Supply, from the coördinate *quī* clause preceding, *coniūrātiōnem esse factam* as the object of *fateātur.*——**Hōc,** abl. sing. m. of the dem. pron. *hīc, haec, hōc;* abl. in the abl. absolute construction with *interfectō; hōc = Catilīnā. Hōc . . . interfectō =* a conditional clause, *sī hīc ūnus interfectus sit, intellegō hanc pestem . . . reprimī posse;* compare the form of the reported condition, ll. 29–33.

Line 34. **autem,** adversative conj.; connects the sentence with the one preceding. *Autem* is the weakest of the adversative conjunctions, and is used (1) in mild antithesis, (2) in contrasted conditions, as in this passage, for *hōc . . . interfecto =* a condition, and is contrasted with *sī iste pervēnerit* above. Often *autem* has no adversative force at all, and is merely connective; cf. the Greek particle δέ.——**ūnō,** abl. sing. m. of the numeral adj. *ūnus, -a, -um;* agrees with *hōc. Ūnus* is often used as a synonym of *sōlus = only, alone,* and here *ūnō = sōlō.*——**interfectō,** abl. sing. m. of *interfectus, -a, -um,* perf. part. pass. of *interficiō, -ere, interfēcī, interfectum,* 3 (*inter + faciō*); agrees with *hōc* in the ablative absolute construction. *Interficere* is the general verb meaning *to kill;* see the synonyms in the note on *occīdit,* Chap. I, l. 38.——**intellegō,** 1st pers. sing. pres. ind. act. of *intellegō, -ere, intellēxī, intellectum,* 3 (*inter + legō*); the subj. *ego* is implied by the personal ending. Observe that *hōc,* l. 33—*posse,* l. 36, is a disguised condition, and that the *apodosis* (i.e. *hanc pestem . . . reprimī, nōn comprimī . . . posse*) is thrown into the acc. and inf. indirect form by *intellegō* here, just as *intellegō,* l. 29, gave indirect form to the condition in the previous sentence. In direct form the condition = *hōc interfectō* (i.e. *sī hīc interfectus erit*), *haec pestis reprimī, nōn comprimī poterit.*——**hanc,** acc. sing. f. of the dem. pron. *hīc, haec, hōc;* agrees with *pestem; hanc pestem = coniūrātiōnem.*

Line 35. **reī,** gen. sing. of *rēs,* f. 5th; poss. gen., limiting *pestem.*——**pūblicae,** gen. sing. f. of the adj. *pūblicus, -a, -um;* agrees with *reī; reī pūblicae* as usual = *of the state, of the commonwealth.*——**pestem,** acc. sing. of *pestis, -is,* f. 3d; subj.-acc. of *posse* in the acc. and inf. construction dependent on *intellegō.* The nouns *pestis* and *pestilentia* are often used in a metaphorical sense with regard to political weakness or danger. Refer to the synonyms given under *pestem,* Chap. I, l. 27.——**paulisper** (*paulum + per*), adv. = *for a little while;* modifies *reprimī. Paulus,* not *paullus,* is read in all the best Mss.; yet with the derivation *paur + los* we should rather expect *paullus,* i.e. assimilation of *r* to *l,* instead of omission. Yet the root may be *pau +* termination *-lus* (= Greek *-ρος; r* and *l* are frequently interchangeable). As *paulus,* so *paulisper* is found in the Mss., e.g. in the Medicean Vergil.——**reprimī,** pres. inf. pass. of *reprimō, -ere, repressī, repressum,* 3 (*re = back + premō = I press*); complementary inf., with *posse.* Observe the difference of meaning between *reprimere* and *comprimere,* upon which the whole force of the sentence rests. *Reprimere = ad tempus continēre = to hold in check for the time being,* whereas *comprimere = plānē cōnficere = to wholly crush,* i.e. beyond all hope of restoration.

36 nōn   in   perpetuum   comprimī   posse.   Quodsī
   not *for*   *all time*   *to be crushed* *to be able.*   *But if*

37 sē   ēiēcerit   sēcumque   suōs   ēdūxerit
  himself he shall cast out and with him his (friends) shall lead out

38 et   eōdem   cēterōs   undique   collectōs
  and *to the same spot* *all other*   *from all parts*   *collected*

39 naufragōs   adgregārit,   exstinguētur
  the castaways   *shall gather together,*   *will be extinguished*

not be repressed for-ever. But if he rushes out of the city and takes his followers with him and herds together in the one spot the rest of the castaways whom he has got to-gether from every

LINE 36. **nōn**, negative adv.; limits *comprimī.* —— **in**, prep.; gov. the acc. *per-petuum ;* the phrase *in perpetuum = for all time ;* cf. *in posteritātem = for the future.* —— **perpetuum**, acc. sing. n. of the adj. *perpetuus, -a, -um (per + root pat = to fly;* cf. *peto = I fall upon, attack, πέτομαι = I fly,* etc.; hence *perpetuus = continual); per-petuum* is substantival, *= perpetuum tempus,* and is governed by the prep. *in.* —— **comprimī**, pres. inf. pass. of *comprimō, -ere, compressī, compressum,* 3 (*con + premō*); complementary or epexegetical, with *posse.* The complementary inf. is used with verbs, e.g. *to dare, seem, begin, attempt,* etc., which imply a further action of the same subject ; see the references in the note on *invenīrī,* Chap. II, l. 44. —— **posse**, pres. inf. of *possum, posse, potuī,* no supine, irreg. (*potis + sum*); agrees with the subj.-acc. *pestem* above. —— **Quodsī** (*Quod + sī*), conj.; followed by the coördinate fut.-perf. tenses *ēiēcerit, ēdūxerit,* and *adgregārit,* as the condition is a logical one respecting the future. Many editors write separately, *Quod sī ; quod* is an adverbial acc. of reference, for which refer to the note on *Quodsī,* l. 15.

LINE 37. **sē**, acc. sing. of the reflexive pron. of the 3d pers., *sē (sēsē),* gen. *suī ;* direct obj. of *ēiēcerit ; sē* refers to the subj. of *ēiēcerit,* i.e. Catiline. —— **ēiēcerit**, 3d pers. sing. fut.-perf. ind. act. of *ēiciō, -ere, ēiēci, ēiectum,* 3 (*ex + iaciō*); of the subj. *hīc* or *īs,* refer-ring to Catiline, is implied by the personal ending ; with *ēiēcerit* supply *ex urbe.* —— **sēcumque** (*sē + cum + que*) *sē* is the abl. sing. of the reflexive pron. *sē,* gen. *suī ;* refers to the subj. of the clause, and is governed by the prep. *cum. Cum* is the prep. + the abl.; gov. *sē,* and appended to it, as regularly to personal pronouns, and usually to the relative. *Que* is the enclitic cop. conj. ; connects the clause (*sī*) *sēcum ēdūxerit* with the clause *sī sē ēiēcerit.* —— **suōs**, acc. of *suī, -ōrum,* m. 2d (substantival m. plur. of *suus, -a, -um,* reflexive poss. adj. of the 3d pers.); direct obj. of *ēdūxerit.* —— **ēdūxerit**, 3d pers. sing. fut.-perf. ind. act. of *ēdūcō, -ere, ēdūxī, -ēductum,* 1 (*ē + dūcō ;* distinguish from *ēdūcō, -āre, -āvī, -ātum,* 1); coördinate with *ēiēcerit,* agreeing with the same subj., and in the same construction.

LINE 38. **et**, cop. conj.; connects the clause (*sī*) *adgregārit* with the clause (*sī*) *ēdūxerit.* —— **eōdem**, abl. sing. n. of *īdem, eadem, idem ; (is + dem),* adv. *= to the same place (eō + -dem);* modifies *adgregārit; eōdem = in Manliana castra.* —— **cēterōs**, acc. plur. m. of the adj. *cēterus, -a, -um* (not found in the nom. sing. m., and rarely used except in the plur. ; *cēterī* and *cētera* are commonly substantival); agrees with *naufragōs.* Synonyms: (1) *reliquī (relinquō = I leave behind) = the rest,* regarded numerically as a remainder ; (2) *cēterī = the rest,* implying contrast ; (3) *aliī =* not *the others,* but *others.* —— **undique** (*unde + que*), adv. + *from all sides* ; modifies *collectōs.* —— **collectōs**, acc. plur. m. of *collectus, -a, -um,* perf. part. pass. of *colligō, -ere, collēgī, collectum,* 3 (*con + legō = I gather together*); agrees with *naufragōs; collectōs* stands in place of a clause *quī undique collectī sunt.*

LINE 39. **naufragōs**, acc. plur. of *naufragī, -ōrum,* m. 2d *= castaways, bankrupts* (substantival m. of the adj. *naufragus, -a, -um = shipwrecked, ruined; nāvis + frangō ;* for the form *nau,* cf. *nauta,* and *ναῦς = a ship, ναύτης = a sailor*); direct object of *adgre-*

direction, not only this political disease (far developed as it is) but also the root and seed of all our sufferings will be put to an end and utterly destroyed.	atque dēlēbitur nōn modo haec tam adulta **40** *and will be destroyed not only this so full grown* reī pūblicae pestis, vērum etiam stirps **41** *of the commonwealth plague, but also the root* ac sēmen malōrum omnium. **42** *and the seed of evils all.*

gārit; cf. Chap. XI, l. 8, *contrā illam naufragōrum ēiectam ac aēbilitātam manum.* The metaphor from shipwreck is a familiar one in English. *Naufragus* = a man financially ruined; *perditus* = a man morally ruined.——**adgregārit** (contraction from *adgregāverit*), 3d pers. sing. fut.-perf. ind. act of *adgregō, -āre, āvī, ātum,* 1 (also written *aggregō,* etc. ; *ad* + *grex* = *a flock,* hence lit. *I add to a flock, collect*); coördinate with *ēdūxerit* and *ēiēcerit* above, agreeing with the same subj., and in the same construction (i.e. part of the *protasis* with *sī*).——**exstinguētur,** 3d pers. sing. fut. ind. pass. of *exstinguō, -ere, exstinxī, exstinxtum,* 3 (*ex* + *stinguō* = lit. *I prick* or *scratch out;* root *stig* = *to puncture,* cf. *stilus* = *a pointed* instrument for writing, *stimulus* = *a goad,* στίζω = *I prick,* στίγμα = *a prick, brand*); agrees with the subj. *pestis,* and understood with *stirps* and *sēmen.*

LINE 40. **atque,** cop. conj. ; connects *exstinguētur* and *dēlēbitur. Atque* is often used to join together synonymous words, esp. verbs.——**dēlēbitur,** 3d pers. sing. fut. ind. pass. of *dēleō, -ēre, -ēvī, -ētum,* 2 (*dē* + root *li* or *ri* = *to flow, pass away;* hence *dēleō* = *I make to pass away, destroy;* from the same root note *rīvus, lītus, lībātiō,* λείφω = *I let flow* or *pour*); coördinate with *exstinguētur;* and agreeing with the same subject.——**nōn,** negative adv. ; *nōn modo* = *not only,* limiting *pestis exstinguētur.*——**modo,** adv. ; in conjunction with *nōn,* as above. *Not only* is expressed by *nōn modo, nōn sōlum,* or *nōn tantum;* of these *nōn tantum* does not occur in Caesar and Sallust, and is comparatively rare in Cicero. On a few occasions in Cicero we find *nōn* alone in the first member, followed by *sed* alone in the second, or by *sed etiam.*——**haec,** nom. sing. f. of the dem. pron. *hīc, haec, hōc;* agrees with *pestis* = *coniūrātiō.*——**tam,** adv. ; modifies *adulta.*——**adulta,** nom. sing. f. of the adj. *adultus, -a, -um* = *fully grown, mature* (in origin perf. part. pass. of *adolēscō, -ere, -ēvī, adultus,* 3); agrees with *pestis.*

LINE 41. **reī,** gen. sing. of *rēs,* f. 5th ; poss. gen., limiting *pestis.*——**pūblicae,** gen. sing. f. of the adj. *pūblicus, -a, -um;* agrees with *reī.*——**pestis,** gen. *pestis,* f. 3d ; nom. sing., subj. of *exstinguētur* and of *dēlēbitur.*——**vērum,** adversative conj. ; connects *pestis* and *stirps ac sēmen.*——**etiam,** adv. ; emphasizes *stirps ac sēmen* (*exstinguētur*). After *nōn modo* (etc.), *sed etiam* and *vērum etiam* are very common ; *sed quoque* is first found in Cicero ; *sed et* (for *sed etiam*) occurs in authors of the silver age.——**stirps,** gen. *stirpis,* f. 3d ; nom. sing., a subj. of *exstinguētur* supplied from the previous clause. *Stirps* = (1) *root, stem,* of a tree or plant ; (2) *race, family;* (3) *offspring;* (4) *source, origin.*

LINE 42. **ac** (shortened form of *atque; ac* is used before consonants, except *g, c, qu*), cop. conj. ; connects *stirps* and *sēmen;* note that *ac* and *atque* often connect words of similar meaning.——**sēmen,** gen. *sēminis,* n. 3d (root *sa, sī* = *to sow;* cf. *serō* = *I sow*); nom. sing., a subj. of *exstinguētur* supplied from the previous clause ; *stirps ac sēmen* express a single idea. *Sēmen* = (1) *seed;* (2) *race,* by metonymy ; (3) *source, origin, essence.*——**malōrum,** gen. plur. of *malum, -ī,* n. 2d (substantival neut. of the adj. *malus, -a, -um;* cf. *malī, -ōrum,* m. 2d = *the bad;* root *mal* = *to be black,* cf. μέλας = *black*); poss. gen., limiting the composite subj. *stirps ac sēmen.*——**omnium,** gen. plur. n. of the adj. *omnis, -e,* 3d ; agrees with *malōrum.* The concluding statement is, of course, only an example of rhetorical exaggeration.

1 XIII. Etenim iam diū, patrēs
　　　　　For 　　*already for a long time,* 　*fathers*

2 cōnscrīptī, in hīs perīculīs coniūrātiōnis
　enrolled, 　*among these* 　*dangers* 　*of conspiracy*

3 īnsidiīsque versāmur, sed
　and (among) plots 　*we have been (lit. are) dwelling,* 　*but*

4 nesciō quō pāctō omnium scelerum ac
　I know not *what* *by means* 　*all* 　*of the crimes* *and*

XIII. For it is now a long time, Conscript Fathers, that we have been living amid these perils and plots of conspiracy; yet somehow or other every form of crime and desperate mad-

LINE 1. **Etenim** (*et + enim*), causal conj. ; connects the sentence with the preceding one. *Etenim* is much used by Cicero, but little by other authors ; it corresponds to the Greek καὶ γάρ = *and for*, with the ellipse of an idea which can be supplied from the context, e.g. *and* it is time that the conspiracy were ended, *for we have long*, etc.—— **iam**, adv. of time ; strengthens *diū*. *Diū* and *dūdum* may be used alone with the *historic* present but it is far more common for them to be intensified by the adv. *iam*, which emphasizes that the point of view is from the present, though the range of view is an unbroken one extending from some point in the past up till now. *Iam* is found in conjunction with other adverbs of time, e.g. *iam nunc, iam tum, iam prīdem, iam aliquandō,* etc. —— **diū** (root *di* or *dyn* = *to shine;* akin to *dūdum, diēs, dīvus,* etc.), adv. of time ; modifies *versāmur.* ——'**patrēs**, voc. plur. of *pater, patris,* m. 3d (root *pa* = *to nourish,* cf. Greek πατήρ) ; the case of address.

LINE 2. **cōnscrīptī**, voc. plur. m. of *cōnscrīptus, -a, -um,* perf. part. pass. of *cōnscrībō, -ere, cōnscrīpsī, cōnscrīptum,* 3 (*con + scrībō*) ; agrees with *patrēs. Cōnscrīptī* serves to distinguish patricians or heads of families who were senators also from those who were not senators, and does not = *patrēs et cōnscrīptī* (as if recording the plebeian additions made in 509 B.C.), for *patricians (and) enrolled* would rather be expressed by *patrēs et adscrīptī.* —— **in**, prep. ; gov. the abl. *perīculīs.* —— **hīs**, abl. plur. n. of the dem. pron. *hīc, haec, hōc;* agrees with *perīculīs.* —— **perīculīs**, abl. plur. of *perīculum, -ī,* n. 2d ; governed by the prep. *in.* —— **coniūrātiōnis**, gen. sing. of *coniūrātiō,* f. 1st (*con + iūrō*) ; poss. gen., limiting *perīculīs* and *īnsidiīs.*

LINE 3. **īnsidiīsque** (*īnsidiīs + que*) : *īnsidiīs* is the abl. of the plur. noun *īnsidiae, -ārum,* f. 1st (from the verb *īnsideō, in + sedeō; īnsidiae* = (1) *ambush,* (2) *plot, snare*) ; governed by the prep. *in;* coördinate with *perīculīs. Que* is the enclitic cop. conj. ; connects *perīculīs* and *īnsidiīs.* As distinguished from *et* and *atque, que* connects two words or ideas between which there is a close internal relation. —— **versāmur**, 1st pers. plur. pres. ind. pass. of *versō, -āre, -āvī, -ātum,* 1 (frequentative form of *vertō*) ; the subj. *nōs* is implied by the personal ending ; the pres. tense is *historic* and is common with *iam diū, iam prīdem,* etc., expressing that an action begun in the past has been going on ever since and is still going on. A. & G. 276, *a* ; B. 259, 4 ; G. 230 ; H. 467, III, 2. The *historic* imperfect is also found with *iam diū* and *iam dūdum,* and only differs from the *historic* present in that the ultimate point of view is in the past, covering a range extending still further to the source in the past. The passive *versor* illustrates the medial or reflexive use of this voice in Latin, corresponding to the regular *middle voice* of Greek verbs. *Versor* = *I turn myself about,* hence *I pass my life, am engaged in, am associated,* or *busy with;* it is accompanied by the abl. with *in;* cf. *in rēpūblicā versārī* = *to be a politician* (lit. *to move about* or *to be busy in the state*). A. & G. 111, *b* ; B. no reference ; G. 218 ; H. 465. —— **sed**, adversative conj. ; connects the sentences *versāmur in perīculīs* and *mātūritās ērūpit.*

LINE 4. **nesciō**, 1st pers. sing. pres. ind. act. of *nesciō, -īre, -īvī* or *-iī, -ītum,* 4 (*ne + sciō*) ; understand the subj. *ego. Nesciō* is not the principal verb of the clause, nor does

ness of long-continued			veteris	furōris	et	audāciae	mātūritās in 5
growth	have	burst	long-standing	of madness	and	of effrontery	the ripeness upon

quō pacto introduce an indirect question, for the subjunct. *ēruperit* would be required instead of the ind. *ērūpit*. *Nesciō* and *quō* must be regarded as a single word (and so it is often written) = *some* (*I know not what*). In fact *nesciō quis* and *nesciō quī, quae, quod* are classed respectively with the indefinite pronouns and indefinite pronominal adjectives; see the note on *quāsdam*, Chap. II, l. 4. Compare *nesciō quō modō* = *somehow or other; nesciō an* = lit. *I know not whether*, i.e. *perhaps, probably.* A few other interrogative expressions are used in a similar parenthetic way with the ind. instead of subjunct., and with similar indefinite sense; cf. *mirum quam* = lit. *marvellous how*, i.e. *marvellously, valdē quam* = *enormously, sānē quam gāvīsus sum* = *I was tremendously glad, mīrum quantum labōrāvit* = lit. *it (is) wonderful, how much he worked!* i.e. *he worked wonderfully.* A. & G. 334, *e*; B. 253, 6; G. 467, REM. I, and NOTE; H. 529, 5, 3). —— **quō**, abl. sing. n. of the interrog. pron. *quis, quae, quid* or of the interrog. adj. *quī, quae, quod;* agrees with *pactō*. —— **pāctō**, abl. sing. of *pāctum, -ī*, n. 2d = (1) *agreement*, (2) as here, *way, manner* (properly substantival neut. of *pāctus*, perf. part. of *paciscor, -i, pāctus sum*, 3 = *I agree, stipulate*); abl. of manner, with the modifier *quō*. Manner is expressed by the abl. with *cum*, but *cum* may be omitted or retained if the noun in the abl. is modified by an adjective. But *cum* is very rarely retained with expressions of manner such as *modō, pāctō* (e.g. *nūllō, modō* or *pāctō*), *ratiōne, rītū, viā*, and with adverbial expressions like *silentiō, iniūriā*, etc. —— **omnium**, gen. plur. n. of the 3d decl. adj. *omnis, -e;* agrees with *scelerum*. —— **scelerum**, gen. plur. of *scelus, sceleris*, n. 3d; poss. gen., limiting *mātūritās*. —— **ac**, cop. conj.; joins *scelerum* and *furōris et audāciae*. The use of the more emphatic conj. *ac* here shows that the two words connected by *et*, viz. *furōris* and *audāciae*, represent one idea.

LINE 5. **veteris**, gen. sing. m. of the 3d decl. adj. *vetus* (akin to ἕτος = *a year;* cf. *vetustus, veterāscō*); agrees with *furōris*. Observe that an adj. frequently agrees only with the nearest of two or more nouns, and is understood with the rest; so here *veteris* must be understood in the fem. with *audāciae*. See *iūcundus*, Chap. VI, l. 31. Synonyms: (1) *vetus* = *old, of old standing*, e.g. *vetus amīcitia;* (2) *antīquus* = *old, ancient*, usually of what was in ancient times but no longer exists; (3) *prīscus* = *old*, with a claim to reverence, e.g. *prīsca sevĕritās; vetustus* = *old*, of something long used and so superior, e.g. *vetusta disciplīna;* (5) *prīstĭnus* = *old, earlier*, as opposed to *praesēns;* (6) *obsolētus* = *old, out of use*, e.g. *verba obsolēta*. —— **furōris**, gen. sing. of *furor*, m. 3d (*furō* = *I rage*); poss. gen., limiting *mātūritās; furōris et audāciae* = poss. genitives, coördinate with *scelerum*. —— **et**, cop. conj.; connects *furōris* and *audāciae*. —— **audāciae**, gen. sing. of *audācia*, f. 1st (from adj. *audāx*, gen. *audācis; audeō* = *I dare*); poss. gen., limiting *mātūritās*. The force of the conjunctions (see *ac* above) would seem to imply that *furōris et audāciae* be taken as one idea = *furōrem audācem*, an instance of *hendiadys;* cf. Chap. I, l. 9, *ōra vultūsque*, and see the note and references under *ōra*. —— **mātūritās**, gen. *mātūritātis*, f. 3d (from the adj. *mātūrus, -a, -um*); nom. sing., subj. of *ērūpit*. Observe the abstract character of this sentence; Caesar would have had a concrete subject. —— **in**, prep.; gov. the acc. *tempus. In tempus* instead of *in tempore* is an instance of the *cōnstrūctiō praegnāns* (pregnant construction, i.e. the combination of two different expressions in one), and = *has* (come *to* and) *burst out upon the time*, etc.; cf. the well-known example from the Acts of the Apostles, Chap. VIII, verse 40, Φίλιππος δὲ εὑρέθη εἰς Ἄζωτον = *Philip was found at Azōtus*, lit. *to Azōtus* (i.e. *Philip* went *to Azōtus* and *was found* there). Prof. Taylor compares (1) a passage with *in* + the abl. from the speech *prō Sullā*, viz. *furōrem ērūpisse in meō cōnsulātū*, i.e. *during my consulship;* (2) a passage from the *prō Murēnā*, viz. *omnia quae per hōc biennium agitātā sunt . . . in hōc tempus ērumpunt*, i.e. *in* + acc., as in our passage.

6 nostrī	cōnsulātūs	tempus	ērūpit.		Quodsī
our	*of consulship*	*the season has burst out.*			*But if*
7 ex	tantō	latrōciniō	iste		ūnus
out of	*so large*	*a herd of brigands*	*that man*		*one*
8 tollētur,		vidēbimur	fortasse	ad	breve
shall be disposed of,		*we shall seem*	*perhaps*	*for*	*short*
9 quoddam		tempus	cūrā	et	metū
some		*time*	*from care*	*and*	*from fear*

forth in full maturity upon the season of my consulship. Now if Catiline alone of all this band of brigands be got rid of, we shall seem perhaps to have secured relief from trouble and anxiety

LINE 6. **nostrī**, gen. sing. m. of the poss. adj. *noster, nostra, nostrum ;* agrees with *cōnsulātūs.* Cicero seems to allude to himself alone in the implied *nōs ;* but he may have been thinking also of his colleague. —— **cōnsulātūs**, gen. sing. of *cōnsulātūs*, m. 4th (the office or period of office of the *cōnsul*) ; subjective gen., limiting *tempus.* —— **tempus**, acc. sing. of *tempus, temporis*, n. 3d (root *tam = to cut ;* hence lit. *a section* of time, then *time,* generally). —— **ērūpit**, 3d pers. sing. perf. ind. act. of *ērumpō, -ere, ērūpī, ēruptum*, 3, trans. and intrans. (root *rup =* Greek λυπ *= to break, to trouble ;* cf. λύπη *= pain*) ; agrees with the subj. *mātūritās.* —— **Quodsī** (*Quod + sī*), conditional particle *= but if ;* followed by *tollētur* in a logical condition respecting the future. For the adverbial acc. *quod*, see the note on *quodsī*, Chap. XII, l. 15.

LINE 7. **ex** (*ē* or *ex* before consonants, *ex* before vowels and *h*) prep. + the abl. ; gov. *latrōciniō*, expressing *partition*, cf. *ūnus mīlitum* and *ūnus ex mīlitibus.* —— **tantō**, abl. sing. n. of the adj. *tantus, -a, -um ;* agrees with *latrōciniō. Ex tantō latrōciniō = ex tot latrōnibus*, or *ex tot latrōnum numerō.* —— **latrōciniō**, abl. sing. of *latrōcinium, -ī*, n. 2d (for a full discussion of the etymology, see *latrōciniō*, Chap. IX, l. 35) ; governed by the prep. *ex.* Observe that the abstract takes the place of the concrete expression ; cf. *servitium* which is sometimes used for *servī, coniūrātiō* for *coniūrātī*, etc., and the following from one of Cicero's letters, *ubi salūtātiō dēflūxit* (*= ubi salūtātōrēs dēflūxērunt*), *litterīs mē involvō = when my stream of morning-callers has flowed away, I surround myself with correspondence.* —— **iste**, nom. sing. m. of the dem. pron. *iste, ista, istud ;* subj. of *tollētur ; iste* refers to Catiline, and expresses contempt. —— **ūnus**, nom. sing. m. of the numeral adj. *ūnus, -a, -um* (gen. *ūnīus*, dat. *ūnī ;* old forms of nom. are *oenus*, and *oinos*) ; agrees with *iste ; ūnus* is often used likē *sōlus.*

LINE 8. **tollētur**, 3d pers. sing. fut. ind. pass. of *tollō, ere, sustulī, sublātum*, 3 irreg. (*sustulī* and *sublātum* are borrowed from *sufferō, sub + ferō ;* root *tal =* Latin *tol, tul = to lift, bear ; tollō, tulī*, and *lātus*, i.e. (*t*)*lātus* are all akin ; cf. *tol-erō*, τλῆναι *= to endure*, πολμάω *= I bear, I dare*) ; agrees with the subj. *iste ; tollētur* is in the *protasis* with *sī. Tollō =* (1) *I lift, bear ;* (2) *I make away with, remove, destroy.* —— **vidēbimur**, 1st pers. plur. fut. ind. pass. of *videō, -ēre, vīdī, vīsum*, 2 (the pass. *videor, ērī, vīsus sum*, 2 = (1) *I am seen*, (2) *I seem*, as here) ; the subj. *nōs* is implied by the personal ending. *Videor* is always used personally, e.g. *it seems that he can do this = haec facere posse vidētur* (lit. *he seems to be able to do this*) ; the 3d pers. sing. is sometimes impersonal, but with the sense *to seem good.* —— **fortasse** (for *fortassis = forte an sī vīs*), adv. *= perhaps ;* modifies *vidēbimur relevātī esse.* Other adverbs meaning perhaps are also derived from *fors :* (1) *forsitan*, a contraction from *fors sit an ;* (2) *forsan*, elliptical for *forsitan. Fortasse, forsitan, forsan*, and *fors sit* are often used with the potential subjunctive, e.g. *forsitan quispiam dīxerit = perhaps some one will say.* —— **ad**, prep. ; gov. the acc. *tempus*, expressing limit of time. —— **breve**, acc. sing. n. of the adj. *brevis, -e*, 3d ; agrees with *tempus.*

LINE 9. **quoddam**, acc. sing. n. of the indef. pron. and adj. *quīdam, quaedam, quiddam* (adjectival neut. *quoddam ; quī + -dam*) ; agrees with *tempus. Quoddam* makes

for some short pe-	esse relevātī ;　perīculum　autem　residēbit 10
riod; but the danger	*to have been relieved ;　the danger　but　will remain behind*
will remain settled	
behind and will be	et　erit　inclūsum　penitus　in　vēnīs　atque 11
shut deep down	*and　will be　shut in　deeply　in　the veins　and*
within the veins and	
vitals of the state.	in　vīsceribus　reī pūblicae.　　Ut　saepe 12
Just as in several in-	*in　the vitals　of the commonwealth.　As　often*

the idea presented by *breve tempus* vaguer still ; see the note on *quīsdam*, Chap. II, l. 4. —— **tempus**, acc. sing. of *tempus, temporis*, n. 3d ; governed by the prep. *ad*. —— **cūrā**, abl. sing of *cūra, -ae*, f. 1st ; abl. of separation, dependent on *relevātī*. The meanings of *cūra* are : (1) *care, attention*, (2) *pursuit, business*, (3) *love, affection*, (4) *anxiety, trouble, sorrow*, as in the text. The last meaning alone is found in the adj. *sēcūrus* (*sē = sine + cūra*) = *free from anxiety*. The root is *sku = to observe ;* cf. *caveō = I am on guard, take care*, ἀκούω = *I hear*. —— **et**, cop. conj. ; connects *cūrā* and *metū*. —— **metū**, abl. sing. of *metus, -ūs*, m. 4th ; abl. of separation, dependent on *relevātī*. See note on *timor*, Chap. I, l. 6.

LINE 10.　**esse relevātī**, perf. inf. pass. of *relevō, -āre, -āvī, -ātum*, 1 (*re + levō = I lift*, hence (1) *I lift up*, (2) *I lighten, mitigate*, (3) *release, set free*, as here) ; complementary or epexegetical inf., predicative with *vidēbimur ;* the part. *relevātī* agrees in gender, number, and case with *nōs*, the implied subj. of *vidēbimur*. Observe that *relevātī esse* is accompanied by the simple abl. without a prep. *dē, ab*, or *ex ;* this is the rule with a few verbs, viz. those which express *setting free, depriving, wanting*, and *removing*. A. & G. 243, *a* ; B. 214, 1 ; G. 390, 2, and NOTE 2 ; H. 414. Usually a prep. is required with other verbs, always with persons, but sometimes in technical and metaphorical combinations the abl. alone is found (esp. after compound verbs). —— **perīculum**, gen. *perīculī*, n. 2d ; nom. sing., subj. of *residēbit*. —— **autem**, adversative conj. ; connects the clause with the one preceding, and adds a contradictory idea. —— **residēbit**, 3d pers. sing. fut. ind. act. of *resideō, -ēre, resēdī*, no supine, 2 (*re = back, behind + sedeō = I sit, settle*) ; agrees with the subj. *perīculum*. Compare Chap. V, l. 43, *resiaēbit in rē pūblicā reliqua coniūrātōrum manus* (i.e. the *sentīna* or *dregs* of the state).

LINE 11.　**et**, cop. conj. ; connects *residēbit* and *erit inclūsum*. —— **erit**, 3d pers. sing. fut. ind. of *sum, esse, fuī ;* coördinate with *residēbit*, and agrees with the same subj. *perīculum*. —— **inclūsum**, nom. sing. n. of *inclūsus, -a, -um*, perf. part. pass. of *inclūdō, -ere, inclūsī, inclūsum*, 3 (*in + claudō*) ; predicative with *erit*, agreeing in gender, number, and case with the subj. *perīculum*. *Erit inclūsum* may be explained : (1) as fut.-perf. tense pass. = *will have been shut in ;* but we should expect the fut. simple *inclūdētur*, corresponding to *residēbit* ; (2) *erit* fut. simple, corresponding to *residēbit*, with *inclūsum* as a quasi-complement representing *a state ;* cf. *amātus fuī*, which differs from *amātus sum* inasmuch as the latter states an action accomplished as a *fact*, while the former describes *a state* which has been experienced. —— **penitus**, adv. ; modifies *inclūsum*. —— **in**, prep. ; gov. the abl. *vēnīs*. —— **vēnīs**, abl. plur. of *vēna, -ae*, f. 1st ; governed by the prep. *in ; in vēnīs . . . reī pūblicae* is an adverbial phrase modifying *inclūsum*. —— **atque**, cop. conj. ; connects *in vēnīs* and *in vīsceribus*.

LINE 12.　**in**, prep. ; gov. the abl. *vīsceribus*. —— **vīsceribus**, abl. plur. of *viscus, vīsceris*, n. 3d (commonly plur. *vīscera, -um*) ; governed by the prep. *in*. Literally *vīscera = the inward parts* of the body, esp. the nobler parts, i.e. heart, lungs and liver, as distinguished from the *intestīna* or lower parts. It was the *vīscera* (= Greek σπλάγχνα) which the soothsayers examined for omens. —— **reī**, gen. sing. of *rēs*, f. 5th ; poss. gen., limiting *vēnīs* and *vīsceribus*. —— **pūblicae**, gen. sing. f. of the adj. *pūblicus, -a, -um ;* agrees with *reī*. —— **Ut**, adv. ; introduces the simile following. The application of the

13	homines	aegri	morbo	gravi,	cum	stances men who are
	men	*sick*	*with a disease*	*serious,*	*when*	suffering from a seri-
14	aestu		febrique	iactantur,	si	aquam
	with the heat and with the fever they toss about,				*if*	*water*
15	gelidam		biberunt,	primo	relevari	
	cold	*they drink (lit. have drunk), at first*			*to be relieved*	

ous disease, tossing about with the heat of fever, appear, if they take a draught of cold water, to be re-

---

metaphor of the human body is too familiar to require comment ; but cf. Catiline's decla-ration that there were two bodies in the state, one weak with a weak head (= the Sen-ate), and the other strong but without a head (= *plebs*); and cf. the allegory of the war between the stomach and the rest of the body, by which in early days the *plebs* was induced to return to Rome. —— **saepe**, adv. ; modifies *relevari videntur.*

LINE 13. **homines**, nom. plur. of *homo, hominis*, m. 3d ; subj. of *videntur*, l. 16 ; *homines* is here = *to people* in an indefinite sense (the French would use the indef. pron. *on*). —— **aegri**, nom. plur. m. of the adj. *aeger, aegra, aegrum ;* agrees with *homines ; aegri morbo gravi = qui morbo gravi aegri sunt.* —— **morbo**, abl. sing. of *morbus, -i*, m. 2d (akin to *morior, mors, marcere = to wither* or *be feeble ;* root *mar = to waste away ;* cf. βροτός = μορτός = *mortal,* μάρανσις = *decay*); abl. of specification, defining *aegri.* A. & G. 253 ; B. 226 ; G. 397 ; H. 424.   Synonyms: (1) *morbus = disease, sickness,* of the whole body ; (2) *aegrotatio* (from *aegrotus*) = *sickness,* with weakness ; note that *aegritudo,* though used by Tacitus like *degrotatio,* usually expresses mental disorder, hence = *sorrow, grief.* —— **gravi**, abl. sing. m. of the adj. *gravis, -e*, 3d (for *gar-uis,* from Latin root *gar, gra* = Greek βαρ, cf. βαρύς = *heavy*); agrees with *morbo.* —— **cum**, tem-poral conj. ; followed by the pres. ind. *iactantur,* expressing frequentative or iterative action.   Remember that *cum* regularly takes the ind. except in the imperf. and pluperf. tenses.   But *cum* iterative = *as often as, whenever,* takes the ind. even in past tenses ; e.g. *cum haec dixerat, manus tollebat = as often as he said these words, he raised his hands.* A. & G. 325 ; B. 288 ; G. 580–585 ; H. 521.   Refer to the note on *cum*, Chap. III, l. 23.

LINE 14. **aestu**, abl. sing. of *aestus, -us*, m. 4th (root *idh* = αιθ = Latin *aed, to burn, shine ;* hence *aestus* is for *aed-tus,* and is akin to *aedes* = (1) lit. *fireplace,* (2) *temple, aestas = summer,* αἶθος = *burning heat,* Ἀιθιοψ = *an Ethiopian*); abl. of the cause, modifying the medial verb *iactantur.* —— **febrique** (*febri + que*) : *febri* is the dat. sing. of *febris, -is*, f. 3d (acc. *febrem* or *febrim ;* abl. usually *febri ;* perhaps akin to *ferveo*); abl. of the cause, like *aestu.   Que* is the enclitic cop. conj. ; connecting the two ablatives *aestu* and *febri.   Aestu febrique = with the fever-heat,* a single idea expressed by two nouns, whereas one noun + a modifier might have served.   This figure is known as *hen-diadys,* i.e. ἕν διὰ δυοῖν = *one by means of two.*   A. & G. 385 ; B. 374, 4 ; G. 698 ; H. 636, III, 2. —— **iactantur**, 3d pers. plur. pres. ind. pass. of *iacto, -are, -avi, -atum*, 1 (fre-quentative of *iacio,* hence = *keep tossing*); agrees with the subj. *ei* understood, referring to the principal subj. *homines.   Iactantur* does not = *are tossed,* with proper passive force, but = *toss themselves about,* with *middle* voice or reflexive force ; cf. *vetor = not I am turned* i.e. by another, but *I turn myself, I turn* (intransitive). —— **si**, conditional particle ; followed by the ind. *biberunt* in a logical condition.   *Si* is practically = *to cum* frequentative above. —— **aquam**, acc. sing. of *aqua, -ae*, f. 1st ; direct obj. of *biberunt.*

LINE 15. **gelidam**, acc. sing. f. of the adj. *gelidus, -a, -um* (from noun *gelu, -us*, n. 4th = *frost, cold ;* cf. Sicilian γέλα); agrees with *aquam.* —— **biberunt**, 3d pers. plur. perf. ind. act. of *bibo, -ere, bibi, bibitum* (rare), 3 (root *pa* or *po* = *drink ;* akin to *poto,* πότος = *a drinking-bout,* πίνω = *I drink*); the implied subj. is a pron. *illi* referring to *homines.*   In general conditions of present time the perf. ind. sometimes takes the place of the pres. in the *protasis ;* in any case *si biberunt* = *cum biberunt,* i.e. *whenever they*

lieved at first, but are	videntur,	deinde	multō	gravius 16
afterwards much more	*seem,*	*afterwards*	*by much*	*more seriously*
seriously and distress-	vehementiusque	adflīctantur,	sīc	hīc morbus, 17
ingly tormented; so	*and more violently*	*are distressed,*	*so*	*this disease,*
this disease which	qui	est	in	rē pūblicā,	relevātus 18
possesses the body	*which*	*is*	*in*	*the commonwealth,*	*(sc. if) relieved*
politic wil!, if it be	istīus		poenā,		vehementius 19
alleviated by this fel-	*of that (fellow)*		*by the punishment,*		*more violently*
low's punishment, as-				
sume a character yet				

drink; the perf. tense expresses instantaneous action, prior in time to *relevārī videntur.* There is another reading *biberint* = the fut. perf. ind. active, but the best Mss. read *biběrunt.* Yet *biberint* might have stood, if the *apodosis* also referred to future (i.e. *relevārī videntur, deinde . . . adflīctābuntur*). —— **prīmō** (abl. neut. sing. of *prīmus, -a, -um;* cf. *prīmum,* adverbial acc. neut. sing. = *firstly* of a series, *at first*), adv. = *at first;* modifies the pred. *relevārī videntur.* —— **relevārī,** pres. inf. pass. of *relěvō, -āre, -āvī, -ātum,* 1 (*re + levō*); complementary inf., in the pred. with *videntur.* Note that the pres. inf. marks the action of *relevārī* and *videntur* as strictly contemporaneous; we may render *think they are being relieved,* as opposed to *think they have been relieved* (which would be expressed by *relevātī esse*).

LINE 16. **videntur,** 3d pers. plur. pres. ind. pass. of *videō, -ēre, vīdī, vīsum,* 2 (*videor* = *I seem*) agrees with the subj. *hominēs.* —— **deinde** (sometimes a dissyllable; *dē +* *inde* = *from that time, then, next, still*), adv.; modifies *adflīctantur.* The counts or points of an elaborated argument are often introduced by the following adverbs, in order: *prīmum, deinde, tum, dēnique.* —— **multō** (abl. neut. sing. of *multus*), adv.; modifies *gravius.* The abl. case marks the measure of difference with compar. and superl. adjectives and adverbs, and with words implying comparison such as *post, ante.* —— **gravius,** adv.; modifies *adflīctantur. Gravius* is the compar. of *graviter* (from adj. *gravis, -e,* 3d); superl. *gravissimē.* The comparative of an adverb = the acc. sing. n. of the comparative of the adjective from which the adverb is formed. A. & G. 92; B. 76, 2, and 77, 1; G. 93; H. 306.

LINE 17. **vehementiusque** (*vehementius + que*): *vehementius* is the compar. of the adv. *vehementer;* modifies *adflīctantur.* The adj. *vehemēns* is probably a lengthened form of *vēmēns* (*vē,* an inseparable particle with negative force + *mēns,* hence *not having mind, unreasonable, violent*). *Que* is the enclitic cop. conj.; connects *gravius* and *vehementius.* —— **adflīctantur,** 3d pers. plur. pres. ind. pass. of *adflīctō, -āre, -āvī, -ātum,* 1 (frequentative form of *adflīgō*); coördinate with *videntur* above, and agrees with the same subj. *hominēs.* —— **sīc** (*sī + ce*), adv. = *so;* used correlatively with *ut,* l. 12. *Ut . . . sīc* (*ita*) = *as . . . so,* with comparative clauses. —— **hīc,** nom. sing. m. of the dem. pron. *hīc, haec, hōc;* agrees with *morbus.* —— **morbus,** gen. *morbī,* m. 2d; nom. sing., subj. of *ingravēscet.*

LINE 18. **qui,** nom. sing. m. of the rel. pron. *quī, quae, quod;* agrees with the antecedent *morbus,* and is subj. of *est.* —— **est,** 3d pers. sing. pres. ind. of *sum, esse, fui;* agrees with the subj. *quī.* —— **in,** prep.; gov. the abl. *rēpūblicā,* expressing *place where.* —— **rē,** abl. sing. of *rēs, reī,* f. 5th; gov. by the prep. *in.* —— **pūblicā,** abl. sing. f. of the adj. *pūblicus, -a, -um;* agrees with *rē.* —— **relevātus,** nom. sing. m. of *relevātus, -a, -um,* perf. part. pass. of *relevō, -āre, -āvī, -ātum,* 1 (*re + levō*); agrees with *morbus. Relevātus* is really a disguised *protasis,* and = *sī relevātus erit.* For the forms which disguised conditions may assume, consult A. & G. 310, esp. *a;* B. 305; G. 600; H. 507, 1–3.

LINE 19. **istīus,** gen. sing. m. of the dem. pron. *iste, ista, istud;* objective gen., with *poenā; istīus* = *Catilīnae.* —— **poenā,** abl. sing. of *poena, -ae,* f. 1st (root *pu = to*

20 vīvīs reliquīs   ingravēscet.   Quārē   more grave and vio-
   (remaining) alive the rest will be aggravated.   *Wherefore* lent while the other
                                           traitors remain alive.

21 sēcēdant improbī, sēcernant sē ā   Wherefore let the dis-
   let withdraw the disloyal men, let them separate themselves from loyal withdraw apart,
                                   let them sever them-
                                   selves from the com-

22 bonīs, ūnum in locum congregentur, pany of the loyal and
   the loyal men, one into place let them herd together, gather like a herd in

---

cleanse; cf. ποινή = *a penalty, pūniō* for *poeniō,* etc.); abl. of the means, modifying *rele-vātus.* —— **vehementius,** comparative adv. (see l. 17); modifies *ingravēscet.*

LINE 20. **vīvīs,** abl. plur. m. of the adj. *vīvus, -a, -um;* agrees with *reliquīs* in the abl. absolute construction; *vīvīs reliquīs* is a disguised condition = *sī reliquī vīvent.* For the abl. absolute construction, refer to the note on *dīmissō,* Chap. IV, l. 38. —— **reliquīs,** abl. plur. m. of the adj. *reliquus, -a, -um (relinquō; reliquī* is substantival = *the rest,* i.e. of the conspirators); in the abl. absolute construction with *vīvīs.* Remember that the abl. abs. = a clause and that it cannot be used of the subj. or obj. of a sentence; in fact, the abl. abs. is independent of the rest of the sentence. —— **ingra-vēscet,** 3d pers. sing. fut. ind. act. of *ingravēscō, -ere,* no perf., no supine, 3 (inceptive form of *ingravō);* agrees with the subj. *morbus.* —— **Quārē** (*Qua,* abl. f. sing. of rel. *quī,* agreeing with *rē;* + *rē*); adv., used as an illative conj.; connects the sentence with what has preceded, and sums up the gist of the argument.

LINE 21. **sēcēdant,** 3d pers. plur. pres. subjunct. act. of *sēcēdō, -ere, sēcessī, sēcessum,* 3 (*sē = apart + cēdō = I go*); agrees with the subj. *improbī;* the subjunct. is *hortatory.* The *hortatory* subjunct. here expresses an exhortation or command; sometimes it expresses a concession; a negative command is introduced by *nē.* The pres. tense or the perf. tense is used for the 3d pers., sing. or plural; the pres. tense for the 1st person; the present for affirmative commands or exhortations in the 2d person; the perfect (less commonly the present) for negative commands in the 2d person. A. & G. 266; B. 274-276; G. 263; H. 484. —— **improbī,** nom. plur. m., substantival, of the adj. *im-probus, -a, -um (in + probus);* subj. of *sēcēdant. Improbī* here is a political technical term. —— **sēcernant,** 3d pers. plur. pres. subjunct. act. of *sēcernō, -ere, sēcrēvī, sēcrētum,* 3 (*sē = apart + cernō = I separate;* root *kar = to separate,* cf. κρίνω = *I separate, judge*); the implied subj. is a pron., e.g. *eī,* referring to *improbī.* Observe the *asynde-ton,* and the vigorous effect of the short, sharp exhortations. The subjunct. is *horta-tive;* cf. *sēcēdant* above. —— **sē,** acc. plur. of the reflexive pron. of the 3d pers. *sē,* gen. *suī;* direct obj. of *sēcernant; sē* refers to the subj. of *sēcernant.* —— **ā,** prep.; gov. the abl. *bonīs,* expressing *separation.*

LINE 22. **bonīs,** abl. plur. m., substantival, of the adj. *bonus, -a, -um;* governed by the prep. *ā. Bonī,* as a political term in Cicero, is used of men who shared his political views, and may be sometimes rendered *the conservatives;* but here it denotes the *loyal* as opposed to the *traitorous (improbī).* —— **ūnum,** acc. sing. m. of the adj. *ūnus, -a, -um;* agrees with *locum.* —— **in,** prep.; gov. the acc. *locum.* —— **locum,** acc. sing. of *locus, -ī,* m. 2d (the plur. is usually neut. *loca, -ōrum = places, district;* sometimes *locī, -ōrum,* m. = *places,* separate and not connected, or *topics* in a literary work); governed by the prep. *in.* —— **congregentur,** 3d pers. plur. pres. subjunct. pass. of *congregō, -āre, -āvī, -ātum,* 1 (*con + grex*); the subj. is a pron. understood referring to *improbī* above; the subjunct. is *hortatory,* as in *sēcēdant* and *sēcernant.* The passive is used with *medial* or *reflexive* force; see the note on *iactantur,* l. 14. The meta-phor of *herding* expresses Cicero's opinion as regards the intelligence and ability of the conspirators.

one spot; in short, as I have already said many times, let them be shut off from us by the city-wall. Let them cease to make treacherous attacks on the consul at his

mūrō	dēnique,	quod	saepe	iam 23
by the wall (of the city)	*finally,*	*which thing*	*often*	*already*
dīxī,	sēcernantur	ā	nōbīs;	dēsinant 24
I have said,	*let them be divided*	*from*	*us;*	*let them cease*
īnsidiārī	domī	suae	cōnsulī, 25
to lie in wait	*at house*	*his own*	*for the consul,*

LINE 23. **mūrō**, abl. sing. of *mūrus, -ī,* m. 2d (root *mu = to enclose, to protect;* akin to *moenia*); abl. of the means or instrument, modifying *sēcernantur.* Synonyms: (1) *moenia = the wall* of a city or fortified place; cf. *mūniō = I fortify;* (2) *mūrus = wall,* the general term; often, as here, used for *moenia;* (3) *pariēs = a party-wall* of a house. ——**dēnique,** adv.; marks the clause as summing up the meaning of the clauses immediately preceding. Synonyms: (1) *dēnique = finally, lastly, at last,* esp. at the end of enumeration or argument, where it gives the pith of what has been under discussion and practically dismisses the subject; (2) *postrēmum* or *postrēmō = finally, lastly,* with emphasis on the fact that something is *last;* opposed to *prīmus;* (3) *tandem = finally, at length,* of what happens after long expectation; (4) *dēmum,* cf. *tum dēmum,* of what might have occurred before, and is late in occurring. —— **quod,** acc. sing. n. of the rel. pron. *quī, quae, quod;* direct obj. of *dīxī. Quod* stands for *id quod,* i.e. agrees in gender and number with *id* understood; *id,* if expressed, = an acc. in explanatory apposition with the idea contained in *mūrō sēcernantur ā nōbīs. Id quod* or simply *quod,* when so used, are parenthetic, i.e. independent of the rest of the sentence. A. & G. 200, *e;* B. 247, 1, *b;* G. 614, REM. 2; 324; 333, NOTE 2; H. 363, 5. For the supplied acc. *id,* see the note and references under *id,* Chap. III, l. 19. —— **saepe,** adv. of time; modifies *dīxī.* ——**iam,** adv. of time; in combination with *saepe* (cf. *iam tum, iam diū,* etc.), modifying *dīxī.*

LINE 24. **dīxī,** 1st pers. sing. perf. ind. act. of *dīcō, -ere, dīxī, dictum,* 3; the subj. *ego* is implied by the personal ending. —— **sēcernantur,** 3d pers. plur. pres. subjunct. pass. (with medial force) of *sēcernō, -ere, sēcrēvī, sēcrētum,* 3 (*sē + cernō*); the implied subj. is a pron. referring to the people denoted by the term *improbī,* l. 21; the subjunct. is *hortatory,* as in the verbs immediately preceding. ——**ā,** prep.; gov. the abl. *nōbīs,* expressing *separation,* as usual in combination with a verb which in itself implies *separation,* viz. *sēcernantur.* —— **nōbīs,** abl. plur. of the 1st personal pron. (sing. *ego,* plur. *nōs*); gov. by the prep. *ā.* —— **dēsinant,** 3d pers. plur. pres. subjunct. act. of *dēsinō, -ere, desiī, dēsitum,* 3 (*dē + sinō*); the implied subj. is a pron. referring to *improbī. Dēsinō* may be either trans. or intrans.; when active, like all verbs of *beginning* and *ending,* it implies a further action of the same subject, and is used with a complementary inf., e.g. *īnsidiārī, circumstāre, obsidēre, comparāre.*

LINE 25. **īnsidiārī,** pres. inf. of the deponent verb *īnsidior, -ārī, -ātus sum,* 1 (from *īnsidiae, -ārum,* f. 1st = *ambush, plot; in + sedeō*); complementary inf., predicative with *dēsinant.* Like many intrans. verbs compounded with *in, ad, ante, con,* etc., *īnsidiārī* governs the dat. of the indirect obj., viz. *cōnsulī.* The allusion is to the attempt of Varguntēius and Cornēlius to murder Cicero at his morning reception on Nov. 7th (or 8th, as Mommsen holds). ——**domī,** locative case of *domus, -ūs* or *-ī,* f. 4th and 2d; expresses *place where,* modifying *īnsidiārī.* There is another form of this locative, viz. *domuī.* When qualified by a poss. pron., *domī (domuī)* is regarded as a quasi-genitive; hence the gen. *suae* following. —— **suae,** gen. sing. f. of the reflexive poss. pron. *suus, -a, -um;* agrees with *domī; suae* refers to the possessor *cōnsulī,* not to the subj. of *dēsinant.* ——**cōnsulī,** dat. sing. of *cōnsul, -is,* m. 3d; indirect obj. of *īnsidiārī.* Observe the impersonal form of the reference to Cicero's danger.

26 circumstāre	tribūnal	praetōris	urbānī,	own house, to sur-
to stand around	*the tribunal*	*of the praetor*	*of the city,*	round the judgment-seat of the city praetor, to beset the
27 obsidēre	cum	gladiīs	cūriam,	malleolōs	senate-house with
to invest	*with*	*their swords*	*the senate-house,*	*firebrands*	swords drawn and

LINE 26. **circumstāre**, pres. inf. act. of *circumstō, -āre, -āvī, -ātum*, 1 (*circum = around + stō = I stand*); complementary inf., predicative with *dēsinant*, like *īnsidiārī* above. Observe the *asyndeton*, i.e. the want of cop. conjunctions to connect in coördination the infinitives *īnsidiārī, circumstāre, obsidēre, comparāre*, each of which states a further action of the subj. of *dēsinant.*——**tribūnal**, acc. sing. of *tribūnal, -is*, n. 3d (like *tribuō* and *tribūnus*, connected with *tribus = a tribe*, originally a third part of the Roman people; root *tri = three*); direct obj. of *circumstāre*. Many intransitive verbs acquire transitive force by composition with the prepositions *ad, ante, ob, trāns, circum*, etc.; cf. *praetereō =* lit. *I go beyond, I pass by.* A. & G. 228, *a*; B. 175, 2, *a*; G. 331; H. 372. There were at this time eight praetors; six of these were presidents of criminal courts, while the remaining two, viz. the *praetor urbānus* and the *praetor peregrīnus* tried civil suits, the former between parties who were both citizens, the latter between parties of whom one or each was a foreigner. The *praetor urbānus* in 63 B.C. was *Lūcius Valerius Flaccus.* The *praetor urbānus* dispensed justice from his *sella curūlis*, which was set upon a raised platform (the *tribūnal*) and was surrounded by seats on a lower level (*subsellia*) for the convenience of those who had legal business to do. In early times the *tribūnal* was situated in the *Comitium*, but toward the close of the republic it was fixed under a portico in the *Forum*. There were, of course, other *tribūnālia* in various parts of Rome, which the other praetors used, according as they were most convenient. The allusion in the present passage is to an attempt of Catiline and his friends to prevent by intimidation the *praetor urbānus* from making a settlement on a civil question of debt.——**praetōris**, gen. sing. of *praetor, -ōris*, m. 3d (see the note on *praetōrem*, Chap. II, l. 13); poss. gen., limiting *tribūnal.*——**urbānī**, gen. sing. m. of the adj. *urbānus, -a, -um* (from *urbs = a city*); agrees with *praetōris.* The *praetor urbānus* was considered superior in dignity to the other praetors, and hence was sometimes called *praetor māior.* The name, but not the powers, of the *praetor urbānus* lasted as long as the Roman empire in the west; even the name of *praetor peregrīnus* fell out of use after Caracalla's time.

LINE 27. **obsidēre**, pres. inf. act. of *obsideō, -ēre, obsēdī, obsessum*, 2 (*ob + sedeō =* lit. *I sit down before*, hence *I beset, invest*); complementary inf., predicative with *dēsinant.* ——**cum**, prep.; gov. the abl. *gladiīs.*——**gladiīs**, abl. plur. of *gladius, -ī*, m. 2d; governed by the prep. *cum. Cum gladiīs* is an idiomatic phrase (apparently belonging to the abl. of accompaniment) *= armātī = under arms;* do not suppose that it expresses the instrument, for this can only be expressed by the abl. without a preposition.——**cūriam**, acc. sing. of *cūria, -ae*, f. 1st; direct obj. of *obsidēre.* The *cūria* here mentioned is the *cūria Hostīlia*, north of the Forum, in which the Senate regularly met, except when it was specially summoned to meet in one or other of the different temples. For meetings of the Senate, and for the various *cūriae*, refer to the note on *locus*, Chap. I, l. 8. ——**malleolōs**, acc. plur. of *malleolus, -ī*, m. 2d (diminutive of *malleus = a hammer*); direct obj. of *comparāre.* A *malleolus* or *firebrand* derives its name from the likeness of its appearance to a *mallet*. It was a missile used in sieges, etc., for setting on fire houses, shipping, etc., belonging to an enemy. It consisted of a mallet-shaped body, with a wire frame, filled with tow and other combustible material which was ignited before the missile was hurled; projecting from this brand was a short shaft with a barbed point, and the missile was so discharged that the arrow-head would stick fast in woodwork, etc., and allow the flames from the tow to do their destructive work.

collect stores of fire-brands and torches for setting fire to the city. In a word, let every man have it printed upon his forehead what his political sympathies are. I promise you this, Con-

et	facēs	ad	īnflammandam	urbem	28
and	torches	for	burning (lit. *to be burnt*)	*the city*	
comparāre :	sit	dēnique	īnscrīptum	in	29
to provide :	*let it be*	*finally*	*inscribed*	*upon*	
fronte	ūnīus	cūiusque,	quid	dē	30
the forehead	*one*	*of each (man),*	*what*	*about*	
rē pūblicā	sentiat.		Polliceor	vōbīs	31
the commonwealth	*he feels.*		*I promise*	*to you*	

LINE 28. **et**, cop. conj. ; connects *malleolōs* and *facēs*.——**facēs**, acc. plur. of *fax, facis*, f. 3d ; direct obj. of *comparāre* ; joined by *et* to *malleolōs*. *Facēs* or *torchēs* = (1) pieces of resinous wood, dipped into oil or pitch and then ignited ; (2) tubes of metal or wattled laths enclosing inflammable materials, such as tow steeped in tallow, pitch, rosin, and the like.——**ad**, prep. ; gov. the acc. *īnflammandam urbem*, expressing *purpose*.——**īnflammandam**, acc. sing. f. of *īnflammandus, -a, -um*, gerundive of *īnflammō, -āre, -āvī, -ātum*, 1 (*in + flammō*) ; agrees with *urbem* in the construction of gerundival attraction. *Ad +* the acc., and *causā +* the gen., of the gerund or gerundive, express *purpose ;* so *ad īnflammandam urbem = ut urbem īnflamment*.——**urbem**, acc. sing. of *urbs, urbis*, f. 3d ; governed by *ad* in the gerundival construction.

LINE 29. **comparāre**, pres. inf. act. of *comparō, -āre, -āvī, -ātum*, 1 (*com + parō*) ; complementary infin., predicative with *dēsinant*.——**sit**, 3d pers. sing. pres. subjunct. of *sum, esse, fuī ;* the true subj. is the clause *quid dē rē pūblicā sentiat*. The subjunct. is *hortatory ;* see the note on *sēcēdant*, l. 21.——**dēnique**, adv. = *in a word ;* concludes the series of exhortations ; see *dēnique*, l. 22.——**īnscrīptum**, nom. sing. n. of *īnscrīptus, -a, -um*, perf. part. pass. of *īnscrībō, -ere, īnscrīpsī, īnscrīptum*, 3 (*in + scrībō*) ; *īnscrīptum + sit* above = the *hortative* perfect, which tense is as common as the pres. subjunct. when the person is third. The phrase recalls the branding of a mark upon runaway slaves.——**in**, prep. ; gov. the abl. *fronte*.

LINE 30. **fronte**, abl. sing. of *frōns, frontis*, f. 3d (Sanskrit *bhru = eyebrow ;* cf. Greek ὀφρύς, and English *brow*) ; governed by the prep. *in*.——**ūnīus**, gen. sing. m. of the numeral adj. *ūnus, -a, -um ;* agrees with *cūiusque*.——**cūiusque**, gen. sing. m. of the indef. pron. *quisque, quaeque, quodque* (adjectival neut. *quodque ; quis + que*) ; poss. gen., limiting *fronte ; ūnus quisque* in combination = *every single one*. Distinguish : (1) *ambō = both*, of two, together ; (2) *uterque = each of two*, singly ; often in apposition with two names, e.g. *Dēmosthenēs et Cicerō, uterque fācundissimus ;* (3) *quisque = each*, of several. Note the idiom of a superl. + *quisque*, e.g. *fortissimus quisque = all the most resolute men*.——**quid**, acc. sing. n. of the interrog. pron. *quis, quae, quid ;* direct obj. of *sentiat*. Observe that *quid* introduces an indirect question, hence the subjunct. *sentiat ;* also that the clause *quid . . . sentiat* is the subj. of *īnscrīptum sit*, to which it is subordinate.——**dē**, prep. = *concerning ;* gov. the abl. *rē pūblicā*.

LINE 31. **rē**, abl. sing. of *rēs, reī*, f. 5th ; governed by the prep. *dē*.——**pūblicā**, abl. sing. f. of the adj. *pūblicus, -a, -um ;* agrees with *rē*.——**sentiat**, 3d pers. sing. pres. subjunct. act. of *sentiō, -īre, sēnsī, sēnsum*, 4 ; understand *quisque*, from *cūiusque* above, as subject ; as often, *sentīre = to hold political views. Quid . . . sentiat* is an indirect question. Indirect questions : (1) are introduced by an interrog. pron., adj., or adv. ; (2) are subordinate to a leading verb or verbal expression, as subj. or obj. ; thus *quid . . . sentiat* is subj. of *sit īnscrīptum*, cf. *sciō quis sīs, quis sīs* being obj. of *sciō ;* (3) the verb of the contained question is subjunct., and conforms to the rule of tense sequence. A. & G. 334 ; B. 300 ; G. 467 ; H. 528, 2, and 529, I.——**Polliceor**, 1st pers. sing. pres. ind. of the deponent verb *polliceor, -ērī, pollicitus sum*, 2 (*port +*

32	hōc,	patrēs	cōnscrīptī,	tantam	in	nōbīs
	this thing,	*fathers*	*enrolled,*	*(that) so great*	*in*	*us*
33	cōnsulibus	fore	dīligentiam,	tantam	in	
	the consuls	*will be* (see NOTE)	*carefulness,*	*so great*	*in*	
34	vōbīs	auctōritātem,	tantam	in	equitibus	
	you	*authority,*	*so great*	*in*	*the knights*	

script Fathers, that such will be the display of zealous assiduity in us consuls, of authority in you senators, of manly bearing

---

liceor = I bid largely; port is an old prep., and = the *po* of compound expressions, serving to denote power or possession or else to emphasize the verbal meaning; cf. *pōnō,* for *pōsnō,* for *pōsinō,* for *port + sinō);* the subj. *ego* is implied by the personal ending. Synonyms: (1) *prōmittere* = lit. *to send forth,* i.e. *to hold out, to promise;* generic, denoting every kind of promise; (2) *pollicērī* (as opposed to *abnuere*) = *to proffer, to voluntarily pledge oneself;* (3) *recipere = 'to pledge oneself,* at the same time guaranteeing the risks and results; cf. Cic., *dē aestāte pollicēris vel potius recipis.* —— **vōbīs,** dat. of *vōs;* indirect obj. of *polliceor.*

LINE 32. **hōc,** acc. sing. n. of the dem. pron. *hīc, haec, hōc;* direct obj. of *polliceor; hōc* is defined by the following appositional acc. and inf. clause *tantam in nōbīs fore dīligentiam, etc. . . . videātis* (ll. 32-38). —— **patrēs,** voc. plur. of *pater, patris,* m. 3d); the case of address. —— **cōnscrīptī,** voc. plur. of *cōnscrīptus, -a, -um,* perf. part. of *cōnscrībō, -ere, cōnscrīpsī, cōnscrīptum,* 3 (*con + scrībō);* agrees with *patrēs;* see the note on *cōnscrīptī,* l. 2. —— **tantam,** acc. sing. f. of the dem. adj. *tantus, -a, -um;* predicative; agrees with the subj.-acc. *dīligentiam.* —— **in,** prep.; gov. the abl. *nōbīs.* —— **nōbīs,** abl. of *nōs,* 2d plur. personal pron.; governed by the prep. *in.*

LINE 33. **cōnsulibus,** abl. plur. of *cōnsul, -is,* m. 3d; in apposition with *nōbīs.* —— **fore,** fut. inf. of *sum, esse, fuī;* agrees with the subj.-acc. *dīligentiam.* The verb *sum* has two forms of the fut. inf., viz. (1) *fore,* (2) *futūrus, -a, -um + esse,* i.e. fut. part. + *esse,* as most fut. infinitives act. are formed. The clause *tantam fore dīligentiam* is in apposition with *hōc,* which is direct obj. of *polliceor;* instead of rendering *I promise such carefulness to be about to be,* etc., it is usual in English to commence the indirect discourse with the word *that,* and turn the Latin inf. into the English ind., e.g. *I promise that there will be such carefulness,* etc. —— **dīligentiam,** acc. sing. of *dīligentia, -ae,* f. 1st (from *dīligēns,* adj. and pres. part. of *dīligō*); subj.-acc. of *fore tantam* in indirect discourse; the acc. and inf. clause = the acc. of the verbal noun, in apposition with the acc. *hōc.* —— **tantam,** acc. sing. f. of the adj. *tantus, -a, -um;* predicative, with *fore* supplied from the coördinate clause preceding; agrees with the subj.-acc. *auctōritātem;* this clause, and the others following with *tantam,* are in apposition with *hōc,* l. 32. The repetition of *tantam* at the beginning of each coördinate clause is an instance of the rhetorical device known as *anaphora.* A. & G. 344, *f;* B. 350, 11, *b;* G. 636, NOTE 4; H. 636, III, 3. —— **in,** prep.; gov. the abl. *vōbīs.*

LINE 34. **vōbīs,** abl. of the 2d personal pron. plur. *vōs;* governed by the prep. *in; in vōbīs,* i.e. in the Senate, as distinguished from the *ōrdō equestris* and the *cīvēs Rōmānī.* —— **auctōritātem,** acc. sing. of *auctōritās, -ātis,* f. 3d; subj.-acc. of *tantam (fore); auctōritātem* here has a general meaning of *authoritative influence,* i.e. making itself felt and respected in the city. —— **tantam,** acc. sing. f. of the adj. *tantus, -a, -um;* predicative, with *fore* understood; agrees with the subj.-acc. *virtūtem.* —— **in,** prep.; gov. the abl. *equitibus.* —— **equitibus,** abl. plur. of *eques, equitis,* m. 3d (*equus = a horse,* hence lit. *a horseman, knight*); governed by the prep. *in.* See the note on *equitēs,* Chap. IV, l. 33. The whole sentence, ll. 31-38, is an appeal to all classes of Roman society to take joint action against the conspirators; the appeal is disguised by the flattering attribution to the Senate, knights, and populace of the qualities which the orator desired them to show.

in our Roman knights,	**Rōmānīs**	**virtūtem,**	**tantam**	**in**	**omnibus** 85

Left column prose:

in our Roman knights, —such the display of unanimity among all loyal citizens, that on Catiline's departure you will see every scheme laid bare, revealed, crushed, and punished. With these

Latin interlinear text:

Rōmānīs virtūtem, tantam in omnibus 85
Roman *worthiness,* *so great* *in* *all*

bonīs cōnsēnsiōnem, ut Catilīnae 86
loyal (citizens) *unanimity,* *that* *of Catiline*

profectiōne omnia patefacta, inlūstrāta, 87
by the departure *all (evils)* *disclosed,* *cleared up,*

oppressa, vindicāta esse videātis. Hisce 88
crushed, *punished* *to be* *you may see.* *These*

LINE 35. **Rōmānīs**, abl. plur. m. of the adj. *Rōmānus, -a, -um;* agrees with the noun *equitibus;* the addition of this epithet often gives a statement a dignified and formal character. —— **virtūtem**, acc. sing. of *virtūs, virtūtis,* f. 3d (= the quality of a *vir*, hence *manly courage*, physical and moral, *virtue*); subj.-acc. of *tantam* (*fore*). —— **tantam**, acc. sing. f. of the adj. *tantus, -a, -um;* predicative with *fore* supplied from above; agrees with the subj.-acc. *cōnsēnsiōnem.* —— **in**, prep.; gov. the abl. *omnibus.* —— **omnibus**, abl. plur. m. of the adj. *omnis, -e,* 3d; agrees with *bonīs.*

LINE 36. **bonīs**, abl. of the plur. noun *bonī, -ōrum,* m. 2d = *patriots, loyal citizens* (substantival mas. of the adj. *bonus, -a, -um;* cf. *bona = property*); governed by the prep. *in.* *Bonī* here includes all true citizens not members of the *ōrdō senātōrius* or of the *ōrdō equestris.* —— **cōnsēnsiōnem**, acc. sing. of *cōnsēnsiō, -ōnis,* f. 3d (from *cōnsentīre* = *to agree together, be one-minded*, con + *sentiō*); subj.-acc. of *tantam* (*fore*); the clause is, like the clauses immediately preceding, an appositive of *hōc*, l. 32. *Cōnsēnsiō* or *unanimity* is the very quality which one may expect not to find in the Roman populace, whose sympathies were very easily stirred and diverted, and whose honesty was never very secure if dishonesty seemed likely to be profitable. —— **ut**, conj.; introducing the adverbial consecutive clause *ut . . . esse videātis.* Adverbial clauses of *result* frequently depend on a principal sentence which contains a dem. word, e.g. *tam, ita, adeō, tālis* or *tantus.* —— **Catilīnae**, gen. sing. of *Catilīna,* m. 1st; poss. gen., limiting *profectiōne.*

LINE 37. **profectiōne**, abl. sing. of *profectiō, -ōnis,* f. 3d (from *profectus*, perf. part. of *proficīscor = I set out*); abl. of the means, modifying *patefacta esse*, etc.; render *on Catiline's departure*, rather than *by Catiline's departure.* —— **omnia**, acc. plur. n. substantival = *everything*, of the adj. *omnis, -e,* 3d; subj.-acc. of the coördinate infinitives following, viz. *patefacta* (*esse*), *inlūstrāta* (*esse*), *oppressa* (*esse*), and *vindicāta esse;* the construction is the objective acc. and inf., dependent on *videātis.* —— **patefacta**, acc. plur. n. of *patefactus, -a, -um,* perf. part. of *patēfīō, patefierī, patefactus sum,* irreg., used as pass. of *patefaciō, -ere, patefēcī, patefactum,* 3 (*pateō + faciō = patēre faciō = I make to be open, I disclose*); agrees with the subj.-acc. *omnia;* supply *esse* from below = the perf. inf. pass. of *patefaciō.* Observe: (1) that when a part of *sum*, making a composite pass. tense, belongs to two or more coördinate verbs, it is frequently expressed only with one (usually, as here, the last) and understood with the rest; (2) that *patefaciō* is one of the few exceptions to the rule that *faciō* becomes *ficiō* in compounds, e.g. *perficiō.* —— **inlūstrāta**, acc. plur. n. of *inlūstrātus, -a, -um,* perf. part. pass. of *inlūstrō* (*illūstrō*), *-āre, -āvī, -ātum,* 1 (*in + lustrō;* hence = *to make bright*, from root *ruk* or *luk* = *to light, shine;* cf. *lūceō, lūx, lūmen,* λύχνος); supply *esse* = the perf. inf. pass. agreeing with the subj.-acc. *omnia.* Observe that the four infinitives here are coördinate, yet are unconnected; a good example of *asyndeton.*

LINE 38. **oppressa**, acc. plur. n. of *oppressus, -a, -um,* perf. part. pass. of *opprimō, -ere, oppressī, oppressum,* 3 (*ob + premō*); supply *esse* = perf. inf. pass., agreeing with the subj.-acc. *omnia.* —— **vindicāta**, acc. plur. n. of *vindicātus, -a, -um,* perf. part. pass. of *vindicō, -āre, -āvī, -ātum,* 1; *vindicāta + esse* following = the perf. inf. pass., agreeing

sentment would over-take me like a flood in the future. But even supposing that such resentment threatened me in all seriousness, neverthe-less I have always been so disposed as	posteritātem *the future time*	redundāret. *should flood over.*	Quodsī *But if*	ea *it (= odium)*	mihi 15 *me*
	māximē *very greatly*	impendēret, *threatened,*	tamen *yet*	hōc *this*	animō 16 *in mind*
	fuī *I have been*	semper, *always,*	ut *that*	invidiam *odium*	virtūte 17 *by virtue*

LINE 15. **posteritātem**, acc. sing. of *posteritās, posteritātis*, f. 3d (from the adj. *pos-terus*, which is from the adv. *post*); governed by the prep. *in; in posteritātem = in posterum tempus. Posteritās* is used in two senses: (1) *the future*, (2) *people of the future, posterity.* —— **redundāret**, 3d pers. sing. imperf. subjunct. act. of *redundo, -āre, -āvī, -ātum,* 1 (*red = re + undō;* = lit. *I surge back; undō = I rise in waves, I surge,* and *unda = a wave,* are from root *ud* or *und = to wet;* cf. ὕδωρ *= water*); agrees with the subj. *quid;* the subjunct. mood is final, following *nē* in dependence on *erat verendum.* The imperf. tense is required, because the principal verb *erat verendum* is historic, and calls for historic sequence in subordinate clauses. A. & G. 286; B. 267, 268; G. 509, *ff;* H. 491. The metaphor is taken from a stream which has burst its banks, flooding the adjacent country. —— **Quodsī**, conj. = *but if;* followed by the imperf. subjunct. *impendē-ret* in the *protasis*, marking the supposition as referring to the present, and therefore un-realized. *Quodsī = quod + sī,* i.e. *sī* introduces the condition, while *quod* is an adverbial acc. of reference, = *as to which,* i.e. *as regards the above.* A. & G. 240, *b;* B. 185, 2; G. 334; H. 453, 6. —— **ea**, nom. sing. f. of the dem. pron. *is, ea, id;* subj. of *impendēret; ea = invidia.* —— **mihi**, dat. sing. of *ego;* dat. of the indirect obj., dependent on *impendē-ret.* Many compounds of *in* (like *impendēre*), *con, prō,* etc., govern the dative of the indirect object.

LINE 16. **māximē** (formed from *māximus,* superl. of the adj. *magnus*), adv.; modi-fies *impendēret.* —— **impendēret**, 3d pers. sing. imperf. subjunct. act. of *impendeō, -ēre,* no perf. no supine, 2 (*in = over, upon,* + *pendeō = I hang*); agrees with the subj. *ea.* Distinguish *impendēret* from *impendēret* (imperf. subjunct. act. of *impendō, -ere, impendī, impensum,* 3, = *I weigh out, expend, employ,* transitive). Observe that the condition is irregular in form: the imperf. subjunct. of the *protasis* marks the hypothesis as an ideal one respecting the present time, and we should expect the imperf. subjunct. also in the *apodosis.* But the orator changes the form of the *apodosis* by an afterthought, with the direct statement *hōc animō semper fuī.* He might just as well have said *quodsī ea mihi impendēret, tamen invidia virtūte parta glōria, nōn invidia esset (ut semper putāvī) = but if hatred threatened me now, yet hatred earned by virtue would be (as I have always thought it) glory, not hatred.* However, it is not uncommon for the *apodosis* to be altered, esp. by the means employed here, viz. the addition of a principal clause, not found in the original form of the condition, or at least only found as a parenthesis, to which the original *apodosis* is made subordinate by alteration to an acc. and inf. or to a substantival subjunct. object clause. —— **tamen**, adv. (used as adversative conj.); strengthens the oppositional force of the statement following. *Tamen* is often used in the *apodosis* of a condition with *quodsī;* cf. ὅμως in the *apodosis* in Greek. —— **hōc**, abl. sing. m. of the dem. pron. *hīc, haec, hōc;* agrees with *animō.* —— **animō**, abl. sing. of *animus, -ī,* m. 2d; abl. of quality, otherwise called descriptive abl., describing the subj. of *fuī.* A. & G. 251; B. 224; G. 400; H. 419, II.

LINE 17. **fuī**, 1st pers. sing. perf. ind. of *sum, esse, fuī;* the subj. *ego* is implied by the personal ending. —— **semper**, adv. of time; modifies the pred. *hōc animō fuī.* —— ut, conj.; followed by the subjunct. *putārem;* the clause *ut . . . putārem* is explana-

18	partam	glōriam,	nōn	invidiam	putārem.
	acquired	*(to be) glory,*	*not*	*odium*	*I thought.*
19	Quamquam		nōnnūllī	sunt	in	hōc
	And yet		*some*	*there are*	*in*	*this*
20	ōrdine,		quī	aut	ea	quae
	order (= Senate),	*who*	*either*	*those things*	*which*
21	imminent	nōn	videant,	aut	ea	quae
	impend	*not*	*see*	*or those things*	*which*

to regard unpopularity incurred by manly conduct as glory, and not as unpopularity. And yet there are some in this Council who either do not see the dangers which are imminent or conceal their perception

tory of *hōc animō.* ——**invidiam,** acc. sing. of *invidia, -ae,* f. 1st; subj.-acc. of *esse,* which must be supplied in the indirect pred. *glōriam esse,* dependent on *putārem* (a *verbum sentiendī*). ——**virtūte,** abl. sing. of *virtūs, virtūtis,* f. 3d (from *vir;* hence (1) *manliness,* (2) *courage,* cf. ἀνδρία = *courage,* from ἀνήρ, gen. ἀνδρός = *a man,* (3) *virtue*); abl. of the means, modifying *partam.*

LINE 18. **partam,** acc. sing. f. of *partus, -a, -um,* perf. part. pass. of *pariō, -ere, peperī, partum,* fut. part. *pariturus,* 3; predicate part., agreeing with *invidiam; invidiam virtūte partam* here = *invidiam quae virtūte parta esset.* ——**glōriam,** acc. sing. of *glōria, -ae,* f. 1st (akin to *clārus*); predicative, complement of *esse* understood. ——**nōn,** negative adv.; limits *invidiam (esse).* ——**invidiam,** acc. sing. of *invidia, -ae,* f. 1st; predicative, complement of *esse* understood. Observe that the subj. of the indirect statement (dependent on *putārem*) is *invidiam,* l. 17; hence the predicate words *glōriam* and *invidiam* (l. 18) take the same case as the subject. A. & G. 176; B. 167, 168; G. 205, 206; H. 360.——**putārem,** 1st. pers. sing. imperf. subjunct. act. of *putō, -āre, -āvī, -ātum,* 1; the subj. *ego* is implied by the personal ending; the subjunct. is consecutive, with *ut,* explaining *hōc animō* above.

LINE 19. **Quamquam,** (*quam + quam*) conj. = *and yet;* connects the sentence with the previous one. *Quamquam,* and less commonly *etsī,* which are usually subordinate conjunctions = *although,* may be used to connect coördinately. ——**nōnnūllī,** (*nōn + nūllī*), nom. plur. m. of the adj. *nōnnūllus, -a, -um; nōnnūllī* is substantival, and subj. of *sunt.* ——**sunt,** 3d pers. plur. pres. ind. of *sum, esse, fuī;* agrees with the subj. *nōnnūllī.* ——**in,** prep.; gov. the abl. *ōrdine.* ——**hōc,** abl. sing. m. of the dem. pron. *hīc, haec, hōc;* agrees with *ōrdine.*

LINE 20. **ōrdine,** abl. sing. of *ōraō, ōrdinis,* m. 3d; governed by the prep. *in; in hōc ōrdine = in senātū.* ——**quī,** nom. plur. m. of the rel. pron. *quī, quae, quod;* agrees with the indef. antecedent *nōnnūllī,* and is subj. of *videant; quī* is generic, i.e. represents a class (= *tālēs ut*), hence followed by the subjunct. *videant.* A. & G. 320; B. 283; G. 631, 2; H. 503, I. Distinguish *quī,* as used here, from *quī,* as used in l. 22. ——**aut,** disjunctive conj.; used correlatively with *aut* below, = *either . . . or.* ——**ea,** acc. plur. n. of the dem. pron. *is, ea, id;* direct obj. of *videant.* ——**quae,** nom. plur. n. of the rel. pron. *quī, quae, quod;* agrees with the antecedent *ea,* and is subj. of *imminent.* Observe that when the antecedent of the rel. clause is not otherwise expressly defined than by the statement made in the rel. clause the antecedent is usually a part of *is, ea, id.*

LINE 21. **imminent,** 3d pers. plur. pres. ind. act. of *immineō, -ēre,* no perf., no supine, 2 (*in + minor*); agrees with the subj. *quae.* Note the ind. mood, which is employed instead of the subjunct., because stress is laid on the *fact* of dangers being imminent; otherwise the rule would require a subjunctive, because the rel. clause is subordinate to the subjunct. in *quī nōn . . . videant.* A. & G. 342; B. 324; G. 629; H. 529, II, NOTE I. ——**nōn,** negative adv.; limits *videant.* ——**videant,** 3d pers. plur. pres. subjunct. act. of *videō, -ēre, vīdī, vīsum,* 2; agrees with the subject *quī* above;

| of what they do see; and it is these men who have fostered Catiline's hopes by their pacific declara- | **vident** *they see* | **dissimulent:** *disguise :* | **quī** *who* | **spem** *the hope* | **Catilīnae** 22 *of Catiline* |
| | **mollibus** *mild* | **sententiīs** *by views* | **aluērunt,** *have fostered,* | **coniūrātiōnemque** *and the conspiracy* | 23 |

the subjunct. is *consecutive*, as regularly with *quī generic* or *characteristic ; see quī above.*——**aut,** disjunctive conj. ; connects *videant* and *dissimulent.*——**ea,** acc. plur. n. of the dem. pron. *is, ea, id;* direct obj. of *dissimulent,* or of *vidēre* in *sē vidēre* supplied.——**quae,** acc. plur. n. of the rel. pron. *quī, quae, quod;* agrees with the antecedent *ea,* and is direct obj. of *vident* following.

LINE 22. **vident,** 3d pers. plur. pres. ind. act. of *videō, -ēre, vīdī, vīsum,* 2 ; the implied subj. of *vident* is a pron. *eī* or *illī,* referring to *nōnnūllī,* l. 19 ; the mood is ind. for the same reason as in the case of *imminent* above (where see note).——**dissimulent,** 3d pers. plur. pres. subjunct. act. of *dissimulō, -āre, -āvī, -ātum,* 1 (for *dissimilō, dis* marking contradiction + *similis* = *like;* the Latin root is *sim,* Greek ἁμ or ὁμ = *like;* cf. *similis, simul, simulō, semel, semper,* and ἅμα, ὁμοιος, ὁμοῦ) ; agrees with the subj. *quī* (generic), l. 20 ; the subjunct. is consecutive and coördinate with *videant.* Synonyms : (1) *simulō* = lit. *I make like, I pretend, I invent,* i.e. that something is which really is not, e.g. (a) + direct obj., *morbum simulāre* = *to feign sickness,* (b) + acc. and inf., *mē aegrōtum esse simulō ;* (2) *dissimulō,* = *I hide, I pretend* that something is not which really is, e.g. (a) + direct obj., *morbum dissimulāre* = *to hide sickness* (feigning health), (b) + acc. and inf., *mē aegrōtum esse dissimulō.* The distinction may be memorized in the following hexameter : *Quae nōn sunt simulō ; quae sunt, ea dissimulantur.*——**quī,** nom. plur. m. of the rel. pron. *quī, quae, quod;* agrees with the antecedent *nōnnūllī,* and is subj. of *aluērunt* and *corrōborāvērunt.* Observe that *quī* here really begins a new sentence, i.e. is purely connective, = *hī autem, but these men;* hence the ind. mood of *aluērunt.* A. & G. 180, *f*; B. 251, 6; G. 610; H. 453.——**spem,** acc. sing. of *spēs, spei,* f. 5th ; direct obj. of *aluērunt.*——**Catilīnae,** gen. sing. of *Catilīna,* m. 1st ; poss. gen., limiting *spem.*

LINE 23. **mollibus,** abl. plur. f. of the adj. *mollis, -e,* 3d (probably for *mov-lis* = (1) *easily moved, pliant;* (2) *weak, uncertain;* (3) *delicate, soft;* root *mav* = Latin *mov, to push out of place;* cf. *mōbilis,* and ἀμείβω = *I change*) ; agrees with *sententiīs.* There is probably no connection between *mollis* and μαλακός. *Mollibus* suggests a rebuke, implying that mild, weak, and conciliatory speeches were made instead of the vigorous and resolute denunciations which the occasion required. It is not necessary to suppose that Cicero suspected treasonable collusion. The reference in *quī spem . . . corrōborāvērunt* is to the time, just before the elections, 63 B.C., when Cicero warned the Senate of danger and when Catiline, called upon to speak, declared that he would lead the people against the infirm Senate. Cicero, in his speech for Mūrēna, laments the Senate's weakness on this occasion, cf. *neque tamen satis sevērē prō reī indignitāte decrēvit.*——**sententiīs,** abl. plur. of *sententia, -ae,* f. 1st (*sentiō*) ; abl. of the means or instrument, modifying *aluērunt. Sententia* is the regular word for the declaration of opinion made by a senator ; the speaker was not compelled to adhere to the subject under discussion, but might speak on any subject of a public nature, hence when it was so desired a party might delay the settlement of a particular question by speaking on extraneous subjects the whole day.——**aluērunt,** 3d pers. plur. perf. ind. act. of *alō, -ere, uī-, altum* or *alitum,* 3 (root *al* = *to nourish;* cf. *alumnus,* ἄν-αλ-τος = *insatiable,* etc.) ; agrees with the subj. *quī.*——**coniūrātiōnemque** (*coniūrātiōnem* + *que*), *coniūrātiōnem* is the acc. sing. of *coniūrātiō, -ōnis,* f. 3d (*con* + *iūrō*) ; direct obj. of *corrōborāvērunt. Que* is the enclitic cop. conj. ; connects the coördinate rel. clauses *quī . . . aluērunt* and (*quī*) *. . . corrōborāvērunt.*

24 **nāscentem   nōn   crēdendō   corrōborāvērunt;**
   growing   not   by believing   have strengthened;

25 **quōrum   auctōritāte   multī,   nōn   sōlum**
   whose   by authority   many men,   not   only

26 **improbī,   vērum   etiam   imperītī,   sī   in**
   the dishonest,   but   also   the inexperienced,   if   upon

tions and strength-ened the conspiracy at its birth by re-fusing to believe in its existence. And guided by their au-thority many others, not the rogues alone but also the unin-

LINE 24. **nāscentem**, acc. sing. f. of *nāscēns, -entis*, pres. part. of the deponent verb *nāscor, nāscī, nātus sum*, 3; agrees with *coniūrātiōnem* and = a temporal clause like *dum nāscitur*.——**nōn**, negative adv.; limits *crēdendō* (not *corrōborāvērunt*).—— **crēdendō**, abl. of the gerund *crēdendum, -ī*, of the verb *crēdō, -ere, crēdidī, crēditum*, 3 (Sanskrit *çrat* or *çrad= trust* + root *dha = to put;* for root *dha =* Latin *da, fa, fac,* cf. *con-dō, ab-dō*, etc.); abl. of the means, modifying *corrōborāvērunt*. The abl. of the gerund or gerundive expresses: (1) *the means*, as above; (2) *cause;* (3) less often, *manner* or *circumstance*. Study the examples in A. & G. 301; B. 339, 1; G. 431; H. 542. *Crēdere* is used: (1) intransitively = *to believe*, with the dat., e.g. *crēdō tibi = I believe, trust in you;* with acc. of neuter pronouns, e.g. *id quod volunt crēdunt;* (2) transitively, in the sense *to commit, entrust, lend*, with the acc. and dat. of the direct and indirect objects respectively.——**corrōborāvērunt**, 3d pers. perf. ind. act. of *corrōborō, -āre, -āvī, -ātum*, 1 (*con + rōborō*, from noun *rōbur*, gen. *rōboris*, n. 3d = *strength;* probably akin to Greek root *ρω* in *ῥώ-ννυμι= I strengthen*); agrees with the subj. *quī*, and is coördinate with *aluērunt*.

LINE 25. **quōrum**, gen. plur. m. of the rel. pron. *quī, quae, quod;* agrees with the antecedent *nōnnūllī* (l. 19) i.e. *nōnnūllī quī coniūrātiōnem corrōborāvērunt*, and is poss. gen., limiting *auctōritāte*. Like *quī* in l. 22, *quōrum* is here connective and begins a new sentence = *nam hōrum auctōritāte*, etc.——**auctōritāte**, abl. sing. of *auctōritās, -ātis*, f. 3d (from *auctor*); abl. of the cause, modifying *dīcerent*. It is more usual for *the cause* of an action to be expressed by the abl. in conjunction with a perf. part. passive, e.g. *quōrum auctōritāte adductī* (*impulsī, incitātī*, etc.). A. & G. 245, and 2, *b*; B. 219; G. 408, and NOTE 2; H. 416. Some editors read *auctōritātem secūtī* for *auctōritāte*.—— *Auctōritāte* here = *on the authority, by the influence;* sometimes *auctōritās* has a special meaning, viz. senatorial *sanction* of a measure which an interposition of veto alone pre-vented from becoming a *senātūs cōnsultum*.——**multī**, nom. plur. m. (substantival) of the adj. *multus, -a, -um;* subj. of *dīcerent. Multi* here = *multī aliī*, i.e. not members of the Senate.——**nōn**, negative adv.; *nōn sōlum* modifies *improbī*.——**sōlum** (acc. neut. sing. of the adj. *sōlus, -a, -um;* cf. adv. *multum, vērum*, etc.), adv.; combines with *nōn* as an adverbial modifier.

LINE 26. **improbī**, nom. plur. m. of the adj. *improbus, -a, -um* (*in = not + probus = honest, virtuous*); agrees with *multī = multī, quī sunt improbī*, or we may consider *improbī* as substantival (= *the dishonest*) and appositive of *multī. Improbī*, evidently refers to followers of the senators *quī ea quae vident dissimulent* (l. 21), i.e. corrupt fol-lowers of corrupt patrons.——**vērum**, adversative conj.; connects and opposes *improbī* and *imperītī*. See the note and references under *tamen*, Chap. I, l. 18.——**etiam** (*et + iam*), adv.; intensifies *imperītī*.——**imperītī**, nom. plur. m. of the adj. *imperītus, -a, -um* (*in = not + perītus = experienced, skilled*); agrees with *multī*, or else substanti-val in apposition. *Imperītī =* the ignorant and politically blind followers of ignorant senators (*quī ea imminent nōn videant*, l. 20).——**sī**, conditional particle; with the pluperf. subjunct. *animadvertissem* of an ideal supposition in regard to past time.—— **in**, prep.; gov. the acc. *hunc*.

formed, would say that I had acted in a savage and tyrannical fashion, if I had inflicted punishment on Catiline. Now, however, I perceive that if he once ar-	hunc	animadvertissem,	crūdēliter	et 27
	this (fellow)	*I had inflicted punishment,*	*cruelly*	*and*
	rēgiē	factum esse	dīcerent.	Nunc 28
	tyrannically	*(it) to have been done*	*would say.*	*Now*
	intellegō,	sī iste,	quō	intendit,	in 29
	I discern,	*if that (fellow)*	*whither*	*he purposes*	*to*

LINE 27. **hunc**, acc. sing. m. of the dem. pron. *hĭc, haec, hŏc ;* governed by the prep. *in ; hunc = Catilīnam.* —— **animadvertissem**, 1st pers. sing. pluperf. subjunct. act. of *animadvertō, -ere, animadvertī, animadversum,* 3 *(animum + advertō)* ; the subj. *ego* is implied by the personal ending ; in the *protasis* with *sī.* The verb *animadvertō* is often written *animum advertō* and = lit. *I turn my mind (attention) towards, I notice, observe ;* see the note on *animadverſīs,* Chap. VIII, l. 41 ; it is followed by the acc. of the direct object. In a judicial sense *animadvertere* is used with *suppliciō* understood = *to notice with punishment, to punish, to inflict punishment on,* and is followed by (a) the acc. of the direct object, (b) by *in* + the acc., in which case emphasis is laid on the attention which has been bestowed on the circumstances of the offence. —— **crūdēliter** (formed from the 3d decl. adj. *crūaēlis, -e ;* root *kru = to be hard ;* cf. *crūdus = unripe, raw*) ; modifies *factum esse.* —— **et,** cop. conj. ; connects *crūdēliter* and *rēgiē.*

LINE 28. **rēgiē** (from the adj. *rēgius, -a, -um ;* from *rēx, rēgis,* m. 3d), adv. ; modifies *factum esse. Rēgiē* is the Latin equivalent for the Greek τυραννικῶς ; the Romans and Greeks found that *kingship* and the rule of a τύραννος (= *despotic ruler*) were opposed to the principles of freedom. The Tarquins had made the word *rēx* odious to Romans, and the description of an action as *rēgium* was always likely to arouse indignation against it ; this feeling lasted long, and showed itself in many secret organizations and conspiracies in the early empire. Compare II, Chap. VII, line 19, *(mē) crūdēlissimum tyrannum exīstimārī velint.* Cicero was exposed to much criticism for his so-called despotic conduct during his consulship ; he speaks in one of his speeches of this, *quī nōs tyrannōs vocās.* —— **factum esse,** perf. inf. of *fīō, fierī, factus sum,* used as pass. of *faciō, -ere, fēcī, factum,* 3 ; understand as subj.-acc. a pron., e.g. *id,* referring to *sī animadvertissem ; factum esse* is obj. of *dīcerent.* —— **dīcerent,** 3d pers. plur. imperf. subjunct. act. of *dīcō, -ere, dīxī, dictum,* 3 ; agrees with the subj. *multī,* l. 25 ; *dīcerent* is the verb of the *apodosis,* and the imperf. tense expresses continuity of action, i.e. *they would have said* and *they would be saying now.* —— **Nunc,** adv. of time ; used partly in a temporal sense and partly to contrast the present with the past, = *now, as it is.*

LINE 29. **intellegō,** 1st pers. sing. pres. ind. act. of *intellegō, -ere, intellēxī, intellectum,* 3 *(inter + legō)* ; the subj. *ego* is implied by the personal ending. See the synonyms and the note under *intellegit,* Chap. I, l. 17. Observe that *intellegō,* as a verb of *perception,* throws the condition following into an indirect form ; hence the *protasis* has the perf. subjunct. *pervēnerit,* and the verb of the *apodosis* is the pres. inf. *fore.* In direct form the condition would be : *sī iste . . . in Manliāna castra pervēnerit* (fut. perf. ind.), *nēmō tam stultus erit* (*quī,* etc.), *nēmō tam improbus quī nōn fateātur.* A. & G. 337, 1 and 2 ; B. 319, A, B ; G. 657 ; H. 527, I. —— **sī,** conditional particle ; introducing a logical condition respecting the future, and followed by the perf. subjunct. *pervēnerit* (= fut. perf. ind. of direct statement). —— **iste,** nom. sing. m. of the dem. pron. of the 2d pers. *iste, ista, istud ;* subj. of *pervēnerit ; iste* refers to Catiline, and has its usual forensic signification of contempt, = *that fellow.* See note on *iste,* Chap. I, l. 3. —— **quō** (abl. n. sing. of *quī*), adv., = *eō quō, thither, whither ;* introduces the clause *quō intendit* as an adverbial modifier of *pervēnerit.* —— **intendit,** 3d pers. sing. pres. ind. act. of *intendō, -ere, intendī, intensum* or *intentum,* 3 *(in + tendō* = lit. *I stretch towards,* hence

30	Manliāna	castra	pervēnerit,	nēminem	tam
	of Manlius	*the camp*	*shall come,*	*no one*	*so*
31	stultum	fore	quī	nōn	videat
	foolish	*to be likely to be*	*who*	*not*	*can see*
32	coniūrātiōnem	esse	factam,	nēminem	tam
	a conspiracy	*to have been*	*made,*	*no one*	*so*
33	improbum	quī	nōn	fateātur.	Hōc
	dishonest	*who*	*not*	*may confess (it). This (man)*	

rives, as he purposes, at the camp of Manlius, there will be no one so dull as not to see that a conspiracy has been set on foot or so shameless as not to acknowledge the reality of it.   Yet,

I aim, purpose, urge, etc.); the implied subj. is *iste,* which is the expressed subj. of *pervēnerit. Quō intendit* is a kind of additional statement made in parenthesis and referring to *in Manliāna castra;* hence, as it might well be left out without disturbing the sentence, the verb is indicative, though the verb of a subordinate clause in indirect speech is properly in the subjunctive. A. & G. 336, 2; B. 314, 1; G. 650; H. 524.——**in,** prep.; gov. the acc. *castra,* expressing *limit of motion.*

LINE 30. **Manliāna,** acc. plur. of the adj. *Manliānus, -a, -um* (formed from the proper noun *Manlius, -ī,* m. 2d; cf. *Sultānus* from *Sulla*); agrees with *castra.*—— **castra,** acc. of the plur. noun *castra, -ōrum,* n. 2d (*castrum, -ī,* n. 2d = *fortress*); governed by the prep. *in.*——**pervēnerit,** 3d pers. sing. perf. subjunct. act. of *perveniō, -īre, pervēnī, perventum,* 4 (*per + veniō*); agrees with the subj. *iste.* For the mood, see the note on *intellegō,* l. 29.——**nēminem,** acc. sing. of *nēmō,* m. 3d, dat. *nēminī (nē + homō;* the gen. and abl. are wanting, and are supplied by *nūllīus,* and *nūllō,* from *nūllus, -a, -um*); subj.-acc. of *fore* in the acc. and inf. object clause of *intellegō; nēminem fore,* etc., is the *apodosis* of the condition introduced by *sī* above. For model sentences and remarks on the form of reported conditions after primary and historic leading verbs, refer to the note on *sī,* Chap. VIII, l. 31.——**tam,** adv.; modifies *stultum. Tam* never modifies verbs, only adverbs and adjectives; use *ita* and *adeō* with verbs.

LINE 31. **stultum,** acc. sing. m. of the adj. *stultus, -a, -um;* agrees with the subj.-acc. *nēminem;* predicative, being the complement of *fore* in the acc. and inf. construction.——**fore,** fut. inf. of *sum, esse, fuī;* agrees with the subj.-acc. *nēminem.* The fut. inf. of *sum* is also formed in the familiar way by means of the fut. part. *futūrus, -a, -um + esse.*——**quī,** nom. sing. m. of the rel. pron. *quī, quae, quod;* agrees with the antecedent *nēminem,* and is subj. of *videat; quī* is equivalent to *ut is,* introducing a clause of result.—— **non,** negative adv.; limits *videat.*——**videat,** 3d pers. sing. pres. subjunct. act. of *videō, ēre, vīdī, vīsum,* 2; agrees with the subj. *quī;* the subjunct. is consecutive, after *quī = ut is.* A. & G. 319; B. 284; G. 552; H. 500.

LINE 32. **coniūrātiōnem,** acc. sing. of *coniūrātiō, -ōnis,* f. 3d (*con + iūrō*); subj.-acc. of *factum esse,* in dependence on the verb of *perception videat.*——**esse factam,** perf. inf. of *fīō, fierī, factus sum,* used as the passive of *faciō, -ere, fēcī, factum,* 3 (root *dha = fa, fac = to put, place, make,* with a large number of derivatives); agrees (the part. *factam* in gender, number, and case) with the subj.-acc. *coniūrātiōnem.* In composite infinitives and composite ind. and subjunct. tenses it is very common for (1) the part. of *sum* to precede the participle, as in this passage, and (2) for other words, often a large number, to separate the participle from the part of *sum.*——**nēminem,** acc. sing. of *nēmō,* m. 3d (see *nēminem,* above); subj.-acc. of *fore tam improbum (fore* being supplied from the preceding coördinate object-clause).——**tam,** adv.; modifies *improbum.*

LINE 33. **improbum,** acc. sing. m. of the adj. *improbus, -a, -um (in = not + probus = upright, honest*); agrees with the subj.-acc. *nēminem,* l. 32; predicative, being the complement of *fore* understood.——**quī,** nom. sing. m. of the rel. pron. *quī, quae, quod;* agrees with the antecedent *nēminem,* and is subj. of *fateātur; quī* introduces a rel.

if Catiline alone be put to death, I discern that this disease which is in the state may be repressed for a short time but can-	autem *however*	ūnō *one*	interfectō *having been killed,*	intellegō *I perceive*	hanc 34 *this*
	reī pūblicae *of the commonwealth*	pestem *plague*		paulisper *for a little while*	reprimī, 35 *to be checked,*

clause of result = *ut is*. In sentences of this kind Cicero prefers *quī nōn* to *quīn* (*quī*, old abl., + *nōn*); *quī nōn* marks the tendency, and *quīn* the result (= *ut nōn*). —— **nōn**, negative adv.; limits *fateātur*. —— **fateātur**, 3d pers. sing. pres. subjunct. of the deponent verb *fateor, fatērī, fossus sum*, 2 (akin to *fārī, fās, fāma,* φημί, φαίνω, etc.); agrees with the subj., *quī*; the subjunct. is consecutive, with *quī* = *ut is*. The perf. of *fateor* is not very often found; indeed the compound *confiteor* is much more used than *fateor*. Supply, from the coördinate *quī* clause preceding, *coniūrātiōnem esse factam* as the object of *fateātur*. —— **Hōc**, abl. sing. m. of the dem. pron. *hīc, haec, hōc*; abl. in the abl. absolute construction with *interfectō; hōc* = *Catilinā. Hōc . . . interfectō* = a conditional clause, *sī hīc ūnus interfectus sit, intellegō hanc pestem . . . reprimī posse;* compare the form of the reported condition, ll. 29–33.

LINE 34. **autem**, adversative conj.; connects the sentence with the one preceding. *Autem* is the weakest of the adversative conjunctions, and is used (1) in mild antithesis, (2) in contrasted conditions, as in this passage, for *hōc . . . interfecto* = a condition, and is contrasted with *sī iste pervēnerit* above. Often *autem* has no adversative force at all, and is merely connective; cf. the Greek particle δέ. —— **ūnō**, abl. sing. m. of the numeral adj. *ūnus, -a, -um;* agrees with *hōc. Unus* is often used as a synonym of *sōlus* = *only, alone,* and here *ūnō* = *sōlō*. —— **interfectō**, abl. sing. m. of *interfectus, -a, -um*, perf. part. pass. of *interficiō, -ere, interfēcī, interfectum*, 3 (*inter + faciō*); agrees with *hōc* in the ablative absolute construction. *Interficere* is the general verb meaning *to kill;* see the synonyms in the note on *occīdit*, Chap. I, l. 38. —— **intellegō**, 1st pers. sing. pres. ind. act. of *intellegō, -ere, intellēxī, intellectum*, 3 (*inter + legō*); the subj. *ego* is implied by the personal ending. Observe that *hōc,* l. 33 — *posse,* l. 36, is a disguised condition, and that the apodosis (i.e. *hanc pestem . . . reprimī, nōn comprimī . . . posse*) is thrown into the acc. and inf. indirect form by *intellegō* here, just as *intellegō,* l. 29, gave indirect form to the condition in the previous sentence. In direct form the condition = *hōc interfectō* (i.e. *sī hīc interfectus erit*), *haec pestis reprimī, nōn comprimī poterit*. —— **hanc**, acc. sing. f. of the dem. pron. *hīc, haec, hōc;* agrees with *pestem; hanc pestem* = *coniūrātiōnem*.

LINE 35. **reī**, gen. sing. of *rēs*, f. 5th; poss. gen., limiting *pestem*. —— **pūblicae**, gen. sing. f. of the adj. *pūblicus, -a, -um;* agrees with *reī; reī pūblicae* as usual = *of the state, of the commonwealth*. —— **pestem**, acc. sing. of *pestis, -is,* f. 3d; subj.-acc. of *posse* in the acc. and inf. construction dependent on *intellegō*. The nouns *pestis* and *pestilentia* are often used in a metaphorical sense with regard to political weakness or danger. Refer to the synonyms given under *pestem*, Chap. I, l. 27. —— **paulisper** (*paulum + per*), adv. = *for a little while;* modifies *reprimī. Paulus,* not *paullus,* is read in all the best Mss.; yet with the derivation *paur + los* we should rather expect *paullus,* i.e. assimilation of *r* to *l,* instead of omission. Yet the root may be *pau + termination -lus* (= Greek -*πος ; r* and *l* are frequently interchangeable). As *paulus,* so *paulisper* is found in the Mss., e.g. in the Medicean Vergil. —— **reprimī**, pres. inf. pass. of *reprimō, -ere, repressī, repressum*, 3 (*re = back + premō = I press*); complementary inf., with *posse*. Observe the difference of meaning between *reprimere* and *comprimere,* upon which the whole force of the sentence rests. *Reprimere* = *ad tempus continēre* = *to hold in check for the time being,* whereas *comprimere* = *plānē cōnficere* = *to wholly crush,* i.e. beyond all hope of restoration.

Dictionaries: The Classic Series. Half morocco. Especially planned for students and teachers in colleges and high schools. Up to the times in point of contents, authoritative while modern as regards scholarship, instantly accessible in respect to arrangement, of best quality as to typography and paper, and in a binding at once elegant and durable. 8x5½ in.

French-English and English-French Dictionary, 1122 pages. $2.00.

German-English and English-German Dictionary, 1112 pages. $2.00.

Latin-English and English-Latin Dictionary, 941 pages. $2.00.

Greek-English and English-Greek Dictionary, 1056 pages. $2.00.

English-Greek Dictionary. Price $1.00.

Dictionaries: The Handy Series. "Scholarship modern and accurate; and really beautiful print." *Pocket Edition.*

Spanish-English and Eng.-Span., 474 pages. $1.00.

Italian-English and Eng.-Ital., 428 pages. $1.00.

New Testament Lexicon. *Entirely new and up-to-date. With a fine presentation of the Synonyms of the Greek Testament.* $1.00.

Liddell & Scott's Abridged Greek Lexicon. With new Appendix of Proper and Geographical names. $1.20.

White's Latin-English Dictionary. $1.20.

White's English-Latin Dictionary. $1.20.

White's Latin-English and Eng.-Lat. Dictionary. $2.25.

Casserly's Latin Prosody. New Edition. 60 cents.

Brooks' Historia Sacra, with First Latin Lessons. Revised, *with Vocabulary,* Price 50 cts. This justly popular volume besides the Epitome Historiæ Sacræ, the Notes, and the Vocabulary, contains 100 pages of elementary Latin Lessons, enabling the teacher to carry the pupil quickly and in easy steps over the ground preparatory to the Epitome Historiæ Sacræ.

Brooks' First Lessons in Greek, *with Lexicon.* Revised Edition. Covering sufficient ground to enable the student to read the New Testament in the Greek. 50c.

Brooks' New Virgil's Aeneid, *with Lexicon.* Revised. Notes, Metrical Index, Map. *With Questions.* $1.50.

Brooks' New Ovid's Metamorphoses, *with Lexicon.* Expurgated for mixed classes. With *Questions.* $1.50.

Handy Literal Translations. Cloth, *pocket*. 50 cts. per vol.

" To one who is reading the Classics, a literal
translation is a convenient and legitimate help:
every well informed person will read the Classics
either in the original or in a translation.

Eighty-nine volumes, viz. : (*Interlinears* other page).

Cæsar's Gallic War. *The Seven Books.* (For *Book I* trans-
    lated *and* completely *parsed*, see other page.)
Cæsar's *Civil* War.
Catullus.
Cicero's Brutus.
Cicero's Defense of Roscius.
Cicero De Officiis.
Cicero On Old Age and Friendship.
Cicero On Oratory.
Cicero On The Nature of The Gods.
Cicero's Orations. *Four vs. Catiline, and others.* (For
    Orations I, II, translated *and parsed*, see other page.)
Cicero's Select Letters.
Cicero's Tusculan Disputations.
Cornelius Nepos, *complete*.
Eutropius.
Horace, *complete*.
Juvenal's Satires, *complete*.
Livy, Books I and II.
Livy, Books XXI and XXII.
Lucretius, *in preparation*.
Martial's Epigrams (*paper*).
Ovid's Metamorphoses, *complete in two volumes*.
Phædrus' Fables.
Plautus' Captivi, and Mostellaria.
Plautus' Pseudolus, and Miles Gloriosus.
Plautus' Trinummus, and Menæchmi.
Pliny's Select Letters, *complete in two volumes*.
Quintilian, Books X and XII.
Roman Life in Latin Prose and Verse.
Sallust's Catiline, and the Jugurthine War.
Seneca on Benefits.
Tacitus' Annals, *the First Six Books*.
Tacitus' Germany and Agricola.
Tacitus' On Oratory.
Terence: Andria, Adelphi and Phormio.
Terence: Heautontimorumeno.
Virgil's Æneid, *the First Six Books*. (For *Book I* translated
    and completely *scanned* and *parsed*, see other page.)
Virgil's Eclogues and Georgics.
Viri Romæ.
Æschines Against Ctesiphon.
Æschylus' Prometheus Bound; Seven vs. Thebes.
Æschylus' Agamemnon.
Aristophanes' Clouds.
Aristophanes' Birds, and Frogs.
Demosthenes' On The Crown.
Demosthenes' Olynthiacs and Philippics.
Euripides' Alcestis, and Electra.
Euripides' Bacchantes, and Hercules Furens.
Euripides' Hecuba and Andromache.
Euripides' Iphigenia In Aulis, In Tauris.
Euripides' Medea.
Herodotus, Books VI and VII.
Herodotus, Book VIII.

Homer's Iliad, *the First Six Books.*
Homer's Odyssey, *the First Twelve Books.*
Isocrates' Panegyric, *in preparation.*
Lucian's Select Dialogues, *two volumes.*
Lysias' Orations. *The only Translation extant.*
Plato's Apology, Crito, and Phædo.
Plato's Gorgias.
Plato's Laches (*paper*).
Plato's Protagoras, and Euthyphron.
Plato's Republic.
Sophocles' Œdipus Tyrannus, Electra, and Antigone.
Sophocles' Œdipus Coloneus.
Thucydides, *complete in two volumes.*
Xenophon's Anabasis, *the First Four Books.* (*Book I,* translated *and* completely parsed, *in prep.* See other page.)
Xenophon's Cyropædia, *complete in two volumes.*
Xenophon's Hellenica, and Symposium (The Banquet).
Xenophon's Memorabilia, *complete.*

———

Freytag's Die Journalisten (*paper*).
Goethe's Egmont.
Goethe's Faust.
Goethe's Hermann and Dorothea.
Goethe's Iphigenia in Tauris.
Lessing's Minna von Barnhelm.
Lessing's Nathan The Wise.
Lessing's Emilia Galotti.
Schiller's Ballads.
Schiller's Der Neffe als Onkel.
Schiller's Maid of Orleans.
Schiller's Maria Stuart.
Schiller's Wallenstein's Death.
Schiller's William Tell.
Corneille's The Cid.
Feuillet's Romance of a Poor Young Man.
Racine's Athalie.,

Completely Parsed Caesar, Vergil, Cicero, etc., *other page.*

Shortest Road to Caesar. Successful elem'y method. 75c.

Caesar's Idioms. Complete, with Eng. equivalents. Pap. 25c.

Cicero's Idioms. As found in "Cicero's Orations." Pap. 25c.

Beginners' Latin Book. Hoch & Bert's. Many improvements over other books for beginners, one being the diagram to illustrate conditional sentences. $1.00.

Beginners' Greek Book. I. P. Frisbee. Complete in itself. Applies the principles of correct teaching to the preparation (in one year) for reading Xenophon's Anabasis. *Fully tested in many schools.* $1.25.

German Texts. With *footnotes* and **Vocabulary:** W. Tell, Jungfrau v. Orleans, Maria Stuart, Neffe als Onkel, Minna v. Barnhelm, Nathan der Weise, Emilia Galotti, Herm. und Dorothea. *Eight vols.* 50 cts. *each.*

Ideophonic Texts. Wilhelm Tell, Act I. $1.00.

ness of long-continued	veteris	furōris et audāciae mātūritās in 5
growth have burst	*long-standing of madness and of effrontery*	*the ripeness upon*

quō pacto introduce an indirect question, for the subjunct. *ērūperit* would be required instead of the ind. *ērūpit*. *Nesciō* and *quō* must be regarded as a single word (and so it is often written) = *some* (*I know not what*). In fact *nesciō quis* and *nesciō quī, quae, quod* are classed respectively with the indefinite pronouns and indefinite pronominal adjectives; see the note on *quāsdam*, Chap. II, l. 4. Compare *nesciō quō modō* = *somehow or other; nesciō an* = lit. *I know not whether*, i.e. *perhaps, probably*. A few other interrogative expressions are used in a similar parenthetic way with the ind. instead of subjunct., and with similar indefinite sense; cf. *mirum quam* = lit. *marvellous how*, i.e. *marvellously, valdē quam* = *enormously, sānē quam gāvisus sum* = *I was tremendously glad, mīrum quantum labōrāvit* = lit. *it (is) wonderful, how much he worked!* i.e. *he worked wonderfully.* A. & G. 334, *e*; B. 253, 6; G. 467, REM. 1, and NOTE; H. 529, 5, 3). —— **quō**, abl. sing. n. of the interrog. pron. *quis, quae, quid* or of the interrog. adj. *quī, quae, quod;* agrees with *pactō.* —— **pāctō**, abl. sing. of *pāctum, -ī*, n. 2d = (1) *agreement*, (2) as here, *way, manner* (properly substantival neut. of *pāctus*, perf. part. of *paciscor, -i, pāctus sum*, 3 = *I agree, stipulate*); abl. of manner, with the modifier *quō.* Manner is expressed by the abl. with *cum*, but *cum* may be omitted or retained if the noun in the abl. is modified by an adjective. But *cum* is very rarely retained with expressions of manner such as *modō, pāctō* (e.g. *nūllō, modō* or *pāctō*), *ratiōne, ritū, viā*, and with adverbial expressions like *silentiō, iniūriā*, etc. —— **omnium**, gen. plur. n. of the 3d decl. adj. *omnis, -e;* agrees with *scelerum.* —— **scelerum**, gen. plur. of *scelus, sceleris*, n. 3d; poss. gen., limiting *mātūritās.* —— **ac**, cop. conj.; joins *scelerum* and *furōris et audāciae.* The use of the more emphatic conj. *ac* here shows that the two words connected by *et*, viz. *furōris* and *audāciae*, represent one idea.

LINE 5. **veteris**, gen. sing. m. of the 3d decl. adj. *vetus* (akin to *ἔτος* = *a year;* cf. *vetustus, veterāscō*); agrees with *furōris.* Observe that an adj. frequently agrees only with the nearest of two or more nouns, and is understood with the rest; so here *veteris* must be understood in the fem. with *audāciae.* See *iūcundus*, Chap. VI, l. 31. Synonyms: (1) *vetus* = *old, of old standing*, e.g. *vetus amīcitia;* (2) *antiquus* = *old, ancient*, usually of what was in ancient times but no longer exists; (3) *prīscus* = *old*, with a claim to reverence, e.g. *prīsca sevēritās; vetustus* = *old*, of something long used and so superior, e.g. *vetusta disciplīna;* (5) *prīstinus* = *old, earlier*, as opposed to *praesēns;* (6) *obsolētus* = *old, out of use*, e.g. *verba obsolēta.* —— **furōris**, gen. sing. of *furor*, m. 3d (*furō* = *I rage*); poss. gen., limiting *mātūritās; furōris et audāciae* = poss. genitives, coördinate with *scelerum.* —— **et**, cop. conj.; connects *furōris* and *audāciae.* —— **audāciae**, gen. sing. of *audācia*, f. 1st (from adj. *audāx*, gen. *audācis; audeō* = *I dare*); poss. gen., limiting *mātūritās.* The force of the conjunctions (see *ac* above) would seem to imply that *furōris et audāciae* be taken as one idea = *furōrem audācem*, an instance of hendiadys; cf. Chap. I, l. 9, *ōra vultūsque*, and see the note and references under *ōra.* —— **mātūritās**, gen. *mātūritātis*, f. 3d (from the adj. *mātūrus, -a, -um*); nom. sing., subj. of *ērūpit.* Observe the abstract character of this sentence; Caesar would have had a concrete subject. —— **in**, prep.; gov. the acc. *tempus. In tempus* instead of *in tempore* is an instance of the *cōnstrūctiō praegnāns* (pregnant construction, i.e. the combination of two different expressions in one), and = *has* (*come to* and) *burst out upon the time*, etc.; cf. the well-known example from the Acts of the Apostles, Chap. VIII, verse 40, Φίλιππος δὲ εὑρέθη εἰς Ἄζωτον = *Philip was found at Azōtus*, lit. *to Azōtus* (i.e. *Philip went to Azōtus and was found there*). Prof. Taylor compares (1) a passage with *in* + the abl. from the speech *prō Sullā*, viz. *furōrem ērūpisse in meō cōnsulātū*, i.e. *during my consulship;* (2) a passage from the *prō Murēnā*, viz. *omnia quae per hōc biennium agitāta sunt . . . in hōc tempus ērumpunt*, i.e. *in* + acc., as in our passage.

6 nostrī	cōnsulātūs	tempus	ērūpit.	Quodsī
our	*of consulship*	*the season has burst out.*		*But if*
7 ex	tantō	latrōciniō	iste	ūnus
out of	*so large*	*a herd of brigands*	*that man*	*one*
8 tollētur,		vidēbimur	fortasse	ad breve
shall be disposed of,	*we shall seem*	*perhaps*	*for*	*short*
9 quoddam	tempus	cūrā	et	metū
some	*time*	*from care*	*and*	*from fear*

forth in full maturity upon the season of my consulship. Now if Catiline alone of all this band of brigands be got rid of, we shall seem perhaps to have secured relief from trouble and anxiety

LINE 6. **nostrī**, gen. sing. m. of the poss. adj. *noster, nostra, nostrum ;* agrees with *cōnsulātūs.* Cicero seems to allude to himself alone in the implied *nōs ;* but he may have been thinking also of his colleague. —— **cōnsulātūs**, gen. sing. of *cōnsulātus*, m. 4th (the office or period of office of the *cōnsul*); subjective gen., limiting *tempus*. —— **tempus**, acc. sing. of *tempus, temporis*, n. 3d (root *tam = to cut ;* hence lit. *a section* of time, then *time*, generally). —— **ērūpit**, 3d pers. sing. perf. ind. act. of *ērumpō, -ere, ērūpī, ēruptum*, 3, trans. and intrans. (root *rup* = Greek λυπ *= to break, to trouble ;* cf. λύπη *= pain*); agrees with the subj. *mātūritās*. —— **Quodsī** (*Quod + sī*), conditional particle *= but if ;* followed by *tollētur* in a logical condition respecting the future. For the adverbial acc. *quod*, see the note on *quodsī*, Chap. XII, l. 15.

LINE 7. **ex** (*ē* or *ex* before consonants, *ex* before vowels and *h*) prep. + the abl. ; gov. *latrōciniō*, expressing *partition*, cf. *ūnus mīlitum* and *ūnus ex mīlitibus*. —— **tantō**, abl. sing. n. of the adj. *tantus, -a, -um ;* agrees with *latrōciniō*. *Ex tantō latrōciniō = ex tot latrōnibus*, or *ex tot latrōnum numerō*. —— **latrōciniō**, abl. sing. of *latrōcinium, -ī*, n. 2d (for a full discussion of the etymology, see *latrōciniō*, Chap. IX, l. 35); governed by the prep. *ex*. Observe that the abstract takes the place of the concrete expression ; cf. *servitium* which is sometimes used for *servī, coniūrātiō* for *coniūrātī*, etc., and the following from one of Cicero's letters, *ubī salūtātiō dēflūxit* (= *ubī salūtātōrēs dēflūxērunt*), *litterīs mē involvō = when my stream of morning-callers has flowed away, I surround myself with correspondence*. —— **iste**, nom. sing. m. of the dem. pron. *iste, ista, istud ;* subj. of *tollētur ; iste* refers to Catiline, and expresses contempt. —— **ūnus**, nom. sing. m. of the numeral adj. *ūnus, -a, -um* (gen. *ūnīus*, dat. *ūnī ;* old forms of nom. are *oenus*, and *oinos*); agrees with *iste ; ūnus* is often used likē *sōlus*.

LINE 8. **tollētur**, 3d pers. sing. fut. ind. pass. of *tollō, ere, sustulī, sublātum*, 3 irreg. (*sustulī* and *sublātum* are borrowed from *sufferō, sub + ferō ;* root *tal* = Latin *tol, tul = to lift, bear ; tollō, tulī*, and *lātus*, i.e. *(t)lātus* are all akin ; cf. *tol-erō*, τλῆναι *= to endure*, πολμάω *= I bear, I dare*); agrees with the subj. *iste ; tollētur* is in the *protasis* with *sī*. *Tollō* = (1) *I lift, bear ;* (2) *I make away with, remove, destroy*. —— **vidēbimur**, 1st pers. plur. fut. ind. pass. of *videō, -ēre, vīdī, vīsum*, 2 (the pass. *videor, ērī, vīsus sum*, 2 = (1) *I am seen*, (2) *I seem*, as here); the subj. *nōs* is implied by the personal ending. *Videor* is always used personally, e.g. *it seems that he can do this = haec facere posse vidētur* (lit. *he seems to be able to do this*); the 3d pers. sing. is sometimes impersonal, but with the sense *to seem good*. —— **fortasse** (for *fortassis = forte an sī vīs*), adv. *= perhaps ;* modifies *vidēbimur relevātī esse*. Other adverbs meaning perhaps are also derived from *fors :* (1) *forsitan*, a contraction from *fors sit an ;* (2) *forsan*, elliptical for *forsitan*. *Fortasse, forsitan, forsan*, and *fors sit* are often used with the potential subjunctive, e.g. *forsitan quispiam dīxerit = perhaps some one will say*. —— **ad**, prep. ; gov. the acc. *tempus*, expressing limit of time. —— **breve**, acc. sing. n. of the adj. *brevis, -e*, 3d ; agrees with *tempus*.

LINE 9. **quoddam**, acc. sing. n. of the indef. pron. and adj. *quīdam, quaedam, quid-dam* (adjectival neut. *quoddam ; quī + -dam*); agrees with *tempus*. *Quoddam* makes

for some short pe-riod; but the danger will remain settled behind and will be shut deep down within the veins and vitals of the state. Just as in several in-	esse relevātī; perīculum autem residēbit 10 *to have been relieved;* *the danger* *but* *will remain behind* et erit inclūsum penitus in vēnīs atque 11 *and* *will be* *shut in* *deeply* *in* *the veins* *and* in vīsceribus reī pūblicae. Ut saepe 12 *in* *the vitals* *of the commonwealth.* *As* *often*

the idea presented by *breve tempus* vaguer still ; see the note on *quāsdam*, Chap. II, l. 4.——**tempus**, acc. sing. of *tempus, temporis*, n. 3d ; governed by the prep. *ad.*——**cūrā**, abl. sing of *cūra, -ae,* f. 1st ; abl. of separation, dependent on *relevātī.* The mean-ings of *cūra* are : (1) *care, attention,* (2) *pursuit, business,* (3) *love, affection,* (4) *anxiety, trouble, sorrow,* as in the text. The last meaning alone is found in the adj. *sēcūrus* (*sē* = *sine* + *cūra*) = *free from anxiety.* The root is *sku* = *to observe ;* cf. *caveō* = *I am on guard, take care,* ἀκούω = *I hear.*——**et**, cop. conj. ; connects *cūrā* and *metū.*——**metū**, abl. sing. of *metus, -ūs,* m. 4th ; abl. of separation, dependent on *relevātī.* See note on *timor,* Chap. I, l. 6.

LINE 10. **esse relevātī**, perf. inf. pass. of *relevō, -āre, -āvī, -ātum,* 1 (*re* + *levō* = *I lift,* hence (1) *I lift up,* (2) *I lighten, mitigate,* (3) *release, set free,* as here); comple-mentary or epexegetical inf., predicative with *vidēbimur ;* the part. *relevātī* agrees in gender, number, and case with *nōs,* the implied subj. of *vidēbimur.* Observe that *relevātī esse* is accompanied by the simple abl. without a prep. *dē, ab,* or *ex ;* this is the rule with a few verbs, viz. those which express *setting free, depriving, wanting,* and *remov-ing.* A. & G. 243, *a* ; B. 214, 1 ; G. 390, 2, and NOTE 2 ; H. 414. Usually a prep. is required with other verbs, always with persons, but sometimes in technical and metaphor-ical combinations the abl. alone is found (esp. after compound verbs).——**perīculum**, gen. *perīculī,* n. 2d ; nom. sing., subj. of *residēbit.*——**autem**, adversative conj. ; con-nects the clause with the one preceding, and adds a contradictory idea.——**residēbit**, 3d pers. sing. fut. ind. act. of *resideō, -ēre, resēdī,* no supine, 2 (*re* = *back, behind* + *sedeō* = *I sit, settle*); agrees with the subj. *perīculum.* Compare Chap. V, l. 43, *resiēbit in rē pūblicā reliqua coniūrātōrum manus* (i.e. the *sentīna* or *dregs* of the state).

LINE 11. **et**, cop. conj.; connects *residēbit* and *erit inclūsum.*——**erit**, 3d pers. sing. fut. ind. of *sum, esse, fuī ;* coördinate with *residēbit,* and agrees with the same subj. *perī-culum.*——**inclūsum**, nom. sing. n. of *inclūsus, -a, -um,* perf. part. pass. of *inclūdō, -ere, inclūsī, inclūsum,* 3 (*in* + *claudō*); predicative with *erit,* agreeing in gender, number, and case with the subj. *perīculum. Erit inclusum* may be explained : (1) as fut.-perf. tense pass. = *will have been shut in ;* but we should expect the fut. simple *inclūdētur,* corresponding to *residēbit ;* (2) *erit* fut. simple, corresponding to *residēbit,* with *inclū-sum* as a quasi-complement representing *a state ;* cf. *amātus fuī,* which differs from *amātus sum* inasmuch as the latter states an action accomplished as a *fact,* while the former describes *a state* which has been experienced.——**penitus**, adv. ; modifies *inclū-sum.*——**in**, prep. ; gov. the abl. *vēnīs.*——**vēnīs**, abl. plur. of *vēna, -ae,* f. 1st ; gov-erned by the prep. *in ; in vēnīs . . . reī publicae* is an adverbial phrase modifying *inclūsum.*——**atque**, cop. conj. ; connects *in vēnīs* and *in vīsceribus.*

LINE 12. **in**, prep. ; gov. the abl. *vīsceribus.*——**vīsceribus**, abl. plur. of *viscus, vīsceris,* n. 3d (commonly plur. *vīscera, -um*); governed by the prep. *in.* Literally *vīscera* = *the inward parts* of the body, esp. the nobler parts, i.e. heart, lungs and liver, as distinguished from the *intestīna* or lower parts. It was the *vīscera* (= Greek σπλάγχνα) which the soothsayers examined for omens.——**reī**, gen. sing. of *rēs,* f. 5th ; poss. gen., limiting *vēnīs* and *vīsceribus.*——**pūblicae**, gen. sing. f. of the adj. *pūblicus, -a, -um ;* agrees with *reī.*——**Ut**, adv. ; introduces the simile following. The application of the

13 hominēs	aegrī	morbō	gravī,	cum
men	sick	with a disease	serious,	when

stances men who are suffering from a serious disease, tossing about with the heat

14 aestū	febrīque	iactantur,	sī	aquam
with the heat and with the fever they toss about,	if	water

of fever, appear, if

15 gelidam	bibērunt,	prīmō	relevārī
cold	they drink (lit. have drunk),	at first	to be relieved

they take a draught of cold water, to be re-

metaphor of the human body is too familiar to require comment ; but cf. Catiline's declaration that there were two bodies in the state, one weak with a weak head (= the Senate), and the other strong but without a head (= *plēbs*); and cf. the allegory of the war between the stomach and the rest of the body, by which in early days the *plēbs* was induced to return to Rome. —— **saepe**, adv. ; modifies *relevārī videntur.*

LINE 13. **hominēs**, nom. plur. of *homō, hominis*, m. 3d ; subj. of *videntur*, l. 16 ; *hominēs* is here = *to people* in an indefinite sense (the French would use the indef. pron. *on*). —— **aegrī**, nom. plur. m. of the adj. *aeger, aegra, āegrum ;* agrees with *hominēs; aegrī morbō gravī = quī morbō gravī aegrī sunt.* —— **morbō**, abl. sing. of *morbus, -ī*, m. 2d (akin to *morior, mors, marcēre = to wither* or *be feeble ;* root *mar = to waste away ;* cf. βροτός = μορτός = *mortal,* μάρανσις = *decay);* abl. of specification, defining *aegrī.* A. & G. 253 ; B. 226 ; G. 397 ; H. 424. Synonyms: (1) *morbus = disease, sickness,* of the whole body ; (2) *aegrōtātiō* (from *aegrōtus) = sickness,* with weakness , note that *aegritūdō*, though used by Tacitus like *aegrōtātiō,* usually expresses mental disorder, hence = *sorrow, grief.* —— **gravī**, abl. sing. m. of the adj. *gravis, -e,* 3d (for *gar-uis,* from Latin root *gar, gra* = Greek βαρ, cf. βαρύς = *heavy);* agrees with *morbō.* —— **cum,** temporal conj. ; followed by the pres. ind. *iactantur,* expressing frequentative or iterative action. Remember that *cum* regularly takes the ind. except in the imperf. and pluperf. tenses. But *cum* iterative = *as often as, whenever,* takes the ind. even in past tenses ; e.g. *cum haec dīxerat, manūs tollēbat = as often as he said these words, he raised his hands.* A. & G. 325 ; B. 288 ; G. 580-585 ; H. 521. Refer to the note on *cum,* Chap. III, l. 23.

LINE 14. **aestū**, abl. sing. of *aestus, -ūs,* m. 4th (root *idh = διθ =* Latin *aed, to burn, shine ;* hence *aestus* is for *aed-tus,* and is akin to *aedēs* = (1) lit. *fireplace,* (2) *temple, aestās = summer,* αἶθος = *burning heat,* Ἀιθίοψ = *an Ethiopian);* abl. of the cause, modifying the medial verb *actantur.* —— **febrīque** (*febrī + que*): *febrī* is the dat. sing. of *febris, -is,* f. 3d (acc. *febrem* or *febrim;* abl. usually *febrī;* perhaps akin to *ferveō);* abl. of the cause, like *aestū. Que* is the enclitic cop. conj. ; connecting the two ablatives *aestū* and *febrī. Aestū febrīque = with the fever-heat,* a single idea expressed by two nouns, whereas one noun + a modifier might have served. This figure is known as *hendiadys,* i.e. ἓν διὰ δυοῖν = *one by means of two.* A. & G. 385 ; B. 374, 4 ; G. 698 ; H. 636, III, 2. —— **iactantur,** 3d pers. plur. pres. ind. pass. of *iactō, -āre, -āvī, -ātum,* 1 (frequentative of *iaciō,* hence = *keep tossing);* agrees with the subj. *eī* understood, referring to the principal subj. *hominēs. Iactantur* does not = *are tossed,* with proper passive force, but = *toss themselves about,* with *middle* voice or reflexive force ; cf. *vetor =* not *I am turned* i.e. by another, but *I turn myself, I turn* (intransitive). —— **sī,** conditional particle ; followed by the ind. *bibērunt* in a logical condition. *Sī* is practically = to *cum* frequentative above. —— **aquam**, acc. sing. of *aqua, -ae,* f. 1st ; direct obj. of *bibērunt.*

LINE 15. **gelidam**, acc. sing. f. of the adj. *gelidus, -a, -um* (from noun *gelū, -ūs,* n. 4th = *frost, cold;* cf. Sicilian γέλα); agrees with *aquam.* —— **bibērunt**, 3d pers. plur. perf. ind. act. of *bibō, -ere, bibī, bibitum* (rare), 3 (root *pa* or *po = drink;* akin to *pōtō,* τότος = *a drinking-bout,* πίνω = *I drink);* the implied subj. is a pron. *illī* referring to *hominēs.* In general conditions of present time the perf. ind. sometimes takes the place of the pres. in the *protasis;* in any case *sī bibērunt = cum bibērunt,* i.e. *whenever they*

lieved at first, but are	videntur,	deinde	multō	gravius 16
afterwards much more	*seem,*	*afterwards*	*by much*	*more seriously*
seriously and distress-				
ingly tormented; so	vehementiusque	adflīctantur,	sīc	hīc morbus, 17
this disease which	*and more violently*	*are distressed,*	*so*	*this disease,*
possesses the body	qui	est	in	rē pūblicā,	relevātus 18
politic will, if it be	*which*	*is*	*in*	*the commonwealth,*	*(sc. if) relieved*
alleviated by this fel-	istīus		poenā,		vehementius 19
low's punishment, as-	*of that (fellow)*		*by the punishment,*		*more violently*
sume a character yet				

drink; the perf. tense expresses instantaneous action, prior in time to *relevārī videntur.* There is another reading *biberint* = the fut. perf. ind. active, but the best Mss. read *biberunt.* Yet *biberint* might have stood, if the *apodosis* also referred to future (i.e. *relevārī videntur, deinde . . . adflīctābuntur*). —— **primō** (abl. neut. sing. of *primus, -a, -um;* cf. *primum,* adverbial acc. neut. sing. = *firstly* of a series, *at first*), adv. = *at first;* modifies the pred. *relevārī videntur.* —— **relevārī,** pres. inf. pass. of *relevō, -āre, -āvī, -ātum,* I (*re + levō*); complementary inf., in the pred. with *videntur.* Note that the pres. inf. marks the action of *relevārī* and *videntur* as strictly contemporaneous; we may render *think they are being relieved,* as opposed to *think they have been relieved* (which would be expressed by *relevātī esse*).

LINE 16. **videntur,** 3d pers. plur. pres. ind. pass. of *video, -ēre, vīdī, vīsum,* 2 (*videor* = *I seem*) agrees with the subj. *hominēs.* —— **deinde** (sometimes a dissyllable; *dē + inde* = *from that time, then, next, still*), adv.; modifies *adflīctantur.* The counts or points of an elaborated argument are often introduced by the following adverbs, in order: *primum, deinde, tum, dēnique.* —— **multō** (abl. neut. sing. of *multus*), adv.; modifies *gravius.* The abl. case marks the measure of difference with compar. and superl. adjectives and adverbs, and with words implying comparison such as *post, ante.* —— **gravius,** adv.; modifies *adflīctantur. Gravius* is the compar. of *graviter* (from adj. *gravis, -e,* 3d); superl. *gravissimē.* The comparative of an adverb = the acc. sing. n. of the comparative of the adjective from which the adverb is formed. A. & G. 92; B. 76, 2, and 77, 1; G. 93; H. 306.

LINE 17. **vehementiusque** (*vehementius + que*): *vehementius* is the compar. of the adv. *vehementer;* modifies *adflīctantur.* The adj. *vehemēns* is probably a lengthened form of *vēmēns* (*vē,* an inseparable particle with negative force + *mēns,* hence *not having mind, unreasonable, violent*). *Que* is the enclitic cop. conj.; connects *gravius* and *vehementius.* —— **adflīctantur,** 3d pers. plur. pres. ind. pass. of *adflīctō, -āre, -āvī, -ātum,* I (frequentative form of *adflīgō*); coördinate with *videntur* above, and agrees with the same subj. *hominēs.* —— **sīc** (*sī + ce*), adv. = *so;* used correlatively with *ut,* l. 12. *Ut . . . sīc (ita)* = *as . . . so,* with comparative clauses. —— **hīc,** nom. sing. m. of the dem. pron. *hīc, haec, hōc;* agrees with *morbus.* —— **morbus,** gen. *morbī,* m. 2d; nom. sing., subj. of *ingravēscet.*

LINE 18. **qui,** nom. sing. m. of the rel. pron. *qui, quae, quod;* agrees with the antecedent *morbus,* and is subj. of *est.* —— **est,** 3d pers. sing. pres. ind. of *sum, esse, fuī;* agrees with the subj. *qui.* —— **in,** prep.; gov. the abl. *rēpūblicā,* expressing *place where.* —— **rē,** abl. sing. of *rēs, reī,* f. 5th; gov. by the prep. *in.* —— **pūblicā,** abl. sing. f. of the adj. *pūblicus, -a, -um;* agrees with *rē.* —— **relevātus,** nom. sing. m. of *relevātus, -a, -um,* perf. part. pass. of *relevō, -āre, -āvī, -ātum,* I (*re + levō*); agrees with *morbus. Relevātus* is really a disguised *protasis,* and = *sī relevātus erit.* For the forms which disguised conditions may assume, consult A. & G. 310, esp. *a;* B. 305; G. 600; H. 507, 1–3.

LINE 19. **istīus,** gen. sing. m. of the dem. pron. *iste, ista, istud;* objective gen., with *poenā; istīus* = *Catilīnae.* —— **poenā,** abl. sing. of *poena, -ae,* f. 1st (root *pu* = *to*

20 vīvīs reliquīs	ingravēscet.	Quārē	more grave and vio-
(remaining) alive the rest	will be aggravated.	Wherefore	lent while the other
			traitors remain alive.
21 sēcēdant improbī,	sēcernant	sē ā	Wherefore let the dis-
let withdraw the disloyal men, let them separate themselves from			loyal withdraw apart, let them sever them- selves from the com-
22 bonīs, ūnum in	locum	congregentur,	pany of the loyal and
the loyal men, one into	place	let them herd together,	gather like a herd in

cleanse; cf. ποινή = a penalty, pūniō for poeniō, etc.); abl. of the means, modifying rele-vātus.——vehementius, comparative adv. (see l. 17); modifies ingravēscet.

LINE 20. vīvīs, abl. plur. m. of the adj. vīvus, -a, -um; agrees with reliquīs in the abl. absolute construction; vīvīs reliquīs is a disguised condition = sī reliquī vīvent. For the abl. absolute construction, refer to the note on dīmissō, Chap. IV, l. 38.—— reliquīs, abl. plur. m. of the adj. reliquus, -a, -um (relinquō; reliquī is substantival = the rest, i.e. of the conspirators); in the abl. absolute construction with vīvīs. Remem-ber that the abl. abs. = a clause and that it cannot be used of the subj. or obj. of a sentence; in fact, the abl. abs. is independent of the rest of the sentence.—— ingra-vēscet, 3d pers. sing. fut. ind. act. of ingravēscō, -ere, no perf., no supine, 3 (inceptive form of ingravō); agrees with the subj. morbus.——Quārē (Quā, abl. f. sing. of rel. quī, agreeing with rē; + rē); adv., used as an illative conj.; connects the sentence with what has preceded, and sums up the gist of the argument.

LINE 21. sēcēdant, 3d pers. plur. pres. subjunct. act. of sēcēdō, -ere, sēcessī, sēcessum, 3 (sē = apart + cēdō = I go); agrees with the subj. improbī; the subjunct. is hortatory. The hortatory subjunct. here expresses an exhortation or command; sometimes it expresses a concession; a negative command is introduced by nē. The pres. tense or the perf. tense is used for the 3d pers., sing. or plural; the pres. tense for the 1st person; the present for affirmative commands or exhortations in the 2d person; the perfect (less commonly the present) for negative commands in the 2d person. A. & G. 266; B. 274-276; G. 263; H. 484.——improbī, nom. plur. m., substantival, of the adj. im-probus, -a, -um (in + probus); subj. of sēcēdant. Improbī here is a political technical term.——sēcernant, 3d pers. plur. pres. subjunct. act. of sēcernō, -ere, sēcrēvī, sēcrētum, 3 (sē = apart + cernō = I separate; root kar = to separate, cf. κρίνω = I separate, judge); the implied subj. is a pron., e.g. eī, referring to improbī. Observe the asynde-ton, and the vigorous effect of the short, sharp exhortations. The subjunct. is horta-tive; cf. sēcēdant above.——sē, acc. plur. of the reflexive pron. of the 3d pers. sē, gen. suī; direct obj. of sēcernant; sē refers to the subj. of sēcernant.——ā, prep.; gov. the abl. bonīs, expressing separation.

LINE 22. bonīs, abl. plur. m., substantival, of the adj. bonus, -a, -um; governed by the prep. ā. Bonī, as a political term in Cicero, is used of men who shared his political views, and may be sometimes rendered the conservatives; but here it denotes the loyal as opposed to the traitorous (improbī).——ūnum, acc. sing. m. of the adj. ūnus, -a, -um; agrees with locum.——in, prep.; gov. the acc. locum.——locum, acc. sing. of locus, -ī, m. 2d (the plur. is usually neut. loca, -ōrum = places, district; some-times locī, -ōrum, m. = places, separate and not connected, or topics in a literary work); governed by the prep. in.——congregentur, 3d pers. plur. pres. subjunct. pass. of congregō, -āre, -āvī, -ātum, 1 (con + grex); the subj. is a pron. understood referring to improbī above; the subjunct. is hortatory, as in sēcēdant and sēcernant. The passive is used with medial or reflexive force; see the note on iactantur, l. 14. The meta-phor of herding expresses Cicero's opinion as regards the intelligence and ability of the conspirators.

one spot; in short, as I have already said many times, let them be shut off from us by the city-wall. Let them cease to make treacherous attacks on the consul at his	mūrō	dēnique,	quod	saepe	iam 23
	by the wall (of the city)	*finally,*	*which thing*	*often*	*already*
	dīxī,	sēcernantur	ā	nōbīs;	dēsinant 24
	I have said,	*let them be divided*	*from*	*us;*	*let them cease*
	īnsidiārī	domī	suae	cōnsulī, 25
	to lie in wait	*at house*	*his own*	*for the consul,*

LINE 23. **mūrō**, abl. sing. of *mūrus, -ī*, m. 2d (root *mu = to enclose, to protect;* akin to *moenia*); abl. of the means or instrument, modifying *sēcernantur*. Synonyms: (1) *moenia = the wall* of a city or fortified place; cf. *mūniō = I fortify;* (2) *mūrus = wall*, the general term; often, as here, used for *moenia;* (3) *pariēs = a party-wall* of a house. —— **dēnique**, adv.; marks the clause as summing up the meaning of the clauses immediately preceding. Synonyms: (1) *dēnique = finally, lastly, at last,* esp. at the end of enumeration or argument, where it gives the pith of what has been under discussion and practically dismisses the subject; (2) *postrēmum* or *postrēmō = finally, lastly,* with emphasis on the fact that something is *last;* opposed to *prīmus;* (3) *tandem = finally, at length,* of what happens after long expectation; (4) *dēmum,* cf. *tum dēmum,* of what might have occurred before, and is late in occurring. —— **quod**, acc. sing. n. of the rel. pron. *quī, quae, quod;* direct obj. of *dīxī. Quod* stands for *id quod,* i.e. agrees in gender and number with *id* understood; *id,* if expressed, = an acc. in explanatory apposition with the idea contained in *mūrō sēcernantur ā nōbīs. Id quod* or simply *quod,* when so used, are parenthetic, i.e. independent of the rest of the sentence. A. & G. 200, *e;* B. 247, 1, *b;* G. 614, REM. 2; 324; 333, NOTE 2; H. 363, 5.   For the supplied acc. *id,* see the note and references under *id,* Chap. III, l. 19. —— **saepe**, adv. of time; modifies *dīxī.* —— **iam**, adv. of time; in combination with *saepe* (cf. *iam tum, iam diū,* etc.), modifying *dīxī.*

LINE 24. **dīxī**, 1st pers. sing. perf. ind. act. of *dīcō, -ere, dīxī, dīctum,* 3; the subj. *ego* is implied by the personal ending. —— **sēcernantur**, 3d pers. plur. pres. subjunct. pass. (with medial force) of *sēcernō, -ere, sēcrēvī, sēcrētum,* 3 (*sē + cernō*); the implied subj. is a pron. referring to the people denoted by the term *improbī,* l. 21; the subjunct. is *hortatory,* as in the verbs immediately preceding. —— **ā**, prep.; gov. the abl. *nōbīs,* expressing *separation,* as usual in combination with a verb which in itself implies *separation,* viz. *sēcernantur.* —— **nōbīs**, abl. plur. of the 1st personal pron. (sing. *ego,* plur. *nōs*); gov. by the prep. *ā.* —— **dēsinant**, 3d pers. plur. pres. subjunct. act. of *dēsinō, -ere, desiī, dēsitum,* 3 (*dē + sinō*); the implied subj. is a pron. referring to *improbī. Dēsinō* may be either trans. or intrans.; when active, like all verbs of *beginning* and *ending,* it implies a further action of the same subject, and is used with a complementary inf., e.g. *īnsidiārī, circumstāre, obsidēre, comparāre.*

LINE 25. **īnsidiārī**, pres. inf. of the deponent verb *īnsidior, -ārī, -ātus sum,* 1 (from *īnsidiae, -ārum,* f. 1st = *ambush, plot; in + sedeō*); complementary inf., predicative with *dēsinant.*   Like many intrans. verbs compounded with *in, ad, ante, con,* etc., *īnsidiārī* governs the dat. of the indirect obj., viz. *cōnsulī.*   The allusion is to the attempt of Varguntēius and Cornēlius to murder Cicero at his morning reception on Nov. 7th (or 8th, as Mommsen holds). —— **domī**, locative case of *domus, -ūs* or *-ī,* f. 4th and 2d; expresses *place where,* modifying *īnsidiārī.*   There is another form of this locative, viz. *domuī.*   When qualified by a poss. pron., *domī* (*domuī*) is regarded as a quasi-genitive; hence the gen. *suae* following. —— **suae**, gen. sing. f. of the reflexive poss. pron. *suus, -a, -um;* agrees with *domī; suae* refers to the possessor *cōnsulī,* not to the subj. of *dēsinant.* —— **cōnsulī**, dat. sing. of *cōnsul, -is,* m. 3d; indirect obj. of *īnsidiārī.*   Observe the impersonal form of the reference to Cicero's danger.

26 circumstāre	tribūnal	praetōris	urbānī,	own house, to sur-
to stand around	*the tribunal*	*of the praetor*	*of the city,*	round the judgment-seat of the city
27 obsidēre	cum	gladiīs	cūriam,	malleolōs	praetor, to beset the senate-house with
to invest	*with*	*their swords*	*the senate-house,*	*firebrands*	swords drawn and

LINE 26. **circumstāre**, pres. inf. act. of *circumstō, -āre, -āvī, -ātum*, I (*circum = around + stō = I stand*); complementary inf., predicative with *dēsinant*, like *īnsidiārī* above. Observe the *asyndeton*, i.e. the want of cop. conjunctions to connect in coördination the infinitives *īnsidiārī, circumstāre, obsidēre, comparāre*, each of which states a further action of the subj. of *dēsinant*.——**tribūnal**, acc. sing. of *tribūnal, -is*, n. 3d (like *tribuō* and *tribūnus*, connected with *tribus = a tribe*, originally a third part of the Roman people; root *tri = three*); direct obj. of *circumstāre*. Many intransitive verbs acquire transitive force by composition with the prepositions *ad, ante, ob, trāns, circum*, etc.; cf. *praetereō =* lit. *I go beyond, I pass by*. A. & G. 228, *a*; B. 175, 2, *a*; G. 331; H. 372. There were at this time eight praetors; six of these were presidents of criminal courts, while the remaining two, viz. the *praetor urbānus* and the *praetor peregrīnus* tried civil suits, the former between parties who were both citizens, the latter between parties of whom one or each was a foreigner. The *praetor urbānus* in 63 B.C. was *Lūcius Valerius Flaccus*. The *praetor urbānus* dispensed justice from his *sella curūlis*, which was set upon a raised platform (the *tribūnal*) and was surrounded by seats on a lower level (*subsellia*) for the convenience of those who had legal business to do. In early times the *tribūnal* was situated in the *Comitium*, but toward the close of the republic it was fixed under a portico in the *Forum*. There were, of course, other *tribūnālia* in various parts of Rome, which the other praetors used, according as they were most convenient. The allusion in the present passage is to an attempt of Catiline and his friends to prevent by intimidation the *praetor urbānus* from making a settlement on a civil question of debt. ——**praetōris**, gen. sing. of *praetor, -ōris*, m. 3d (see the note on *praetōrem*, Chap. II, l. 13); poss. gen., limiting *tribūnal*.——**urbānī**, gen. sing. m. of the adj. *urbānus, -a, -um* (from *urbs = a city*); agrees with *praetōris*. The *praetor urbānus* was considered superior in dignity to the other praetors, and hence was sometimes called *praetor māior*. The name, but not the powers, of the *praetor urbānus* lasted as long as the Roman empire in the west; even the name of *praetor peregrīnus* fell out of use after Caracalla's time.

LINE 27. **obsidēre**, pres. inf. act. of *obsideō, -ēre, obsēdī, obsessum*, 2 (*ob + sedeō =* lit. *I sit down before*, hence *I beset, invest*); complementary inf., predicative with *dēsinant*. ——**cum**, prep.; gov. the abl. *gladiīs*.——**gladiīs**, abl. plur. of *gladius, -ī*, m. 2d; governed by the prep. *cum*. *Cum gladiīs* is an idiomatic phrase (apparently belonging to the abl. of accompaniment) *= armātī = under arms;* do not suppose that it expresses the instrument, for this can only be expressed by the abl. without a preposition.——**cūriam**, acc. sing. of *cūria, -ae*, f. 1st; direct obj. of *obsidēre*. The *cūria* here mentioned is the *cūria Hostīlia*, north of the Forum, in which the Senate regularly met, except when it was specially summoned to meet in one or other of the different temples. For meetings of the Senate, and for the various *cūriae*, refer to the note on *locus*, Chap. I, l. 8. ——**malleolōs**, acc. plur. of *malleolus, -ī*, m. 2d (diminutive of *malleus = a hammer*); direct obj. of *comparāre*. A *malleolus* or *firebrand* derives its name from the likeness of its appearance to a *mallet*. It was a missile used in sieges, etc., for setting on fire houses, shipping, etc., belonging to an enemy. It consisted of a mallet-shaped body, with a wire frame, filled with tow and other combustible material which was ignited before the missile was hurled; projecting from this brand was a short shaft with a barbed point, and the missile was so discharged that the arrow-head would stick fast in woodwork, etc., and allow the flames from the tow to do their destructive work.

collect stores of fire-brands and torches for setting fire to the city. In a word, let every man have it printed upon his fore-head what his politi-cal sympathies are. I promise you this, Con-	et	facēs	ad	īnflammandam	urbem 28
	and	*torches*	*for*	*burning* (lit. *to be burnt*)	*the city*
	comparāre:		sit	dēnique	īnscrīptum	in 29
	to provide:		*let it be*	*finally*	*inscribed*	*upon*
	fronte	ūnīus		cūiusque,	quid	dē 30
	the forehead	*one*		*of each (man),*	*what*	*about*
	rē pūblicā		sentiat.		Polliceor	vōbīs 31
	the commonwealth		*he feels.*		*I promise*	*to you*

LINE 28. et, cop. conj.; connects *malleolōs* and *facēs.* —— **facēs**, acc. plur. of *fax, facis*, f. 3d; direct obj. of *comparāre;* joined by *et* to *malleolōs*. *Facēs* or *torches* = (1) pieces of resinous wood, dipped into oil or pitch and then ignited; (2) tubes of metal or wattled laths enclosing inflammable materials, such as tow steeped in tallow, pitch, rosin, and the like. —— **ad**, prep.; gov. the acc. *īnflammandam urbem*, express-ing *purpose.* —— **īnflammandam**, acc. sing. f. of *īnflammandus, -a, -um*, gerundive of *īnflammō, -āre, -āvī, -ātum*, 1 (*in + flammō*); agrees with *urbem* in the construction of gerundival attraction. *Ad* + the acc., and *causā* + the gen., of the gerund or gerundive, express *purpose;* so *ad īnflammandam urbem* = *ut urbem īnflamment.* —— **urbem**, acc. sing. of *urbs, urbis*, f. 3d; governed by *ad* in the gerundival construction.

LINE 29. **comparāre**, pres. inf. act. of *comparō, -āre, -āvī, -ātum*, 1 (*com + parō*); complementary infin., predicative with *dēsinant.* —— **sit**, 3d pers. sing. pres. subjunct. of *sum, esse, fuī;* the true subj. is the clause *quid dē rē pūblicā sentiat.* The subjunct. is *hortatory;* see the note on *sēcēdant*, l. 21. —— **dēnique**, adv. = *in a word;* concludes the series of exhortations; see *dēnique*, l. 22. —— **īnscrīptum**, nom. sing. n. of *īnscrīptus, -a, -um*, perf. part. pass. of *īnscrībō, -ere, īnscrīpsī, īnscrīptum*, 3 (*in + scrībō*); *īnscrīptum + sit* above = the *hortative* perfect, which tense is as common as the pres. subjunct. when the person is third. The phrase recalls the branding of a mark upon runaway slaves. —— **in**, prep.; gov. the abl. *fronte*.

LINE 30. **fronte**, abl. sing. of *frōns, frontis*, f. 3d (Sanskrit *bhru* = *eyebrow;* cf. Greek ὀφρύς, and English *brow*); governed by the prep. *in.* —— **ūnīus**, gen. sing. m. of the numeral adj. *ūnus, -a, -um;* agrees with *cūiusque.* —— **cūiusque**, gen. sing. m. of the indef. pron. *quisque, quaeque, quidque* (adjectival neut. *quodque; quis + que*); poss. gen., limiting *fronte; ūnus quisque* in combination = *every single one.* Distinguish: (1) *ambō* = *both*, of two, together; (2) *uterque* = *each of two*, singly; often in appo-sition with two names, e.g. *Dēmosthenēs et Cicerō, uterque fācundissimus;* (3) *quisque* = *each*, of several. Note the idiom of a superl. + *quisque*, e.g. *fortissimus quisque* = *all the most resolute men.* —— **quid**, acc. sing. n. of the interrog. pron. *quis, quae, quid;* direct obj. of *sentiat.* Observe that *quid* introduces an indirect question, hence the sub-junct. *sentiat;* also that the clause *quid . . . sentiat* is the subj. of *īnscrīptum sit*, to which it is subordinate. —— **dē**, prep. = *concerning;* gov. the abl. *rē pūblicā*.

LINE 31. **rē**, abl. sing. of *rēs, reī*, f. 5th; governed by the prep. *dē.* —— **pūblicā**, abl. sing. f. of the adj. *pūblicus, -a, -um;* agrees with *rē.* —— **sentiat**, 3d pers. sing. pres. subjunct. act. of *sentiō, -īre, sēnsī, sēnsum*, 4; understand *quisque*, from *cūiusque* above, as subject; as often, *sentīre* = *to hold political views.* *Quid . . . sentiat* is an indirect question. Indirect questions: (1) are introduced by an interrog. pron., adj., or adv.; (2) are subordinate to a leading verb or verbal expression, as subj. or obj.; thus *quid . . . sentiat* is subj. of *sit īnscrīptum*, cf. *sciō quis sīs, quis sīs* being obj. of *sciō;* (3) the verb of the contained question is subjunct., and conforms to the rule of tense sequence. A. & G. 334; B. 300; G. 467; H. 528, 2, and 529, I. —— **Polliceor**, 1st pers. sing. pres. ind. of the deponent verb *polliceor, -ērī, pollicitus sum*, 2 (*port +*

32	hōc,	patrēs	cōnscrīptī,	tantam	in	nōbīs	script Fathers, that
	this thing,	*fathers*	*enrolled,*	*(that) so great*	*in*	*us*	such will be the dis-
33	cōnsulibus		fore	dīligentiam,	tantam	in	play of zealous assidu-
	the consuls		*will be* (see NOTE)	*carefulness,*	*so great*	*in*	ity in us consuls, of
34	vōbīs	auctōritātem,		tantam	in	equitibus	authority in you sena-
	you	*authority,*		*so great*	*in*	*the knights*	tors, of manly bearing

liceor = *I bid largely; port* is an old prep., and = the *po* of compound expressions, serving to denote power or possession or else to emphasize the verbal meaning; cf. *pŏnō*, for *pŏsnō*, for *pŏsinō*, for *port + sinō*); the subj. *ego* is implied by the personal ending. Synonyms: (1) *prōmittere* = lit. *to send forth*, i.e. *to hold out, to promise;* generic, denoting every kind of promise; (2) *pollicērī* (as opposed to *abnuere*) = *to proffer, to voluntarily pledge oneself;* (3) *recipere* = *to pledge oneself,* at the same time guaranteeing the risks and results; cf. Cic., *dē aestāte pollicēris vel potius recipis.* —— **vōbīs,** dat. of *vōs;* indirect obj. of *polliceor.*

LINE 32. **hōc,** acc. sing. n. of the dem. pron. *hīc, haec, hōc;* direct obj. of *polliceor;* *hōc* is defined by the following appositional acc. and inf. clause *tantam in nōbīs fore dīligentiam, etc. . . . videātis* (ll. 32-38). —— **patrēs,** voc. plur. of *pater, patris,* m. 3d); the case of address. —— **cōnscrīptī,** voc. plur. of *cōnscrīptus, -a, -um,* perf. part. of *cōn-scrībō, -ere, cōnscrīpsī, cōnscrīptum,* 3 (*con + scrībō*); agrees with *patrēs;* see the note on *cōnscrīptī,* l. 2. —— **tantam,** acc. sing. f. of the dem. adj. *tantus, -a, -um;* predicative; agrees with the subj.-acc. *dīligentiam.* —— **in,** prep.; gov. the abl. *nōbīs.* —— **nōbīs,** abl. of *nōs,* 2d plur. personal pron.; governed by the prep. *in.*

LINE 33. **cōnsulibus,** abl. plur. of *cōnsul, -is,* m. 3d; in apposition with *nōbīs.* —— **fore,** fut. inf. of *sum, esse, fuī;* agrees with the subj.-acc. *dīligentiam.* The verb *sum* has two forms of the fut. inf., viz. (1) *fore,* (2) *futūrus, -a, -um + esse,* i.e. fut. part. + *esse,* as most fut. infinitives act. are formed. The clause *tantam fore dīligentiam* is in apposition with *hōc,* which is direct obj. of *polliceor;* instead of rendering *I promise such carefulness to be about to be,* etc., it is usual in English to commence the indirect discourse with the word *that,* and turn the Latin inf. into the English ind., e.g. *I promise that there will be such carefulness,* etc. —— **dīligentiam,** acc. sing. of *dīligentia, -ae,* f. 1st (from *dīligēns,* adj. and pres. part. of *dīligō*); subj.-acc. of *fore tantam* in indirect discourse; the acc. and inf. clause = the acc. and inf. of the verbal noun, in apposition with the acc. *hōc.* —— **tantam,** acc. sing. f. of the adj. *tantus, -a, -um;* predicative, with *fore* supplied from the coördinate clause preceding; agrees with the subj.-acc. *auctōritātem;* this clause, and the others following with *tantam,* are in apposition with *hōc,* l. 32. The repetition of *tantam* at the beginning of each coördinate clause is an instance of the rhetorical device known as *anaphora.* A. & G. 344, *f*; B. 350, 11, *b*; G. 636, NOTE 4; H. 636, III, 3. —— **in,** prep.; gov. the abl. *vōbīs.*

LINE 34. **vōbīs,** abl. of the 2d personal pron. plur. *vōs;* governed by the prep. *in;* *in vōbīs,* i.e. in the Senate, as distinguished from the *ōrdō equestris* and the *cīvēs Rōmānī.* —— **auctōritātem,** acc. sing. of *auctōritās, -ātis,* f. 3d; subj.-acc. of *tantam (fore); auctōritātem* here has a general meaning of *authoritative influence,* i.e. making itself felt and respected in the city. —— **tantam,** acc. sing. f. of the adj. *tantus, -a, -um;* predicative, with *fore* understood; agrees with the subj.-acc. *virtūtem.* —— **in,** prep.; gov. the abl. *equitibus.* —— **equitibus,** abl. plur. of *eques, equitis,* m. 3d (*equus* = *a horse,* hence lit. *a horseman, knight*); governed by the prep. *in.* See the note on *equitēs,* Chap. IV, l. 33. The whole sentence, ll. 31-38, is an appeal to all classes of Roman society to take joint action against the conspirators; the appeal is disguised by the flattering attribution to the Senate, knights, and populace of the qualities which the orator desired them to show.

Rōmānīs	virtūtem,	tantam	in	omnibus **35**
Roman	*worthiness,*	*so great*	*in*	*all*
bonīs	cōnsēnsiōnem,		ut	Catilīnae **36**
loyal (citizens)	*unanimity,*		*that*	*of Catiline*
profectiōne	omnia	patefacta,		inlūstrāta, **37**
by the departure	*all (evils)*	*disclosed,*		*cleared up,*
oppressa,	vindicāta	esse	videātis.	Hisce **38**
crushed,	*punished*	*to be*	*you may see.*	*These*

In our Roman knights, —such the display of unanimity among all loyal citizens, that on Catiline's departure you will see every scheme laid bare, revealed, crushed, and punished. With these

LINE 35. **Rōmānīs**, abl. plur. m. of the adj. *Rōmānus, -a, -um ;* agrees with the noun *equitibus ;* the addition of this epithet often gives a statement a dignified and formal character. —— **virtūtem**, acc. sing. of *virtūs, virtūtis,* f. 3d (= the quality of a *vir,* hence *manly courage,* physical and moral, *virtue*); subj.-acc. of *tantam (fore).* —— **tantam,** acc. sing. f. of the adj. *tantus, -a, -um ;* predicative with *fore* supplied from above ; agrees with the subj.-acc. *cōnsēnsiōnem.* —— **in,** prep. ; gov. the abl. *omnibus.* —— **omnibus,** abl. plur. m. of the adj. *omnis, -e,* 3d ; agrees with *bonīs.*

LINE 36. **bonīs,** abl. of the plur. noun *bonī, -ōrum,* m. 2d = *patriots, loyal citizens* (substantival mas. of the adj. *bonus, -a, -um ;* cf. *bona = property*); governed by the prep. *in. Bonī* here includes all true citizens not members of the *ōrdō senātōrius* or of the *ōrdō equestris.* —— **cōnsēnsiōnem,** acc. sing. of *cōnsēnsiō, -ōnis,* f. 3d (from *cōnsenīre* = *to agree together, be one-minded, con + sentiō*); subj.-acc. of *tantam (fore);* the clause is, like the clauses immediately preceding, an appositive of *hōc,* l. 32. *Cōnsēnsiō* or *unanimity* is the very quality which one may expect not to find in the Roman populace, whose sympathies were very easily stirred and diverted, and whose honesty was never very secure if dishonesty seemed likely to be profitable. —— **ut,** conj. ; introducing the adverbial consecutive clause *ut . . . esse videātis.* Adverbial clauses of *result* frequently depend on a principal sentence which contains a dem. word, e.g. *tam, ita, adeō, tālis* or *tantus.* —— **Catilīnae,** gen. sing. of *Catilīna,* m. 1st ; poss. gen., limiting *profectiōne.*

LINE 37. **profectiōne,** abl. sing. of *profectiō, -ōnis,* f. 3d (from *profectus,* perf. part. of *proficīscor = I set out*); abl. of the means, modifying *patefacta esse,* etc. ; render *on Catiline's departure,* rather than *by Catiline's departure.* —— **omnia,** acc. plur. n. substantival = *everything,* of the adj. *omnis, -e,* 3d ; subj.-acc. of the coördinate infinitives following, viz. *patefacta (esse), inlūstrāta (esse), oppressa (esse),* and *vindicāta esse ;* the construction is the objective acc. and inf., dependent on *videātis.* —— **patefacta,** acc. plur. n. of *patefactus, -a, -um,* perf. part. of *patefīō, patefierī, patefactus sum,* irreg., used as pass. of *patefaciō, -ere, patefēcī, patefactum,* 3 (*pateō + faciō = patēre faciō = I make to be open, I disclose*); agrees with the subj.-acc. *omnia ;* supply *esse* from below = the perf. inf. pass. of *patefaciō.* Observe : (1) that when a part of *sum,* making a composite pass. tense, belongs to two or more coördinate verbs, it is frequently expressed only with one (usually, as here, the last) and understood with the rest ; (2) that *patefaciō* is one of the few exceptions to the rule that *faciō* becomes *ficiō* in compounds, e.g. *perficiō.* —— **inlūstrāta,** acc. plur. n. of *inlūstrātus, -a, -um,* perf. part. pass. of *inlūstrō (illūstrō), -āre, -āvī, -ātum,* 1 (*in + lustrō ;* hence = *to make bright,* from root *ruk* or *luk = to light, shine ;* cf. *lūceō, lūx, lūmen, λύχνος*); supply *esse* = the perf. inf. pass. agreeing with the subj.-acc. *omnia.* Observe that the four infinitives here are coördinate, yet are unconnected ; a good example of *asyndeton.*

LINE 38. **oppressa,** acc. plur. n. of *oppressus, -a, -um,* perf. part. pass. of *opprimō, -ere, oppressī, oppressum,* 3 (*ob + premō*); supply *esse* = perf. inf. pass., agreeing with the subj.-acc. *omnia.* —— **vindicāta,** acc. plur. n. of *vindicātus, -a, -um,* perf. part. pass. of *vindicō, -āre, -āvī, -ātum,* 1 ; *vindicāta + esse* following = the perf. inf. pass., agreeing

39 ōminibus, Catilīna, cum summā   reī pūblicae
    with omens,   Catiline,   with   supreme of the commonwealth

40 salūte,   cum   tuā   peste   ac   perniciē
    safety,   with   your own destruction   and   .   ruin

41 cumque   eōrum   exitiō,   quī   sē   tēcum
    and with   of those men the overthrow,   who   themselves   with you

prophetic words, Catiline, go forth, and bring complete deliverance to the state, ruin and death upon yourself, and destruction upon those who have allied them-

with the subj.-acc. *omnia.* ——**esse**, pres. inf. of *sum;* forms the composite perf. inf. pass. with the participles preceding. ——**videātis**, 2d pers. plur. pres. subjunct. act. of *videō, -ēre, vīdī, vīsum,* 2 ; understand the subj. *vōs* (implied from *vōbīs,* l. 31). The subjunct. is consecutive, expressing *result* after *ut,* l. 36. The sentence *polliceor . . . videātis* is Cicero's forecast of the fate of the conspiracy ; cf. *hīsce ōminibus.* ——**Hīsce**, abl. plur. n. of *hīce, haece, hōce (hīc, haec, hōc +* the dem. suffix *-ce,* which adds emphasis and is pointedly deictic) ; agrees with *ōminibus.* With *hīce* compare the French *ce-ci = this here.* In classical Latin the only cases in which *-ce* is added to *hīc* are : *hōsce, hāsce, hūiusce,* and *hīsce. Ille* and *iste* also combine with *ce,* and *istuc* is the more common neut. sing. of *iste* than *istud.* The final letter *c* of *hīc, haec, hōc* is really a shortened form of *ce.*

LINE 39. **ōminibus**, abl. plur. of *ōmen, ōminis,* n. 3d (earlier form *osmen,* from *ōs, ōris,* n. 3d = *the mouth*) ; *hīsce ōminibus* may be explained (1) as abl. of accompaniment, with *cum* omitted (*cum* is often omitted in military phrases) ; (2) as abl. absolute, lit. *the omens being such;* we may render *with such prophetic words,* in reference to the preceding sentence. Like Eastern peoples, the Romans always tried to discover the will of the gods on the subject before embarking on any enterprise of importance. Prof. Ramsay remarks : "The various signs which were believed to indicate the disposition of the Supreme Powers were comprehended under the general name of *ōmina.* There was scarcely any sight or sound connected with animate or inanimate nature which might not, under certain circumstances, be regarded as yielding an *ōmen.*" The most common ominous signs for good or bad were those afforded by thunder and lightning, victims' entrails, and the cries, flight, and feeding of birds. ——**Catilīna**, voc. sing. of *Catilīna, -ae,* m. 1st ; the case of address. ——**cum**, prep. ; gov. the abl. *salūte* expressing the *attendant circumstances* of the departure. We should in English render *to the salvation of the state,* etc. A. & G. 248, *a* ; B. 221, 222 ; G. 392 ; H. 419, I, and 1. ——**summā**, abl. sing. f. of the adj. *summus, -a, -um,* superl. of *superus, -a, -um* (from the adv. *super;* the compar. adj. is *superior;* another form of the superl. is *suprēmus*) ; agrees with *salūte.* ——**reī**, gen. sing. of *rēs,* f. 5th ; poss. gen., limiting *salūte.* ——**pūblicae**, gen. sing. f. of the adj. *pūblicus, -a, -um;* agrees with *reī.*

LINE 40. **salūte**, abl. sing. of *salūs, -ūtis,* f. 3d ; governed by the prep. *cum.* ——**cum**, prep. ; gov. the ablatives *peste* and *perniciē* expressing *accompaniment* of circumstance. ——**tuā**, abl. sing. f. of the poss. adj. *tuus, -a, -um;* agrees with *peste* and understood with *perniciē;* the poss. adj. always takes the place of a poss. gen. of a personal pronoun. ——**peste**, abl. sing. of *pestis, -is,* f. 3d ; governed by the prep. *cum.* For *pestis, perniciēs,* and synonyms, refer to the note on *pestem,* Chap. I, l. 27. ——**ac** (abbreviation of *atque*), cop. conj. ; as often, connects synonyms, viz. *peste* and *perniciē.* ——**perniciē**, abl. sing. of *perniciēs, perniciēī,* f. 5th (*per + nex;* cf. *necō,* 1) ; governed by the prep. *cum;* coördinate with *peste.*

LINE 41. **cumque** (*cum + que*): *cum* is the prep. + the abl. ; gov. *exitiō,* expressing *accompaniment* of circumstance. *Que* is the enclitic cop. conj. ; connects the adverbial phrase *cum exitiō* with the adverbial phrases with *cum* preceding. The ablative of *accompaniment* is a branch of the abl. of *manner;* the ablatives here modify the pred.

selves with you in every kind of wickedness and heinous crime — go forth to begin your shameless and abominable warfare. Thou, Juppiter, who wast here established in effigy by	omnī *every*	scelere *in crime*	parricīdiōque *and in murder*	iūnxērunt, *have united,*	42
	proficīscere *set out*	ad *to*	impium *impious*	bellum *a war*	ac *and*	nefārium. *heinous.*	43
	Tū, *Thou,*	Iuppiter, *Juppiter,*	quī *who*	īsdem *with the same (auspices)*	quibus *which*	44

proficīscere. —— **eōrum**, gen. plur. m. of the dem. pron. *is, ea, id;* poss. gen., limiting *exitiō.* The gen. case of *is, ea, id,* supplies the place of a poss. pron. of the 3d person. —— **exitiō**, abl. sing. of *exitium, -ī,* n. 2d; governed by the prep. *cum.* —— **quī**, nom. plur. m. of the rel. pron. *quī, quae, quod;* agrees with the antecedent *eōrum,* and is subj. of *iūnxērunt* in its own clause. —— **sē**, acc. plur. of *sē (sēsē),* gen *suī,* reflexive pron. of the 3d pers. (sing. or plur. all genders); direct obj. of *iūnxērunt; sē* refers back to the subj. *quī,* i.e. denotes the same persons. —— **tēcum** (*tē + cum*) : *tē* is the abl. sing. of *tū;* governed by the prep. *cum;* the abl. is *sociative. Cum* is the prep. + the abl.; gov. *tē. Cum* is regularly enclitic with the personal and reflexive pronouns, and usually with the relative.

LINE 42. **omnī**, abl. sing. n. of the 3d decl. adj. *omnis, -e;* agrees with *scelere.* —— **scelere**, abl. sing. of *scelus, sceleris,* n. 3d ; abl. of the means, modifying *iūnxērunt; scelere parricīdiōque* expresses the bond which was instrumental in uniting the conspirators together. —— **parricīdiōque** (*parricīdiō + que*) : *parricīdiō* is the abl. sing. of *parricīdium, -ī,* n. 2d ; abl. of the means, coördinate with *scelere.* For the derivation and meaning of *parricīdium,* see the note on *parricīdiō,* Chap. VII, l. 40. *Que* is the enclitic cop. conj.; joins *scelere* and *parricīdiō* together. —— **iūnxērunt**, 3d pers. plur. perf. ind. act. of *iungō, -ere, iūnxī, iūnctum,* 3 (root *yu, yug = ζυγ = jug, to bind, join;* cf. *iugō, iugum, iūs, ζεύγνυμι = I join, ζύγον = a yoke,* etc.); agrees with the subj. *quī.*

LINE 43. **proficīscere**, 2d pers. sing. pres. imperative of the deponent verb *proficīscor, proficīscī, profectus sum,* 3 (inceptive of *proficiō; prō +* root *fic = to set one's self forward*); the subj. *tū* is implied by the personal ending. —— **ad**, prep.; gov. the accusative *bellum.* —— **impium**, acc. sing. n. of the adj. *impius, -a, -um (in = not + pius = dutiful);* agrees with *bellum. Impietās* includes all offences of disrespect towards or actual crime against one's parents, one's country, and the gods. —— **bellum**, acc. sing. of *bellum, -ī,* n. 2d (for *du-ellum,* from *duo;* cf. English *duel*), governed by the prep. *ad.* —— **ac**, cop. conj.; connects the attributes *impium* and *nefārium.* —— **nefārium**, acc. sing. n. of the adj. *nefārius, -a, -um* (from noun *nefās; ne + fās;* cf. *fārī,* etc.); agrees with *bellum;* joined by *ac* to *impium.*

LINE 44. **Tū**, gen. *tuī;* nom. sing. of the 2d personal pron., subj. of *arcēbis,* l. 50. *Tū* is emphatic ; the nom. of the personal pronouns is only expressed for purposes of emphasis of contrast. As he spoke, Cicero would turn towards the statue of *Iuppiter Stator* in the temple. This address to Jupiter is a fitting close to the powerful speech which the orator has delivered. —— **Iuppiter**, voc. sing. of *Iuppiter,* gen. *Iovis,* m. 3d ; the case of address. *Iuppiter* stands for *Iovis + pater; Iovis,* with collateral form *Diovis,* was the earlier form of the nominate. The root is *di, div,* or *dyu = to shine;* cf. *diēs, dīvus, Diāna, δῖος,* and esp. Ζεύς, stem Δις, gen. Διός. The word is more correctly spelt in Latin with *pp,* but it would be pedantic in English to make a change from the single *p* which English literature has caused to appear more familiar. —— **quī**, nom. sing. m. of the rel. pron. *quī, quae, quod;* agrees with the antecedent *tū,* and is subj. of *cōnstitūtus es* in its own clause. The clause *quī . . . es cōnstitūtus* is elliptical, and = *quī īsdem auspiciis, quibus haec urbs cōnstitūta est, es cōnstitūtus.* —— **īsdem**, abl. plur. n. of the

45 haec	urbs	auspiciis	ā	Rōmulō	Romulus with the
this	*city*	*(with) auspices*	*by*	*Romulus*	same sacred rites that inaugurated this
46 es cōnstitūtus,		quem Statōrem	hūius	urbis	city's foundation,
wast established,		*whom the Establisher*	*this*	*of city*	thou whom we call

dem. pron. *īdem, eadem, idem* (for *is, ea, id* + -*dem*); agrees with *auspiciis*. Note: (1) that *m* changes to *n* before *d*, e.g. acc. sing. *eundem, eandem ;* gen. plur. *eōrundem, eārundem ;* (2) that the nom. mas. plur. has 2 forms, *eīdem* and *iīdem,* sometimes *īdem ;* (3) that the dat. and abl. plur. = *eīsdem, iīsdem,* or a contraction of the latter to *īsdem. The same as* may be rendered (a) by *īdem* with *qui* (cf. *īsdem quibus* in this passage); (b) *īdem* with *atque* (*ac*), e.g. *eadem ac tū cupiō* = *I desire the same as you ;* (c) *īdem* + *ut ;* (d) *īdem* + *cum* (prep.), e.g. *eadem tēcum cupiō.* A. & G. 234, NOTE 2 ; B. 341, I, *c*); G. 310, REM. 2 ; H. 451, 5. —— *quibus,* abl. plur. n. of the rel. pron. *qui, quae, quod ;* agrees with the antecedent *auspiciis,* or we may consider *auspiciis* part of the rel. clause with *quibus* by attraction. The ablatives *īsdem auspiciis* and *quibus* belong to the wide class which embraces *manner, means,* and *accompaniment ;* it is better perhaps to style them ablatives of *accompaniment.*

LINE 45. **haec,** nom. sing. f. of the dem. pron. *hīc, haec, hōc ;* agrees with *urbs.* —— **urbs,** gen. *urbis,* f. 3d; nom. sing., subj. of *constitūta est* understood in the rel. clause introduced by *quibus.* —— **auspiciis,** abl. plur. of *auspicium, -ī,* n. 2d (*auspex,* gen. *auspicis,* m. 3d); abl. of accompaniment ; *auspiciis* seems to be attracted into the rel. clause with *quibus,* and so *auspiciis* must be understood with *īsdem ; īsdem quibus . . . auspiciis* = *īsdem auspiciis quibus. Auspicium* = *augury from birds, auspices ;* the derivation is *avis* = *a bird* + *speciō,* hence *auspex* (for *avispex*) = *a bird-seer.* Compare *auceps* (for *aviceps, avis* + *capiō*) = *a bird-catcher ; augur* (*avis* + Sanskrit *gar* = *to make known*) = *soothsayer ;* and Sanskrit *vis* = *a bird.* The Indo-European root *avi* may be assumed = Greek *ὄρι* = *ὄϊ ;* cf. *οἰ-ωνό-s* = *a large bird.* The auspices were always taken (i.e. ominous signs were observed, esp. from the cries, flight, etc. of birds) before any important private or public business was entered upon, e.g. the *comitia centuriāta* never met unless favorable auspices had been previously taken. —— **ā,** prep. ; gov. the abl. *Rōmulō,* expressing *agency ; ā Rōmulō* modifies *es constitūtus* and also *constitūta est* understood (see note on *urbs* above). —— **Rōmulō,** abl. sing. of *Rōmulus, -ī,* m. 2d ; governed by the prep. *ā. Rōmulus* was the mythical founder of Rome. His name is clearly an invention to explain the name of the city *Rōma* (which is for *Srouma* = *the stream-town*); cf. *Hellēn,* invented to explain *Hellēnes,* etc. etc. According to the legend *Rōmulus* was the son of *Mars* and *Rhaea Sylvia ;* in company with his brother *Remus,* he was exposed to die in the Tiber, but was saved and suckled by a she-wolf. The two brothers eventually slew the usurper *Amūlius,* and then began to build Rome, in the course of which task a quarrel arose and *Rōmulus* killed his brother. After his death or disappearance, *Rōmulus* was worshipped under the name of *Quirīnus.*

LINE 46. **es cōnstitūtus,** 2d pers. sing. perf. ind. pass. of *cōnstituō, -ere, -uī, -ūtum,* 3 (*con* + *statuō*); agrees with the subj. *quī ;* when the antecedent of the rel. is a personal pron., the verb of the rel. clause takes the person of the pronominal antecedent (so *tū . . . quī* in this passage). Observe that the *statue* is addressed directly, *thou who wast set up.* The statement *quī īsdem auspiciis,* etc., is not literally correct, for Rōmulus did not vow the erection of the temple when Rome was being built but some time afterwards, viz. during the Sabine war ; moreover, the temple was not built till very much later, viz. 294 B.C. —— **quem,** acc. sing. m. of the rel. pron. *quī, quae, quod ;* agrees with the antecedent *tū,* l. 44, and is direct obj. of *nōmināmus* in its own clause. —— **Statōrem,** acc. sing. of *stator, -ōris,* m. 3d (cf. *sistō* = *I make to stand,* and *ἵστημι ;* the root is *sta,* as in *stō* = *I stand*); objective complement of the verb *nōmināmus.* Remember that

Lightning Source UK Ltd.
Milton Keynes UK
UKOW05f1452050915

258083UK00014B/1416/P